Dynamic Social Network Modeling and Analysis

Workshop Summary and Papers

Ronald Breiger, Kathleen Carley, and Philippa Pattison

Committee on Human Factors
Board on Behavioral, Cognitive, and Sensory Sciences
Division of Behavioral and Social Sciences and Education

NATIONAL RESEARCH COUNCIL
OF THE NATIONAL ACADEMIES

THE NATIONAL ACADEMIES PRESS
Washington, D.C.
www.nap.edu

THE NATIONAL ACADEMIES PRESS 500 Fifth Street, N.W. Washington, DC 20001

NOTICE: The project that is the subject of this report was approved by the Governing Board of the National Research Council, whose members are drawn from the councils of the National Academy of Sciences, the National Academy of Engineering, and the Institute of Medicine. The members of the committee responsible for the report were chosen for their special competences and with regard for appropriate balance.

This work relates to Department of Navy grant N00014-02-1-0997 issued by the Office of Naval Research to the National Academy of Sciences. The United States Government has a royalty-free license throughout the world in all copyrightable material contained in the publications. Any opinions, findings, and conclusions or recommendations expressed in this material are those of the author(s) and do not necessarily reflect the views of the Office of Naval Research.

International Standard Book Number 0-309-08952-2 (Book)
International Standard Book Number 0-309-51916-0 (PDF)

Library of Congress Catalog Card Number 2003107509

Additional copies of this report are available from National Academies Press, 500 Fifth Street, N.W., Lockbox 285, Washington, DC 20055; (800) 624-6242 or (202) 334-3313 (in the Washington metropolitan area); Internet, http://www.nap.edu.

Printed in the United States of America

Suggested citation: National Research Council. (2003). *Dynamic Social Network Modeling and Analysis: Workshop Summary and Papers*, Ronald Breiger, Kathleen Carley, and Philippa Pattison. Committee on Human Factors. Board on Behavioral, Cognitive, and Sensory Sciences, Division of Behavioral and Social Sciences and Education. Washington, DC: The National Academies Press.

PLANNING SUBCOMMITTEE FOR THE WORKSHOP ON DYNAMIC SOCIAL NETWORK MODELING AND ANALYSIS

DANIEL R. ILGEN (*Chair*), Department of Psychology and Department of Management, Michigan State University, East Lansing

JOHN M. CARROLL, Center for Human-Computer Interaction, Virginia Polytechnic Institute and State University, Blacksburg

MARTHA GRABOWSKI, Department of Decision Sciences and Engineering Systems, Rensselaer Polytechnic Institute; and Information Systems Programs, LeMoyne College

ANNE S. MAVOR, *Senior Staff Officer*
SUSAN R. McCUTCHEN, *Research Associate*

COMMITTEE ON HUMAN FACTORS

RAJA PARASURAMAN (*Chair*), Department of Psychology, Catholic University

JOHN M. CARROLL, Center for Human-Computer Interaction, Virginia Polytechnic Institute and State University, Blacksburg

ROBYN DAWES, Department of Social and Decision Sciences, Carnegie Mellon University

COLIN G. DRURY, Department of Industrial Engineering, State University of New York, Buffalo

DONALD FISHER, Department of Mechanical and Industrial Engineering, University of Massachusetts, Amherst

MARTHA GRABOWSKI, Department of Decision Sciences and Engineering Systems, Rensselaer Polytechnic Institute; and Information Systems Programs, LeMoyne College

PETER A. HANCOCK, Department of Psychology, University of Central Florida, Orlando

DANIEL R. ILGEN, Department of Psychology and Department of Management, Michigan State University, East Lansing

RICHARD J. JAGACINSKI, Department of Psychology, Ohio State University, Columbus

BONNIE E. JOHN, Human-Computer Interaction Institute, School of Computer Science, Carnegie Mellon University

KURT KRAIGER, Department of Psychology, University of Tulsa, Oklahoma

WILLIAM S. MARRAS, Institute for Ergonomics and Department of Industrial, Welding, and Systems Engineering, Ohio State University, Columbus

RICHARD W. PEW, BBN Technologies, Cambridge, Massachusetts

ROBERT G. RADWIN, Department of Biomedical Engineering, University of Wisconsin, Madison

KARLENE ROBERTS, Haas School of Business, University of California, Berkeley

KIM J. VICENTE, Cognitive Engineering Laboratory and Department of Mechanical and Industrial Engineering, University of Toronto

GREG L. ZACHARIAS, Charles River Analytics, Cambridge, Massachusetts

ANNE S. MAVOR, *Director*
SUSAN R. McCUTCHEN, *Research Associate*

Preface

The Committee on Human Factors was established in 1980 by the Commission on Behavioral and Social Sciences and Education. Over the years, the committee has pursued a wide range of topics dealing with theoretical and methodological issues and with the application of principles of human behavior and performance to the design of systems. Recent interests have included modeling individual and organizational behavior, networks and remote collaboration, and contributions of the behavioral and organizational sciences to ensuring national security.

Within this context, the Committee on Human Factors was asked by the Office of Naval Research to hold a workshop on social network modeling and analysis and to examine the potential of research in this area for application to national security issues. In response, a subgroup of the committee was appointed by the National Research Council to plan and organize the workshop. Key participants were identified and asked to write papers and make presentations. Many of the papers focused on current developments in the science of social network modeling and several discussed various applications, including national security. Part I of this document is a summary of the major themes and the research issues and prospects that emerged from the presentations and discussions. Part II contains the papers as submitted.

I would like to thank Rebecca Goolsby from the Office of Naval Research for supporting this effort and for her interest, insights, and helpful suggestions. I would also like to extend our appreciation to National Research Council staff Anne Mavor and Susan McCutchen for their assistance in planning and organizing the workshop.

Part I, the workshop summary, has been reviewed in draft form by individuals chosen for their diverse perspectives and technical expertise, in accordance with procedures approved by the Report Review Committee of the National Research Council. The purpose of this independent review is to provide candid and critical comments that will assist the institution in making its published report as sound as possible and to ensure that the report meets institutional standards for objectivity, evidence, and responsiveness to the charge. The review comments and draft manuscript remain confidential to protect the integrity of the process. We thank the following individuals for their review of Part I of this report: Kari Chopra, Aptima, Inc., Washington, DC; Patrick Doreian, Department of Sociology, University of Pittsburgh; and Charles M. Macal, Center for Complex Adaptive Systems Simulation, Argonne National Laboratory, Argonne, IL.

Although the reviewers listed above provided many constructive comments and suggestions, they were not asked to endorse the content of the document nor did they see the final draft of the report before its release. The review of this report was overseen by Paul Holland, Statistical Theory and Practice, Educational Testing Service, Princeton, NJ. Appointed by the National Research Council, he was responsible for making certain that an independent examination of this report was carried out in accordance with institutional procedures and that all review comments were carefully considered. Responsibility for the final content of this report rests entirely with the authors and the institution.

Daniel Ilgen, *Chair*
Planning Subcommittee

Contents

PART I: WORKSHOP SUMMARY 1

Introduction, 3
Workshop Sessions and Themes, 3
Research Issues and Prospects, 11

PART II: WORKSHOP PAPERS 15

Opening Address

Emergent Themes in Social Network Analysis: Results, Challenges, Opportunities 19
Ronald L. Breiger

Session I: Social Network Theory Perspectives

Finding Social Groups: A Meta-Analysis of the Southern Women Data 39
Linton C. Freeman

Autonomy vs. Equivalence Within Market Network Structure? 78
Harrison C. White

Social Influence Network Theory: Toward a Science of Strategic Modification of Interpersonal Influence Systems 89
Noah E. Friedkin

Information and Innovation in a Networked World 101
David Lazer

Session II: Dynamic Social Networks

Informal Social Roles and the Evolution and Stability of Social Networks 121
Jeffrey C. Johnson, Lawrence A. Palinkas, and James S. Boster

Dynamic Network Analysis 133
Kathleen M. Carley

Accounting for Degree Distributions in Empirical Analysis of Network Dynamics 146
Tom A.B. Snijders

Polarization in Dynamic Networks: A Hopfield Model of Emergent Structure 162
Michael W. Macy, James A. Kitts, and Andreas Flache

Local Rules and Global Properties: Modeling the Emergence of Network Structure 174
Martina Morris

Social Networks: Threat Networks and Threatened Networks 187
H. Eugene Stanley and Shlomo Havlin

Session III: Metrics and Models

Sensitivity Analysis of Social Network Data and Methods: Some Preliminary Results 197
Stanley Wasserman and Douglas Steinley

Spectral Methods for Analyzing and Visualizing Networks: An Introduction 209
Andrew J. Seary and William D. Richards

Statistical Models for Social Networks: Inference and Degeneracy 229
Mark S. Handcock

The Key Player Problem 241
Stephen P. Borgatti

Balancing Efficiency and Vulnerability in Social Networks 253
Elisa Jayne Bienenstock and Phillip Bonacich

Data Mining on Large Graphs 265
Christopher R. Palmer, Phillip B. Gibbons, and Christos Faloutsos

Session IV: Networked Worlds

Data Mining in Social Networks 289
David Jensen and Jennifer Neville

Random Effects Models for Network Data 303
Peter D. Hoff

Predictability of Large-Scale Spatially Embedded Networks 313
Carter T. Butts

Using Multi-Theoretical Multi-Level (MTML) Models to Study Adversarial Networks 324
Noshir S. Contractor and Peter R. Monge

Identifying International Networks: Latent Spaces and Imputation 345
Michael D. Ward, Peter D. Hoff, and Corey Lowell Lofdahl

Summary: Themes, Issues, and Applications

Linking Capabilities to Needs 363
Kathleen M. Carley

APPENDIXES

A Workshop Agenda 373

B Biographical Sketches 376

PART I

Workshop Summary

Workshop Summary

INTRODUCTION

In the summer of 2002, the Office of Naval Research asked the Committee on Human Factors to hold a workshop on dynamic social network modeling and analysis. The primary purpose of the workshop was to bring together scientists who represent a diversity of views and approaches to share their insights, commentary, and critiques on the developing body of social network analysis research and application. The secondary purpose of the workshop was to assist government and private-sector agencies in assessing the capabilities of social network analysis to provide sound models and applications for current problems of national importance, with a particular focus on national security. Some of the presenters focused on social network theory and method, others attempted to relate their research or expertise to applied issues of interest to various government agencies. This workshop is one of several activities undertaken by the National Research Council that bears on the contributions of various scientific disciplines to understanding and defending against terrorism—a topic raised by Bruce M. Alberts, president of the National Academy of Sciences, in his annual address to the membership in April 2002.

The workshop was held in Washington, D.C., on November 7-9, 2002. Twenty-two researchers were asked to prepare papers and give presentations. The presentations were grouped into four sessions, each of which concluded with a discussant-led roundtable discussion among presenters and workshop attendees on the themes and issues raised in the session. The sessions were: (1) Social Network Theory Perspectives, (2) Dynamic Social Networks, (3) Metrics and Models, and (4) Networked Worlds. The opening address was presented by workshop chair Ronald Breiger, of the University of Arizona; Kathleen Carley, of Carnegie Mellon University, offered closing remarks summarizing the sessions and linking the work to applications in national security. Part II of this report contains the opening address, the closing remarks, and the papers as provided by the authors. The agenda and biographical sketches of the presenters are found in the appendixes.

This summary presents the major themes developed by the presenters and discussants in each session and concludes with research issues and prospects for both the research and applications communities.

WORKSHOP SESSIONS AND THEMES

Overall, the workshop provided presentations on the state of the art in social network analysis and its potential contribution to policy makers. The papers run the gamut from the technical to the theoretical, and examine such application areas as public health, culture, markets, and politics. Throughout the workshop a number of themes emerged, all based on the following understandings:

- Both network theory and methodology have expanded rapidly in the past decade.
- New approaches are combining social network analysis with techniques and theories from other research areas.
- Many of the existing tools, metrics, and theories need to be revisited in the context of very large scale and/or dynamic networks.
- The body of applied work in social networking is growing.

Several common analytical issues underlie much of the research reported. First, traditional social network analysis is "data greedy"—very detailed data are required on all participants. Questions to be addressed in the analysis of these data concern how to estimate the data from high-level indicators, how sensitive the measures are to missing data, and how network data can be collected rapidly and/or automatically. Furthermore, advances require the development of additional shareable data sets that capture heretofore understudied aspects such as large-scale networks, sampling errors, linkages to other types of data, and over-time data. Second, traditional social network analysis (especially prior to the last couple of decades)[1] has focused on static networks, whereas much of the work discussed here focuses on the processes by which networks change or emerge. While ongoing data collection and analysis are providing key new insights, researchers need new statistical methods, simulation models, and visualization techniques to handle such dynamic data and to use these data to reason about change. Third, social network theories are beginning to outstrip the measures and data. For example, theories often posit ties as being flexible, probabilistic, or scaled; most data and metrics, however, are still based on binary data.

Session I: Social Network Theory Perspectives

Presenters and Papers

Discussant: Ronald Breiger

1. Linton C. Freeman, *Finding Social Groups: A Meta-Analysis of the Southern Women Data*
2. Harrison C. White, *Autonomy vs. Equivalence Within Market Network Structure?*
3. Noah E. Friedkin, *Social Influence Network Theory: Toward a Science of Strategic Modification of Interpersonal Influence Systems*
4. David Lazer, *Information and Innovation in a Networked World*

Themes

The papers in this session illustrate the breadth of areas that can be addressed by social network analysis. On one hand, the work can be used to explain, predict, and understand the behavior of small groups and the influence of group members on one another, as seen in the work of Freeman and Friedkin. On the other hand, social network analysis can be "writ large" and applied at the market or institutional level, as described in the papers by White and Lazer. Regardless of network size, all four papers demonstrate that a structural analysis that focuses on connections can provide insight into how one person, group, or event can and does influence another. These people or groups or events cannot, and do not, act in an autonomous fashion; rather, their actions are constrained by their position in the overall network, which is in turn constrained by the other networks and institutions in which they are embedded (the overall ecology). Further, the papers presented in this session review the range of methodologi-

[1]Early work on dynamic modeling was done by P.S. Holland and S. Leinhardt (A dynamic model for social networks, *Journal of Mathematical Sociology* 5:5-20, 1977).

cal approaches and styles of analysis that are compatible with a social network approach. Unlike many other scientific methods, the social network approach can be used with ethnographic and field data (Freeman), experimental laboratory data (Friedkin), historical examples (White), and policy/technology evaluation (Lazer).

Freeman provided a framework for assessing comparative analyses of a long-standing object of sociological theory—the small social collectivity characterized by interpersonal ties. White integrated theoretical perspectives on a network-based sociology of markets and firms. Friedkin advocated applications of social influence network theory to problems of network modification. Lazer considered governance questions arising from the "informational efficiency" of different network architectures (spatial, organizational, emergent) and the prospects of "free riding"—governments becoming complacent about innovating in the hope that another government will bear the cost of a successful innovation. Three major themes crosscut these papers and the resultant discussion.

Scaling up and uncertainty. How well do the different analytical techniques and algorithms "scale up" to large networks with hundreds or thousands of actors and multiple types of relations? Perhaps a more useful phrasing of this question is, *Under what conditions* and *for which analytical purposes* do models of social networks scale up, and how well do existing techniques deal with uncertainty in information? Spirited discussion arose in response to the question of whether the same social network model may be posed at "micro" and "macro" levels of social organization, or whether scaling up must involve the addition of substantially more complex representation of social structure within the network model.

White's model requires the analyst to account explicitly for the varied circumstances of particular industries. In his work, markets constructed among firms in networks are mapped into a space of settings with interpretable parameters that govern the ratio of demand to producers' costs; key parameters pertain to growth in volume and to variation in product quality. White's model is also distinctive in treating uncertainty not as a technical problem implicated in parameter estimation (statistical models being a main concern of the second and third sessions of this workshop), but as a substantive force that drives the evolution of ranking and manipulation as organizing features of a space of markets. During discussion, White expressed the view that scaling up is indeed a formidable challenge.

Friedkin, on the other hand, felt that the only practical constraint on social influence models is the problem of data-gathering ability. Friedkin's social influence network theory describes an influence process in which members' attitudes and opinions on an issue change recursively as the members revise their positions by taking weighted averages of the positions of influential fellow members. One example of an application would be producers who eye, and orient to, their competitors while figuring out the cost of their product, as in White's market model. The mathematics is general—Friedkin suggested applications to the modification of group structure such that, for example, outcomes are rendered less sensitive to minor changes in influence structure or to initial opinions of group members. However, Friedkin's model focuses on convergent interpersonal dynamics rather than on the structuring of qualitatively distinct network outcomes, as in White's market ecology.

Network outcomes. Both Lazer and Friedkin argued that the partial structuring of interdependence, a definitive aspect of social networks, must be taken into account in theorizing the production of outcomes. Taking innovative information, such as knowledge of policies or innovations that work as a desired network outcome, Lazer's paper asks how interdependence can be governed in large and complex systems. Lazer develops the argument that, where the production of information requires costly investment, there is a paradoxical possibility that the more efficient a system is at spreading information, the less new information the system might generate. This suggests that in networked (as distinct from hierarchical) worlds, incentives should be provided to continue experimenting with innovations.

Breiger suggested the benefits of a comparative reading of Lazer's paper and Friedkin's: In Friedkin's model the dependent variable is actor opinions at equilibrium; in Lazer's, it is knowledge created by or held by actors. Can the free riding that motivates Lazer's rational actors be usefully applied to suggest processes that structure the interior of Friedkin's influence networks? Conversely, can Friedkin's model provide a concrete format for specifying Lazer's theories of information interdependency?

Meta-analysis of network analysis methods. Freeman was able to locate 21 analyses of the same data set (concerning the participation of women in social events in a southern city in the 1930s). He examined these studies by use of a form of meta-analysis, but it is an unusual form in that multiple analytic techniques are applied to a single data set. There is an underlying dimension on which the analytic methods converge, and the several most effective techniques allow identification of a single (and, in this convergent sense, most informed) description of the data. Generally, the "best" of these 21 analytic procedures agree more with one another than with the anecdotal description supplied by the original data gatherers. The possibility is raised that in certain circumstances (perhaps in cases where the various methods applied yield results that are not too far from the true network structure) the intensive application of multiple analytic methods may compensate for problems in data quality.

Session II: Dynamic Social Networks

Presenters and Papers

Discussant: Stanley Wasserman

1. Jeffrey C. Johnson, *Informal Social Roles and the Evolution and Stability of Social Networks* (coauthors Lawrence A. Palinkas and James S. Boster)
2. Kathleen M. Carley, *Dynamic Network Analysis*
3. Tom A.B. Snijders, *Accounting for Degree Distributions in Empirical Analysis of Network Dynamics*
4. Michael W. Macy, *Polarization in Dynamic Networks: A Hopfield Model of Emergent Structure* (coauthors James A. Kitts and Andreas Flache)
5. Martina Morris, *Local Rules and Global Properties: Modeling the Emergence of Network Structure*
6. H. Eugene Stanley, *Threat Networks and Threatened Networks: Interdisciplinary Approaches to Stabilization and Immunization* (coauthor Shlomo Havlin)

Themes

The papers in this session address the evolution, emergence, and dynamics of network structure. Methods range across ethnography and participant observation, statistical modeling, simulation studies, and models employing computational agents. The methods are not mutually exclusive and were often used together to create a more complete understanding of the dynamics of social networks. Four themes emerged from these papers and the roundtable discussion.

What makes networks effective or ineffective? This theme added an explicitly dynamic focus to the "network outcomes" theme of the previous session. Various factors were considered, including the presence or absence of certain roles, structural characteristics (patterns of ties), and connections to other networks. The cross-cultural ethnographies of network evolution conducted by Jeffrey Johnson and his colleagues demonstrate that group dynamics can vary dramatically from one group to another even within the same physical and cultural setting and in the presence of similar organizational goals and formal structure. Johnson et al., studying Antarctic research station teams, found five features of emergent social roles that are associated with the evolution of effective networks: heterogeneity (such that members' roles fit in with one another), consensus (agreement on individuals' status and function), redundancy (such that removal of a single actor still ensures proper functioning, avoiding vulnerability), latency (promoting adaptive responses to unforeseen events), and isomorphism of formal and informal social roles (promoting agreement on group goals and objectives). The studies make use of quantitative modeling of network structures over time as well as direct observation over extended periods.

Multiagent network models are featured in the dynamic network analysis of Kathleen Carley and in the computational modeling of Michael Macy and his colleagues. Carley has formulated a highly distinctive approach to the dynamic modeling of social networks. Her simulation models and her formulation of ties among actors as probabilistic (such that connections can go away, get stronger, or change in strength dynamically over time) rather than deterministic allow her to investigate how networks may endeavor to regain past effectiveness (or to "regrow") to make up for destabilizing losses. "What if" exercises allow theoretical exploration of assumptions that an analyst makes about network vulnerabilities and about alternative distributions of resources, with reference to the system the analyst has constructed. For example, Carley found that removal of the most central node might leave a network less vulnerable than removal of an emergent leader.

Macy et al. studied conditions in which a group might be expected to evolve into increasingly antagonistic camps. Their computational model allows the manipulation of qualities attributed to agents—for example, their tendency to focus on a single issue, the degree of their conviction, and their rigidity or openness to influence from others. A surprising finding of this simulation study is that global alignment along a single polarizing definition of opposing ideologies is facilitated by ideological flexibility and open-mindedness among local constituents, as seen in the elegantly simple system of actors and relations postulated by the type of neural network employed by Macy et al.

Researchers in the statistical physics community have recently focused attention on "scale-free" social networks, characterized, as Eugene Stanley pointed out in his presentation, by a power-law distribution of ties emanating from the nodes, loosely analogous to an airline route map showing a very small number of well-connected "hubs" and many less well-connected nodes. It has been proven that scale-free networks are optimally resilient to random failure of individuals; Stanley and Havlin point out at the same time, however, that such networks are highly susceptible to deliberate attack. Under the assumption that social networks of people exposed to disease have the scale-free property, the authors review possible strategies for immunization.

Dynamics of local structure. The papers presented by Macy and by Carley also speak effectively to another theme that crosscut many of the papers in this session: the advancement of modeling techniques that focus on behavior among small sets of actors and on the implications of such local behavior for the evolution of a network macro-structure. This theme provides a dynamic cast to the ideas of "scaling up" presented in the first session. Computational models of social networks are precisely about exploring the evolution of whole systems on the basis of rules (such as when an actor should form a tie with another) and endowments postulated at the level of individual actors.

Coming from quite a different direction, that of the formulation of models that allow the fit of models to data to be assessed within a statistical context, Snijders' paper reports an investigation of network evolution on the basis of a stochastic, actor-oriented model that embeds discrete-time observations in an unobserved continuous-time network evolution process. Just one arc is added or deleted at any given moment, and actors are assumed to try to obtain favorable network configurations for themselves.

The paper by Martina Morris continues the focus on relating local rules to global structure, relying on empirical data (from sexual partner networks) and statistical modeling as well as simulations. Her question was whether the overall network structure can be explained by recourse to a small number of partnership formation rules that operate on the local, individual level. Two such rules were evinced in selective mixing patterns, such as the degree of matching on race or age, and the timing/sequencing of partnership formation (e.g., serial monogamy versus concurrency). Morris linked network data to network simulation by means of a statistical modeling framework: statistical models for random graphs as implemented via the Markov chain Monte Carlo (MCMC) estimation method. Putting together local rules and simulations based on random graph (statistical) methods allows empirical modeling of global networks on the basis of local properties.

Key features of networks in modeling evolution. Physicists including Stanley and Havlin, who have made many recent contributions to the modeling of scale-free networks, are interested in the dynamic evolution of degree distributions (number of ties emanating from each node). Sociologists tend to emphasize that other features of the network are also of great importance in network evolution, including the degree of transitivity (which is one way of measuring hierarchy), cyclicity (a hierarchy-defeating principle), segmentation into subgroups, and so on. In his paper, Snijders demonstrates that it is possible to formulate a model for network evolution in which the evolutionary process of the degree distribution is decoupled from other, arguably important, features of the network's evolution such as those mentioned above. Snijders' paper elaborates a statistical context within which the contribution of each of several features of network evolution might be comparatively assessed. Carley's paper elaborates mechanisms for evolution that draw on nonstructural properties such as individual learning and resource depletion, as well as exogenous changes such as the removal of specific nodes.

Simulation and computational-actor models versus validation and statistical models. A lively roundtable discussion of the six papers in this session focused in particular on the preceding theme and on the relative merits of conceptual modeling versus validation techniques. It was argued, on one hand, that an emphasis on validation is healthy because the analyst can be in a position to distinguish real patterns from mere noise or from wishful thinking. On the other hand, it was argued that simulations can help an analyst to explore the logic of postulated mechanisms that may be driving an empirical result, and to explore realms of the possible rather than predicting the future of a specific event or action. Such predictions are generally not possible outcomes of simulation studies. It was argued that each broad project approach (statistical rigor and simulations that explore various insights) is valuable, as are efforts to integrate them more closely. As more data become publicly available to the social networking community, they can be used to improve both simulation and statistical techniques.

Session III: Metrics and Models

Presenters and Papers

Discussant: Philippa Pattison

1. Stanley Wasserman, *Sensitivity Analysis of Social Network Data and Methods: Some Preliminary Results* (coauthor Douglas Steinley)
2. Andrew J. Seary and William D. Richards, *Spectral Methods for Analyzing and Visualizing Networks: An Introduction*
3. Mark S. Handcock, *Assessing Degeneracy in Statistical Models for Social Networks*
4. Stephen P. Borgatti, *The Key Player Problem*
5. Elisa Jayne Bienenstock and Phillip Bonacich, *Balancing Efficiency and Vulnerability in Social Networks*
6. Christos Faloutsos, *ANF: A Fast and Scalable Tool for Data Mining in Massive Graphs* (coauthors Christopher R. Palmer and Phillip B. Gibbons)

Themes

The papers in this session present methodological developments at the forefront of efforts to construct statistical models and metrics for understanding social networks. Although a number of papers in the other sessions also contributed significantly to this effort, a key distinction between these papers and those in the other sessions is that they focus on what can be learned if we only have network data. At least four important themes guiding the development of new models and metrics can be identified.

Exploratory data analysis (EDA) for networks. The first is the development of techniques that fall under the broad class of methods for exploratory data analysis (EDA) for networks. Such methods include descriptive measures and analyses that assist in summarizing and visualizing properties of networks and in investigating the dependence of such measures on other network characteristics. Under this general heading, Seary and Richards provided a comprehensive review of what can be learned from spectral analyses of matrices related to the adjacency matrix of a network. They also illustrated the application of these analyses to empirical networks using the computer program NEGOPY (a key concept in this program is that of liaisons). Faloutsos summarized a number of relationships between node measures (such as degree of connectivity and the "hop exponent") and their frequency in power-law terms and presented a fast algorithm for computing the approximate neighborhood of each node. Wasserman and Steinley presented the first stages of a study designed to explore the "sensitivity" of network measures by assessing the variation in some important network statistics (e.g., degree centralization, "betweenness" centralization, and proportion of transitive triads) as a function of specified random graph distributions.

Model development and estimation. The second guiding theme is the value of developing plausible models for social networks whose parameters can be estimated from network data. Mark Handcock outlined the general class of exponential random graph models and presented a compelling analysis of difficulties associated with estimating certain models within the class. He showed how model degeneracy—the tendency for probability mass to be concentrated on just a few graphs—interferes with approaches to apply standard simulation-based estimation approaches, and he described an important alternative model parameterization in which such problems can be handled.

Impact of network change on network properties. A third theme underlying the work presented in this session is the importance of understanding how different measures of network structure change following "node removal" or "node failure." For example, Borgatti considered two versions of the "key player" problem: Given a network, find a set of k nodes that, if removed, maximally disrupts communication among remaining nodes or is maximally connected to all other nodes. He proposed distance-based measures of fragmentation and reach as relevant to these two versions of the key-player problem and presented an algorithm for optimizing the measures as well as several applications.

Bienenstock and Bonacich contrasted the notions of efficiency and vulnerability in networks, and of random and strategic attack, and examined the efficiency and resilience of four network forms—random, scale-free, lattice, and bipartite—under both forms of attack. A distance-based efficiency measure—similar to Borgatti's fragmentation measure—was proposed and vulnerability was measured as the average decrease in efficiency of the network after a sequence of successive attacks. Bienenstock and Bonacich found that, of the class of networks assessed, scale-free networks were most susceptible to attack, and lattice and bipartite models with a small proportion of random ties offered the best balance of efficiency and resilience.

Finally, Faloutsos examined three types of network node failure: random, in order of degree, and in order of approximate neighborhood size. He argued that the Internet at the router level was robust in the case of random node failure but sensitive to the other two forms.

In the roundtable discussion, it was noted that the research topic of network vulnerability appears to be an emerging area in which there are many useful, and usefully interrelated, results, with reference in particular to the papers by Borgatti and by Bienenstock and Bonacich in this session, as well as to those by Carley and by Stanley and Havlin in the previous session. Fast algorithms such as those developed by Faloutsos and colleagues are necessary to extend these investigations to very large contexts such as the Internet.

Processes or flows on networks. A fourth theme is the importance of distinguishing the structure of a network from the different types of dynamic processes or flows that the network might support. Borgatti described a framework for distinguishing different interpersonal processes (e.g., disease transmission, dissemination of knowledge) that might involve network partners and considered the implications of such distinctions for analyses of network structure.

Session IV: Networked Worlds

Presenters and Papers

Discussant: David Lazer

1. Alden S. Klovdahl, *Social Networks in Contemporary Societies*
2. David Jensen, *Data Mining in Social Networks* (coauthor Jennifer Neville)
3. Peter D. Hoff, *Random Effects Models for Network Data*
4. Carter T. Butts, *Predictability of Large-Scale Spatially Embedded Networks*
5. Noshir S. Contractor, *Using Multi-Theoretical Multi-Level (MTML) Models to Study Adversarial Networks* (coauthor Peter R. Monge)
6. Michael D. Ward, *Identifying International Networks: Latent Spaces and Imputation* (coauthor Peter D. Hoff and Corey Lowell Lofdahl)

Themes

The papers in this session focus on the modeling of large-scale social networks. It is important to stress that tools and data sets for addressing large-scale networks are still in their infancy. An overarching concern is the extent to which standard social network metrics provide information in large-scale networks. A related need is publicly available, large-scale network data sets that can serve as examples for systematic comparative methodological analysis. Four themes emerged from the papers and the roundtable discussion in this session.

Understanding the structure of large-scale networks. Klovdahl's paper demonstrates how social structure can be exploited to obtain a sample of a large-scale network. In random-walk sampling, a small set of persons is randomly sampled from a large population and interviewed; from the contacts provided by each interviewee, one is randomly selected for an interview, and this process is repeated until chains of (say) length 2 are constructed. In essence, this procedure allows observation of random sets of *connected* nodes, which provide the basis for statistical inferences of the structural properties of large networks.

The feature of structure addressed in the paper by Butts is geographical distance, which he discusses as a robust correlate of interaction (e.g., most participants in the 9/11 airplane hijackings were from a particular, relatively small region of Saudi Arabia). His paper models the predictive power of geographical distance in large-scale, spatially embedded networks, and argues that in many realistic situations distance explains a very high proportion of variability in tie density.

Understanding processes in large-scale networks. What are the processes that sustain large networks? Why do people maintain, dissolve, and reconstitute communication links as well as links to information? Contractor and Monge systematically reviewed large bodies of empirical literature and distilled many propositions concerning the maintenance and dissolution of links. To date, much research on social networks has looked at just one of these mechanisms at a time. Ironically, however, many of the mechanisms contradict one another. For example, creating a tie with someone because many others do so is consistent with social contagion theory but contradicts self-interest theories that suggest the marginal return from an additional tie would be slight. In their larger project, Contractor and Monge develop a framework that tests multiple theories such as these at multiple levels, allowing many theories to be brought to bear on the same data set.

Understanding data on large-scale networks. Papers by several participants present models, methods, and illustrative analyses oriented toward the study of large-scale networks. Jensen and Neville joined social network analysis with data mining and related techniques of machine learning and knowledge discovery in order to investigate large networks. At the intersection of statistics, databases, artificial intelligence, and visualization, data mining techniques have been extended to relational data. One example, useful in detecting cell phone fraud, is that fraudulent telephone numbers are likely to be not one but two degrees away (because various phone numbers are stolen but they tend to be used to call the same parties). Jensen's and Neville's paper reports their effort to predict an outcome (the success of a film) on the basis of a data set that interlinks features of a large network (such as movies, studios, actors, and previous awards). Whereas recent work in machine learning and data mining has made impressive strides toward learning highly accurate models of relational data, Jensen and Neville suggest that cross-disciplinary efforts that make good use of social network analysis and statistics should lead to even greater progress.

Hoff presented random effects modeling for social networks, which provide one way to model the statistical dependence among the network connections. The models assume that each node has a vector of latent characteristics and that nodes relate preferentially to others with similar characteristics. Hoff employs a Markov chain Monte Carlo (MCMC) simulation procedure to estimate the model's parameters.

Ward, Hoff, and Lofdahl report in their paper an application of Hoff's latent spaces model to data on interactions among primary actors in Central Asian politics over an 11-year period ending in 1999, based on 1 million iterations of the MCMC estimation procedure using geographic distance as the only covariate. Countries closer together in the dimensional space resulting from model estimation were predicted to have a higher probability of connection. Imputation techniques were investigated and found to predict ties that were not sampled. The paper provides a favorable initial application of the latent spaces model to a data context of interest.

A final observation from the resultant discussion concerned the similarities (which are very great) as well as the differences (which are nonetheless consequential) among the various statistical models, notably those of Handcock's and Hoff's papers as well as the random graph models presented by Wasserman, Pattison, and colleagues. In brief, the similarities concern the increased focus on formulating parametric models for random graphs within the exponential family. The differences pertain to different paths taken in the estimation of model parameters.

Understanding the adversary versus understanding ourselves. In the roundtable discussion, Lazer began his remarks by considering, in the post-9/11 context, the contributions that network analysis might make to decision makers who confront security challenges and suggested that the first problem to be considered is that of understanding the adversary. Severe information overload coupled with a great deal of missing or nonexistent data and the need for quick, real-time decisions are factors that hamper efforts to understand an adversary's vulnerabilities. Social network models cannot always lead an analyst to make a prediction that has perfect accuracy, but they can certainly improve the process of making such predictions by identifying relevant linkages and related sources of uncertainty that may be easily overlooked. For example, the paper by Ward and his colleagues provides a major extension to the usual international relations models that paradoxically ignore relational structures. Further, Butts was able in his paper to project the likely structure of a network based on a small amount of publicly available information.

Lazer then turned to the question of understanding ourselves, arguing that a different set of challenges is implicated in this second concern. Here the needs center around questions of who needs to coordinate, communicate, and cooperate. Challenges concern critical self-evaluation (turf issues, organizational cultures, entrenched constituencies), design challenges (including needs for security as well as coordination), and the ability to be up and running in real-time, emergent situations. An opportunity in this area is that there are many more chances to gather data. Therefore, in contrast to a project designed to understand the adversary's vulnerabilities, there are perhaps more obvious openings for data-analytic approaches and for rigorous research.

RESEARCH ISSUES AND PROSPECTS

In this final section we identify near-term prospects for improving social networks research that emerged from the workshop papers and discussion. In doing so we focus on three areas: formulation of models; data and measurement; and research relevant to national security needs. The concerns and questions that we identify, while voiced by various workshop participants speaking as individuals, do not represent conclusions or recommendations of the workshop itself.

Formulation of Models

Networks "Plus": Generalized Relational Structures

The social network community has often found it useful to view social networks as "skeletal" abstractions of a much richer social reality. An important question, though, is whether the extent to which attempts to model and quantify network properties can rely on the network observations alone or whether they would instead be enhanced by additional information about actors and ties and their embedding in other social forms (the constellation of which might be termed "generalized relational data structures"). In other words, to what extent do we need to develop a more systematic (and quantitative) understanding of such generalized relational data structures, such as the meta-matrix approach? Such an understanding could lead to the development of models and analytic approaches that reflect the social context in which networks reside and the interaction of network processes with other aspects of this reality, including the background, intentions, and beliefs of the actors involved and the cultural and geographical settings in which they find themselves. Breiger raised similar points in his opening address.

Processes on Networks

An important reason to examine network structure is that such examination provides an understanding of the constraints and opportunities for social and cognitive processes enacted through network ties. Yet there is a limited understanding of the extent to which we can predict the course of social and cognitive processes from network topology alone. Should we be engaging in empirical and methodological programs of study that enable us to articulate more clearly the relationship between network structure and various types of social processes in which we are interested? Research presented at this workshop demonstrates that models in which the network ties and other network-based diffusion or contagion processes coevolve significantly expand our ability to understand, interpret, and predict social and cognitive behavior. Further work involving empirical analysis, simulation, and statistical modeling in this area seems to hold particular promise.

Scaling Up

An evident theme emerging from Sessions I (Social Network Theory Perspectives) and II (Dynamic Social Networks) is the potential value of juxtaposing methods used to describe large-scale networks, primarily in physics and computer science, with methods for evaluating models for social networks at a smaller scale, primarily in the social sciences. A number of statistical models that have been developed for social networks of medium size have attempted to express network structure as the outcome of regularities in interactive interpersonal processes at a "local" level. Can we extend the focus of such statistical modeling approaches to develop theoretically principled and testable models for social networks at a larger scale and in the process evaluate some of the claims emerging from the more descriptive analyses? A number of network theories are based on cognitive principles and small-group social theory. As we move to large-scale networks does this microlevel behavior still appear, or does the variance inherent in human action cause such microbehavior to be lost as macrolevel bases for relations become visible?

Model Development and Evaluation

In addition to extending models to include richer sources of relational data, how can we best incorporate potentially more complex dependence structures and longitudinal observations? Can we develop measurement models for ties and structural models for networks that take account of measurement and sampling issues? Can we also develop more rigorous and diagnostic approaches to model evaluation? How can simulation studies be best utilized to contribute to the resolution of questions of model specification and evaluation for evolving networks? Can we evaluate the fit of power laws more carefully; indeed, can we construct *and evaluate* models predicting the emergence of scale-free networks? Furthermore, can we extend and possibly integrate the very different and distinctive programs of fruitful work currently being done (and presented at the workshop in papers by Carley, Faloutsos et al., Friedkin, Macy et al., Morris, Snijders, and Stanley and Havlin) in order to build models for the coevolution of network ties, actor orientations, and actor affiliations?

Modeling: Estimation and Evaluation

Significant issues that emerged from the workshop session on dynamic social networks are the complementarity of simulation from complex models for dynamic and interactive network-based processes (in order to understand model behavior) and the task of formulating models in such a way that model parameters can be estimated from observed data and model fit can be carefully evaluated. The potential value of developing, estimating, and evaluating models in conjunction with empirical data is evident, and a major research domain is the development of models for network observations that will allow us to close the gap between what can be hypothesized from simulation-based explorations of theoretical positions and what can be verified empirically from well-designed network studies.

Data and Measurement

The Design of Network Studies: Sampling Issues and Data Quality

A significant set of issues surrounds the question of network sampling. Although only a few presentations in this workshop directly addressed questions of sampling, such issues were always close to the surface. Networks rarely have boundaries, and almost all empirical networks have been based on sampling decisions or sampling outcomes of some form. A principled means for handling sampling issues would be very valuable and indeed is a natural extension of model-based formulations. Several factors that might be considered here include (1) the biases inherent in the collection of nodes and ties obtained by a given sampling procedure, (2) the tendency to over- or undersample certain types of relations, and (3) the extent to which such errors are uniformly distributed over the network or focused in some portion of the overall network.

Related issues concern missing data, unreliable data, and data arising from actors (ranging from school children to corporate executives) who may strategically misreport their ties. Methods for analyzing network data exhibiting these properties include intensive application of multiple analytic procedures to compensate for problems of data quality (see Freeman's paper and related discussion in Session I above); addition of actors by means of random-walk sampling (see discussion of Klovdahl's presentation in Session IV); and the possibility that missing links can be implied by the existence of other linkages, as reviewed in the section entitled "Data Quality and Network Sampling" in Breiger's opening address.

Important questions to address include: What methodological steps can be taken to minimize the consequences of missing nodes and tie measurement errors? Can we deal with missing data in model construction and develop model-based approaches to estimate missing data? Would it be prudent to develop more effective measurement strategies for each tie of interest, as well as models for the measurement of ties? How can we go about providing evidence for the validity of network measurement? Further, should we focus more effort on characterizing the multifaceted nature of network ties?

Network Estimation

It is important to note that most network studies are done in a "data greedy" fashion, with the result that the underlying network is mapped out or sampled at a fairly high level of accuracy. This is practical in some contexts, such as situations in which archival or observational data are available and reliable; however, it is likely to be highly impractical in many other contexts. Thus, it would be useful to specify systematically the classes or dimensions of networks that exhibit fundamentally different behavior. Which high-level indicators can be used to determine the location of an unobserved network of interest in this space of possibilities? In other words, what can be done to provide a first-order estimate of the shape of the unobserved network? What kinds of questions can be answered by having even this high-level estimate? Basic research both on characterizing the impact of networks and on their fundamental form would be useful in this regard.

Exploratory Data Analysis

In light of the issues summarized above, it will be important to consider how we can augment descriptive analyses of networks so as to incorporate information from other sources (e.g., node attributes, orientations and locations, tie properties, group and organizational affiliations). More generally, can we extend these approaches to more complex and longitudinal relational data structures, and can they be developed so as to assist in the evaluation and development of model-based approaches? Many visualization tools provide valuable means for the simultaneous presentation of relational and other data forms, but can their capacities be further enhanced? In relation to the notion of *resistance* of network statistics, is special treatment required for certain network concepts?

For example, many network analyses have been based on the role of cut points and bridge ties, observations that lead to statistics that may be inherently nonresistant (e.g., number of components, reachability, etc.). Should researchers identify observations associated with lack of resistance (e.g., investigate their measurement quality)?

Research Relevant to National Security

Impact of Network Change on Network Properties

What is learned by integrating an understanding of network "interventions" with a model-based approach? One of the core features of social networks is arguably their potential to self-organize, which is especially likely in response to an intervention. Research presented at this workshop illustrates the potential for network models, both simulation and mathematical, to be used to foreshadow the probable network response to various types of interventions such as the removal of a node that is high in centrality or cognitive load, a "key player." This work suggests that, to be effective, strategies for altering networks need to be tailored to the processes by which the networks change, recruit new members, and diffuse goods, messages, or services.

Stabilization and Destabilization Strategies

Basic research is needed to determine the set of factors that influence network stabilization and destabilization strategies. Papers in each of the workshop's four sessions address these concerns. A problem analogous to the "key player" problem that was not addressed at the workshop but is equally critical is the problem of the "key tie." Can we develop metrics to identify key ties and the impact of their removal or addition on the overall behavior of the network? What are the basic properties that make a group, an organization, or a community resilient, efficient, and adaptive? Can we identify network structures or roles in networks that optimize these properties? While the research on dynamic networks, both empirical and simulation, suggests that this is possible, there is still much work to be done. Can we combine our analysis of the consequences of network change with a model-based understanding of measurement error? Can we identify a program of empirical research that would evaluate predictions about the impact of diverse types of intervention under different levels and types of error?

Closing the Gap

As Carley emphasized in her closing address, the ideas, measures, and tools being developed by network analysts hold promise with respect to the needs of the defense and intelligence community. However, there is still a large gap. Fundamental new science on dynamic networks under varying levels of uncertainty is needed. To fill this gap, Carley suggested that new research featuring empirical studies, metrics, statistical models, computer simulations, and theory building are all needed.

How can the gap between scientific research on networks and national needs be narrowed? Carley put forward four proposals. First, universities need to produce more master's and Ph.D. students who are trained in social network analysis and who enter government work. Second, illustrative data sets that are suitable for dissemination within the community of networks researchers and that suggest the types of problems faced by the defense and intelligence community need to be made publicly available. Third, effort needs to be made to establish a dialogue with social networks researchers in which the needs of the defense and intelligence community can be articulated without compromising national security. Finally, academicians in this research area need to continue to strive for clarity in the articulation of the practical implications of their theoretical results.

PART II

Workshop Papers

Note: Part II contains the papers as submitted to the workshop.

OPENING ADDRESS

Emergent Themes in Social Network Analysis: Results, Challenges, Opportunities

Ronald L. Breiger
University of Arizona

On behalf of the Workshop participants, I thank Anne Mavor (Director, Committee on Human Factors, National Research Council / National Academy of Sciences) and Rebecca Goolsby (US Office of Naval Research) for organizing this Workshop.

After a brief introduction to network analysis, I will identify the results of this enterprise to date, emphasizing major themes that have emerged. I will then turn to scientific and research challenges that I see on the immediate horizon, and to those I perceive just beyond that horizon. Finally, I will point to opportunities.

Thinking about social networks is ubiquitous and of long standing. It may be said that kinship was the first social science, in that various peoples' own cultural constructions of their networks of kinship relations have seemed always to mix observation with analysis and with proclamation (White, 1992: 290; Freeman, 2003). The 17th-century philosopher, Spinoza, derived scores of logically interrelated propositions about a system that has the characteristics of a basic social network situation, a system consisting of multiple relations—such as loving, hatred, and envy—among multiple actors (notably an acting person, an other, and an object).[1] Spinoza's system is in many respects remarkably similar to the 20th-century theory of cognitive balance[2] that forms the backdrop to several papers presented at this Workshop. In Spinoza's conception, actors change their initial opinions on the basis of network structure, as in some contemporary forms of social influence modeling (see, e.g., Carley's and Friedkin's papers included in this volume), and multiple relations are key (which is the sense in which balance theory provides one foundation for the paper of Macy et al.). A science of networks did not emerge from Spinoza's speculative endeavor, or from the many others like it that are precursors of contemporary network studies. Lacking was a commitment to the systematic observation and modeling of actual behavior.

Military thinkers, too, have long found it natural to plan in terms of relations and forces. Clausewitz ([1832] 1976: 484) articulated a structuralist vision of warfare, writing that "in war, more than anywhere else, it is the whole that governs all the parts, stamps them with its character, and alters them radically." Keeping the dominant characteristics of both belligerents in mind, "out of these characteristics a certain center of gravity develops, the hub of all power and movement, on which everything else depends" (pp. 595-96). In countries subject to domestic strife, Clausewitz continued, the center of gravity is generally the capital city. Among alliances, it lies in "the community of interest," and in popular uprisings it is "the personalities of the leaders and public opinion." It is "against these that our energy should be directed" (p. 596). In sharp contrast to a concentrated network of forces, some more contemporary conflicts feature protagonists who seek to "attain decisive strategic advantage by exploitation of the strength of dispersed forces" (Boorman, 1969: 171). Two centuries after Clausewitz, social network modeling is aiding in a reformulation of the "center of gravity" concept so that it is applicable to extended command and control architectures (Dekker, 2001), and social network models of both concentrated and dispersed forces inform thinking about information warfare (Pew and Mavor, 1998:301-19), netwars (Arquilla and Ronfeldt, 2001), and the destabilization of networks (Carley et al., 2001).

Freeman (2003) presents a monographic treatment of the history of social network analysis; brief overviews are also available (Scott, 2000: 7-37; Wellman, [1988] 1997: 21-29). At the present time, the field is a recognized academic specialty pursued by a cross-disciplinary network of sociologists, anthropologists, organization analysts, social psychologists, physicists, statisticians, mathematicians, communication experts, and people from many other fields. Network analysts have a membership organization,[3] professional journals,[4] and a variety of university centers of research. Network researchers are likely to agree with anthropologist Mary Douglas (1973: 89) that "in a complex society, networks are the minimum level at which social relations can be investigated." Four characteristics of the contemporary paradigm on network analysis are identified by Freeman (2003): motivation by a structural intuition about specific relationships linking social actors; grounding in systematic empirical data; heavy reliance on graphic imagery; and use of mathematical and/or computational models.

Results

Especially from the 1960s onward, major advances as well as cumulative building of analytical methods and research findings have led to productive results in social network modeling. Overviews and full treatments are available elsewhere.[5] I will briefly identify six distinctive themes of network analysis that have emerged in recent decades.

1. Measures on nodes, arcs, and whole networks have been developed to exploit a variety of relational insights. For example, the "centrality" of an actor (call him Ego) as measured by the number of ties he receives from other actors is a notion that is quite distinct from the same actor's degree of "centrality" on the basis of the number of shortest paths through the network that connect pairs of actors and that include Ego as an intermediary. (This is the distinction between "degree" and "betweenness" variants of centrality; e.g., Freeman, 1979.) "Constraint" is a measure of the extent to which Ego is tied to people who are invested in other of Ego's contacts (Burt, 1992). The extent to which the acquaintance sets of two connected individuals overlap has been captured by the faction of triplets in a network that are transitive (Holland and Leinhardt, 1975), recently reintroduced as the "clustering coefficient" of Watts and Strogatz (1998). And entire networks may be characterized by their "density" of ties (the proportion of possible relationships among the actors that are observed to exist).

2. Analyses of role interlock have exploited the interpenetration of multiple networks (such as "liking" and "disliking") on a given population of actors. Boorman and White (1976) model role interlock by use of algebraic semigroups and homomorphisms; examples include the study of "strength of weak ties" among advice-seeking on community affairs, business partnerships, and social relations of the community influentials in two small cities (Pattison, 1993: 254). Recent studies of role interlock have made use of innovative statistical models for network analysis, as in Lazega and Pattison's (2001) study of work relations, advice-seeking, and friendship among partners and associates in three offices of a US law firm.

3. Concepts of equivalence form the link between the individual-level data on ties and connections, and the overall network macro-structure. Lorrain and White (1971: 80) sought to locate "sets of individuals ... who are placed similarly with respect to all other sets of individuals, to the extent that total relations and flows are captured by the aggregation of detailed relations consonant with those equivalence sets of individuals." Structural equivalence captures sets of actors each of whom has identical relations to all actors in a network of multiple types of tie. Automorphic equivalence identifies actors who have the same relation to similar types of others. (A good metaphoric example of automorphic equivalence is the quarterbacks of opposing football teams). More general forms of equivalence have also been developed (see, e.g., Batagelj et al., 1992; Borgatti and Everett, 1992; Pattison, 1993) and applied in studies such as Van Rossem's (1996) analysis of international diplomatic, military, and economic exchanges. Statistical estimation of models of network macro-structure has been an area of considerable progress (Nowicki and Snijders, 2001).

4. Duality refers to the idea (for example) that interpersonal networks based on common membership in groups may be turned "inside out" to reveal networks among groups based the number of members they share (Breiger, 1974; Pattison and Breiger, 2002). Thus, in addition to defining networks on persons, networks may be defined on linkages between different levels of structure. An example and extensions appear in Mische and Pattison's (2000) three-level study of social movement activists, their organizational memberships, and various projects in which they engaged. Statistical modeling of affiliation data has been developed and applied to study appearances of Soviet political elites at official and social events for 8 years during the Brezhnev era (Faust et al., 2002). Innovative sampling schemes and analytical frames have been developed for dual network situations (McPherson, 2001).

5. The study of social influence links networks of social relations to attitudes and behaviors of the actors (Marsden and Friedkin, 1994: 3; Robins et al., 2001). Analysts of social influence model how an actor's attitudes or opinions are adjusted to those of the others who have some influence on the actor (DeGroot, 1974). Friedkin formal theory (1998) models the equilibrium outcomes of influence processes and leads to testable predictions of opinion change. From a different perspective, one viewing an organization's members as interdependent entrepreneurs who cultivate status competition, Lazega (2001) studies collective action and the evolution of mechanisms for self-governance among peers in a "collegial" (non-hierarchical) organization. In their Workshop paper included in this volume, Michael Macy and his collaborators demonstrate how the study of evolving group polarization can benefit from the modeling of actors as computational agents.

6. Models and methods for visualizing networks have improved strikingly since Jacob Moreno introduced the sociogram in 1934. At that time the basic idea was to represent social actors by circles and relationships by arrows connecting the circles. Increasingly in recent times (see Freeman 2000), the barrier between visualization and formal modeling has been disappearing, as more powerful techniques for representation continue to be developed.

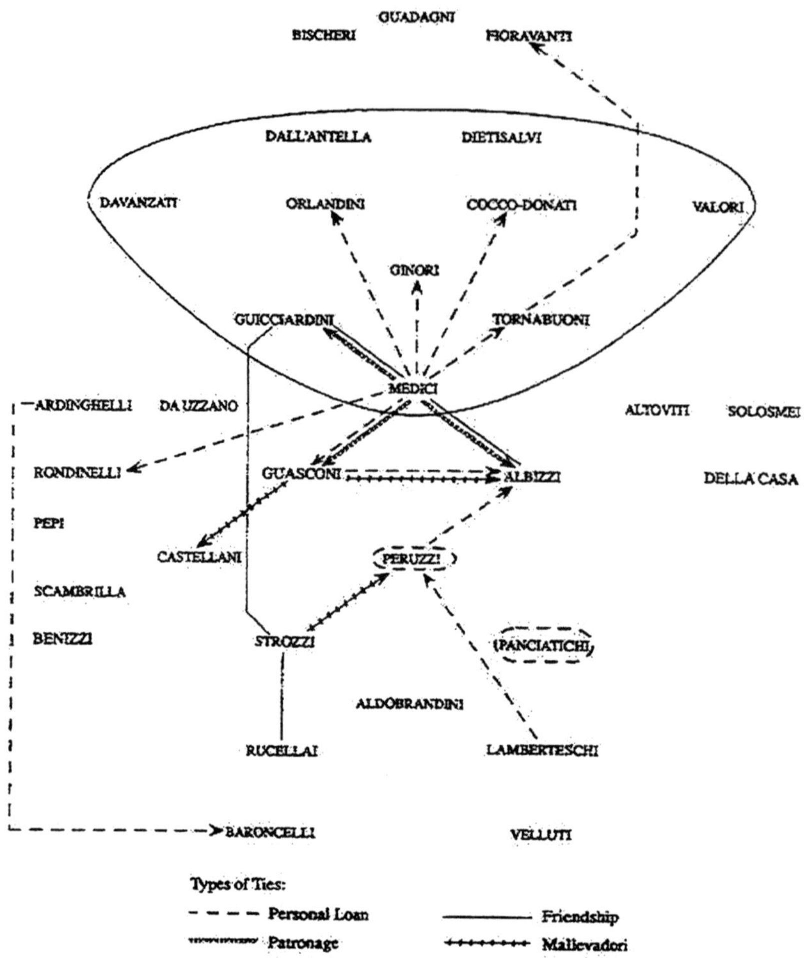

Figure 1. Florence network macro-structure. SOURCE: Figure 2.b on p. 1277 in J.F. Padgett and C.K. Ansell, in Robust Action and the Rise of the Medici, 1400-1434, *American Journal of Sociology* 98:1259-1319, 1993. Reprinted by permission.

An illustration of how various of these themes might combine in a research application is provided by Padgett and Ansell's (1993) study of the rise of the Medici family in fifteenth-century Florence. The data came (in some cases directly, in others via the work of historians) from the extensive archives in Florence, including tax assessments for the years 1403 and 1427 and a wealth of kinship, marriage, business, and census records. The data reflected in Figure 1 pertain to 92 families.

With respect to multiple networks: The graph in Figure 1 reports relations (coded separately) of personal loans, patronage, friendship (coded by historians from extensive personal letters that have been preserved), and the posting of surety bonds in another's behalf in order to guarantee good behavior. By hypothesis, each network reports a potentially different quality of relation, with the entire set of relations serving to comprise the structure.

With respect to types of equivalence: Padgett and Ansell develop a method for aggregating the 92 families into structurally equivalent sets relying heavily on their external ties with outsiders, as well as on their internal relations. Figure 1 thus reports a macro-structure, a reduced-form visualization of the network of relations among the identified aggregates of families.

With respect to network measures: The authors report that, among the Medicean families at the top of Figure 1, Freeman's measure of "betweenness" centrality (C_B) is .362 for intermarriages among the families; for the remaining families in the figure, it is a much lower .198. The import is that the Medici family connected many other families that had few ties among themselves; they served as a hub for this portion of the structure.

The authors' interpretation is roughly as follows. The traditional oligarchical families portrayed in the lower portion of Figure 1 were highly interconnected. Dense ties, however, did not lead to cohesive collective action in time of crisis, given the many status equals among the oligarghs, each with a plausible claim to leadership. In sharp contrast, the Medici family stood as the gateway from its followers to the rest of the structure. This was an extraordinarily centralized "star" or "spoke" system, with very few direct relations among the Medici partisans. Thus, the rise of the Medici corresponded to a network strategy in which their follwers were kept structurally isolated from one another (see also Padgett, 2001).

In my summary characterization of the results of social network analysis, I have recourse to the subtitle of Wasserman and Faust's (1994) 800-page compendium: "Methods and Applications." I believe we now have a productive array of distinctive tools with which to build impressive analyses along many lines of inquiry. Before we move to a qualitatively higher level of progress in theoretical development, certain extant challenges will have to be met, and it is to these that I now turn.

Challenges on the Horizon

Here I focus on scientific and research challenges on the immediate horizon, in the areas of statistical modeling, data quality, and network sampling. A number of Workshop participants are in the process of making breakthroughs in these areas.

Statistical Modeling

Statistical analysis of network ties is both important and difficult. It is important (among other reasons) because it can allow us to distinguish pattern from random noise, and because it enables us to assess comparatively a variety of hypotheses about the structures that underlie or generate the network data that we observe. It is difficult because the units of observations (such as the tie from person A to B and those from A to C and from B to A) are not independent.

Efforts dating from the 1930s to model the distribution of ties received by actors in social networks (such as the binomial model of Paul Lazarsfeld's reported in Moreno and Jennings, 1938) recognized that "a change in position of one individual may affect the whole structure."[6] A major line of investigation in the 1970s (e.g., Holland and Leinhardt, 1975) sought network inferences from a more realistic embedding of non-independent relationships within triads of social actors. In a major breakthrough, Holland and Leinhardt (1981) formulated an exponential family of models (which they termed the p_1 family) that provided estimation of the probability of an observed network conditioned on the number of ties sent and received by each actor (and the network's overall density) and, simultaneously, on the two-person configurations (mutual, asymmetric, and null-choice dyads) among the actors. Application of the model led to some substantively important research, for example on decision-making in organizational fields (Galaskiewicz and Wasserman, 1989).

Three problems with the p_1 model were to motivate further work. First, the advances of Holland and Leinhardt's 1981 model entailed a return to the assumption of dyadic independence (the assumption, e.g., that person A's choice of B is independent of A's choice of C), which is surely unrealistic in many contexts. Second, because p_1 is essentially a null model, its ability to characterize actual network data was poor. Third, degrees of freedom for assessing the overall fit of these model often depended on the number of actors in the network, thus violating the usual assumptions about asymptotics in maximum likelihood estimation.

Recent work constituting fully a new breakthrough, however, has allowed the assumption of dyadic independence to be rendered unnecessary in new families of more realistic models based on hypotheses about the precise nature of network dependencies.[7] These new models, as formulated in particular by Wasserman, Pattison, and Robins (Wasserman and Pattison, 1996; Pattison and Wasserman, 1999; Robins et al., 1999) go under the name of random graph models or p^* models. Formulating applications of these models to diverse network contexts, as well as issues pertaining to estimation of the models, characterizes major challenges for current network research. Because a number of papers presented at this Workshop pertain to these challenges, I will continue with a brief characterization of such models.[8]

It is useful for those without a strong statistics background to keep in mind that these random graph (or p^*) models encode hypotheses that "you can get your hands on," hypotheses concerning definite features of observed social relations. Each such model asserts that a specific collection of simple, concrete structures (termed "configurations") compose the network as a whole. Single networks as well as networks of multiple types of relation (such as co-worker and socializing, in Lazega and Pattison's 2001 study of 71 partners and associates in a law firm with offices in three cities) may be modeled with this approach.

There is also an equilibrium aspect to these random graph models, in that the presence or absence of each possible tie in the network is estimated conditioning on the rest of the data. It may be the case that, once these configurations are specified by an analyst, very standard methods of estimation ("logit regression") are applicable. However, the resulting estimates do not satisfy some of the usual assumptions (they are pseudo-likelihood estimates rather than full maximum likelihood), and this point has occasioned a good deal of additional work, some of which is reported at this Workshop.

Several of the Workshop papers included in this volume may be located with respect to the challenges of statistical modeling that I have reviewed. In his paper, Mark Handcock investigates some of the consequences (for what he terms the degeneracy of the estimation process) that result from the use of pseudo-likelihood estimation. He makes use of simulation methods, known as Markov Chain Monte Carlo (MCMC) methods, that allow estimation of parameters such that the estimates are constrained to the non-degenerate part of the model space. In his paper, Peter Hoff reviews an approach (a form of generalized linear mixed-effects models) that he and his colleagues see as having particularly feasible means of exact parameter estimation. An application of this approach—to modeling political interactions of the primary actors in Central Asian politics over the period 1989-1999—is presented in the paper of Michael Ward and Peter Hoff in this volume.

Tom Snijders has developed a model for the statistical evaluation of network dynamics that has a certain relation to the random graph (p*) models (see Snijders, 2001: 388-89). In his Workshop paper included in this volume Snijders applies his model to the study of network evolution and, in particular, to the evolution of a network's degree distribution (the number of ties implicating each actor). Degree distribution has been the central focus of recent models of social networks that have been formulated by physicists (see Watts and Strogatz, 1998, and also the papers in this volume by Eugene Stanley and by Christos Faloutsos). One of Snijders' principal findings—that there is no general straightforward relation between the degree distribution on one hand and structural aspects of evolution on the other—continues the debate on the importance of degree distributions and, in particular, on whether such distributions provide a major key to (or even a "universal law" governing) the evolution of social networks.

In Snijders' paper as well as the paper of Martina Morris, the question of what sorts of parameterizations are appropriate for statistical models of social networks comes strongly to the foreground. Stanley Wasserman and Douglas Steinley begin building a framework for analysis how sensitive the results of network analysis are to the peculiarities of the dataset as well as to the parameters the analyst is attempting to estimate. Their paper in this volume reports, for example, that interaction between different graph statistics (such as centralization and transitivity) is crucial for robustness of estimation.

Elisa Jayne Bienenstock and Phillip Bonacich turn robustness from a technical issue to a substantive one. In their Workshop paper they report a simulation study of different network configurations (pinwheels, lattices, and so on). Their major measures are network efficiency and vulnerability. They find for example that centralized communication networks are more efficient but also more vulnerable to selective attacks on their most central members.

In another contribution that seeks to turn robustness from a technical issue to a substantive one, Stephen Borgatti's Workshop paper develops two versions of what Borgatti terms the key player problem: finding a set of nodes which, if removed, would maximally disrupt communication among the remaining nodes (KPP-1), and finding a set of nodes that is maximally connected to all other nodes (KPP -2).

The Workshop paper authored by Andrew Seary and William Richards reviews eigenvector decomposition methods for network analysis. Their paper also moves in the direction of investigating conditions for network stability and its disruption, as with their report of a result from spectral decomposition that may be used to solve the longstanding problem of dividing a network into two sets with minimal connectivity between them.

Pattison and Robins (2002; see also Robins et al., 2001) have explored various sorts of non-network information that can be incorporated into random-graph models—information such as actor attributes, affiliations of persons with groups, and spatial layouts. Research on the relation between geographic spatial arrangements and social networks is rapidly advancing

(Faust et al., 1999). In his paper for this Workshop, Carter Butts presents some fundamental results on the relation of physical distance to network evolution. At least implicitly, this work seems beneficial for the formulation of spatially oriented random graph models.

Data Quality and Network Sampling

Social networks have been measured in many ways, and the available research indicates that these can make some claim to being reliable, though certainly imperfect, measures (Marsden, 1990: 456). A continuing challenge for network analysts is the formulation of methods for the study of network data that are less than pristine with respect to reliability and validity. Applications of network modeling to situations of increasing realism have heightened concerns about missing data, data that seem unreliable, and actors (ranging from schoolchildren to corporate executives) who may be behaving strategically in reporting or concealing their ties to others. Related challenges concern the representativeness of network data. Network analysts, including a number of Workshop participants, are currently engaged in confronting these challenges.

Linton Freeman's paper for this Workshop reports a meta-analysis of twenty-one methods applied to a single affiliation network. Assuming that there is a "true" answer to the question of whether each pair of persons belongs together in the same group, Freeman employs a procedure—termed consensus analysis (Batchelder and Romney, 1988)—that allows (simultaneously) the pooling of results from the twenty-one methods to uncover the most likely candidates for "true" answers, and also quantitative assessment of the "competence" of each of the twenty-one methods. Freeman's paper thus suggests that, in some situations (perhaps those in which the various methods applied are in the vicinity of the correct analysis of a structure), intensive application of multiple analytical methods can compensate for data that are less than perfect.

In her Workshop paper, Martina Morris is particularly interested in two rules governing partner selection in sexual transmission networks: concurrency (number of partners) and mixing (the extent to which both partners share an attribute, such as race). These are examples of network properties that can be measured with "local" network sampling strategies; they do not require data on all relations of all people in a network. Going further, Morris writes that "if simple local rules [such as concurrency and mixing] govern partner selection, then these also determine the aggregate structure in the network: What looks like an unfathomably complicated system is, in fact, produced by a few key local organizing principles." In her paper included in this volume, Morris combines this "local rules" approach with random graph models and simulation strategies to understand the emergence of overall network structuring.

Robins, Pattison, and Woolcock (2002) provide random graph (p*) models for network data containing non-respondents, without having to assume that the respondents missing are a random sample. An earlier effort along a somewhat similar line is that of Friedkin (1998: 77-78).

Cognitive social structure (Krackhardt, 1987; see also Carley and Krackhardt, 1996) is an analytical approach associated with a distinctive format of data collection. Each individual in a network is asked to provide reports of whether each individual has a relationship with each other. Thus, each individual reports a full matrix of data. This approach has implications for the analysis of data quality.[9] Define there to be "consensus" (Krackhardt, 1987: 117) on the tie from person i to person j if at least a stipulated fraction of all network members report that i indeed sends that tie to j. This allows a calibration of self-reports against the reports of others.

In his Workshop paper included in this volume, Alden Klovdahl reviews studies that employ random walk sampling designs, which involve random selection of a very small number of individuals from a large population. Each person is interviewed in order to obtain (among other things) a list of network associates. One of these is randomly selected to be the next person interviewed, and so forth. Klovdahl discusses in his paper how he used just 180 interviews (60 random walks of 2 steps each) to study network properties of a city of a quarter-million people.

All of the above efforts respond to the challenge of analyzing network data that is of less than perfect quality. It will also be useful to encourage studies (such as the one of Costenbader and Valente, 2002) of the comparative performance of network measures (such as various measures of actor centrality) in the presence of increasing amounts of missing data.

Challenges Just Over the Horizon

I will now turn to scientific and research challenges that I envision as just beyond our current horizon. These concern efforts to significantly extend, or to generalize or to move beyond, the social networks paradigm as outlined in the first major section above. Here too, the Workshop participants are among those leading the way.

1. There is increasing interest in moving beyond the analysis of social networks to consider questions of how such analyses relate to design issues. Principles of network governance may be extended to the consideration of how criminal or terrorist networks might function most effectively (Milward and Raab, 2002). Asking what makes a network effective, Arquilla and Ronfeldt (2001: 324-43) point to five levels: organizational (where leadership resides; how hierarchical dynamics may be mixed in with network dynamics), narrative (not simply a "line" with a "spin," but grounded expression of participants' experiences, interests, and values), doctrinal (for example, preference for a leaderless form), technological (for example, use of couriers or the internet to connect people), and social (for example, the use of kinship or bonding experiences as bases for trust). In his Workshop paper included in this volume, David Lazer is concerned with governance issues involved in information diffusion among policy agencies. In their Workshop paper, Noshir Contractor and Peter Monge raise the question of how theories of underlying network dynamics need to be modified to be applicable to the study of adversarial networks. Of particular interest, Contractor and Monge formulate numerous testable hypotheses drawn from a wide range of substantive theories, all pertaining to modeling the emergence of networks within their multi-theoretical, multi-level (MTML) model.

2. Dynamic Network Analysis (DNA) is the name that Kathleen Carley gives to her highly distinctive, highly innovative effort to push the envelope on network analysis. Not

directly related to models of network dynamics such as Snijders' (reviewed in the previous section), Carley's approach has three hallmarks. First, it is meta-matrix, in a dramatic extension of the "duality" concept discussed in the first section above. The meta-matrix includes matrices relating people to people (social networks), people to knowledge (knowledge networks), people to events (attendance networks), events to each other (temporal ordering), and more. Second, the ties in the meta-matrix are defined probabilistically, on the basis of cognitive inferencing or cognitive change models or Bayesian updating techniques. Third, Carley's approach employs multi-agent network models; for example, learning mechanisms are specified and used to dynamically adjust networks as the computational agents in them attend events, learn new information, or are removed from the network. One principal focus of Carley's approach is the cognitive, and to a lesser extent the social, processes by which the networks in the meta-matrix evolve.

As is Kathleen Carley, Michael Macy is a leader in the area of self-organizing networks and computational agents. In his Workshop paper coauthored with James Kitts and Andreas Flache, Macy *et al.* model evolving polarization of group opinion space. They report some surprising disjunctions between interactions among the actors, on one level, and the emerging group structuring, on the other.

3. "At the beginning of the 21st century, a maverick group of scientists is discovering that all networks have a deep underlying order and operate according to simple but powerful rules. This knowledge promises to shed light on the spread of fads and viruses, the robustness of ecosystems, the vulnerability of economies—even the future of democracy." Thus reads the dust jacket of a recent popularized account (Barabási, 2002) of work by several researchers trained in physics who have developed distinctive lines of modeling for social (and other) networks. Beginning with regular structures on the one hand and random structures on the other, researchers within this new tradition (Watts and Strogatz, 1998) show that introducing small changes into the "regular" structure leads to massive change—this is the "small world" network with a few "shortcuts" that bridge the structure. Researchers in this tradition emphasize power-law distributions of choices made by actors (this is the "scale-free" property), according to which a very few actors have a great many ties (in rough analogy to route maps of airlines that have "hub" systems). These writers demonstrate that such networks have important implications for diffusion of diseases and for many other properties such as those alluded to in the quotation at this paragraph's beginning.

In their paper for this Workshop, E. Eugene Stanley and Shlomo Havlin review advances in the modeling of scale-free networks and related work, and they propose a trajectory of future research aimed at understanding how to optimize the stability of threatened netoworks. And the Workshop paper of Christos Faloutsos and his co-authors reviews a wide range of results concerning power laws applied to network data, in research that combines network analysis and graph mining. I believe that these papers should be read in conjunction with that of Snijders, who argues (convincingly, in my view) for the desirability of a dynamic modeling context that explicitly incorporates features (such as transitivity, cyclicity, and subgrouping) in addition to the degree distribution that is emphasized in physicists' models.

4. Moving beyond a structural approach to social network analysis by directly engaging cultural issues is a challenge that is increasingly attracting attention.[10] The emphasis of network analysis on formal aspects of social structure often seems the opposite of a concern for culture and cognition; indeed, in the early work on structural equivalence "the cultural and social-psychological meanings of actual ties are largely bypassed .... We focus instead on interpreting the patterns among types of tie" (White et al. 1976: 734). However, over the past decade a fusion of concern across structural modeling and problems of culture, cognition, action, and agency has been among the most important developments for an influential segment of the community of networks researchers.

An important spur to network thinking about culture and cognition was White's rethinking of network theory in his 1992 volume *Identity and Control*. White now wrote of agency as "the dynamic face of networks," as motivating "ways of ... upend[ing] institution[s] and ... initiat[ing] fresh action" (pp. 315, 245). White (1992) considered discursive "narratives" and "stories" to be fundamental to structural pursuits, writing that "stories describe the ties in networks" and that "a social network is a network of meanings" (pp. 65, 67). Emirbayer and Goodwin (1994), who characterized *Identity and Control* in exactly this way (p. 1437), went on to prod network analysts to conceptualize more clearly the role of "ideals, beliefs, and values, and of the actors that strive to realize them" (p. 1446). A more extensive review of this direction for extending social network research is provided in Breiger (2003).

The Workshop paper of Jeffrey Johnson, Lawrence Palinkas, and James Boster moves in a sense in the "opposite" direction: extending rigorous structural conceptions into the analysis and interpretation of cross-cultural studies on the evolution of informal group roles in Antarctic research stations. One finding for example is that groups that have a rich mix of informal role properties fare better.

5. Actor-Network Theory (ANT) is an orientation within the "post-modern" branch of contemporary science studies. The term "actor-network" is intended to mark the difficulties in establishing clear boundaries between network actors and connections, between agency and structure, and between network actors and those who analyze networks (Law and Hassard, 1999). Research within this tradition includes Latour's ([1984] 1988) rewriting of the history of Louis Pasteur as the interpenetration of networks of strong microbes with networks of weak hygienists, viewing the microbes as "a means of locomotion for moving through the networks that they wish to set up and command" (p. 45). This line of work has had no influence at all on social network analysts. There may however be some potential in developing formal, analytic models that incorporate insights from this tradition concerning the bridging of ties and connections, structure and agency, and reflexivity (relations between analysts and network actors).

Opportunities

I will conclude by summarizing my discussion of results and challenges, and by pointing to opportunities.

As to results, we now have a large number of spectacularly useful methods and applications. We have numerous studies of real-world processes. There is a remarkable degree of consensus among researchers on the fundamentals of the approach, and a notable cumulation of results.

The challenges that I see concern the development of research syntheses at the theory-data interface. We need improved network statistical models. We need to further the development of models that are at once validated, robust, and concerned with network dynamics. We need to continue to improve methods for dealing with network sampling. We need to continue to explore ways to significantly extend, or to generalize, or to move beyond the static social networks paradigm, by embedding network models and research within the wider array of concerns that I have sketched in the preceding section.

This Workshop will play an important role in furthering the kind of communication and interchange that is necessary, among many of the leading researchers in the field. In pointing to future opportunities, I will paraphrase David Lazer's paper, hoping that he won't mind that I take one of his conclusions slightly out of context, a conclusion that he labels a counterintuitive governance prescription. In my version, the conclusion is that as research groups receive more information regarding what other research groups are doing, incentives for all such groups to continue innovating, and thus creating knowledge, should be increased. Our opportunities lie in joining resources with innovation in pursuing the scientific challenges that confront us.

Endnotes

[1] For example, Proposition 35 in Spinoza's Ethic ([1677] 1923) reads: "If I imagine that an object beloved by me is united to another person by the same, or by a closer bond of friendship than that by which I myself alone hold the object, I shall be affected with hatred towards the beloved object itself, and shall envy that other person."

[2] Fritz Heider, who formulated balance theory in the 1940s, writes that he came to the theory by reading and reconsidering Spinoza's work (Heider, 1979).

[3] The International Network for Social Network Analysis (INSNA), web address http://www.sfu.ca/~insna/.

[4] Social Networks (published by Elsevier), the Journal of Social Structure (an electronic journal, available on-line at http://www2.heinz.cmu.edu/project/INSNA/joss/), and Connections (published by INSNA).

[5] See in particular the monographic reviews of Wasserman and Faust (1994), DeGenne and Forsé ([1994] 1999), and Scott (2000) as well as the succinct overviews of Wellman ([1988] 1997) and Breiger (2003).

[6] Information in this and the following paragraphs is condensed from the review of statistical modeling of networks in Breiger (2003).

[7] The analyst is allowed to specifiy dependencies among any ties in the network that share a node.

[8] See also the introduction in Anderson et al. (1999) as well as the cited papers of Wasserman, Pattison, and Robins.

[9] I am grateful to Philippa Pattison for reminding me of this point.

[10] This paragraph and the next draw directly on Breiger (2003).

References

Anderson, Carolyn J., Stanley Wasserman, and Bradley Crouch (1999) "A p^* primer: Logit models for social networks." Social Networks 21: 37-66.

Arquilla, John, and David Ronfeldt (2001). Networks and Netwars: The Future of Terror, Crime, and Militancy. Santa Monica, CA: RAND.

Barabási, Albert-László (2002). Linked: The New Science of Networks. Cambridge, MA: Perseus Publishing.

Batagelj, Vladimir, Patrick Doreian, and Anuška Ferligoj (1992). "An Optimizational Approach to Regular Equivalence." Social Networks 14: 121-135.

Batchelder, William H., and A. Kimball Romney (1988). "Test Theory without an Answer Key." Psychometrika 53: 71-92.

Boorman, Scott A. (1969). The Protracted Game: A Wei-Ch'i Interpretation of Maoist Revolutionary Strategy. New York: Oxford University Press.

Boorman, Scott A., and Harrison C. White (1976). "Social structure from multiple networks: II. Role structures." American Journal of Sociology 81:1384-1446.

Borgatti, Stephen P., and Martin G. Everett. (1992) "The Notion of Position in Social Network Analysis." Pp. 1-35 in Peter V. Marsden (ed.), Sociological Methodology 1992. London: Basil Blackwell.

Breiger, Ronald L. (1974). "The Duality of Persons and Groups." Social Forces 53: 181-90.

Breiger, Ronald L. (2003). "The Analysis of Social Networks." In Melissa Hardy and Alan Bryman, eds., Handbook of Data Analysis. London: Sage Publications, Ltd., in press.

Burt, Ronald S. (1992) Structural Holes: The Social Structure of Competition. Cambridge, MA: Harvard University Press.

Carley, Kathleen M., and David Krackhardt (1996). "Cognitive Inconsistencies and Non-Symmetric Friendship." Social Networks 18: 1-27.

Carley, Kathleen M., Ju-Sung Lee and David Krackhardt (2001). "Destabilizing Networks." Connections 24(3): 31-34.

Clausewitz, Carl von. ([1832] 1976). On War, tr. Michael Howard and Peter Paret. Princeton, NJ: Princeton University Press.

Costenbader, Elizabeth, and Thomas Valente (2002). The Effect of Sampling on Centrality Measures. Unpublished paper, Department of Preventative Medicine, University of Southern California.

DeGenne, Alain, and Michel Forsé ([1994] 1999). Introducing Social Networks. London: Sage Publications.

DeGroot, M.H. (1974) "Reaching a Consensus." Journal of the American Statistical Association 69: 118-121.

Dekker, Anthony (2001). "Applying Social Network Analysis Concepts to Military C4ISR Architectures." Connections 24 (3): 93-103.

Douglas, Mary (1973). Natural Symbols. Baltimore: Penguin Books.

Emirbayer, Mustafa, and Jeff Goodwin (1994). "Network Analysis, Culture, and Agency." American Journal of Sociology 99: 1411-53.

Faust, Katherine, B. Entwisle, R.R. Rindfuss, S.J. Walsh, & Y. Sawangdee, "Spatial Arrangement of Social and Economic Networks Among Villages in Nang Rong District, Thailand," Social Networks 21 (1999): 311-37.

Faust, Katherine, Karin E. Willert, David D. Rowlee and John Skvoretz (2002). "Scaling and Statistical Models for Affiliation Networks: Patterns of Participation among Soviet Politicians during the Brezhnev Era." Social Networks 24: 231-59.

Freeman, Linton C. (1979). "Centrality in Social Networks I. Conceptual Clarification." Social Networks 1: 215-39.

Freeman, Linton C. (2000). "Visualizing Social Networks." Journal of Social Structure 1 (electronic journal).

Freeman, Linton C. (2003). The History of Social Network Analysis. Unpublished manuscript. School of Social Sciences, University of California–Irvine.

Friedkin, Noah E. (1998). A Structural Theory of Social Influence. Cambridge University Press.

Galaskiewicz, Joseph, and Stanley Wasserman (1989). "Mimetic and Normative Processes wihin an Interorganizational Field: An Empirical Test." Administrative Science Quarterly 34: 454-479.

Heider, Fritz (1979). "On Balance and Attribution." Pp. 11-23 in Paul W. Holland and Samuel Leinhardt (eds.), Perspectives on Social Network Research. New York: Academic Press.

Holland, Paul W., and Samuel Leinhardt (1975). "Local structure in social networks." Pp. 1-45 in David R. Heise (ed), Sociological Methodology 1976. San Francisco: Jossey-Bass.

Holland, Paul W., and Samuel Leinhardt (1981). "An Exponential Family of Probability Distributions for Directed Graphs." Journal of the American Statistical Association 76:33-65.

Krackhardt, David (1987). "Cognitive Social Structures." Social Networks 9: 109-34.

Latour, Bruno ([1984] 1988) The Pasteurization of France, tr. Alan Sheridan and John Law. Cambridge, MA: Harvard University Press.

Law, John, and John Hassard, eds. (1999). Actor Network Theory and After. Oxford: Blackwell.

Lazega, Emmanuel (2001). The Collegial Phenomenon: The Social Mechanisms of Cooperation among Peers in a Corporate Law Partnership. Oxford University Press.

Lazega, Emmanuel, and Philippa E. Pattison (2001). "Social Capital as Social Mechanisms and Collective Assets: The Example of Status Auctions Among Colleagues." Pp. 185-208 in Nan Lin, Karen Cook, and Ronald S.Burt (eds.), Social Capital: Theory and Research. New York: Aldine de Gruyter.

Lorrain, François P., and Harrison C. White (1971). "Structural Equivalence of Individuals in Social Networks." Journal of Mathematical Sociology 1: 49-80.

Marsden, Peter V. (1990). "Network Data and Measurement." Annual Review of Sociology 16: 435-63.

Marsden, Peter V., and Noah E. Friedkin (1994). "Network Studies of Social Influence." Pp. 3-25 in Stanley Wasserman and Joseph Galaskiewicz (eds.), Advances in Social Network Analysis. Thousand Oaks, CA: Sage.

McPherson, J. Miller (2001) 'Sampling strategies for the arts: A hypernetwork approach', *Poetics* 28: 291-306.

Milward, H. Brinton, and Jörg Raab (2002). "Dark Networks: The Structure, Operation, and Performance of International Drug, Terror, and Arms Trafficking Networks." Unpublished paper, School of Public Administration and Policy, University of Arizona.

Mische, Ann, and Philippa E. Pattison (2000) "Composing a civic arena: Publics, projects, and social settings." *Poetics* 27: 163-194.

Moreno, Jacob L., and Helen H. Jennings (1938). "Statistics of Social Configurations." Sociometry 1:342-374.

Nowicki, Krzysztof, and Tom A.B. Snijders (2001). "Estimation and Prediction for Stochastic Blockstructures." Journal of the American Statistical Association 96: 1077-1087.

Padgett, John F. (2001). "Organizational Genesis, Identity, and Control: The Transformation of Banking in Renaissance Florence." Pp. 211-57 in James E. Rauch and Alessandra Casella (eds.), Networks and Markets. New York: Russell Sage Foundation.

Padgett, John F., and Christopher K. Ansell (1993). "Robust Action and the Rise of the Medici, 1400-1434." American Journal of Sociology 98: 1259-1319.

Pattison, Philippa E. (1993). Algebraic Models for Social Networks. Cambridge: Cambridge University Press.

Pattison, Philippa E., and Ronald L. Breiger (2002). "Lattices and Dimensional Representation: Matrix Decompositions and Ordering Structures." Social Networks 24: 423-44.

Pattison, Philippa , and Garry Robins (2002). "Neighborhood-Based Models for Social Networks." Pp. 301-37 in Sociological Methodology 2002, ed. R.M. Stolzenberg. Boston: Blackwell.

Pattison, Philippa, and Stanley Wasserman (1999). "Logit Models and Logistic Regressions for Social Networks: II. Multivariate Relations." British Journal of Mathematical and Statistical Psychology 52: 169-193.

Pew, Richard W., and Anne S. Mavor, eds. (1998). Modeling Human and Organizational Behavior: Application to Military Simulations. Washington, DC: National Academy Press.

Robins, Garry, Peter Elliott and Philippa Pattison (2001). "Network Models for Social Selection Processes." Social Networks 23: 1-30.

Robins, Garry, Philippa Pattison, and Peter Elliott (2001). "Network Models for Social Influence Processes." Psychometrika 66: 166-90.

Robins, Gary, Philippa Pattison, and Stanley Wasserman (1999). "Logit Models and Logistic Regressions for Social Networks, III: Valued Relations." Psychometrika 64:371-394.

Robins, Garry, Philippa Pattison, and Jodie Woolcock (2002). "Missing Data in Networks: Exponential Random Graph (p*) Models for Networks with Non-Respondents." Unpublished paper, Department of Psychology, University of Melbourne, Australia.

Scott, John (2000). Social Network Analysis: A Handbook, 2nd ed. London: Sage.

Snijders, Tom A.B. (2001). "The Statistical Evaluation of Social Network Dynamics." Pp. 361-95 in Sociological Methodology 2001, edited by Michael E. Sobel and Mark P. Becker. Cambridge, MA: Blackwell 31: 361-95.

Spinoza, Benedict de. ([1677] 1923). Ethic, tr. W. Hale White. Oxford University Press.

Van Rossem, Ronan (1996). "The World System Paradigm as General Theory of Development: A Cross-National Test." American Sociological Review 61: 508-27.

Wasserman, Stanley, and Katherine Faust (1994). Social Network Analysis: Methods and Applications. New York: Cambridge University Press.

Wasserman, Stanley, and Philippa Pattison (1996). "Logit Models and Logistic Regressions for Social Networks: I. An introduction to Markov Graphs and p*." Psychometrika 61: 401-425.

Watts, Duncan J., and Steven H. Strogatz, "Collective Dynamics of 'Small-World' Networks." Nature 393 (1998): 440-42.

Wellman, Barry ([1988] 1997). "Structural Analysis: From Method and Metaphor to Theory and Substance." Pp. 19-61 in Barry Wellman and S.D. Berkowitz (eds.), Social Structures: A Network Approach. Greenwich, CT: JAI Press.

White, Harrison C. (1992). Identity and Control: A Structural Theory of Social Action. Princeton, NJ: Princeton University Press.

White, Harrison C., Scott A. Boorman, R.L. Breiger (1976). "Social Structure from Multiple Networks: I. Blockmodels of Roles and Positions." American Journal of Sociology **81**: 730-780.

SESSION I

Social Network Theory Perspectives

Photograph by Ben Shahn, Natchez, MS, October, 1935

Library of Congress, Prints & Photographs Division, FSA-OWI Collection, [reproduction number, LC-USF33-006093-M4]

Finding Social Groups: A Meta-Analysis of the Southern Women Data[1]

Linton C. Freeman
University of California, Irvine

1. Introduction

For more than 100 years, sociologists have been concerned with relatively small, cohesive social groups (Tönnies, [1887] 1940; Durkheim [1893] 1933; Spencer 1895-97; Cooley, 1909). The groups that concern sociologists are not simply categories—like redheads or people more than six feet tall. Instead they are social collectivities characterized by interaction and interpersonal ties. Concern with groups of this sort has been—and remains—at the very core of the field.

These early writers made no attempt to specify exactly what they meant when they referred to groups. But in the 1930s, investigators like Roethlisberger and Dickson (1939) and Davis, Gardner and Gardner (1941) began to collect systematic data on

[1] The author owes a considerable debt to Morris H. Sunshine who read an earlier draft and made extensive suggestions all of which improved this manuscript.

interaction and interpersonal ties. Their aim was to use the data both to assign individuals to groups and to determine the position of each individual—as a core or peripheral group member. But, to assign individuals to groups and positions, they needed to specify the sociological notions of group and position in exact terms.

Over the years a great many attempts have been made to specify these notions. In the present paper I will review the results of 21 of these attempts. All 21 tried to specify the group structure in a single data set. And 11 of the 21 also went on and attempted to specify core and peripheral positions.

My approach to this review is a kind of meta-analysis. Schmid, Koch, and LaVange (1991) define meta-analysis as "... a statistical analysis of the data from some collection of studies in order to synthesize the results." And that is precisely my aim here. A typical meta-analysis draws on several data sets from a number of independent studies and brings them together in order to generalize their collective implications. Here I am also trying to discover the collective implications of a number of studies. But instead of looking at the results produced by several data sets, I will be looking at the results produced by several different analytic methods.

In this meta-analysis I will compare the groups and the positions that have been specified by investigators who examined data collected by Davis, Gardner and Gardner (1941) [**DGG**] in their study of southern women. My comparison draws on a number of techniques, including consensus analysis (Batchelder and Romney, 1986, 1988, 1989), canonical analysis of asymmetry (Gower, 1977) and dynamic paired-comparison scaling (Batchelder and Bershad, 1979; Batchelder, Bershad and Simpson, 1992). I will address two questions: (1) do the several specifications produce results that converge in a way that reveals anything about the structural form of the data? And, (2) can we learn anything about the strengths and weaknesses of the various methods for specifying groups and positions?

2. Southern Women Data Set

In the 1930s, five ethnographers, Allison Davis, Elizabeth Stubbs Davis, Burleigh B. Gardner, Mary R. Gardner and J. G. St. Clair Drake, collected data on stratification in Natchez, Mississippi (Warner, 1988, p. 93). They produced the book cited above [**DGG**] that reported a comparative study of social class in black and in white society. One element of this work involved examining the correspondence between people's social class levels and their patterns of informal interaction. **DGG** was concerned with the issue of how much the informal contacts made by individuals were established solely (or primarily) with others at approximately their own class levels. To address this question the authors collected data on social events and examined people's patterns of informal contacts.

In particular, they collected systematic data on the social activities of 18 women whom they observed over a nine-month period. During that period, various subsets of these women had met in a series of 14 informal social events. The participation of women in events was uncovered using "interviews, the records of participant observers, guest lists, and the newspapers" (**DGG**, p. 149). Homans (1950, p. 82), who presumably had been in touch with the research team, reported that the data reflect joint activities like, "a day's work behind the counter of a store, a meeting of a women's club, a church supper, a card party, a supper party, a meeting of the Parent-Teacher Association, etc."

This data set has several interesting properties. It is small and manageable. It embodies a relatively simple structural pattern, one in which, according to **DGG**, the women seemed to organize themselves into two more or less distinct groups. Moreover, they reported that the positions—core and peripheral—of the members of these groups could also be determined in terms of the ways in which different women had been involved in group activities.

At the same time, the **DGG** data set is complicated enough that some of the details of its patterning are less than obvious. As Homans (1950, p. 84) put it, "The pattern is frayed at the edges." And, finally, this data set comes to us in a two-mode—woman by event—form. Thus, it provides an opportunity to explore methods designed for direct application to two-mode data. But at the same time, it can easily be transformed into two one-mode matrices (woman by woman or event by event) that can be examined using tools for one-mode analysis.

Because of these properties, this **DGG** data set has become something of a touchstone for comparing analytic methods in social network analysis. Davis, Gardner and Gardner presented an intuitive interpretation of the data, based in part on their ethnographic experience in the community. Then the **DGG** data set was picked up by Homans (1950) who provided an alternative intuitive interpretation. In 1972, Phillips and Conviser used an analytic tool, based on information theory, that provided a systematic way to reexamine the **DGG** data. Since then, this data set has been analyzed again and again. It reappears whenever any network analyst wants to explore the utility of some new tool for analyzing data.

3. The Data Source

Figure 1, showing which women attended each event, is reproduced from **DGG** (p. 148). **DGG** examined the participation patterns of these women along with additional information generated by interviews. As I discussed in Section 1 above, they had two distinct goals in their analysis: (1) they wanted to divide women up into groups within on the basis of their co-attendance at events, and (2) they wanted to determine a position—in the core or periphery—for each woman. As they put it (p. 150):

> Where it is evident that a group of people participate together in these informal activities consistently, it is obvious

that a clique[2] had been isolated. Interviewing can then be used to clarify the relationship. Those individuals who participate together most often and at the most intimate affairs are called *core members*; those who participate with core members upon some occasions but never as a group by themselves alone are called *primary members*; while individuals on the fringes, who participate only infrequently, constitute the *secondary members* of a clique.

Names of Participants of Group I	Code Numbers and Dates of Social Events Reported in *Old City Herald*													
	(1) 6/27	(2) 3/2	(3) 4/12	(4) 9/26	(5) 2/25	(6) 5/19	(7) 3/15	(8) 9/16	(9) 4/8	(10) 6/10	(11) 2/23	(12) 4/7	(13) 11/21	(14) 8/3
1. Mrs. Evelyn Jefferson	×	×	×	×	×	×		×	×					
2. Miss Laura Mandeville	×	×	×		×	×	×	×						
3. Miss Theresa Anderson		×	×	×	×	×	×	×	×					
4. Miss Brenda Rogers	×		×	×	×	×	×	×						
5. Miss Charlotte McDowd			×	×	×		×							
6. Miss Frances Anderson			×		×	×		×						
7. Miss Eleanor Nye					×	×	×	×						
8. Miss Pearl Oglethorpe						×		×	×					
9. Miss Ruth DeSand					×		×	×	×					
10. Miss Verne Sanderson							×	×	×			×		
11. Miss Myra Liddell								×	×	×		×		
12. Miss Katherine Rogers								×	×	×		×	×	×
13. Mrs. Sylvia Avondale							×	×	×	×		×	×	×
14. Mrs. Nora Fayette						×	×		×	×	×	×	×	×
15. Mrs. Helen Lloyd							×	×		×	×	×		
16. Mrs. Dorothy Murchison								×	×					
17. Mrs. Olivia Carleton									×		×			
18. Mrs. Flora Price									×		×			

Figure 1. Participation of the Southern Women in Events

Unfortunately, the data as presented in Figure 1 are not definitive. Indeed, two pages after presenting their data, **DGG** (p. 150) presented them again in another format. Their second version of the data is reproduced here as Figure 2. I have added annotations showing important comparative features in red.

The existence of that second presentation raises a problem; the data shown in Figure 1 do not agree with those shown in Figure 2. Specifically, in Figure 2 woman 15 was reported to have been a participant in events 13 and 14, but she was not so reported in Figure 1. In addition, in Figure 2 woman 16 was reported as participating in events 8, 9, 10 and 12. But in Figure 1, she was reported to have been a participant only in events 8 and 9. The extra events reported in Figure 2 but missing in Figure 1 are outlined in red.

[2] Note that **DGG** wrote before "clique" was defined as a technical term by Luce and Perry (1949). **DGG** used the word "clique" to mean what I am calling a "group."

We are faced with a dilemma then. Are we to believe the data presented in Figure 1 or those presented in Figure 2? Homans (1950) was the first to use these data in a secondary analysis. He reported additional details that suggest that he was probably in touch with the original research team. And in his report he used the data as they are displayed in Figure 1.

Moreover, there is additional ancillary evidence for the correctness of the data as presented in Figure 1. It turns out that there is a contradiction in the presentation of Figure 2 that makes it difficult to accept the data presented there as correct. Compare, for example, the participation patterns displayed by the two women designated with red arrows in Figure 2: woman 11 and woman 16. According to Figure 2, these two women displayed identical patterns of participation. Yet, in that figure, woman 11 was classified as a primary member of her "clique" while woman 16 was called secondary. This contradiction implies that the correct data are those shown in Figure 1.

Type of Membership	Members	Events and Participations													
		1	2	3	4	5	6	7	8	9	10	11	12	13	14
Clique I: Core......	1	C	C	C	C	C	C	–	C	C					
	2	C	C	C	–	C	C	C	C	–					
	3	–	C	C	C	C	C	C	C	C					
	4	C	–	C	C	C	C	C	C	–					
Primary...	5			P	P	P	–	P	–	–					
	6			P	–	P	P	–	P	–					
	7					P	P	P	P	–					
Secondary.	8					–	S	–	S	S					
Clique II: Secondary.	9					S	–	S	S	S					
	10							S	S	S	–	–	S		
Primary...	11							–	P	P	P	–	P		
	12							–	P	P	P	–	P	P	P
Core......	13							C	C	C	C	–	C	C	C
	14						C	C	–	C	C	C	C	C	C
	15							C	C	–	C	C	C	C	C
Secondary.	16								S	S	S	–	S		
	17									S	–	S			
	18									S	–	S			

Figure 2. Participation of the Southern Women in Events

Most analysts have apparently reached this conclusion. Most have used the data as shown in Figure 1. A few, however, have analyzed the data as presented in Figure 2, and this produces a problem for any attempt to compare the results of one analysis with those of another. When the two analyses are based on the use of different data sets comparisons are, of course, not possible.

I have assumed that the "correct" data are those shown in Figure 1. For the relatively small number of results that have been produced by analyses of the data of Figure 2, I have asked the original analysts to redo their analyses using the Figure 1 data or I have redone them myself.

4. Finding Groups and Positions in the DGG Data

4.1 Davis, Gardner and Gardner's Intuition-Based Groups (DGG41)

In their own analysis Davis Gardner and Gardner did not use any systematic analytic procedures. They relied entirely on their general ethnographic knowledge of the community and their intuitive grasp of the patterning in Table 1 to make sense of the data. As Davis and Warner (1939) described it, they drew on "... records of overt behavior and verbalizations, which cover more than five thousand pages, statistical data on both rural and urban societies, as well as newspaper records of social gatherings ..."

DGG drew on all this material and used it both to assign the women to groups and to determine individuals' positions within groups. They indicated that the eighteen women were divided into two overlapping groups. They assigned women 1 through 9 to one group and women 9 through 18 to another. They assigned three levels in terms of core/periphery participation in these groups. They defined women 1 through 4 and 13 through 15 as core members of their respective groups. Women 5 through 7 and 11 and 12 they called primary. Women 8 and 9 on one hand and 9, 10, 16, 17 and 18 on the other were secondary. Note that woman 9 was specified as a secondary member of both groups because, they said, "in interviews" she was "claimed by both" (**DGG**, p. 151).

4.2 Homans' Intuition-Based Analysis (HOM50)

Like Davis, Gardner and Gardner before him, Homans (1950) interpreted these data from an intuitive perspective. Unlike those earlier investigators, however, Homans did not have years of ethnographic experience in Natchez to draw upon. His intuitions, therefore, had to be generated solely by inspecting the **DGG** data and, presumably, by conversations with the ethnographers.

Homans implied that he had re-analyzed the data using a procedure introduced by Forsyth and Katz (1946) whom he cited. Forsyth and Katz had suggested permuting the rows and columns of a data matrix so as to display its group structure as clusters around the principal diagonal of the matrix (upper left to lower right). Their procedure required that both the rows and columns be rearranged until—as far as possible—more or less solid blocks of non-blank cells are gathered together. Such blocks of cells, they suggested, represent "well-knit" groups.

It is doubtful that Homans actually used the Forsyth and Katz procedure. **DGG** had already arranged the matrix in such a way that it displayed group structure. Seemingly they had anticipated the Forsyth and Katz approach by six years. Homans, then, did not rearrange the data matrix at all; he simply copied the arrangement of Figure 1, exactly as it was reported by **DGG**.

In any case, after inspecting the arrangement shown in Figure 1, Homans grouped 16 of the women and distinguished two levels of core and peripheral positions. In his report Homans (p. 84) report wrote:

> . . . we generalize these observations by saying that the 18 women were divided into two groups. The pattern is frayed at the edges, but there is a pattern. The first seven women, Evelyn through Eleanor, were clearly members of one group; numbers 11 through 15, Myra through Helen, were just as clearly members of another. Some women participated about equally with both groups but not very much with either; Pearl [woman 8] is an example. And some participated, though not very often, only with the second group. Pearl, Olivia, Flora [women 8, 17 and 18] and their like are marginal group members.

This statement is somewhat ambiguous. It does assign women 1 through 8 to one group and 11 through 15, along with 8, 17 and 18 to the other. Because woman 8 (Pearl) is assigned to both, the two groups overlap. In addition Homans characterized women 8, 17 and 18 to "marginal positions" but it is difficult to know whet he intended by the phrase "and their like." His statement, moreover, makes no mention at all of woman 9 (Ruth) or woman16 (Dorothy). They were simply not assigned to either group or to any position.

4.3 Phillips and Conviser's Analysis Based on Information Theory (P&C72)

Phillips and Conviser (1972) were the first to use a systematic procedure in the attempt to uncover the group structure in the **DGG** data.[3] They reasoned that a collection of individuals is a group to the extent that all of the members of the collection attend the same social events. So, to examine the **DGG** data, they needed an index of the variability of attendance. They chose the standard information theoretic measure of entropy, **H** (Shannon, 1964). **H** provides an index of the variability of a binary (yes/no) variable. In this case, it was applied to all the women (and all the events) in the **DGG** data. Thus, **H** was used to provide an index of the degree to which different collections of women attended different sets of events (and different sets of events attracted different collections of women).

Phillips and Conviser set about to find groups by comparing various ways of partitioning the women into subsets. They argued that any given partitioning produced social groups if the entropy **H** summed for all of the subsets was less than the entropy for

[3] It should be noted that Phillips and Conviser attributed the southern women data to Homans. Nowhere in their paper did they acknowledge **DGG**.

the total set of women. In such an event, the women assigned to each subset would be relatively homogeneous with respect to which events they attended.

They evaluated the utility of any proposed partitioning by calculating the information theoretic measure **α**. **α** is an index of the degree to which the overall entropy of the total collectivity **H** is reduced by calculating the value $\mathbf{H_i}$ within each of the **i** designated subsets and summing the results (Garner and McGill, 1956). **α** is large when all the women who are classed into each subset are similar with respect to their attendance patterns. It is maximal only when the within-subset patterns are all identical.

To employ this approach, then, it is necessary to partition the women in all possible ways, calculate **α** for each partitioning, and see which partitioning produces the largest value.

There is, however, a major difficulty with this approach. The number of possible partitionings grows at an exponential rate with an increase in the number of individuals examined. The number grows so rapidly that the partitions cannot all be examined, even with as few as 18 women to be considered.

So Phillips and Conviser worked out a way to simplify the problem. Like Homans, they cited again the procedure suggested by Forsyth and Katz (1946). That procedure rearranges the rows and columns in the data matrix in such a way that women who attended the same events and events that were attended by the same women are grouped together. When this is done, only those women who are close together in the matrix are eligible to be in the same group. That being the case, only those relatively few partitionings that include or exclude individuals in successive positions in the data matrix need to be considered.

As I indicated above, the **DGG** data had already been arranged in the desired order by the original authors. So, like Homans, Phillips and Conviser did not actually have to rearrange them. They could proceed directly to partitioning. They began by partitioning the women into two classes (1 versus 2 through 18, 1 and 2 versus 3 through 18, 1 through 3 versus 4 through 18, etc.). They reported that, of all these two-group partitions, the split of 1 through 11 versus 12 through 18 yielded the largest value of **α**.

In checking their results, however, I discovered that their result was based on an error in calculation. When I recalculated I discovered that the maximum value of **α** is actually achieved with the 1 through 9 versus 10 through 18 split. This approach simply partitions; it cannot distinguish core or peripheral positions, nor can it permit overlapping.

4.4 Breiger's Matrix Algebraic Analysis (BGR74)

Breiger (1974) used matrix algebra to show that the original two-mode, woman by event, **DGG** data matrix could be used to generate a pair of matrices that are, mathematically, dual. First, multiplying the original matrix by its transpose produces a woman by woman matrix in which each cell indicates the number of events co-attended by both the row and the column women. Second, multiplying the transpose by the original matrix yields an event-by-event matrix where each cell is the number of women who attended both the row event and the column event. The woman-by-woman matrix is shown in Figure 3.[4] And its dual, the event-by-event matrix, is shown in Figure 4.

		1 E	2 L	3 T	4 B	5 C	6 F	7 E	8 P	9 R	10 V	11 M	12 K	13 S	14 N	15 H	16 D	17 O	18 F
1	EVELYN	8	6	7	6	3	4	3	3	3	2	2	2	2	2	1	2	1	1
2	LAURA	6	7	6	6	3	4	4	2	3	2	1	1	2	2	2	1	0	0
3	THERESA	7	6	8	6	4	4	4	3	4	3	2	2	3	3	2	2	1	1
4	BRENDA	6	6	6	7	4	4	4	2	3	2	1	1	2	2	2	1	0	0
5	CHARLOTTE	3	3	4	4	4	2	2	0	2	1	0	0	1	1	1	0	0	0
6	FRANCES	4	4	4	4	2	4	3	2	2	1	1	1	1	1	1	1	0	0
7	ELEANOR	3	4	4	4	2	3	4	2	3	2	1	1	2	2	2	1	0	0
8	PEARL	3	2	3	2	0	2	2	3	2	2	2	2	2	2	1	2	1	1
9	RUTH	3	3	4	3	2	2	3	2	4	3	2	2	3	2	2	2	1	1
10	VERNE	2	2	3	2	1	1	2	2	3	4	3	3	4	3	3	2	1	1
11	MYRA	2	1	2	1	0	1	1	2	2	3	4	4	4	3	3	2	1	1
12	KATHERINE	2	1	2	1	0	1	1	2	2	3	4	6	6	5	3	2	1	1
13	SYLVIA	2	2	3	2	1	1	2	2	3	4	4	6	7	6	4	2	1	1
14	NORA	2	2	3	2	1	1	2	2	2	3	3	5	6	8	4	1	2	2
15	HELEN	1	2	2	2	1	1	2	1	2	3	3	3	4	4	5	1	1	1
16	DOROTHY	2	1	2	1	0	1	1	2	2	2	2	2	2	1	1	2	1	1
17	OLIVIA	1	0	1	0	0	0	0	1	1	1	1	1	1	2	1	1	2	2
18	FLORA	1	0	1	0	0	0	0	1	1	1	1	1	1	2	1	1	2	2

Figure 3. The One-Mode, Woman by Woman, Matrix Produced by Matrix Multiplication

		1 E1	2 E2	3 E3	4 E4	5 E5	6 E6	7 E7	8 E8	9 E9	10 E10	11 E11	12 E12	13 E13	14 E14
1	E1	3	2	3	2	3	3	2	3	1	0	0	0	0	0
2	E2	2	3	3	2	3	3	2	3	2	0	0	0	0	0
3	E3	3	3	6	4	6	5	4	5	2	0	0	0	0	0
4	E4	2	2	4	4	4	3	3	3	2	0	0	0	0	0
5	E5	3	3	6	4	8	6	6	7	3	0	0	0	0	0
6	E6	3	3	5	3	6	8	5	7	4	1	1	1	1	1
7	E7	2	2	4	3	6	5	10	8	5	3	2	4	2	2
8	E8	3	3	5	3	7	7	8	14	9	4	1	5	2	2
9	E9	1	2	2	2	3	4	5	9	12	4	3	5	3	3
10	E10	0	0	0	0	0	1	3	4	4	5	2	5	3	3
11	E11	0	0	0	0	0	1	2	1	3	2	4	2	1	1
12	E12	0	0	0	0	0	1	4	5	5	5	2	6	3	3
13	E13	0	0	0	0	0	1	2	2	3	3	1	3	3	3
14	E14	0	0	0	0	0	1	2	2	3	3	1	3	3	3

Figure 4. The One-Mode, Event by Event, Matrix Produced by Matrix Multiplication

---

[4] Breiger renamed **DGG**'s "Myra." He listed her as "Myrna" in his tables and diagrams. Breiger's designation has been picked up in a number of later works—including the data set released as part of the **UCINET** program (Borgatti, Everett and Freeman, 1992).

After examining the woman by woman matrix Breiger's conclusion was that ". . . everyone was connected to virtually everyone else." It was difficult, therefore, to separate the women into subgroups. So, in order to do that he turned to the dual, event by event, matrix. He reasoned that ". . . only those events that have *zero* overlap with at least one other event are likely to separate the women into socially meaningful subgroups." He found that events 6, 7, 8 and 9 were all linked to all of the other events; they contained no zero entries. So he eliminated their columns from the original two-mode data matrix. When those four columns were eliminated, women 8 and 16 were not participants in any of the remaining events so they were dropped from the analysis.

The next step was to recalculate a new woman-by-woman matrix from the reduced woman by event matrix from which the four linking events and the two uninvolved women had been removed. He then dichotomized the reduced data matrix and determined its clique[5] structure. The result was a clear separation of the women into three cliques, two of which overlapped. Women 1 through 7 plus woman 9 formed one clique, women 10 through 15 formed another. In addition, women 14, 15, 17 and 18 formed a third. Thus, the latter two groups overlapped; women 14 and 15 were members of both the second and the third cliques. Breiger's procedure, then, permits the generation of more than two groups and it allows groups to overlap. But like the Phillips and Conviser approach, it cannot assign core or peripheral positions.

4.5 Breiger, Boorman and Arabie's Computational Analysis (BBA75)

Breiger, Boorman and Arabie (1975) reported on a new computational technique, **CONCOR**, designed for clustering binary relational data. **CONCOR** partitions the points in a graph into exactly two similarity classes, or blocks. Such blocks result when a data matrix can be permuted in such a way that some rectangular areas of the permuted matrix contain mostly ones, and other rectangular areas are predominately filled with zeros.

CONCOR begins with a data matrix, for example, the **DGG** women by event data. Then, using only the rows (women) or only the columns (events) CONCOR calculates either a row-by-row or column-by-column matrix of ordinary Pearsonian correlations. Then the rows (or columns) in this correlation matrix are again correlated and this process is repeated, again and again, until all the correlations are uniformly either plus or minus one. The convergence to correlations to plus or minus one seems always to occur. And the result is partitioning of the original data into two relatively homogeneous groups.

The application of **CONCOR** to the women (rows) of the **DGG** data set produced a partition. Women 1 through 7 and 9 were assigned to one group and 10 through 18 along with 8 were assigned to the other. Like the information theoretic approach used by

---

[5] Here the term "clique" is used in the technical sense. It is a maximal complete subset (Luce and Perry, 1949).

Phillips and Conviser, **CONCOR** partitions the data. That means that **CONCOR**'s results cannot assign core or peripheral positions nor can they display groups that overlap.

4.6 Bonacich's Boolean Algebraic Analysis (BCH78)

Bonacich (1978) focused on the same duality that Breiger had noted, but he used a different algebraic tool. Instead of using Breiger's matrix algebra, Bonacich drew on Boolean algebra to specify both homogeneous groups of women and homogenous groups of events.

Bonacich began with the two-mode data set reported by **DGG**. His aim was to find a procedure for simplifying the data in such a way that—as much as possible—all the unions (**a** or **b**), intersections (**a** and **b**) and complements (not **a**) contained in the original data are preserved. Like Breiger, he drew on the duality between women and events. He strategically selected a subset of events (3, 8 and 12) that permitted him to divide the women into two groups in terms of their attendance at those events. The first group contains women 1, 2, 3, 4, 5 and 6 who were present at Event 3. The second group contains women 10, 11, 12, 13 and 15 who attended Event 12. Most of the women from both groups (all but woman 5 from the first group and woman 14 from the second group) also attended Event 8 along with four others. So, because they avoided attending event 8—that "bridged" between the two groups—Bonacich reasoned that they were "purer" representatives of their groups. He therefore defined women 5 and 14 as occupants of the central, or core, positions in their respective groups.

The approach used by Bonacich, then, divided the women into two groups and it also determined core and peripheral group members. But, because it ignored all but three events, it eliminated one-third of the women (7, 8, 9, 16, 17 and 18) from the analysis.

4.7 Doreian's Analysis Based on Algebraic Topology (DOR79)

Doreian (1979) drew on Atkin's (1974) algebraic topology in order to specify subgroups and positions in the **DGG** data. Atkin's model defines each event as the collection of women who attended it. Dually, each woman is defined as the collection of events she attended.

From the perspective of Atkin's model, two women are assumed to be connected to the degree that they are linked through chains of co-attendance. Women **A**, **B** and **C** form a chain at level 5 if a woman **A** co-attends 5 events with woman **B** and **B** attended 5 events with **C.** Then, even if **A** and **C** never attended any event together, all three are put together and their connection is assigned a level of 5. Doreian used this procedure to uncover the patterning of connections among the **DGG** women.

Women who form chains linked by co-attendance at 4 or more events, are divided into two groups. One contains women 1, 2, 3, 4, 5, 6, 7 and 9. The other includes women 10, 11, 12, 13, 14 and 15. Moreover, by considering subsets of women who were connected at higher levels, Doreian was able to specify degrees of co-attendance ranging from the core to the periphery according of each group. His results place women 1 and 3 in the core of the first group, followed by 2 and 4 at the next level and 5, 6, 7 and 9 at the third. In the second group there were only two levels. Women 12, 13 and 14 were core, and 10, 11 and 15 were placed at the second level.

4.8 Bonacich's Use of Singular Value Decomposition (BCH91)

Bonacich (1991) used a form of singular value decomposition (SVD) to uncover groups in the **DGG** data. SVD is a tool from linear algebra. It is closely related to principal components analysis. Richards and Seary (1997) described the procedure:

> . . . choose a set of axes in the multidimensional space occupied by the data and *rotate* them so that the first axis points in the direction of the greatest variability in the data; the second one, perpendicular to the first, points in the direction of greatest remaining variability, and so on. This set of axes is a coordinate system that can be used to describe the relative positions of the set of points in the data. Most of the variability in the locations of points will be accounted for by the first few dimensions of this coordinate system.

SVD can be used to analyze either one-mode or two-mode data. In this case, Bonacich applied it directly to the two-mode, women by events, data set. And he proposed that the first of the new transformed axes reveals both overall group structure and individual positioning. Individuals who displayed similar patterns of attendance at events are assigned similar scores on that axis. Moreover, that first axis is bipolar—it assigns both positive and negative scores to individuals. Bonacich indicated that women with positive values belong in one group and those with negative values in the other. The magnitudes of individual scores—positive or negative—can be taken as indices of core versus peripheral group membership. A large score associated with a woman indicates that she tended to present herself only at those events that were attended by other members of her own group and that she avoided events that were attended by members of the other group.

One of Bonacich's groups included women 1 through 9, and the other women 10 through 18. The order for the first group placed woman 5 in the core, followed by 4, 2, 1 and 6 together, and 3, 7, 9, and 8 in that order. In the second group, women 17 and 18 were together at the core, followed by 12, 13 and 14 together, then 11, 15, 10, and 16 in that order.

4.9 Freeman's Analysis Based on G-Transitivity (FRE92)

Freeman (1992) was the first to analyze the **DGG** data in a strictly one-mode form. Like Breiger (1974) he used matrix multiplication to produce the woman-by-woman matrix shown above in Figure 3. The cells in that figure show the number of events co-attended by the row-woman and the column-woman. The cells in the principal diagonal indicate the total number of events attended by each woman.

Freeman's analysis was based on an earlier suggestion by Granovetter (1973), hence the name, G-Transitivity. Granovetter focused on the strengths of the social ties linking individuals. He argued that, given three individuals **A**, **B** and **C** where both **A** and **B** and **B** and **C** are connected by strong social ties, then **A** and **C** should be at least weakly tied. Freeman assumed that the frequency of co-attendance provided an index of tie strength. He developed a computational model that works from the larger frequencies of co-attendance to the smaller. It determines a critical level of co-attendance below which the data violate Granovetter's condition. At the level just below the critical one, there is at least one triple where an **A** and a **B** are tied at that level, **B** and some **C** are tied at that level, but **A** and **C** have no tie at all. But at the critical level and all higher levels, the condition is met; so all ties that involve co-attendance at or above that critical level are, in Granovetter's sense, strong.

Applied to the **DGG** data this procedure divided fifteen of the eighteen women into two groups. The first contained women 1 through 7 and 9. The second contained women 10 through 16. Within each of those groups each woman was connected to every other woman on a path involving only strong ties. But there were no strong ties linking women across the two groups. Thus, this method could uncover groups in the **DGG** data set, but it could not distinguish between cores and peripheries. Moreover, this procedure was unable to assign group membership to women 8, 17 and 18.

4.10 Everett and Borgatti's Analysis Based on Regular Coloring (E&B93)

In an earlier paper Everett and Borgatti (1991) had defined regular equivalence in terms of graph coloring. Let the vertices of a graph represent social actors and the edges represent a symmetric relation linking pairs of actors. The neighborhood of a vertex is the set of other vertices that are directly connected to that vertex. Each vertex is assigned a color. Then any subset of vertices can be characterized by its spectrum, the set of colors assigned to its members.

Assigning colors to vertices partitions the actors into equivalence sets. And those equivalence sets are regular when all the vertices are colored in such a way that they are all embedded in neighborhoods with the same spectrum.

Everett and Borgatti (1993) used the concept of hypergraphs to generalize their regular coloring to two-mode data sets. And Freeman and Duquenne (1993) restated that generalization in simpler terms, referring only to ordinary bipartite graphs.

This approach draws on the duality of two-mode data. Women are connected only to events and *vice versa*. So the women are assigned colors from one spectrum and the events are assigned colors from another. Women are regularly equivalent when they participate in events that are regularly equivalent. Events are regularly equivalent when they have participants who are regularly equivalent. To simplify their analysis, Everett and Borgatti dropped four women (8, 16, 17 and 18). The remaining 14 women were partitioned into two regular equivalence classes, and, at the same time, the events were partitioned into three classes: Any women who attended any of events 1 through 5 and also any of events 6 through 9 were assigned to one class. Those women who attended any of events 6 through 9 and also any of 10 through 14 were assigned to the other class. The resulting partitioning of the fourteen women assigned women 1 through 7 along with 9 to one group and women 10 through 15 to the other. No assignments to core or peripheral positions were made.

4.11 Two Groupings Resulting from Freeman's Use of a Genetic Algorithm (FR193 and FR293)

Freeman (1993) produced another one-mode analysis of the DGG data. He began with the definition of group proposed by Homans (1950) and Sailer and Gaulin (1984). They defined a group as a collection of individuals all of whom interact more with other group members than with outsiders.

To explore this idea, Freeman used the same one-mode woman-by-woman matrix of frequencies that he had used in his earlier analysis of G-transitivity. He assumed that the women who co-attended the same social events would almost certainly have interacted. So he took this matrix as an index of interaction.

To find groups, then, one might examine all the possible partitionings of these 18 women and find any that meet the Homans-Sailer-Gaulin condition. But, in the discussion of the approach used by Phillips and Conviser above, the impossibility of searching through all the partitionings was established. Phillips and Conviser avoided the problem by limiting their search to only a small subset of the possible partitionings. Freeman (1993) took another approach. He drew on a search optimization algorithm to enhance the probability of finding partitionings that yield groups.

Freeman search was based on Holland's (1962) genetic algorithm. This approach emulates an actual evolutionary process in which pseudo-organisms "adapt" to the demands of an environmental niche. In this case, each pseudo-organism was associated with a particular partitioning of the 18 women. The niche was defined in terms of the Homans-Sailer-Gaulin definition of group. And the "fitness" of each grouping was evaluated in terms of the extent to which it approached that condition.

The search for an optimum partitioning was enhanced by allowing those partitionings with the highest fitness to crossbreed. In that way they produced another generation of "offspring" partitionings, each with some of the traits of their two parents.

And, to avoid getting the whole process locked into some less than optimal pattern, each partitioning in the new generation was subjected to a small chance of a mutation that would vary its structure.

The **DGG** data were entered into the genetic program and 500 runs were made. Two solutions that met the Homans-Sailer-Gaulin criterion were uncovered. The first, that occurred 327 times, found the same optimum revealed in the corrected Phillips and Conviser analysis. It grouped women 1 through 9 together and women 10 through 18 together. The second pattern occurred less frequently. It turned up 173 times and assigned women 1 through 7 to one group and women 8 through 18 to the other. These were the only partitions that displayed more interaction within groups than between groups.

4.12 Two Solutions Provided by Freeman and White's Galois Lattice Analysis (FW193 and FW293)

Freeman and White (1993) drew on another algebraic tool. They used Galois lattices to uncover groups and positions in the **DGG** data. Mathematically, a Galois lattice (Birkhoff, 1940) is a dual structure. It displays the patterning of women in terms of the events that each attended. And at the same time it shows the patterning of events in terms of which women attended each. Moreover it shows the containment structure of both the women and the events. A woman **A** "contains" another **B** if never attends an event where **A** is not present. And an event **X** contains event **Y** if no woman is present at **Y** who is not also present at **X**.

A Galois lattice, therefore, permits the specification of classes of events. And it allows us to define subsets of actors in terms of those event classes. Overall, it allows an investigator to uncover all the structure that was displayed in the earlier algebraic work by Breiger (1974) and Bonacich (1978), without the necessity of choosing arbitrary subsets of events in order to classify the women.

Freeman and White first reported the structure that was revealed by examining the overall lattice. Those results assigned women 1 through 9 and 16 to one group and women 10 through 18 to the other. Woman 16, then, was a member of both groups. Core and peripheral positions were assigned according to the patterning of containment. At the core of the first group were women 1, 2, 3 and 4. Women 5, 6, 7, and 9 were in the middle. And woman 16 was peripheral. The core of the second group contained women 13, 14 and 15. Women 10, 11, 12, 17 and 18 were in the middle, and again woman 16 was peripheral.

Freeman and White's second analysis was based on examining the two sub-lattices of women that were generated by the partitioning of events in the overall lattice. Two sets of events, 1 through 5 and 10 through 14 shared no common actors. So Freeman and White examined the sub-lattices generated by considering only these events.

This is exactly the event set that Breiger used in his matrix algebraic analysis described above. And its overall results are similar to those produced by Breiger.

This second analysis excluded women 8 and 16 who had not attended any of these ten events. It produced two non-overlapping groups that contained the remaining sixteen women. One group included women 1 through 7 along with 9. And the other included women 10 through 15 along with 17 and 18. Woman 1 was at the core of her group, followed by 2, 3 and 4 at the next level, then 5, then 6, and finally 7 and 9 together at the periphery. Woman 14 was at the core of her group, followed by 12, 13 and 15 at the next level, 11, 17 and 18 next, and finally by woman 10 at the extreme periphery.

4.13 Borgatti and Everett's Three Analyses (BE197, BE297 and BE397)

As part of a broad examination of techniques for the analysis of two-mode data, Borgatti and Everett (1997) used three procedures for finding groups in the **DGG** data. They began by constructing a one-mode *bipartite* matrix of the **DGG** data. A bipartite matrix represents a graph in which the nodes can be partitioned in such a way that all the ties in the graph connect nodes that fall in one partition with nodes that fall in the other; there are no within partition ties. The bipartite matrix produced by Borgatti and Everett is shown in Figure 5. The partition is between women and events. All the ties go from women to events or from events to women. There are neither woman-woman ties nor are there any event-event ties.

		1 E	2 L	3 T	4 B	5 C	6 F	7 E	8 P	9 R	10 V	11 M	12 K	13 S	14 N	15 H	16 D	17 O	18 F	19 E	20 E	21 E	22 E	23 E	24 E	25 E	26 E	27 E	28 E	29 E	30 E	31 E	32 E
1	EVELYN	0	0	0	0	0	0	0	0	0	0	0	0	0	0	0	0	0	0	1	1	1	1	1	1	0	1	1	0	0	0	0	0
2	LAURA	0	0	0	0	0	0	0	0	0	0	0	0	0	0	0	0	0	0	1	1	1	0	1	1	1	1	0	0	0	0	0	0
3	THERESA	0	0	0	0	0	0	0	0	0	0	0	0	0	0	0	0	0	0	0	1	1	1	1	1	1	1	1	0	0	0	0	0
4	BRENDA	0	0	0	0	0	0	0	0	0	0	0	0	0	0	0	0	0	0	1	0	1	1	1	1	1	1	0	0	0	0	0	0
5	CHARLOTTE	0	0	0	0	0	0	0	0	0	0	0	0	0	0	0	0	0	0	0	0	1	1	1	0	1	0	0	0	0	0	0	0
6	FRANCES	0	0	0	0	0	0	0	0	0	0	0	0	0	0	0	0	0	0	0	0	1	0	1	1	0	1	0	0	0	0	0	0
7	ELEANOR	0	0	0	0	0	0	0	0	0	0	0	0	0	0	0	0	0	0	0	0	0	0	1	1	1	1	0	0	0	0	0	0
8	PEARL	0	0	0	0	0	0	0	0	0	0	0	0	0	0	0	0	0	0	0	0	0	0	0	1	0	1	1	0	0	0	0	0
9	RUTH	0	0	0	0	0	0	0	0	0	0	0	0	0	0	0	0	0	0	0	0	0	0	1	0	1	1	1	0	0	0	0	0
10	VERNE	0	0	0	0	0	0	0	0	0	0	0	0	0	0	0	0	0	0	0	0	0	0	0	0	1	1	1	0	0	1	0	0
11	MYRA	0	0	0	0	0	0	0	0	0	0	0	0	0	0	0	0	0	0	0	0	0	0	0	0	0	1	1	1	0	1	0	0
12	KATHERINE	0	0	0	0	0	0	0	0	0	0	0	0	0	0	0	0	0	0	0	0	0	0	0	0	0	1	1	1	0	1	1	1
13	SYLVIA	0	0	0	0	0	0	0	0	0	0	0	0	0	0	0	0	0	0	0	0	0	0	0	0	1	1	1	1	0	1	1	1
14	NORA	0	0	0	0	0	0	0	0	0	0	0	0	0	0	0	0	0	0	0	0	0	0	0	1	1	0	1	1	1	1	1	1
15	HELEN	0	0	0	0	0	0	0	0	0	0	0	0	0	0	0	0	0	0	0	0	0	0	0	0	1	1	0	1	1	1	0	0
16	DOROTHY	0	0	0	0	0	0	0	0	0	0	0	0	0	0	0	0	0	0	0	0	0	0	0	0	0	1	1	0	0	0	0	0
17	OLIVIA	0	0	0	0	0	0	0	0	0	0	0	0	0	0	0	0	0	0	0	0	0	0	0	0	0	0	1	0	1	0	0	0
18	FLORA	0	0	0	0	0	0	0	0	0	0	0	0	0	0	0	0	0	0	0	0	0	0	0	0	0	0	1	0	1	0	0	0
19	E1	1	1	0	1	0	0	0	0	0	0	0	0	0	0	0	0	0	0	0	0	0	0	0	0	0	0	0	0	0	0	0	0
20	E2	1	1	1	0	0	0	0	0	0	0	0	0	0	0	0	0	0	0	0	0	0	0	0	0	0	0	0	0	0	0	0	0
21	E3	1	1	1	1	1	1	0	0	0	0	0	0	0	0	0	0	0	0	0	0	0	0	0	0	0	0	0	0	0	0	0	0
22	E4	1	0	1	1	1	0	0	0	0	0	0	0	0	0	0	0	0	0	0	0	0	0	0	0	0	0	0	0	0	0	0	0
23	E5	1	1	1	1	1	1	1	0	1	0	0	0	0	0	0	0	0	0	0	0	0	0	0	0	0	0	0	0	0	0	0	0
24	E6	1	1	1	1	0	1	1	1	0	0	0	0	0	1	0	0	0	0	0	0	0	0	0	0	0	0	0	0	0	0	0	0
25	E7	0	1	1	1	1	0	1	0	1	1	0	0	1	1	1	0	0	0	0	0	0	0	0	0	0	0	0	0	0	0	0	0
26	E8	1	1	1	1	0	1	1	1	1	1	1	1	1	0	1	1	0	0	0	0	0	0	0	0	0	0	0	0	0	0	0	0
27	E9	1	0	1	0	0	0	0	1	1	1	1	1	1	1	0	1	1	1	0	0	0	0	0	0	0	0	0	0	0	0	0	0
28	E10	0	0	0	0	0	0	0	0	0	0	1	1	1	1	1	0	0	0	0	0	0	0	0	0	0	0	0	0	0	0	0	0
29	E11	0	0	0	0	0	0	0	0	0	0	0	0	1	1	0	1	1	0	0	0	0	0	0	0	0	0	0	0	0	0	0	0
30	E12	0	0	0	0	0	0	0	0	0	1	1	1	1	1	1	0	0	0	0	0	0	0	0	0	0	0	0	0	0	0	0	0
31	E13	0	0	0	0	0	0	0	0	0	0	0	1	1	1	0	0	0	0	0	0	0	0	0	0	0	0	0	0	0	0	0	0
32	E14	0	0	0	0	0	0	0	0	0	0	0	1	1	1	0	0	0	0	0	0	0	0	0	0	0	0	0	0	0	0	0	0

Figure 5. One-Mode Bipartite Representation of the DGG Data

Borgatti and Everett defined an object on this matrix called an *n-biclique*. Like an n-clique, an n-biclique is a maximal complete subgraph in which no pair of points is at a distance greater than **n**. In this case, they were interested only in such bicliques where **n** = 2.

Since women are connected to events, a 2-bicliques must include both women and events. It could include a one-step connection from at least one woman to at least one event and another one-step connection from those events to at least one other woman. Or it might include a one-step connection from at least one event to at least one woman and another one-step connection from those women to at least one other event. Originally, Luce and Perry (1949) had required that a clique contain at least three objects. Borgatti and Everett generalized that requirement and specified that their 2-bicliques must contain at least three women *and* at least three events.

Of the 68 2-bicliques, only 22 contained 3 or more women and 3 or more events. Women 8, 16, 17 and 18 were not included in any of these bicliques. Everett and Borgatti recorded the pattern of overlap among the 22 cliques and then used the average method of Johnson's (1967) hierarchical clustering to define groups, cores and peripheries on the matrix of overlaps. Their results reveal two groups. One contains women 1 through 7 and 9. The other contains women 10 through 15. Women 3 and 4 are the core of the first group. They are followed by 2, 1, 7, 6, 9 and 5 in that order. Women 12 and 13 are the core of the second group. They are followed in order by 11, 14 10 and 15.

Borgatti and Everett used the same bipartite data in a second approach. There they used a search algorithm to find the two-group partitioning that maximized the fit between the observed data and an idealized pattern. In their idealized pattern all within-group ties are present and no between-group ties are present. An optimal partition is sought using Glover's (1989) *tabu search* algorithm, and the fit of any partition is measured by correlation between that partition and the ideal. The result was a simple partition of all the women and all the events. The positions of individuals were not calculated. The tabu search found that the best two-group partition for the women was 1 through 9 and 10 through 18.

In their third analysis Borgatti and Everett used the regular two-mode **DGG** data. Here again they sought an optimal partitioning. And again the criterion for an optimum was correlation between a particular partitioning and the ideal that contained solid blocks of zero ties between groups and one ties within groups. Like Freeman (1993), Borgatti and Everett used a genetic algorithm to search for an optimum. But, while Freeman's search was made on the one mode woman by woman data, Borgatti and Everett searched the two mode, woman by event data. The result of their application of the genetic algorithm assigned women 1 through 9 to one group and 10 through 18 to the other.

4.14 Skvoretz and Faust's p* Model (S&F99)

Skvoretz and Faust (1999) explored the ability of **p***, a family of structural models proposed by Wasserman and Pattison (1996) to uncover the important structural properties of the **DGG** data. Skvoretz and Faust developed several models in which various conditioning factors were used in the attempt to reproduce the patterning of the **DGG** data from a small number of parameters. Their best fitting model embodied three key parameters, all concerned with bridging ties. One parameter was based on the number of triads in which two actors were linked by an event. The second was based on the number of triads in which two events were linked by an actor. And the third took into account the distances between pairs of events as measured by the number of actors on the shortest path linking them.

Together, these parameters did a good job of capturing the tendency of these women to attend those events that brought the same sets of individuals together, again and again. These three factors, then, were included in a model that predicted the likelihood that each woman attended each event. In effect, Skvoretz and Faust used the **p*** model to produce an idealized version of the **DGG** data, one that removed minor perturbations and—hopefully—captured the essence of the overall pattern of attendance. They produced, in effect, an "improved" version of the **DGG** data.

In order to uncover the group structure in this idealized data set, I clustered the data produced by the model using Johnson's (1967) complete link hierarchical clustering algorithm. That algorithm produces an ordering among sets of women by linking first those who were assigned the closest ties according to the **p*** model, then proceeding to the next lower level and so on. The results divide the women into two groups, and they assign core and peripheral positions in those groups. One group included women 1 through 9 and the other women 10 through 15 as well as 17 and 18. Woman 16 was not included in either group. The two positional orderings were: 1 and 3, 2, 4, 5, 6, 7, 9, 8 for the first group and 12 and 13, 14, 15, 11, 10, and finally 17 and 18 together at the extreme periphery for the second.

4.15 Roberts' Singular Value Decomposition of Dual Normalized Data (ROB00)

Roberts (2000) calculated a "marginal free" (Goodman, 1996) two-mode analysis of the **DGG** data. He pre-processed the data using the classical iterative proportional fitting algorithm (Deming and Stephan, 1940). This produced a "pure pattern" (Mosteller, 1968) in which all differences in row and column marginals were eliminated. The two-mode data transformed to constant marginals are shown in Figure 6.

		1 E1	2 E2	3 E3	4 E4	5 E5	6 E6	7 E7	8 E8	9 E9	10 E10	11 E11	12 E12	13 E13	14 E14
1	EVELYN	0.349	0.349	0.078	0.174	0.025	0.019	0.000	0.005	0.002	0.000	0.000	0.000	0.000	0.000
2	LAURA	0.414	0.415	0.093	0.000	0.030	0.023	0.021	0.006	0.000	0.000	0.000	0.000	0.000	0.000
3	THERESA	0.000	0.522	0.117	0.260	0.037	0.028	0.027	0.007	0.003	0.000	0.000	0.000	0.000	0.000
4	BRENDA	0.523	0.000	0.117	0.261	0.037	0.028	0.027	0.007	0.000	0.000	0.000	0.000	0.000	0.000
5	CHARLOTTE	0.000	0.000	0.265	0.591	0.085	0.000	0.060	0.000	0.000	0.000	0.000	0.000	0.000	0.000
6	FRANCES	0.000	0.000	0.616	0.000	0.197	0.150	0.000	0.038	0.000	0.000	0.000	0.000	0.000	0.000
7	ELEANOR	0.000	0.000	0.000	0.000	0.375	0.285	0.268	0.072	0.000	0.000	0.000	0.000	0.000	0.000
8	PEARL	0.000	0.000	0.000	0.000	0.000	0.729	0.000	0.184	0.087	0.000	0.000	0.000	0.000	0.000
9	RUTH	0.000	0.000	0.000	0.000	0.501	0.000	0.358	0.096	0.046	0.000	0.000	0.000	0.000	0.000
10	VERNE	0.000	0.000	0.000	0.000	0.000	0.000	0.320	0.086	0.041	0.000	0.000	0.554	0.000	0.000
11	MYRA	0.000	0.000	0.000	0.000	0.000	0.000	0.000	0.052	0.025	0.588	0.000	0.335	0.000	0.000
12	KATHERINE	0.000	0.000	0.000	0.000	0.000	0.000	0.000	0.006	0.003	0.072	0.000	0.041	0.439	0.439
13	SYLVIA	0.000	0.000	0.000	0.000	0.000	0.000	0.023	0.006	0.003	0.070	0.000	0.040	0.428	0.428
14	NORA	0.000	0.000	0.000	0.000	0.000	0.024	0.023	0.000	0.003	0.069	0.005	0.039	0.419	0.419
15	HELEN	0.000	0.000	0.000	0.000	0.000	0.000	0.160	0.043	0.000	0.486	0.034	0.277	0.000	0.000
16	DOROTHY	0.000	0.000	0.000	0.000	0.000	0.000	0.000	0.678	0.322	0.000	0.000	0.000	0.000	0.000
17	OLIVIA	0.000	0.000	0.000	0.000	0.000	0.000	0.000	0.000	0.376	0.000	0.624	0.000	0.000	0.000
18	FLORA	0.000	0.000	0.000	0.000	0.000	0.000	0.000	0.000	0.376	0.000	0.624	0.000	0.000	0.000

Figure 6. DGG Data After Roberts' Iterative Proportional Fitting

Roberts then subjected the transformed data to a singular value decomposition. The result is a procedure like correspondence analysis or principal components analysis, but one in which *all* of the marginal effects have been removed. The groups produced linked women 1 through 9 and 10 through 18. Women 1 and 12 are in the cores of the two groups. Woman 1 is followed by 2, 3 and 4 who are tied at the next level. They are followed by 5, 6, 7, 9, and 8 in that order. Woman 12 is followed by 13, 14, 11, 15, 10 and 16 in that order. And finally women 17 and 18 are grouped together at the extreme periphery of the second group.

4.16 Osbourn's VERI Procedure for Partitioning (OSB00)

Osbourn (1999) is a physicist who conducted experimental research on visual perception. His experiment examined how individuals perceived collections of points presented on a two-dimensional plane and categorized them into clusters. His empirical results suggested that individuals rescale a dumbbell-shaped area around each pair of points in the plane. An individual clusters a pair of points together if and only if no other point falls in the dumbbell-shaped area between them. That result was used to determine the threshold for grouping as a function of variations in the separation of pairs of points. That threshold was called the visual empirical region of influence (**VERI**).

Osbourn generalized these results and they have been used to produce an all-purpose clustering and pattern recognition algorithm. The algorithm turns out to have important applications that deal with a wide range of complex phenomena. The model has successfully been applied in a number of areas. Among them it has been applied to interpretation of inputs of odors reported by mechanical "noses," and it has been used to interpret pictures of brain tissue produced by magnetic resonance imagery (**MRI**).

The publications include general descriptions of the **VERI** procedure, but they do not specify the details. So when, in the year 2000, I met Osbourn I asked him if I might try **VERI** on the one-mode woman-by-woman version of the **DGG** data. Because my data were not based on measured physical data, he concluded that it would be necessary to develop a special form of the algorithm. He did exactly that and sent me a program that was specifically designed to tolerate data that were not scaled.

I tried his adapted algorithm on the **DGG** data, but it was limited. It could only do one partitioning—splitting the women into two groups at a point that, according to the **VERI** criterion, provided the most dramatic separation. That partitioning assigned women 1 through 16 to one group and women 17 and 18 to the other.

4.17 Newman's Weighted Proximities (NEW01)

In analyzing data on co-authorship, Newman (2001) constructed a weighted index of proximity for two-mode data. He assigned each author of a publication a weight inversely proportional to the number of co-authors he or she had in that publication. This weighting was based on the assumption that a large collection of co-authors might be less well connected to each other than a small collection.

Newman had reported his general approach, but, like Osbourn, he had not spelled out the details of his weighting scheme. But I had already noticed that the bridging events in the **DGG** data (E6 through E9) were larger than the other events, therefore such weighting had intuitive appeal for those data. Therefore, I asked Newman to run his weighting algorithm on the **DGG** data, and he obliged. The results were a transformation of the **DGG** data that took his differential weighting into account.

As in the case of the Skvoretz and Faust result described above, I needed a way to convert the Newman data into groups and positions. Just as I did above, I used the complete link form of Johnson's (1967) hierarchical clustering to do that conversion. The clustering algorithm divided the women into a group containing women 1 through 7 and 9 and another with woman 8 along with women 10 through 18. It placed women 1 and 2 at the core of their group. They were followed, in order, by 3, 4, 6, 5, and 7 and 9 tied for the peripheral position. The core of the other group contained 13 and 14. They were followed by 12, 11, 15 and 10 in that order, then 17 and 18 were placed together and finally 8 and 16 were together at the extreme periphery.

That completes the review of 21 analyses of the **DGG** data. All of those analyses—either directly or indirectly—have specified groups among the women. In addition, 11 of them have indicated women's positions in the core or periphery. The question for the next section, then, centers on an examination of what we can learn by considering all of these results together and conducting a meta-analysis.

5. Meta-Analysis of the Results

In Section 4, twenty-one analytic procedures produced two kinds of substantive results when they were applied to the **DGG** data. In every case, groups were specified and individuals were assigned to those groups. And eleven procedures went on to specify various levels of core and peripheral positions and to assign individuals to those positions. The next two sections will review and analyze these two kinds of results. Section 5.1 will deal with groups and Section 5.2 will examine positions.

In each of these sections, meta-analysis will be used to try to answer the two questions posed in Section 1 above: (1) By considering all of the results together, can we come up with an informed description of the group structure revealed in the **DGG** data? And (2), can we distinguish between those analytic tools that were relatively effective and those that were less effective in producing that description?

5.1 Finding Groups

The classifications of women into groups by each of the 21 procedures described in Section 4 yields a 21 by 153 matrix. The 21 rows represent the analytic procedures and the 153 columns represent the unordered pairs of women [(1,2), (1,3) . . . (17,18)]. But, since there is a good deal of agreement among the procedures and since no procedure generated more than two groups, we can simplify their presentation. Figure 7 shows the whole pattern of assignment of women to groups.

In Figure 7 the 18 columns represent the 18 women. And the 21 rows refer to the 21 analytic procedures. A woman in each cell is designated by a "**W**." Groups are designated by colors. All the red "**W**s" in a given row were assigned to the same group by the procedure designated in that row. All the blue ones were assigned to a second group. And in the fourth row there are green "**W**'s" that were assigned to a third group. Any woman who was assigned to two groups by the procedure in question, received a pair of color codes.

		1	2	3	4	5	6	7	8	9	10	11	12	13	14	15	16	17	18
1	DGG41	W	W	W	W	W	W	W	W	WW	W	W	W	W	W	W	W	W	W
2	HOM50	W	W	W	W	W	W	W	WW			W	W	W	W	W		W	W
3	P&C72	W	W	W	W	W	W	W	W	W	W	W	W	W	W	W	W	W	W
4	BGR74	W	W	W	W	W	W	W		W	W	W	W	W	WW	WW		W	W
5	BBA75	W	W	W	W	W	W	W	W	W	W	W	W	W	W	W	W	W	W
6	BCH78	W	W	W	W	W	W				W	W	W	W	W	W			
7	DOR79	W	W	W	W	W	W	W		W	W	W	W	W	W	W			
8	BCH91	W	W	W	W	W	W	W	W	W	W	W	W	W	W	W	W	W	W
9	FRE92	W	W	W	W	W	W	W		W	W	W	W	W	W	W	W		
10	E&B93	W	W	W	W	W	W	W		W	W	W	W	W	W	W			
11	FR193	W	W	W	W	W	W	W	W	W	W	W	W	W	W	W	W	W	W
12	FR293	W	W	W	W	W	W	W	W	W	W	W	W	W	W	W	W	W	W
13	FW193	W	W	W	W	W	W	W	W	W	W	W	W	W	W	W	WW	W	W
14	FW293	W	W	W	W	W	W	W		W	W	W	W	W	W	W		W	W
15	BE197	W	W	W	W	W	W	W		W	W	W	W	W	W	W			
16	BE297	W	W	W	W	W	W	W	W	W	W	W	W	W	W	W	W	W	W
17	BE397	W	W	W	W	W	W	W	W	W	W	W	W	W	W	W	W	W	W
18	S&F99	W	W	W	W	W	W	W	W	W	W	W	W	W	W	W		W	W
19	ROB00	W	W	W	W	W	W	W	W	W	W	W	W	W	W	W	W	W	W
20	OSB00	W	W	W	W	W	W	W	W	W	W	W	W	W	W	W	W	W	W
21	NEW01	W	W	W	W	W	W	W	W	W	W	W	W	W	W	W	W	W	W

Figure 7. Group Assignments by 21 Procedures

What we need here is a way to evaluate the pattern displayed in Figure 7. Batchelder and Romney (1986, 1988, 1989) developed a method called *consensus analysis* that will do just that. Consensus analysis was originally designed to analyze data in which a collection of subjects answered a series of questions. It is based on three assumptions: (1) there is a "true" (but not necessarily known) answer to each question, (2) the answers provided are independent from question to question and (3) all the questions are equally difficult. Given these assumptions, consensus analysis uses the patterning of agreements among subjects to estimate both the "true" answer to each question and the "competence" of each subject. "True" answers are determined by the overall consensus of all the subjects. And the "competence" of a given subject is a function of the degree to which that subject provides answers that are close to the consensual answers.

For each pair of women, each analytic tool was, in effect, asked a kind of true/false question: does this pair of women belong together in the same group? And each analytic tool answered that question—yes or no—for each of the 153 pairs of women.

Thus, consensus analysis can be used to address both questions of interest in the current context. It can determine the "true" answers and it can determine the "competence" of each procedure. It uses an iterative maximum likelihood procedure to estimate the "true" answers. For these data, the answer sheet is shown in Figure 8. There, a woman are in a row is classified as a member of the same group as a woman in a column if there is a 1 in their cell. The bold entries show complete agreement among the 21 procedures. All in all, there are 25 pairs of women where all 21 analytic procedures agreed that they should be placed together. But even in those cases where there was less than total agreement, the probability of misclassification approached zero very closely. The very worst case was the estimate that woman 8 and woman 9 belonged together; in that case the maximum likelihood probability of error was .0008. According to this figure, then, the consensus of the analytic procedures is to assign women 1 through 9 to one group and women 10 through 18 to the other.

	2	3	4	5	6	7	8	9	10	11	12	13	14	15	16	17	18
1	1	1	1	1	1	1	1	1	0	0	0	0	0	0	0	0	0
2		1	1	1	1	1	1	1	0	0	0	0	0	0	0	0	0
3			1	1	1	1	1	1	0	0	0	0	0	0	0	0	0
4				1	1	1	1	1	0	0	0	0	0	0	0	0	0
5					1	1	1	1	0	0	0	0	0	0	0	0	0
6						1	1	1	0	0	0	0	0	0	0	0	0
7							1	1	0	0	0	0	0	0	0	0	0
8								1	0	0	0	0	0	0	0	0	0
9									0	0	0	0	0	0	0	0	0
10										1	1	1	1	1	1	1	1
11											1	1	1	1	1	1	1
12												1	1	1	1	1	1
13													1	1	1	1	1
14														1	1	1	1
15															1	1	1
16																1	1
17																	1

Bold font indicates that all 21 algorithms put this pair together

Figure 8. The Groupings Estimated by Consensus Analysis

Estimates of the "competence" of the 21 analytic procedures are obtained using factor analysis. First, the number of matches in the answers to the 153 questions is calculated for each pair of procedures. Then the covariance in those answers is calculated for each pair. And finally, loadings on the first principal axis are determined using singular value decomposition.

The first axis of each—matches and covariance—provides an index of competence. These two indices are useful in estimating the competence of procedures only if they are in substantial agreement. In this case the correlation between the axis based on matches and that based on covariances was .967. This suggests that the patterning of agreements is robust and that the results are not simply an artifact of the computational procedures.

The estimates of competence based on matches are shown in Figure 9. These are probably overestimates because of the large number of zeros in the data matrix. Nonetheless, because of their high correlation with covariances, they can be taken as monotonically linked to the success of each procedure in approximating the consensus classifications shown in Figure 9.

	Code	Analysis	Closeness to the Matching Criterion
1	DGG41	Davis, Gardner and Gardner, Ethnography	0.920
2	HOM50	Homans, Intuition	0.854
3	P&C72	Phillips and Conviser, Information Theory	0.968
4	BGR74	Breiger, Algebra	0.933
5	BBA75	Breiger, Boorman and Arabie, CONCOR	0.927
6	BCH78	Bonacich, Boolean Algebra	0.841
7	DOR79	Doreian, Algebraic Topology	0.923
8	BCH91	Bonacich, SVD	0.968
9	FRE92	Freeman, G-Transitivity	0.926
10	E&B93	Everett and Borgatti, Regular Coloring	0.916
11	FR193	Freeman, Genetic Algorithm 1	0.968
12	FR293	Freeman, Genetic Algorithm 2	0.842
13	FW193	Freeman and White, Galois Lattice	0.917
14	FW293	Freeman and White, Galois Sub-Lattice	0.954
15	BE197	Borgatti and Everett, Bi-Clique	0.916
16	BE297	Borgatti and Everett, Taboo Search	0.968
17	BE397	Borgatti and Everett, Genetic Algorithm	0.968
18	S&F99	Skvoretz and Faust, p* Model	0.957
19	ROB00	Roberts, SVD with Normalization	0.968
20	OSB00	Osbourn, VERI Algorithm	0.543
21	NEW01	Newman, Weighted Co-Attendance	0.932

Figure 9. The "Competence" Scores of the 21Analytic Procedures

Figure 9 shows variation in the degree to which the various methods produce group assignments that meet this new criterion. Method 20, Osbourn's **VERI** algorithm is dramatically poorer than any of the others. And at the opposite extreme, six of the methods, 3 (Phillips and Conviser's information theory), 8 (Bonacich's correspondence analysis), 15 (Borgatti and Everett's taboo algorithm), 11 (Freeman's first genetic algorithm solution), 16 (Borgatti and Everett's tabu search), 16 (Borgatti and Everett's genetic algorithm) and 19 (Roberts' correspondence analysis) are tied for the best performance. They are followed very closely by two additional methods, 18 (Skvoretz and Faust's **p*** analysis) and 14 (Freeman and White's Galois sub-lattice). All in all, then, we have eight methods that perform very well. They all assigned individuals to groups in a way that is in substantial agreement with the assignments uncovered by consensus analysis.

One area in which the analytic devices displayed no consensus at all has to do with overlap in-group memberships. Only four of the methods reviewed displayed overlapping groups. **DGG** and Homans both relied on intuition, so they could easily specify women who bridged between the groups they reported. **DGG** proposed that woman 9 was a member of their two groups: women 1 through 9 and 9 through 18. Homans saw woman 8 as a bridge between a group that included women 1 through 8 and one containing women 8, 11, 12, 13, 14, 15, 17 and 18. Breiger's analysis was based in part on cliques. Thus, it could, and did allow overlaps. His method suggested that there were three groups, two of which overlapped. One group involved women 1 through 9, a second involved women 10 through 15. And his third group included women 14 and 15 again, along with 17 and 18. Finally, the lattice analysis also allowed overlaps. Freeman and White found that, in lattice terms, woman 16 bridged between their two groups (women 1 through 9 plus 16 in the first, and women 10 through 18 in the second).

Clearly, there is nothing resembling a consensus in these reports of overlap. In fact, the closest thing there is to agreement can be found in the reports by **DGG** and Homans on one hand and the two solutions by Freeman using the genetic algorithm (**FR193** and **FR293**). The two Freeman solutions agreed that women 1 through 7 were a group, as were women 10 through 18. Women 8 and 9 were assigned to the first group by one solution and to the second group by the other. One possible interpretation of these results is that women 8 and 9 were both bridges between groups. This suggests that the lattice analysis supports both the **DGG** designation of woman 9 and the Homans designation of woman 8 as bridges. But beyond that, little can be generalized about these results. When it came to dealing with group overlap, these analyses certainly did not agree.

5.2 Specifying Positions: Core and Periphery

Next we turn to the question of the assignment of individuals to core and peripheral positions. In this case we are limited because only 11 of the analytic procedures produced such assignments. The designation of core and peripheral positions by those 11 procedures is shown in Figure 10. In each procedure, core and peripheral orders were assigned within each group. The first groups are shown on the left and the second groups on the right. Within each group, core/peripheral positions are shown left to right. The vertical lines show the divisions specified by the procedure. In the case of **DGG41**, for example, women 1, 2, 3 and 4 were at the core. They were followed by 5, 6 and 7. And finally, 8 and 9 were farthest from the core.

<table>
<tr><th></th><th>First Group</th><th>Second Group</th></tr>
<tr><td>DGG41</td><td>1 2 3 4 | 5 6 7 | 8 9</td><td>13 14 15 | 11 12 | 9 10 16 17 18</td></tr>
<tr><td>HOM50</td><td>1 2 3 4 5 6 7 | 8</td><td>11 12 13 14 15 | 8 17 18</td></tr>
<tr><td>BCH78</td><td>5 | 1 2 3 4 6</td><td>14 | 10 11 12 13 15</td></tr>
<tr><td>DOR79</td><td>1 3 | 2 4 | 5 6 7 9</td><td>12 13 14 | 10 11 15</td></tr>
<tr><td>BCH91</td><td>5 | 4 | 2 | 1 6 | 3 | 7 | 9 | 8</td><td>17 18 | 12 | 13 14 | 1 | 15 | 10 | 16</td></tr>
<tr><td>FW193</td><td>1 2 3 4 | 5 6 7 8 9 | 16</td><td>13 14 15 | 10 11 12 17 18 | 16</td></tr>
<tr><td>FW293</td><td>1 | 2 3 4 | 5 | 6 | 7 9</td><td>14 | 12 13 15 | 11 17 18 | 10</td></tr>
<tr><td>BE197</td><td>3 4 | 2 | 1 | 7 | 6 | 9 | 5</td><td>12 13 | 11 | 14 | 10 | 15</td></tr>
<tr><td>S&F99</td><td>1 3 | 2 | 4 | 5 | 6 | 7 | 9 | 8</td><td>12 13 | 14 | 15 | 11 | 10 | 17 18</td></tr>
<tr><td>ROB00</td><td>1 | 2 | 4 | 3 | 5 | 6 | 7 | 9 | 8</td><td>12 | 13 | 14 | 11 | 15 | 10 | 16 | 17 18</td></tr>
<tr><td>NEW01</td><td>1 2 | 3 | 4 | 6 | 5 | 7 9</td><td>13 14 | 12 | 11 | 15 | 10 | 17 18 | 8 16</td></tr>
</table>

Figure 10. Core/Periphery Assignments by the 11Analytic Procedures

In dealing with groups, consensus analysis was used to determine the "true" assignment of women to groups. That grouping drew upon the information provided by all the analytic devices considered simultaneously. In dealing with core and peripheral positions, it would be useful to be able to establish a similar criterion for the "true" positions in which to place individuals. But, unfortunately, consensus analysis could not be used here. The analytic devices displayed too much variability in assigning core and peripheral positions. Moreover, with only 11 analytic tools making assignments, there were fewer data points from which to generate reliable estimates.

As an alternative, I used two analytic tools. One is *canonical analysis of asymmetry* (Gower 1977; Freeman, 1997) and the other is *dynamic paired-comparison scaling* (Batchelder and Bershad, 1979; Batchelder, Bershad and Simpson, 1992; Jameson, Appleby and Freeman, 1999).

These two tools offer alternative ways of establishing the "true" or "best" ordering of individuals given something less than complete agreement among the eleven methods. The problem is simplified somewhat by partitioning the original 18 by 18 matrix. The "answer sheet" in Figure 8 above defined women 1 through 9 as one group and 10 through 18 as another. The assignments to core and peripheral positions reflect this division. All in all the eleven methods compared 537 ordered pairs of women in terms of which woman was nearer the core. Of these, 533 comparisons involved women from the same group; only four compared women from different groups. Therefore, since the overall pattern reflects the presence of the same groups that were specified above, I analyzed core/periphery positioning separately for each of those two groups. The core/periphery matrix for the first group is shown in Figure 11. That for the second is shown in Figure 12.

	1	**2**	**3**	**4**	**5**	**6**	**7**	**8**	**9**
1	0	4	4	5	8	8	9	7	9
2	2	0	3	3	8	9	9	7	9
3	1	3	0	3	7	7	8	6	8
4	2	2	2	0	8	8	9	7	9
5	2	2	2	2	0	5	5	6	6
6	0	0	1	0	2	0	5	6	7
7	0	0	0	0	1	1	0	6	5
8	0	0	0	0	0	0	0	0	0
9	0	0	0	0	1	0	0	4	0

Number of times the row woman was judged more central than the column woman

Figure 11. Matrix of Frequencies of Assignment to a "Closer to the Core" Position by 11 Analytic Procedures for the First Group of Nine

	1	2	3	4	5	6	7	8	9
1	0	0	0	0	0	1	4	3	3
2	7	0	0	0	1	4	5	5	5
3	8	7	0	2	4	6	5	6	6
4	9	9	3	0	3	6	5	7	7
5	10	9	5	2	0	8	5	7	7
6	7	4	2	0	0	0	5	7	7
7	0	0	0	0	0	0	0	1	1
8	2	1	1	1	1	1	3	0	0
9	2	1	1	1	1	1	3	0	0

Number of times the row woman was judged more central than the column woman

Figure 12. Matrix of Frequencies of Assignment to a "Closer to the Core" Position by 11 Analytic Procedures for the Second Group of Nine

These two data sets were first subjected to canonical analysis of asymmetry. As it is used here, the canonical analysis is based on an on/off—all or none—model. Each cell $\mathbf{X}_{ij}$ in the data matrix is compared with its counterpart $\mathbf{X}_{ji}$. Whichever is the larger of the two is set equal to ½ and the smaller is set equal to -½. If the two are equal, both are set to 0. Thus, either woman i is closer to the core than woman j, woman j is closer than i, or neither is closer.

The resulting matrix is called *skew-symmetric*. A skew-symmetric matrix displays an important property when it is analyzed using singular value decomposition. If a linear order is present, the first two axes of the output form a perfect arc around the origin. The arc arranges the points from the one at the extreme core to the one at the most extreme periphery.

The results for the data of Figures 11 and 12 both formed perfect arcs. They ordered the women in each of the two groups as shown in the third column of Figure 13. Those results show that the canonical all or none approach produces clear results. Women 5 and 6 fall at the same level, as do women 17 and 18. Other than these two positional ties, the canonical analysis displays a linear order for each of the two groups. It places woman 1 in the first group and woman 13 in the second in the extreme core positions. And it places women 8 and 16 in the extreme peripheries of their respective groups.

The other procedure, paired-comparison scaling, is not based on an all or none model. Instead, it provides real valued dominance scores that are sensitive to the proportion of judgments in which each woman is assigned a position nearer the core than each of the others. This approach is based on Thurstone's (1927) method of paired comparisons. Again we begin by comparing each cell $\mathbf{X}_{ij}$ in the data matrix with its counterpart $\mathbf{X}_{ji}$. Only this time we do not convert the numbers to dichotomous values. Instead, we convert them to probabilities:

$$P_{ij}=X_{ij}/(X_{ij}+X_{ji}).$$

These probabilities, then, are used to determine the core/periphery order.

Normal distribution assumptions are used to assign an initial level to each woman. Her initial level is determined by the number of others with whom she was compared, and the number of those comparisons in which she was determined to be nearer the core. These initial levels are then used in a recursive equation to assign each woman a final

Label	Woman	Rank on Canonical Analysis	Rank on Paired-Comparison
1	EVELYN	1	1
2	LAURA	2	2
3	THERESA	3	3
4	BRENDA	4	4
5	CHARLOTTE	5.5	5
6	FRANCES	5.5	6
7	ELEANOR	7	7
8	PEARL	9	9
9	RUTH	8	8
10	VERNE	6	6
11	MYRA	5	5
12	KATHERINE	3	3
13	SYLVIA	1	1
14	NORA	2	2
15	HELEN	4	4
16	DOROTHY	9	9
17	OLIVIA	7.5	7.5
18	FLORA	7.5	7.5

Figure 13. The Core-Periphery Rankings Assigned to Each Group of Women by the Two Scaling Procedures

level in the hierarchy. These final levels depend on the same two factors listed above. And, in addition, they depend on the number of comparisons in which a given woman was judged farther from the core and the average level of all those with whom she was compared

These calculations are repeated, again and again, each time adjusting for the changed values of the average levels of others. Finally, they converge and further computations are unnecessary. The final result is a scaling. Each woman is assigned a numerical score that represents her position in the continuum from core to periphery. The rank orders produced by this scaling are shown in the fourth column in Figure 13.

These two calculations involve approaches that are quite different. So it is heartening to discover that they order the women almost identically. The only difference is found in the first group. The canonical analysis shows a tie between woman 5 and woman 6, but the paired-comparison analysis places woman 5 closer to the core than woman 6.

To evaluate the effectiveness of each of the 11 orders provided by the analytic procedures, I used **gamma. Gamma** provides an order-based measure of agreement. I compared each of the orders suggested by the procedures with the idealized orders provided by canonical analysis and paired-comparison analysis.

Because the two idealized orders are so similar, their **gammas** with the orders produced by the analytic procedures were, of course, nearly identical. The results for both the canonical and the paired-comparison standards are shown in Figure 14.

For both model-based standards, Homans' order produced the highest gamma. One must be careful, however, in looking at these values because different **gamma** calculations may be built on vastly different numbers of observations. In this case, the value of 1.0 associated with Homans' work was based on only 17 comparisons in the order of the women. In contrast the values associated with the two analyses by Newman were based on 58 and 59 comparisons respectively. Because Homans' report contained relatively less information about who was in the core and who was peripheral, it generated fewer predictions about positions. The predictions it did make happened to agree with the positional information produced by both criteria. But the Newman analyses both produced large numbers of predictions, and they were still mostly in agreement with those produced by the criteria.

Beyond Newman, the orders produced by Davis, Gardner and Gardner themselves, by Doreian, by Freeman and White in their first analysis, and by Skvoretz and Faust are consistently in agreement with the criteria. Their **gammas** are all above .9 and they are all based on at least 43 comparisons. At the opposite extreme, both Bonacich analyses and the Borgatti and Everett bi-clique analysis do not agree very well with the criteria.

ID	Code	Analysis	Gamma with Cannonical	Number of Comps	Gamma with Paired-Comparison	Number of Comps
1	DGG41	Davis, Gardner and Gardner, Ethnog.	0.962	52	0.923	52
2	HOM50	Homans, Intuition	1.000	17	1.000	17
6	BCH78	Bonacich, Boolean Algebra	-0.111	9	0.000	10
7	DOR79	Doreian, Algebraic Topology	0.929	28	0.929	28
8	BCH91	Bonacich, Correspondence Analysis	0.313	67	0.324	68
12	FW193	Freeman and White, Full Lattice	0.953	43	0.953	43
13	FW293	Freeman and White, Sub-Lattice	0.867	45	0.870	46
14	BE197	Borgatti and Everett, Bi-Clique	0.385	39	0.350	40
17	S&F99	Skvoretz and Faust, p*	0.932	59	0.933	60
18	ROB00	Roberts, Correspondence Analysis	0.844	64	0.846	65
20	NEW01	Newman, Weighted Co-Attendance	0.966	58	0.932	59

Figure 14. Gammas Showing the Degree to which 11 Analyses Agreed with the Two Standards in Assigning Individuals to Core and Peripheral Positions

So again, we have been able to uncover something close to a consensus—this time with respect to core and peripheral positions. And we have again been able to find out something about the extent to which each of the analytic procedures approaches that consensus.

6. Summary and Discussion

6.1 Assignment to Groups

Each of the 21 analyses reported here assigned the **DGG** women to groups. Consensus analysis determined the agreement among the assignments. It turned out that there was a strong core of agreement among most of the analytic devices. The agreement was substantial enough to allow the model to be used specify a partition of the women into groups—one that captured the consensus of all the analyses. At the same time, the consensus analysis was also able to provide ratings of the "competence" of each of the analytic procedures.

The consensual assignment of women to groups and the "competence" ratings of the analytic methods were reported above. The "competence" scores were reflected in the first axis of an singular value decomposition of the matches generated by the methods in assigning pairs of women to the same or to different groups. In that earlier examination I reported only the first axis. But here, it is instructive to examine the second and third axes. They are shown in Figure 15.

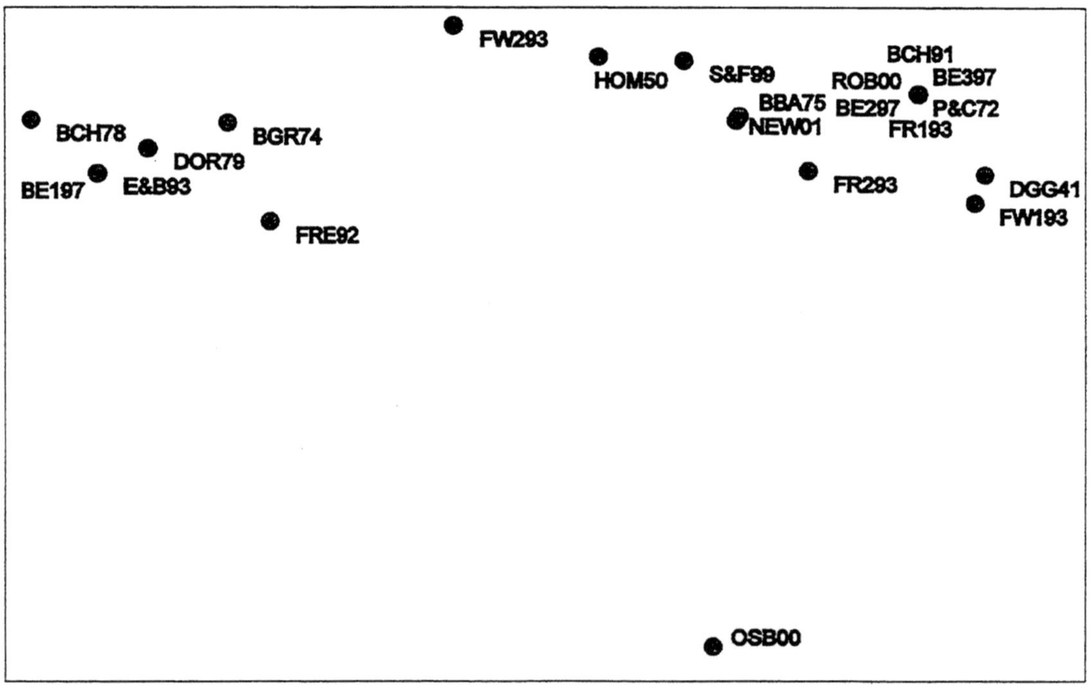

Figure 15. Axes 2 and 3 Produced by the Singular Value Decomposition of the Matches in the Assignments of Women

The arrangement of points representing the analytic methods in Figure 15 tells a good deal about both the partitioning of women to groups and the competence of the methods. The consensus put women 1 through 9 in the first group and women 10 through 18 in the second. In Figure 15, the basis for determining why this was the "best" partition becomes apparent. That partition was specified exactly by six of the analytic procedures: **P&C72** (The corrected version of Phillips and Conviser's information theoretic algorithm), **BCH91** (Bonacich's correspondence analysis), **FR193** (Freeman's first genetic algorithm solution), **BE297** (Borgatti and Everett's taboo search), **BE397** (Borgatti and Everett's genetic algorithm) and **ROB00** (Roberts' correspondence analysis of normalized data). These analyses are all placed at a single point at the upper right of the figure.

Other analyses that produced results that were quite close to that ideal pattern are clustered closely around that point. For example, **BBA75** and **NEW01** produced the same pattern with only one exception. They both assigned woman 8 to the second group. **FR292** assigned both women 8 and 9 to the second group. **DGG41** put woman 9 in both groups. And **FW193** put woman 16 in both. Finally, **S&F99** deviated only by failing to include woman 16 in either group. Thus, in addition to the six "perfect" partitionings, six additional procedures came very close to the ideal and are clustered in the region surrounding these "perfect" solutions. This clustering is the key. It shows a clear consensus around the 1-9, 10-18 division. This consensus is really remarkable in view of the immense differences among the analytic procedures used.

Figure 16 re-labels all the points such that their departure from the "perfect" partitioning is displayed. Note that the 1-9, 10-18 partition is labeled "**PERFECT**." Note also that departures from that ideal are generally placed farther from the **PERFECT** point as the degree of their departure grows. They are, moreover, segregated in terms of the kinds of departure they embody. All the points that fall on the left of the vertical axis involve methods that failed to assign two or more of the women to groups. Overall, those points are arranged in such a way that those falling further to the left are those that are missing more women. Immediately to the right of the vertical, are the methods that located women in the "wrong" group. And their height indicates the number of women classified in "error." All the way to the right are the methods that assigned women to both groups. And, to the degree that they assigned more women in that way, they are farther to the right. Finally, it should be noted that there are two analyses that assigned women to multiple groups on the left. But it is clear from their placement that this analysis was more responsive to their inability to place women in groups than it was to their dual assignments.

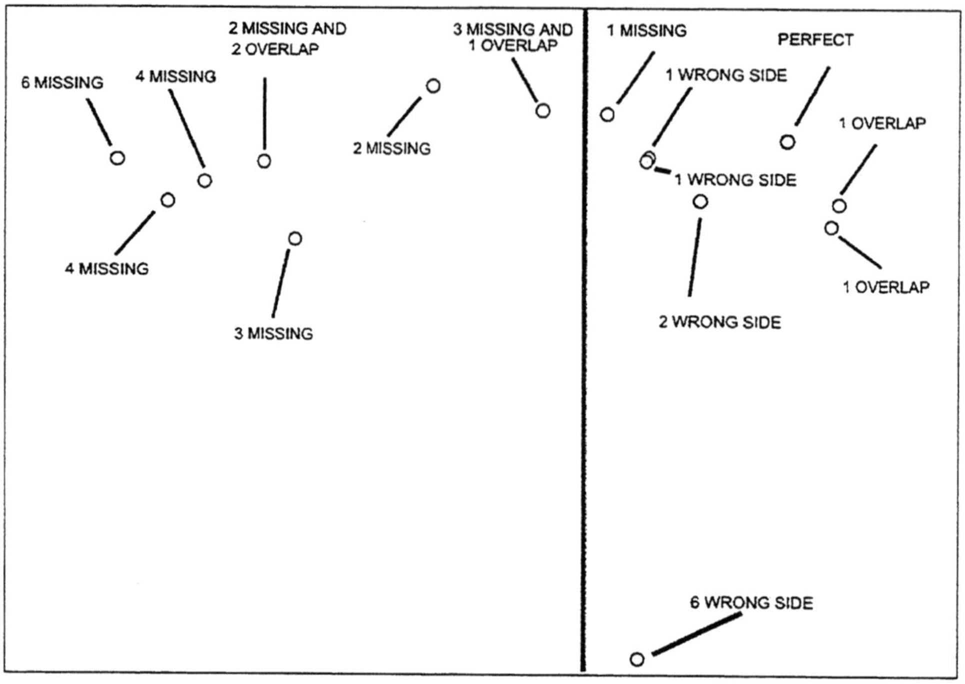

Figure 16. Axes 2 and 3 of the Matches Labeled by Structural Form

Overall, then, it is clear that there was a consensus about assigning women to groups. Six methods agreed, and most of the others departed relatively little from that agreed-upon pattern.

6.2 Positions in Groups

In assigning positions to individuals, I used two, quite different, scaling techniques. One was based on a dominance model. For each pair of women **A** and **B**, the model placed **A** closer to the core than **B**, if and only if more procedures placed **A** closer to the core than **B**. The other was probability-based. It placed **A** closer to the core than **B** with some probability based on the proportion of procedures that placed **A** closer to the core than **B**.

Despite their differences, the results of these two methods turned out to be almost identical. They were similar enough that either could be taken as providing something very close to an optimum assignment of individuals to positions. The effectiveness of each of the analytic procedures was evaluated by their monotone correlations with these optima. The results were very similar; the correlation between the gammas produced by the dominance model and those produced by the probability model was .983. So, even with without consensus among the procedures, I was able to find the agreed-upon order—core to periphery—and to evaluate the ability of each method to uncover that order.

6.3 A Final Word

As a whole I believe that this meta-analysis has been productive. As far as assigning women to groups was concerned, the results were dramatic. When it came to assigning women to positions, the results were less dramatic, but still fairly convincing. We end, then, with four strong results: (1) We have a consensual partitioning of women into groups. (2) We have a consensual assignment of women into core and peripheral positions. (3) We have a rating of the methods in terms of their competence in assigning women to groups. And (4) we have a rating of the methods in terms of their ordinal correlations with the standard positional assignments.

I would like to wind up with two additional comparisons of the analytic procedures examined here. These final comparisons will be restricted to the published analyses of the **DGG** data; they will not include the unpublished analyses involving my use of Osbourn's **VERI** or the analysis Newman ran at my request.

The first comparison is based on time. Figure 17 shows the average competence ratings of procedures published at various points of time. The data in Figure 17 show an interesting secular trend. There has been a slow but consistent trend toward increasing competence through time. Thus, the overall tendency in published reports using the **DGG** data is clearly in the direction of greater competence.

In addition, it is possible to make some generalizations about the adequacy of the various kinds of analytic procedures that have been used to find groups and positions using the **DGG** data. Six procedures (**BGR74**, **BCH78**, **DOR79**, **E&B93**, **FW193** and **FW293**) all took essentially algebraic approaches. Five (**P&C72**, **FR193**, **FR293**, **BE197** and **BE297**) used various algorithms to search for an optimal partition. Three analyses (**BBA75**, **BCH91** and **ROB00**) employed various versions of singular value decomposition. Two (**DGG41** and **HOM50**) were based simply on the authors' intuititions. And three developed unique approaches. One (**FRE92**) looked at a kind of transitivity. A second (**BE197**) dealt with overlapping bicliques. And the third (**S&F99**) developed a statistical model.

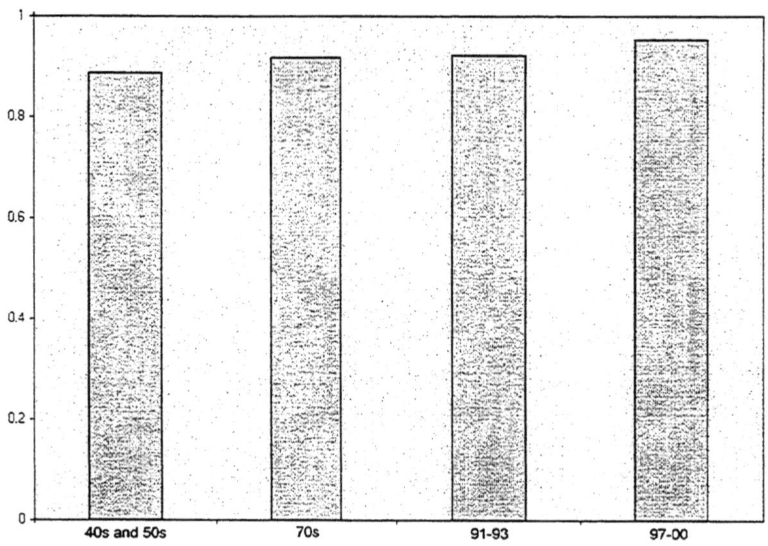

Figure 17. Competences of the Procedures Over Time

All in all, then, we have used seven distinct classes of procedures in analyzing the **DGG** data. Figure 18 shows the relative success of each class in terms of its average competence.

Procedure	N	Average Score
Statistical Model	1	0.957
Eigen Structure	3	0.954
Optimal Partition	5	0.941
Transitivity	1	0.926
Cliques	1	0.916
Algebraic Duality	6	0.914
Intuition	2	0.887

Figure 18. Average Competences of the Various Classes of Procedures

A number of features of Figure 17 are worth noting. First, the statistical model of the **DGG** data developed by Skvoretz and Faust was the winner. It won despite the fact that, unlike most of the other procedures, it was not explicitly designed to uncover groups. Group structure emerged as a sort of bi-product of a broader structural analysis.

The statistical model is not, however, the undisputed champion. It is followed so closely by the three singular value decomposition analyses, that it has to share the crown with them. And the five partitioning programs are right up there near the top.

There seems to be a step between all those procedures and the next three. Clearly transitivity, bicliques and the algebra-based approaches did not do as well. And, finally, the intuitive judgments fall at the bottom. In part that position is due to the vagaries of Homans' report, but **DGG** themselves did very little better. This result is particularly interesting given the fact that Davis, Gardner and Gardner's interpretation of their own data is often taken as privileged. The assumption has been that because they had a huge amount of ethnographic experience in the community, **DGG** had an edge—they somehow knew the "true" group structure. But, particularly in the light of the present results, there is no compelling reason to award **DGG** any special exalted status *vis-à-vis* their ability to assign individuals to groups. Indeed, their very intimacy with these 18 women might have led to various kinds of biased judgments.

References

Batchelder, W. H. and N. J. Bershad
1979 The statistical analysis of a Thurstonian model for rating chess players. Journal of Mathematical Psychology, 19:39–60.

Batchelder, W. H., N. J. Bershad and R. S. Simpson
1992 Dynamic paired-comparison scaling. Journal of Mathematical Psychology, 36:185–212.

Batchelder, W. H. and A. K. Romney
1986 The statistical analysis of a general Condorcet model for dichotomous choice situations. In B. Grofman and G. Owen (Eds.) Information Pooling and Group Decision Making. Greenwich, Connecticut: JAI Press, Inc.

Batchelder, W. H. and A. K. Romney
1988 Test theory without an answer key. Psychometrika 53:71-92.

Batchelder, W. H. and A. K. Romney
1989 New results in test theory without an answer key. In E. Roskam (Ed.) Advances in Mathematical Psychology Vol. II. Heidelberg New York: Springer Verlag.

Birkhoff, G.
1940 Lattice theory. New York: American Mathematical Society.

Bonacich, P.
1978 Using boolean algebra to analyze overlapping memberships.

Sociological Methodology 101-115.

Bonacich, P.
1990 Simultaneous group and individual centralities. Social Networks 13:155-168.

Borgatti, S. P. and M. G. Everett
1997 Network analysis of 2-mode data. Social Networks 19:243-269.

Borgatti, S. P., M. G. Everett and L. C. Freeman
1991 UCINET IV, Version 1.0. Reference Manual. Columbia, SC: Analytic Technologies.

Breiger, R. L.
1974 The duality of persons and groups. Social Forces 53:181-190.

Breiger, R. L., S. A. Boorman and P. Arabie
1975 An algorithm for clustering relational data, with applications to social network analysis and comparison to multidimensional scaling. Journal of Mathematical Psychology 12:328-383.

Cooley, C. H.
1909 Social Organization. New York: C. Scribner's sons.

Davis, A., B. B. Gardner and M. R. Gardner
1941 Deep South. Chicago: The University of Chicago Press.

Davis, A. and W. L. Warner
1939 A comparative study of American caste. In Race Relations and the Race Problem. (Ed.) E. T. Thompson. Durham: Duke University Press.

Deming, W. E. and F. F. Stephan
1940 On a least squares adjustment of a sampled frequency table when the expected marginal totals are known. Annals of Mathematical Statistics 11:427-444.

Doreian, P.
1979 On the delineation of small group structure. In H. C. Hudson, ed. Classifying Social Data, San Francisco: Jossey-Bass.

Durkheim, É.
[1893] 1933 The division of labor in society. Translated by G. Simpson. New York: Free Press.

Everett, M. G. and S. P. Borgatti
1992 An Extension of regular colouring of graphs to digraphs, networks and hypergraphs. Social Networks 15:237-254.

Forsyth, E. and L. Katz
1946 A matrix approach to the analysis of sociometric data. Sociometry 9: 340-347.

Freeman, L. C.
1993 On the sociological concept of "group": a empirical test of two models. American Journal of Sociology 98:152-166.

Freeman, L. C.
1994 Finding groups with a simple genetic algorithm. Journal of Mathematical Sociology 17:227-241.

Freeman, L. C.
1997 Uncovering organizational hierarchies. Computational and Mathematical Organization Theory 3:5-18

Freeman, L. C. and V. Duquenne
1993 A note on regular colorings of two mode data. .Social Networks 15:437-442.

Freeman, L. C. and D. R. White
1994 Using Galois lattices to represent network data. In Sociological Methodology 1993. P. Marsden, ed. Pp. 127-146. Cambridge, MA: Blackwell.

Garner, W. R. and W. J. McGill
1956 The relations between information and variance analyses. Psychometrika 21: 219-228.

Glover, F.
1989 Tabu search.-- Part 1. ORSA Journal on Computing 1: 190-206.

Goodman, L. A.
1995 A single general method for the analysis of cross-classified data: Reconciliation and synthesis of some methods of Pearson, Yule, and Fisher, and also some methods of correspondence analysis and association analysis. Journal of the American Statistical Association 91: 408-428.

Gower, J.C.
1976 The Analysis of asymmetry and orthoganality. In J. Barra, F. Brodeau

and G. Romier (Eds.), Recent Developments in Statistics, North Holland, Amsterdam.

Granovetter, M.
1973 The strength of weak ties. American Journal of Sociology 81: 1287-1303.

Holland, J. H.
1962 Outline for a logical theory of adaptive systems. Journal of the ACM, 9:297-314.

Homans, G. C.
1950 The Human Group. New York: Harcourt, Brace and Company.

Jameson, K. A., M. C. Appleby and L. C. Freeman
1998 Finding an appropriate order for a hierarchy based on probabilistic dominance. Animal Behaviour 57:991-998.

Johnson, S. C.
1967 Hierarchical clustering schemes. Psychometrika 32:241-254.

Koch, G. G. and L. M. LaVange
1991 An overview of statistical issues and methods of meta-analysis Journal of Biopharmaceutical Statistics 1:103-120

Luce, R. D., and A. Perry
1949 A method of matrix analysis of group structure," Psychometrika, 14:95-116.

Mosteller, F.
1968 Association and estimation in contingency tables. Journal of the American Statistical Association 63: 1-28.

Newman, M.
2001 The structure of scientific collaboration networks. Proceedings of the National Academy of Science 98:404-409.

Osbourn, G. C.
1999 Clustering, pattern recognition and augmentation of data visualization using VERI algorithm. Invited talk, American Statistical Society Meeting.

Phillips, D. P. and R. H. Conviser
1972 Measuring the structure and boundary properties of groups: Some uses of information theory. Sociometry 35:235-254.

Richards, W. and A. Seary
1996 Introduction to eigen analysis of networks. Paper presented at the INSNA Sunbelt Meeting, San Diego. http://www.sfu.ca/~richards/Pages/wdr97.htm

Roberts, J. M. Jr.
2000 Correspondence analysis of two-mode networks. Social Networks 22:65-72.

Roethlisberger, F. J. and W. J. Dickson
1939 Management and the Worker: An Account of a Research Program Conducted by the Western Electric Company, Hawthorne Works, Chicago. Cambridge, Mass.: Harvard University Press.

Sailer, L. D., and S. J. C. Gaulin
1984 Proximity, sociality and observation: the definition of social groups. American Anthropologist, 86, 91-98.

Shanon, C. E.
1963 The mathematical theory of communication. In C. E. Shannon and W. Weaver, The Mathematical Theory of Communication. Urbana: University of Illinois Press.

Skvoretz, J. and K. Faust
1999 Logit models for affiliation networks. Sociological Methodology 29:253-280.

Spencer, H.
1895-97 The Principles of Sociology. 3d ed., New York: D. Appleton.

Thurstone, L. L.
1927 A law of comparative judgment. Psychological Review 34:273-286.

Tönnies, F.
[1855] 1936 Fundamental Concepts of Sociology (Gemeinschaft und gesellschaft). Translated and supplemented by C. P. Loomis. New York: American Book Company.

Warner, M.
1987 W. Lloyd Warner: Social Anthropologist. New York: Publishing Center for Cultural Resources.

Wasserman, S. and P. Pattison
1997 Logit models and logistic regressions for social networks: I. An introduction to Markov graphs and p*. Psychometrika, 60:401-426.

Autonomy vs. Equivalence Within Market Network Structure?

Harrison White --Notes, November 2002

Results from three authors—Burt, Podolny, and White— will be melded, yielding surprising answers to this title question.

PART I. SETUP

Structural Holes proposes formulae for direct and indirect constraints, and back-constraints, upon dickering of ego with all alters in ego's observed network. With dollar volume of transaction as tie strength, Ron Burt adapts these principled formulae for log regression fitting across the 500 or so four-digit SIC markets in the 1970s American economy. The constraints are gathered into an overall measure of structural autonomy—Straut—and entrepreneurial success is measured by net income to ego market. His Figure 2.8 illustrates the worst, nightmare context for ego.

Podolny theorizes the conditions in which single producers (in a finance market) will seek status in this market of theirs versus when instead they will dicker à la Burt—around their alters' anxiety of being constrained versus ego's uncertainty in choosing a right offer. Figure P is his 2x2.

Markets from Networks predicts emergence of a ranked set of producers as a market to subdue their Knightian uncertainty of sales downstream, when their cost schedules stack in the same order as buyers' valuations of their qualities. The producers must offer equally good tradeoffs of their quality status versus the volume committed to, and then each can find a unique optimum niche along the observed schedule of producer revenue by volume across that market.

> So I cannot apply Burt's formulas for Straut, since I fold into a cost schedule all the charges for procurements from diverse markets upstream to the volume y delivered across all buyers downstream by a producer, in return for revenues, call them worth W(y). Whereas Burt aggregated the producers as a market, even though he can keep the flows from markets upstream separate from flows to markets downstream.
>
> On the other hand I predict, I don't assume as given, the sizes of the ties to ego once these are aggregated into total inflow and outflow to that producer. And I predict, not just observe, the profitability to each producer.
>
> Both my predictions draw simultaneously on measures from upstream, from downstream, and from the producer set in between, not just from buyer and seller as two "sides."

In *Structural Holes*, Burt (his Chapter 6) applies an approximate, aggregate version of this White model, alongside his Straut measures, to the industry data and concludes that they fit together, partially. I offered a very crude version of Burt's entrepreneur (my Chapter 5), with the same conclusion.

But the phenomenologies remain unreconciled: the joining is ad hoc. Podolny provides the insight to meld them: **That is the goal of this paper.**

PART II. COMBINING INSIGHTS

Podolny like Burt deals with just two sides and invokes complementary uncertainties of egos and alters.

Crucial groundwork comes from the earlier Burt book (1983), where he still troubles to keep procurement ties and sales ties distinct instead of symmetrizing the ties as he does in *Structural Holes*. From his fittings there (Table 2.5) to the national data:

(1) The contribution to Straut from market procurement ties with upstream is much less so that Podolny's looking only at alters downstream is a reasonable fit.

(2) The backlash, against ego Straut, from alters exploiting weak binding among the firms within ego market is as substantial as the exploiting of structural holes downstream by ego market. So this market is shown to be a distinct operative level of actor—albeit untheorized, merely ad hoc insertion, in Burt.

This justifies calling on Podolny's framing, Figure P.

Markets from Networks lays out varieties of market not as a 2x2 table but as a two-dimensional MAP: see the diagram, where the vertical axis parameter, call it v, scales valuation of volume y by downstream over against valuation of y by ego as cost from upstream for volume produced. The horizontal axis parameter, call it u, analogously is ratio of valuation downstream of distinctive quality of product versus cost upstream required for that level of quality.

> The market mechanism runs off a profile of worth W by volume y committed to as choice set by producers. Feedback from observations by producers and others is the fuel. The mechanism is sited with appropriately simple descriptions of cost and attraction schedules. Producers engage in a self-consistent search for optimal niche on a viable schedule.
>
> Predictions of robustness of the profile vary with location in MAP, as do the volumes and profitabilities predicted across any particular set of qualities for producers.
>
> (1) The outcome profile, being an equilibrating between competing variabilities, each local, necessarily is path dependent, which fits well with the Burt vision of dickering a la Straut. The path index, k, is a single number, which may be plus or minus.

(2) Only for one median path, indexed by k = 0, can closed formulae replace messy numerical algorithms, guiding qualitative exploration.

(3) In this special case k = 0, each producer has the same profitability percentage (though not revenue), which also makes for easy comparison with Burt's treatment only of aggregate markets.

Four regions of MAP are demarcated by the line at v = 1 together with the diagonal for v = u. So just these two parameters, v and u, tell much about outcomes even without knowing the producers particular locations on quality, effected through different investments for facilities. Descriptors for the general sort of market found in each region are entered in MAP.

Now we can apply to Podolny for guidance.
Alter uncertainty—that is downstream uneasiness about their deal-making, is surely going to increase with the extent of their being more eager for given quality than producers are to supply it at that volume. Thus the diagonal should be the split line with alter uncertainty high on the lower diagonal region. So Podolny would have (Hypothesis 1) a rank based market form such as W(y) activated down and right from the diagonal.

Ego uncertainty—that is producers' concerns about how best to handle their business—surely will be exacerbated when v is greater than unity which means that downstream eagerness for volume is not conveniently kept in check by cost-based reluctance of producers. So Podolny would have (Hypothesis 2) ad hoc Burt maneuvering take over markets in contexts in the region above the horizontal line v = 1.

Presto, we replicate the topology of Poldolny's insightful 2x2, but with changed interpretation of cells: see the second MAP.

The Low-Low cell Podolny has as pure competition, say wheat markets without much structuring by either rank or maneuver. But the W(y) feedback rank model has it as the basic ordinary sort of production market—and yet exposed also, for path indexed b negative value of k, to dissolution into chaotic maneuver a la Burt.

The lower right cell, High-Low, Podolny argues is premier context for rank market, such as his house roofing. But White locates regional road haulage as prototype there and shows a contradiction between context, which indeed favors rank market, and feedback mechanism, which is prey to cheating by low-quality aspirants for producer slots and thus induces some Burt dickering.

The upper left cell, Low-High, Podolny has as premier context for Burt maneuver. The W(y) feedback model agrees, but with the proviso that for a limited class of paths, a rank market can establish itself, disciplining producers.

These insights can refine results from Burt, too. Note the huge scatter in Burt's graphs of market outcomes versus Straut.

According to Burt's results, constraint on alters is heavily increased by perceived extent of joint action by the producer set that they confront—Burt uses the conventional Four Leading Firms' share of market as measure.

And *Markets from Networks* derives how such concentration (using the more general Gini index) will vary with location in MAP. It is opposite in the bottom half from the top half!: the sort of result one can expect from non-linear feedback.

More basic still, Burt has the profitability of ego and its four-firm concentration going up together. Whereas the W(y) model says they vary oppositely, though with opposite polarity for v>1 and v<1.

I suggest that if markets that do go primarily with W(y) are separated from those that are "catch as catch can" entrepreneurial, the scatter in Burt's results will lessen because these opposite predictions are segregated out of overall results.

PART III. A THIRD DIMENSION

However, the deepest results concern the remaining cell:

The High-High upper right box maps into the upper right triangle labeled CROWDED: This is in W(y) terms a viable stable market, and yet also a super-market in outcomes, rather than the unstable market intuited by Podolny with High-Risk Debt as example. Podolny's two hypotheses clash for this cell, whereas the W(y) feedback model shows that the two tendencies can reinforce—but only in terms of a further, third dimension to MAP not mentioned earlier.

This third dimension both explicates the CROWDED triangle of MAP and thus the High-High cell for Podolny. And at the same time it rescues a contribution of Burt's from his own discard pile.

The third dimension, labeled x, measures aggregate impacts on valuations by buyers downstream of the ego market from their awareness of other markets lying cross-stream. Both the markets upstream from a given market and the markets downstream are reflected in the MAP dimensions u and v. There are, besides, maybe hundreds of markets with no discernible influence, direct or indirect, on the given one. But there usually are a number of others which are to some extent structurally equivalent to the given one: that is have a somewhat similar pattern of what producers and/or markets they buy from and sell to—call them "cross-stream."

Cross-stream markets are a weakened form of the structural equivalence exhibited by the set of producer firms being ranked by quality within the given market.

So it makes sense to call *x* a measure of generalized substitutability.

Now comes my claim: This x substitutability has impact upon W(y) market size analogous to the impact of secondary structural holes upon Straut in Burt's theory of markets.

Burt is ingenious and persistent in formulating this leveraging upon dickering through intermediary ties: see Figure 2.8 and associated formulae. Yet Burt largely discards such impacts on several grounds:

It is hard to trace networks completely enough to permit measurement, except for government generated censuses of ties: in the chapters where Burt treats individual managers rather than markets of firms, Burt could not come up with any of the needed data.

It is not clear conceptually how to model impact of secondary structural holes upon his dependent variable of profitability.

So prediction from W(y) of the impact of substitutability x upon market size can suggest how much Burt is missing by discarding secondary holes.

After all, the really extraordinary outcome is that W(y) markets can ever be stable in the High-High cell, the CROWDED triangle in MAP. The prediction is that markets in this region are stabilized only through an appreciable degree of substitutability x induced by cross-stream markets.

In other words, my challenge to Podolnys' characterization of High-High context comes only through effects of cross-stream markets, analogous to Burt's second-order structural holes. Once again this shows how a feedback model can deepen and enrich insights.

Substitutability is being included in only a crude and approximate way, as seen by use of just one parameter as sufficient descriptor. The benefit is that explicit prediction formulae can be derived. This is a complex and multi-stage procedure, which is laid out fully in my ISERP Working Paper 02-02, available on the Web from the Columbia site.

There are two final surprising predictions.

(1) **For most of the contexts laid out as points in the parameter space MAP, as the substitutability x from cross-stream markets grows, the aggregate size of the W(y) market (assuming it is reachable by a viable path and so can exist) actually increases!!**

But the quantitative impact generally is slight, which is conformable with Burt's discard.

(2) **There is however an exception for much of the High-High cell, that is, for CROWDED markets**. Figure 8 from my Working Paper 02-92 shows the two possible curves for aggregate

market size (sum of revenues across producers) versus substitutability x. The upper, exceptional curve applies within MAP in and only in a central cone within High-High, CROWDED region. In this cone the aggregate market size decreases as substitutability increases, just as one might intuit from the siphoning away by the cross-stream markets. But surprise #1 above shows that the intuition is not generally reliable for such complex feedback situations.

Putting all this together, the larger surprise is that the most distinctive, profitable and possibly common market—especially, as it turns out, for new product markets—is sustainable only through the hidden support of cross-stream markets, Burt's second order holes. That is, the CROWDED markets (analyzed at length in Chapters 6 and 7 of White, 1992) exist by sufferance, predictable sufferance, of second order maneuvering.

There is much else to explicate. Besides k, there is another historical descriptor (tau) built into the W(y) model, and each should impact on predictions about dickering versus market profile discipline, plus there are other extensions and generalization, including possible to Small World analyses. There are hosts of other directions to explore in Burt's writings and in a cascade of articles by Podolny and co-workers. And each of us point to still other authors contributing to the emerging network based sociology of markets and firms.

References

Burt, Ronald S. 1992. *Structural Holes: The Social Structure of Competition.* Cambridge: Harvard University Press.

Podolny, Joel M. 2001. "Networks as the Pipes and Prisms of the Markets." *American Journal of Sociology.*

White, Harrison C. 2002. *Markets from Networks.* Princeton: Princeton University Press.

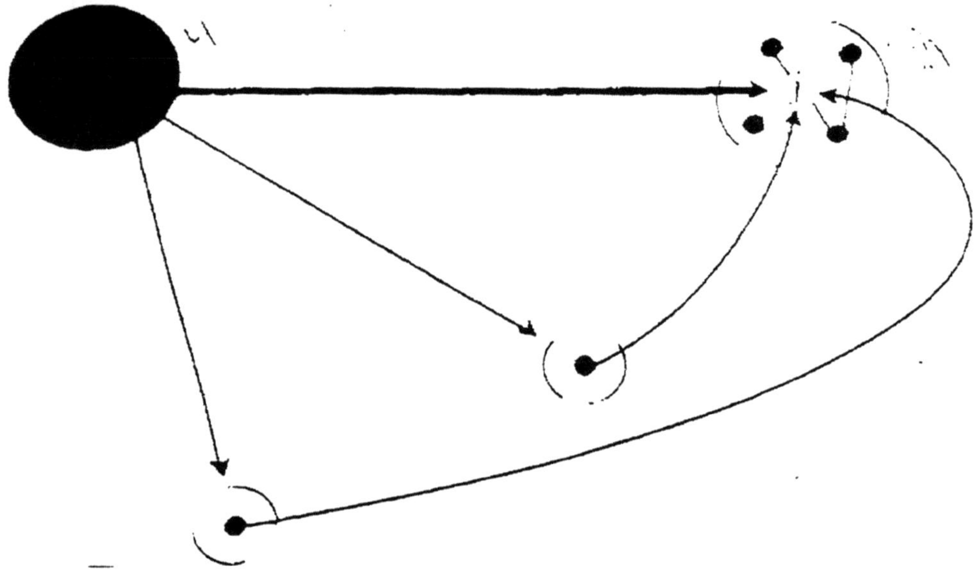

Conditions Limiting i's Entrepreneurial Negotiation in the Relationship with j

(1) P_{ij} is high

(2) P_{jq} arc high

(3) $( )_j$ is high

(4) O_j is low

Figure 2.8 The entrepreneur's nightmare

Ego uncertainty	Alter uncertainty: LOW	Alter uncertainty: HIGH
HIGH	e.g., vaccine production	e.g., high-yield debt
LOW	e.g., wheat	e.g., house roofing

Figure P. Podolny 2x2 table

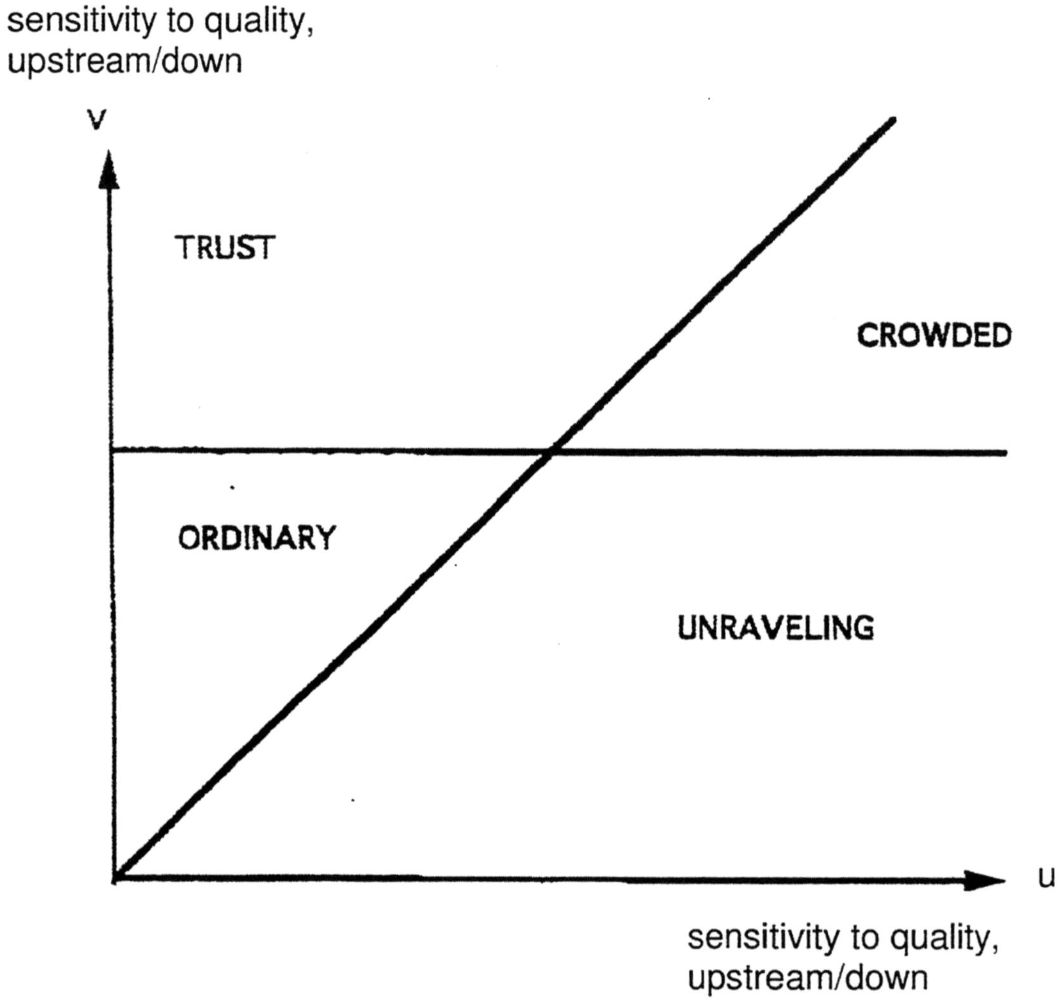

MAP with varieties of markets

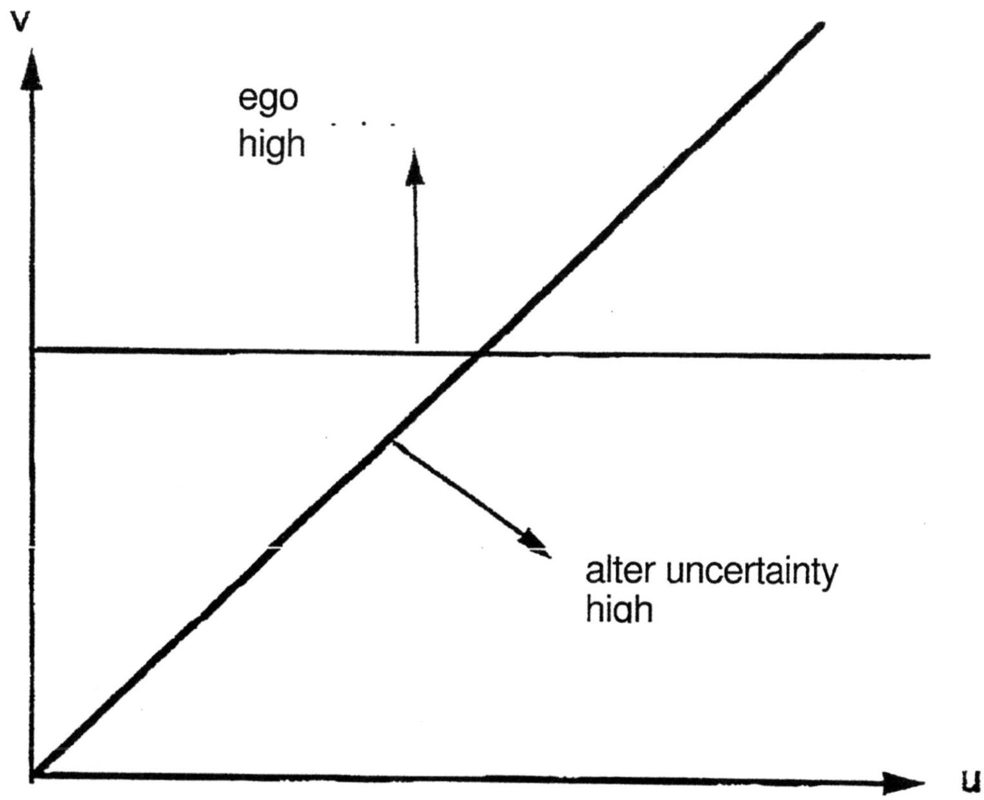

MAP with Podolny gradients in uncertainty

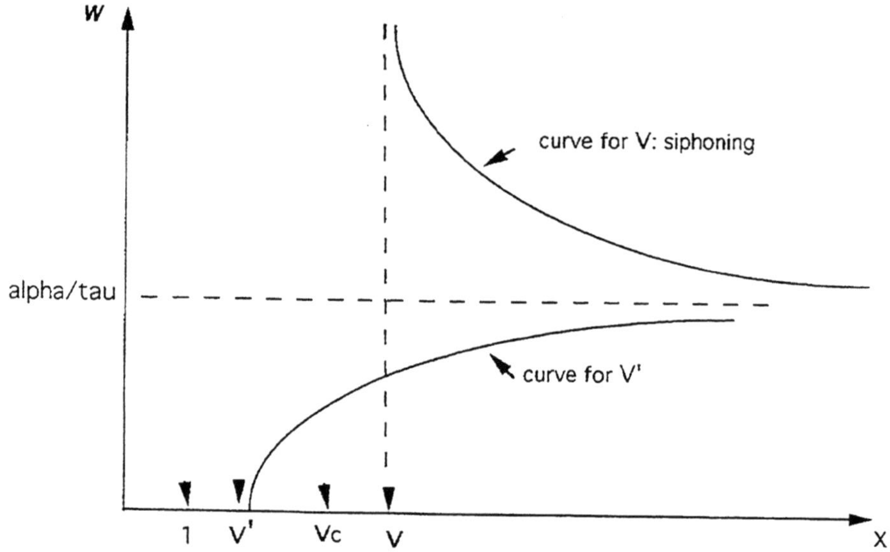

Figure 8. Graphs of market revenue ***W*** versus substitutability, x, given critical size Vc, for two fixed value of V. The curve for V' shows backward siphoning.

Social Influence Network Theory: Toward a Science of Strategic Modification of Interpersonal Influence Systems[1]

Noah E. Friedkin
Department of Sociology
University of California, Santa Barbara

Abstract

Social influence network theory is a mathematical formalization of the process of interpersonal influence that occurs in groups, affects persons' attitudes and opinions on issues, and produces interpersonal agreements, including group consensus, from an initial state of disagreement. The theory also may be employed to predict the consequences of particular modifications of a social influence system. A description of social influence network theory is presented. Using network data from a field study of a policy group, simulated modifications of an influence system and the consequences of these modifications are described. The illustration introduces a large subject: the development of a scientific basis for constructing and modifying the social structures of groups so that the expected outcomes of the influence system of a group will be close to desirable optimal outcomes for the group with some pre-specified degree of reliability. Toward the development of such a science and within the framework of social influence network theory, some key lines of research are outlined that are related to the operation and structural dynamics of interpersonal influence networks and that, in my view, would advance the development of a science concerned with the strategic modification of interpersonal influence systems.

[1] Direct all correspondence to Professor Noah E. Friedkin, Department of Sociology, University of California, Santa Barbara, CA 93106. Email: **friedkin@soc.ucsb.edu**.
URL: http://www.soc.ucsb.edu/faculty/friedkin/

1.1 INTRODUCTION

In this paper I briefly describe a formal theory of the formation of attitudes and opinions, including the production of consensus, in a network of interpersonal influences. This theory has been advanced in successive generalizations from the 1950s to the present by social psychologists and mathematicians concerned with developing a formal model of how consensus is produced in groups through interpersonal interactions (DeGroot 1974; French 1956; Friedkin and Johnsen 1990; 1999; Harary 1959). The theory incorporates an assumption on which there has been a remarkable convergence of independent theoretical work: that persons integrate conflicting attitudes and opinions as if they were utilizing a "cognitive algebra" of weighted averaging (Anderson 1981). The integration is triggered by the display of differences of opinion and the susceptibility of persons to interpersonal influences (in essence, a social comparison trigger) in which the pursuit of "correct" or "satisficing" positions on an issue takes into account the current positions of others on the issue. Persons' efforts to integrate discrepant influences and to form socially validated positions on issues often occur in a structural context, that is, in a more or less complexly configured network of interpersonal influences. This network has profound effects on the course of the opinion change process and the revised positions that persons may settle on. The content of persons' equilibrium positions on an issue, the efficiency with which this content is produced, and the relative net influence of each group member on others depend on the structure of the influence network in the group. Social influence network theory describes how a network of interpersonal influence enters into the process of interpersonal influence on attitudes and opinions in a group, and it allows an analysis of the way in which the structure of the influence network of the group has shaped individual and group-level outcomes.

Social influence network theory offers a distinctly sociological perspective on the attitude and opinion change process; it is a realization of a *structural* social psychology that was at the core of social psychological work in psychology in the 1950s and 1960s, during the flowering of the group dynamics field, but that currently is not being addressed by the more cognitively-oriented generation of psychologists. Festinger, French, Newcomb, and Cartwright, among other founding members of modern social psychology, were *social network analysts* who sought to build a theoretical foundation for social psychology in which network structures figured prominently; these social psychologists understood the potential importance of social networks in the development of a science of group dynamics but their agenda was derailed by the cognitive revolution in psychology. Social network analysis has grown rapidly since the 1970s, especially in sociology and anthropology and, most recently, in schools of business. The line of work on social influence network theory that is the focus of the present paper is a continuation of the classical agenda of the group dynamics field to understand the mechanisms and structures entailed in the process of attitude and opinion change and consensus production in groups.

The present paper is a first effort to bring social influence network theory to bear on the development of a scientific basis for constructing and modifying the social structures of groups so that the expected outcomes of the influence system of a group can be made close to desirable optimal outcomes for the group with some pre-specified degree of reliability. My treatment is schematic and introductory. First, I briefly describe social influence network theory. Second, using network data from a field study of a policy group, I describe several simulated modifications of an influence system and the consequences of these modifications. Third, within the framework of social influence network theory, lines of research are outlined that are related to the operation and structural dynamics of interpersonal influence networks and that, in my view, would advance the development of a science concerned with the strategic modification of interpersonal influence systems.

1.2 SOCIAL INFLUENCE NETWORK THEORY

There are several lines of work in social psychology on so-called "combinatorial" theories of consensus formation and group decision-making that focus on how agreements are formed in groups when there is an initial state of disagreement on an issue (Davis 1973; Friedkin and Johnsen 1990; 1999; Latane 1981; 1996; Laughlin 1980; Stasser, Kerr, and Davis 1989; Witte and Davis 1996). My colleague, Eugene Johnsen, and I have developed one of these combinatorial theories—social influence network theory (Friedkin 1991; 1998; 1999; Friedkin and Johnsen 1990; 1997; 1999).

Social influence network theory includes as special cases French's formal theory of social power (French 1956; Harary 1959) and DeGroot's consensus formation model (Berger 1981; Chatterjee and Seneta 1977; DeGroot 1974). The theory has close formal relationships with the rational choice model of group decision making proposed by Lehrer and Wagner (Lehrer and Wagner 1981; Wagner 1982; 1978), the social decision scheme model for quantitative judgments proposed by Davis (1996), and the information integration model of group decision making proposed by Graesser (1991). The theory is formally consistent with Anderson's weighted averaging model of information integration (Anderson 1981; Anderson 1991; Anderson and Graesser 1976). It also has a close formal relationship with an interdisciplinary tradition in statistics that includes work in geography, political science, and sociology on models of the interdependence of persons and spatial units (Anselin 1988; Doreian 1981; Duncan and Duncan 1978; Duncan, Haller, and Portes 1968; Erbring and Young 1979; Friedkin 1990; Marsden and Friedkin 1994; Ord 1975).

Social influence network theory describes an influence process in a group of N persons in which the members' attitudes and opinions on an issue change as they revise their positions by taking *weighted averages* of the influential positions other members:

$$y_i^{(t+1)} = a_i\left(w_{i1}y_1^{(t)} + w_{i2}y_2^{(t)} + \ldots + w_{iN}y_N^{(t)}\right) + (1-a_i)y_i^{(1)} \quad (1)$$

for $t = 1,2,\ldots$ and each of the N persons in the group, $i = 1,2,\ldots,N$. The opinions of persons at time t are $y_1^{(t)}, y_2^{(t)}, \ldots, y_N^{(t)}$ and their initial opinions are $y_i^{(1)}, y_2^{(1)}, \ldots, y_N^{(1)}$. The set of influences of the group members on person i is $\{w_{i1}, w_{i2}, \ldots, w_{iN}\}$, where $0 \le w_{ij} \le 1$, and $\sum_j w_{ij} = 1$. The *susceptibility* of person i to the influence of others is a_i, where $0 \le a_i \le 1$ and $a_i = 1 - w_{ii}$. Thus, a person's susceptibility is equated to the aggregate weight of the interpersonal influences on him or her (i.e., $a_i = \sum_{j \ne i} w_{ij}$). Social influence network theory rests on a model of how individuals cognitively integrate conflicting opinions, Eqn. (1), but the outcome of this process depends on the *social structure* in which the process occurs. This social structure consists of the set of members' initial positions, interpersonal influences, and susceptibilities to influence.

In a group of N persons, the system of equations described by Eqn. (1) can be represented as

$$\mathbf{y}^{(t+1)} = \mathbf{AWy}^{(t)} + (\mathbf{I} - \mathbf{A})\mathbf{y}^{(1)} \quad (2)$$

for $t = 1,2,\ldots$, where $\mathbf{y}^{(t)}$ is a $N \times 1$ vector of persons' opinions on an issue at time t, $\mathbf{W} = [w_{ij}]$ is a $N \times N$ matrix of interpersonal influences, and $\mathbf{A} = \mathrm{diag}(a_1, a_2, \cdots, a_N)$ is a $N \times N$ diagonal matrix of persons' susceptibilities to interpersonal influence on the issue.

Under suitable conditions, this process transforms persons' initial opinions into a set of equilibrium opinions:

$$\mathbf{y}^{(\infty)} = \mathbf{V}\mathbf{y}^{(1)} \qquad (3)$$

where $\mathbf{V} = [v_{ij}]$ is a matrix of reduced-form coefficients, describing the total or net interpersonal effects that transform the initial opinions into equilibrium opinions. The coefficients in **V** are nonnegative $(0 \le v_{ij} \le 1)$ and each row of V sums to unity $(\sum_j v_{ij} = 1)$. Hence, v_{ij} gives the *relative weight* of the initial opinion of person *j* in determining the final opinion of person *i* for all *i* and j. If **I-AW** is nonsingular, then from Eqn. (2) $\mathbf{V} = (\mathbf{I} - \mathbf{AW})^{-1}(\mathbf{I} - \mathbf{A})$. More generally, since $\mathbf{V}^{(t)} = (\mathbf{AW})^t + \left[\sum_{k=0}^{t-1} (\mathbf{AW})^k\right](\mathbf{I} - \mathbf{A})$, for $t = 1,2,\ldots$, **V** can be estimated numerically for a sufficiently large t when $\lim_{t\to\infty} \mathbf{V}^{(t)}$ exists.

All equilibrium opinions will be in range of the group members' initial opinions. Equilibrium opinions may settle on the mean of group members' initial opinions; they may settle on a compromise opinion that differs from the mean of initial opinions; they may settle on an initial opinion of a group member; or they may settle on altered opinions that do not form a consensus. When a consensus is formed in a group, **V** will commonly have the form of a stratification of individual contributions,

$$\mathbf{V} = \begin{bmatrix} v_{11} & v_{22} & \cdots & v_{NN} \\ v_{11} & v_{22} & \cdots & v_{NN} \\ \vdots & \vdots & \vdots & \vdots \\ v_{11} & v_{22} & \cdots & v_{NN} \end{bmatrix},$$

in which each person's initial opinion makes a particular relative contribution to the emergent consensus. The production of consensus is a *special case* of a larger domain of group outcomes encompassed by social influence network theory, in which stable patterns of disagreements may be formed. Thus, the theory satisfies Horowitz's criterion that "any serious theory of agreements and decisions must at the same time be a theory of disagreements and the conditions under which decisions cannot be reached" (1962, p. 182).

Abelson (1964) was frustrated to find that consensus was an *inevitable* outcome in the broad class of mathematical models that he examined, and he turned to simulation models in order to account for equilibrium disagreements. Similarly, the most prominent combinatorial theories in psychology today either do not deal with an account of disagreement (Davis 1996) or they rely on simulation models (Gigone and Hastie 1996; Latane 1996; Stasser 1988). I believe that it is one of the more *useful* prejudices of the scientific community that simulation models should be maintained as a last resort, after analytical approaches have been exhausted or appear to be intractable. Thus, I abandoned work on a simulation model of attitude and opinion change when it became apparent that a simpler mathematical model would suffice. In this light, an important contribution of social influence network theory is its demonstration that both consensus and disagreement are consistent with an analytically tractable mathematical model.

1.3 ILLUSTRATIVE MODIFICATIONS OF THE INFLUENCE SYSTEM OF A POLICY GROUP

I now briefly report some findings from a study of school board policy groups that will illustrate one way in which influence systems may be modified to change the systems' outcomes (Friedkin Forthcoming). In this application, the formal model described by Eqn. (1) was adapted for an account of a binary opinion—the preferences of school board policy group members for a flat or compensatory allocation of a school district's resources to schools that differ in the average academic achievement of the students. The flat preference stipulates that schools should receive resources proportionate to the number of students in a school regardless of their average academic performance. The compensatory preference stipulates that schools with low average academic performance should receive more resources than some schools with a higher average performance. Relational, attitudinal and demographic data were collected on five policy groups. In each group, the membership was defined on the basis of a snowball sampling procedure that included all persons (school board members, school district personnel, and community members) who were reported to be influential in school board decisions during the year preceding our inquiry. Among the 267 policy group members who were surveyed, the sample was roughly evenly split between persons who preferred a compensatory or a flat allocation pattern; there was virtual consensus that high performance schools should not be over-rewarded at the expense of low performance schools.

With data on social network relations (discussion, advice, friendship ties) occurring among the policy group members, I employed a technique described in Friedkin (1998) to obtain a measure of the influence network, **W**. Given a measure of the influence network and equilibrium opinions, $\mathbf{Y}^{(\infty)}$, "backward" estimates were obtained for the unobserved *initial* resource allocation preferences of the group members, $\mathbf{Y}^{(1)}$. More precisely, estimates of the unobserved preferences were obtained for the small subgroup of members whose opinions were influential in determining equilibrium preferences. The preferences of non-influential members cannot be estimated with this approach and, in any case, are irrelevant to an understanding of group outcomes. The core subgroup of influentials in each of the policy groups was comprised mainly of key central office staff members in the school district (the superintendent and other high-level school district administrators), and among these administrators there was disagreement on the preferred resource allocation pattern for the district. The interpersonal influences of the core members were projected throughout the network to the other members, including most of the school board members, and the *cross-pressures* from the disagreement among the influentials produced, in each group, a distribution of resource allocation preferences that was roughly evenly split between a flat and compensatory preference.

I was able to show with a simulation that the equilibrium distribution of allocation preferences is susceptible to substantial modification; i.e., that a change in the initial preference of a core influential could produce a substantial shift in the equilibrium distribution of group members' resource allocation preferences; see Table 1. The simulated modifications were of two sorts: (a) a neutralization of a person's preference in which the person became *indifferent* rather than positive or negative about a flat or compensatory pattern, and (b) a reversal of preference in which a person switched positions from positive to negative, or vice versa. Of course, reversals of positions had stronger impacts than neutralizations, but it is surprising how *much* of an impact neutralization sometimes had on the equilibrium distribution.

Table 1. Effects of a Simulated Change in the Estimated Initial Position of Each Core Member on the Expected Proportion of the Group Favoring the Flat (F) versus Compensatory (C) Allocation at Equilibrium

Core Member's ID # & Role	Estimated Initial Position	Observed Equilibrium Position	Effect of a Neutralization of ID's Position on the Distribution of Issue Positions	Effect of a Switch of ID's Position on the Distribution of Issue Positions
			% Flat	
Group A (61% Flat)				
4 School Board	-7.28	C	76	85
15 Central Office	-5.76	C	82	92
29 Central Office	-3.60	C	75	84
21 Central Office	5.82	F	39	21
34 Central Office	10.25	F	21	6
40 Community	7.10	F	53	44
Group B (46% Flat)				
4 Central Office	-2.00	C	52	58
15 Central Office	-2.66	C	57	67
41 Central Office	-2.22	C	55	63
46 Central Office	-1.92	C	54	61
49 Central Office	-2.32	C	52	58
60 Principal	-11.39	C	57	67
17 Central Office	12.98	F	10	2
Group C (54% Flat)				
32 Central Office	-132.28	C	93	95
36 Central Office	-5.78	C	78	90
50 School Board	-7.21	C	69	80
51 Central Office	-23.04	C	93	95
39 Central Office	45.10	F	1	0
43 Principal	8.55	F	42	31
Group D (67% Flat)				
25 Central Office	-3.79	C	86	95
49 Central Office	-267.44	C	98	98
8 Central Office	1.18	F	66	64
26 Central Office	10.35	F	24	8
58 School Board	26.95	F	3	2
Group E (49% Flat)				
9 School Board	-7.97	C	58	65
20 Central Office	-3.67	C	62	73
22 Central Office	-23.91	C	92	95
51 Central Office	-2.50	C	59	68
66 Principal	-3.51	C	60	69
19 Central Office	3.00	F	40	31
65 Community	44.51	F	3	2

1.4 TOWARD A SCIENCE OF STRATEGIC MODIFICATION OF INTERPERSONAL INFLUENCE SYSTEMS

A science of strategic modifications of influence systems requires clarity on desirable goals, a technology for producing structural modifications, an understanding of the possible multiple unintended effects of a modification on the relevant structure of the situation, and a confident grasp on the theoretical underpinnings of the dynamic features of the influence system. I now turn to a discussion of various outcomes of influence systems that might be optimized, the modifications of influence systems that might be feasible, key problems that need to be addressed, and lines of research that might be developed on these key problems.

1.4.1 Manipulatable Outcomes

Some influence networks are not consistent with the production of consensus, or even with the production of a degree of agreement (e.g., a majority opinion) that is sufficient to allow a collective decision. Strategic modifications of an influence system can be designed that will produce a consensus across a variety of issues, or at least a sufficient amount of agreement to allow decisions to be made.

Some influence systems will produce consensus with great difficulty over a range of issues that arise. Holding constant the initial relative positions of group members on issues, the efficiency of consensus production in a group depends on the structure of the influence network. Strategic modifications of an influence structure can be designed that will produce consensus more efficiently across a variety of issues, or at least with a sufficient degree of efficiency as the circumstances warrant.

Some groups reach consensus too quickly, short-circuiting a careful consideration of alternative positions on an issue. The overly-rapid convergence to agreement has been referred to as groupthink (Janis 1982), and it appears to be associated with centralized influence networks and homogeneous distributions of initial positions on an issue. Social influence network theory predicts that equilibrium opinions are always in the range of the distribution of initial opinions; hence, some heterogeneity of initial positions is crucial to a thorough vetting of an issue. In groups that regularly deal with judgmental issues, for which proper deliberation is important, strategic modifications of a group's influence system can be designed to slow down the process of convergence to consensus and to maximize the degree of initial diversity of opinion, consistent with a sufficient degree of efficiency.

In some groups, issues of control by a person or subgroup are crucial. Control loss in organizational hierarchies is a ubiquitous phenomenon that occurs whenever influence is transmitted indirectly from a single authoritative source to a large number of persons via a series of subordinate authorities. We have recently analyzed this phenomenon from the perspective of social influence network theory and shown how control loss may be mitigated by the addition of lateral lines of influence among subordinates (Friedkin and Johnsen 2002). The general point is that strategic modifications of an influence structure can be designed that will produce a consensus that is more closely representative of the initial preferences of authoritative sources.

The influence system of a group may be made more robust in the sense that its outcomes are less sensitive to minor changes in the influence structure or initial opinions. For instance, if the goal were to develop a robust influence system that is *insensitive* to a switch or neutralization of the position of any *one* person, then the strategic problem would be to find a feasible change in the influence structure of the group that would make its influence system less sensitive to such idiosyncratic opinion changes. For a fixed pattern of interpersonal influence among the initial positions of group members, the influence network can be made more robust so that net relative effects of initial positions are less sensitive or vulnerable to minor perturbations of initial opinion or interpersonal influence.

The foregoing outcomes are illustrative of goals that might be viewed as desirable under particular circumstances. In this brief treatment, I do not believe that I have come close to exhausting the potential number of manipulatable outcomes.

1.4.2 Feasible Modifications

Modifications of an influence system can be made in different ways. The initial attitudes and opinions, $\mathbf{Y}^{(1)}$, of one or more members may be modified. The direct interpersonal influences, **W**, including susceptibilities, **A**, may be modified, holding the structure of nonzero weights in **W** constant; that is, this type of modification would not alter who influences whom, but only the relative weight of some of these influences. Feasible structural modifications also include changes in the persons who are involved in the influence network: the addition of one or more new members who have particular configurations of interpersonal influences or the loss of one or members. Structural modifications also include changes in the pattern of nonzero interpersonal influences: the addition of new lines of influence, or the loss of extant lines. In some influence systems, slight changes may have large effects; in other systems, obtaining a different outcome from the system might require gross restructuring. Any single set of modifications may affect outcomes other than the particular outcome that is being optimized.

1.4.3 Key Problems

Sets of applied and theoretical problems need to be addressed in order to develop a scientific basis for modifying influence systems. I describe three problems.

First, there is the practical problem of developing a technology for generating particular modifications of persons' initial attitudes or opinions and their susceptibilities and interpersonal influences. Some of the structural components of influence systems may be more feasible to manipulate than others.

Second, there is the problem of ascertaining the precision and reliability of the model and measures that are employed to predict attitude and opinion changes in interpersonal influence networks. Models and measures need not be precisely accurate, but they should not be seriously misleading; hence we must have *a priori* estimates of the reliability and precision of the predictions that the model and measures allow.

Third, there is the problem of building a model of structural interdependency that can be dovetailed with social influence network theory. The social structural components of a group may be interdependent, so that making a change in one component (e.g., an initial position, a susceptibility, an interpersonal influence) may generate changes in other parts of the structure. If *ceteris paribus* is not a feasible assumption, then we must have a reliable prediction of the consequences of making changes in a structure for the other relevant parts of the structure.

1.4.4 Lines of Research

Certain lines of research are suggested by the problems that I have just sketched. I do not intend to make a global assessment about what lines of work are most important in the field of social network analysis. The lines of work that I describe are important only in the context of an application of social influence network theory to the development of a science of strategic modification of influence systems.

First, there should be fundamental work on the mathematical framework of social influence network theory that would test and refine its assumptions about the influence process. My colleague, Eugene Johnsen, and I have published some work on this problem (Friedkin 1999; Friedkin and Johnsen 1999), and we are hoping to continue to do more work on it. Second, methodological work needs to be done on the measurement of persons' susceptibilities and interpersonal influences. March and Simon's work (March 1955; 1956; Simon 1953) on the measurement of interpersonal influence has not been pursued, and my call for more work by social psychologists on the measurement of influence networks (Friedkin 1990) has not had much of an effect either. I regard the structural measures of susceptibility and interpersonal influence that I have developed (Friedkin 1998) as the beginning of what should be a concerted effort to fill an arbitrarily large $N \times N$ matrix with valid and reliable measures of persons' susceptibilities and interpersonal influences.

Third, theoretical and empirical work on structural interdependencies also is important, because such work shows how a change in one component of a social structure generates changes in other components. There are extant research programs that deal with interdependency but interdependency is a vague concept that can be defined in different ways, not all of which bear on the application of social influence network theory. In terms of the application of social influence network theory, the relevant interdependencies are defined by two constructs $\mathbf{Y}^{(1)}$ and $\mathbf{W}$ and concern the effects of a change in any part of these constructs on the other parts of either or both of these constructs. My collaborator and I have recently completed a project (Friedkin and Johnsen Forthcoming) in which the evolution of an influence network is described in terms of persons' initial set of sentiments about one another as attitudinal objects. Hence, changes in the initial sentiment structure, $\mathbf{Y}^{(1)}$, may affect the entire structure of $\mathbf{W}$.

A research program on an applied science of influence networks cannot be pursued without a broad appreciation of the various *types* of work that are important in its development. The program includes applied work on the technology of making modifications, methodological work on the development of measures of persons' susceptibilities and interpersonal influences, mathematical work on model development and refinement, experimental work that probes the merits of basic assumptions, and field studies that allow an assessment of the reliability and precision of the model's predictions.

1.5 CONCLUSIONS

The broad line of research that is represented by social influence theory, involving the formal modeling of interpersonal influence processes as they are played out in a social network, is in the classical tradition of group dynamics that was initiated by Festinger, French, Newcomb, and Cartwright, among others. It was a tradition, I might add, that was very strongly supported at one time by the Office of Navel Research (Guetzkow 1951), one of the sponsor's of the present symposium on social networks. Thus, an applied science of influence of networks is not a new or odd proposal in any sense; it is an attempt to revisit and revitalize a line of work on influence networks in social psychology that has been sidetracked by the cognitive revolution in psychology and by the "cultural turn" in sociology. My hope is that the present paper will serve as a useful platform for the future development of an applied science of influence networks that is based on a formal theory of how influence networks operate to shape persons' attitudes and opinions.

Although the mathematical structure of social influence network theory is simple, the specified process is consistent with a number of previous independent efforts to model the process of interpersonal influence. Indeed, the theoretical convergence on roughly the same mechanism is a remarkable development in the social sciences. For this reason, it is important to find out whether or not this basic mechanism is correct and, if not, whether it can be refined or should be replaced. The potential domain of application of social influence network theory is large. My collaborator and I are presently engaged in developing the theory's applications to the literature on group dynamics in psychology and sociology. Some of this work has already appeared (Friedkin 1999; 2001; Friedkin and Johnsen 1999). The present paper outlines a largely undeveloped potential application in which the theory would be employed, in an Operations Research mode (Hillier and Lieberman 1995), to analyze and control extant social structures. In the practical world, theoretical tools are rarely entirely correct, but they may be applied with the understanding that the friction and stress generated by unexpected results provide an opportunity for learning new things about fundamental mechanisms, and that trial-and-error is usually implicated in the development of any good theory.

1.6 REFERENCES

Abelson, R.P. 1964. "Mathematical Models of the Distribution of Attitudes under Controversy." Pp. 142-160 in *Contributions to Mathematical Psychology*, edited by N. Frederiksen and H. Gulliksen. New York: Holt, Rinehart & Winston.

Anderson, Norman H. 1981. *Foundations of Information Integration Theory*. New York: Academic Press.

—. 1991. "Contributions to Information Integration Theory." Hillsdale, NJ: Lawrence Erlbaum.

Anderson, Norman H. and Cheryl C. Graesser. 1976. "An Information Integration Analysis of Attitude Change in Group Discussion." *Journal of Personality and Social Psychology* 34:210-222.

Anselin, Luc. 1988. *Spatial Econometrics: Methods and Models*. Dordrecht: Kluwer Academic.

Berger, R.L. 1981. "A Necessary and Sufficient Condition for Reaching a Consensus Using DeGroot's Method." *Journal of the American Statistical Association* 76:415-418.

Chatterjee, S. and E. Seneta. 1977. "Towards Consensus: Some Convergence Theorems on Repeated Averaging." *Journal of Applied Probability* 14:89-97.

Davis, James H. 1973. "Group Decision and Social Interaction: A Theory of Social Decision Schemes." *Psychological Review* 80:97-125.

—. 1996. "Group Decision Making and Quantitative Judgments: A Consensus Model." Pp. 35-59 in *Understanding Group Behavior: Consensual Action by Small Groups*, edited by E. H. Witte and J. H. Davis. Mahwah, NJ: Lawrence Erlbaum.

DeGroot, Morris H. 1974. "Reaching a Consensus." *Journal of the American Statistical Association* 69:118-121.

Doreian, Patrick. 1981. "Estimating Linear Models with Spatially Distributed Data." Pp. 359-388 in *Sociological Methodology*, edited by S. Leinhardt. San Fransico: Jossey-Bass.

Duncan, Beverly and Otis Dudley Duncan. 1978. "Interaction of Spouses with Respect to an Unobserved Attitude." Pp. 291-296 in *Sex Typing and Social Roles*. New York: Academic.

Duncan, Otis Dudley, Archibald O. Haller, and Alejandro Portes. 1968. "Peer Influences on Aspirations: A Reinterpretation." *American Journal of Sociology* 74:119-137.

Erbring, Lutz and Alice A. Young. 1979. "Individuals and Social Structure: Contextual Effects as Endogenous Feedback." *Sociological Methods & Research* 7:396-430.

French, John R. P. , Jr. 1956. "A Formal Theory of Social Power." *The Psychological Review* 63:181-194.

Friedkin, Noah E. 1990. "Social Networks in Structural Equation Models." *Social Psychology Quarterly* 53:316-328.

—. 1991. "Theoretical Foundations for Centrality Measures." *American Journal of Sociology* 96:1478-1504.

—. 1998. *A Structural Theory of Social Influence*. Cambridge: Cambridge University Press.

—. 1999. "Choice Shift and Group Polarization." *American Sociological Review* 64:856-875.

—. 2001. "Norm Formation in Social Influence Networks." *Social Networks* 23:167-89.

—. Forthcoming. "Influence Networks in School Board Policy Groups: An Analysis of Resource Allocation Preferences." in *Social Organization of Schooling*, edited by L. Hedges and B. Schneider. New York: Russell Sage Foundation.

Friedkin, Noah E. and Eugene C. Johnsen. 1990. "Social Influence and Opinions." *Journal of Mathematical Sociology* 15:193-206.

—. 1997. "Social Positions in Influence Networks." *Social Networks* 19:209-222.

—. 1999. "Social Influence Networks and Opinion Change." *Advances in Group Processes* 16:1-29.

—. 2002. "Control Loss and Fayol's Gangplanks." *Social Networks* 24:395-406.

—. Forthcoming. "Attitude Change, Affect Control, and Expectation States in the Formation of Influence Networks." *Advances in Group Processes*.

Gigone, Daniel and Reid Hastie. 1996. "The Impact of Information on Group Judgment: A Model and Computer Simulation." Pp. 211-251 in *Understanding Group Behavior: Consensual Action by Small Groups*, edited by E. H. Witte and J. H. Davis. Mahwah, NJ: Lawrence Erlbaum.

Graesser, Cheryl C. 1991. "A Social Averaging Theorem for Group Decision Making." Pp. 1-40 in *Contributions to Information Integration Theory*, vol. 2, edited by N. H. Anderson. Hillsdale, NJ: Lawrence Erlbaum.

Guetzkow, Harold. 1951. "Groups, Leadership and Men." Pittsburgh: Carnegie Press.

Harary, Frank. 1959. "A Criterion for Unanimity in French's Theory of Social Power." Pp. 168-182 in *Studies in Social Power*, edited by D. Cartwright. Ann Arbor, MI: Institute for Social Research.

Hillier, Frederick S. and Gerald Lieberman, J. 1995. *Introduction to Operations Research*. New York: McGraw-Hill.

Horowitz, Irving L. 1962. "Consensus, Conflict and Cooperation: A Sociological Inventory." *Social Forces* 41:177-188.

Janis, I. L. 1982. *Groupthink: Psychological Studies of Policy Decisions and Fiascoes*. Boston: Houghton Mifflin.

Latane, Bibb. 1981. "The Psychology of Social Impact." *American Psychologist* 36:343-356.

—. 1996. "Dynamic Social Impact: The Creation of Culture by Communication." *Journal of Communication* 46:13-25.

Laughlin, Patrick R. 1980. "Social Combination Processes of Cooperative Problem-Solving Groups on Verbal Intellective Tasks." Pp. 127-155 in *Progress in Social Psychology*, edited by M. Fishbein. Hillsdale, NJ: Erlbaum.

Lehrer, Keith and Carl Wagner. 1981. *Rational Consensus in Science and Society*. Dordrecht: D. Reidel.

March, James G. 1955. "An Introduction to the Theory and Measurement of Influence." *American Political Science Review* 49:431-451.

—. 1956. "Influence Measurement in Experimental and Semi-Experimental Groups." *Sociometry* 19:260-271.

Marsden, Peter V. and Noah E. Friedkin. 1994. "Network Studies of Social Influence." Pp. 3-25 in *Advances in Social Network Analysis*, edited by S. Wasserman and J. Galaskiewicz. Thousand Oaks, CA: Sage.

Ord, K. 1975. "Estimation Methods for Models of Spatial Interaction." *Journal of the American Statistical Association* 70:120-126.

Simon, Herbert A. 1953. "Notes on the Observation and Measurement of Political Power." *Journal of Politics* 15:500-516.

Stasser, Garold. 1988. "Computer Simulation as a Research Tool: The DISCUSS Model of Group Decision Making." *Journal of Experimental Social Psychology* 24:393-422.

Stasser, Garold, Norbert L. Kerr, and James H. Davis. 1989. "Influence Processes and Consensus Models in Decision-Making Groups." Pp. 279-326 in *Psychology of Group Influence*, edited by P. B. Paulus. Hillsdale, N.J.: Lawrence Erlbaum.

Wagner, C. 1982. "Allocation, Lehrer Models, and the Consensus of Probabilities." *Theory and Decision* 14:207-220.

Wagner, Carl. 1978. "Consensus through Respect: A Model of Rational Group Decision-Making." *Philosophical Studies* 34:335-349.

Witte, Erich H. and James H. Davis. 1996. "Understanding Group Behavior: Consensual Action by Small Groups." Mahwah, New Jersey: Lawrence Erlbaum.

Information and Innovation in a Networked World[1]

David Lazer
John F. Kennedy School of Government

The potential for the diffusion of information regarding successful governmental (international, national or subnational) innovation has increased enormously in recent years. Information from geographically distant locales is often simply a click away, where networks of intergovernmental information exchange are spontaneously emerging. The intertwining of information technology and globalization – extends the pool of accessible innovations and lowers the barriers for their diffusion. (Bernstein & Cashore, 2000; Coleman & Grant, 1998; Coleman & Perl, 1999; Evans & Davies, 1999)

This diffusion process has enormous potential for increasing public welfare, by allowing location B to adopt the successful innovation in location A. There is, however, a potential dark side to the increased diffusion of information. First, as information diffuses more efficiently, it becomes more of a public good. As the publicness of information increases, so does the likelihood of free riding. There is an incentive for each government to allow another government to take the risks of innovation, and then to simply adopt the successful innovations. Second, in complex policy areas, the diffusion process may be too efficient: resulting in either premature convergence on a non-optimal policy, or eliminating policy alternatives that while not optimal in the present, might be in the future.

The governance implication is that in the networked world special attention must be given to increase governments' incentives to experiment and innovate. (Moon & Bretschneider, 1997)

This paper will be organized as follows. First, it will briefly discuss some distinctive features of the diffusion process in the public sector. Second, it will analyze the "informational efficiency" of different types of networks. Third, it will examine the potential for informational free riding in the networked world. Fourth, it will study the paradoxical possibility that the more efficient the system is at spreading information, the less information the system might contain. Finally, it will discuss the implication for governance: how does one design a system that is efficient at "spreading the word" while encouraging experimentation?

Inter-organizational diffusion of innovation

Networked governance is in vogue (e.g., O'Toole 1997, Rhodes 1997). By "networked governance" I mean a system of interdependent sovereign units. Thus, one might think of the relationships among nations as networked governance (although typically with the threat of violence removed—Keohane and Nye 2000; Slaughter 2000). One might also think of the relationship among local governments as "networked", and

---

[1] This material is based upon work supported by the National Science Foundation under Grant No. 0131923. Any opinions, findings, and conclusions or recommendations expressed in this material are those of the author(s) and do not necessarily reflect the views of the National Science Foundation.

even agencies within the federal government as effectively "networked" in that that hierarchy within the federal government intrudes little on the basic independence of federal agencies—especially where it comes to issues around coordination and cooperation with other agencies. In the US, due to both shared powers within the federal government, and a system of dual sovereignty between state and federal government, the networked nature of government has been an accepted feature of governance since the founding of the republic (although not with that vocabulary). As we move into the 21st century there is an increased awareness that the networked nature of governance is universal—in systems that heretofore might have been considered models of hierarchy (e.g., the British—Rhodes 1997) or anarchy (i.e., the international system).

Elsewhere I have argued that three strands of interdependence are coordinative, cooperative, and informational (Lazer 2001; Lazer and Mayer-Schoenberger 2002). For each of these interdependencies there are large literatures which can and should be mapped into the ideas around networked government, and descriptive and normative theories of "networked government" developed. In this paper I will develop the informational dimension.

The presence of the informational aspect of networked government is that policy generates potential informational externalities. When a policy actor adopts a policy, that adoption and subsequent experience conveys information to other policy actors. Some of those choices may be a matter of public record (statutes and regulations) and in principle accessible to all, and other important information will remain private. Policy actors thus simultaneously suffer from information overload and information deprivation. Actors need to adopt both network strategies—selective attention to help sift the public information and access private information—and internal filtering strategies to eliminate the large majority of information that is publicly available.

One may therefore usefully construe the universe of policy actors as a set of nodes among which there is a set of evolving connections. Over these connections flows information and attention about adoption success and failure, and just raw data. It is the assertion of this paper that this architecture matters, that some architectures are better at facilitating information transfer than others, and that it is necessary to understand how this structure emerges. The next section of the paper discusses the general processes by which networks emerge, and what the likely consequences for information diffusion in the emergent structure.

There exists, of course, a substantial body of literature on the diffusion of policy innovations – and adjacent topics such as policy networks, policy transfer, and policy convergence. (e.g., Abrahamson & Rosenkopf, 1997; Bennett, 1991; Berry, 1994; Berry & Berry, 1992; Coleman, 1994; Coleman & Grant, 1998; Dolowitz, 2000; Dolowitz & Marsh, 1996 & 2000; Evans & Davies, 1999; Gray, 1973 & 1994; Hubner, 1996; Kogut & Zander, 1995; Mintrom, 1997a & 1997b; Mintrom & Vergari, 1998; Robertson, Swan, & Newell, 1996; Savage, 1985; Schenk, Dahm, & Sonje, 1997; Seeliger, 1996; Stone, 2000; Valente, 1995 & 1996; Walker, 1969, Weenig, 1999)

Similarly, there is a large literature on the diffusion of innovations through inter-organizational networks within and between corporations. (Atkinson & Bierling, 1998; Coleman & Grant, 1998; Dolowitz & Marsh, 2000; Dyer & Nobeoka, 2000; Evans & Davies, 1999; Gupta & Govindarajan, 1991; Kogut & Zander, 1992 & 1995; Liebeskind et al., 1996; Nooteboom, 1999; Radaelli, 2000; Robertson, Swan, & Newell, 1996; Rom, Peterson, & Scheve, 1998; Seeliger, 1996; Weale et al., 1996) This literature suggests that a tremendous amount of information flows through inter-organizational networks (typically measured through overlap of corporate boards).

This voluminous research examines the process of diffusion, how innovation evolves as it diffuses, the characteristics of early versus late adopters, etc. (Rogers 1995). The objective of this paper is to consider what are the generic processes by which the architecture of diffusion of emerges—the network; what the normative implications of different architectures; and what is distinctive about diffusion among public organizations. Information diffusion through intergovernmental networks is quite different on certain dimensions from diffusion in the private sector. First, in the private sector, many innovations are proprietary, thus increasing both the cost of adopting an innovation, as well as the likelihood of the innovation in the first place, since the innovator may extract most of the benefits of that innovation.[2] The profit motive also means that the innovator has an incentive to spread information about the innovation. Second, where innovations are not proprietary, a corporation has an incentive to keep information secret from competitors as long as possible. The public sector, in contrast, has relatively little incentive to suppress information about successful innovations. Third, with survival less of an issue, and relative performance more difficult to measure, bureaucratic inertia is likely a greater barrier to adopting successful innovations in the public sector than in the private. Fourth, many policy makers are likely "proselytizers"—moved to innovate and to spread the word in order to increase their impact on society.

There is therefore substantial potential for diffusion of successful policy innovations, both intra and internationally. The question asked here is what is the impact of the shift from local to global informational networks. The next section examines the role that the structure of the informational network plays in the speed with which information spreads in a system.

The architecture of the network

First, a few definitions: A *node* is a unit which may contain and pass on information. It may be an individual or an organization. In this paper, I will largely focus on public sector actors, but at the end will speculate what the implications are for public-private partnerships. A connection between two nodes means that there is some passing of information between those nodes. At its broadest definition, it may mean that some actors are just selectively paying attention to other actors (e.g., everyone is paying attention to California's experience in electricity deregulation). At its narrowest (and more typical) definition, it means that there is a private exchange of information among a subset (at least two) actors. An *informational network* is a set of connections among nodes. It is useful to distinguish among three kinds of informational networks: spatial, organizational, and emergent.

---

[2] Although spillovers occur not just in the public sector but in the private as well, despite the protection of intellectual property law. Baumol (1999) for example, estimates that innovators retain only approximately 10% of the gains from their innovations.

A *spatial network* is a network whose dyadic connections are determined by proximity: each actor speaks exclusively to other actors in its neighborhood. For example, in figure 1, A communicates only with its four immediate neighbors to the north, south, east, and west.

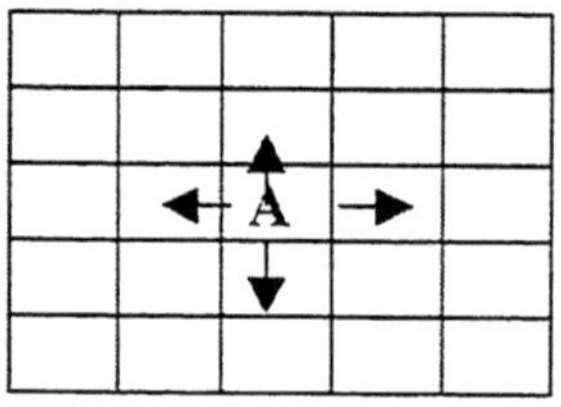

Figure 1: Example of a spatial network

The probability of communication between any two actors is strongly related to how close they are to each other. The relationship between distance and communication, of course, is vastly more complicated than characterized by the lattice in figure 1. As noted above, the Great Plains excepted, geography is typically not as smooth as characterized in figure 1. These irregularities affect the costs of communication between any two nodes. Distance is also partially a social construct. The probability that two local jurisdictions communicate is probably affected by whether they are in the same state, for example.

Finally, communication frequency is not a linear function of distance. As a general matter, communication drops off precipitously with distance (McPherson 2001).

An *organizational network* is simply the communications that result from the groupings within the organization (Mintzberg 1992). That is, the formal organizational chart is typically related to the architecture of the informational network. If faculty, for example, are grouped into departments, communication will typically be higher within those departments, in part because of a functional interdependence, in part because the institution then structures serendipity—departments will often be grouped together, departmental meetings guarantee that paths will cross, etc.

Both of these network archetypes are flawed at spreading information. Spatial networks are often broken by spatial "chasms"— mountains, rivers, or climate in a geographic context, buildings in an organizational context, railroad tracks and highways within communities— between which little information flows. Further, even in the absence of these discontinuities a purely grid-type of network, such as in figure 1, would only slowly (if inexorably) spread information. If one assumed that it takes one period to spread information to a node's immediate four neighbors, it would take eight periods for a piece of information to spread from one corner of the system to the other.

Similarly, organizational networks are often characterized by dysfunctional chasms—communication within stovepipes but not between. In fact, the "networked" organization, cross-functional teams, the matrix form, etc, etc, is often seen as an antidote to the stovepipes of the organizational chart. However, as discussed below, organic (emergent) network structure have their own disfunctions.

Serendipity is the underlying principle of *emergent networks*. Emergent networks result from the myriad of decisions by individual nodes to pay attention or not pay attention, by pairs of nodes to form a relationship, and by larger numbers of nodes to create formal or informal groupings that then form the basis for larger scale communication. The assumption I make here is that these decisions are made on an egoistic basis, made in a boundedly rational fashion. It is this "think locally, act locally" assumption that can result in outcomes that at the systemic level are suboptimal. There are a number of fairly robust patterns that have been observed in a wide range of social networks: the emergence of cliques, power-laws of connectedness, homophily, powerful core-periphery tendencies, each of which is discussed in the context of governance networks.

Cliques: Networks often break down into cliques, where there is a much higher density of communication within cliques than between. Thus, for example, a tie between A and B and a tie between B and C predicts a tie between A and C (Davis 1967). There are a variety of reasons why cliques might emerge. For example, B's tie to A and C might facilitate a tie between A and C. Cliques might also emerge out of a functional need to collectively produce something that all benefit from, and for which a certain scale is required (e.g., a pick up softball game). Informationally, it might also be more efficient to share information within a group than dyadically (reducing repetition and redundancy).

Cliques might also be epiphenomenal: the result of homophily or proximity. As discussed below, similarity and proximity predict communication. If A is similar/close to B and C, then it is likely that B and C are similar and close to each other.

Scale free networks: Notably, in networks where nodes have no constraints on communication the frequency at the node level of any given level of connectedness of a node is proportional to the inverse of that level of connectedness, raised to some power (i.e., "power law" distributed, also known as scale free networks—see other contributions to this volume). In essence, the more connected, the less frequent. In a power law world, the well connected are vastly more connected than the average connected nodes, and thus play a vastly disproportionate role in the flow of information in the system. Such a power law distribution has been observed with respect to websites, citation frequencies (Price 1976), and, surprisingly, number of sexual partners. One suspects, in the policy world, that particular exemplar policies emerge with the bulk of attention; thus, policymakers look disproportionately at California's experiences in deregulation, Wisconsin's experiences with welfare reform, etc.

Power law frequency distributions tend to emerge from stochastic growth processes, where the growth of any particular observation is proportionate to its size (e.g., the growth rate of small units is about the same as large units—e.g. Simon 1956).

These hubs, in a power law world, play a disproportionate role. One could imagine (as discussed below) that they help systems overcome problems in diffusing and processing information that would likely result from the other types of processes enumerated here (and probably do, to a certain extent—see small world section below). One could imagine that hubs are the nodes with the highest processing capacity, and serve as instruments to aggregate and re-disseminate information (and they probably do, to a certain extent—see information aggregation section below). However, the conditions under which they typically arise limits their potential as conduits of information—since for most of the cases enumerated above, the well connected nodes only send information, and do not receive. That is, one might imagine a power law world where the exceptionally well connected received as much as they sent; however, in the policy world, it seems unlikely, for example, that California pays as much attention (and then retransmits) the experiences of others as much as others pay attention to California.

Homophily: It does turn out that birds of a feather do tend to flock together. Similarity turns out to be a strong predictor of communication across a wide variety settings (McPherson 2001). There are a number of likely explanations for this. First, similar actors will be more likely to have useful information for each other. Imagine moving to a new city: would it make any sense to talk to someone who had a much larger income than you, and thus could afford a much more expensive house? Similarly, one might expect that policymakers would do best to pay attention to those in similar circumstances. Second, especially in political contexts, there are strategic reasons to share information more with those with similar preferences. Information assists actors in achieving their goals. If the goals of another individual are opposed to your goals, you would be unlikely to share information with them.

Cores and peripheries: Emergent networks often will have a "rich get richer" dynamic. Assume that nodes have unequal access to private information. Those nodes with more private information will be more desirable as partners with which to exchange information. If all nodes have constraints on how much they communicate (this does not apply to attention networks, for example) then the node with the most information will be in the greatest demand to form ties with. It would presumably choose ties with those who have the most private information. Those with less information would be in a less of a position to be so picky. Out of a process where the most informed choose the most informed, the moderately informed will be left with each other to choose to communicate with, and the least informed to choose each other. That is, the network will have a well-informed core, that distributes information internally, and a less-informed periphery, with occasional leakage of information from core to periphery. Thus, while the diffusion of information has the potential to reduce informational inequalities in a system, it will potentially just replicate those inequalities.

This tendency will be exacerbated by the fact that nodes that are the most informed will often have the capacity to form more connections. If connectedness were roughly proportional to the informedness of nodes, it is conceivable that the spread of information would (while raising the absolute informedness of everyone) actually exacerbate the informational inequalities in the system. One would expect that out of such a scenario would emerge a highly informed and interconnected core, and a highly uninformed and unconnected periphery.

Small worlds

Emergent networks thus tend to result in clusters of nodes which are highly similar to each other, within which there are many connections, and between which there are very few connections. Clearly, this is not an effective architecture for spreading information. Might networks automatically adjust themselves so as to reduce the worst effects of this inefficient configuration? For example, Burt (1995) enumerates the competitive advantage actors can achieve by bridging these "structural holes" in the network. One might imagine the larger the advantage, the greater the likelihood that actors will seek to close these holes. There are a number of obstacles to this, however, especially in the public sector. The combination of cheap intra-clique communication and lack of property rights may discourage such communication. By their very nature, cliques allow for accidental (and inexpensive) collisions. The lack of property rights means that a node that seeks extra-clique communication that brings novel information may pay a high price for novel information, where the benefits quickly diffuse to the entire clique.[3] Those nodes that do not attempt to bridge the structural holes will actually fair better, under these circumstances, than those that do. An additional deterrent to inter-clique communication is that inter-clique information may be less reliable, because the communicators have fewer reputational concerns. If they pass on inaccurate information, there are few/no consequences, since the two nodes are not embedded in the same social structure (Granovetter 1985, Uzzi 1996).

The above analysis suggests that it is likely that organizational, spatial, and emergent informational networks in the public sector world will tend to be inefficient at spreading information. However, what may be true of each of these networks may not be true of the networks together, as the "small world" findings of Watts and Strogatz (1998) illuminate. What these findings demonstrate that is that while a highly structured network (e.g., the lattice) is not effective at spreading information, and a purely random network (e.g., where the probability of a tie between A and B is uncorrelated with the probability of a tie between any other dyad in the system), an overlay of structure and random networks is very effective at spreading information. This is indicative of a more general phenomenon: *cross-cutting types of networks are typically more effective at spreading information than equally dense networks of a single type.*

A simple illustration will demonstrate why. Consider the network represented by figure 2, where each actor communicates with its immediate four neighbors.

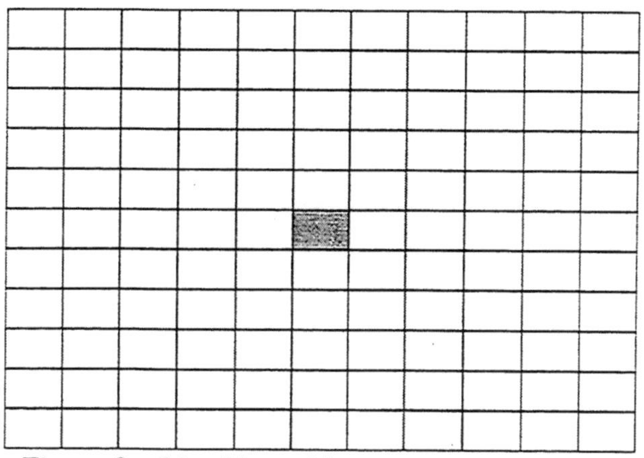

Figure 2: 11 x 11 world

Assume, now, that the actor in the middle of the chess board has a successful innovation, which is then adopted by its four neighbors, which is in turn adopted by each of their neighbors, and so on. It will take 10 rounds of communication before the whole system has adopted the innovation. By comparison, a "random-collision" network, where actors

[3] Obviously, this is a critical assumption that will differ in different systems.

randomly "collide" with four other actors each round, will take just 4 rounds before the whole (99+%) system has adopted the innovation.[4]

A spatial network is inefficient at spreading information simply because the informed are spending most of their time communicating with other informed actors. Only at the periphery of the informed set of actors is information actually spreading.

An overlay of an emergent network on a spatial network is potentially far more effective at spreading information than just a spatial network, for the simple reason that the emergent network will provide bridges between the regions (or, alternatively, the spatial network will provide bridges between the cliques), thus increasing the proportion of the uninformed in communication with the informed.[5]

A minor elaboration of the above example will illustrate why. Imagine, now, that while all actors still communicate with all other actors, the actor in the middle of the chessboard communicates also with an actor in the distant corner.[6] What impact will adding just this one tie to the 242 that already exist have on the speed with which the innovation spreads? It will take *40% less time for innovation to spread.* Alternatively, what is the impact of simply accentuating the existing spatial network by doubling the neighborhood with which an actor communicates? Increasing the number of neighborhood ties by 242 is only slightly more effective than adding one non-neighborhood tie-- the time it would take for an innovation to spread drops by 50%.

Figure 3 presents the rate of diffusion for four diffusion models: random-collision, spatial with 4 neighbors, spatial with 8 neighbors, and spatial with 4 neighbors + one non-spatial tie.

---

[4] Note that this is a very different notion of a "random network" than Watts and Strogatz (1998) use.

[5] Note that this general observation works with any cross-cutting networks—e.g., two emergent networks, two organizational networks, etc. The key is that each network have a logic that is orthogonal to the other network.

[6] In this scenario I am assuming that the chess board "wraps around"; i.e., the actors on the top communicate with the parallel actor on the bottom; actors on the left communicate with the parallel actor on the right.

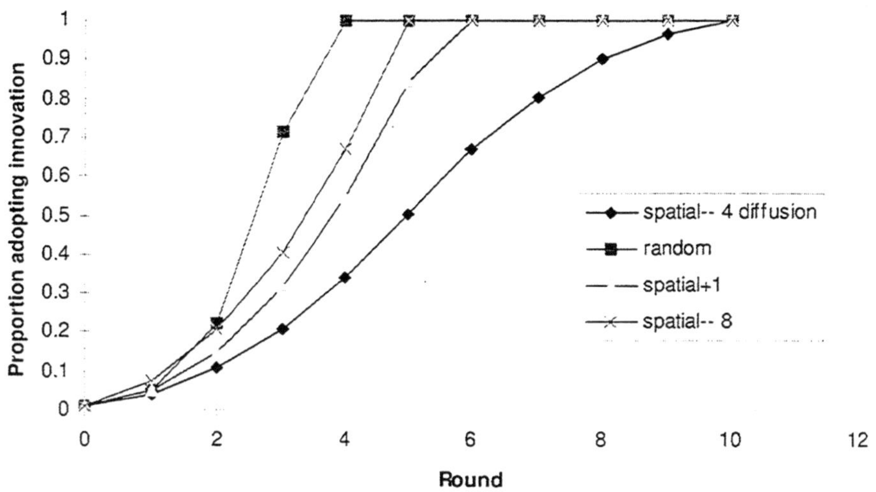

Figure 3: Four modes of diffusion

The above analysis highlights how even the slight overlay of one network on another can dramatically increase the rate of the diffusion of information in that network. It also demonstrates how technologies that reconfigure the logics of the networks in a system can have effects disproportionate to their use.

Producing information

The second key dimension of an informational network is the production of information by the network nodes. Does the architecture of the network affect the incentives to produce information? Yes—and there is a potential downside to a more informationally efficient system, however. Generally, the absence of property rights discourages investment in producing information in the public sector (although see caveats to this general proposition below).[7] A system that is more effective at spreading information may further aggravate this. Specifically, governments may become more complacent with respect to innovating, in the hope that someone else will bear the costs of a successful innovation.

An illustration highlights why this might happen. Imagine a potential innovation that yields \$1.10 worth of benefits and costs \$1.00 to produce if a government produces the initial innovation, or is free if some other government produces the innovation. Assume, further, that there are 100 governments. In the absence of any information diffusion (call this the "island scenario"), every government will spend \$1.00, and produce \$1.10 worth of benefits, for a total of \$110 of benefits for \$100 of costs. In the networked world where there is rapid diffusion of information, assume that there is an initial innovator, that spends the initial \$1.00, and reaps \$.10 worth of net benefits. All other states then adopt the innovation, for \$1.10 worth of net benefits. From the systemic

[7] See Strumpf forthcoming; Rose-Ackerman 1980.

point of view, that $1.00 of cost has yielded $109.10 of net benefits, as compared to just $10 in the previous scenario. From a systemic point of view, this is an enormous success. From 99 governments point of view, this is an enormous success. For the 100th government, this is, in absolute terms, exactly the same as the island scenario.

The networked world scenario is therefore pareto superior to the island scenario. However, it is not a stable scenario if you assume that the choice to innovate is endogenous. If you assume (1) that each government is choosing whether to innovate: and (2) that governments are in part benchmarked by each other's performance (Beslsy and Case 1995) and that therefore the innovation decision, over the long run, is itself modeled on the decisions of the governments that produce the highest net benefits, the equilibrium scenario is *zero* innovation by any government-- 0 net benefits.[8]

The impact of free riding is particularly acute because the benefits of an innovation would be so much greater in the networked scenario-- in fact, innovations that result in net absolute losses for an innovator could result in welfare gains for the system. If one assumes that the initial costs of an innovation are F, the costs of adoption for each government after the initial innovator are c, the benefits for each government from that innovation are B, and N governments benefit from that innovation, then the innovation would result in net benefits if $N*(B - c) - F > 0$. For example, if $N = 100$, $c = 0$, $B = \$1.10$, that innovation would produce net systemic benefits even if $F = \$109$. The innovator, however, would face net losses of $107.90. If the innovator retained rights to its information, then it could, in principle, extract many of the benefits that everyone else in the system receives.

The danger of free riding is determined, in part, by whether governments have different underlying preferences with respect to a potential innovation. Free riding is a great danger where "one size fits all"-- governments have identical preferences. It is no danger if each government requires a unique solution (of course, in this latter scenario, there is no benefit to the networked world either).

The possibility of free riding may be reduced to the extent that policy makers are "proselytizers", valuing the possibility that their innovation will spread. If one assumes that, rather than being egoists, policy makers are proselytizers, then the rate of innovation in the networked scenario will be greater than the rate of innovation in the island scenario. That is, those who seek to maximize their impact on the world rather than their jurisdiction will have greater opportunities to affect a networked world.

The Rabbit and the Hare

A second danger in the highly networked world is that some diversity of policy solutions will be lost, to the detriment of the system. The decision to attempt an innovation will rely in part on a government's assessment of the innovations adopted by other states, and whether there is a consensus in the system as to what best practice is. In a poorly networked world, a government will occasionally look at what a small number of other governments are doing-- if none have a clearly superior alternative, that government may experiment. A successful innovation somewhere in the system will spread slowly,

---

[8]More technically, "no innovation" is an evolutionarily stable strategy-- see Axelrod 1984.

resulting in continued experimentation in the rest of the system during a slow "take off" period. If that innovation is the optimal solution this is clearly dysfunctional; however, if it is not, the continued experimentation in the rest of the system may uncover a better solution.

Alternatively, even if the successful innovation is optimal, it may not be optimal in the future, and maintaining a diversity of approaches would therefore be healthy. Heterogeneity is a systemic property that may yield benefits to all within a system. Adherence to unconventional and suboptimal policies today may provide diversity in the system for all to benefit from tomorrow. It also serves as a platform to experiment from. Excellent policy solutions may only differ from policy disasters on a few dimensions. A world where everyone rapidly converges to "best practice" will likely have better policy outcomes in the short run than a world where everyone experiments in different "neighborhoods" of the policy space and then only slowly converge to best practice. However, the latter world will have more experimentation and may be more likely to produce better policy outcomes in the long run.[9]

A classic example of premature convergence is the convergence on the QWERTY layout of keyboards. Early in the typewriter industry, there was substantial diversity of key layout. The QWERTY layout was originally designed to slow typing to prevent the mechanical jamming of the typewriter, and, over time, through a diffusion process, the QWERTY layout became standard. While the mechanical jamming of typewriters is no longer a problem, the QWERTY standard remains.[10] One might hypothesize that QWERTY-type of outcomes are more likely in an informationally efficient system.

The likelihood of A adopting B's innovation should drop as the similarity of A and B's policy objectives drops, since B's innovation would presumably be tailored to its policy objectives. Heterogeneity in underlying policy objectives should therefore help maintain a diversity of policy approaches (although limit the benefits to policy diffusion as well).

Aggregating information

The third dimension to thinking about informational networks is how well that network *aggregates* information. Bad information as well as good spreads in informational networks. A more efficient network at spreading information is also a more efficient network at spreading fads, manias, etc. As the information cascade literature demonstrates, in a system where adoption is the only thing that one actor can observe about another can easily result in the spread of misinformation (Strang and Macy 2001). Essentially, if one imagines that each node in the system has private information about the value of an innovation, but that this private information can be outweighed by the observation of the adoption decisions of others, then all it might take for the system to get rolling in the wrong direction is for a few of the initial adopters to have incorrect signals. At that point, the private information of subsequent adopters is outweighed by

---

[9] See March (1991) more generally on the trade off between exploration and exploitation.

[10] See David 1986. Also see Liebowitz and Margolis (1990) for a critique of David's analysis, which debunks Dvorak as a superior alternative to QWERTY (although does not demonstrate that QWERTY is an optimal layout of keys).

what they observe others to have adopted, resulting in a potential bandwagon going in the wrong direction.

These potential bandwagon effects might be ameliorated by a number of potential dynamics. First, potential adopters could pool their private information regarding an innovation. Given a large enough set of nodes sharing their private evaluations, this pooled knowledge could outweigh the information conveyed by a "bandwagon" (since, actually, bandwagons do not convey that much information). Second, adopters might send information about their experiences. That is, not only is adoption information conveyed, but success/failure information. This would vastly increase the amount of information conveyed in the adoption process; and every bandwagon would contain the seeds of its own destruction since the bandwagon would create a body of data about its failings. The potential of success/failure information to eliminate bandwagons depends on (1) the lag between adoption and success/failure data; (2) whether such data are even generated by the process (as noted above). It is in fact not in the interest of adopters to produce data that demonstrate that they chose failing policies. There is an incentive to suppress negative feedback, and, even worse, to suppress any feedback at all in fear that it could be negative.

Parallel processing

The vision sometimes conveyed of networks is that they distribute the informational load over the many nodes within the system, as compared to an hierarchical system, which overloads the top node. It is not at all clear that such a network would emerge organically, however, or that the ideal configuration differs greatly from an hierarchy. Imagine the following scenario: each node receives a signal about the state of the world—let's say a quantitative estimate of something of importance to the system. Each node has a certain processing capacity—let's say a capacity to "average" its information and the information of 10 other nodes. What would be the most efficient organization of the system? An hierarchy, where at the bottom of the hierarchy nodes were grouped by 10, each communicating with one node above it, which averaged the 10 bits of information along with its own. This layer would be identically organized in groups of 10 passing information upwards. This structure would continue iteratively upwards, until the single top node averaged the information from its immediate 10 subordinates.

Would such structures emerge organically, without centralized intervention? It seems unlikely. The hierarchical structure described above is, arguably, at best, a very hard to reach equilibrium, if one posits that the nodes are seeking to maximize their own informedness. The reason for this is that there is little reason for nodes to communicate with the nodes below them, as compared to the nodes above them, or at their own level. Consider the nodes one level down from the top. A pair of nodes at this level, given the opportunity to switch one communication from one of their subordinates each to each other, would certainly improve the quality of information they were receiving. The one caveat here (and the reason why the hierarchy is a potential equilibrium) is that if one assumes that the top node "broadcasts" its solution once it has calculated it, none of its subordinates will have the incentive to deviate from their communication pattern, since it would be detrimental to the quality of this signal. However, there is no smooth path to that equilibrium, because the actors that emerged as more central would have an incentive to drop their ties to less central nodes, which would undermine the hierarchical structure outlined above.

Institutions in the middle

There are potential institutions that can play an aggregating role. In particular, one might imagine institutions that have both high processing capacity and high levels of connectedness. For example, the federal government might play the role of a central node that processes the experiences of the states, develops and disseminates best practices. However, arguably, the federal government focuses more of its analytical capacities on developing its own mandates, rather than enabling state and local governments develop their policies.

There are also a variety of national organizations of local and state governments (the National Governors Association, the National Conference of State Legislatures, the National District Attorneys Association, etc). There exist also various international organizations that serve (in a network sense) a similar function, such as the Organization of Economic Cooperation and Development, the World Bank, etc. In the US context, however, these organizations often have a somewhat limited desire to serve as a conduit of information, in significant part because they really act as industry associations—representing their collective needs to the outside world, rather than facilitating the smooth flow of information among their members. In fact, the reason for this is that these two objectives are at odds: facilitating the smooth flow of information, aggregating information into studies of best practice, etc, in fact means picking the practices of a small number of members as winners and the rest as losers. Such a strategy might quickly undermine the support of such an organization.[11]

Finally, academia plays a potential role as a central node—collecting, comparing, and critically examining the practices of many jurisdictions.

The organizational nexus: networks, markets, and hierarchies

Markets, networks, and hierarchies offer different mechanisms to deal with the issues around information diffusion, creation, and aggregation. Networks rely on reciprocity and embeddedness to regulate the behavior of their members. They are relatively poor at dealing with complex chains of exchange—for example, where A has something B needs, and C has something A needs, and B has something C needs. In this scenario, the network cannot be sustained by reciprocity or reputation, but instead may at best be supported a complicated system of arbitrage. Networks, in the absence of markets and property rights, may do poorly at encouraging significant investment in new information, because of the lack of control of that information once it is produced.

Markets institutions standardize goods along salient dimensions, offer a standard for exchange (money). Supporting institutions, such as property rights, also encourage

[11] I thank Robert Behn for this point. Notably, some of the international organizations are exceptions. Arguably, this is in part because of the political irrelevance of those organizations. Further, in many of these cases—the international development organizations—critical examination is not of donor countries, but of recipients.

production of information (although at the cost of efficiency in the monopoly rights conveyed). People thus write books, develop new medicines, create new software, in the expectation that the properties of the goods will somehow be captured by dimensions that have emerged as salient in the market (of course, these dimensions are themselves highly contested). Markets work less well at supporting transactions where the properties of the good is not easily captured by the dimensions that the market has defined. Consider the vast array of little bits of information, gossip, etc, exchanged in informational networks: "the biggest difficult we encountered in implementation was…" "the next division chief is going to be…" etc. These non-standard bits of information, essential to the operation of any system, would be impossible to put valuations on (or far too costly). Instead, this type of information exchange is governed by reciprocity, norms, etc.

Hierachies (by which I mean authority structures), have a variety of mechanisms to deal with the issues raised above. At the simplest level, information sharing and information production can simply be commanded. Thus, if A is in a position to discover something, A is ordered to do so. If A has information B would find useful, A is ordered to share information. Of course, such a system would typically put demands that would quickly outstrip the capacity of the apex an organization.

There are other, less blunt, authority tools. Hierarchies standardize behavior and information, facilitating information flow. Hierarchies also create the public goods for information exchange—e.g., infrastructure. Hierarchies can also recognize and reward information production and information sharing ex post, a less difficult task than doing it a priori.

A particular system will generally operate by multiple institutional logics. The prescriptive question is whether there is a match between what a particular institutional logic is effective at, and what it is being asked to do.

Conclusion: how to maintain innovation.gov?

The objective of this paper has to be view the intergovernmental network as an informational network: each node producing information and potentially transferring information to other nodes. The shift from relatively geographically bound networks to global networks should greatly increase the informational efficiency of international policy networks. Yet, by increasing the rate at which successful innovations spread through the system, globalization may discourage policy experimentation due to free riding and premature policy convergence. This suggests a counter-intuitive governance prescription: as governments receive more information regarding what other governments are doing, incentives for all governments to continue experimenting (and thus creating information) should be increased.

References:

Abrahamson, E., & Rosenkopf, L. 1997. "Social Network Effects on the Extent of Innovation Diffusion: A Computer Simulation," *Organization Science*, 8: 289-309.

Atkinson, M. M., Bierling, G. 1998. "Is there convergence in provincial spending priorities?," *Canadian Public Policy*, 24: 71-89.

Axelrod, Robert (1984). *The Evolution of Cooperation*. New York: Basic Books.

Baumol, William J. (1999). Pareto optimal sizes of innovation spillovers. Working paper, Starr Center for Applied Economics, New York University.

Bennett, C. J. 1991. "How States Utilize Foreign Evidence," *Journal of Public Policy*, 11: 31-54.

Bernstein, S., & Cashore, B. 2000. "Globalization, four paths of internationalization and domestic policy change: The case of ecoforestry in British." *Canadian Journal of Political Science*, 33: 67-99.

Berry, F. S. 1994. "Seizing Up State Policy Innovation Research," *Policy Studies Journal*, 22: 442-456.

Berry, F. S., & Berry, W. D. 1990. "State Lottery Adoptions as Policy Innovations: An Event History Analysis," *American Political Science Review*, 84: 395-415.

Burt, Ronald. 1995. *Structural Holes: The Social Structure of Competition*. Belknap Press.

Case, Anne, and Timothy Besley. 1995. "Incumbent Behavior: Vote Seeking, Tax Setting, and Yardstick Competition." *American Economic Review* 85: 24-45.

Coleman, W. D. 1994. "Policy convergence in banking: a comperative study," *Political Studies*, XLII, 274-299.

Coleman, W. D., & Grant, W. P. 1998. "Policy convergence and policy feedback: Agricultural finance policies in a globalizing era," *European Journal of Political Research*, 34: 225-247.

Coleman, W. D., & Perl, A. 1999. "Internationalized policy environments and policy network analysis," *Political Studies*, 47: 691-709.

Davis, James A. 1970. "Clustering and Hierarchy in Interpersonal Relations: Testing Two Graph Theoretical Models on 742 Sociomatrices." American Sociological Review 35: 843-851.

Dolowitz, D. P. 2000. "Special issue on policy transfer - Introduction," *Governance*, 13: 1-4.

Dolowitz, D. P., & Marsh, D. 1996. "Who learns what from whom: a review of the policy transfer literature," *Policy Studies*, 44: 343-357.

Dolowitz, D. P., & Marsh, D. 2000. "Learning from abroad: The role of policy transfer in contemporary policy-making," *Governance*, 13: 5-24.

Dyer, J. H., & Nobeoka, K. 2000. Creating and managing a high-performance knowledge-sharing network: The Toyota case, *Strategic Management Journal*, 21: 345-367.

Evans, M., & Davies, J. 1999. "Understanding policy transfer: A multi-level, multi-disciplinary perspective," *Public Administration*, 77: 361-385.

Granovetter, Mark. 1985. Economic action and social structure: The problem of embeddedness. American Journal of Sociology, 91(3): 481-510.

Gray, V. 1973. "Innovation in the states: A Diffusion Study," *American Political Science Review*. 67: 1174-1185.

Gray, V. 1994. "Competition, Emulation, and policy Innovation," L. C. Dodd & C. Jillson, Washington, DC: CQ Press.

Gupta, A. K., & Govindarajan, V. 1991. "Knowledge flows and the structure of control within multinational corporations," *Academy of Management Review*, 16: 768-792.

Hubner, H. 1996. "Decisions on innovation and diffusion and the limits of deregulation," *Technovation*, 16: 327-339.

Keohane, Robert, and Joseph Nye. 2000. *Power and Interdependence*, 3rd edition, Addison-Wesley.

Kogut, B., & Zander, U. 1995. "Knowledge and the speed of the transfer and imitation of organizational capabilities – an empirical test," *Organization Science*, 6: 76-92.

Lazer, David. 2001. "Regulatory Interdependence and International Governance," *Journal of European Public Policy*: 474-492.

Lazer, David, and Viktor Mayer-Schoenberger. 2002. "Governing Networks," *Brooklyn Journal of International Law*, 27, number 3: 819-851.

Liebeskind, J. P., Oliver, A. L., Zucker, L. & Brewer, M. 1996. "Social networks, learning, and flexibility: Sourcing scientific knowledge in new biotechnology firms," *Organization Science*, 7: 428-443.

Liebowitz, Steve and Stephen Margolis. 1990. "The Fable of the Keys." *Journal of Law and Economics* 33: 1-24.

March, James. 1991. "Exploration and exploitation in organizational learning." *Organization Science*, 2(1): 71-87

McPherson, M., Smith-Lovin, L., & Cook, J. M. 2001. Birds of a feather: Homophily in social networks. Annual Review of Sociology, 27: 415-444.

Mintrom, M. 1997a. "Policy entrepreneurs and the diffusion of innovation," *American Journal of Political Science*, 41: 738-770.

Mintrom, M. 1997b. "The state-local nexus in policy innovation diffusion: The case of school choice," *Publius*, 27: 41-59.

Mintrom, M., & Vergari, S. 1998. "Policy networks and innovation diffusion: The case of state education reforms," *Journal of Politics*, 60: 126-148.

Henry Mintzberg. 1992. *Structure in Fives: Designing Effective Organization.* Prentice Hall.

Moon, M. J., & Bretschneider, S. 1997. "Can state government actions affect innovation and its diffusion?: An extended communication model and empirical test," *Technological Forecasting and Social Change*, 54: 57-77.

Nooteboom, B. 1999. "Innovation and inter-firm linkages: new implications for policy," *Research Policy*, 28: 793-805.

O'Toole, Laurence J., Jr., "Treating Networks Seriously: Practical and Research-based Agendas in Public Administration. *Public Administration Review* 57, 1 (January-February 1997):45-52

Price, D. J. de Solla. 1976. "A general theory of bibliometric and other cumulative advantage processes", *J. Amer. Soc. Inform. Sci.* 27: 292-306.

Radaelli, C. M. 2000. "Policy transfer in the European Union: Institutional isomorphism as a source of legitimacy," *Governance*, 13: 25-43.

Rhodes, R.A.W. 1997. *Understanding Governance: Policy Networks, Governance, Reflexivity and Accountability*, Open University Press.

Robertson, M., Swan, J., & Newell, S. 1996. "The role of networks in the diffusion of technological innovation," *Journal of Management Studies*, 33: 333-359.

Rogers, E. 1995. *Diffusion of Innovations*, 4th edition, New York, NY: Free Press.

Rom, M. C., Peterson, P. E., & Scheve, K. F. 1998. "Interstate competition and welfare policy," *Publius*, 28: 17-37.

Rose-Ackerman, Susan. 1980. "Risk Taking and Re-election: Does Federalism Promote Innovation?" *Journal of Legal Studies* 9: 593-616.

Savage, R. L. (ed.) 1985. Special issue. "Policy Diffusion in a Federal System," *Publius*, 15: 1-27.

Schenk, M., Dahm, H., & Sonje, D. 1997. "The importance of social networks concerning the diffusion of new communication technology," *Kölner Zeitschrift für Soziologie und Sozialpsychologie*, 49: 35-.

Seeliger, R. 1996. "Conceptualizing and researching policy convergence," *Policy Studies Journal*, 24: 287-306.

Simon, Herbert. 1955. "On a class of skew distribution functions," *Biometrika*, 42:425-440.

Slaughter, Anne-Marie. 2000. "Agencies on the Loose: Holding Government Networks Accountable," in George Bermann, Matthias Herdegen, and Peter Lindseth (eds), Transatlantic Regulatory Cooperation.

Stone, D. 2000. "Non-governmental policy transfer: The strategies of independent policy institutes," *Governance*, 13: 45-70.

Strang, David, and Michael Macy. 2001. "'In Search of Excellence': Fads, Success Stories, and Adaptive Emulation" *American Journal of Sociology*, 106.

Strumpf, Kenneth. Forthcoming. "Does Government Decentralization Increase Policy Innovation?" *Journal of Public Economics*.

Brian Uzzi. 1996. The Sources and Consequences of Embeddedness for the Economic Performance of Organizations: The Network Effect. *American Sociological Review* 61: 674-698.

Valente, T. W. 1996. "Social network thresholds in the diffusion of innovations," *Social Networks*, 18: 69-89.

Valente, T. W. 1995. *Network models of the diffusion of innovations*, Cresskill, NJ: Hampton Press.

Walker, J. L. 1969. "The Diffusion of Innovations Among the American States," *American Political Science Review*, 63: 880-899.

Duncan Watts and Steven Strogatts. 1998, Collective dynamics of 'small-world' networks, Nature 393:440-42.

Weale, A., Pridham, G., Williams, A., & Porter, M. 1996. "Environmental administration in six European states: Secular convergence or national distinctiveness?," *Public Administration*, 74: 255-274.

Weenig, M. W. H. 1999. "Communication networks in the diffusion of an innovation in an organization," *Journal of Applied Social Psychology*, 29: 1072-1092.

SESSION II

Dynamic Social Networks

Informal Social Roles and the Evolution and Stability of Social Networks[1]

Jeffrey C. Johnson, East Carolina University

Lawrence A. Palinkas, University of California San Diego

James S. Boster, University of Connecticut

Introduction

From a series of cross-cultural studies on the evolution of group or network structure in Antarctic research stations it is evident that despite similarity in natural environments (e.g., cold, isolation), organizational goals (e.g., conducting science), formal organizational structure, physical settings, group size, and duration of isolation across years group dynamics can vary dramatically from one group to another even within the same physical and cultural settings (Johnson et al. in press; Johnson et al. 2002). Thus, network dynamics are largely a function of both formal and informal factors (e.g., the emergence of informal social roles) that have variable effects on the patterns of interaction and connection among network actors and ultimately on such things as performance, productivity, morale, and individual psychological well-being.

An important distinction needs to be made between formal, informal, and latent social roles in networks. Formal social roles are those proscribed by groups, organizations, or cultures and are reflected in the designation of formal positions (e.g., manager, CEO). Although formal aspects of groups are certainly important, much of network dynamics are the result of informal influences and the interaction between formal and informal processes. Although early work in organization studies recognized a link between latent and informal roles in organizations (Gouldner 1957; Becker and Geer 1960) there is a fundamental difference between the two. Whereas all latent roles are informal, not all informal roles are latent. In this sense there are informal, as well as formal social roles, that are visible and active throughout a group's existence. On the other hand, there are informal social roles that can be dormant or hidden emerging only when circumstances or conditions warrant (e.g., due to external or internal events). The presence or absence of informal social roles and the nature of hidden, dormant, or latent roles all have an impact on a network's emergent properties. Emergent properties here refer to the emergence of higher level group phenomena, such as cohesion or other global structural properties, that stem from the characteristics of lower level constituent entities, such as the mix of individual actors. The focus of this this paper is the relationship between these emergent properties and the evolution of network structures as they relate to such things as network stability, adaptability, and robustness.

In a study of the relationship between informal social roles and emergent properties of networks Johnson et al. (in press) found that the evolution of globally coherent networks in Antarctic winter-over groups was associated with group consensus on the presence of critically important informal social roles (e.g., expressive leadership) where global coherence is the extent to which a network forms a single group composed of a unitary core and periphery as opposed to being fragmented into two or more subgroups. Conversely, the evolution of multiple subgroups was associated with the absence of consensus on informal social roles, above all the critically important role of instrumental leader and the lack of role redundancy in expressive leadership. Thus the nature, multiplicity, and coincidence of both formal and informal social roles in networks can have an impact on the evolution and stability of network structures. More importantly, however, these network structures all have implications for such group outcomes as productivity, group morale, efficiency, individual psychological well-being, group communication, and group conflict (Johnson et al. 2002).

Although there are a wide range of informal role properties and structural correlates we will concentrate on 5 primary forms. Table 1 summarizes these properties in terms of the implications of their presence or absence for group functioning in terms of their effect on network structure. Each of these properties will be discussed in more or less detail in the examples that follow. Briefly, role complementarity is important for diminishing role competition and conflict. Whereas we may want homogeneity in the backgrounds of group members in order to diminish any bases for intra-group divisions (white collar vs. blue collar), role complementarity or heterogeneity is desirable since it helps ensure that group member's roles fit in with one another (Johnson et al. in press). Role consensus, or agreement on informal roles, reflects a lack of role competition and conflict in that there is agreement on the set or sets of actors performing such roles. For some of these informal roles, redundancy is important in that removal of a single actor in a set of multiple roles still ensures proper role function. As later examples will show, lack of replacement may leave groups structurally vulnerable due to the loss of critically important roles that function to foster group coherence or cohesion. Similarly, unforeseen internal or external events that threaten groups may require latent or hidden informal roles that function to maintain structural integrity during these events, in a sense informal roles in reserve being called on in times of need. Finally, the overlap between formal and informal leadership is important for producing group consensus on the group's instrumental goals and objectives and for reducing role competition for leadership. A more in-depth discussion of these properties can be found in Johnson and Finney (1986) and Johnson et al. (in press).

Table 1. Consequences of the presence or absence of network informal role properties.

Informal Role Properties	**Presence**	**Absence**
Role Complementarity	People fit in with one another	Role Homogeneity: Role competition/conflict ("Too many chiefs and not enough Indians")
Role Consensus	Agreement on individual status, role, and function	Role collisions leading to group divisions
Role Redundancy	For certain informal roles can enhance network adaptability	Structural Vulnerability
Role Latency	Promotes adaptive responses to unforeseen events	Structural Vulnerability
Formal/Informal Role Isomorphism	Promotes agreement on group goals and objectives	Role collisions leading to group divisions

Informal Roles and Emergent Properties: Examples of the Ties That Bind

In a dynamic world there is no guarantee of group or network stability over time despite the best intentions of formal organizational efforts (Johnson and Parks 1998). Groups are, in a sense, constantly under attack from both within and from the outside. Interpersonal tensions, for example, always have the potential to tear at the very fabric of group structures from within, inhibiting adaptation to changing circumstances and thereby have the potential to lead to divisive and less cohesive or coherent groups (Johnson et al. in press). Different forms of deviance can work to either integrate or divide group structure (Johnson and Miller 1983; Johnson et al. in press; Dentler and Ericksen 1959). Outside events or organizations can also present threats in terms of such things as withholding resources or outside meddling in internal group affairs that can also impact a group's ability to adapt to changing conditions. Although these outside influences can sometimes serve as group reference points that can foster group cohesion (i.e., internal group alliance to fight outside threats in an *us* versus *them* mentality) such phenomena tend to be short-lived, and once such threats are diminished tend to exacerbate preexisting tensions and conflicts (Johnson and Finney 1986). In either case, the ability of a group to respond to such challenges depends on number of important factors.

Example 1: The Emergence of the Latent Informal Social Role of 'Court Jester'

We now turn to an example of a latent informal social role that contributed to positive group function during a time of external threat. Johnson and Miller (1983) and Johnson and Finney (1986) described the function of the informal social role of 'court-jester' for fostering group cohesion during periods of stress in both fishers in an isolated fish camp in Alaska and in Antarctic expeditions. What makes these examples important is the presence of informal latent social roles that fostered the emergence of group coherence during a stressful event.

Every spring fishermen travel to Bristol Bay, Alaska in the pursuit of king, sockeye, and dog salmon, among other species. The fishing is crowded, competitive, and has historically been very lucrative. Bristol Bay, an arm of the Bering Sea, is extremely isolated and the purchasing, processing, and marketing of salmon has traditionally been dominated by a small set of oligopolistic firms. Within recent times, however, fishers have gained more power due to increasing competition from outside firms and the organization of fishers under the Alaska Independent Fishermen's Marketing Association. Most fishers are associated with large firms staying in bunkhouses within canneries or in fish camps during the salmon season (2-3 months). One such fish camp was owned and operated by a large, powerful firm. The fish camp was multi-ethnic but dominated by a large group of Italians who had mostly emigrated from Sicily to the U.S in the 1960's. The network of interest consists of 16 Italian boat captains. A more detailed ethnographic background for this example can be found in Johnson and Miller (1983).

In a multidimensional scaling of unconstrained judged similarity pile sort data among the 16 captains (not shown) two distinct groups were clear based mostly on bunkhouse residence with the group from bunkhouse 2 being highly among residents while those from bunkhouse 1 had moderate density (Johnson and Miller 1983). There were a number of important exceptions including a fisher who lived in bunkhouse 1 but who interacted most frequently with fishers in bunkhouse 2 and a fisher who lived in bunkhouse 2 but socialized in bunkhouse 1. Another important actor is "fisher 1" who was described by captains during the pile sort task as "the bridge between the two groups" and "belonging to everyone". Fisher 1 is the focal point in this example.

Table 2 shows the timeline of events leading up to the emergence and disappearance of the role of court jester over the course of the fishing season. Initially fishers are extremely busy during the period before the opening of sockeye season preparing boats and gear. During this period there is little free time and fishers work throughout the long Alaskan days (daylight until after midnight). Just prior to opening, the fishers begin to negotiate season prices with firms. If prices have not been settled prior to season opening, the fishers will strike until a satisfactory price can be negotiated. In the year of this study, the strike was quite bitter and protracted (2 weeks of a 4 week season) creating an extremely stressful atmosphere (e.g., captains could gross more than $10,000 a day). With the preparations for the season mostly completed the fishers had little to occupy their time during the strike, contributing further to potential conflicts among and between fishers and management.

Table 2. Timeline for the emergence and disappearance of the role of court jester.

Preparation for salmon season (May-June)	Strike Begins (approx 1 week before season opening)	Season Opens, Strike Still in Effect (Tension, Boredom)	Court Jester Role Emerges	Strike Ends/Fishing Begins (just prior to the season peak)	Court Jester Role disappears	Role Rewarded with over limit fish

During this strike period fisher 1 emerged in the role of court jester and provided hours of comic relief for the fishers of both bunkhouses. Fishers from bunkhouse 1, for example, would come to bunkhouse 2 to engage in a number of activities one of which included a mock funeral and burial in the tundra for fisher1 (Johnson and Miller 1983). Thus, fisher 1 provided comic relief and brought fishers together in positive face to face interactions thereby diminishing chances for intra-group conflicts during this particularly stressful period.

Once fish prices were settled, the role of court jester receded as fishers immersed themselves in their fishing activities. However, despite the lack of need, for this role the role was still recognized as being important to the function of the group. During the remainder of the season fisher 1 received over limit fish transfers from a wide range of fishers as a reward for his role as court jester. The receivers were primarily from bunkhouse 2 with the exception of fisher1 (i.e., reflecting the relative status of members of the respective bunkhouses). Among receivers, fisher 1 had a unique status and role in the group reflected in his high indegree centrality in the fish transfer network. Although he received fish from a wide range of fishers he tended to receive small amounts, generally being at the bottom of the list behind those related by kinship to the giver. This network of Italians was highly interconnected through kinship, and fisher 1 had no kinship relation to any other members of the group, either captains or crew (Johnson and Miller 1983).

There are a number of structural factors and actor characteristics that facilitated the emergence of role of court jester with respect to fisher 1:

- Lower Status actor living in the higher status bunkhouse,
- Worst fisher in the camp (deviant in terms of productivity norms ala Homans (1974)),
- No kinship relations to the group,
- Willingness to be the brunt of jokes and pranks

These structural and individual features allowed fisher 1 to play the role of court jester without the fear of violating norms, despite his formal status as fishing captain. What was important in this case was his informal position and role as court jester bridged the gap between the two bunkhouses during a time of extreme stress, thus significantly contributing to the group's structural integrity. Although there were certainly other forces, such as extensive kinship relations, that also fostered group cohesion, the role of court jester encouraged actual face-to-face interactions at a particularly critical time.

Example 2: The Bridging Informal Role of Clown in Antarctic Groups

The next example of a bridging informal role comes from research on the group dynamics of Antarctic winter-over crews at the Amundsen-Scott South pole Station. Three separate years at the station were studied throughout the Austral winter in which station crews were isolated for approximately 9 months. Network data, informal role data and morale and psychological data were collected on a monthly basis throughout the 9 months of the winter. Similar to the example above we concentrate on the role of 'clown'. However, in this case the informal role of clown was recognized throughout winter in each of the three years studied. The role term itself was derived from in-depth interviews with former winter-overs prior to the beginning of the study (see Johnson and Weller 2002 for a discussion). This term and 10 other informal role terms (e.g., social director, work leader, peacemaker) were a part of a informal role sentence completion task in which respondents were asked to associate each of his or her fellow winter-over crewmembers with each of the 11 informal role terms.

Figure 1 shows a series of graphs revealing the connections among winter-over crew from year A in the middle of winter (July) one of the most stressful periods of the winter-over period (Palinkas et al. 1998, 2000a, 2000b, 2001, 2002; Johnson et al. 2002). The series of network graphs reveals the important bridging function of the clown role during this year (more than 67 % of the crew nominated this actor for the role of 'clown/comedian'). This role was particularly important in maintaining connections between trades crew (i.e., the contractors) and scientists (i.e., primarily NSF grantees). The trades and scientists, often jokingly referred to by the trades crew as "beakers" (as in laboratory beaker), a distinction that has historically been a potential source of intra-group conflicts in Antarctic winter-over groups.

What this series dramatically reveals is that the clown role functioned to bridge relations between the two major social categories in the station. The crewmember who played this role was central to a wide range of both trade and science crew. With respect to trade crew he linked different segments among members of the trades themselves, particularly the two isolates to the lower left in graph II. Similarly, he provided a link between the major cluster of scientists in the upper right of the graph both with other scientists, particularly the isolated science personnel, and the primary trades contingent.

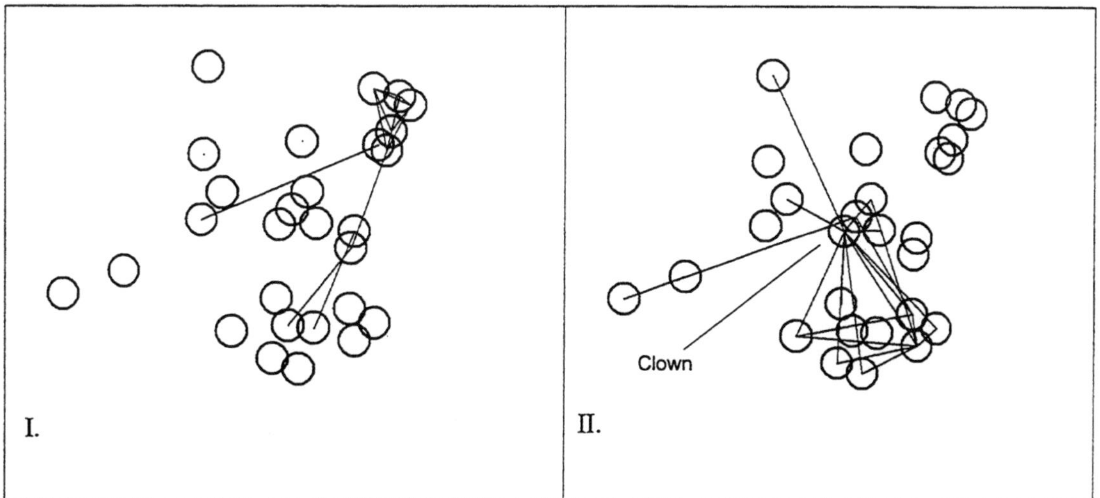

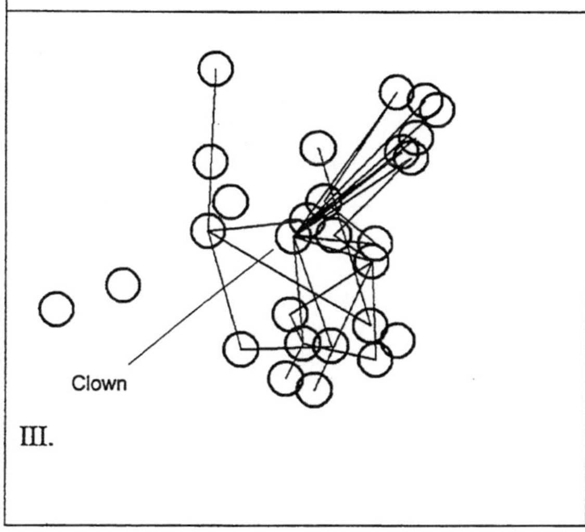

Figure 1. The network structure in the middle of the winter (July) derived from a stacked correspondence analysis of the ratings of social interaction during each of the 9 winter months. Edges are shown for $r_{ij} > 4$, where r ranges between 0 and 10. The graphs show (I) ties among scientists in the middle of winter for year A, (II) ties among trades in the middle of winter with clown role highlighted, and (III) ties between scientists and trades in the middle of winter with clown role highlighted

In addition to the clown noted in Figure 4, there were several other crewmembers who were nominated as clowns by winter's end in year A, 2 with high consensus (consensus $c>0.66$) and 4 with moderate consensus ($0.33<c<0.67$). Of the remaining 2 years, year B had high consensus on 3 individuals in the role of clown while year C had only moderate consensus on one crew member in this informal role. Further, year C had high consensus on one crew member in a negative deviant role, while the remaining 2 years had limited negative deviance with the exception of moderate consensus on one deviant role in year

A. Thus, Years A and B displayed a high degree of role redundancy with respect to the informal role of clown. This stands in stark contrast to year C where this informal role was largely absent.

Example 3: Expressive Leadership, Role Redundancy, and Adaptability

In this example we examine the consequences of the degree of expressive leadership available to groups. What separates expressive from instrumental leadership is the arena in which each operates. Whereas instrumental leadership generally deals with achieving organizational goals and objectives related to work, expressive leadership, as its name entails, involves leadership and direction in a variety of mostly non-work realms. Expressive leaders, referred to in the study as social directors, organized events that were primarily expressive or leisure oriented (e.g., dinner parties, theme costume parties, sports competitions, dance lessons, etc.). These events brought people of various backgrounds together in face-to-face interactions that were of a positive nature.

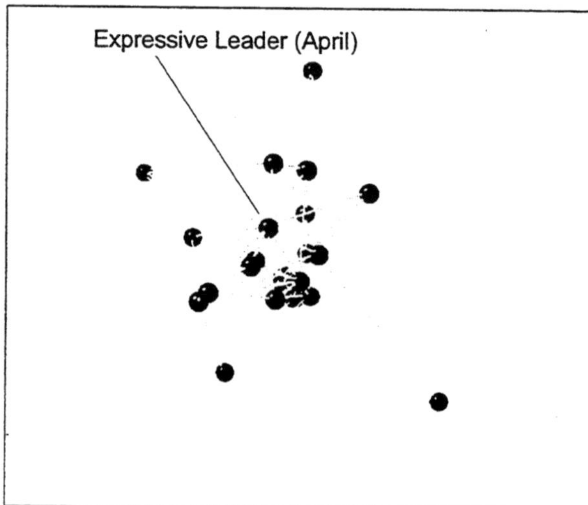

Figure 2a. Graph showing the position of the single expressive leader two months after the start of the Austral winter for year C. Edges are shown for $r_{ij} > 4$, where r ranges between 0 and 10.

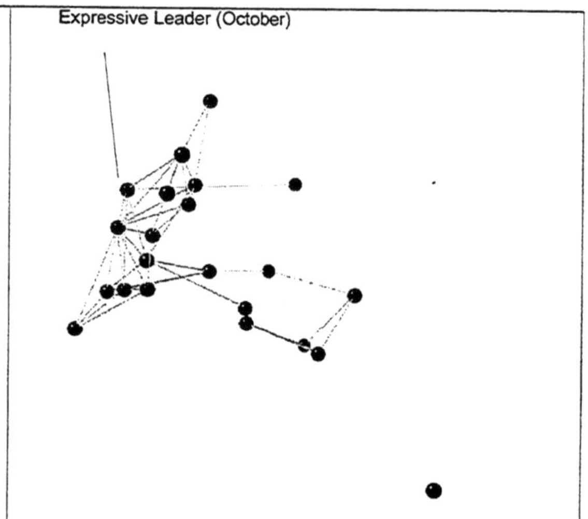

Figure 2b. Graph showing the position of the earlier nominated expressive leader at the end of the winter for year C. Edges are shown for $r_{ij} > 4$, where r ranges between 0 and 10.

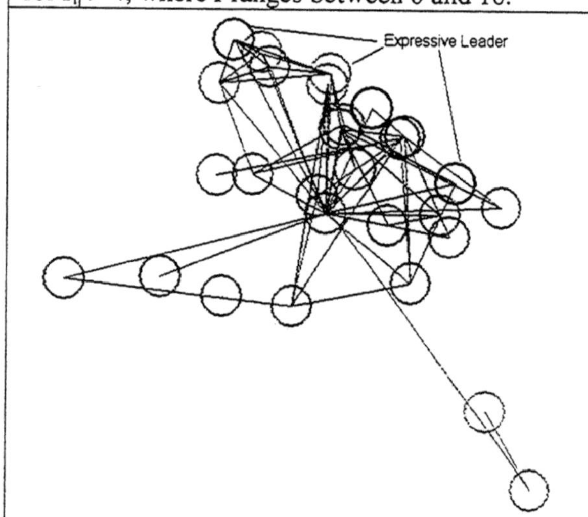

Figure 2c. The network structure in the middle of the winter (July) for year A derived from a stacked correspondence analysis of the ratings of social interaction during each of the 9 winter months. Edges are shown for $r_{ij} > 4$, where r ranges between 0 and 10. The graph shows the position of the 3-crew members who were highly nominated as expressive leaders.

Figures 2a & 2b show the position of the single expressive leader for year C in the beginning and end of the Austral winter. In the beginning of the winter this actor is central to the group bridging connections between science and trades crewmembers. However, by the end of the winter this crewmember had become less central and the group had fragmented into several subgroups with two primary divisions being between science and trades crew.

This single expressive leader for this year dropped out of most group interactions in about the middle of winter because of problems with harassment, particularly from one crewmember (see discussion on negative deviant roles above). Whereas this expressive leader was an organizer of social events and dinner parties in the earlier months of the winter, by mid-winter this crewmember had dropped out of most social activities, particularly as the important organizer of events that functioned to bring group members together in face-to-face interactions. Thus, just at the time when the integrating functions of expressive leadership were most needed (mid-winter), this crewmember went into relative social isolation and the expressive leadership role was lost with no one to fill that important informal role. Paralleling this decline in the presence of expressive leadership, the group structure began to fragment into various subgroups (see discussion below on instrumental leadership).

In contrast to year C, year A had 3 crewmembers in the role of expressive leader (Figure 2c). In each case these expressive leaders provided crucial bridges between science and trades crewmembers. For example, the expressive leader at the top left (a science crew member) was central to the science subgroup and connected to the clown role (a trades crewmember) at the center of the network. In any event these 3 crew members helped in organizing events, dinner parties, sports competitions, dance lessons, card games, etc., all activities that increased chances for face-to-face interactions across all crew members. Of the 3 years of the study, this winter-over crew had the most extra-work related activities of any year. It should also be noted that role redundancy in this case lessened the potential vulnerability of this important role in that elimination of a single expressive role still afforded chances for the remaining expressive leaders to perform this critically important function. Thus, this year had a number of informal roles in reserve that could be called on in times of need.

Example 4: Isomorphism Between Formal and Informal Instrumental Leadership

In the final example we look at the important relationship between informal and formal instrumental leadership. Johnson et al. (in press) discuss the importance of the overlap in the formal and informal instrumental leadership roles for proper group function. The idea is that the overlap between the two roles diminishes chances for role competition within a group for the important leadership role, whether formal or informal.

Figure 3 shows the final group structures for the three years and the position of the formal station managers in each of the networks in the final month of the winter. There are a number of striking features with respect to the placement of formal managers in the network structure. For year A, the station manager is embedded in the middle of a rather cohesive network. The station manger for year B is also central to the structure but in a much less cohesive or coherent structure. Finally, year C finds the station manager less central in the network that is divided into three primary network subgroups.

As might be expected from the differences of the network positions of the three station mangers there are also differences on the overlap between formal and informal instrumental leadership. By winter's end 100 percent of the crew in year A nominated the formal station manager as the informal work leader with moderate consensus on informal work leadership for two other crewmembers. For year B, there was high consensus for the station manager as also filling the role of informal work leader with moderate consensus on one other crewmember. For year C, however, there was a lack of high consensus on an informal work leader and there was moderate consensus on three crewmembers including the station manager. Thus, in years A and B in terms there was high agreement with respect to the station manager as informal work leader, reflecting a considerable degree of role consensus. The moderate agreement for three crew for year C, on the other hand, reflects role competition for instrumental leader that included the station manager. It should be noted that initially year C had high consensus on the station manager as the exclusive informal instrumental leader. This is important in that the lack of extensive informal role properties in this year allowed for potential problems in the future stemming from interpersonal conflicts and external threats of various kinds. Good leadership alone cannot produce stable, productive groups. It requires a combination of informal roles, all improving the chances for the evolution of cohesive and productive groups.

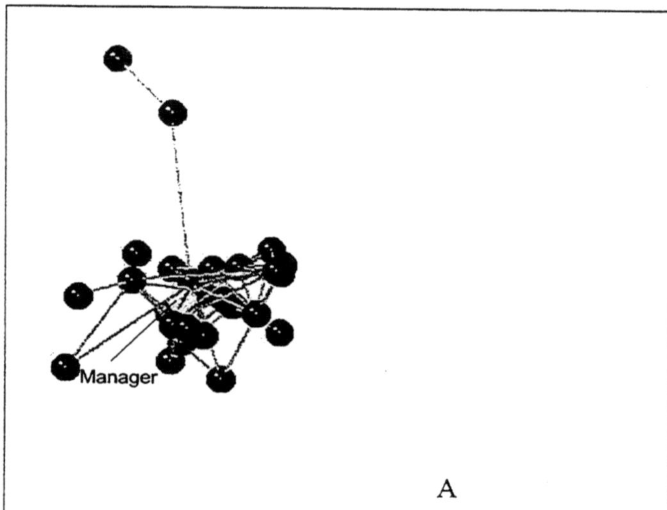

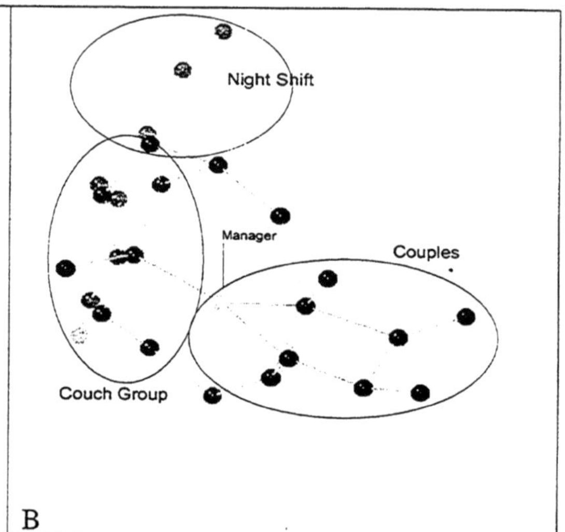

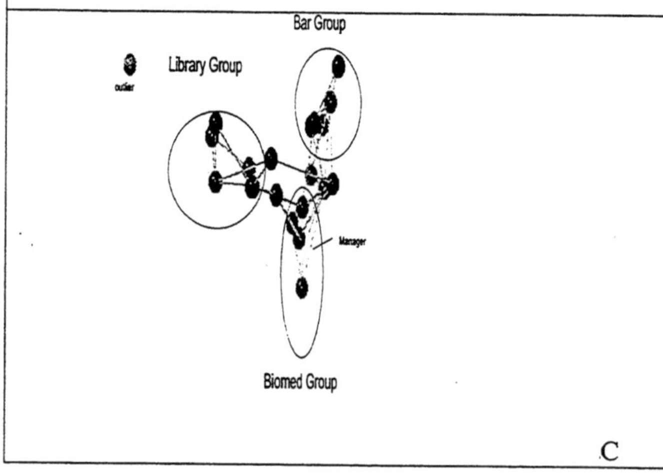

Figure 3. Final (October) group structures for winter-over crews for the 3 showing the position of station manager and the delineation of groups as determined by the winter-overs in in-depth interviews (from a correspondence analysis of the ratings of interaction). Year A formed a single group (global coherence), while years B and C had varying degrees of subgroups. Year C had subgroups determined primarily on the basis of a science versus trades split. The library group consisted mostly of scientists while the bar group consisted of trades crew members (e.g., carpenters, plumbers, mechanics, etc.) [from Johnson et al., in press]

Informal Role Properties and Group Outcomes

In this section we examine the consequences of the informal role properties discussed above. In an earlier paper, Johnson et al. (in press) demonstrated that informal role properties of these winter-over groups were important for understanding the evolution of coherent group structures. Globally coherent structures were associated with role consensus, role heterogeneity, expressive leadership, functional deviance, and an overlap between formal and informal instrumental leadership, while local coherence (presence of network fragmentation) was associated with the lack of extensive informal social roles, negative deviance, and role competition for instrumental leadership. In this case, year A's structure evolved to be highly coherent over time, year B's structure was moderately coherent, while year C's structure became locally coherent over time, fragmenting into several subgroups (Figure 3). Aside from these structural consequences of informal role properties, what effect do these factors have on such things as group morale, psychological well-being, and group productivity?

Figure 4 is a graph of changes in 'overall morale' of group members over the 9 months of the winter. Whereas there is no significant difference between years initially [$F=2.297$, $p<0.2$] there is a dramatic decline in morale for year C over the 8.5 months of the winter. Although each year experiences a downward trend in morale as mid-winter approaches, year C shows a much more dramatic decline relative to the other two years. In a two way repeated measures analysis of variance there is a significant difference between years [$F=19.375$, $p<0.0001$] in overall morale. More importantly, however, there is an interaction effect between year and month [$F=2.495$, $p<0.002$] indicating significantly different linear trends in morale over the winter. Although year A declines slightly in morale as the winter progresses, by August (when the sun first appears) the trend is upward. This is in contrast to the other two years that experience further downward movements in morale only rebounding at the end of the winter-over in anticipation of station opening. However, this trend is much larger for year C than year B.

A further example of the consequences of differences in informal role structures across the 3 years can be seen in a comparison of anger and tension/anxiety over the winter. Figure 5 is a scatter plot of the relationship between group means for tension/anxiety and anger over the winter gained from the profile of mood states (POMS) instrument that was administered on a monthly basis (Palinkas et al. 1998, 2000a, 2000b, 2001, 2002; Johnson et al. 2002). A 68 percent confidence ellipse is shown for each of the years. Year A has the least variation in these psychological measures over the course of the winter and has the lowest overall values across the three groups. Year C has somewhat more variability in these psychological indices over the winter and is the most extreme overall in values over the winter months. Year B has a high degree of variation over the winter and is in between the other years in terms of the magnitude of psychological indices.

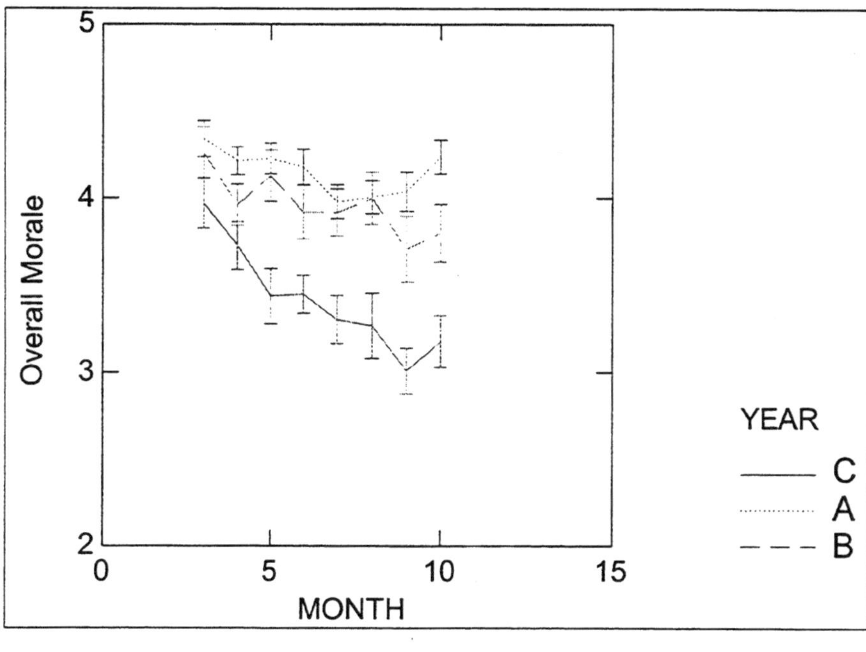

Figure 4. Comparison of "overall morale" over the Austral winter across the three years of South Pole crews (intervals shown as standard errors)

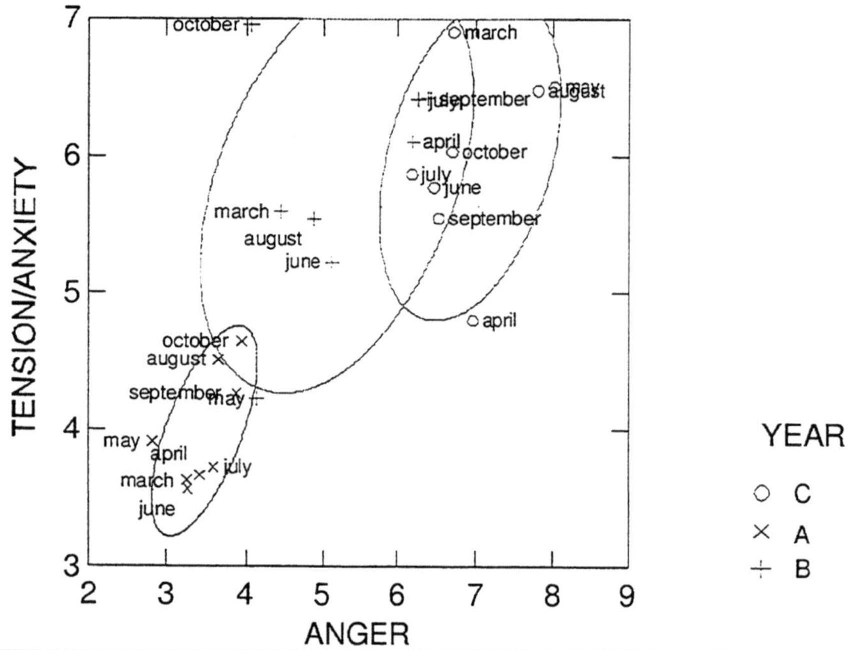

Figure 5. Relationship between anger and tension/anxiety over the 8 months for the three years studied (years are encompassed by 68 percent confidence level ellipses).

Table 3 summarizes the comparison between the three years with respect to the informal role properties discussed above. Year A had by far the richest combination of role properties, followed by year B. Year C lacked many of the informal role properties that are hypothesized as important for the proper functioning of groups. It is clear from this analysis that the presence of informal role properties lead to more desirable group outcomes. Year A had higher levels of morale and lower levels of tension, anxiety, and anger. This was followed by year B that had more moderate levels of informal role properties and correspondingly lower levels of morale and higher levels of anger, tension, and anxiety. Year C actually started with the most coherent structure of the three years at the beginning of winter (Johnson et al. in press) but the structure fragmented into several subgroups over the course of the winter that mostly reflected the trades versus science categories. Although year C initially displayed a cohesive structure, it lacked the informal role properties needed to effectively deal with the inevitable internal and external threats faced by groups (e.g., negative deviance, interpersonal conflicts, meddling from outside agents or agencies).

Table 3. Summary of informal role properties present in the 3 years at the South Pole Station by winter's end.

Informal Role Properties	**Year A**	**Year B**	**Year C**
Role Complementarity	High	Moderate	Low
Role Consensus	High	High	Low
Role Redundancy	High	High-Moderate	Low*
Role Latency	Moderate	Moderate	Low
Role Isomorphism	High	Moderate	Low

*Redundancy is low in terms of expressive leadership but high in terms of instrumental leadership leading to role competition for the work leadership position

Concluding Remarks: Informal Roles and Implications for Network Evolution, Stability, and Adaptability

This paper provided a brief discussion and examples of the importance of the recognition of the informal and latent role properties of networks for understanding network evolution and change particularly with respect to the direction of change (i.e., the evolution of network fragmentation or coherence). The examples above have suggested that groups that have a rich mix of informal role properties fair better in terms of both the evolution and stability of group cohesion or coherence. In addition, these properties appear to enhance the ability of groups to adapt to a number of both internal and external threats to group structure and function. Whereas this research has largely been interested in the factors that keep networks together (e.g., cohesion, coherence) and productive, such an understanding can similarly be used to achieve just the opposite, the fragmentation or disruption of network structures. Steve Borgatti (this conference) has been concerned with the removal of nodes and its effect on network fragmentation and inter-node distances. Kathleen Carley has recently examined the importance of node insertion in disrupting network structures and the importance of extra-network information in predicting network change and adaptability (e.g., a talk at the Cambridge Colloquium Complexity and Social Networks in December 2001). In either case, an understanding of the relationship between structural properties and role properties of the kind discussed here can aid in producing more informed theories on network fragmentation and disruption. It is important, for example, to know not only the network or nodal properties of actors, but also their informal role properties. Such combined information can lead to a deeper understanding of the potential impacts of both node removal (e.g., the removal of expressive leaders that bridge various categories of actors) and insertion (e.g., increased role competition for instrumental leader) on network structures. This entails knowledge of related but distinctly different forms of social structural data.

The examples described here have been relatively simplistic in that they involved well-bounded and enduring groups with little or no movement in or out of the network. Despite their simplicity, however, such examples can help inform us about the importance of informal role properties across a wider range of network contexts. Further research is needed on the types of informal role properties at work in networks in other settings (e.g., terrorist networks). In addition, we need a better theoretical understanding of the structural correlates of these informal role properties and their ultimate effect on network evolution and stability.

Footnotes

1. This research was supported by the National Science Foundation grants BNS-9011351 and OPP-9610231. In addition, a portion of this work was sponsored by a grant from the National Aeronautics and Space Administration grant NAG-5-4571. We would like to warmly thank the winter-over crews of South Pole Station for their kindness, friendship, and generous cooperation.

References

H.S. Becker and B. Geer. Latent culture: A note on the theory of latent social roles. Administrative Science Quarterly, Volume 5, Issue 2 Sep. 1960, 304-313.

R.A. Dentler and K.T. Erickson. The function of deviance in small groups. Social Problems, 1959, 99-107

A.W. Gouldner. Cosmopolitans and locals: Towards an analysis of latent social roles. Administrative Science Quarterly, Volume 2, Issue 3 Dec. 1957, 281-306.

G. Homans (1974). Social Behavior, 2nd edn, New York: Harcourt Brace Jovanovich.

J.C. Johnson and S. Weller. Elicitation Techniques in Interviewing. (2002) In Handbook of Interview Research (J. Gubrium and J. Holstein, eds.), pp 491-514, Sage:Newbury Park.

J.C. Johnson and M.L. Miller. "Deviant Social Positions in Small Groups: the Relation Between Role and Individual," Social Networks 5:51-69, 1983.

J.C. Johnson and B.R. Finney. "Structural Approaches to the Study of Groups in Space: A Lookat Two Analogs," Journal of Social Behavior and Personality 1(3):325-347, 1986.

J.C. Johnson, J. Boster, and L. Palinkas. "Social Roles and the Evolution of Networks in Isolatedand Extreme Environments. The Journal of Mathematical Sociology (In Press).

J.C. Johnson and D. Parks. "Communication Roles, Perceived Effectiveness, and Satisfaction in an Environmental Management Program." Journal of Computational and Mathematical Organization Theory VOL 4(3) 223-239, 1998.

J. C. Johnson, L.A. Palinkas,., J. S. Boster, S. Rakusa-Suszczewski, V. P. Klopov, X. Quan Fu, and Usha Sachdeva. Network Evolution, Social Roles, and Well-being in Isolated Groups: A Cross-Cultural Comparison. . Paper presented at the Scientific Committee for Antarctic Research (SCAR) meeting, Shanghai, China, July 2002.

L.A. Palinkas, E.K.E. Gunderson, J.C. Johnson, and A. Holland,. "Behavior and Performance on long Duration Space Flights: Evidence from Analog Environments." Aviation, Space, and Environmental Medicine Vol. 71, No. 49: September 2000.

L.A. Palinkas, E.K.E. Gunderson, A. Holland, C. Miller, and J.C. Johnson. "Predictors of Behavior and Performance in Extreme Environments: The Antarctic Space Analogue Program." Aviation, Space, and Environmental Medicine Vol. 71, No. 41: 1-7, April 2000.

L.A. Palinkas, J.C. Johnson, J.S. Boster, and M. Houseal. Longitudinal Studies of Behavior and Performance During a Winter at the South Pole. Aviation, Space, and Environmental Medicine 69(1) 73-77, 1998.

L.A. Palinkas, J.C. Johnson, and J.S. Boster. Social Support and Depressed Moods in Isolated and Confined Environments. In The proceedings of the 52nd International Astronautical Congress, IAF/IAA-010G3.b.01, Oct. 2001.

L. A. Palinkas, J. C. Johnson., J.S. Boster, S. Rakusa-Suszczewski, V. P. Klopov, X. Quan Fu, U. Sachdeva. Cultural Differences in Mood and Social Support in Antarctica. Paper presented at the Scientific Committee for Antarctic Research (SCAR) meeting, Shanghai, China, July 2002.

Dynamic Network Analysis

Kathleen M. Carley
Institute for Software Research International
Carnegie Mellon University

Abstract

Dynamic network analysis (DNA) varies from traditional social network analysis in that it can handle large dynamic multi-mode, multi-link networks with varying levels of uncertainty. DNA, like quantum mechanics, would be a theory in which relations are probabilistic, the measurement of a node changes its properties, movement in one part of the system propagates through the system, and so on. However, unlike quantum mechanics, the nodes in the DNA, the atoms, can learn. An approach to DNA is described that builds DNA theory through the combined use of multi-agent modeling, machine learning, and meta-matrix approach to network representation. A set of candidate metric for describing the DNA are defined. Then, a model built using this approach is presented. Results concerning the evolution and destabilization of networks are described.

Acknowledgement

The research reported herein was supported by the National Science Foundation NSF IRI9633 662, the Office of Naval Research (ONR) Grant No. N00014-97-1-0037 and Grant No. 9620.1.1140071, Additional support was provided by the NSF IGERT 9972762 for research and training in CASOS and by the center for Computational Analysis of Social and Organizational Systems at Carnegie Mellon University (http://www.casos.ece.cmu.edu). The views and conclusions contained in this document are those of the authors and should not be interpreted as representing the official policies, either expressed or implied, of the Office of Naval Research, the National Science Foundation or the U.S. government.

Dynamic Network Analysis

Terrorist organizations have network structures that are distinct from those in typical hierarchical organizations – they are cellular and distributed. While most commanders, politicians and intelligence agents have at least an intuitive understanding of hierarchies and how to affect their behavior, they have less of an understanding of how to even go about reasoning about dynamic networked organizations (Ronfelt and Arquilla, 2001). It is even more difficult for us to understand how such networks will evolve, change, adapt and how they can be destabilized.

Clearly social network analysis can be applied to the study of covert networks (Sparrow, 1991). Many are stepping forward suggesting that to understand these networks we just need to "connect the dots" and then isolate the "key actors who are often defined in terms of their "centrality" in the network. To an extent, this is right. However, it belies the difficulty of "connecting the dots" in terms of mining vast quantities of information, pattern matching on agent characteristics for people who go under multiple aliases, and still ending up with information the may be intentionally misleading, inaccurate, out-of-date, and incomplete. Further, this belies the difficulty in "knowing" who is the most central when you have at best only a sample of the network. Finally, and critically, this approach does not contend with the most pressing problem – the underlying network is dynamic. Just because you isolate a key actor today does not mean that the network will be destabilized and unable to respond. Rather, it is possible, that isolating such an actor may have the same effect as cutting off the Hydra's head; many new key actors may emerge (Carley, Lee and Krackhardt, 2001).

To understand the dynamics of terrorist, and indeed any, network we need to understand the basic processes by which networks evolve. Moreover, we have to evaluate isolation strategies in the face of an evolving network and in the face of missing information. To ignore either the dynamics or the lack of information is liable to lead to erroneous, and possibly devastatingly wrong, policies. Taking in to account both the dynamics and the lack of information should engender a more cautious approach in which we can ask, "if we do x what is likely to happen?"

Limitations to Traditional SNA

Traditionally, social network analysis (SNA) has focused on small, bounded networks, with 2-3 types of links (such as friendship and advice) among one type of node (such as people), at one point in time, with close to perfect information. To be sure there are a few studies that have considered extremely large networks, or two types of nodes (people and events), or unbounded networks (such as inter-organizational response teams); however, these are the exception not the norm. However, such studies are still the exception not the rule. Further, while it is understood, at least in principle how to think about multi-modal, multi-plex, dynamic networks, the number of tools, the interpretation of the measures, and the illustrative studies using such "higher order" networks are still in their infancy relative to what is available for simpler networks. Finally, many of the tools do not scale well with the size of the network or degrade gracefully with errors in the network; e.g., they may be too computationally expensive or too sensitive to both type 1 and 2 errors. What is needed is a dynamic network analysis theory and toolkit. We are working to develop such a tool kit and the associated metrics and decision aids. In this paper, one such tool, DyNet is described and used to examine various isolation strategies.

Dynamic Network Analysis

Recently there have been a number of advances that extend SNA to the realm of dynamic analysis and multi-color networks. There are three key advances: 1) the meta-matrix, 2) treating ties as probabilistic, and 3) combining social networks with cognitive science and multi-agent systems. These advances result in a dynamic network analysis.

Meta-Matrix: Carley (2002) combined knowledge management, operations research and social networks techniques together to create the notion of the meta-matrix – a multi-color, multiplex representation of the entities and the connections among them. The Meta-matrix is an extension and generalization of the PCANS approach forwarded by Carley and Krackhardt (1999) that focused on people, resources and tasks. For our purpose, the entities of interest are people, knowledge/resources, events/tasks and organizations – see table 1. This defines a set of 10 inter-linked networks such that changes in one network cascade into changes in the others; relationships in one network imply relationships in another. For example, co-membership in an organization or co-attendance at an event for two people suggests a tie in the social network between these two people. A group, such as a terrorist network, can be represented in terms of an overtime sequence of such networks. In fact, any organization or group can be represented in this fashion and we have used this representation on numerous occasions to characterize actual organizations and to predict their ability to adapt.

All graph theory and network measures can be defined in terms of whether they can or have been applied to which cells. Further, on the basis of this meta-matrix new metrics can be developed that better capture the overall importance of an individual, task, or resource in the group. An example of such a metric is cognitive load – the effort an individual has to employ to hold his role in the terrorist group - and it takes in to account, who he interacts with, which events he has been at, which organizations he is a member of, the coordination costs of working with others in the same organization or at the same event or in learning from an earlier event or training for an upcoming event. A large number of such metrics have been developed and analyzed in terms of their ability to explain the evolution, performance, and adaptability of dynamic networks.

A key difficulty from a growth of science perspective, is that as we move from SNA to DNA the number, type, complexity, and value of measures changes. A core issue for DNA is what are the appropriate metrics for describing and contrasting dynamic networks. Significant new research is needed in this regard. To date, our work suggests that a great deal of leverage can be gained in describing networks by focusing on measures that utilize more of the cells in the meta-matrix. For example, cognitive load, which measures the cognitive effort and individual has to do at one point in time has been shown to be a valuable predictor of emergent leadership (Carley and Ren, 2001). Cognitive load is a complex measure that takes into account the number of others, resources, tasks the agent needs to manage and the communication needed to engage in such activity. In addition, we find that for any of the cells in the meta-matrix, particularly for large scale networks, many of the standard graph level measures have little information content as the network grows in size (Anderson, Butts and Carley, 1999) and/or are highly correlated with each other. A set of measures that are generally not correlated, scale well, and are key in characterizing a network are the size of the network (number of nodes), density (either as number of ties or the typical social network form number of ties/number of possible ties), homogeneity in the distribution of ties (e.g., the number of clusters or subcomponents, the variance in centrality), rate of change in nodes, and rate of change in ties. The point is not that these are the only measures needed to characterize dynamic networks. The point is that these are a candidate set that have value and that as a field we need to develop a small set of metrics that can be applied to networks, regardless of size, to characterize the dynamics.

Table 1. Meta-Matrix

	People	Knowledge/Resources	Events/Tasks	Organizations
People	Social network	Knowledge network	Attendance network	Membership network
Knowledge/Resources		Information network	Needs network	Organizational capability
Events/Tasks			Temporal ordering	Institutional support or attack
Organizations				Inter-organizational network

Probabilistic Ties: The ties in the meta-matrix are probabilistic. Various factors affect the probability, including the observer's certainty in the tie and the likelihood that the tie is manifest at that time. Bayesian updating techniques (Dombroski and Carley, 2002), cognitive inferencing techniques, and models of social and cognitive change processes (Carley, 2002; Carley, Lee and Krackhardt, 2001) can be used to estimate the probability and how it changes over time. We are in the process of exploring techniques for combining the cognitive inferencing with the cognitive change process models.

Multi-Agent Network Models: A major problem with traditional SNA is that the people in the networks are not treated as active adaptive agents capable of taking action, learning, and altering their networks. There are several basic, well known, social and cognitive processes that influence who is likely to interact with whom: relative similarity, relative expertise, and co-worker. Carley uses multi-agent technology in which the agents use these mechanisms, learn, take part in events, do tasks to model organizational and social change. The dynamic social network emerges from these actions. The set of networks linking people, knowledge, tasks and other groups or organizations co-evolve. Carley, Lee and Krackhardt (2001) use simple learning mechanisms to dynamically adjust networks as the agents in them attended events, learned new information, or were removed from the network. In DyNet, described herein, additional mechanisms center on agent isolation are also considered.

DNA has a wide range of applications. For example, this approach is being used to examine the likely impact of unanticipated events in the VISTA project (Diedrich et al, forthcoming), the possible effects of biological attacks on cities in BioWar (Carley et al, 2002), in evaluating CIO response strategies to denial of service attacks (Chen, 2002), and evaluating information security within organizations – ThreatFinder Project (Carley, 2001). See also www.casos.ece.cmu.edu current projects and working papers.

Dynamic Network Theory

To move beyond representation and method, we need to ask, "How do networks change?" What are the basic processes? From the meta-matrix perspective, the processes are easy – things that lead to the adding and dropping of nodes and/or relations – see table 2. Again, no claim is being made that the processes listed in table 2 cover the complete spectrum; rather, they illustrate the types of node change processes that need to be postulated. A full theory of dynamic networks needs to speak to such mechanisms.

Table 2. Basic Change Processes for Nodes in the Meta-Matrix

People	Knowledge/Resources	Events/Tasks	Organizations
Birth	Innovation	Goal Change	Organizational birth
Death	Discovery	Re-engineering	Organizational death
Promotion	Forgetting	Development of new technology	Mergers
Mobility	Consumption	Stop usage of technology	Acquisitions
Recruitment			Legislation of new entity
Incarceration			
Isolation			

Similarly, there are a set of processes that lead to the addition and removal of relations. Basic processes are cognitive, social and political in nature. Cognitive processes have to do with learning and forgetting, the changes that occur in ties due to changes in what individuals know. Social changes occur when one agent or organization dictates a change in ties, such as when a manager re-assigns individuals to tasks. Finally, political changes are due to legislation that effect organizations and the over-arching goals. To illustrate what is meant, a limited number of such processes are described in Table 3. Further, and this should be obvious, processes that add or eliminate nodes also affect relations to/from that node. For example, if all individuals in a society forget a particular piece of information that knowledge node, no longer exists and all connections from people to it are now eliminated.

Table 3. Change Processes for Relations in the Meta-Matrix				
	People	Knowledge/ Resources	Events/ Tasks	Organizations
People	Motivation to Interact Change in access	Learning Acquisition	Re-assignment	Mobility Recruitment
Knowledge/ Resources		Discovery Analogical reasoning	Innovation	IP development
Events/Tasks				Re-engineering Out-sourcing
Organizations				Alliances Coalitions

DyNet

The purpose of the DyNet project is to develop the equivalent of a flight simulator for reasoning about dynamic networked organizations. Through a unique blending of computer science, social networks and organization theory we are creating a new class of tools for managing organizational dynamics. The core tool is DyNet – a reasoning support tool for reasoning under varying levels of uncertainty about dynamic networked and cellular organizations, their vulnerabilities, and their ability to reconstitute themselves. Using DyNet the analyst would be able to see how the networked organization was likely to evolve if left alone, how its performance could be affected by various information warfare and isolation strategies, and how robust these strategies are in the face of varying levels of information assurance.

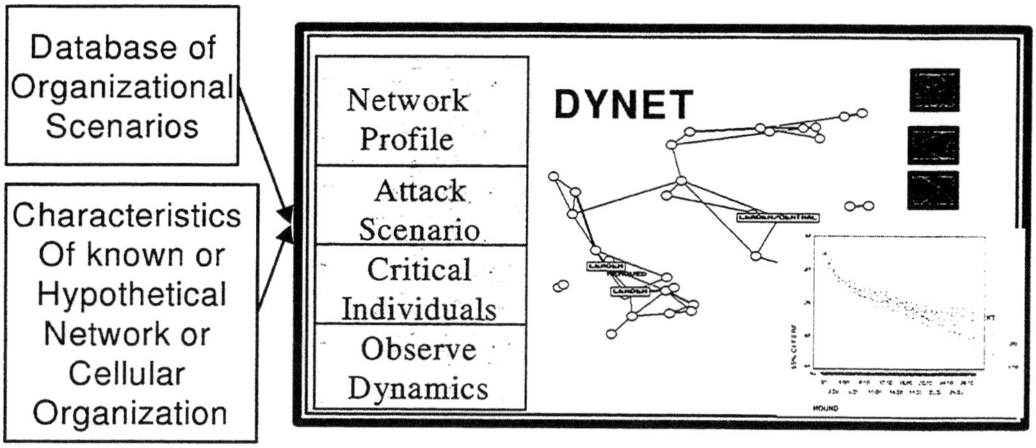

Figure 1. DYNET: A desktop tool for reasoning about dynamic networked and cellular organizations.

DyNet is intended to be a desktop system that can be placed in the hands of intelligence personnel, researchers, or military strategists. Through hands-on what if analysis the analysts will be able to reason in a what –if fashion about how to build stable adaptive networks with high performance and how to destabilize networks. There are many applications for such a tool including: threat assessment; assessing information security risks in corporations; intel training; simulation of the red team in a gaming situation, and estimation of efficacy of destabilization policies. Currently an alpha version exists as a batch program (no visualization) and it has been used to evaluate simple isolation strategies. The system can handle data on real networks.

The DyNet tool is a step toward understanding how networks will evolve, change, adapt and how they can be destabilized. The goal will be to incorporate all of the evolutionary mechanisms previously discussed. DyNet, which is a computer model of dynamic networks, can also be thought of as the embodiment of a theory of dynamic networks. The focus of this theory is on the cognitive, and to a lesser extent, social processes by which the networks in the meta-matrix evolve. The basic cognitive forces for change in DyNet are learning, forgetting, goal-setting, and motivation for interaction. The basic social forces for change are recruitment, isolation, and to a limited extent the initiation of rumors and training.

The basic motivations for interaction are relative similarity, relative expertise or some combination of the two. Relative similarity is based on the fundamental finding of homophilly, the tendency of interacting partners to be similar. Arguments surrounding this fundamental process include the need for communicative ease, comfort, access, and training. Relative expertise is based on the fundamental finding that when in doubt people will turn they view as experts for information. Arguments surround this fundamental processes include the need to acquire, desire to minimize search, desire to optimize information, and so on. Other basic motivations such as the need to exhibit competence and the need to coordinate have also been identified and will be added to DyNet but are not in the current system.

Among the attrition strategies are removal of the most "central" individual, removal of the individual with the highest cognitive load, and removal of individual's at random. User's can control the frequency and severity of such attrition strategies. Previous studies using this system have shown that a) it is difficult to completely destabilize a network, b) that the best strategy depends on the structure of the network, and c) attrition strategies vary in whether there effectiveness is enhanced or diminished by removing multiple agents at once or sequentially (Carley, 2002).

Agents can be distinguished based on fixed characteristics such as race, family and gender, and on knowledge (or training). Further, the agents can operate in a world without information technology or augmented by access to email, web pages, or manuals. Access to others can be restricted, as might be the case when operatives live in different countries. Performance metrics include task completion, accuracy, energy for tasks, information diffusion, and group cohesion. Finally, the basic networks can be extracted continually in order to see the system evolve. Among the networks that can be extracted are the knowledge network, the overall social network, the emotive or "friendship" networks, and the acquisition or "advice" network. The network evolutionary strategies include learning (during interaction), forgetting, personnel attrition, misinformation, and changing task demands. DyNet offers the user the choice of entering specific networks or entering network characteristics (such as size and density).

Results

Using DyNet a series of virtual experiments were run. These experiments were designed to examine the interaction between network structure, dynamics (particularly in response to isolation), and the information that the observer has on which to base the isolation strategies. In figure 2, a very high level conceptualization of these differences is shown. Three possible isolation strategies: isolating individuals at random, isolating those who are the most central (degree centrality), and isolating those with the highest cognitive load are shown relative to a specific organization and networks within it. Given that the networks are evolving at issue is which of these strategies will be the most effective? Further, we might ask, if the social network was different, e.g., less hierarchical, would that matter?

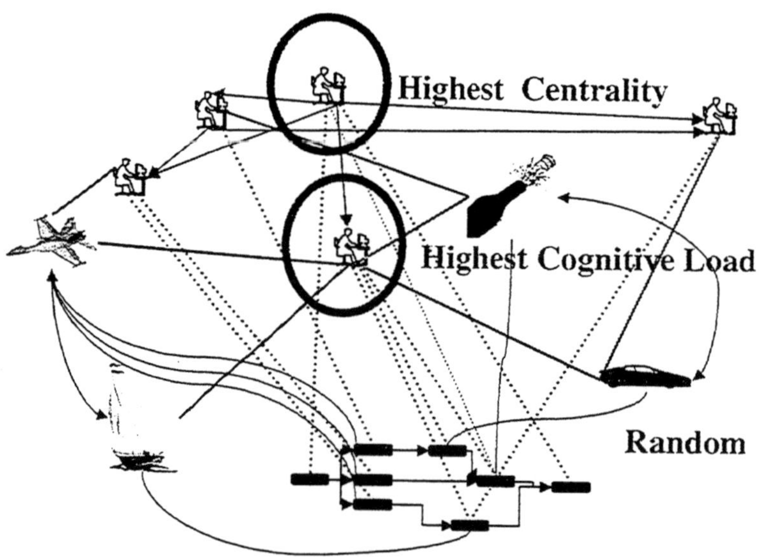

Figure 2. Structure, Isolation and Dynamics

The Structure of the Network Matters

The first finding, and it is quite robust, is that the structure of the network matters. That is, random networks in which the relations are distributed in an independent and identical fashion, hierarchies, and cellular networks all evolve quite differently, require different strategies to destabilize, have different abilities to diffuse information, and exhibit different performance for the same task. In Figures 3 and 4, this difference is illustrated with respect to the networks ability to recover from isolation strategies. In figure 3 we see the impact of the three isolation strategies on a random iid network and in figure 4 the impact of the same strategies on a cellular network. As an aside, the particular cellular network simulated here is one whose features map onto available information about covert networks, such as the cells are completely connected internally and cell size ranges from 3-10 members. In these figures not only do we see that the isolation strategies vary in their effectiveness based on the structure of the network they are attacking, but in addition, cellular networks are able to recover from the attacks.

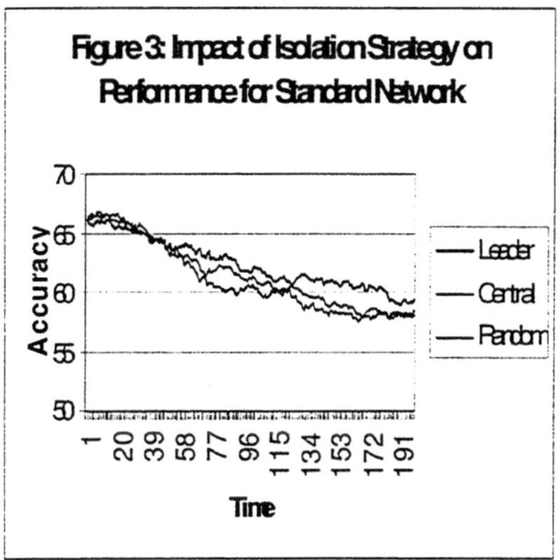

Figure 3: Impact of Isolation Strategy on Performance for Standard Network

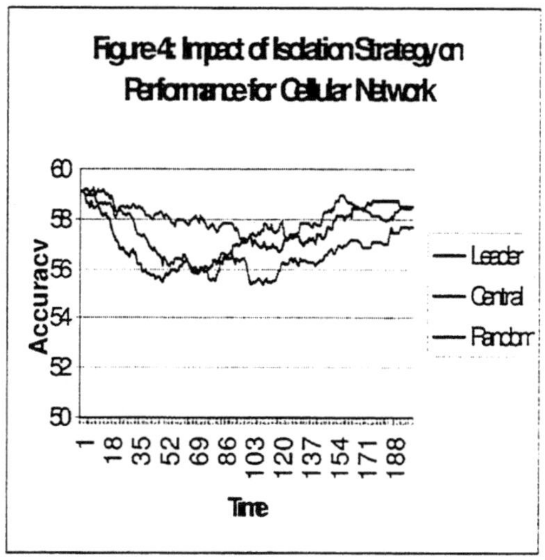

Figure 4: Impact of Isolation Strategy on Performance for Cellular Network

Networks Can Heal Themselves

A second key finding is that networks are generally able to heal themselves. That is isolation of a node that links disparate groups together typically does not leave those groups disconnected. Rather the basic social and cognitive processes outlined lead individuals to seek alternative contact points to interact with. For example in Figure 5 we see on the left a network where the person with the highest cognitive load, the emergent leader was isolated. A consequence is that multiple new leaders emerge, each of whom ends up being more directive than the original leader. Healing is not guaranteed and in fact depends on the underlying structure, the cultural basis for interaction, the degree of isolation, the frequency of isolation, and the strategy for isolation. For example, as was seen in Figure 4, cellular networks heal themselves regardless of which isolation strategy is used against it. In this case, the cell structure of the network enables the network as a to engage in what appears as "meta-learning," i.e., learning how to recover from unanticipated attrition. Cellular networks, which are the structure most like those used by terrorist organizations, are very difficult to destabilize. The reasons are complex, but a key factor is that such network structures are able to heal relatively faster than other structure both in terms of the re-emergence of leaders and in terms of performance recoveries after personnel have been removed.

Full Information is Not Necessary

In the foregoing two examples, we saw the impact of destabilization strategies on network without considering "how is it that we know what we know?" Or in other words, "if we are not sure what the underlying network looks like, how confident can we be in our predictions about how to destabilize it?" Notice, that in traditional SNA, typically we have close to full information. For covert networks we do not. Information may be missing because we don't know some of the nodes – the people involved, or because we don't know some of the relations.

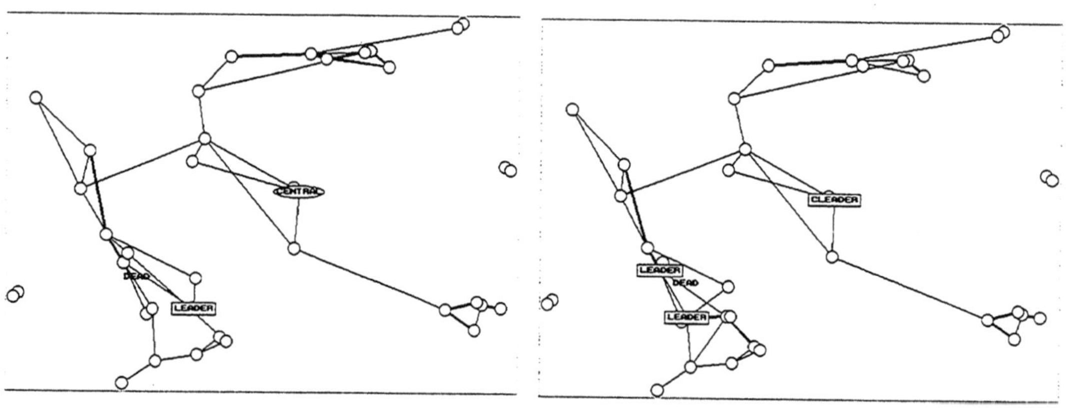

Figure 5. The network before (left) and after (right) the isolation of the leader.

Figure 6. The impact of incomplete information about who is in the network.

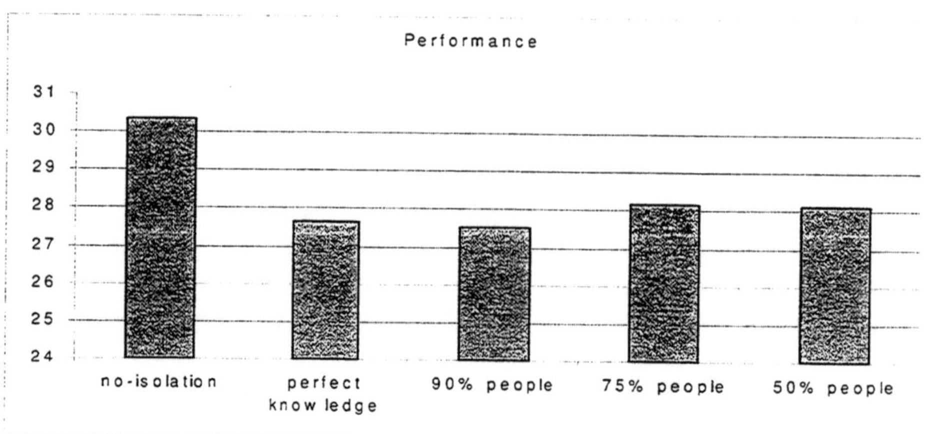

In Figure 6 we see the impact of not knowing al the nodes. Here we see the comparison of no attack, versus the average impact of isolating personnel (across the three isolation strategies) under conditions of full information, knowing 90% of the nodes, 75% and only 50%. Clearly having close to perfect or perfect knowledge means that more effective isolation strategies are found. Note, however, that any isolation is better than none, assuming our goal is to degrade the performance and that we don't need perfect information to be quite effective.

Now, consider the case where we don't have perfect information about the relations. One way for this to occur is if we don't know all the knowledge or resources that are available to the network. In figure 7 we see the impact of having imperfect knowledge of the relations as a function of how much do we know about the other entities, in this case what there is for the other to know. Here we see that we actually do better knowing less. This is due to the interaction between what we know and the isolation strategy. Essentially, when we don't really know the underlying social and knowledge network we may overestimate the primacy of a person, who although not the key in terms of degree centrality, is more central in terms of cognitive load. Thus, in effect, less knowledge makes both the centrality and the cognitive load strategies more similar resulting in on average lower performance due to the fact that cellular networks are more devastated by the extraction of such emergent leaders, at least in the short run. Further, reduced information about relations makes all isolation strategies more mixed thus inhibiting the ability of the opponent to engage in meta-learning.

Figure 7. The impact of incomplete information about what people know.

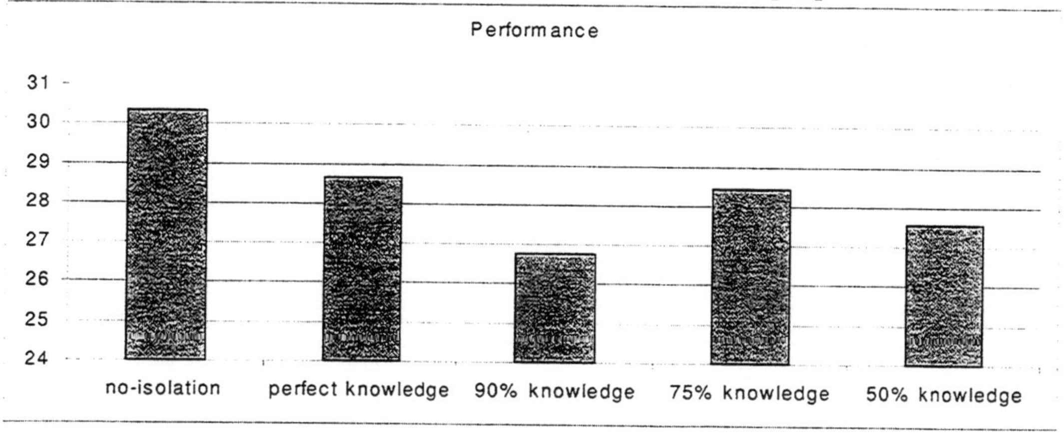

Summary

Thinking about networks from a dynamic perspective is absolutely essential to understanding the modern world. An approach toward dynamic networks has been outlined. There are several distinctive hallmarks to this approach. First, in contrast to other multi-agent work, the agents we describe are in actual social networks. Here, the networks and the agents co-evolve. Secondly, the web of affiliations connects not just agents, but agents and other entities such as knowledge, tasks and organizations. The agents described here in are more cognitively realistic than the typical a-life agents. They are also more socially realistic in terms of interaction than the typical e-commerce agents as the agents we use are boundedly rational rather than optimizers. Another distinction compared to most systems is that DyNet can take real networks as input.

In contrast to traditional SNA, DNA considers the role of the agent in terms of processes and not just position. That is, the agents can do things – communicate, store information, learn. Further, the networks are dynamic and changing even as the agents change. The links are probabilistic, the networks multi-colored and multi-plex to the extent that the set of networks combine in to one complex system where changes in one sub-network inform and constrain changes in the others, often leading to error cascades. Finally, DNA explores the sensitivity of the measures and the impacts to error.

The approach, theory, and results described here are illustrative. Clearly much work needs to be done before we have a complete understanding of network dynamics. Are there likely to be other change mechanisms than those currently in DyNet – to be sure. However, since all human action is cognitively mediated – it is unlikely that such mechanisms will not be derivable, at a basic level from what the physical and physiological constraints, what the agent knows, the basic learning and information processing mechanisms, and the way in which groups, organizations and institutions store such information. To create a truly dynamic network theory we need to create the equivalent of a quantum dynamics for the socio-cognitive world, where the fundamental entities, the people, unlike atoms, have the ability to learn.

References

Anderson, Brigham S., Carter Butts & Kathleen M. Carley, 1999, "The Interaction of Size and Density with Graph-Level Measures" to Social Networks. " Social Networks. 21: 239-267.

Butts, C. 2000. "Network Inference, Error, and Informant (In)Accuracy: A Bayesian Approach," to appear in Social Networks

Carley K. (1990). ``Group Stability: A Socio-Cognitive Approach," in Lawler E., Markovsky B., Ridgeway C. and Walker H. (Eds.), Advances in Group Processes}, JAI Press, Greenwich, CN.

Carley, Kathleen M. & Yuqing Ren, 2001, "Tradeoffs Between Performance and Adaptability for C3I Architectures." In Proceedings of the 2001 Command and Control Research and Technology Symposium. Conference held in Annapolis, Maryland, June, 2001. Evidence Based Research, Vienna, VA.

Carley, Kathleen M. 1999, "On the Evolution of Social and Organizational Networks." In Steven B. Andrews and David Knoke (Eds.) Vol. 16 special issue of Research in the Sociology of Organizations. on "Networks In and Around Organizations." Greenwhich, CN: JAI Press, Inc. Stamford, CT, pp. 3-30.

Carley, Kathleen M. 2002, "Inhibiting Adaptation" In Proceedings of the 2002 Command and Control Research and Technology Symposium. Conference held in Naval Postgraduate School, Monterey, CA. Evidence Based Research, Vienna, VA.

Carley, Kathleen M. 2002, "Smart Agents and Organizations of the Future" The Handbook of New Media. Edited by Leah Lievrouw & Sonia Livingstone, Ch. 12 pp. 206-220, Thousand Oaks, CA, Sage.

Carley, Kathleen M. Ju-Sung Lee and David Krackhardt, 2001, Destabilizing Networks, Connections 24(3):31-34.

Diedrich, Frederick J., Kathleen M. Carley, Jean MacMillan, Keith Baker, MAJ Jerry L. Schlabach, LTC J, Victor Fink, forthcoming, VISualization of Threats and Attacks (VISTA) in Urban Environments" Military Intelligence Professional Bulletin

Krackhardt, David & Kathleen M. Carley, 1998, "A PCANS Model of Structure in Organization" Pp. 113-119 in Proceedings of the 1998 International Symposium on Command and Control Research and Technology. Conference held in June. Monterray, CA. Evidence Based Research, Vienna, VA.

Ronfeldt, D. and J. Arquilla. September 21, 2001. "Networks, Netwars, and the Fight for the Future," First Monday, Issue 6 No. 10. online: http://firstmonday.org/issues/issue6_10/ronfeldt/index.htm.

Skvoretz, J. 1990. "Biased Net Theory: Approximations, Simulations, and Observations," Social Networks, Vol. 12. pp. 217-238

Sparrow, M. (1991). The application of network analysis to criminal intelligence: An assessment of the prospects. Social Networks 13:251-274.

Accounting for Degree Distributions in Empirical Analysis of Network Dynamics

Tom A.B. Snijders
University of Groningen *

December 2002

Abstract

Degrees (the number of links attached to a given node) play a particular and important role in empirical network analysis because of their obvious importance for expressing the position of nodes. It is argued here that there is no general straightforward relation between the degree distribution on one hand and structural aspects on the other hand, as this relation depends on further characteristics of the presumed model for the network. Therefore empirical inference from observed network characteristics to the processes that could be responsible for network genesis and dynamics cannot be based only, or mainly, on the observed degree distribution.

As an elaboration and practical implementation of this point, a statistical model for the dynamics of networks, expressed as digraphs with a fixed vertex set, is proposed in which the outdegree distribution is governed by parameters that are not connected to the parameters for the structural dynamics. The use of such an approach in statistical modeling minimizes the influence of the observed degrees on the conclusions about the structural aspects of the network dynamics.

The model is a stochastic actor-oriented model, and deals with the degrees in a manner resembling Tversky's Elimination by Aspects approach. A statistical procedure for parameter estimation in this model is proposed, and an example is given.

---

*Tom A.B. Snijders, ICS, Department of Sociology, Grote Rozenstraat 31, 9712 TG Groningen, The Netherlands, email <t.a.b.snijders@ppsw.rug.nl>. The preparation of this work has profited from stimulating discussions with Philippa Pattison and Mark Handcock and from participation in NIH grant 1 R01 DA12831-01A1, "Modeling HIV and STD in Drug User and Social Networks". I am very grateful to Jeffrey Johnson for putting at my disposal the data used in the example, and giving permission to use them here.

I. Introduction

Consider a social network with the focus on one relation represented by a directed graph (digraph), referring to the nodes as actors (which could be individual humans or other primates but also, e.g., companies or websites). In such a network, the degrees represent an important aspect of network structure. The outdegree of an actor, defined as the number of ties from this actor to other actors, reflects the total amount of activity of the actor in this network, which could be dependent on the importance of the network for this actor, the average costs and benefits for this actor of having outgoing ties, and, if the outgoing ties are based on self-reports, the actor's response tendencies or constraints of the data collection methods. The indegree of an actor, defined as the number of ties from others to this actor, will reflect the importance and easiness for the others of extending a tie to this particular actor, etc. The importance of the degrees as an aspect of network structure is generally recognized (e.g., Wasserman and Faust, 1994; Albert and Barabási, 2002). Degrees refer directly to the individual actors, which gives them an interesting position combining structural and individual relevance. Degrees often are constraints in, but also consequences of, the processes that generate networks and determine network dynamics.

This has led to various proposals to control for degrees in the statistical evaluation of networks. One possibility for doing this is to test observed network characteristics for the null hypothesis defined as the uniform distribution given the outdegrees, the $\mathcal{U} \mid X_{i+}$ distribution, or the uniform distribution given the in- as well as the outdegrees, denoted the $\mathcal{U} \mid X_{i+}, X_{+i}$ distribution (Wasserman, 1977; Wasserman & Faust, 1994; Snijders, 1991, 2002b). How to generate such graphs was studied by Snijders (1991) with a focus on Monte Carlo simulation methods for the directed case, and by Molloy and Reed (1995) who proposed a simulation method for the undirected case which also can be fruitfully used to obtain asymptotic results for sparse undirected graphs with a given degree sequence. Various ways to take account of the degree distribution in the context of the p^* model of Wasserman & Pattison (1996) were discussed in Snijders & van Duijn (2002). Stimulated by observations of the long-tailed nature of the degree distributions of links in the worldwide web, Barabási and Albert (1999) proposed models for network dynamics (modeled as undirected graphs with a growing number of vertices) in which the creation of new links depends strongly on the current degrees, and is random conditional on the current degree vector. Newman, Strogatz, and Watts (2001) and Newman, Watts and Strogatz (2002) derived various asymptotic properties of random undirected graphs with given degree sequences. They followed the mentioned literature in underlining the importance of studying for empirical networks whether observed network structure can be accounted for by the degree sequence plus randomness; if the answer is negative, there is evidence for structural mechanisms in addition to the degrees.

It is argued here that the degree distribution is a primary characteristic for the structure of digraphs but many other features, such as transitivity, occurrence of cycles, segmentation into subgroups, etc., are also of great importance. Although the degree distribution may pose constraints to the values of these other structural features (Snijders, 1991; Newman, Strogatz, and Watts, 2001; Newman, Watts and Strogatz, 2002), it does not determine them and an empirical focus on degrees exclusively would close our eyes to much that network analysis can tell us. This paper presents a two-step model for network dynamics, in which the determination of the outdegrees is separated from the further determination of network structure. This gives a greater flexibility in modeling, and allows to model structural network dynamics without contamination by unfortunate assumptions about the dynamics of the outdegrees.

II. A two-step model for network dynamics: first outdegrees, then network structure

This paper is concerned with the statistical modeling of network evolution for data consisting of two or more repeated observations of a social network for a given fixed set of actors, represented by a directed graph with a given vertex set. When proposing statistical models for network evolution, theoretical credibility of the model has to be combined with empirical applicability. The stochastic actor-oriented model of Snijders (2001, 2003), extended to networks of changing composition by Huisman & Snijders (2003), tried to do just this, embedding the discrete-time observations in an unobserved continuous-time network evolution process in which the network changes in small steps where just one arc is added or deleted at any given moment. The network changes are determined stochastically in steps modeled by random utility models for the actors.

The present paper adapts this model to have more freedom in fitting observed distributions of outdegrees. The following features of the earlier model are retained. The model is a stochastic process in continuous time, in which the arcs in the network can change only one at the time. It is actor-oriented in the sense that the model is described in such a way that network changes take place because actors create a new outgoing tie, or withdraw an existing outgoing tie. The actor who changes an outgoing tie is designated randomly, with probabilities that may depend on the actors' characteristics as reflected by covariates and by network positions. Given that an actor changes some tie, (s)he selects the tie to be changed according to a random utility model, which is based on effects reflecting network structure (e.g., transitivity).

The precise way in which it is determined stochastically which actor will make a change, and what is the change to be made, is defined differently than in the earlier papers, so as to allow modeling a diversity of degree distributions in a more natural way. The focus here is on the distribution of the outdegrees; of course, by reversing direction, this can be applied equally well to modeling the distribution of the indegrees. The model proposed here is composed of two substeps in a manner comparable to Tversky's (1972) *Elimination by Aspects* approach. In the first substep, the actor is chosen, and the actor decides whether to create a new outgoing tie, or to delete an existing tie. In the second step, if the result of the first substep was to add a tie, the actor chooses to which of the other actors the new tie will be created; and if the first substep led to the decision to delete a tie, the actor chooses which existing tie will be withdrawn. Thus, the first aspect that the actor takes into consideration is his or her outdegree; the second aspect is the further position of the actor in the network structure.

Notation

The network is represented by a directed graph on n vertices with adjacency matrix $x = (x_{ij})$, where x_{ij} indicates whether there is a tie directed from actor i to actor j $(i, j = 1, ..., n)$ (in which case $x_{ij} = 1$) or not ($x_{ij} = 0$). The diagonal is formally defined by $x_{ii} = 0$. It is supposed that a time-series $x(t), t \in \{t_1, ..., t_M\}$ of social networks is available where the t_m are strictly increasing and $M \geq 2$. These observed networks are regarded as M discrete observations on a stochastic process $X(t)$ on the space of all digraphs on n vertices, evolving in continuous time. This process is taken to be left-continuous, i.e.,

$$X(t) = \lim_{t' \uparrow t} X(t') \quad \text{for all } t.$$

The state of the network immediately after time t is denoted

$$X(t^+) = \lim_{t' \downarrow t} X(t') \ .$$

No assumption of stationarity is made for the marginal distributions of $X(t)$, and therefore the first observation $x(t_1)$ is not used to give direct information on the distribution of this stochastic process, but the statistical analysis conditions on this first observed network.

Summation is denoted by replacing the summation index by a $+$ sign: e.g., x_{i+} is the outdegree and x_{+i} the indegree of actor i.

Model definition: rates of change

At random moments, one of the actors i is 'permitted' to change one of his or her outgoing tie variables X_{ij}. For the different actors, these random moments are independent conditionally given the present network. The rate, in the time interval $t_m \leq t < t_{m+1}$, at which actor i *adds* a tie is denoted $\rho_m \lambda_{i+}(\alpha, x)$; the rate at which this actor *deletes* a tie is $\rho_m \lambda_{i-}(\alpha, x)$. Here x is the current network and α is a parameter indicating how the rate function depends on the position of i in the current network (e.g., as a function of the outdegree or indegree of i) and/or on covariates, if these are available. The multiplicative parameters ρ_m depend on m (the index number of the observation interval) to be able to obtain a good fit to the observed amounts of change between consecutive observations. Together, these two change rates imply that for actor i, during the time interval $t_m \leq t < t_{m+1}$, these random moments of change follow a non-homogeneous Poisson process with intensity function

$$\lambda_i(x) = \rho_m\big(\lambda_{i+}(\alpha, x) + \lambda_{i-}(x, \alpha)\big) , \tag{1}$$

conditional on $X(t) = x$. Given that actor i makes a change at moment t, the probability that the changes amounts to creating a new tie is

$$\begin{aligned} &\mathrm{P}\{X_{i+}(t^+) = X_{i+}(t) + 1 \,|\, \text{change by actor } i \text{ at time } t, X(t) = x\} \\ &= \frac{\lambda_{i+}(\alpha, x)}{\lambda_{i+}(\alpha, x) + \lambda_{i-}(x, \alpha)} . \end{aligned} \tag{2}$$

This separation between the rates of adding and deleting ties allows to focus specifically on the distribution of the degrees.

Model definition: objective function

Given that actor i makes a change at some moment t for which the current network is given by $X(t) = x$, the particular change made is assumed to be determined by the so-called *objective function* – which gives the numerical evaluation by the actor of the possible states of the network – together with a random element – accounting for 'unexplained changes', in other words, for the limitations of the model. This objective function could be different between the creation of new ties and the deletion of existing ties. Denote these two objective functions by $f_{i+}(\beta, x)$ and $f_{i-}(\beta, x)$, respectively. These functions indicate what the actor strives to maximize when adding or deleting ties, respectively; they depend on a parameter vector β. In a simple model specification, it can be assumed that $f_{i+} \equiv f_{i-}$. (This corresponds to a zero gratification function in the model of Snijders, 2001).

The way in which the objective functions and a random element together define the changes in the outgoing relation of actor i is defined as follows. Suppose that at some moment t, actor i changes one of his outgoing relations. The current state of the network is $x(t)$. At this moment, actor i determines the other actor j to whom he will change his tie variable x_{ij}. Denote by $x(i \rightsquigarrow j)$ the adjacency matrix that results from x when the single element x_{ij} is changed into $1 - x_{ij}$ (i.e., from 0 to 1 or from 1 to 0). If at moment t actor i *adds* a tie, then he chooses the other actor j, among those for which $x_{ij} = 0$, for which

$$f_{i+}(\beta, x(i \rightsquigarrow j)) + U_i(t, x, j)$$

is maximal; where $U_i(t, x, j)$ is a random variable, indicating the part of the actor's preference not represented by the objective function, and assumed to be distributed according to the type 1 extreme value distribution with mean 0 and scale parameter 1 (Maddala, 1983). Similarly, if at moment t actor i *deletes* a tie, then he chooses the other actor j, among those for which $x_{ij} = 1$, for which

$$f_{i-}(\beta, x(i \rightsquigarrow j)) + U_i(t, x, j)$$

is maximal. The type 1 extreme value distribution is conventionally used in random utility modeling (cf. Maddala, 1983); it yields the choice probabilities for j given by the multinomial logit (or potential function) expressions

$$p_{ij+}(\beta, x) = \frac{(1 - x_{ij}) \exp\left(f_{i+}(\beta, x(i \rightsquigarrow j))\right)}{\sum_{h=1, h\neq i}^{n} (1 - x_{ih}) \exp\left(f_{i+}(\beta, x(i \rightsquigarrow h))\right)} \qquad (j \neq i) \qquad (3)$$

for adding a tie, and

$$p_{ij-}(\beta, x) = \frac{x_{ij} \exp\left(f_{i-}(\beta, x(i \rightsquigarrow j))\right)}{\sum_{h=1, h\neq i}^{n} x_{ih} \exp\left(f_{i-}(\beta, x(i \rightsquigarrow h))\right)} \qquad (j \neq i) \qquad (4)$$

for deleting a tie.

The specification of the objective function is discussed extensively in Snijders (2001). It is proposed there to use objective functions f_{i+} and f_{i-} of the form

$$f_i(\beta, x) = \sum_k \beta_k \, s_{ik}(x), \qquad (5)$$

where the β_k are statistical parameters and the s_{ik} are network statistics. A basic network statistic is the number of reciprocated relations

$$s_{ik}(x) = \sum_j x_{ij}\, x_{ji} \; . \tag{6}$$

Network closure, or transitivity, can be expressed by various terms in the objective function, e.g., by the number of transitive patterns in i's relations (ordered pairs of actors (j,h) to both of whom i is related, while also j is related to h),

$$s_{ik}(x) = \sum_{j,h} x_{ij}\, x_{ih}\, x_{jh} \; ; \tag{7}$$

or by a negative effect for the number of other actors at geodesic distance equal to 2,

$$s_{ik}(x) = \sharp\{j \mid d_x(i,j) = 2\} \; , \tag{8}$$

where $d_x(i,j)$ is the oriented geodesic distance, i.e., the length of the shortest directed path from i to j. Many other examples of possibly relevant functions s_{ik} are proposed in Snijders (2001).

Intensity matrix

The intensity matrix $q(x,y)$, for $x \neq y$, of the continuous-time Markov chain defined by this model, indicates the rate at which the current value x changes into the new value y. Since relations here are allowed to change only one at a time, the intensity matrix can be represented by the change rates $q_{ij}(x)$, from x to $x(i \leadsto j)$ for $j \neq i$, defined by

$$q_{ij}(x) = \lim_{dt \downarrow 0} \frac{\mathrm{P}\{X(t+dt) = x(i \leadsto j) \mid X(t) = x\}}{dt} \; .$$

The model definition given above corresponds to an intensity matrix given by

$$q_{ij}(x) = \begin{cases} \rho_m\, \lambda_{i+}(\alpha, x)\, p_{ij+}(\beta, x) & \text{for } x_{ij} = 0 \\ \rho_m\, \lambda_{i-}(\alpha, x)\, p_{ij-}(\beta, x) & \text{for } x_{ij} = 1. \end{cases} \tag{9}$$

III. Rate functions and stationary distributions

In a simple model definition, the rates λ_{i+} and λ_{i-} depend only on the outdegree of actor i. This will be assumed henceforth, and it implies that the outdegree processes $X_{i+}(t)$ are independent continuous-time random walks on the set $\{0, \ldots, n-1\}$. For the sake of brevity, and with a slight abuse of notation, denote the rates of adding and withdrawing ties by $\lambda_+(s)$ and $\lambda_-(s)$, where $s = x_{i+}$ is the outdegree of actor i. Thus, $\lambda_+(x_{i+})$ is shorthand for $\lambda_{i+}(\alpha, x)$ and similarly for $\lambda_-(x_{i+})$. It is assumed that these rates are strictly positive except for the boundary conditions $\lambda_-(0) = \lambda_+(n-1) = 0$.

The network evolution model is not necessarily assumed to be stationary, and indeed it is likely that in empirical observations, networks often will be far from the stationary distributions of the corresponding evolution processes. It is interesting nevertheless to consider the stationary distribution of the process, as this indicates the direction into which the evolution is going. The probability distribution $p(s)$ on the set $\{0, \ldots, n-1\}$ is the stationary distribution for the random walk process of the outdegrees if and only if

$$p(s)\, \lambda_+(s) \;=\; p(s+1)\, \lambda_-(s+1) \quad \text{for } 0 \le s \le n-2. \tag{10}$$

(This follows directly from the fact that this is the condition for detailed balance, cf. Norris, 1997.)

As a benchmark situation, it is instructive to consider the stationary distribution of the outdegrees in the actor-oriented model of Snijders (2001) with the very simple objective function $f_i(x) = \beta_1\, x_{i+}$. In this model, the choice of which actor changes an outgoing tie variable is made strictly randomly. In this model also, the outdegrees of the different vertices are independent stochastic processes. This model can be obtained in the formulation of the present paper by defining

$$\begin{aligned} \lambda_{i+}(s) &= \frac{(n-s-1)\, \exp(\beta_1)}{(n-s-1)\, \exp(\beta_1) + s\, \exp(-\beta_1)} \\ \lambda_{i-}(s) &= \frac{s\, \exp(-\beta_1)}{(n-s-1)\, \exp(\beta_1) + s\, \exp(-\beta_1)}\,, \end{aligned}$$

as can be checked from the intensity matrices (see (5) and (8) in Snijders, 2001, and (9), (3), (4) above). This implies

$$\begin{aligned} &\frac{\lambda_{i+}(s)}{\lambda_{i-}(s+1)} \\ &\qquad = \frac{(n-s-1)\, \exp(\beta_1)}{(s+1)\, \exp(-\beta_1)} \, \frac{(n-s-2)\, \exp(\beta_1) + (s+1)\, \exp(-\beta_1)}{(n-s-1)\, \exp(\beta_1) + s\, \exp(-\beta_1)} \end{aligned}$$

which is close to $p(s+1)/p(s)$ for the binomial distribution with denominator $n-1$ and succes probability $\exp(2\,\beta_1)/(1+\exp(2\,\beta_1))$. Thus, for this model, the outdegrees are for $t \to \infty$ close to binomially distributed with these parameters.

The change rates λ_{i+} and λ_{i-} together reflect two aspects of the evolution process of the outdegrees: the *distributional tendency*, i.e., the equilibrium distribution towards which the outdegree distribution tends; and the *volatility*, i.e., how quickly the ties are changing. It follows from (10) that the distributional tendency depends on $\xi(s)$, defined by

$$\xi(s) = \frac{\lambda_{i+}(s)}{\lambda_{i-}(s+1)} . \tag{11}$$

It is mathematically convenient to express the volatility by

$$\nu(s) = \lambda_{i+}(s) + \lambda_{i-}(s+1) . \tag{12}$$

These definitions imply that the rates are given by

$$\begin{aligned} \lambda_{i+}(s) &= \frac{\nu(s)\,\xi(s)}{1+\xi(s)}, \\ \lambda_{i-}(s) &= \frac{\nu(s-1)}{1+\xi(s-1)} . \end{aligned} \tag{13}$$

With these definitions, p is the stationary distribution if and only if

$$\xi(s) = \frac{p(s+1)}{p(s)} \qquad s = 0, \dots , n-2. \tag{14}$$

For the purpose of statistical modeling, it is necessary to consider parametric families of distributions p. If $p(s)$ is a member of an exponential family

$$p(s) = p_0(s) \exp\left(\alpha' t(s) - \psi(\alpha)\right)$$

where $t(s)$ is a vector of sufficient statistics, α is a parameter vector, and $\psi(\alpha)$ is a normalizing constant, then this yields

$$\xi(s) = \frac{p_0(s+1)}{p_0(s)} \exp\left(\alpha(t(s+1) - t(s))\right) . \tag{15}$$

E.g., for a truncated Poisson distribution ($p_0(s) = 1/s!$, $t(s) = s$), this becomes

$$\xi(s) = \frac{1}{s+1} e^{\alpha} = \exp\left(\alpha - \log(s+1)\right) . \tag{16}$$

For a truncated power distribution ($p_0(s) = 1$, $t(s) = \log(s+1)$, $\alpha < 0$), the rate functions are

$$\xi(s) = \left(\frac{s+2}{s+1}\right)^{\alpha} \approx \exp\left(\frac{\alpha}{s+1}\right) . \tag{17}$$

The Poisson distribution is short-tailed, corresponding to $\xi(s)$ becoming small as s gets large, in contrast to the long-tailed power distribution, for which $\xi(s)$ becomes close to 1.

A model containing the tendencies toward either of these distributions as submodels is obtained by defining

$$\xi(s) = \exp\left(\alpha_1 - \alpha_2 \log(s+1) - \frac{\alpha_3}{s+1}\right) . \tag{18}$$

For the volatility function $\nu(s)$, the dependence on s could be linear, analogous to what was proposed in Snijders (2001). This is unattractive, however, if one considers digraphs with arbitrarily large numbers n of vertices. A hyperbolic function, tending to a finite constant as s grows indefinitely, seems more attractive: e.g.,

$$\nu(s) = \left(1 + \alpha_4 \frac{1}{s+1}\right) , \tag{19}$$

where the restriction must be made that $\alpha_4 > -1$. The functions ξ and ν can also be made to depend on covariates, e.g., through an exponential link function.

IV. Parameter estimation

For the estimation of parameters of this type of network evolution models for observations made at discrete moments $t_1, \ldots, t_M$, Snijders (2001) proposed an implementation of the method of moments based on stochastic approximation, using a version of the Robbins-Monro (1951) algorithm. The method of moments is carried out by specifying a suitable vector of statistics of the network and determining (in this case, approximating) the parameters so that the expected values of these statistics equal the observed values. To apply this approach, statistics must be found that are especially informative about these parameters.

First consider the parameters of ξ. For a model of the general exponential form (15), e.g., (18), the statistic $t(S)$ is a sufficient statistic for the limiting distribution, and therefore it seems advisable to use the statistic $\sum_i t(X_{i+}(t_{m+1}))$, or for multiple observation periods

$$\sum_{m=1}^{M-1} \sum_{i=1}^{n} t(X_{i+}(t_{m+1})) \ . \tag{20}$$

For model (18), some simplifying approximations may be used; e.g., for parameter α_2, this can be based on Stirling's formula. This leads for the three parameters in this model to the fitting statistics

$$\begin{gathered}\sum_{m=1}^{M-1} \sum_{i=1}^{n} X_{i+}(t_{m+1}) \\ \sum_{m=1}^{M-1} \sum_{i=1}^{n} (X_{i+}(t_{m+1}) + \tfrac{1}{2})\big(\log(X_{i+}(t_{m+1}) + 1) - 1\big) \\ \sum_{m=1}^{M-1} \sum_{i=1}^{n} \log(X_{i+}(t_{m+1})) \ .\end{gathered} \tag{21}$$

For the parameters in the volatility function ν, the same approach can be taken as in Section 7.4 of Snijders (2001). This leads for parameter ρ_m to the statistic

$$\sum_{i,j=1}^{n} |\, X_{ij}(t_{m+1}) \ - \ X_{ij}(t_m) \,| \tag{22}$$

and for parameter α_4 in (19) to the statistic

$$\sum_{m=1}^{M-1} \sum_{i,j=1}^{n} \frac{|\, X_{ij}(t_{m+1}) \ - \ X_{ij}(t_m) \,|}{X_{i+}(t_m) + 1} \ . \tag{23}$$

V. Example

As a numerical example of the analysis, the dynamics of a network of political actors is considered, based on a study by Johnson and Orbach (2002). The data used here are from a second and third wave of data collection between 46 actors, most of whom the same individuals as those in the first wave of which results are presented in Johnson and Orbach (2002). They are self-reported dyadic interaction data, rated on a 0-10 scale which here was dichotomized as 0-6 vs. 7-10. Space limitations prohibit doing justice to the richness of the original data and the social processes involved in the network dynamics.

Preliminary analyses indicated that there is evidence for a network closure effect, expressed better by the number of geodesic distances equal to two, cf. (8), than by the number of transitive triplets, see (7); and that there is evidence for a gender popularity effect. Sets of estimates are presented here for two corresponding models, differing as to how the degrees are modeled. The first model is according to the specification in Snijders (2001), with a constant rate function and without the differentiation between adding and withdrawing ties proposed in the present paper. The objective function is specified as

$$\begin{aligned} f_i(\beta, x) &= \beta_1 \, x_{i+} + \beta_2 \sum_j x_{ij} \, x_{ji} + \beta_3 \, \#\{j \mid d_x(i,j) = 2\} \\ &\quad + \beta_4 \sum_j x_{ij} \, z_j \end{aligned}$$

where z_j indicates the gender of actor j. The second model follows the specification proposed above. Preliminary analyses showed that a good fit is obtained by using model (18) with $\alpha_2 = \alpha_3 = 0$. The volatility function is held constant, $\nu \equiv 1$. The objective function here is defined as

$$\begin{aligned} f_{i+}(\beta, x) = f_{i-}(\beta, x) &= \beta_2 \sum_j x_{ij} \, x_{ji} + \beta_3 \, \#\{j \mid d_x(i,j) = 2\} \\ &\quad + \beta_4 \sum_j x_{ij} \, z_j \end{aligned}$$

(note that in this model, it is meaningless to include a term $\beta_1 \, x_{i+}$ in the objective function; the role that this term has in the earlier model is here taken over by the rate function). The parameter estimates, obtained from the SIENA program (version 1.98; see Snijders & Huisman, 2002) are presented in Table 1. Gender is coded 1 (female) vs. 0 (male), and centered in the program by subtracting the average value of 0.17.

Parameters can be tested by approximate z-tests based on the t-ratios (parameter estimate divided by standard error). Using this procedure, all effects mentioned in Table 1 are significant ($p < .001$). The fit of the two models can be compared by considering the fitted distributions of the degree sequences. A rather subtle way of doing at this is to look at the observed ranked outdegrees and their fitted distributions. Figures 1 and 2 show, for these two models, the observed ranked outdegrees combined with simulated 90-% intervals for the distributions of the ranked outdegrees. Figure 1 indicates a poor fit: the distributions of the 9 highest outdegrees in the fitted model are concentrated on too low values compared to the observed highest outdegrees; in the middle low range, the fitted distribution of the ranked

Table 1. Parameter estimates for two model fits for the Johnson-Orbach political actor data (waves 2-3).

Effect	*Model 1* par.	*Model 1* (s.e.)	*Model 2* par.	*Model 2* (s.e.)
Rate factor (ρ_1)	23.09		22.78	
Rate function: ξ				
Outdegrees (α_1)			-0.57	(0.07)
Objective function				
Outdegrees	−1.14	(0.19)		
Reciprocated ties	1.37	(0.11)	1.77	(0.23)
Indirect relations	−0.50	(0.21)	−0.62	(0.30)
Gender (F) popularity	0.28	(0.10)	0.39	(0.11)

outdegrees is too low compared to the observations. Combined, this implies that the fitted outdegree distribution is too closely peaked about its mean value. On the other hand, Figure 2 indicates a good fit for the second model, each observed ranked outdegree being situated within the 90-% interval of its fitted distribution.

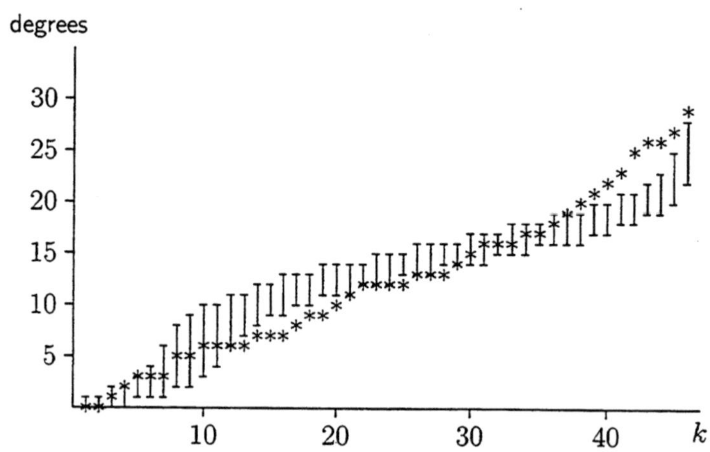

Fig. 1. Observed (∗) and 90% intervals for ranked outdegrees, Model 1. (k = rank)

The parameter estimates and standard errors in Table 1 for both models point to the same conclusions. In the network dynamics there is clear evidence for reciprocity of choices, for a network closure effect, and for a greater popularity of female actors. (A gender similarity effect also was tested, but

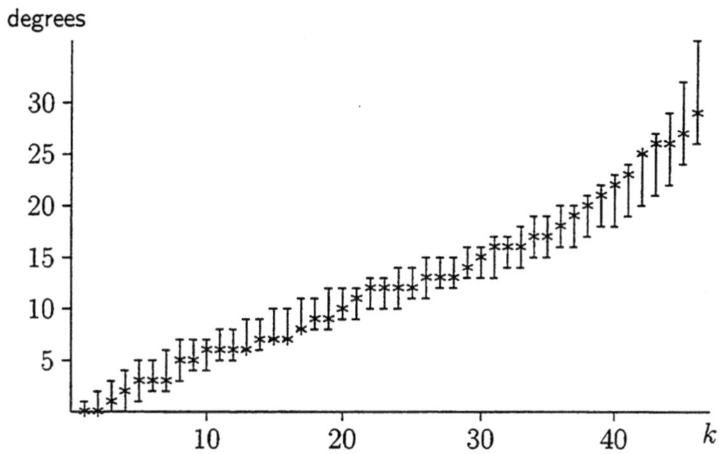

Fig. 2. Observed (*) and 90% intervals for ranked outdegrees, Model 2. (k = rank)

this was not significant.) If there would have been important differences between the results of the two models, then model 2 would have been the more trustworthy, given that it shows a better fit for the outdegree distribution.

VI. Discussion

The degree distribution is an important characteristic of networks and has received much attention in recent work. However, attention for the degrees should be combined with sufficient attention paid to other aspects of network structure. The current paper proposes a modification of the model presented in Snijders (2001), addressing the following points of criticism that could be addressed to the earlier model. First, it may be hard to specify the earlier model in a way that gives a satisfactory fit for the very skewed degree distributions that are sometimes empirically observed (cf. the many examples mentioned in Newman, Strogatz, and Watts, 2001). The model proposed here gives almost unlimited possibilities with respect to the outdegree distribution that is generated. Second, the extrapolation properties of the earlier model may be unrealistic in the sense that, depending on the parameters of the model, letting the model run on for a long hypothetical time period may lead to unrealistic phase transitions. More specifically, similarly to what is explained in Snijders (2002a), the earlier model can be specified so that quite a good fit is obtained for the evolution over a limited time period of a network with, say, a rather low density and a relatively high amount of transitivity, but that the graph evolution process so defined will with probability one lead to an 'explosion' in the sense that at some moment, the graph density very rapidly increases to a value of 1 and remains 1, or almost 1, for a waiting time that is infinite for all practical purposes. (A closely related property, but for the case of a graph evolution process where the number of vertices tends to infinity, was noticed by Strauss, 1986. This phenomenon also resembles the phase transitions known for the Ising model and other spatial models in statistical physics discussed, e.g., in Newman and Barkema, 1999.) Such phase transitions can be avoided in the model proposed below because the outdegree distribution is determined independently of the further structural network properties.

A third reason, of a more theoretical nature, for proposing this model, is to demonstrate that quite plausible models are possible for digraph evolution in which the distribution of the outdegrees is dissociated completely from the other structural network properties such as transitivity and subgroup formation. This implies that we can learn little about the processes leading to transitivity and related structural properties of graphs and digraphs by looking only at degree distributions, or by limiting attention to network evolution processes that are based only on degrees.

REFERENCES

Albert, R., and Barabàsi, A.-L. (2002). Statistical mechanics of complex networks. *Review of modern physics*, 74, 47–97.

Barabàsi, A.-L., and Albert, R., (1999). Emergence of scaling in random networks. *Science*, 286, 509–512.

Huisman, M.E., and T.A.B. Snijders. 2003. Statistical analysis of longitudinal network data with changing composition. *Submitted for publication.*

Johnson, J.C., and M.K. Orbach. 2002. Perceiving the Political Landscape: Ego Biases in Cognitive Political Networks. *Social Networks*, 24, 291 – 310.

Maddala, G.S. 1983. *Limited-dependent and qualitative variables in econometrics.* Cambridge: Cambridge University Press.

Molloy, M., and B. Reed. 1995. A critical point for random graphs with a given degree sequence. *Random Structures and Algorithms*, 6, 161–179.

Newman, M.E.J., and Barkema, G.T. (1999). *Monte Carlo methods in statistical physics.* Oxford: Clarendon Press.

Newman, M.E.J., Strogatz, S.H., and D.J. Watts. 2001. Random graphs with arbitrary degree distributions and theor applications. *Physical Reviews E 64*, 026118.

Newman, M.E.J., Watts, D.J., and Strogatz, S.H. 2002. Random graph models of social networks. *Proceedings of the National Academy of Sciences*

USA, 99, 2566–2572.

Norris, J.R. 1997. *Markov Chains*. Cambridge: Cambridge University Press.

Robbins, H., and S. Monro. 1951. A stochastic approximation method. *Annals of Mathematical Statistics*, 22, 400 – 407.

Snijders, T.A.B. 1991. Enumeration and simulation methods for 0-1 matrices with given marginals. *Psychometrika*, **56**, 397–417.

Snijders, T.A.B. 2001. The Statistical Evaluation of Social Network Dynamics. M.E. Sobel and M.P. Becker (eds.), *Sociological Methodology-2001*, 361–395. Boston and London: Basil Blackwell.

Snijders, T.A.B. 2002a. Markov Chain Monte Carlo Estimation of Exponential Random Graph Models. *Journal of Social Structure* vol. 3 no. 2.

Snijders, T.A.B. 2002b. Manual for ZO version 2.3. Groningen: ICS, University of Groningen.
Obtainable from http://stat.gamma.rug.nl/snijders/socnet.htm .

Snijders, T.A.B. 2003. Models for Longitudinal Network Data. In: P.J. Carrington, J. Scott, and S. Wasserman (eds.), *Models and Methods in Social Network Analysis*. New York: Cambridge University Press, in preparation.

Snijders, T.A.B., and Huisman, J.M. 2002. *Manual for SIENA version 1.95*. Groningen: ICS, University of Groningen.
Obtainable from http://stat.gamma.rug.nl/snijders/socnet.htm .

Snijders, T.A.B., and van Duijn, M.A.J. 2002. Conditional maximum likelihood estimation under various specifications of exponential random graph models. Pp. 117–134 in Jan Hagberg (ed.), *Contributions to Social Network Analysis, Information Theory, and Other Topics in Statistics; A Festschrift in honour of Ove Frank*. University of Stockholm: Department of Statistics.

Strauss, D. 1986. On a general class of models for interaction. *SIAM Review*, 28, 513–527.

Tversky, A. 1972. Choice by elimination. *Journal of Mathematical Psychology*, 9, 341–367.

Wasserman, S. 1977. Random directed graph distributions and the triad census in social networks. *Journal of Mathematical Sociology*, 5, 61–86.

Wasserman, S., and K. Faust. 1994. *Social Network Analysis: Methods and Applications*. New York and Cambridge: Cambridge University Press.

Wasserman, S., and P. Pattison. 1996. Logit models and logistic regression for social networks: I. An introduction to Markov graphs and p^*. *Psychometrika*, 61, 401 – 425.

Polarization in Dynamic Networks: A Hopfield Model of Emergent Structure

Michael W. Macy, Cornell University; James A. Kitts, University of Washington; Andreas Flache, University of Groningen; Steve Benard, Cornell University

ABSTRACT

Why do populations often self-organize into antagonistic groups even in the absence of competition over scarce resources? Is there a tendency to demarcate groups of "us" and "them" that is inscribed in our cognitive architecture? We look for answers by exploring the dynamics of influence and attraction between computational agents. Our model is an extension of Hopfield's attractor network. Agents are attracted to others with similar states (the principle of homophily) and are also influenced by others, as conditioned by the strength and valence of the social tie. Negative valence implies xenophobia (instead of homophily) and differentiation (instead of imitation). Consistent with earlier work on structural balance, we find that networks can self-organize into two antagonistic factions, without the knowledge or intent of the agents. We model this tendency as a function of network size, the number of potentially contentious issues, and agents' openness and flexibility toward alternative positions. Although we find that polarization into two antagonistic groups is a unique global attractor, we investigate the conditions under which uniform and pluralistic alignments may also be equilibria. From a random start, agents can self-organize into pluralistic arrangements if the population size is large relative to the size of the state space.

INTRODUCTION: GROUP POLARIZATION

Why do populations often self-organize into antagonistic groups even in the absence of competition over scarce resources? Is there a tendency to demarcate groups of "us" and "them" that is inscribed in our cognitive architecture? We look for answers by exploring the dynamics of influence and attraction between computational agents.

Our model builds on recent work using agent-based models of cultural convergence and differentiation (1,2,3). Scholars contend that the abundance of social groups containing highly similar actors is due to dual processes of attraction and social influence. Formal models generally assume that each agent chooses interaction partners that are similar to itself, while social interaction also leads agents to adopt each other's traits and thus grow more similar. In this positive feedback loop, a minimal initial similarity increases the probability of interaction which then increases similarity.

This process of consolidation (4) will presumably continue until all agents engaged in mutual interaction have converged to unanimity. While this self-reinforcing dynamic seems to imply a "melting pot," or inexorable march toward homogeneity, scholars have shown that global diversity can survive through impermeable barriers to interaction between distinct subcultures. If bridge ties between groups are entirely absent, then this local convergence can indeed lead to global differentiation, in spite of cultural conformity among the individual agents. Stable minority subcultures persist because of the protection of structural holes created by cultural differences that preclude interaction. Given such barriers, homogenizing tendencies actually reinforce rather than eliminate diversity.

The models thus predict social stability only where a population is entirely uniform or where agents cluster into mutually exclusive uniform subpopulations that are oblivious to one another. This global pluriformity depends on the assumption that interaction across these boundaries is impossible. Any allowance for interaction between dissimilar agents, no matter how rare, leads diversity to collapse into global homogeneity. This also reflects earlier analytical results obtained with models of opinion dynamics in influence networks (21,22,23). Abelson proved that a very weak condition is sufficient to guarantee convergence of opinions to global uniformity: The network needs to be "compact," such that there are no subgroups that are entirely cut off from outside influences. This apparently ineluctable homogeneity in fully connected networks led Abelson (21, p. 153) to wonder "... what on earth one must assume in order to generate the bimodal outcome of community cleavage studies?"

We will pursue this interest in cleavages, or structural bifurcations, as an alternative explanation for both the disproportionate homogeneity in social groups and the persistence of diversity across groups. First let us revisit the generative processes, the psychological and behavioral foundations of attraction and social influence.

These models of convergence implement one of the starkest regularities in the social world: "homophily," or the tendency for each person to interact with similar others (5, 6, 7). Several explanations for homophily have been proposed. Social psychologists posit a "Law of Attraction" based on an affective bias toward similar others (8; see also 9,10,11,12). Even disregarding such an emotional bias, structural sociologists (3,2,14) point to the greater reliability and facility of communication between individuals who share vocabulary and syntax as an inducement for homophilous relations.

Others counter that homophily is the spurious consequence of social influence, as in classic research on "pressures to uniformity" (16,17,18) and recent work in social networks (19,20). Even if relations are held constant in an exogenously clustered social network, social influence from network neighbors will lead to local homogeneity, without the need to assume homophilous interaction.

Scholars have thus overwhelmingly attributed homophily in observed social networks to some combination of differential attraction and social influence, where agents choose similar partners and partners grow more similar over time. Much less attention has been directed to an alternative explanation – that homophily is largely a byproduct of its antipole. It is not so much attraction to those who are similar that produces group homogeneity but repulsion from those who are different. Xenophobia leads to the same emergent outcome as attraction between similar actors: disproportionate homogeneity in relations. In fact, Rosenbaum (15) argues that many experimental findings of homophily in relations may have spuriously represented this effect of repulsion from those who are different.

The most sustained treatment of positive and negative ties has appeared in the literature on Balance Theory. Following Heider (24), scholars have assumed that actors are motivated to maintain "balance" in their relations, such that two actors who are positively tied to one another will feel tension when they disagree about some third cognitive object. Formally, we can think of this as a valued graph of agents A and B along with object X, where the graph will be balanced only when the sign product $A*B*X$ is positive. For example, if A and B are positively tied but A positively values X and B negatively values X, then the graph is imbalanced. In order for this dissonance to resolve and result in a stable alignment, there will either be a falling out between A and B or one (but not both) of these actors will switch evaluations of X. A parallel process operates if the tie between A and B is negative.

A prolific line of research – Structural Balance Theory (32) – has examined a special case of Heider's model, where the object X is actually a third actor, C. The model simply extends to triadic agreement among agents A, B, and C, where balance obtains when the sign product of the triad A-B-C is positive. This formalizes the adage that a friend of a friend or an enemy of an enemy is a friend, while an enemy of a friend or a friend of an enemy is an enemy. Extended to a larger network, it is well known that the elemental triadic case suggests a perfect separation of two mutually antagonistic subgroups.

Our model integrates the attraction-influence feedback loop from formal models of social convergence with the bivalent relations in Balance Theory. Following Nowak and Vallacher (29), the model is an application of Hopfield's attractor network (25, 26) to social networks. Like Heider's Balance Theory, an important property of attractor networks is that individual nodes seek to minimize "energy" (or dissonance) across all relations with other nodes. As we will see, this suggests self-reinforcing dynamics of attraction and influence as well as repulsion and differentiation.

More precisely, this class of models generally uses complete networks, with each node characterized by one or more binary or continuous *states* and linked to other nodes through endogenous *weights*. Like other neural networks, attractor networks learn stable configurations by iteratively adjusting the weights between individual nodes, without any global coordination. In this case, the weights change over time through a Hebbian learning rule (27): the weight w_{ij} is a function of the correspondence of states for nodes i and j over time. To the extent that i and j tend to occupy the same states at the same time, the tie between them will be increasingly positive. To the extent that i and j occupy discrepant states, the tie will become increasingly negative.

Extending recent work (30), we apply the Hopfield model of dynamic attraction to the study of polarization in social networks. In this application, observed similarity/difference between states determines the strength and valence of the tie to a given referent.

MODEL DESIGN

In our application of the Hopfield model, each node has N-1 undirected ties to other nodes. These ties include weights, which determine the strength and valence of influence between agents. Formally, social pressure on agent i to adopt a binary state s (where $s = \pm 1$) is the sum of the states of all other agents j, conditioned by the weight (w_{ij}) of the dyadic tie between i and j ($-1.0 < w_{ij} < 1.0$):

$$P_{is} = \frac{\sum_{j=1}^{N} w_{ij} s_j}{N-1}, j \neq i \tag{1}$$

Thus, social pressure ($-1 < P_{is} < 1$) to adopt s becomes increasingly positive as i's "friends" adopt s (s=1) and i's "enemies" reject s (s=-1). The pressure can also become negative in the opposite circumstances. The model extends to multiple states in a straightforward way, where [1] independently determines the pressure on agent i for each binary state s.

Strong positive or negative social pressure does not guarantee that an agent will accommodate, however. It is effective only if i is willing and able to respond to peer influence. If i is closed-minded or if a given trait is not under i's control (e.g., ethnicity or gender), then no change to s will occur. Let v classify states as fixed (v=0) or free (v=1) and X represent an exogenous determination of s. We then find i's propensity π to adopt state s as a cumulative logistic function of social pressure:

$$\pi_{is} = \frac{v_s}{1+e^{-10P_{is}}} + (1-v_s)X_i \tag{2}$$

Agent i adopts s if $\pi > 0.5 + \chi\varepsilon$, where χ is a random number ($-0.5 < \chi < 0.5$) and ε is an exogenous error parameter ($0 \leq \varepsilon \leq 1$). At one extreme, ε=0 produces deterministic behavior, such that any social pressure above the trigger value always leads to s=1 and pressure even slightly below the trigger value always leads to s=-1. Following Harsanyi (31), ε>0 allows for a "smoothed best reply" in which pressure levels near the trigger point leave the agent relatively indifferent and thus likely to explore behaviors on either side of the threshold.

In the Hopfield model, the path weight w_{ij} changes as a function of similarity in the states of node i and j. Weights begin with uniformly distributed random values, subject to the constraints that weights are symmetric ($w_{ij}=w_{ji}$). Across a vector of K distinct states s_{ik}, (or the position of agent i on issue k), agent i compares its own states to the observed states of another agent j and adjusts the weight upward or downward corresponding to their aggregated level of agreement or disagreement. Based on the correspondence of states for agents i and j, their weight will change at each discrete time point t in proportion to a parameter λ, which defines the rate of structural learning ($0<\lambda<1$):

$$w_{ij,t+1} = w_{ijt}(1-\lambda) + \frac{\lambda}{K}\sum_{k=1}^{K} s_{jkt}s_{ikt}, j \neq i \tag{3}$$

As correspondence of states can be positive (agreement) or negative (disagreement), ties can grow positive or negative over time, with weights between any two agents always symmetric. Note that both processes – adjustment of social ties and adjustment of behavior – seek to maximize balance in relations between any two agents across their vectors of states. Given an initially random configuration of states and weights, these agents will search for a profile that minimizes dissonance across their relations.

METHODS

We tested the dynamics of network polarization by manipulating three agent-level behavioral rules: *flexibility*, *broad-mindedness*, and *open-mindedness*:

1. Rigid vs. flexible (a.k.a. "waffling"): the extent to which the state adoption decision is stochastic near indifference, ranging from ε=0 (agent *i* always picks the strictly preferred position even when almost indifferent) to ε=1 (*i* adopts state *s* with propensity π_{is}).
2. Narrow- vs. broad-minded: the multiplexity of the state space, that is, the number of salient cross-cutting dimensions that agents consider in evaluating each other.
3. Closed- vs. open-minded: the proportion of these salient dimensions that can be affected by social pressure, with a minimum of at least one free state. A fixed state can be a position on an issue about which an agent is strictly uncompromising. It can also be an attribute that is difficult to change, such as ethnicity or gender.

Thus, we consider a range of stylized character profiles for agents, ranging from "extremists" who focus on ascriptive differences and are rigidly narrow- and closed-minded, to more broad-minded "moderates" who tend to waffle on the issues, and are open to influence (and/or focused on behavior rather than ascriptive traits).

We measure network polarization as the degree of segregation among mutually exclusive cohesive subgroups of agents, measured after all weights and states have converged to equilibrium. This measure is based on the graph theoretical LS-set (32). An LS-set is a subset of agents who have stronger ties to members within the subset than they have to members outside the subset.* For the cohesive subgroups thus identified, we calculated their segregation in terms of the normalized difference between the average internal tie strength and the average tie strength between the subgroup and its complement. To obtain an overall polarization score, we generated all partitionings of the graph into mutually exclusive cohesive subgroups and took from these the average segregation of all subgroups in the most segregated partitioning.

We allowed each experimental condition to repeat for 1000 iterations, which was sufficient for almost all conditions to arrive at an equilibrium. Only equilibrium outcomes (converged solutions) were analyzed. For all the experiments, we set the structural learning rate (λ) at 0.5, which means that agents consider current states equally with previous impressions in determining the tie weight for the next (arbitrary) time interval.† Each parameter combination was repeated 20 times, yielding a total of 44,000 observations.

---

* More technically, for each of the subsets of an LS-set, average tie strength between members of the subset and its complement within the LS set is higher than the average tie strength to members outside the LS set. We first identified subgroups of agents that agree on those states that they are free to change. We then searched through coalitions of these subgroups to find maximal LS-sets in the graph defined by agreement on free states. Finally, we used these LS-sets to identify the maximally segregated partitioning of the network, based on the relational weights (which reflect agreement on all states -- fixed and free).

† Qualitative patterns shown appear to be robust to a very broad range of assumptions about the learning rate, though extremely low learning rates make waiting for convergence impractical.

RESULTS

Experiment 1 tests the effects on network polarization of agent broad-mindedness, while holding flexibility and openness constant (ε=0 and ν=1). With zero flexibility and no fixed states, network dynamics converged to equilibrium in every case. Network polarization is measured as the degree of segregation in the most segregated equilibrium partitioning of the weight graph into mutually exclusive cohesive subgroups. Maximum segregation (1.0) occurs in a perfectly bifurcated network, composed of exactly two internally cohesive and mutually antagonistic groups. Broad-mindedness is operationalized as multiplexity, or the number of dimensions in the state space. Intuitively, we would expect polarization to be most likely in a world where agents focus single-mindedly on one highly salient issue, and indeed, Figure 1 confirms the intuition. What is surprising, however, is that network polarization can also be caused by *too many* salient issues. With 100 agents scattered over a state space larger than 2^5, the dynamics quickly approach the bifurcation we would expect in a single-issue population. As N declines, the non-monotonic effect becomes less pronounced. For N>100, the U-shape function is little changed but the critical value of K increases, from 5 dimensions with N<100 to 11 dimensions with N=300.

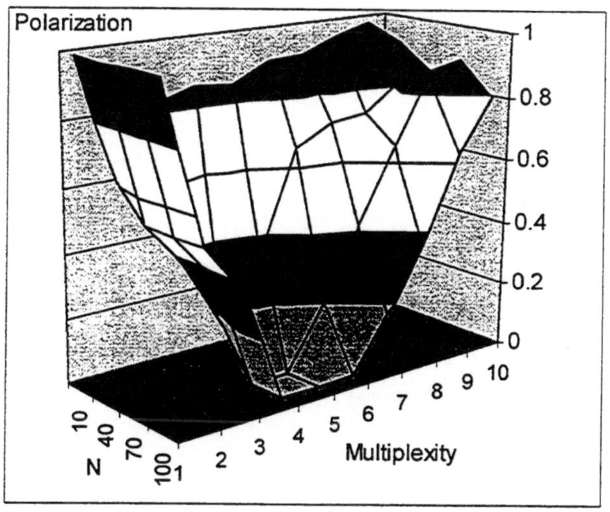

Figure 1. Effect of network size (10≤N≤100) and agent multiplexity (1≤K≤10) on network polarization (with ε=0 and ν=1).

Experiment 1 assumes rigidly deterministic agents (ε=0) who never explore alternative positions, even when they approach indifference. It also assumes that agents are willing and able to change all positions in response to social influence (ν=1), which would not be the case, for example, if race or ethnicity were a salient dimension of social differentiation. Experiment 2 relaxes these assumptions under conditions that make polarization relatively unlikely, namely, that there are at least five dimensions of differentiation (see Figure 1).‡ Intuitively, we might

‡ Fewer than five dimensions also constrains the ability to manipulate the relative number of dimensions that agents can alter.

expect less network polarization in a population that is less rigid and more polarization in a population that is less open-minded. The surprising result is that the effect is quite the opposite.

Figure 2 displays the polarizing effects of flexibility and open mindedness in greater detail. As in Experiment 1, polarization is based on the relational partition that maximizes segregation of the weight graph among coalitions of distinct subgroups in the matrix of free states. Flexibility is simply the error level, ranging from ε=0 (always pick the strictly preferred position) to ε=1 (adopt the position with propensity π). Openness is the proportion of K states that are affected by social pressure (or $\Sigma v_s/K$), where there must always be at least one free state. Results were averaged over 20 replications of each treatment condition, in which N ranged from 10 to 100 and K ranged from 5 to 10 (hence openness ranged from 0.2 to 1.0).

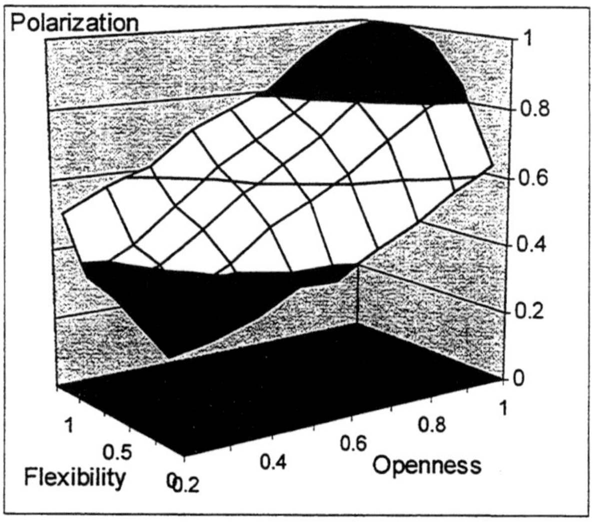

Figure 2. Effect of agent flexibility ($0 \leq \varepsilon \leq 1$) and open-mindedness ($\Sigma v_s/K$) on network polarization (with K=[5…10], N=[10…100]).

The surprising result is that polarization sharply increases with flexibility across all levels of openness. A population of "hardliners" (who never reveal ambivalence by waffling on the issues) is generally less prone to become polarized. Less surprisingly, polarization also increases with openness to social influence, for the simple reason that agents cannot alter their fixed states as a way of reducing dissonance in their relations. Note that Figure 2 is based only on equilibrium outcomes. As flexibility increases, the rate of convergence declines, due to the destabilizing effects of stochasticity. If we include nonconverged outcomes (coded with zero polarization), the effect of flexibility goes from convex to concave when most states are fixed, and when all states are free, the effect becomes non-monotonic, with polarization declining at maximum flexibility. In other words, with maximum flexibility and openness, the network is less likely to develop stable factions, but if this should happen, the number of factions is almost certain to be two.

DISCUSSION

With binary agent states, the dynamics of homophilous influence and xenophobic differentiation create an energy landscape in which there is only one basin of attraction, polarization. Any configuration with more than two cohesive subgroups represents global tension for a reason that is readily apparent: A binary state precludes the ability to hold a position that differs from each of two opposing positions. As the number of dimensions increases, it is possible for many more than two unique combinations to persist at equilibrium, but for each, there must always be some similarity with all other combinations except one. Surprisingly, as these combinations explode, they lead not to pluralism but to polarization. The mechanism is similar to that identified by Axelrod. The more opportunities for neighborhoods to be linked via overlapping positions, the higher the probability they will find a way to coalesce.

The key variable here is the density of the population distribution across the state space. When there are many agents but few dimensions, then, from a random start, every possible combination of states (corresponding to "ideologies" if the states are variable and to "identities" if the states are fixed) will find multiple incumbents. The presence of identical neighbors (as well as dissimilar antipodes who serve as negative referents) creates strong pressures to remain loyal to a shared set of states. This resistance to change can then support a pluriform equilibrium. Increasing the number of dimensions expands the set of possible combinations, allowing groups to mobilize around a variety of configurations of states. Accordingly, polarization initially declines with increasing multiplexity. However, if population density in the state space falls below a critical level (either due to low population or high multiplexity), it becomes impossible for every distinct vector of states to find an incumbent. The sparseness of the population relative to the number of unique positions in state space requires that some agents begin with neither allies (who overlap perfectly) nor enemies (who overlap not at all). These agents lack sufficient pressure to stick to their guns and will thus be pulled into coalitions with agents who overlap partially with their positions. As the multiplexity of the state space increases, equilibria increasingly depend on a delicate balance, where a distribution of agents on ideologies and identities needs to be found that corresponds to the distances between positions, such that they are not so close to each other that they are pulled together and not so far apart that they are pushed toward the opposite pole. In this higher range, increasing multiplexity makes it more difficult for pluriform configurations to persist, such that collapse into a simple bifurcation becomes the most likely alternative.

Flexibility promotes polarization by the same process. Network self-organization can become trapped in high-energy pluriform equilibria that are nevertheless a local minimum of the energy landscape, as depicted in Figure 3. Agents who express ambivalence by "waffling" on the issues can disturb these local solutions, allowing the system to continue searching for the global attractors. Thus, increased flexibility washes out the non-monotonic effect of multiplexity evident in Figure 1. Flexibility leads to polarization even when agents attend to multiple dimensions of differentiation that would otherwise produce the cross-cutting cleavages characteristic of a pluriform society.

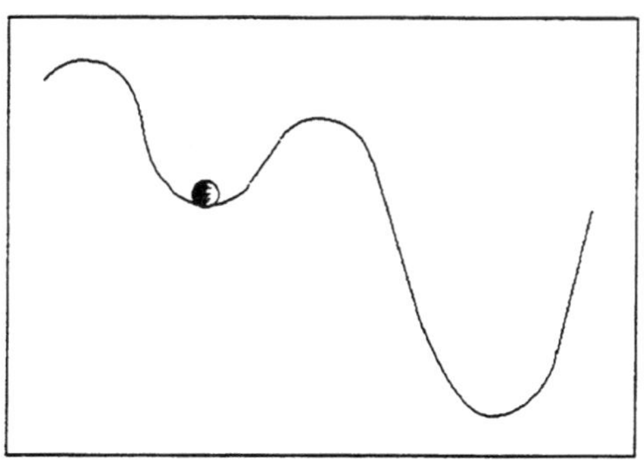

Figure 3. How agent volatility allows the network to find a lower energy minimum – hence greater polarization.

Homogeneity is also a stable equilibrium of the model, but this equilibrium cannot obtain unless we preclude negative weights and negative influence (as in the earlier models of cultural convergence and differentiation discussed above). If we initialize the model at homogeneity, it will remain there indefinitely. However, from a random start, the system cannot find the single-group solution without falling into an inescapable trap of in-group/out-group hostility. Further, a sufficient exogenous perturbation will disturb the unitary equilibrium and yield a two-group solution, but the reverse shift is much more difficult to obtain and is extremely unlikely.

To explore this interpretation further, we measured the energy level of equilibria by summing over the product of agreement and tie strength across all dyads in the weight graph. As expected, we found that networks with perfect polarization in two opposing camps had an energy level of zero, while energy levels increased with the number of different positions in the state space that co-existed at equilibrium. That analysis examined tension in dyads for the variety of converged configurations. A continuous index of graph balance (35), assessing balance in triads and cycles of any higher length, yielded the same conclusion. Equilibria with either one or two internally cohesive groups represent maximum balance, while convergence at any higher number of groups implies imbalanced relations in the social network.

CONCLUSIONS AND IMPLICATIONS

This study has explored polarizing tendencies of a self-organizing network, using a Hopfield model of dynamic attraction. The project integrates Axelrod's positive feedback model of influence-interaction with a bivalent model of social relations and cognitive balance. The Hopfield model emulates well-known processes of homophily, xenophobia, and influence from positive and negative referents. Thus, we may account for emergent social phenomena with a rigorous and parsimonious model, including only basic behavioral principles that have been broadly supported in experimental work.

The results have interesting implications for the notion of "structural balance" in social relations. Although the agents in this model are clearly designed to maintain balance in their behaviors with both positive and negative referents, this assumption is not "wired in" to the relations themselves, as it is in Structural Balance Theory. That is, two agents *A* and *B* feel no direct need for consistency in their relations with a third agent *C*. Indeed, *A* has no knowledge of the *B-C* relationship and thus no ability to adjust the *A-B or A-C* relations so as to balance the triad. Notably, the results show that triads (or cycles of any length) do tend to become balanced over time as agents seek balance in their dyadic relations. However, there is no guarantee in this model that they will achieve a globally optimal state in structural balance, and we also observe equilibrium outcomes where more than two subgroups persist indefinitely. This outcome cannot be reconciled with Structural Balance Theory, which predicts that system-level stability can only occur when the group either has become uniform or has polarized into two internally cohesive and mutually antipathetic cliques.

The model also has interesting implications for Social Identity Theory (36), which posits an in-group bias toward those who share a salient trait, prejudice against the out-group, and a tendency to ignore or change discrepant traits. The Hopfield model produces dynamic networks that self-organize into a similar pattern, but without a higher-order cognitive framework of social categories. In fact, these agents are not even aware that they belong to "groups" at all. This demonstrates the possibility that in-group/out-group differentiation and antagonism are emergent properties of network self-organization and are not inscribed in agents' cognitive architectures as assumed by identity theorists. In effect, the model demonstrates a *distributed* representation of the formation of social identities, which are not reducible to *local* representations in the minds of individual agents.

Finally, the model offers an important methodological demonstration. The results show how analytical methods focusing on equilibria may be misleading for prediction of opinion distributions that are likely to obtain. An analysis of possible equilibria clearly shows that more multiplexity and larger population size increase the number of possible pluriform equilibria, i.e. opinion configurations in which for all agents and all issues the aggregated pressures to stick to one's opinion exceed the aggregated pressures to change. However, our computational model showed that despite a larger number of theoretically possible equilibria, these conditions decreased the number of equilibria that were actually reached by the opinion dynamics. The reason is that equilibrium analysis fails to take into account the structural learning process through which outcomes are selected. In structural learning, equilibria become increasingly unlikely as the complexity of the coordination process increases. As a consequence, the computational model identifies polarization as the global attractor in a multiplex opinion space, an important substantive result that is overlooked by static equilibrium analysis.

Previous theoretical work has emphasized the global stability of social homogeneity, where convergence to unanimity is an almost irresistible force in closely interacting populations. If it is possible for some ties to be negative, our model suggests instead that a social structure is most stable when the network self-organizes along a single dimension of differentiation which thus determines a clear "right" and "wrong" choice on all behavioral dimensions. In comparison, social homogeneity is highly brittle.

ACKNOWLEDGEMENT

The research was supported by a grant to the first author from the U.S. National Science Foundation (SES-0079381). The research of the third author was made possible by a fellowship of the Royal Netherlands Academy of Arts and Sciences.

REFERENCES

1. Axelrod, Robert. 1997. "The Dissemination of Culture: A Model with Local Convergence and Global Polarization." *Journal of Conflict Resolution* 41: 2023-226.
2. Mark, N. 1998. "Beyond individual differences: Social differentiation from first principles." *Am Soc Rev* 63:309-330.
3. Carley, K. 1991. "A theory of group stability." *Am Soc Rev* 56:331-54.
4. Latane, B. 2000. "Pressures to uniformity and the evolution of cultural norms." Pp. 189-215 in *Computational Modeling of Behavior in Organizations: The Third Scientific Discipline*, edited by D. R. Ilgen and C. L. Hulin.
5. Cohen, J. M. 1977. "Sources of Peer Group Homogeneity." *Soc Ed* 50:227-41.
6. Kandel, D.B. 1978. "Homophily, Selection, and Socialization in Adolescent Friendships." *Am Jour Soc* 84:427-36.
7. Verbrugge, L.M. 1977. "The structure of adult friendship choices." *Social Forces* 56:576-97.
8. Byrne, D. E. 1971. *The Attraction Paradigm*. New York: Academic Press.
9. Newcomb, T.M. 1961. *The Acquaintance Process*. New York: Holt, Rhinehart & Winston.
10. Hoffman, I.R. & Maier, N.R.F. 1966. "An experimental reexamination of the similarity-attraction hypothesis." *Jour of Pers & Soc Psy* 3:145-152.

11. Homans, G.C. 1950. *The Human Group*. New York: Harcourt Brace.
12. Lott, A.J. & Lott, B.E. 1965. "Group cohesiveness as interpersonal attraction: A review of relationships with antecedent and consequent variables." *Psy Bul* 64:259-309.
13. Fararo, T.J. & Skvoretz, J. 1987. "Unification research programs: Integrating two structural theories." *Am Jour Soc* 92: 1183-1209.
14. Mayhew, Bruce H., J. Miller McPherson, Thomas Rotolo, and Lynn Smith-Lovin. 1995. "Sex and Race Homogeneity in Naturally Occurring Groups." *Social Forces* 74:15-52.
15. Rosenbaum, M.E. 1986. "The repulsion hypothesis: On the non-development of relationships." *Jour of Pers & Soc Psy* 51: 1156-1166.
16. Cartwright, D. & Zander, A. (1968) "Pressures to uniformity in groups: An introduction." Pp. 139-151 in *Group Dynamics: Research and Theory*, edited by Dorwin Cartwright and Alvin Zander. New York, NY: Harper & Row.
17. Festinger, L. 1950. "Informal social communication." *Psy Rev* 57:271-282.
18. Schachter, S. 1951. "Deviation, rejection, and communication." *Jour Abnormal Soc Psy* 46:190-207.
19. Friedkin, N.E. 1984. "Structural cohesion and equivalence explanations of social homogeneity." *Soc Meth & Res* 12:235-261.
20. Marsden, P.V. & Friedkin, N.E. 1993. "Network studies of social influence." *Soc Meth & Res* 22:127-151.
21. Abelson, R.P. 1964. Mathematical Models of the Distribution of Attitudes Under Controversy. Pp. 142-160 in: Frederiksen, N. & Gulliken, H. (eds.): *Contributions to mathematical psychology*. Holt, Rinehart & Winston, New York.
22. Harary, F. 1959. "A criterion for unanimity in French's theory of social power." In *Studies in social power*, edited by D. Cartwright, 168-82. Ann Arbor: Institute for Social Research.
23. French, J. R. P. Jr. 1956. "The formal theory of social power." *Psy Rev* 63: 181-94.
24. Heider, F. 1958. *The Psychology of Interpersonal Relations*. New York: Wiley.
25. Hopfield, John J. 1982. "Neural networks and physical systems with emergent collective computational abilities." *Proc Nat Acad Sci* 79:2554-8.
26. Hopfield, J. J. and D. W. Tank. 1985. ""Neural" Computation of Decisions in Optimization Problems." *Bio Cybernetics* 52:141-152.
27. Hebb, D. O. (1949), The Organisation of Behavior: A Neuropsychological Approach. John Wiley and Sons, New York, NY.
28. Nowak, A., Lewenstein, M, & Tarkowski, W. 1993. "Repeller neural networks." *Phys Rev* 48:1491-8.
29. Nowak, A. & Vallacher, R. 1997 "Computational social psychology: Cellular automata and neural network models of interpersonal dynamics." in S. Read and L Miller, eds. *Connectionist Models of Social Reasoning and Social Behavior*. Mahwah, NJ: Larence Erlbaum.
30. Kitts, J.A., M.W. Macy, & Flache, A. 2000. "Structural learning: Attraction and conformity in task-oriented groups." *Comp Math Org Theory*,5:129-145.
31. Harsanyi, J. 1973. Games with randomly disturbed payoffs. *International Journal of Game Theory* 2:1-23.
32. Cartwright, D. & Harary, F. 1966. "Structural balance: A generalization of Heider's theory." *Psy Rev* 63:277-93.
33. Davis, J.A. 1967. "Clustering and structural balance in graphs." *Human Rel* 20:181-187.

34. Wasserman, S. & Faust, K. 1994. *Social Network Analysis: Methods and Applications*. Cambridge: Cambridge University Press.
35. Cartwright, D. & Gleason, T.C. 1966. "The number of paths and cycles in a digraph." *Psychometrika*. 31: 179-199.
36. Tajfel, H.& Turner, J.C. 1986. "The social identity theory of intergroup relations." in *Psychology of Intergroup Relations*, edited by S. Worchel and W. G. Austin. Chicago, IL: Nelson-Hill

Local Rules and Global Properties: Modeling the Emergence of Network Structure

Martina Morris[1]
University of Washington
Departments of Sociology and Statistics

Abstract

This paper reviews the interaction between theory and methods in the field of network analysis. Network theory has traditionally sought to use social relations to bridge what social scientists refer to as the micro-macro gap: understanding how social structures are formed by the accumulation of simple rules operating on local relations. While early network methods reflected this goal, the bulk of the methods developed later and popularized in computer packages were more descriptive and static. That is beginning to change again with recent developments in statistical methods for network analysis. One particularly promising approach is based on exponential random graph models (ERGM). ERGM were first applied in the context of spatial statistics, and they provide a general framework for modeling dependent data where the dependence can be thought of as a neighborhood effect. The models can be used to decompose overall network structural properties into the effects of localized interaction rules; the traditional concern of the field. An example is given using an HIV transmission network.

Where do networks come from?

There are really two questions implied in this simple query. The first is about the underlying process that gives rise to the patterns of links among nodes in the population – this requires us to think about a dynamic model that links local processes to a global outcome. The second is the inverse question: how to infer the underlying process from the patterns we observe – this requires statistical methods for sampling, estimation and inference. Network theory was explicitly focused on the first question. The current developments in the field are making progress on the second. And the most well developed and commonly used methods in the field, while not particularly well suited to answering either question, have provided some important intermediate tools.

Modern (post 1940) social network theory explicitly focused on the link between local dynamics and global structures. One root can be traced back to social anthropology and exchange theory. In this research, the focus is on how rules governing permissible

[1] This work was supported in part by NIH grants R01 HD41877-01 and R01 DA12831-02.

exchange partners (for, e.g., gift giving, or marriage) cumulate up to determine the overall structure and stability of an exchange system (White 1963; Levi-Strauss 1969; Yamagishi and Cook 1993; Bearman 1996). Another root can be traced back to the social psychology and balance theory. In this research, the focus is on the how the requirement of balance for positive and negative affect among three actors – e.g., my enemy's friend is my enemy – cumulates up (Heider 1946; Granovetter 1979; Chase 1982). In both cases, the key findings have been that some simple local rules may lead to overall network structures that display striking regularities, like linear hierarchies, stable cliques, or stable cycles of exchange. Other rules do not have these systemically stable impacts, and this distinction leads to an evolutionary hypothesis about the differential survival of rules over time, i.e., to links with game theory.

Given this early focus, one might have expected the field to develop a methodology for systematically exploring such dynamics, but this did not happen. Nor did the inverse statistical problem, of inferring the rules from the patterns, receive much attention. It is tempting to attribute this to inadequate computing and statistical tools available at the time (from the 1940s to the 1980s). And to the impact of the progress made in the (less demanding) linear model framework. Whatever the reason, however, the methodology that did develop in the field of network analysis focused on static descriptive measures, rather than the dynamic model.

The descriptive approach drew inspiration from mathematical graph theory, using tools from linear algebra to manipulate the adjacency matrix, and focusing on issues of clustering and connectivity. These tools have become the heart of the field, providing a rich framework for thinking about networks and a wide range of summary measures to represent both the network position occupied by specific nodes, and the overall network structure. Almost all of the classic network measures – paths, cycles, density, centrality, structural equivalence, cliques, blockmodels, role algebras and bicomponents -- owe their development to researchers working with these descriptive tools. Textbooks and computer packages for network analysis typically have these measures at their core. They have become the common language for network analysis, defining the basic features of networks and helping to develop our intuitions about the complex relational structures we seek to understand.

The statistical issues – developing principled methods for estimation from samples, and quantifying the uncertainty in the estimates – have been addressed in a limited way in this descriptive context by eschewing traditional model-based statistical methods. Model-based methods rely on the assumption of independent observations to obtain tractable likelihood-based estimation and inference. In network analysis, independence is not something one would want to assume, since understanding the dependence among observations is actually the primary task. The growth in computing power has given rise to statistical methods that rely on resampling rather than likelihood inference, e.g., the bootstrap, jackknife, and permutation tests. These have been readily adopted by network analysts, finding their way into tests like quadratic assignment procedures (QUAP) for sociomatrix regression. In recent years, Markov Chain Monte Carlo (MCMC) algorithms have been developed for complex estimation problems, and these are now providing the tools needed to return to a model-based framework.

Statistical Models for Networks

Progress in model-based statistical methods for network analysis has picked up momentum in recent years, due to a combination of theoretical developments, advances in statistical computing, and innovations in data collection. Model-based statistical estimation and inference would seem to offer exactly the right tools to answer the original inverse question raised above, because it is based on an underlying stochastic model of the population process. To be useful, however, two things are needed: (1) an appropriate model for the process and the dependencies in it, and (2) a method of estimation that works with dependent observations.[2] This would seem to be fairly straightforward, but the history of the field makes it clear it is not.

There is general agreement that the exponential family of distributions provides a good framework for modeling the probability that a random graph (or sociomatrix) $\boldsymbol{X}$ takes the observed value x. Holland and Leinhardt (1981) were the first to propose using this model for networks, noting that it was a natural form because the sufficient statistics were explicitly tied to parameters of interest, like indegree, outdegree, mutuality and etc. The general form of the model is given by:

$$P(X = x) = \exp\left\{\sum_{i=1}^{IJ} \theta_{ij}' f(x_{ij})\right\} / c(x) \tag{1}$$

where the sufficient statistics, $f(x_{ij})$, are typically counts of links and of products of links, the θ_{ij} are the parameters of interest, and $c(x)$ is a normalizing constant. This model had been proposed 20 years earlier by Bahadur (1961) as a general representation for multivariate binomial distributions. It is a completely general model, and can fit any graph perfectly by using all $\binom{n}{2} - 1$ possible parameters (where n is the number of nodes). One can think of the sufficient statistics as defining the neighborhood of dependence. Conditional on the rest of the graph, the dependence between observations is restricted to the other points in this neighborhood. The heart of the modeling effort is to specify (and test) parsimonious representations of the neighborhood. To focus on this, we will strip equation (1) down to its modeling core:

$$\sum_{i=1}^{IJ} \theta_{ij}' f(x_{ij}) \tag{2}$$

and work through the models that have been proposed in various contexts.

Much of the statistical theory for ERGM was developed and applied in the context of spatial statistics by Besag (1974). The simplest spatial models represent observations as points on a lattice, and assume that only the nearest neighbors have an influence on the status of a site. For example, imagine an agricultural plot, divided into a grid along two orthogonal axes (see Figure 1).

---

[2] It is important to keep in mind that the unit of analysis here is the link, not the node, and the dependence is between links, not between nodes.

Figure 1. A lattice model for a "nearest neighbor" spatial process. The dark site in the center is the site whose status is of interest; the grey sites indicate the neighborhood of dependence.

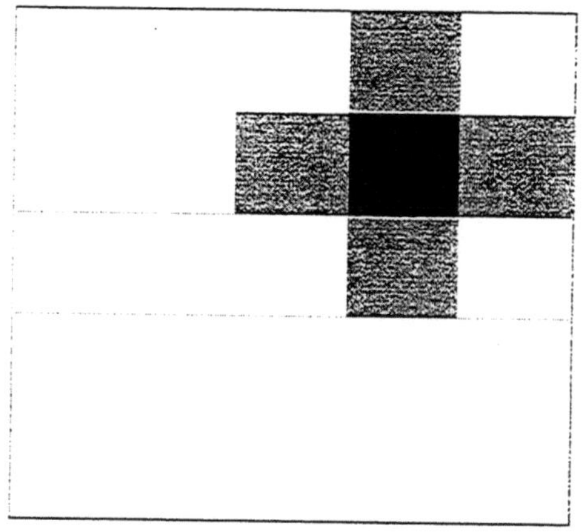

Each square in the grid has 4 adjacent sites in its neighborhood. Nearest neighbor ERGM models mimic the classic Ising model from statistical mechanics, representing the status of a site (say, infected with a fungus) as a function of:

$$\alpha\sum_{i,j} x_{i,j} + \rho\sum_{i,j} x_{i,j}x_{i+k,j+k} \qquad k = \{-1,1\} \tag{3}$$

The spatial dependence among sites is captured by ρ, which is considered a nuisance parameter, and the parameter of interest is α, which represents the spatially adjusted propensity for infection.

When applying these spatial models to networks, both similarities and differences in the nature of the data should be kept in mind. In both cases, the data are often represented in matrix form – the lattice and the adjacency (or socio-) matrix. But the meaning of the indices that order the matrix are quite different. The "site" in the spatial context is a dyad (not a person) in the network context. The Cartesian coordinates that define the grid in the spatial context become persons in the network context. This latter difference has important implications. In the spatial context, the spatial metric is exogeneous, and the lattice is fixed. In the network context, the rows and columns of the adjacency matrix have no intrinisic ordering, and may be permuted at will without changing the pattern of ties among persons, or the neighborhoods that define dependence. While physical space may influence the pattern of ties, it is not the only factor. As a result, the notion of "space" in network models is largely endogeneous and neighborhoods are typically not defined in terms of proximity in the matrix. Because the nature of the "spatial" dependence is the primary focus of interest in network analysis, the parameters that define this dependence are not nuisance parameters, but the parameters of most interest. This also changes the kinds of models that are appropriate for networks. The models can be based on exogeneous non-spatial attributes of the nodes (e.g., age, race, sex, etc.), or on the propensity for certain kinds of configurations in the network (e.g., triad effects, cycles and paths). Alternatively, the models may seek to represent neighborhoods in terms of a completely endogeneously defined latent space (with methods similar in spirit to earlier blockmodeling (White, Boorman et al. 1976)). Each of these approaches can be found in the literature.

The first application of ERGM like models to networks was Holland and Leinhardt's *p1* model for directed graphs. The core of this model takes the form:

$$\sum_{i=1}^{n}\alpha_i x_{i+} + \sum_{j=1}^{n}\beta_j x_{+j} + \rho\sum_{i<j} x_{ij}x_{ji} \qquad (4)$$

The model represents the process that gives rise to the graph as a function of the node-specific outdegree and indegree propensities, the α_i and β_j parameters, and a uniform propensity, ρ, for ties to be reciprocated. A number of key features of the ERGM framework are visible in this simple model.

First, the network statistics that drive the model are simple functions of links, and the neighborhood represented by the statistics is easy to read from functional forms. In much the same way that a standard cross-tabulation can be decomposed into marginal and interaction effects, this model uses marginal and interaction-type terms to distinguish between dyad-independent and dyad-dependent effects. Terms that are based on marginal sums represent effects that operate on each dyad independently. In this model, the basic indegree and outdegree terms are of this sort. Marginal effects can also be used to represent groups of nodes defined by exogeneously given attributes, and the patterns of selective mixing among the groups (this will be shown below). Used in this way, the attributes define a social distance metric that establishes a generalized kind of neighborhood. Terms that are based on products of links, on the other hand, represent dependence between the links. In this model, the only dependence between links is within-dyad – the tendency for mutual ties – so this model is still referred to as a *dyadic independence* model. But products of non-reciprocal links are a fairly straightforward generalization, and models with these terms are referred to as dyadic dependence models. Examples include products of triads of various kinds (a direct formalization of the balance theory hypotheses), and all manner of larger component sizes and structures. In each case, the sufficient statistic will be the sum of the products of sets of links that are eligible for the specific configuration of interest, and the parameter will represent whether this configuration happens more or less likely than one would expect by chance. The size and structure of the configuration indicates the nature of the neighborhood.

Second, one can also catch a glimpse of the two key mechanisms for reducing the number of parameters in these models: one is to limit the number of configurations represented as having an effect on the probability of the graph, the other is to impose "homogeneity constraints" on isomorphic configurations. In this model the number of configurations is quite small – instars, outstars, and mutual dyads. But the homogeneity constraints are only imposed on the mutuality parameter; indegree and outdegree parameters remain node-specific. As the population grows large, the number of parameters will also grow. This is somewhat like a fixed-effect model in economics, where a term is fit to every respondent in a setting with repeated measures. Here, as there, these are essentially nuisance parameters.

Homogeneity constraints are often imposed for parsimony, but they can also be used to represent exogenous covariates. For example, one can specify group-specific, rather than individual-specific parameters for indegree and for outdegree (Fienberg, Meyer et al. 1985; Wang and Wong 1987):

$$\sum \alpha_k \sum_{i \in k} x_{i+} + \sum \beta_l \sum_{j \in l} x_{+j} + \sum \phi_{kl} \sum_{i \in k, j \in l} x_{ij} + \rho \sum x_{ij} x_{ji} \qquad k = 1, \ldots G; l = 1, \ldots G \tag{5}$$

There are now G indegree and outdegree parameters, rather than N. This can lead to a substantially more parsimonious model if the number of groups is much smaller than the number of persons. The ϕ parameters are used to specify the level of mixing within and between groups. As in other log-linear modeling settings, the mixing can also be parsimoniously modeled to represent patterns of interest (Morris 1991).

The next extension of ERGM in networks took on the task of modeling dyadic dependence. The ability to model dyadic dependence is the single most important feature of the ERGM framework, both because it is theoretically appealing, and because it is statistically innovative. The range of possibilities it opens up, however, is daunting. Without the physical space embedding, the notion of "neighborhood" is pretty much unconstrained. Frank and Strauss (Frank and Strauss 1986) were the first to exploit the more general form of the ERGM to represent dyadic dependence in the context of networks. The approach they took was a natural, if somewhat mechanical, first step: links are dependent if they share a node. The neighborhood is Markovian in the sense that links must be directly adjacent to be dependent, so Frank and Strauss referred to the model as the Markov Graph. Using the Hammersley-Clifford theorem, the sufficient statistics for this model can be shown to be products of links that represent the stars of various sizes in the graph, and triangles. A "star" is a cluster of links with a single central node. For an undirected graph the general Markov model is:

$$\sum_{k=1}^{n-1} \sigma_k s_k + \sum \tau_{ijk} x_{ij} x_{jk} x_{ki} \tag{6}$$

where s_k represents a star of size k, so a product of k links. Frank and Strauss then investigate a simpler version of the Markov model, restricting the configurations to s_1 and s_2 -- edges and 2-stars, and imposing an homogeneity constraint on the triangle parameter τ. Wasserman and Pattison (Wasserman and Pattison 1996; Pattison and Wasserman 1999) returned to the more general form, which they christened p*, in honor of Holland and Leinhardt's pioneering work.

The models above are based on explicit measured covariates, though in some cases the covariates are themselves part of the process being modeled. Another approach, with roots in classic multivariate analysis, seeks instead to represent the latent, unmeasured space implied by the pattern of network ties. In this purely descriptive model, the aim is to find a latent space in which the probability of a tie varies with the distance between the two nodes (Hoff, Raftery et al. 2002). Conditional on this metric, the dyads are independent.

$$\alpha - \left| z_i - z_j \right| \tag{7}$$

The z parameters represent the latent spatial locations, and need to be estimated. Without further dimensional reduction, the number of parameters required to map this latent space becomes quite large. More parsimonious representations can be tested. Explicit covariates can also be added.

Despite the enormous flexibility the ERG framework has brought to the field, virtually all of the published applications of these models have either used a variant of the original *p1* model, or the simplified Markov graph. This is somewhat curious, as both are pretty mechanical renderings of what one might think of as the "neighborhood" of influence, and neither is particularly well suited to representing the kinds of processes traditionally of interest to network modelers.

The lack of model development is probably due to the extremely challenging technical problems that accompany the estimation of these models.[3] Another problem is the lack of data, or at least of the type of data currently required. None of the models has been specified in a way that missing data can be handled, so it is still necessary to have the equivalent of census data on a network – data on every node and every link. Such data do exist, but they are not common, and this has been a major obstacle to all forms of network analysis. Finally, it may also be that our ability to think, empirically, in terms of positions and network structure has atrophied as we have waited for the right tools to become available. Whatever the reason, there has been remarkably little application of these modeling tools to data.

Models are the bridge between theory and data. And while there is a certain attraction to simple abstract forms, like Markov graphs, small world graphs, or scale free networks, the simplification we seek will be embedded in each substantive context. In the rest of this paper, I will show how these models can be used to formalize the investigation of how a global network structure might cumulate up from simple local rules in a specific case.

[3] Other papers in this volume will be addressing these in detail, so they do not need to be covered here.

From local rules to global structures: Partnership networks and the spread of HIV

Over the past two decades, the epidemic of HIV has challenged the epidemiological community to rethink its paradigms for understanding the risk of infectious disease transmission, both at the individual level, and at the level of population transmission dynamics. Opinion has rapidly converged on the central importance of partnership networks. Because people acquire infections from their partners, it is not only a person's own behavior that puts them at risk, but the behavior of their partners, and more generally, the persons to whom they are indirectly connected by virtue being connected to their partner. At the individual level the risk of infection is determined by position in the overall transmission network. While individual behavior plays a primary role in establishing this position, it is not the exclusive determinant. To some extent, even the notion of "individual behavior" itself is open to question here, since all behaviors can only be adopted with a willing partner, which has important implications for both modeling and behavioral intervention strategies. At the aggregate level, too, transmission dynamics are strongly affected by networks. The network of partnerships channels the spread of an infection through a population, amplifying or impeding the spread relative to a hypothetical randomly mixing population. At both the individual and the population level then, our ability to quantify the risk of transmission for HIV or other sexually transmitted or blood-borne infections, depends on our ability to measure and summarize the transmission network.

One of the greatest obstacles to using network analysis in this context is the complete data requirement. In the context of the sexual and needle-sharing networks that matter for HIV, such data collection is impossible. The question, then, is whether we can explain the overall network structure with a small number of partnership formation rules that operate at the local individual level. If this is true, it will radically simplify data collection needs, and give network analysis a central place in the tools of sexually transmitted infection (STI) research and intervention.

There is some reason to think that such local rules may govern the network structures of interest. At the population level, the findings from recent mathematical modeling suggest that two general types of structures are important: selective mixing patterns among different groups (Hethcote and Van Ark 1987; Sattenspiel 1987; Garnett and Anderson 1993; Morris 1996), and the timing and sequence of partnership formation (Watts and May 1992; Morris and Kretzschmar 1997). These general insights come from different types of mathematical simulations, including both simple deterministic differential equations (sometimes called compartmental models) and stochastic microsimulations of a population of interacting individuals (sometimes called "agent based models").

Mixing refers to assortative and disassortative biases in the joint distribution of partners' attributes. Examples include the degree of matching on race, age, sex, social status, sexual orientation or level of sexual activity. Assortative biases can create patchy, clustered networks, which tends to increase the speed of spread within groups, and slow the spread between them. If the groups also vary in activity level, the resulting distribution of infection can be very uneven. In the extreme, prevalence may rise to high endemic levels in some groups, while other groups remain infection free. Disassortative biases typically have the opposite effect, ensuring rapid spread to all groups. For example, preferential linking between highly active persons and less active persons ensures that the latter are reached more quickly in the epidemic. An example of this is the traditional double standard, where men can have multiple partners, but women only one.

The timing and sequence of partnership formation refers to the pattern of start and end dates for partnerships over an individual's lifetime. If the partnership intervals defined by these dates are strictly sequential, the pattern is called serial monogamy. If the intervals overlap, the pattern is called concurrency. Serial monogamy retards the spread of infection in two primary ways: it locks the pathogen in a partnership for some time after transmission, and it ensures that only later partners are at indirect risk from earlier ones. With concurrency, by contrast, one's partner can have other partners, who in turn have other partners, and so on. Instead of a monogamous population of dyads and isolates, concurrency creates a potentially large connected component for rapid pervasive spread. In addition, because earlier partners need not be dropped as later partners are added, the infection can be spread both in both directions: from earlier to later partners, and from later to earlier ones.

Almost all of our understanding of the effects of these network patterns on HIV spread have been based on simulation. And with few exceptions, the simulations have created network effects indirectly, by varying parameters of some convenient mathematical function to produce a change in the simulated networks. Network patterns are thus *outcomes* of the model, rather than inputs. This strategy has been enormously valuable for orienting research, and it laid the groundwork for future progress. But it has also limited our ability to place this work on a firm empirical footing, and to quantify the risk in any specific network.

Linking network data to network simulation requires a statistical bridge: a modeling framework that enables the key structural parameters to be estimated from network data, so that these can be used to directly drive a simulation. ERGMs have the potential to do this.

The simplest network statistic is the total number of links, represented as $\sum_{i=\{1,...,n\},j<i} x_{ij}$, which provides information on the *density* of the network – in this context, the level of partnership activity in the population. The level of *concurrency* is represented by statistics for the "nodal degree distribution" – the number of persons with 0, 1, 2, or more partners (and one could test either parametric or non-parametric forms of these distributions). A simple *selective mixing* on a discrete characteristic (e.g., race) would be represented by the count of dyads in which both partners have the same attribute. One can also parameterize cycles of various sizes (e.g., triangles, 4-cycles, etc.), and with parameters that make the temporal dependence explicit. This enables one to model how in the network evolves over time. These parameters and others can be fit simultaneously, which provides a uniform metric for establishing their relative strength, and examining their correlation. What this statistical model provides, then, is a

systematic method for summarizing the key structural features of an empirical network, with a framework for comparison and testing.

While estimation techniques are often of little interest to non-statisticians, this case is an exception. The constant in equation (1) requires a calculation that makes simple maximum likelihood estimation impossible for graphs larger than about 20 nodes. To avoid this, early applications of these models used an approximation called maximum pseudolikelihood estimation (MPLE). The problem was that the estimates produced by MPLE were of unknown quality. In the last few years, researchers have turned instead to computationally intensive Monte-Carlo Markov Chain (MCMC) estimation methods, which allow the true likelihood function to be maximized. In addition to providing more accurate estimates, this approach is particularly interesting for our purposes because the MCMC method effectively simulates the network in order to maximize the likelihood. We can, however, just as easily use the MCMC algorithm to simulate the network *given* the parameter estimates, and this provides the ideal solution to the problem of linking network data to the network simulation. One can estimate the network parameters from data, and then use the same model, with the empirically based parameter estimates, to drive a simulation of the network with an infection spreading through it. The MCMC algorithm provides the engine for both tasks. This makes it possible for the first time to directly control the network structures in a simulation so that they "look like" the networks we observe in different data sets.

A Model-Based Hypothesis

We are now in a position to test a different kind of hypothesis about the role of networks on disease spread. The research of the previous decade has suggested that attribute-based mixing and levels of concurrency have a large impact on network structure and transmission dynamics. Now we can ask whether these are the only features that matter.

One the one hand, there is a good theoretical basis for this hypothesis. For the type of partnerships that spread STI it seems reasonable to presume that people make decisions about which partners to choose based on preferences and norms that operate at the local level. That is, we choose partners because they are the right sex, age, race and status, and we often care if they have other partners. It is unlikely that people form partnerships thinking "If I choose this partner I can shorten the number of steps between me and a randomly chosen person on the west coast" or "I'd like to complete as many 5-cycles as possible with a single partnership". This may seem obvious at one level, but the implications may not be as obvious, and they are quite striking. If simple local rules govern partner selection, then these also determine the aggregate structure in the network: what looks like an unfathomably complicated system is, in fact, produced by a few key local organizing principles. By extension, these simple local rules are also, therefore, the key behavioral determinants of disease transmission dynamics on the network.

There are also important practical implications of this hypothesis. Both mixing and concurrency are network properties that can be measured with local network sampling strategies. If it turns out that these two local rules explain most of the variation in network structure that is relevant to disease spread, then we have a simple inexpensive way to measure network vulnerability routinely in public health surveillance. And they describe simple behavioral rules that people can be taught to recognize and change.

So the last piece of the puzzle is to determine how to test the hypothesis that mixing and concurrency contain all of the information we need to know to evaluate the spread potential in a network. We seek a "goodness of fit" test, but one that is tailored to what we want to fit.

Transmission potential in a network is determined by the network connectivity. Connectivity can be measured in a number of ways, but two simple measures are the properties of *reachability* (is person *i* connected to person *j* by a path of some length?) and *distance* (what is the length of that path?). Reachability and distance represent epidemiologically relevant "higher order" network properties that simple models should be able to reproduce. We can develop fit statistics based on these higher order network statistics to test the models that include parameters only for mixing and concurrency. This makes it possible to test whether the local organizing features represented in the model reproduce the larger structural features of the network. We can therefore develop formal tests for the hypothesis that mixing and concurrency capture the epidemiologically relevant variation in network structure. We can also use the MCMC simulation engine to verify whether these features are sufficient for establishing the epidemic potential in a network.

Conclusion

The new tools for network modeling provide us with the ability to empirically test a question that has both important practical implications, and deep theoretical roots. The generalizable findings from this work will not necessarily be monolithic. There is no reason to think that attribute mixing and concurrency are the local rules that drive all network structure. What is generalizable, though, is that the models for networks should be rooted in the scientific context that they seek to explain. For this, one does not need a one size fits all approach, one needs a flexible class of models that can be tested against data in principled ways. ERGMs provide the basis for this kind of empirically-based network analysis, and should become widely used in the years to come.

References

Bahadur, R. R. (1961). A representation of the joint distribution of responses to n dichotomous items. Studies in Item Analysis and Prediction. H. Solomon. Stanford, California, Stanford University Press: 158-168.

Bearman, P. S. (1996). "Generalized Exchange." Amer J Soc **102**(5): 1383-1415.

Besag, J. (1974). "Spatial interaction and the statistical anaylsis of lattice systems." Journal of the Royal Statistical Society Series B **36**: 192-236.

Chase, I. D. (1982). "Dynamics of hierarchy formation: the sequential development of dominance relationships." Behaviour **80**: 218-40.

Fienberg, S. E., M. M. Meyer, et al. (1985). "Statistical analysis of multiple sociometric relations." Journal of the American Statistical Association **80**: 51-67.

Frank, O. and D. Strauss (1986). "Markov Graphs." JASA **81**: 832-842.

Garnett, G. and R. Anderson (1993). "Contact tracing and the estimation of sexual mixing patterns: the epidemiology of gonococcal infections." Sex Transm Dis **20**(4): 181-91.

Granovetter, M. (1979). The theory gap in social network analysis. Perspectives in Social Network Analysis. P. Holland and S. Leinhardt. New York, Academic.

Heider, F. (1946). "Attitudes and Cognitive Organzation." Journal of Psychology **21**(January): 107-112.

Hethcote, H. and J. Van Ark (1987). "Epidemiological Models for Heterogeneous Populations: Proportionate Mixing, Parameter Estimation, and Immunization Programs." Math. Biosc. **84**: 85-118.

Hoff, P. D., A. E. Raftery, et al. (2002). "Latent space approaches to social network analysis." Journal of the American Statistical Association **97**(460): 1090-1098.

Holland, P. and S. Leinhardt (1981). "An exponential family of probability distributions for directed graphs." JASA **77**: 33-50.

Levi-Strauss, C. (1969). The Elementary Structures of Kinship (orig. 1949). Boston, Beacon Press.

Morris, M. (1991). "A log-linear modeling framework for selective mixing." Math Biosc **107**: 349-77.

Morris, M. (1996). Behavior change and non-homogeneous mixing. Models for Infectious Human Diseases: Their Structure and Relation to Data. V. Isham and G. Medley. Cambridge, Cambridge University Press. **6**: 236-49.

Morris, M. and M. Kretzschmar (1997). "Concurrent partnerships and the spread of HIV." AIDS **11**: 641-8.

Pattison, P. E. and S. Wasserman (1999). "Logit models and logistic regressions for social networks, II. Multivariate relations." British Journal of Mathematical and Statistical Psychology **52**: 169-194.

Sattenspiel, L. (1987). "Epidemics in nonrandomly mixing populations: A simulation." Amer. J. Phys. Anthro. **73**: 251-265.

Wang, Y. J. and G. Y. Wong (1987). "Stochastic blockmodels for directed graphs." JASA **82**: 8-19.

Wasserman, S. and P. Pattison (1996). "Logit models and logistic regressions for social networks: I. An introduction to Markov graphs and p*." Psychometrika **60**(401-426).

Watts, C. H. and R. M. May (1992). "The Influence of Concurrent Partnerships on the Dynamics of HIV/AIDS." Math Biosc **108**: 89-104.

White, H. C. (1963). An Anatomy of Kinship. Englewood Cliffs, Prentice Hall.

White, H. C., S. A. Boorman, et al. (1976). "Social structure from multiple networks, I: Blockmodels of roles and positions." American Journal of Sociology **81**: 730-80.

Yamagishi, T. and K. Cook (1993). "Generalized exchange and social dilemmas." Soc Psych Quarterly **56**(4): 235-48.

Social Networks: From Sexual Networks to Threatened Networks

H. Eugene Stanley[1] and Shlomo Havlin[2]

[1] Center for Polymer Studies and Department of Physics
Boston University, Boston, MA 02215, USA

[2] Minerva Center and Department of Physics
Bar-Ilan University, Ramat Gan, Israel

Abstract. Our scientific goal is to uncover common principles governing the behavior of a range of social networks. Our practical goal is to use this understanding to develop specific strategies to destroy threat networks and, in parallel, to develop specific strategies to defend threatened social networks against attack. There are recent hints that progress toward achieving both goals can be achieved applying new approaches from modern statistical physics to social network structure and dynamics.

1 Introduction

Populations, which can be viewed as networks of social acquaintances, are vulnerable to disease epidemics such as AIDS. Any random immunization of people against such disease attacks is problematic because it must encompass almost the entire population in order to successfully stop the spreading epidemic [1–5]. Other types of social networks are organizations, e.g., security agencies, in which working relations are represented by links. To be effective, these organizations must be stable and allow rapid data flow in the network. We have begun addressing these problems — using concepts and tools of both social sciences and statistical and nonlinear physics — by designing more stable social network structures, enabling them to resist both random and intentional attacks. For this purpose, we need to better understand the topological structures of existing social networks, and to improve our understanding of transport in such systems.

Our methods in statistical physics are based on relatively new concepts, such as correlated site-bond percolation theory [6–10]. The applications of percolation theory range from predicting the amount of oil that can be extracted from an underground reservoir, to understanding the network formation mechanism involved in the hardening of a boiled egg. The use of percolation theory has already proven valuable in the study of social networks. The Bar-Ilan group has generalized percolation theory in order to analyze the structure and stability of general networks under random failures [11] and intentional attacks [12]. Based on this generalization, we are following up on a novel approach for designing new social networks that are more resilient to attack. We are also developing methods based on the percolation approach [13] that will enable us to immunize populations more effectively against different types of epidemics.

2 Recent Advances on Scale-Free Social Networks

Very recent analysis of social networks, as well as many other networks (such as trust networks and sexual networks), reveals that some of these networks display the important property of being scale-free [6,2,14], i.e., there is a very wide distribution of the number of links per vertex. Most vertices have a small number of connections. However, there are a small number of vertices that have a very large number of connections, and there are vertices in the full range between these extremes. Further, it seems that there is a possible explanation for this scale-free behavior [2,15], and that the results for sexual networks extend to other social networks [16].

Our groups are studying the structure of a wide range of social network types [17], and are building mathematical models and tools for large social networks [13]. In studies conducted about the stability of scale-free social networks, it was proven that these networks are optimally resilient to the random failure of individuals [11]. Even if almost all elements of a network malfunction, a large fraction of the individuals will be left connected, allowing continuing interactions between a large fraction of the population. This situation is unlike that of homogeneous networks, in which such a failure will break the entire network into small, unconnected islands. On the other hand, a deliberate, successful attack on the most-connected elements in the network will lead to failure of the entire network after only a small fraction of nodes have been targeted [12]. Further, studies show that search can be conducted in such heterogeneous networks in a much more efficient way than in homogeneous networks [18].

A connection exists between (a) the stability of a network and (b) the propagation of disease. Heterogeneous networks are prone to the rapid spread of epidemics. If the individuals to be immunized are chosen randomly, spreading is unavoidable, even if almost all individuals in the network are immunized. However, if the individuals to be immunized are chosen using "smart" strategies, it becomes possible to reduce the number of infected individuals to almost zero. Using models, it is possible to forecast the consequences of epidemic outbursts and to try to control them. It is established that random immunization of a large fraction of the population fails to prevent epidemics of diseases that spread upon contact between infected individuals; for example, Malaria requires 99% of the population to be immunized in order to stop epidemic spreading [4,5]. On the other hand, targeted immunization of the most-connected individuals requires global knowledge of the topology of the social network in question, rendering 99% immunization impractical. We recently proposed an effective strategy, based on the immunization of a small fraction of *acquaintances* of randomly-selected individuals, that prevents epidemics without requiring global knowledge of the social network [19].

3 Recent Advances on Traffic Flow in Networks

We are adapting recent results on traffic flow to social network analysis. In 1994, Leland et al. [20] found that Ethernet LAN traffic is self-similar; "bursts" occur on every time scale. These findings show that long-range correlations in the interval times of arriving packets and extreme variability (or infinite limit of the variance). Paxson and Floyd [21] have found evidence for self-similarity of Wide Area Network (WAN) Traffic, and showed the failure of Poisson modeling in this case. New empirical findings challenge the validity of the traditional queuing models, and new models have since been proposed. In contrast to the above measurements, Takayasu et al. [22–24] have measured a $1/f$ power spectrum only at the critical point of a phase transition, and it is still not clear whether the flow is always self-similar in such networks. They found finite correlation times in the fluctuations of network traffic, and identified phase transitions between "sparse" and "jam" phases of the network.

The empirical phenomena mentioned above can influence the design of control schemes for traffic. However, the empirical description of the traffic is not yet complete. As the Bar-Ilan group has demonstrated recently in the case of vehicular traffic [25], a careful nonlinear statistical analysis of measured data may lead to the finding of several congested phases. One of our goals is to clarify this issue, and one method that we will use in the analysis of measured time series is Detrended Fluctuation Analysis (DFA). DFA was developed by the Boston group [26] and has been successfully applied by us and others to many systems, e.g., to DNA sequences [27,28], the analysis of climate changes [29,30], heart rate variability [31–34], economics [35], and even prime numbers [36]. One of the advantages of this method is its ability to detect long-range correlations in the records in the presence of trends and other nonstationarities.

4 Characteristic Properies of Real Networks

4.1 Classification of Real Networks

We have developed a method that classifies complex real-world networks according to their statistical topological properties [17]. By studying a wide range of different types of networks, we find evidence for the occurrence of three classes of small-world networks:

(a) scale-free networks,
(b) broad-scale networks, characterized by a connectivity distribution that has a power-law regime followed by a sharp cut-off;
(c) single-scale networks, characterized by a connectivity distribution with a fast-decaying tail.

4.2 Percolation

A percolation approach for general networks has been developed, with surprising results for scale-free networks [11–13]. The network is fully resilient to the random failure of sites and is extremely vulnerable to intentional attack. This analytical approach is being developed to study realistic social networks—e.g., where known correlations between individuals are included—where the measured clustering property and real geographical distance, measured experimentally, are being taken into account. Preliminary findings show that the geographical effect has a strong influence on the stability and transport of the network [37–39].

4.3 Structural and Transport Properties of Networks

We are studying several topological properties of networks—e.g., clustering and correlations. Some preliminary results already exist, such as the work on clustering in trust networks [40]. The clustering coefficient [41,42], which quantifies the extent to which nodes adjacent to a given node are linked, seems not to be affected when the network collapses. This may be relevant to terrorist organizations that are comprised of small, strongly-connected cells that are connected to each other by a few, highly-connected individuals [43]. The clustering was found to be important also in electric power networks, e.g., the power grid in the Western States in which the clustering coefficient is significantly larger than that of random networks. A useful method to quantify correlations (by measuring assortative tendencies, i.e., the tendency of high-degree vertices to associate preferentially with other high-degree vertices) was suggested recently by Newman [44].

We have preliminary results extending these studies to other real social networks. We are also studying the degree distribution for sites at a given distance from the most-connected site [45]. We are also studying the effect of geographical distance in real networks. This information is important for evaluating the stability and the immunization threshold. We are also analyzing the transport properties of data flow in social networks. We are applying DFA analysis and multifractal analysis [46] to better understand transport in complex social networks. We also are developing structural and transport modeling that will enable a better understanding of the structure and transport in such networks.

4.4 Optimizing the Stability of Threatened Networks

We are using the analytical approach we developed to calculate the percolation threshold for a given network [11,12], in order to design topologies that improve the stability of scale-free networks under both random failures and intentional attacks. This is being done by calculating the percolation threshold while keeping the average number of links for an individual in the network constant (for safety and security reasons) and then varying parameters such as the form of the degree distribution, the type of correlations, and the clustering coefficients. We are also testing the effect of geographical distances on the stability of scale free networks. This will enable us to propose ways to design more stable networks and to improve the stability of existing networks.

4.5 Immunization of Networks

Random immunization fails to prevent epidemics of diseases that spread in populations upon contact between infected individuals [4,5]; the same is true for immunization of computers against viruses [47]. Unless almost the entire system is immunized, the virus continues to spread through the population or computer network. To deal with this problem, the Bar-Ilan group has developed an analytical method that can accurately determine, for various scenarios, the threshold needed to stop spreading epidemics [13]. Among these possible scenarios are (i) immunizing people who are acquaintances of an infected individual and (ii) immunizing only those people who are acquaintances of at least two infected individuals.

Our recent results on social networks are complemented by analogous strategies for protecting other threatened networks, such as communication networks. For example, the Bar-Ilan group has already demonstrated that, in scale-free uncorrelated networks, if we immunize the neighbors of randomly-chosen sites, the critical threshold can be reduced by a factor of five [19]. This result has dramatic practical implications.

Our analytical approach is enabling us to study efficient immunization strategies in more realistic networks where, e.g., correlations, clustering effects, and geographical topology are taken into account. The immunization approach is also helping to develop methods to disintegrate targeted organizations, since by removing the nodes that are most relevant for immunity, the targeted network will collapse.

5 Possible Contributions of Social Network Research

(a) We are improving the tentative explanation [15] of scale-free social networks, and develop a better understanding of the range of social networks that are scale-free [16].
(b) We are developing a better understanding of the topological structures and the tomography of threatened social networks.
(c) We are developing new algorithms to improve the stability and safety of threatened networks. We are designing networks for optimal resistance to epidemics, malfunctions and attacks, and we are designing efficient and secure algorithms for organizational data flow.
(d) We are designing efficient methods for effective "immunization" that will greatly reduce spreading in threatened networks—the same mathematics describes spread of infectious agents in social networks, or "viruses" in communication networks. These methods will also help to identify weaknesses and thereby protect threatened networks.

6 Discussion

We are seeking to test whether concepts and methods of statistical physics such as scaling and percolation theory can be usefully applied to social networks, with special emphasis on social networks such as sexual networks and threatened networks. Many of the primary methods being used in our network research have been developed by our research group. These include the analytical percolation approach to general networks [11–13], the efficient immunization theory [19,13], and the DFA method [26]. We also were among the first to identify scale-free networks in certain social systems and sexual networks [14–16], and we developed an approach for classifying network topologies [17].

Acknowledgments

We thank Y. Åberg, L. A. N. Amaral, C. Edling, K. Fukuda, and F. Liljeros for collaborations on which a part of this paper is based, and ONR N00014 02 1 1033 for support.

References

1. R. Albert, H. Jeong and A.-L. Barabási, "Attack and Error Tolerance of Complex Networks," *Nature* **406**, 378–382 (2000).
2. R. Albert and A.-L. Barabási, "Statistical Mechanics of Complex Networks," *Rev. Mod. Phys.* **74**, 47–97 (2002).
3. S. N. Dorogovtsev and J. F. F. Mendes, "Evolution of Networks," *Adv. in Phys.* **51**, 1079–1187 (2002).
4. R. M. Anderson, and R. M. May, *Infectious Diseases of Humans* (Oxford University Press, Oxford, 1991).
5. A. L. Lloyd and R. M. May, "How Viruses Spread among Computers and People," *Science* **292**, 1316–1317 (2001).
6. H. E. Stanley, "Scaling, Universality, and Renormalization: Three Pillars of Modern Critical Phenomena," Reviews of Modern Physics **71**, S358–S366 (1999).
7. A.-L. Barabási, *Linked: The New Science of Networks* (Perseus Publishing, Cambridge, 2002).
8. H. E. Stanley, J. S. Andrade, S. Havlin et al., "Percolation Phenomena: A Broad-Brush Introduction with Some Recent Applications to Porous Media, Liquid Water, and City Growth," Physica A **266**, 5–16 (1999).
9. A. Bunde and S. Havlin, eds., *Fractals and Disordered Systems* (Springer, New York, 1996).
10. D. ben-Avraham and S. Havlin, *Diffusion and Reactions in Fractals and Disordered Systems* (Cambridge University Press, Cambridge, 2000).
11. R. Cohen, K. Erez, D. ben-Avraham, and S. Havlin, "Resilience of the Internet to Random Breakdown," Phys. Rev. Lett. **85**, 4626 (2000).
12. R. Cohen, K. Erez, D. ben-Avraham, and S. Havlin, "Breakdown of the Internet under Intentional Attack," Phys. Rev. Lett. **86**, 3682 (2001).
13. R. Cohen, S. Havlin, and D. ben-Avraham, "Structural Properties of Scale-Free Networks" in *Handbook of Graphs and Networks: From the Genome to the Internet*, edited by S. Bornholdt and H. G. Schuster (Wiley-VCH, Berlin, in press, 2002).
14. F. Liljeros, C. R. Edling, L. A. N. Amaral, H. E. Stanley, and Y. Åberg, "The Web of Human Sexual Contacts," Nature **411**, 907–908 (2001) cond-mat/0106507.
15. L. A. N. Amaral, C. R. Edling, F. Liljeros, and H. E. Stanley, "Mechanisms for the Formation of a Web of Sexual Contacts" (preprint).
16. F. Liljeros, L. A. N. Amaral, and H. E. Stanley, "Scale-Invariance in the Growth of Voluntary Organizations," Europhys. Lett. (submitted).

17. L. A. N. Amaral, A. Scala, M. Barthélemy, and H. E. Stanley, "Classes of Behavior of Small-World Networks," Proc. National Academy of Sciences **97**, 11149–11152 (2000).
18. L. A. Adamic, R. M. Lukose, A. R. Punyani, and B. A. Huberman, "Search in Power Law Networks," Phys. Rev. E **64**, 046135 (2001).
19. R. Cohen, D. ben-Avraham, and S. Havlin, "Efficient Immunization of Populations and Computers," cond-mat/0207387 (2002).
20. W. E. Leland, M. S. Taqqu, W. Willinger, and D. V. Wilson, "On the Self-Similar Nature of Ethernet Traffic (Extended Version)," IEEE/ACM Trans. Netw. **2**, 1 (1994).
21. V. Paxson and S. Floyd, "Wide Area Traffic: The failure of Poisson Modeling," IEEE/ACM Trans. Netw. **3**, 226 (1995).
22. K. Fukuda, H. Takayasu, and M. Takayasu, "Spatial and Temporal Behavior of Congestion in Internet Traffic," Fractals **7**, 23 (1999).
23. M. Takayasu, H. Takayasu, and K. Fukuda, "Dynamic Phase Transition Observed in Internet Traffic Flow," Physica A **277**, 248 (2000).
24. M. Takayasu, H. Takayasu, and K. Fukuda, "Application of Statistical Physics to Internet Traffic," Physica A **274**, 140 (1999).
25. E. Tomer, L. Safonov, and S. Havlin, "Presence of Many Stable Nonhomogeneous States in an Inertial Car-Following Model," Phys. Rev. Lett. **84**, 382 (2000).
26. C. K. Peng, S. Havlin, H. E. Stanley, and A. L. Goldberger, "Quantification of Scaling Exponents and Crossover Phenomena in Nonstationary Heartbeat Time Series" [*Proc. NATO Dynamical Disease Conference*], edited by L. Glass, Chaos **5**, 82–87 (1995).
27. C.-K. Peng, S. V. Buldyrev, S. Havlin, M. Simons, H. E. Stanley, and A. L. Goldberger, "On the Mosaic Organization of DNA Sequences," *Phys. Rev. E* **49** (1994) 1691–1695.
28. S. V. Buldyrev, A. L. Goldberger, S. Havlin, R. N. Mantegna, M. E. Matsa, C.-K. Peng, M. Simons, and H. E. Stanley, "Long-Range Correlation Properties of Coding and Noncoding DNA Sequences: GenBank Analysis" Phys. Rev. E **51**, 5084–5091 (1995).
29. A. Bunde, H. J. Schellnhuber, and J. Kropp, eds., *The Science of Disasters: Climate Disruptions, Heart Attacks, and Market Crashes* (Springer-Verlag, Berlin, 2002).
30. R. B. Govindan, D. Vyushin, A. Bunde, S. Brenner, S. Havlin, and H. J. Schellnhuber, "Global Climate Models Violate Scaling of the Observed Atmospheric Variability," Phys. Rev. Lett. **89**, 028501 (2002).
31. A. Bunde, S. Havlin, J. W. Kantelhardt, T. Penzel, J. H. Peter, and K. Voigt, "Correlated and Uncorrelated Regions in Heart-Rate Fluctuations during Sleep," Phys. Rev. Lett. **85**, 3736–3739 (2000).
32. J. W. Kantelhardt, E. Koscielny-Bunde, H.H.A. Rego, S. Havlin, and A. Bunde, Physica A **294**, 441 (2001).
33. K. Hu, Z. Chen, P. Ch. Ivanov, P. Carpena, and H. E. Stanley, "Effect of Trends on Detrended Fluctuation Analysis" Phys. Rev. E **64**, 011114-1 – 011114-19 (2001) physics/0103018.
34. Z. Chen, P. Ch. Ivanov, K. Hu, and H. E. Stanley, "Effect of Nonstationarities on Detrended Fluctuation Analysis" Phys. Rev. E **65**, 041107-1 to 041107-15 (2002). physics/0111103.
35. Y. Liu, P. Gopikrishnan, P. Cizeau, M. Meyer, C.-K. Peng, and H. E. Stanley, "The statistical properties of the volatility of price fluctuations" Phys. Rev. **60**, 1390-1400 (1999).

36. P. Kumar, P. Ch. Ivanov, and H. E. Stanley, "Statistical Physics and Prime Numbers" (preprint).
37. A. F. Rozenfeld, R. Cohen, D. ben-Avraham, and S. Havlin, "Scale-Free Networks on Lattices," Phys. Rev. Lett. xx, xxx–xxx (2003) cond-mat/0205613.
38. R. Cohen and S. Havlin, "Ultra Small World in Scale-Free Networks," Phys. Rev. Lett. xx, xxx–xxx (2003) cond-mat/0205476 (2002).
39. D. ben-Avraham, A. F. Rozenfeld, R. Cohen, and S. Havlin, "Geographical Embedding of Scale-Free Networks," cond-mat/0301504 (2003).
40. X. Guardiola et al., "Macro- and Microstructure of Trust networks," cond-mat/020640 (2002).
41. D. J. Watts and S. H. Strogatz, "Collective Dynamics of 'Small-World' Networks," Nature **393**, 440–442 (1998).
42. D. J. Watts, *Small Worlds: The Dynamics of Networks between Order and Randomness* (Princeton University Press, Princeton, 1999).
43. V. E. Krebs, "Mapping Networks of Terrorist Cells," Connections **24**, 43–52 (2002).
44. M. E. J. Newman, "Assortative Mixing in Networks," cond-mat/0205405 (2002).
45. R. Cohen, D. Doler, S. Havlin, T. Kalisky, O. Mohryn, and Y. Shavitt, "On the Tomography of Networks and Multicart Trees," Tech. Report TR 2002-49, Hebrew University, Israel.
46. P. Ch. Ivanov, L. A. Nunes Amaral, A. L. Goldberger, S. Havlin, M. G. Rosenblum, Z. Struzik, and H. E. Stanley, "Multifractality in Human Heartbeat Dynamics," Nature **399**, 461 (1999).
47. R. Pastor-Sattoras and A. Vespignani, "Epidemic Dyanamics and Endemic States in Compex Networks," Phys. Rev. E **63**, 066117 (2001).

SESSION III

Metrics and Models

Sensitivity Analysis of Social Network Data and Methods: Some Preliminary Results

Stanley Wasserman and Douglas Steinley
University of Illinois at Champaign-Urbana

Abstract

Four social network indices are examined in depth – degree centralization, betweenness centralization,transitivity, and efficiency. This study uses Monte Carlo techniques and standard random graph distributions to generate graphs. We seek to establish the groundwork for a general theory of resistance of network statistics.

Social network analysis has been used for the past seventy years to advance research in the social and behavioral sciences. Major breakthroughs over the past ten years, both substantive and methodological, have allowed this paradigm to greatly expand its usefulness, especially in communication, broadly defined (including internet research), organizational science, and epidemiology. The focus of this research is on the application of the paradigm to policy issues, especially those arising governmentally, and the study and expansion of standard methodology to these very important research questions. There are several major methodological questions under study:

- What are the effects, and more importantly, the implications, of measurement error on social networks?
- What can be done to control for the lack of independence of interaction measurements taken on the respondents (a common problem with egocentered networks)?
- Are there better methods for analyzing longitudinal networks, their composition and structure, than generalized linear models?

Social network analysis is discussed in detail in Wasserman and Faust (1994); further, theoretical concerns are highlighted in Monge and Contractor (2003). Applications of the paradigm to many substantive disciplines, as well as discussion of how networks have advanced these disciplines, can be found in Wasserman and Galaskiewicz (1994). *Recent* methodological developments are described in Carrington, Scott, and Wasserman (2003), written to update Wasserman and Faust (1994) by presenting advances made during the 1990's after the publication of Wasserman and Faust (1994). We will assume that most of the material presented in Wasserman and Faust (1994) is known to the reader.

Our research program has a variety of components. We first focus attention on two areas:

This research was supported by grants from the National Science Foundation (#ITS99-80189), and the Office of Naval Research (#N00014-02-1-0877). *email* addresses: stanwass@uiuc.edu; steinley@s.psych.uiuc.edu. Affiliations: Department of Psychology, Department of Statistics, and The Beckman Institute for Advanced Science and Technology.

• Robustness and resistance of network statistics and measures

• Study of the effects of measurement error (in a variety of different forms) on standard analyses

Four important statistics are: measures of connectivity (quantifying how much actors are "tied together"), actor centrality, counts of bridges, numbers and frequencies of cohesive subgroups, and the efficiency of a network.. We will look carefully at how these descriptive network statistics can be used in substantive context, and comment on their mathematical definitions, their statistical properties, their error-proneness, and their general resistance to sampling designs.

This presentation uses standard distribution theory for graphs and directed graphs (thereby allowing for parameter estimation, unlike nonconventional computational models with probabilistic assumptions). We sample from these distributions, and study the effects of modifications of distribution assumptions on the variability of standard statistics. Such studies are but a first step in a complete robustness and resistance theory for social networks.

Introduction

We begin with a graph, single set of nodes $\mathcal{N}$, and a set of lines. Here, we will only be interested in graphs, not digraphs. It is common to use this mathematical concept to represent a *social network*, a set of n actors and a collection of r social relations that specify how these actors are related to one another.

Here, we let $r = 1$, focusing just on networks with single, nondirected relations, and assuming that relational ties take on just two values.

We let $\mathcal{N} = \{1, 2, \ldots, g\}$ denote the set of actors, and $\mathcal{X}$ denote a particular relation defined on the actors. Specifically, $\mathcal{X}$ is a set of ordered pairs recording the presence or absence of relational ties between pairs of actors. This social relation can be represented by a $g \times\ g$ matrix $\mathbf{X}$, with elements

$$X_{ij} = \begin{cases} 1 \text{ if } (i,j) \in \mathcal{X}, \\ 0 \text{ otherwise.} \end{cases}$$

We will use a variety of graph characteristics and statistics throughout this presentation

Distribution theory

The first step for any probabilistic model of a network is to construct a dependence graph. Such a device allows us to distinguish among the many possible graph probability distributions, which can often be characterized by considering which relational ties are assumed to be statistically independent.

We define a dependence graph (as it applies to network relational variables) and then show how it can distinguish among basic graph distributions (such as those described in Wasserman and Faust, 1994, chapter 13). This dependence graph is also the starting point for the Hammersley–Clifford Theorem (Besag, 1974), which posits a very general probability distribution for these network random variables using the postulated dependence graph. The exact form of the dependence graph depends on the nature of the substantive hypotheses about the social network under study; we briefly discuss several such hypotheses.

Theory

Any observed single relational network may be regarded as a realization $\mathbf{x} = [x_{ij}]$ of a random two-way binary array $\mathbf{X} = [X_{ij}]$. In general, the entries of the array $\mathbf{X}$ cannot be assumed to be independent; consequently, it is helpful to specify a dependence structure for the random variables $\{X_{ij}\}$ as originally suggested by Frank and Strauss (1986).

The dependence structure for these random variables is determined by the *dependence graph* $\mathcal{D}$ of the random array $\mathbf{X}$. $\mathcal{D}$ is itself a graph whose nodes are elements of the index set $\{(i,j); i,j \in \mathcal{N}, i \neq j\}$ for the random variables in $\mathbf{X}$, and whose edges signify pairs of the random variables that are assumed to be conditionally dependent (given the values of all other random variables).

More formally, a dependence graph for a univariate social network has node set

$$\mathcal{N}_D = \{(i,j); i,j \in \mathcal{N}, i \neq j\}.$$

The edges of $\mathcal{D}$ are given by

$$\mathcal{E}_D = \{((i,j),(k,l)), \text{ where } X_{ij} \text{ and } X_{kl} \text{ are not conditionally independent}\}.$$

This specific dependence graph is a version of an *independence* graph, as it is termed in the graphical modelling literature (for example, Lauritzen, 1996; Robins, 1997); see Robins (1998) for an extended discussion of the application of graphical modelling techniques to social network models.

We also note that all of these concepts and definitions can be extended to multirelational networks (Robins and Pattison, 2002) without too much difficulty. A recent, thorough review of these ideas can be found in the trio of papers (Wasserman and Robins, 2002; Robins and Pattison, 2002; and Koehly and Pattison, 2002) written for the Carrington, Scott, and Wasserman (2003) volume.

Distributions

As Frank and Strauss (1986) observed for univariate graphs and associated two–way binary arrays, several well–known classes of distributions for random graphs may be specified in terms of the structure of the dependence graph. Pattison and Wasserman (2001) and Wasserman and Pattison (2000) note that there are three major classes — Bernoulli graphs and conditional uniform graph distributions, Dyadic dependence distributions, and p^*. Other probabilistic graph models are described by Bollobas (1985), although the primary focus in the mathematics literature is on asymptotic behavior of various graph statistics as the size of the node set increases (whereas typically in social network analysis we wish to analyze social networks on a fixed node set).

The assumption of conditional independence for all pairs of random variables representing distinct relational ties (that is, X_{ij} and X_{kl} are independent whenever $i \neq k$ and $j \neq l$) leads to the class of Bernoulli graphs (Frank and Nowicki, 1993). The dependence graph for such a distribution has no edges; it is empty. A Bernoulli graph assumes complete independence of relational ties; the probability that the tie $i \rightarrow j$ is present is P_{ij}. If $P_{ij} = 0.5$ for all ties, the distribution is often referred to as the uniform random (di)graph distribution, U. All (di)graphs are equally likely to occur; hence the uniform probability aspect of the distribution. A more general Bernoulli graph distribution fixes the P_{ij} at P; each edge can be viewed as the outcome of a biased coin toss, with probability P of a "success".

The uniform distribution U conditions on no graph properties, while the uniform distribution $U|L$, statistically conditions on the number L of edges in the graph. All (di)graphs with $L = l$

lines (arcs) are equally likely; (di)graphs with $L \neq l$ lines (arcs) have probability 0. There are many other conditional uniform distributions, including the classic $U|MAN$ distribution which fixes the counts of the dyad states and assumes that all digraphs with the specified dyad census are equally likely, and $U|\{X_{i+}\}, \{X_{+j}\}$ which fixes the outdegrees and indegrees. Many such conditional uniform distributions are described in Chapter 13 of Wasserman and Faust (1994). Some of these distributions have simple dependence graphs; for example, the $U|\{X_{i+}\}$ distribution, which fixes only the outdegrees, has a dependence graph with edge set $\mathcal{E}_D = \{((i,j),(i,k))$, for all $j \neq k$ for every $i\}$.

The assumption of conditional dependence of X_{ij} and X_{kl} if and only if $\{k,l\} = \{j,i\}$ leads to the class of dyad dependence models (see Wasserman, 1987; Wasserman and Pattison, 2000), the second family of graph distributions mentioned above. These "multinomial dyad" distributions assume all dyads are statistically independent, but the states of any specific dyad are not. It postulates substantively interesting parameterizations for the probabilities of the various dyad states. The dependence graph for such distributions has an edge set with edges connecting only the two random variables withing each dyad: $\mathcal{E}_D = \{((i,j),(j,i))$, for all $i \neq j\}$. This class of models was termed p_1 by Holland and Leinhardt (1977, 1981), and has a long history (see Chapters 15 and 16 of Wasserman and Faust 1994). Although for some parameterizations it is easy to fit, its assumption of independence across dyads is not terribly realistic.

p^*

For an observed network, which we consider to be a realization $\mathbf{x}$ of a random array $\mathbf{X}$, we assume the existence of a dependence graph $\mathcal{D}$ for the random array $\mathbf{X}$.

There are, of course, general dependence graphs, with arbitrary edge sets. Such dependence graphs yield a very general probability distribution for a(di)graph, which we have termed p^*. Such distributions belong to a very general exponential family; they are often referred to as *exponential random graph models* (perhaps a misnomer, since nearly all distributions can be rearranged into an exponential form).

One very general dependence graph, for which this distribution was first developed, assumes conditional independence of X_{ij} and X_{kl} if and only if $\{i,j\} \cap \{k,l\} = \emptyset$. This type of dependency resembles a Markov spatial process, so these dependencies were defined as a Markov graph by Frank and Strauss (1986). This p^* family of distributions has been extended in many ways, and estimates of its parameters scrutinized.

The Hammersley–Clifford theorem (Besag, 1974) establishes that a probability model for $\mathbf{X}$ depends only on the cliques of the dependence graph $\mathcal{D}$. As mentioned, application of the Hammersley–Clifford theorem yields a characterization of $Pr(\mathbf{X} = \mathbf{x})$ in the form of an exponential family of distributions, as discussed in detail, in for example, Wasserman and Robins (2002).

For our sensitivity analyses, we will postulate various, albeit simple, dependence graphs, and adopt the associated probability distribution, in order to study the effects of node and line removals on graph statistics.

Network statistics

An important concern in social network studies is the *connectivity* of a network. Connectivity measures how much actors are tied together within a network. For example, using sexual networks and disease simply for illustrative purposes, actors are unlikely to contract HIV via sexual intercourse if they are not tied to others (i.e., they are isolates). These isolates can, in fact, help to deter the spread of the disease. Conversely, networks with greater connectivity are more likely to include actors who will contract the disease due to more prevalent sexual interactions. Connectivity is also important to terrorist networks because it determines how much information can be 'transmitted' throughout a network. Lack of connectivity (i.e., isolation) can harm individuals. Although connectivity in general is a very important consideration, connectivity is dependent on time. In other words, relationships are continually beginning and ending, in a persistent state of flux. Such continual change influences the spread of information among a set of actors. There are many different connectivity measures; here, we focus on balance (frequency of transitive triads).

Centrality is also an important network measurement for most network relations. Trotter, Rothenberg, and Coyle (1995) suggest that the centrality of network members to determine the 'gatekeepers' of the network – those who function as important links within the network, linking together otherwise unconnected nodes (Freeman, 1980). Laumann, Gagnon, Michael, and Michaels (1994) define these central members as the 'core group' of a network. The number of core members within a network can substantially affect the spread of information throughout a network. A simple measure of actor degree (the number actors adjacent to a 'focal' actor) can determine which actors serve as core members. Structural characteristics of actors are also very important. In studies on terrorism, degree centrality and prestige indices would aid in finding individuals who 'determine' the sending and receiving of information. They also can help 'locate' important subgroups such as core and periphery networks, which have important consequences for individuals in these subgroups. Measures of centralization combine actor–level indices, and are straightforward to investigate.

Trotter, et al. (1995) and Laumann, et al. (1994) also discuss the importance of bridges to the connectivity of a network. A bridge is an individual (or group of individuals) that spans two disconnected subgroups. Such network measures can help to identify those people who are crucial to the connectedness of a terrorist network (usually referred to as cutpoints, see Wasserman and Faust, 1994, Ch. 4). For example, actor betweenness centrality indices could help to identify those network members who link actors to some type of influential sub-network. In this situation, the bridge member functions to 'monitor' the flow of support/information/resources within the network.

Bienenstock and Bonacich (2002) and Borgatti (2002) recently introduced a new measure to describe the efficiency of a network. Efficiency measures the average distance between all pairs of nodes in a network. When all possible pairs of nodes are connected, the efficiency of the network is equal to unity; when all of the nodes are isolates the efficiency of the network is equal to zero. Borgatti (2002) indicates that efficiency may be the key measure to consider when deciding which nodes to delete from the network in order to maximize the impact of the deletion. This especially seems to be the case when the resources used for node deletion are limited.

Sensitivity analyses

Many analyses of standard social network data sets involve summarizing the relational data with a substantively-meaningful, carefully chosen set of network statistics. Many researchers do not go the "model route", and simply focus attention on this small set of statistics, perhaps including these statistics as explanatory variables in linear models with actor measurements as responses. One hope in such studies is that the chosen statistics are not only meaningful, but are "good" statistically. But this hope begs us to ask the question: "How robust and resistant are typical, network (multirelational) statistics"?

Thus, our concern here is the robustness of network statistics, such as those theoretically relevant to the substantive applications of interest here, and to the presence or absence of particular relational ties or actors. In statistics, robustness is defined as how well a parameter estimate behaves when basic assumptions (particularly distributional assumptions) are violated. Resistance is usually defined as how well statistics behave when data become "messy", full of outliers and "ugly" observations. Since most social network studies are not parametric, resistance is perhaps the more important concern. Shouldn't a network analyst know how well his or her analysis is going to "hold up" or "behave" if some modeling assumptions change, or if some of the data are "ugly" or removed?

We term the study of resistance of network statistics *sensitivity analysis*, as it is often called in the statistical modelling literature. It should be obvious that sensitivity analyses of standard network statistics are desparately needed. For example, focus on centrality as one of these network statistics – one of the methodological tools used by the majority of network analysts, and, as mentioned earlier, a substantively-meaningful way of looking at most types of networks. It is straightforward to study how various centrality measurements change when certain ties in a relation are altered. This study can be done systematically and scientifically and should yield valuable information into the resistance of centrality indices. Statisticians have been designing studies such as these (to investigate the resistance and robustness of, say, parameter estimates) for many years. Is it not time to do the same for network analysis? All of the alterations to the relation will be made in the context of policy networks (especially those that are egocentered, longitudinal, and multirelational) so that the findings will indeed reflect what could occur in the real world.

Monte Carlo Technique

In order to study the resistance of various statistics, "artificial" sociomatrices for a nondirected relation were generated. We were concerned with three key aspects of the sociomatrix.

1. First, the number of actors (nodes) is considered. For this preliminary study, two network sizes, 10 and 25, were considered.

2. Second, the density of the sociomatrices was varied. The values of the density were determined by the maximum number of dyads ($\frac{g\times(g-1)}{2}$) possible for each sociomatrix. Starting at zero, these values were allowed to vary in steps of .1(max(dyads)). For example, for a network with 10 actors, max(dyads) = 45. Therefore, the stepsize is 5 (.1(45), after rounding). So, for a network with 10 actors, the number of ties considered were 0, 5, 10, 15, 20, 25, 30, 35, 40, and 45.

3. All matrices were generated randomly from $U|L$. For a fixed g, the appropriate number of ties were randomly assigned to the lower triangles. Following the lower triangular assignment, the sociomatrices were symmetrized.

4. Finally, 1,000 random sociomatrices were generated for each condition.

Results

Degree Centralization

The characteristics of degree centralization do not depend on the size of the network, but rather the density of the network. Furthermore, degree centralization is not monotonically related to the density of the network. In addition, when density is fixed, the observed value of degree centralization is *extremely* discrete. For example, with 10 actors and a density of 0.44, only five different values of degree centralization were observed. Table 1 provides the results for degree centralization when 10 actors are considered (the pattern of results for 25 actors was very similar). Extreme discreteness of of degree centralization is observed; specifically, it is seen that no more

Table 1: Mean and Variances of Distributions–Degree Centralization

# of Actors	# of Lines	Mean Degree Centralization	Variance	# Mass points
10	5	0.2037	0.0058	3
	10	0.2615	0.0091	5
	15	0.2874	0.0101	5
	20	0.3022	0.0100	5
	25	0.2926	0.0086	4
	30	0.2668	0.0072	3
	35	0.2243	0.0046	2
	40	0.1386	0.0000	1

than five probability mass points are observed for any given density (eight were the most observed when 25 actors were considered). Both network sizes indicate the same nonmonotonic relationship between density and degree centralization (Figure 1 indicates that the underlying distribution governing this relationship may be approximated by a binomial distribution). In any case, this may indicate that the density of the network, not the size, has the greatest effect on degree centralization.

Figure 1. Degree centrality by density for 10 actors (1,000 sociomatrices)

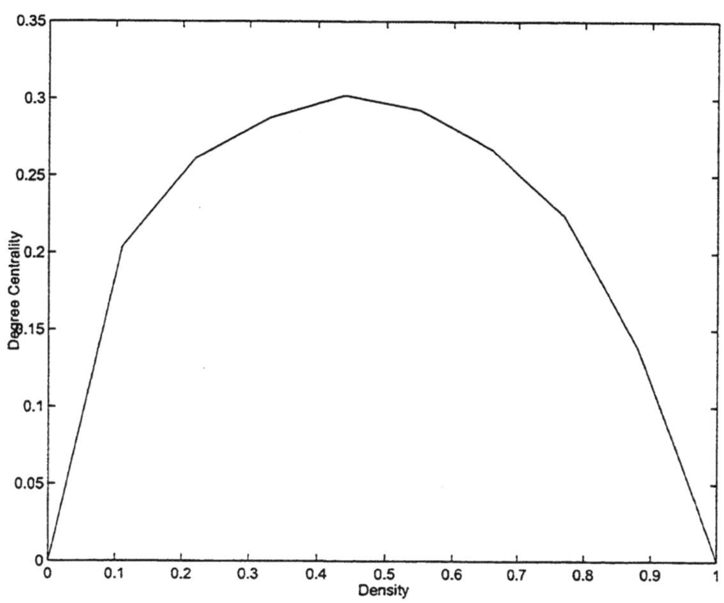

Table 2: Mean and Variances of Distributions–Betweenness Centralization

# of Actors	# of Lines	Mean Betweenness Centralization	Variance	# Mass points
10	5	0.0708	0.0020	33
	10	0.2280	0.0077	833
	15	0.2109	0.0072	960
	20	0.1666	0.0049	911
	25	0.1143	0.0024	661
	30	0.0640	0.0007	545
	35	0.0302	0.0001	581
	40	0.0084	0.0000	66

Betweenness Centralization

Like degree centralization, betweenness centralization is not dependent upon the size of the network but the density of the network. For both network sizes, the betweenness measure has a peak at a density between 0.1 and 0.2 and then proceeds to sharply decline as density increases. Table 2 indicates the results when 10 actors were examined (the same pattern was observed when the 25 actor sociomatrices were examined). A key difference between degree centralization and betweenness centralization is that the latter is not nearly as discrete. Even though several values of betweenness were observed, the small variance indicates that the values were not extremely different. Figure 2 indicates a skewed relationship between density and betweenness. Although the same skewness is present at both sizes of sociomatrices examined, the peak tends to move towards the y-axis as size increases. Figure 2 indicates that this relationship might be approximated by an F-distribution.

Balance

Balance is unlike the other two network statistics. As would be guessed, balance increases as density increases. A peculiar trait of balance is that for several small values of density it is close to zero. The exponential increase does not tend to occur until density is about 0.3 (this is observable in Table 3). Figure 3 further indicates the exponential relationship between balance and density within the sociomatrices (this relationship is the same for both network sizes) This phenomenon was observed for both network sizes studied.

Efficiency

Efficiency behaves in a similiar same manner as balance. As the density of the network increases, efficiency increases as well (this pattern of behavior was observed for both network sizes studied). This type of behavior is clear from the definition of efficiency. However, what is striking is the rapid, inverse exponential increase. This increase begins almost immediately as density increases from zero. Figure 4 indicates the initial inverse exponential relationship that eventually becomes a linear relationship when density is approximately 0.40. The only difference between the

Figure 2. Group betweenness by density for 10 actors (1,000 sociomatrices)

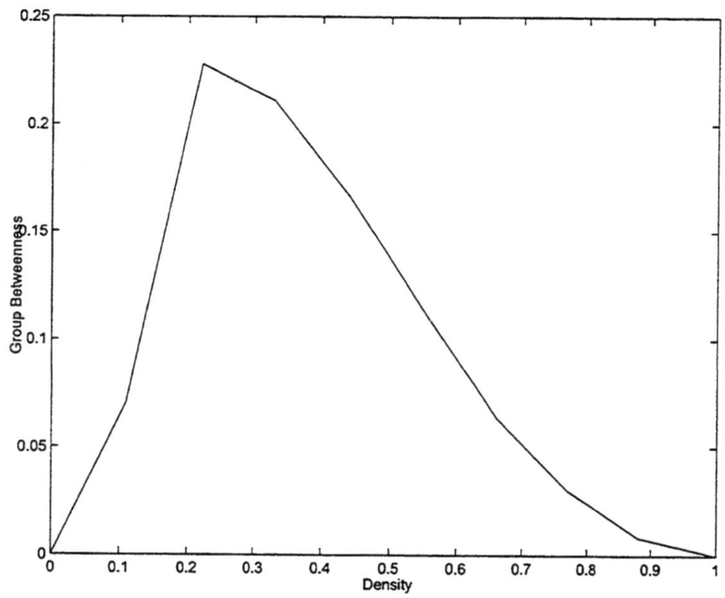

Table 3: Mean and Variances of Distributions–Balance

# of Actors	# of Lines	Mean Balance	Variance	# Mass points
10	5	0.0006	0.0000	2
	10	0.0085	0.0001	4
	15	0.0319	0.0002	10
	20	0.0808	0.0003	15
	25	0.1619	0.0004	18
	30	0.2847	0.0004	16
	35	0.4608	0.0003	15
	40	0.6965	0.0001	9

networks of 10 actors and the networks of 25 actors is the initial inverse exponential relationship is smoother in the larger sociomatrices.

Discussion

This paper begins building the framework for the analysis of resistance and sensitivity in social networks. This is accomplished through the generation of several thousand random sociomatrices with known distributions. Calculating graph statistics for the networks with known structure reveals several key features inherent in social networks.

Figure 3. Balance by density for 10 actors (1,000 sociomatrices)

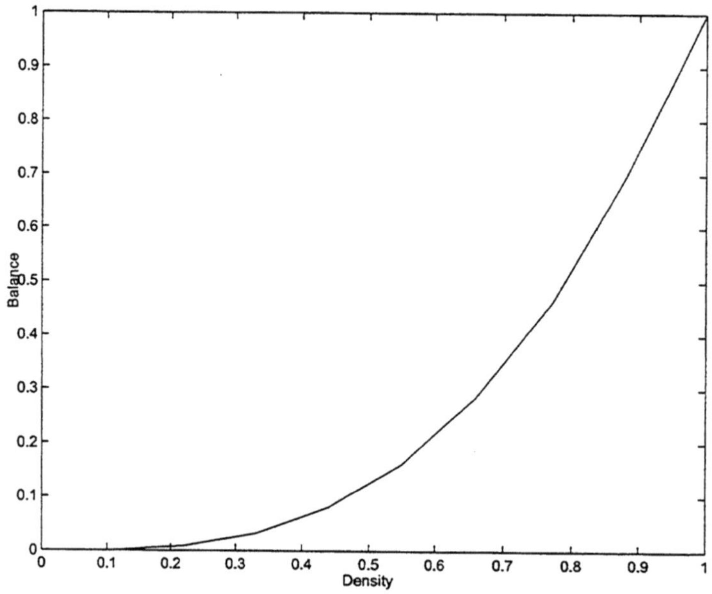

First, regardless of the network statistic, the measurement is not linearly related to the centrality of the network. Second, none of the measurements are related to centrality in the same manner or to the same degree. These two characteristics pose several interesting questions for future research.

Primarily, the interaction between the different graph statistics is crucial in determining overall sensitivity of a network. These interactions will also have an impact on determining the configuration that will lead to the optimum amount of resistance or vulnerability of a network. In addition, by establishing regular features to be expected in networks of various size and density, it will be possible to determine if a given observed network is abnormal. This observed abnormality

Table 4: Mean and Variances of Distributions–Efficiency

# of Actors	# of Lines	Mean Efficiency	Variance	# Mass points
10	5	0.1621	0.0000	2
	10	0.4413	0.0001	4
	15	0.6115	0.0002	10
	20	0.7087	0.0003	15
	25	0.7757	0.0004	18
	30	0.8332	0.0004	16
	35	0.8889	0.0003	15
	40	0.9444	0.0001	9

Figure 4. Efficiency by density for 10 actors (1,000 sociomatrices)

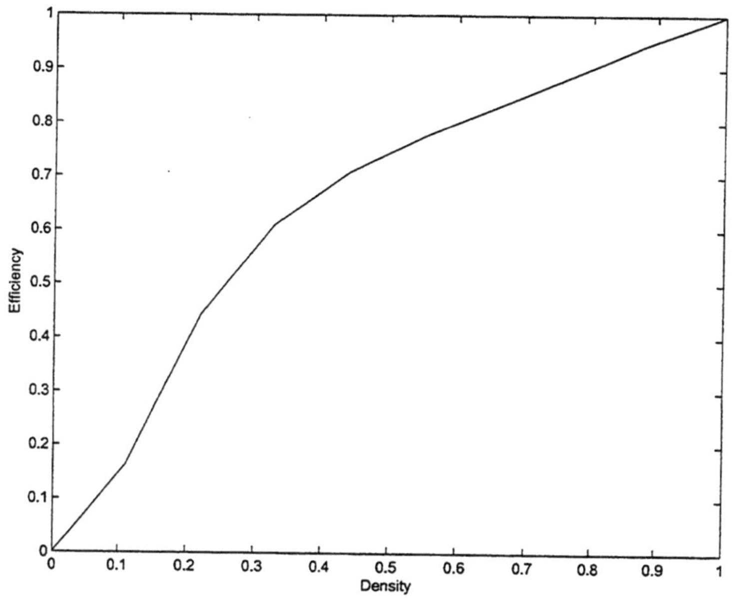

may indicate different possibilities such as: non-observed actors, non-observed links, or networks based on different underlying distributions.

Furthermore, the non-uniformity of the network statistics, as related to centrality, indicates the need to study other graph statistics in more detail. Finally, all of the work presented here will be generalized to directed graphs and additional statistics will be examined (instars, outstars, etc.). In addition to this generalization, analytical derivations of the simulation results will be pursued. This approach will possibly lead to approximating phenomena in the field of social networks with underlying statistical distributions in the same manner that is used in several other fields.

References

Besag, J.E. (1974). Spatial interaction and the statistical analysis of lattice systems (with discussion). *Journal of the Royal Statistical Society, Series B. 36*, 192–236.

Bienenstock, E. J., and Bonacich, P. (2002). Balancing efficiency and vulnerability in social networks. *Paper presented at the National Academy of Science Workshop on Social Network Analysis, Washington, D.C. (November, 2002).*

Bollobas, B. (1985). *Random Graphs.* London: Academic Press.

Borgati, S. P. (2002). The key player problem. *Paper presented at the National Academy of Science Workshop on Social Network Analysis, Washington, D.C. (November, 2002).*

Carrington, P.J., Scott, J., and Wasserman, S. (eds.) (2003). *Models and Methods in Social Network Analysis.* New York: Cambridge University Press.

Frank, O., and Nowicki, K. (1993): Exploratory statistical analysis of networks. In J. Gimbel, J. W. Kennedy, and L. V. Quintas (eds.), *Quo Vadis Graph Theory? A Source Book for Challenges and Directions.* Amsterdam: North-Holland. (also *Annals of Discrete Mathematics.*

55, 349–366.)

Frank, O., and Strauss, D. (1986). Markov graphs. *Journal of the American Statistical Association. 81*, 832–842.

Freeman, L. (1980). The gatekeeper, pair-dependency, and structural centrality. *Quality and Quantity. 14*, 585–592.

Holland, P.W., and Leinhardt, S. (1977). Notes on the statistical analysis of social network data.

Holland, P. W., and Leinhardt, S. (1981). An exponential family of probability distributions for directed graphs. *Journal of the American Statistical Association. 76*, 33–65 (with discussion).

Koehly, L.M., and Pattison, P. (2002). Random graph models for social networks: Multiple relations or multiple raters. In Carrington, P.J., Scott, J., and Wasserman, S. (eds.) *Models and Methods in Social Network Analysis.* New York: Cambridge University Press.

Laumann, E.O., Gagnon, J.H., Michael, R.T., and Michaels, S. (1994). *The Social Organization of Sexuality.* Chicago: University of Chicago Press.

Lauritzen, S. (1996). *Graphical Models.* Oxford: Oxford University Press.

Monge, P., and Contractor, N. (2003). *Theories of Communication Networks.* New York: Oxford University Press.

Pattison, P., and Wasserman, S. (2001). Social network models, statistical. In Smelser, N.J., and Baltes, P.B. (eds.) *International Encyclopedia of the Social and Behavioral Sciences.* London: Elsevier Science.

Robins, G.L. (1997). Graphical modelling. *Chance. 10*, 37–40.

Robins, G.L. (1998). *Personal Attributes in Inter-personal Contexts: Statistical Models for Individual Characteristics and Social Relationships.* Unpublished doctoral dissertation, Department of Psychology, University of Melbourne.

Robins, G.L., and Pattison, P. (2002). Interdependencies and social processes: Dependence graphs and generalized dependence structures. In Carrington, P.J., Scott, J., and Wasserman, S. (eds.), *Models and Methods in Social Network Analysis.* New York: Cambridge University Press.

Trotter II, R.T., Rothenberg, R.B., and Coyle, S. (1995). Drug abuse and HIV prevention research: Expanding paradigms and network contributions to risk reduction. *Connections. 18*, 29–45.

Wasserman, S. (1987). Conformity of two sociometric relations. *Psychometrika. 52*, 3-18.

Wasserman, S., and Faust, K. (1994). *Social Network Analysis: Methods and Applications.* New York: Cambridge University Press.

Wasserman, S., and Galaskiewicz, J. (1994) (eds). *Advances in Social Network Analysis: Research from the Social and Behavioral Sciences.* Newbury Park, CA: Sage Publications.

Wasserman, S., and Pattison, P. (2000). Statistical models for social networks. In Kiers, H., Rasson, J., Groenen, P., and Schader, M. (eds). *Studies in Classification, Data Analysis, and Knowledge Organization..* Heidelberg: Springer–Verlag.

Wasserman, S., and Pattison, P. (2002). *Multivariate Random Graph Distributions.* Springer Lecture Note Series in Statistics.

Wasserman, S., and Robins, G.L. (2002). Introduction to random graphs, dependence graphs, and p^*. In Carrington, P.J., Scott, J., and Wasserman, S. (eds.), *Models and Methods in Social Network Analysis.* New York: Cambridge University Press.

Spectral methods for analyzing and visualizing networks: an introduction

Andrew J. Seary and William .D. Richards
School of Communication
Simon Fraser University
Burnaby BC Canada V5A-1S6
seary@sfu.ca richards@sfu.ca

Abstract

Network analysis begins with data that describes the set of relationships among the members of a system. The goal of analysis is to obtain from the low-level relational data a higher-level description of the structure of the system which identifies various kinds of patterns in the set of relationships. These patterns will be based on the way individuals are related to other individuals in the network. Some approaches to network analysis look for clusters of individuals who are tightly connected to one another; some look for sets of individuals who have similar patterns of relations to the rest of the network. Other methods don't "look for" anything in particular — instead, they construct a continuous multidimensional representation of the network in which the coordinates of the individuals can be further analyzed to obtain a variety of kinds of information about them and their relation to the rest of the network.

One approach to this is to choose a set of axes in the multidimensional space occupied by the network and *rotate* them so that the first axis points in the direction of the greatest variability in the data; the second axis, orthogonal to the first, points in the direction of greatest remaining variability, and so on. This set of axes is a coordinate system that can be used to describe the relative positions of the set of points in the data. Most of the variability in the locations of points will be accounted for by the first few dimensions of this coordinate system. The coordinates of the points along each axis will be an *eigenvector*, and the length of the projection will be an *eigenvalue*. The set of all eigenvalues is the *spectrum* of the network.

Spectral methods (eigendecomposition) have been a part of graph theory for over a century. Network researchers have used spectral methods either implicitly or explicitly since the late 1960's, when computers became generally accessible in most universities. The eigenvalues of a network are intimately connected to important topological features such as maximum distance across the network (diameter), presence of cohesive clusters, long paths and bottlenecks, and how random the network is. The associated eigenvectors can be used as a natural coordinate system for graph visualization; they also provide methods for discovering clusters and other local features. When combined with other, easily obtained network statistics (e.g., node degree), they can be used to describe a variety of network properties, such as degree of robustness (i.e., tolerance to removal of selected nodes or links), and other structural properties, and the relationship of these properties to node or link attributes in large, complex, multivariate networks.

We introduce three types of spectral analysis for graphs and describe some of their mathematical properties. We discuss the strengths and weaknesses of each type and show how they can be used to understand network structure. These discussions are accompanied by interactive graphical displays of small (n=50) and moderately large (n=5000) networks. Throughout, we give special attention to sparse matrix methods which allow rapid, efficient storage and analysis of large networks. We briefly describe algorithms and analytic strategies that allow spectral analysis and identification of clusters in very large networks (n>1,000,000).

Introduction

A standard method in statistics for handling multivariate data is to find the directions of maximum variability, usually of variance-covariance or correlation matrices. These directions are called Principal Coordinates or *eigenvectors,* while the relative importance of each direction is represented by numbers called *eigenvalues*. (Jolliffe, 1986) Finding this coordinate system may be accomplished by a series of *rotations* (although this is not the most efficient method) that end up pointing along the direction of maximum variability, with the second largest maximum variability at right angles, and so on. As a result, the data matrix is reduced to a diagonal matrix, with diagonal entries corresponding to the *importance* (*eigenvalue*) of each direction (*eigenvector*). The collection of *all* eigenvalues is called the *spectrum*. One goal is to reduce the problem so that only the most important dimensions (those with the largest eigenvalues) contain most of the variability. Implicit in these methods (variance-covariance or correlation) is that some kind of "expected" or "background" signal has been subtracted: in the case of variances, these would be the means of each variable in the original data matrix. To find these *eigenvectors* and *eigenvalues* we need to solve the *eigenvalue equation*:

$$\mathbf{E}\,\mathbf{e} = \varepsilon\,\mathbf{e}$$

(we will derive this equation below) which states that along the direction represented by vector **e**, multiplication by data matrix **E** does not change the direction, but only the length (where ε may be any number, including 0).[1] The related pair (ε,**e**) is called an *eigenpair* of matrix **E**.

A *network* or *graph* G(V,E) is a set of *nodes* V (points, vertices) connected by a set of *links* E (lines, edges). We will consider networks that are *binary* (edges have logical value 1 if an edge exists, 0 if not), *symmetric* (an edge from node *i* to *j* implies an edge from node *j* to *i*), *connected* (there is a set of edges connecting any two nodes, consequently only one *component*), and *without self-loops* (no edges between i and i). We may represent such a network as the *adjacency* matrix **A** = **A**(G) with:

1 in row *i*, column *j* if *i* is connected to *j*,

0 otherwise.

We will not directly discuss *weighted* networks, where the entries for an edge may be a number other than 1, although most of the results that follow generalize to such networks. For many "real world" networks, **A** consists mostly of 0's: it is *sparse*. We will discuss efficient ways of storing and manipulating **A** using *sparse methods*.

Associated with **A** is the *degree distribution* **D**, a diagonal matrix with row-sums of **A** along the diagonal, and 0's elsewhere. **D** describes how many connections each node has. We call the number of nodes, m, the *order* of G and it is equal to the number of rows or columns of **A**. We represent the number of edges by |E|. We will also introduce two other matrices related to **A**:

- the *Laplacian:* $\mathbf{L} = \mathbf{D} - \mathbf{A}$
- the *Normal:* $\mathbf{N} = \mathbf{D}^{-1}\mathbf{A}$

and will discuss the properties of the spectrum and associated eigenvectors of **A**, **L**, and **N**.

---

[1] We have introduced some notation which will be followed throughout:

- matrices are represented by bold capitals: **D**
- (column-)vectors are represented by bold lower case: **e**
- inner products of vectors are represented as $\mathbf{e}^T\mathbf{e} = n$ (a scalar) where $\mathbf{e}^T$ is the transpose of **e**.
- outer products of vectors are represented as $\mathbf{e}\mathbf{e}^T = \mathbf{M}$ (a matrix)
- eigenvalues are represented by greek letters, usually with some relationship to the latin letters representing a matrix and an eigenvector. E.g.,(α_i, $\mathbf{a}_i$) is an eigenpair of adjacency matrix **A**.

Distances and diameter:

One important property of a network is the set of *distances* between any pair of nodes *i* and *j*; that is, the least number of links between any pairs *i* and *j*. One way of calculating this is to take *powers* of the matrix **A** as follows:

1st power **A** = **A** by definition gives a matrix of all pairs of nodes linked to each other.

2nd power = **AA** has a non-zero in row *i* column *j* if *j* is two steps away from *i*. Since *i* is 2 steps away from itself, the diagonal *i,i* entry counts the number of these 2-steps.

3rd power = **AAA** has a non-zero entry in row *i* column *j* if *j* is 3 steps away from *i*.

Eventually, some power of **A**, say $\mathbf{A}^N$, will consist of entirely non-zero entries, meaning every node has been reached from every other node. We call N the *diameter* of the graph: the longest possible path between any pair of nodes.

This is a very inefficient way of calculating the diameter of a graph for two reasons:

1) calculating each power of **A** requires m^3 calculations

2) as more nodes are reached, the powers of **A** become less sparse until eventually no 0's remain: the amount of storage required approaches m^2.

If we continue taking powers of **A**, an interesting thing happens: all the columns become multiples of each other. Taking higher powers of **A** corresponds to taking longer "walks" along the edges and we can interpret this as a "loss of memory" about where we started from (Lovasz, 1995). We will see why this happens soon, as well as other examples of this phenomenon.

We can approach this problem another way by the properties of the *spectral decompositon* of **A** (Parlett, 1980). Let α_i be the eigenvalues of **A** and $\mathbf{a}_i$ the corresponding eigenvectors, with $\alpha_0 \geq \alpha_1 \geq \alpha_2 \ldots \geq \alpha_{m-1}$ and $\|\mathbf{a}_i\| = 1$ (the eigenvectors are *normalized* to length 1). Then the spectral decomposition of **A** is:

(1) $\mathbf{A} = \Sigma_i (\alpha_i)\mathbf{a}_i \mathbf{a}_i^T$ where $\mathbf{a}_i \mathbf{a}_i^T$ is an m×m matrix defining a 1-dimension subspace and $(\mathbf{a}_i \mathbf{a}_i^T)^N = \mathbf{a}_i \mathbf{a}_i^T$ if $i=j$; $\mathbf{a}_i \mathbf{a}_j^T = \mathbf{0}$ if $i \neq j$

therefore $\mathbf{A}^N = \Sigma_i (\alpha_i)^N \mathbf{a}_i \mathbf{a}_i^T$ for any power N, and this allows an easy way of calculating powers of **A**, assuming we have already calculated all the eigenpairs $(\alpha_i, \mathbf{a}_i)$.

Another important property of the spectral decomposition is the *approximation* property. If we take the first k of the eigenpairs $(\alpha_i, \mathbf{a}_i)$, then $\mathbf{A}_k = \sum_{i=0}^{k} \alpha_i \mathbf{a}_i \mathbf{a}_i^T$ is the *best least-squares approximation* to **A**, meaning that we have captured most of the variability of **A** in the important eigenpairs. For example, we can *estimate* an *upper bound* for the diameter using the second-largest eigenvalue α_1 (Chung, 1989):

$$\mathrm{Diam}(G) \leq \lceil \ln(m-1)/\ln(k/\alpha_1) \rceil$$

Unfortunately, this bound applies only to k-*regular* networks (all degrees = k = α_0). We will get better bounds for general networks using different spectra. Nevertheless, this bound does show one relationship between the spectrum and an important property like diameter. In particular, when k/α_1 is *large* (there is a large *gap* between the first two eigenvalues), the upper bound on diameter is *small*, so all distances are short.

The Power Method and Sparse methods:

Using **(1)** and eigenpair (α_0 , $\mathbf{a}_0$) we can see why taking taking large enough powers of **A** results in columns that are multiples of one another – in fact, multiples of eigenvector $\mathbf{a}_0$. This is the basis of the *Power method* (Hotelling, 1933) for finding eigenpairs. We have mentioned that taking powers of matrix **A** is not efficient, so we introduce a representation and methods that are far more efficient.

A very simple way of storing and manipulating a sparse matrix **A** is to use a *link list* representation, which stores only the non-zero entries of **A** as a list of pairs *i,j* for each link in **A**. We could then calculate the diameter of **A** by starting at *i*=1 and following each link until we have reached every node, repeat for *i*=2, and save the maximum number of steps. This requires about m|E| operations (Aho, *et al.*, 1987) and a very moderate amount storage equal to 2|E|. We can now use **(1)** to devise a very efficient version of the Power Method for finding the largest eigenpair:

Starting with some random vector **p** normalized to length 1:

Repeat $\mathbf{p'} \leftarrow \mathbf{Ap}$, $\mathbf{q} \leftarrow \mathbf{p}$, $\mathbf{p} \leftarrow \mathbf{p'}$ until **p** is no longer changing in direction.

Then the largest eigenpair of **A** is (**p**/**q**, **p**). There are some bookkeeping details: **Ap** uses the link list representation, and the entries of **p'** must be adjusted in size after each multiplication (for details see Richards & Seary, 2000), but the method will always work for any matrix *without repeated eigenvalues*, which is generally the case for social networks.

If we want more eigenpairs, we can iterate with

$$\mathbf{p'} \leftarrow \mathbf{Mp} - \alpha_0 \mathbf{a}_0 \mathbf{a}_0^T$$

to get the second, and with

$$\mathbf{p'} \leftarrow \mathbf{Mp} - \alpha_0 \mathbf{a}_0 \mathbf{a}_0^T - \alpha_1 \mathbf{a}_1 \mathbf{a}_1^T$$

to get the third, and so on, without destroying sparsity. However, we must store the (α_i, $\mathbf{a}_i$) eigenpairs somewhere; the procedure is subject to loss of precision on a computer; and the iterations may converge slowly if α_i / α_{i-1} is close to 1. There are better methods, such as Lanczos iteration (Parlett *et al.*,1982) which converge very rapidly and do not have problems with loss of precision.

Some network invariants:

Some properties of **A** remain unchanged (*invariant*) under the series of orthogonal rotations that diagonalize **A** (eigendecomposition). We will relate these to some *network invariants* of **A**.

The eigenvalues of any symmetric matrix **M** are the roots of the *characteristic polynomial*:

$$x^m + c_1 x^{m-1} + c_2 x^{m-2} + c_3 x^{m-3} \ldots + c_{m-1}$$

Therefore, $c_1 = \alpha_0 + \alpha_1 + \ldots + \alpha_{m-1}$ (sum over all eigenvalues) of **A**;

$c_2 = \alpha_0 \alpha_1 + \alpha_0 \alpha_2 \ldots + \alpha_0 \alpha_{m-1} \ldots + \alpha_{m-3} \alpha_{m-1} + \alpha_{m-2} \alpha_{m-1}$ (sum over all pairs);

$c_3 = \alpha_0 \alpha_1 \alpha_2 + \alpha_0 \alpha_1 \alpha_3 + \ldots + \alpha_{m-3} \alpha_{m-2} \alpha_{m-1}$ (sum over all triples)

The *trace* of a matrix is the sum of the entries on the diagonal, and this is invariant under orthogonal rotations. Since **A** has trace of 0 (no self-loops), $c_1 = 0$. The sum of product pairs is equal to minus the number of edges so that $c_2 = -|E|$. Most important is c_3 which is twice the number of triangles in G. Higher coefficients are related to cycles of length 4, 5,... although they also contain contributions for shorter cycles (Biggs, 1993). It appears that the eigenvalues of **A** encode information about the cycles of a network as well as its diameter. We will see related results for the other two spectra.

A *bipartite* network is one that can be partitioned so that the nodes in one part have connections only to nodes in the other part, and vice-versa. Such a network cannot have odd cycles (of any length) and hence no triangles. This means *all* the odd coefficients c_{2k-1} must be 0. It can also be shown (Biggs, 1993) that, in bipartite networks, the eigenvalues occur in pairs with opposite signs, so that $\alpha_0 = -\alpha_{m-1}$ and so on. Bipartite networks can be used to represent *two-mode networks* (Wasserman & Faust, 1994), for example the network relating people and the events they attend.

These results scratch the surface of the information contained in the spectrum of **A** for k-regular graphs. For general graphs, we need to turn to other spectra.[2]

The Laplacian spectrum:

The Laplacian of a network was originally discovered by Kirchoff (1847). There are a number of definitions and derivations, perhaps the most revealing due to Hall (1970), who was interested in situating the nodes of any network so that total edge lengths are minimized.

He considers the problem of finding the *minimum* of the weighted sum

(2) $z = 1/2\sum_{i,j}(x_i - x_j)^2 a_{ij}$

where a_{ij} are the elements of the adjacency matrix **A**. The sum is over all pairs of squared distances between nodes *which are connected*, and so the solution should result in nodes with large numbers of inter-connections being clustered together.

Equation **(2)** can be re-written as:

$$= 1/2\sum_{i,j}(x_i^2 - 2x_i x_j + x_j^2) a_{ij} \qquad = 1/2\sum_i x_i^2 a_{ij} - 1/2\sum_{i,j} 2x_i x_j a_{ij} + 1/2\sum_j x_j^2 a_{ij}$$

$$= \sum_i x_i^2 a_{ij} + \sum_i \sum_{i,j} x_i x_j a_{ij} \qquad = \mathbf{X^T L X}$$

where $\mathbf{L = D - A}$ is the Laplacian. In addition to this, Hall supplies the condition that $\mathbf{X^T X} = 1$, i.e., the distances are normalized. Using Lagrange multipliers (a standard method for solving problems with constraints), we have:

$$\mathbf{z = X^T L X - \lambda X^T X}$$

and to minimize this expression, we take derivatives with respect to X to give:

(3) $\mathbf{LX - \lambda X} = 0$ or $\mathbf{LX = \lambda X}$

which is the eigenvalue equation. It is not hard to show that $\lambda_0 = 0$ with $\mathbf{1}_0 = \mathbf{1}$, the constant (or *trivial*) eigenvector, and that $0 = \lambda_0 \leq \lambda_1 \leq \ldots \lambda_{m-1}$. For **L**, the most "important" eigenvectors belong to the smallest eigenvalues (Pothen, *et al.*, 1990).

It turns out that the discrete network Laplacian shares many important properties with the well-known continuous Laplacian *operator* ∇^2 of mathematical physics. This has led to an explosion of research and results, mostly concerned with λ_1 (Bein, 1991).

The definition of **L** shows that there is no loss of sparsity (except for the diagonal) and that the sparse methods mentioned earlier can be applied to find all or some of the eigenpairs. The requirement that we must find the *smallest* eigenpairs is easily overcome by subtracting a suitably large constant from the diagonal of -**L** (which subtracts that constant from the eigenvalues without changing the eigenvectors).This guarantees that the first eigenpairs returned by the Power Method or Lanczos iteration are associated with the smallest eigenvalues of **L**.

[2] Similar results may be obtained from the *moments* of the eigenvalue distribution (Farkas. *et al.*, 2001; Gho, *et al.*, 2001)

Some of the coefficients of the characteristic polynomial of **L** have an easy interpretation:

c_1 = Trace(**L**) = 2|E| (i.e., twice the number of edges)

$c_{m-1} = 0$ (since 0 is an eigenvalue)

$| m\, c_{m-1} | = \lambda_0 \lambda_1 ... \lambda_{m-1} + \lambda_0 \lambda_2 ... \lambda_{m-1} + ... + \lambda_1 \lambda_2 ... \lambda_{m-1} = \lambda_1 \lambda_2 ... \lambda_{m-1}$ = the number of *spanning trees* of G (this is the Matrix-tree theorem of Kirchoff, 1847).

In general, the eigenvalues of **L** encode information about the *tree-structure* of G (Cvetkovic, *et al.*, 1995). The spectrum of **L** contains a 0 for every connected component. There is no such direct way to find the number of components of a network from the spectrum of **A**. There is also a bound on diameter related to λ_{m-1} and λ_1 for general graphs from Chung, *et al.*, (1994):

$$\mathrm{Diam}(G) \le \lceil \cosh^{-1}(m-1) / \cosh^{-1}((\lambda_{m-1} + \lambda_1)/(\lambda_{m-1} - \lambda_1)) \rceil$$

Intuitively, if λ_1 is close to 0, the graph is almost disconnected, while if $\lambda_1 >> \lambda_0$ (an eigenvalue gap) the diameter is small.

The Normal spectrum:

We can repeat the same argument as Hall to derive the Normal spectrum, with the normalization constraint that $\mathbf{X}^T\mathbf{D}\mathbf{X} = 1$ (Seary & Richards, 1995) to give:

$\mathbf{LX} = \mu\, \mathbf{DX}$, or assuming that **D** can be inverted,

$$\mathbf{D}^{-1}\mathbf{LX} = \mathbf{D}^{-1}(\mathbf{D} - \mathbf{A})\mathbf{X} = (\mathbf{I} - \mathbf{D}^{-1}\mathbf{A})\mathbf{X} = \mu\, \mathbf{X}$$

where **I** is an *identity* matrix of proper size. In fact, we usually take the defining equation to be

$$\textbf{(4)}\quad \mathbf{D}^{-1}\mathbf{AX} = \mathbf{NX} = \nu\, \mathbf{X} \quad \text{with} \quad \mathbf{D}^{-1}\mathbf{A} = \mathbf{N} \quad \text{and} \quad \nu = 1 - \mu$$

since adding an identity matrix shifts the eigenvalues by 1 without changing the eigenvectors. Note that for connected networks **D** not only has an inverse, it also has an inverse *square root* $\mathbf{D}^{-1/2}$.

The *Normal* matrix **N** has a number of interesting properties:

1) It is a *generalized* Laplacian (with a different definition of orthonormality)
2) It therefore has a *trivial* eigenvector $\mathbf{n}_0$ with eigenvalue $\nu_0 = 1$
3) The spectrum of **N** is bounded by $1 = \nu_0 \ge \nu_1 ... \ge \nu_{m-1} \ge -1$
4) The rows of **N** sum to 1 (it is a *stochastic* matrix)
5) The spectrum of **N** contains a 1 for every connected component
6) The eigenvalue -1 only occurs if G is bipartite, in which case all eigenvalues occur in pairs.
7) **N** has been rediscovered a number of times: generalized or combinatorial Laplacian (Dodziuk & Kendall, 1985; Chung,1995); Q-spectrum (Cvetkovic, *et al.*,1995).

The descriptive name Normal is suggested by points 2) - 5), although it is not standard terminology.

It is easy to see that there is no loss of sparsity in the definition of **N**. Each 1 in row *i* is simply replaced by $1/\mathbf{D}_{ii}$ and the 0's are unchanged, but **N** is no longer symmetric. However, the matrix $\mathbf{D}^{-1/2}\mathbf{A}\,\mathbf{D}^{-1/2}$ is *similar* to **N** (has the same eigenvalues) and we can apply the sparse methods described above to solve for the eigenpairs (ν_i, $\mathbf{e}_i$) and then calculate $D^{-1/2}\, \mathbf{e}_i = \mathbf{n}_i$ to get the corresponding eigenvectors without losing precision or sparsity.

For **N**, the coefficients of the characteristic equation are harder to interpret except in special cases, but the eigenvalues encode information about *both* the cycle *and* tree structure of G

(Cvetkovic, *et al.*, 1995). Some examples:

$c_1 = \text{Trace}(\mathbf{N}) = 0$

$c_3 = c_{2k-1} = 0$ (no triangles or other odd cycles) if G is bipartite

$\Pi_i \deg(i)/\Sigma_i \deg(i)\ \Sigma_{i=1}(1-v_i)$ = number of spanning trees of G

In the last example we see how details of the degree distribution are *also* encoded in the spectrum. Fan Chung uses this to derive two remarkable bounds (see Chung, 1995 for details):

$$Diam(G) \leq \max \left[\frac{\cosh^{-1}\sqrt{\dfrac{vol\,\overline{X}\ vol\,\overline{Y}}{vol\,X\ vol\,Y}}}{\cosh^{-1}\dfrac{(v_{n-1}+v_1)}{(v_{n-1}-v_1)}} \right] \qquad \min_{i\neq j} dist(X_i, X_j) = \max_{i\neq j} \left[\frac{\ln\sqrt{\dfrac{vol\,\overline{X}_i\ vol\,\overline{X}_j}{vol\,X_i\ vol\,X_j}}}{\ln\dfrac{(v_{n-1}+v_k)}{(v_{n-1}-v_k)}} \right]$$

where vol X is the total number of edges in a subset of nodes $X \subset V$ and $\overline{X}$ is V-X. Chung's first bound applies to *any* graph (regular or not) and is much tighter than the previous bound (for the Laplacian). Intuitively, if v_1 is close to 1, the network has a long path or is almost disconnected, and if $v_1 << 1$, the diameter is small.

Chung's second bound describes the distance between subsets for any number k of subsets, based on the kth eigenvalue. The result suggests that we can use the eigenvalues to estimate how many subsets we should look for in a network without forcing distances that are too short (and hence too many subsets).

Interpreting the Spectra:

Many important properties of the spectrum of **A**(G) where G is k-regular are true for **L**(G) and **N**(G), even when G is not regular. Another way of looking at this is that these properties of **A** are true because the spectrum of **A** is simply related to those of **L** and **N** for regular graphs: ($\alpha_i = k-\lambda_i = v_i/k$ for k-regular graphs, with the corresponding eigenvectors being identical). In other words, both **L** and **N** are more natural function of graphs. This point of view is shared by the authors of recent papers on the Laplacian (Grone, *et al.*, 1990, 1994). Mohar (1991) presents a collection of important results relating to the spectrum and eigenvectors of L. Chung (1995) has written several papers and a book about **N**.

We return to the goal expressed in the opening paragraph. We would like to find the most important global features of a network, after accounting for what could be considered "expected" for a random network with the same number of nodes and edges. The biggest problem with interpreting the spectrum of **A** is the lack of an "expected" eigenvector (again, except for k-regular graphs). There is a lot of literature on the so-called "main eigenvectors" of **A**: those which have a *projection* on the "all-ones" vector (e.g., Harary & Schwenk, 1979), but the results remain hard to interpret (Cvetkovic and Rowlinson,1990). Both **L** and **N** have an "expected" all-ones eigenvector for which the interpretation is clear (though different in each case).

To interpret **L**, we turn to physical analogy and the relation to ∇^2 as discussed by Friedman (1993). He considers a graph G as a discrete *manifold* (surface) subject to "free" boundary conditions.[3] For illustration, consider ∇^2 as the spatial part of the wave equation (Fisher, 1966,

[3] no external constraints need to be satisfied

Chavel, 1984). Think of a fishing net subject to no forces. It just lies there at 0 energy with nothing happening. As we subject it to regular oscillations, the net vibrates with the most highly-connected regions moving together. Friedman shows how the Hilbert Nodal theorem (Courant & Hilbert, 1965) can be applied to a discrete network, which generalizes Fiedler's result (described below): the kth eigenvector divides the network into no more than k+1 *disconnected* components.[4]

To interpret **N**, we have a number of choices:

1) **N** is the Laplacian for a network of nodes, each *weighted* by its degree

2) **N** is the transition matrix of a Markov Chain for a simple random walk on the nodes

3) $\mathbf{N}^2$ is similar to the χ^2 matrix, thus treating **A** as a *contingency table*

The first leads to a physical analogy similar to that for **L**, so we consider 2) and 3):

The Normal spectrum and Random walks:

Specifically, we consider nearest-neighbour random walks on a network (Lawler & Sokal, 1988). Define the probability-transition matrix for such a walk as

$$\mathbf{N} = \mathbf{D}^{-1}\,\mathbf{A}$$

Then the probability of moving from vertex *i* to any vertex adjacent to *i* is uniform. **N** is a row-stochastic matrix, and the random walk is a Markov chain. In this case **1** (the trivial all-ones eigenvector) is related to the *stationary state* of the Markov Chain: the probability is $1 = \nu_0$ that such a probability distribution is eventually reached.[5] The vector $\mathbf{p}_0 = \mathbf{1}^T\,\mathbf{N} = \mathbf{N}^T\,\mathbf{1}$ is the stationary state, and it is *proportional* to the degree distribution. The second eigenpair (ν_1, $\mathbf{n}_1$) has become important in the analysis of *rapidly mixing* Markov chains – those that reach the stationary state quickly (Sinclair, 1995). From the previous discussion it should not be surprising that these are associated with $\nu_1 << 1$ (a large eigenvalue gap), which means that the walk quickly "forgets" where it started.[6] Moreover, when ν_1 is close to 1, there must be parts of the network that are hard to reach in a random walk, implying long paths or a nearly disconnected network.

Normal spectrum and χ^2:

The χ^2 matrix is defined in terms of the row and column *marginals* (sums). A typical element is $(\text{Observed}_{ij} - \text{Expected}_{ij})^2 / \text{Expected}_{ij}$ which is not sparse. For a sparse network **A**, consider χ which has a typical element $(\text{Observed}_{ij} - \text{Expected}_{ij}) / \sqrt{\text{Expected}_{ij}}$ where

$$\text{Expected}_{ij} = \frac{\deg(i)\deg(j)}{\sum \deg(i)}$$

---

[4] This interpretation of the eigenvectors may be even more useful when considering ∇^2 as the spatial part of the *Diffusion* equation (for example, when considering diffusion of innovation or disease).

[5] A problem can arise with bipartite graphs: $\mathbf{p}_0$ does not exist since the chain oscillates between the two sets of vertices (period = 2). Probabilists deal with this by a simple trick: divide **N** by 2 and add a self-loop of probability 1/2 to every vertex: $\mathbf{N}' = \mathbf{I}/2 + \mathbf{N}/2$ The eigenvalues of **N'** are then: $1 = \nu'_0 \le \nu'_1 \le \ldots \le \nu'_{m-1} \le 0$ so that $\nu' = (1+\nu)/2$ and again the eigenvectors are not affected. In effect, this suppresses *all* negative eigenvalues. However, negative eigenvalues are useful for directed and bipartite networks.

[6] As we saw, $\mathbf{A}^K$ shows a similar phenomenon, but there is no simple relation to **D**, due to "leakage" from all the "main eigenvectors" (Cvetkovic, *et al.*, 1988)

We can write χ as: $\frac{O}{\sqrt{E}} - \sqrt{E}$ so that non-zero elements of **A** become $A_{ij} / \sqrt{E_{ij}}$ while the 0 terms are unaffected, maintaining sparsity. The second term corresponds to the trivial eigenvector which can be dealt with separately. In matrix notation $\chi = \mathbf{D}^{-1/2}\mathbf{A}\,\mathbf{D}^{-1/2}$ which has eigenpairs $(\nu_i, \mathbf{D}^{1/2}\mathbf{n}_i)$ Thus we have

(5) $\chi^2 = \Sigma_{j=1} \nu_i^2 / \Sigma_i a_{ij}$ (omitting the ν_0=1 expected term for $\mathbf{n}_i = \mathbf{1}$)

This equation shows how much each dimension contributes to χ^2 which is a measure of *dependence* between rows and columns. In this interpretation, if ν_1 is small ($\nu_1 << \nu_0 = 1$), then χ^2 is also small: there is no relation between rows and columns of **A**, and so there is no "signal" above the expected "background". If ν_1 is close to 1, then χ^2 will be large and there is a relation between rows and columns of **A**, with the first eigenvector pointing in the direction of the maximum variability in χ^2. If $\nu_2, \nu_3, \ldots \nu_k$ are also large, we need k+1 eigenvectors to describe the patterns in the χ^2 matrix. With **(5)** we can tell how many eigenvectors we need to explain most of the χ^2 of the network.[7]

Compositions

The *Kronecker product* of two binary matrices $\mathbf{A}_1$ and $\mathbf{A}_2$ makes a *copy* of $\mathbf{A}_1$ for each 1 in $\mathbf{A}_2$. It is well-know that for two matrices $\mathbf{A}_1$ and $\mathbf{A}_2$ of order m_1 and m_2 the eigenpairs of the Kronecker product $\mathbf{A}_1 \otimes \mathbf{A}_2$ *behave well* (West, 1996):

If $\mathbf{A}_1$ has eigenpairs $(\alpha_i, \mathbf{a}_i)$ and $\mathbf{A}_2$ has eigenpairs $(\beta_j, \mathbf{b}_j)$, then

$\mathbf{A}_1 \otimes \mathbf{A}_2$ has eigenpairs $(\{\alpha_i \times \beta_j\}, \{\mathbf{a}_i \otimes \mathbf{b}_j\})$

It is also well-known that $\mathbf{A}_1$ and $\mathbf{A}_2$ behave well under *Cartesian sum*:

$\mathbf{A}_1 \oplus \mathbf{A}_2 = \mathbf{A}_1 \otimes \mathbf{I}_2 + \mathbf{A}_2 \otimes \mathbf{I}_1$ (where $\mathbf{I}_1$ and $\mathbf{I}_1$ are identity matrices of appropriate size) has eigenpairs $(\{\alpha_i + \beta_j\}, \{\mathbf{a}_i \otimes \mathbf{b}_j\})$.

The Laplacian **L** also behaves well under Cartesian sum. For $\mathbf{L}_1 \oplus \mathbf{L}_2$ the eigenpairs are $(\{\lambda_i + \kappa_j\}, \{\mathbf{l}_i \otimes \mathbf{k}_j\})$

This fact is used by Pothen, *et al.*, (1990) to study the Laplacian of grids, which are Cartesian sums of paths. Further, the eigenvalues of $\mathbf{L}_1$ and $\mathbf{L}_2$ always contain a $\lambda_0 = 0$ with corresponding constant eigenvector, so that the corresponding eigenpairs of $\mathbf{L}_1 \oplus \mathbf{L}_2$ are $(\lambda_i+0, \mathbf{l}_i \otimes \mathbf{1})$. The term $\mathbf{l}_i \otimes \mathbf{1}$ means that the components of $\mathbf{l}_i$ are *replicated* m_2 times. Since the Cartesian sum of two paths is a grid, this produces a perfectly rectangular representation (Fig. 1b). The Laplacian is therefore a useful tool in problems involving regular grids (or hypergrids). However, **N** does *not* behave well under Cartesian sum (Fig. 1c).

The Laplacian does *not* behave well under Kronecker product. However, the Normal spectrum *does* (Chow, 1997), so that $\mathbf{N}_1 \otimes \mathbf{N}_2$ has eigenpairs

$(\{\nu_i \times \mu_j\}, \{\mathbf{n}_i \otimes \mathbf{m}_j\})$

Further, the eigenvalues of $\mathbf{N}_1$ and $\mathbf{N}_2$ always contain a $\nu_0 = 1$ with corresponding constant eigenvector, so that the corresponding eigenpairs of $\mathbf{N}_1 \otimes \mathbf{N}_2$ are $(\nu_i \times 1, \mathbf{n}_i \otimes \mathbf{1})$. The term $\mathbf{n}_i \otimes \mathbf{1}$ means that the components of $\mathbf{n}_i$ are *replicated* m_2 times. Because all the coordinates are the same within each copy, this produces *clustering* of the components of $\mathbf{N}_1 \otimes \mathbf{N}_2$ for these eigenvectors.

[7] While PCA results tell how much of the variance each dimension accounts for, the Normal eigenvalues tell how much of the network's chi-squared each eigenvector (dimension) accounts for.

It appears that the behaviour under Kronecker product explains why both the Adjacency and Normal eigenvectors are good at detecting both on- and off-diagonal *blocks* (clusters of edges).

Visualization

The Laplacian can **L** provide good visual representations of graphs which are Cartesian products (such as grids and hypercubes); while **N** can provide good visual representations of graphs which are Kronecker products (such as graphs consisting of blocks). The reasons for this are suggested above and have mostly to do with the behaviour of eigenpairs which are sums and products with 0 and 1, respectively. For graphs that are not k-regular, eigenpairs of **A** do not provide such good representations since, in general, there is no constant (expected, trivial) eigenvector to combine with.

Another way of describing these results is to consider the relationship between the eigenvector components for a node and those it is connected to (Seary & Richards, 1999). It is evident from the definition of eigendecomposition that (where "u~v" means "u is connected to v")

(6) $\mathbf{a}_i(u) = \Sigma_{u\sim v}\, \mathbf{a}_i(v)/\alpha_i$ for eigenpair i of **A**

(7) $\mathbf{l}_i(u) = \Sigma_{u\sim v}\mathbf{l}_i(v)/(\lambda_i\text{-deg}(u))$ for eigenpair i of **L**

(8) $\mathbf{n}_i(u) = \Sigma_{u\sim v}\mathbf{n}_i(v)/(\nu_i\times\text{deg}(u))$ for eigenpair i of **N**

Note that **A** has no control for node degree. Consider the effect for "important" eigenpairs: ($|\alpha| \approx k \gg 1$, $\lambda \approx 0$ and $|\nu| \approx 1$) when deg(u) is small, **a**(u) will be folded toward the origin, while **l**(u) and **n**(u) will sit further *away* from the origin than its neighbours. This effect makes it difficult to interpret visual representations based on **A**, except for k-regular graphs where all three spectra are essentially the same (Fig. 1)

The equation for $\mathbf{n}_i$ shows that for ν_i near 1, each node is approximately *at the centroid* of those it is connected to. The exact difference from the centroid for node *u* of eigenvector $\mathbf{n}_i$ is:

$$\mathbf{n}_i(u)\text{-}\ \Sigma_{u\sim v}\mathbf{n}_i(v)/\text{deg}(u)) = (1-\nu_i)\mathbf{n}_i$$

For important eigenvalues ν_i near 1, this produces very good visualization properties. In addition, the eigenvector representation may be combined with derived properties such as *betweenness* (Freeman, 1979) to produce very helpful displays of large networks (Brandes *et al.*, 2001)

Interpreting the eigenvectors

1. Partitions

Powers (1988) and others have shown how eigenvectors of **A** can be used to find partitions of highly connected subsets (clusters) of nodes, but these methods are not as general or as clear as those derived from **L** or **N**.

The first non-trivial eigenvector $\mathbf{l}_1$ of **L** is the subject of extensive literature (Lubotzky, 1994; Alon & Millman,1985). Fiedler (1975) first suggested that the eigenvector $\mathbf{l}_1$ associated with the *second-smallest* eigenvalue λ_1 could be used to solve the *min-cut* problem: separate the network into two approximately equal sets of nodes with the fewest number of connections between them, based on the *signs* of the components of $\mathbf{l}_1$.[8] In fact, more recent derivations of **L** use the min-cut property as a starting point (Walshaw, *et al.*, 1995) and the results are used to partition compute-intensive problems into sub-processes with minimal inter-process communication (Pothen, *et al.*, 1990). This technique is called *Recursive Spectral Bisection* (Simon, 1991). Other researchers have used $\mathbf{l}_2$, $\mathbf{l}_3$

[8] Hagen also uses deviations from median

and higher eigenvectors to produce multi-way partitions of networks (Hendrickson & Leland, 1995).

The graph bisection problem (Mohar & Poljak.,1991) is to find two nearly equal-sized subsets $V_1, V_2 \subset V$ such that $cut(V_1,V_2) = \Sigma_{ij}\, a_{ij}$ is minimized, where $i \in V_1$, $j \in V_2$. (i.e. nodes in V_1 and V_2 have few connections to each other).

This problem is known to be NP-hard (Garey & Johnson, 1979), but a good approximation is given by the *signs* of $\mathbf{l}_1$ (Walshaw & Berzins,1995). This gives two sets of nodes of roughly the same size, but has no control for the number of *edges* in each part, and so any clustering of nodes is a *side-effect* of the partition.

However, we can add an additional constraint that the number of edges in each part also be roughly equal by *weighting* the node sets by their total degrees. This is exactly what a partition based on $\mathbf{n}_1$ from **N** gives us, since it $\mathbf{n}_1$ points in the direction of *maximum variability* in χ^2 (Greenacre, 1984).[9] Similarly, further partitions based on $\mathbf{n}_2$, $\mathbf{n}_3$, ...will also produce sets of nodes with a large number of edges in common (as long as v_2, v_3, ...make significant contributions to χ^2). Partitions based on *positive* eigenvalues will produce blocks *on the diagonal* of **A** of edges associated with each set of nodes, while those based on *negative* eigenvalues produce nearly bipartite *off-diagonal* blocks (which occur in pairs if the network is symmetric) (Seary & Richards,1995).

2. Clustering

Ideally, the important eigenvectors should be at least *bimodal* to induce clustering based on sign-partitions, and often they are *multi-modal* (Hagen ,1992), suggesting that standard clustering methods can be used on the coordinates of these vectors. Equations (7) and (8) show that **L** and **N** place nodes approximately at the centroids of their neighbours. For **N**, the distances are actually measured in χ^2 space, meaning that nodes with very similar *patterns* of connections will be close together (Benzecri, 1992). This clustering happens with either positive or negative eigenvalues (on- or off-diagonal). The latter are important in *nearly bipartite* networks with few triangles (Fig. 3).

3. Problems

Farkas, *et al*., (2001) and Goh, *et al*., (2001) report that the important eigenvectors of **A** are very *localized* on nodes of high degree, and suggest that this effect may be used to distinguish certain types of networks. This effect does not occur for **L** or **N** (fig. 2), since each include some control for degree, and so far no similar results for distinguishing network types have been reported for these spectra. The biggest problem for **L** and **N** is their sensitivity to "long paths", especially to pendant trees attached to the main body of the network (Seary & Richards, 2000). For **N**, these may be interpreted as nodes that are hard to reach (distant) in a random walk. For long paths *internal* to a network, this effect is actually an advantage, since these cycles are detected as "locally bipartite" and emphasized in important eigenvectors. Nodes on such paths can have a large effect on global properties such as diameter (Fig. 3-4).

Two-mode networks

Two-mode networks mix two different kinds of nodes and connections. A simple example is an affiliation network such as people and the events they attend. We could be interested in finding sets of people with events in common (or, equivalently, sets of events attended by the same people): this is an example of *co-clustering*. Affiliation networks can be represented by bipartite graphs for which **A** and **N**

---

[9] see Dhillon (2001) for a formal derivation and proof

are most suited, since they have symmetric spectra for these (the eigenvalues occur in pairs with opposite sign). Because of this we don't need the entire bipartite matrix: we can work with the rectangular representation, and infer the missing parts of the eigendecomposition. If we assume m_1 people and m_2 events, the resulting eigenvectors consist of m_1 components for people followed by m_2 components for events. The resulting blocks will be strictly off-diagonal and once again the eigenvectors of **N** provide a superior solution by maximizing χ^2. In fact, this solution is identical to that provided by Correspondence Analysis, a statistical technique for finding patterns in 2-mode data (Benzecri, 1992).

Partial Iteration

For large networks, it is not necessary or desirable to calculate the entire eigendecomposition. For *very* large networks, it may not be possible in terms of time and space to calculate even a *few* eigenpairs. Nevertheless, it is possible to get at a large amount of the global and local network structure by partially iterating using the Power Method. A few iterations of $\mathbf{N} = \mathbf{D}^{-1}\mathbf{A}$, with each iteration placing nodes at the means of their neighbours, will produce a *mixture* of the most important eigenvectors. Consider the spectral representation

$$\mathbf{N}^K = \Sigma_i(v_i)^K \mathbf{n}_i \mathbf{D} \mathbf{n}_i^T$$

We know that $(\mathbf{n}_i\mathbf{D}\mathbf{n}_i^T)^K = \mathbf{n}_i\mathbf{D}\mathbf{n}_i^T$ for all K, so the contributions of eigenvectors with small v_i quickly drop out as these $(v_i)^K$ approach 0. This means that $\mathbf{N}^K$ is dominated by the dimensions with v_i near 1. We start with a random vector, and quickly (6-10 iterations) produce such a mixture. Moody (2001) describes a procedure in which this process is repeated a number of times, each producing a slightly different mixture of the important eigenvectors (Fig 5). The results are then passed to a standard cluster analysis routine (such as k-means, Ward's method) to find any clusters of nodes.

Further analysis

The method of partial iteration of **N** has been used for years in the program NEGOPY (Richards and Rice, 1981; Richards, 1995), as the first step in a more complex analysis. A key concept in NEGOPY is that of *liaisons*. These are nodes which do not have most of their connections with members of a cohesive cluster of nodes, but rather act as connections *between* clusters (Fig 3-4). Often it is the liaisons that provide the connections that hold the whole network together. Finding the liaisons requires detailed knowledge about the members of (potential) clusters and *their* connections, and is not an immediate result of a partition based on eigenvectors or clustering methods. Nevertheless, eigendecomposition methods – full or partial – are an excellent strategy to begin such analysis.

Future prospects

More work needs to be done on the categorization of networks based on important eigenpairs of **L** and **N**. Recent reports (Koren, *et al.*, 2002; Walshaw, 2000) suggest we might not need to resort to partial methods after all; we can find important eigenpairs exactly for enormous networks ($m>10^5$) using "small" amounts of time and memory by first *reducing* the network in some way by sampling, solving the reduced eigenproblem, then interpolating back up with a very good "first guess" for the Power Method. Preliminary tests show that this should work equally well for Lanczos iteration.

References

Aho, A., Hopcroft, J., & Ullman, J. (1997). *Data structures and algorithms* Addison-Wesley.

Alon, N. and Millman, V. (1985). λ_1, Isoperimetric Inequalities for Graphs, and Superconcentrators. *J. Comb. Theory B.* 38: 73-88.

Barnard S. and Simon, H. (1994). Fast Implementation of Recursive Spectral Bisection for Partitioning Unstructured Problems. *Concurrency: Practice and Experience* 6(2): 101-117.

Benzecri, J-P. (1992). *Correspondence Analysis Handbook,* Marcel Dekker Inc.

Bien, F. (1989). Constructions of Telephone Networks by Group Representations. *Notices of the Am. Math. Soc.* 36: 5-22.

Biggs, N. (1993). *Algebraic Graph Theory.* Cambridge University Press.

Brandes, U., Cornelsen, S. (2001). Visual Ranking of Link Structures, *Lecture notes in Computer Science,* 2125, Springer-Verlag.

Chavel, I. (1984). *Eigenvalues in Riemannian Geometry,* Academic Press.

Chow, T.Y. (1997). The Q-spectrum and spanning trees of tensor products of bipartite graphs", *Proc. Am. Math. Soc.,* 125(11): 3155-3161.

Courant, R. and Hilbert, D. (1966). *Methods of Mathematical Physics.* Interscience Publishers.

Cvetkovic , D., Doob, M., and Sachs, H. (1995). *Spectra of Graphs.* Academic Press.

Cvetkovic, D., Rowlinson, P. (1990). The largest eigenvalue of a graph: a survey. *Linear and Multilinear Algebra.* 28: 3-33.

Cvetkovic, D., Doob, M. Guttman, I, Torgasev, A. (1988). *Recent results in the theory of graph spectra,* North Holland.

Chung, F.K.R.(1988). Diameters and Eigenvalues, *J. Am. Math. Soc.* 2(2): 187-196.

Chung, F.K.R, Faber, V.& Manteuffel, T.A. (1994). An upper bound in the diameter of a graph from eigenvalues associated with its Laplacian, *SIAM J. Disc. Math.* 7(3): 443-457.

Chung, F.K.R. (1995). *Spectral Graph Theory,* CBMS Lecture Notes, AMS Publication.

Dhillon, I.S. (2001). Co-clustering documents and words using bapartite spectral graph partitioning, UT CS Technical Report #TR 2001-05.

Diaconis, P. and Stroock, D. (1991). Geometric Bounds for Eigenvalues of Markov Chains, *Ann. Appl. Prob.* 1: 36-61.

Dodziuk, J. and Kendall, W. S. (1985). Combinatorial Laplacians and Isoperimetric Inequality. In K. D. Ellworthy (ed.). *From Local Times to Global Geometry,* Pitman Research Notes in Mathematics Series 150: 68-74

Farkas, I., Derenyi, I., Barabasi, A-L., Viscek, T. (2001). Spectra of "Real-world" graphs: beyond the semi-circle law, cond-mat/100235

Fiedler, M. (1973). Algebraic Connectivity of Graphs, *Czech. Math. J.* 23: 298-305.

Fisher, M. (1966). On hearing the shape of a drum, *J. Combin. Theory,* 1: 105-125.

Freeman, L. (1979). Centrality in social networks: Conceptual clarification, *Social Networks,* 1: 215-239.

Freidman, J. (1993). Some Geometrical Aspects of Graphs and their Eigenfunctions. *Duke Mathematical Journal,* 69: 487-525.

Garey, M., Johnson, D. (1979). *Computers and Intractability.* W. H. Freeman.

Goh, K-I., Kahng, B. Kim, D. (2001). Spectra and eigenvectors of scale-free networks, cond-mat/0103337.

Greenacre, M., (1984). *Theory and Application of Correspondence Analysis.* Academic Press.

Grone, R., Merris, R. and Sunder, V. (1990). The Laplacian Spectrum of a Graph. *SIAM J. Matrix Anal. App.* 11(2): 218-238.

Grone, R. and Merris, R. (1994). The Laplacian Spectrum of a Graph II. *SIAM J. Discrete Math.* 7(2): 221-229.

Hagen, L. (1992). New Spectral Methods for Ratio Cut Partitioning and Clustering, *IEEE Trans. CAD,* 11(9): 1074-1085.

Hall, K. (1970). R-dimensional Quadratic Placement Algorithm, *Management Sci.* 17: 219-229.

Harary, F. & Schwenk, A. (1979). The spectral approach to determining the number of walks in a graph, *Paciific J. Math.* 80: 443-449.

Hendrickson,B. and Leland, R. (1995). An improved spectral graph partitioning algorithm for mapping parallel computations. *SIAM J. Comput. Sci.* 16(2): 452-469.

Hotelling, H. (1933). Analysis of a complex of statistical variables into pricipal components, *J. Educ. Psychol.* 24: 417-441, 498-520.

Joliffe, I.T.. (1986). *Principal Components Analysis*, Springer-Verlag, New York.

Kirchoff, G. (1847). Über die Auflösung der Gleichungen.... *Ann. Phys.Chem*, 72: 497-508.

Koren, Y. Carmel, L., Harel, D. (2002). ACE: a fast multiscale eigenvector computation for huge graphs, *IEEE Symposium On Information Visualization.*

Lawler, G. F. and Sokal, A. D. (1988). Bounds on the L^2 Spectrum for Markov Chains and Markov Processes: a Generalization of Cheeger's Inequality, *Trans. Amer. Math. Soc.* 309: 557-580.

Lovasz, L. (1995). Random Walks, Eigenvalues and Resistance, Handbook of Combinatorics, Elsevier, 1740-1745.

Lubotzky, A. (1994). *Discrete Groups, Expanding Graphs, and Invariant Measures*, Birkhauser.

Mohar, B. (1991). The Laplacian Spectrum of Graphs. In Alavi, Chartrand, Ollermann and Schwenk (eds.). *Graph Theory Combinatorics and Applications*, Wiley, 871-898.

Mohar, B., Poljak, S. (1991). Eigenvalues and the Max-cut Problem, *Czech. Math. J.* 40: 343-352.

Moody, J. (2001). Peer influence groups: identifying dense clusters in large networks, *Soicla Networks*, 23: 261-283.

Parlett, B. (1980). *The Symmetric Eigenvalue Problem*, Prentice-Hall.

Parlett, B., Simon, H. and Stringer, L. (1982). On Estimating the Largest Eigenvalue with the Lanczos Algorithm. *Mathematics of Computation.* 38(157): 153-165.

Pothen, A., Simon, H, and Liou, K-P., (1990). Partitoning Sparse Matrices with Eigenvalues of Graphs. *SIAM J. Matrix Anal. App.* 11(3): 430-452.

Powers, D. (1988). Graph partitioning by eigenvectors. *Linear Algebra Appl.* 101: 121-133.

Richards, W.D. & Seary, A.J. (2000). Eigen Analysis of Networks, *J. Social Structure.* http://www.heinz.cmu.edu/project/INSNA/joss/index1.html

Richards, W.D. and Rice, R. (1981). The NEGOPY Network Analysis Program, *Social Networks*, 3(3): 215–224.

Richards, W.D.(1995). *NEGOPY 4.30 Manual and user's Guide*. School of Communication, SFU. http://www.sfu.ca/~richards/Pdf-ZipFiles/negman98.pdf

Seary, A.J. & Richards, W.D. (2000). Negative eigenvectors, long paths and p*, Paper presented at INSNA XX, Vancouver BC. http://www.sfu.ca/~richards/Pages/longpaths.pdf

Seary, A.J. and Richards, W.D. (1998). Some Spectral Facts. Presented at INSNA XIX, Charleston. http://www.sfu.ca/~richards/Pages/specfact.pdf

Seary, A.J. and Richards, W.D. (1995). Partitioning Networks by Eigenvectors. Presented to European Network Conference, London. Published in Everett, M.G. and Rennolls, K. (eds). (1996). *Proceedings of the International Conference on Social Networks,* Volume 1: Methodology. 47-58.

Simon,H. (1991). Partitoning of Unstructured Problems for Parallel Processing. *Computing Systems in Eng.* 2(2/3): 135-148.

Sinclair, A. (1993). *Algorithms for Random Generation and Counting*, Birkhauser

Walshaw, C. (2000). A multilevel algorithm for force-directed graph drawing, *Proc. Graph Drawing 2000,* Lecture Notes in Computer Science, 1984: 171-182.

Walshaw, C. and Berzins, M. (1995). Dynamic Load-balancing for PDE Solvers on Adaptive Unstructured Meshes, *Concurrency: Practice and Experience.* 7(1): 17-28.

Wasserman, S. & Faust, K. (1994). *Social Network Analysis,* Cambridge

West, D. B. (1996). *Introduction to graph theory*, Prentice Hall, 1996.

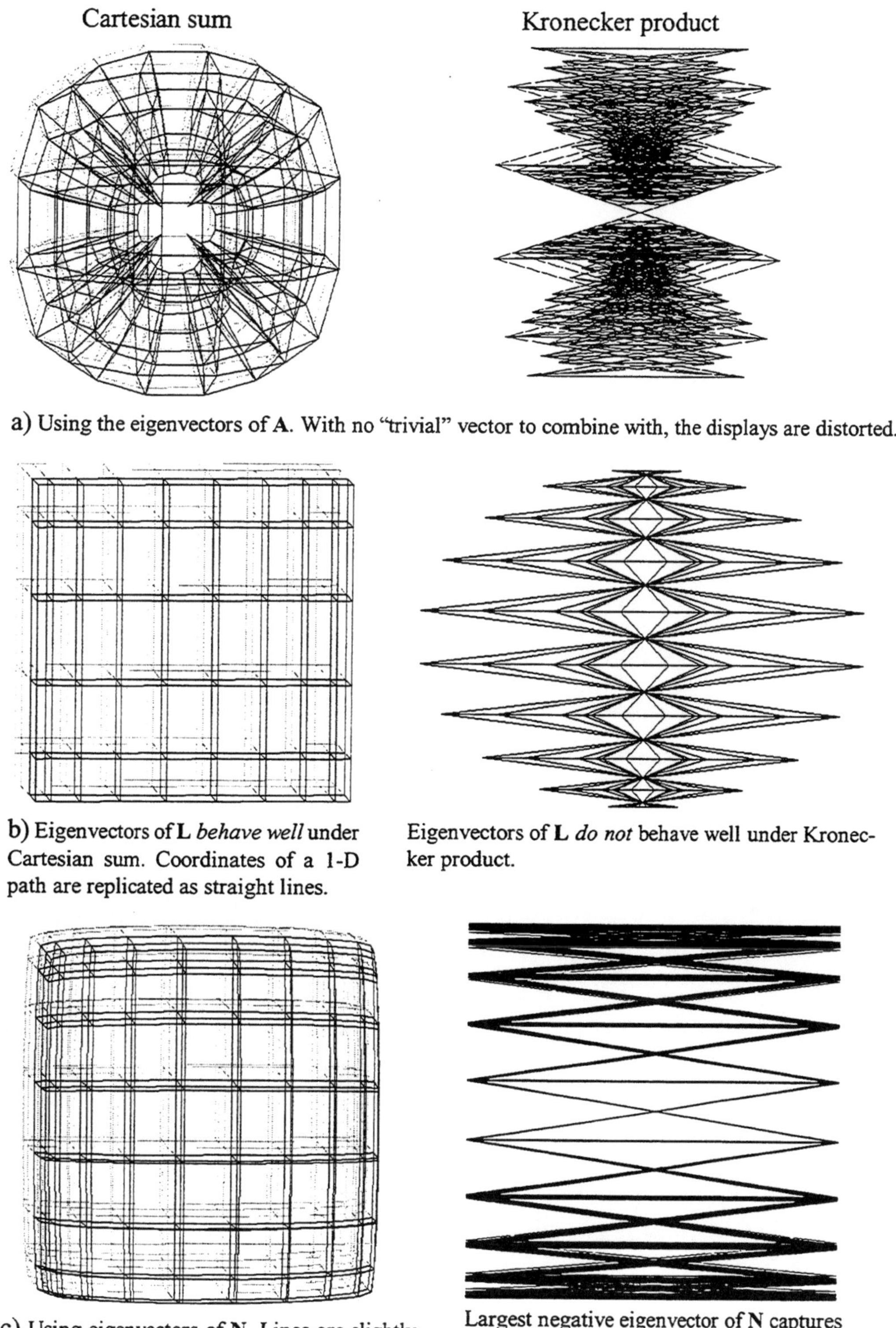

a) Using the eigenvectors of **A**. With no "trivial" vector to combine with, the displays are distorted.

b) Eigenvectors of **L** *behave well* under Cartesian sum. Coordinates of a 1-D path are replicated as straight lines.

Eigenvectors of **L** *do not* behave well under Kronecker product.

c) Using eigenvectors of **N**. Lines are slightly curved, so the cube is slightly distorted.

Largest negative eigenvector of **N** captures bipartiteness perfectly.

Figure 1. Six views of a 6 x 8 x 10 grid. Left: as the Cartesian sum of three paths producing a three-dimensional grid. Right: as the Kronecker product producing a bipartite graph.

a) The first 3 eigenvectors of **N** produce clusters of nodes. These are labelled with the resulting partition into 4 blocks, along with the liaisons. The central liaison is of high degree and holds the network together. The figure is slightly rotated to show the clusters.

b) Adjacency matrix permuted by partition numbers. The blocks have no interconnections, and the network is held together by the liaisons (right and bottom).

Figure 2. Two views of a small social network with 145 nodes. (Data Source: L. Koehly)

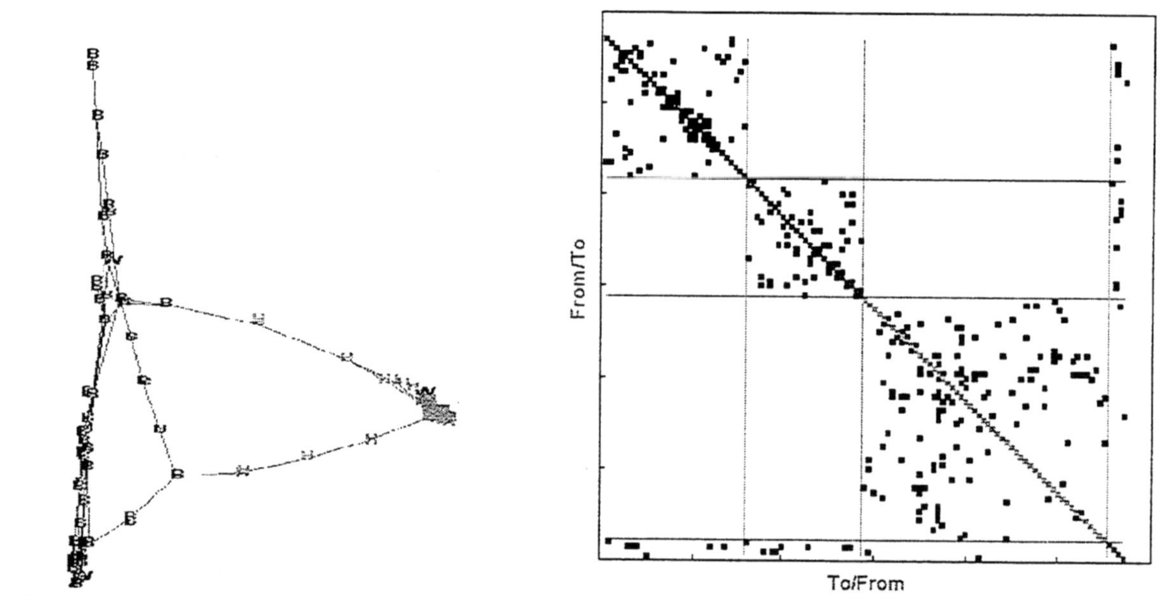

a) The first 3 eigenvectors of **N**. The 3rd eigenvalue is negative, since there are very few triangles in the rightmost cluster. The labelling is by ethnic group, which shows a close relation to structure. There are only two connections between the two main ethnic groups.

b) Adjacency matrix permuted by partition numbers. In this case the liasons are of *low* degree.

Figure 3. Two views of a small social network of drug users with 114 nodes. (Data Source: Scott Clair)

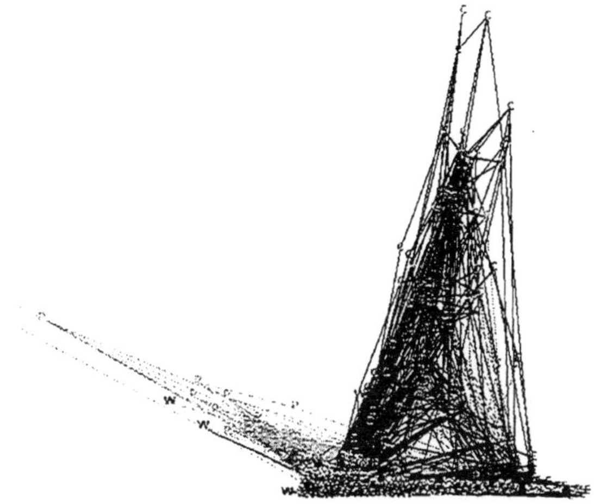

a. This figure shows the close relation between the first 3 eigenvectors of **N** and four needle exchange sites, which are used to label the nodes. The figure is rotated to make this clear.

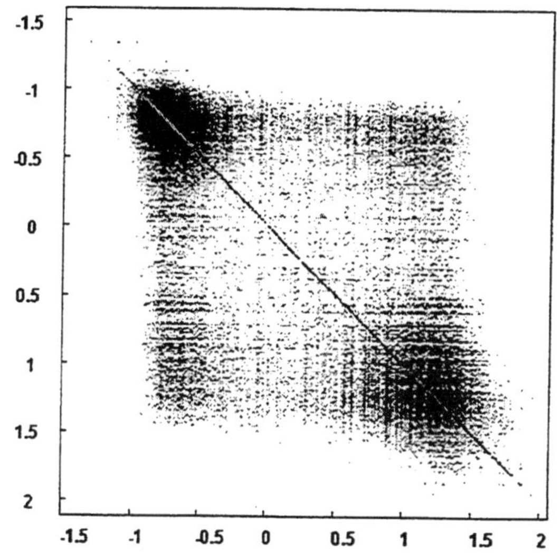

b. This figure is like an Adjacency matrix, except links are located by the *coordinates* of the first eigenvector of **N**. The network is dominated by exchanges *within* sites E and W.

Figure 4. Two views of a needle exchange network. (Data Source: T. Valente and R. Foreman). This network is moderately large (N=2736) and roughly *scale-free* (k≈1.7). The eigenvectors of **A** are dominated by nodes of high degree (>100).

a) Close-up of clusters formed by the first 3 eigenvectors of **N**, labelled by construction.

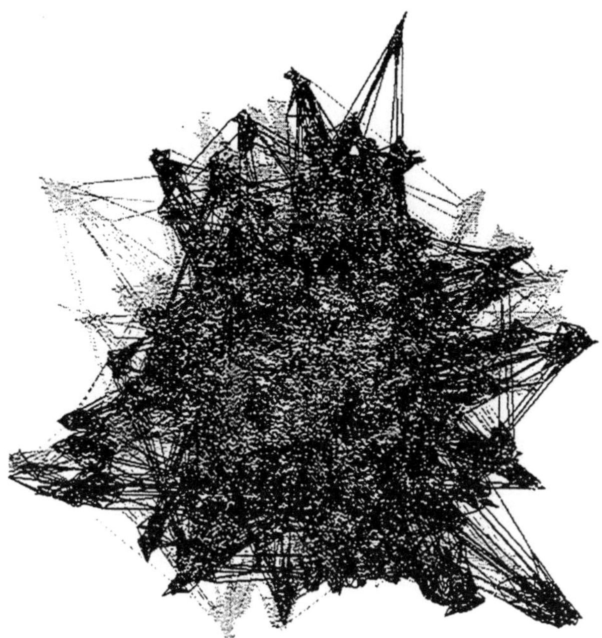

b) Clusters formed by placing each node at the centroid of its neighbours, iterating 8 times with 3 random starts (multiple partial iteration). Labelled by construction.

Figure 5. A moderately large (N=20,000) artificial network (Data Source: J. Moody) constructed for testing purposes. The network was constructed from tightly connected groups of 50 nodes, each group then loosely connected in sets of 8, with 400 of these even more loosely connected into a single component.

APPENDIX (Glossary, examples, facts and definitions)

adjacency matrix: A network (graph) may be represented by a matrix of zeros and ones, with a one indicating that two nodes are connected (adjacent), and a zero otherwise. In a weighted graph, the ones may be replaced by other positive numbers (e.g., a distance or cost).
A sample adjacency matrix is shown below. See *link list*

	a	b	c	d	e	f	g	h	
a	0	1	1	1	0	0	0	0	a has connections to b,c,d
b	1	0	1	1	0	0	0	0	b has connections to a,c,d
c	1	1	0	1	0	0	0	0	...etc...
d	1	1	1	0	0	0	0	0	
e	0	0	0	0	0	0	1	1	
f	0	0	0	0	0	0	1	1	
g	0	0	0	0	1	1	0	0	
h	0	0	0	0	1	1	0	0	

Adjacency spectrum: The adjacency matrix of a graph, like any matrix, may be subject to an eigen decomposition. In graph theory, the resulting set of eigenvalues is referred to as ***the*** graph spectrum, in analogy to the continuous spectrum from continuous spectral analysis methods such as Fourier analysis. In Fourier analysis, the spectrum is understood to refer to the weighting of sines and cosines, whereas the discrete graph spectrum (eigenvalues) are weights of eigenvectors with unknown functional form. We sometimes use the term eigenpair refer to both eigenvalues and eigenvectors. Since there are other spectra associated with graphs, we refer to this one as the Adjacency or Standard spectrum.

block: A block may be contrasted with a clique in the sense that the former are defined as sets of nodes that have similar patterns of links to nodes in other sets, while the latter is a set of nodes that have most of their links to other nodes in their set. All cliques are blocs, but some blocks are not cliques. One of the aims of blockmodelling is to identify roles by clustering the nodes so that those with similar patterns of connections are next to one another in the matrix. The members of each block perform similar roles in the network.

block model: a higher-level description of a network, where roles (or blocks) are represented by a simplified graph. For the matrix above, a block model would be:

1 0 0
0 0 1
0 1 0

Cartesian sum: A form of graph composition, which forms more complex graphs from simpler ones. Cartesian sum may be expressed in terms of Kronecker product as:

$$\mathbf{A}_1 \oplus \mathbf{A}_2 = \mathbf{A}_1 \otimes \mathbf{I}_2 + \mathbf{A}_2 \otimes \mathbf{I}_1$$ (where $\mathbf{I}_1$ and $\mathbf{I}_1$ are identity matrices of appropriate size)

As an example, the Cartesian sum of two paths is a rectangular grid.

clique: In graph theory, a clique is a sub-graph in which all nodes are connected to each other. In social networks, a clique is a set of nodes with most of their connections with other members of the clique. This would generally correspond to an informal role (e.g, friendship). In the above matrix {a,b,c,d} form a clique.

cluster: A collection of points that are "close" to each other in some sense. Many definitions (and related techniques) are available. For networks, we should also insist that the points share connections, either within the cluster (clique) or with another cluster (see block model).

component: If a graph is connected, it consists of a single component. A disconnected graph does not have a path between any pair of nodes, and may consist of several components.

connected: If there is a path between every pair of nodes in a graph, the graph is said to be connected. A disconnected graph does not have a path between any pair of nodes, and so distances (and diameters) cannot be defined, except within each component.

distance: For graphs, the distance between nodes is defined as the smallest number of links connecting them. Also called geodesic distance.

diameter: the largest geodesic distance between any pair of nodes in a graph

gap: The term gap or spectral gap refers to large distances in the spectrum of eigenvalues, particularly between 0 and the second-smallest (Laplacian) or between 1 and the second-largest in absolute value (Normal). A small gap means that a graph can be disconnected with few edge-cuts; a large gap means there are many paths between sets of nodes.

global vs local methods: In graph theory, a local method is one that examines only a few neighbours of a node. A global method is one which examines the entire graph, such as an eigendecomposition.

Kronecker product: A form of graph composition, which forms more complex graphs from simpler ones. An example of the Kronecker product is:

$$\begin{matrix}1&1\\1&0\end{matrix} \otimes \begin{matrix}1&0\\0&1\end{matrix} = \begin{matrix}1&0&1&0\\0&1&0&1\\1&0&0&0\\0&1&0&0\end{matrix}$$

where every 1 in the first matrix has been replaced by a complete copy of the second matrix. In this example the first matrix is a block model, not a graph.

Lanczos iteration: a generalization of the power method which allows calculation of a specified number of eigenpairs without loss of precision or orthogonality. Currently one of the best methods for eigendecomposition of large systems.

Laplacian spectrum: The eigenvalues (and eigenvectors) of a matrix formed by subtracting the adjacency matrix from a diagonal matrix of node degrees. The eigenvalues are non-negative, with a "trivial" (constant) eigenvector of eigenvalue 0. This discrete analogue of the continuous Laplacian shares a great many of its important properties. For this reason, it has become the focus of much research in the last decade.

liaisons: according to NEGOPY, these come in two types. *Direct* liaisons are individuals who have most of their interaction with members of groups, but not with members of any one group. They provide direct connections between the groups they are connected to. *Indirect* liaisons are individuals who do not have most of their interaction with members of groups. They provide indirect or 'multi-step' connections between groups by connecting Direct Liaisons, who have direct connections with members of groups (Richards, 1995).

link: A pair of nodes with some connection between them. In graph theory, links are also called edges or lines. In social networks, links are often called ties.

link list: A sparse format for storing information in a network. Only the pairs of nodes that are connected are in the link list. For symmetric graphs, only one pair is needed for each link. For weighted graphs, a third column may be used to hold the weights. For the symmetric adjacency matrix shown above, the link list is:

1 2
1 3
1 4
2 3
...and so on...

localized: As applied to an eigenvector means that most of the coordinates are near zero, and only a few have large values. Coordinates may be either positive or negative, and the eigenvectors are normalized to make the sum of squares of components 1, so the sum of 4th powers is generally used as a measure of localization. If this sum is near 1 only a small number of coordinates are important. If it is near 1/m, then all nodes contribute to the eigenvector.

neigbourhood: all the nodes which are connected to a given node. May be extended to all nodes connected to a *set* of nodes, but not including the original set.

NEGOPY: (NEGative entrOPY) (Richards and Rice, 1981, Richards, 1995) is a computer program designed to find clique structures. It uses a random starting vector, and multiplies it by the row-normalised adjacency matrix, subtracting off row means. Usually 6-8 such iterations are performed, resulting in a vector which is a mixture of the the important Normal eigenvectors (Richards and Seary, 1997). This vector is then scanned for potential clique structures, which are tested against the original network and for some statistical properties (e.g., variance in the node degrees). Sparse matrix methods are used throughout, allowing large networks to be analysed rapidly.

node: An object that may have some kind of connection (link) to another object. In some cases, nodes are people, organizations, companies, countries, etc. In graph theory nodes are also called vertices and points. In social networks, nodes are often called actors.

normal spectrum: The eigenvalues (and eigenvectors) of a row-normalised adjacency matrix. This matrix is row-stochastic, and similar to a symmetric matrix, so its eigenvalues are real and less than or equal to 1 in absolute value. It is closely related to the Laplacian (indeed, it may be defined to be the Laplacian in the χ^2 metric defined by the node degrees).

partition: A partition of a graph is a division of the nodes into a collection of non-empty mutually exclusive sets. A partition of the adjacency matrix shown above could be: {a,b,c,d}, {e,f,g,h}, so that there are no links between the nodes in each part of the partition.

sparse matrix techniques: In analysis of networks with more than 50 or 60 members, it is usually the case that each node is connected to only a fraction of the others. The adjacency matrix for such networks contain mostly zeroes, which indicates the absence of links. In these situations, it far is easier to work with a list of the links (link list) that are present, rather than the whole matrix which contains many times more numbers. Any array (such as an adjacency matrix) which consists mostly of some default number (usually zero) may be treated as a sparse matrix. Since this value is known, it does not need to be stored as part of the array. This allows the array to be stored in a much more efficient manner, e.g., for an adjacency matrix, we only need to store the links (pairs of nodes) when they exist. For a weighted adjacency matrix, we also need to store the values of the weights, one for each link. Many matrix operations (e.g., multiplying a matrix by a vector) can utilize this more efficient storage to run much faster as well. Sparse matrix techniques are those which avoid any manipulation of the matrix that would affect the sparseness property (e.g., taking the inverse will generally do this, as will correlating each row or column with all the others). It is quite possible to find eigenvalues and eigenvectors using sparse techniques.

spectral analysis or methods: Loosely speaking, another term for eigendecomposition. Mathematically speaking, a general term referring to any re-statement of some function in terms of a set of basis functions (e.g. sines and cosines for Fourier analysis). The spectrum is the weights of these basis functions. The Fourier transform is especially useful in mathematical physics since the sines and cosines (or e^z for complex z) are eigenfunctions of the ubiquitous derivative and integral operators. The terms function, operator and eigenfunction have the discrete analogues of vector, matrix and eigenvector.

Standard spectrum: see Adjacency spectrum

Statistical Models for Social Networks: Inference and Degeneracy

Mark S. Handcock
Department of Statistics
Center for Statistics and the Social Sciences
University of Washington
Box 354322
Seattle, WA 98195-4322, USA
January 18, 2003

Abstract

This paper presents recent advances in the statistical modeling of random graphs that have an impact on the representation of social networks. We also consider issues related to the estimation of random graph models. For concreteness the focus is cross-sectional social networks.

Statistical exponential family models (Wasserman and Pattison, 1996) are a generalization of the Markov random graph models introduced by Frank and Strauss (1986), which in turn derived from developments in spatial statistics (Besag, 1974). These models recognize the complex dependencies within relational data structures.

To date, the use of stochastic graph models for networks has been limited by three interrelated factors: the complexity of realistic models, lack of use of simulation studies, and a poor understanding of the properties of inferential methods.

We discuss these factors and related issues of the degeneracy of inference for commonly promoted models. As a cornerstone of this development we present a Markov Chain Monte Carlo (MCMC) algorithm for general random graph models. We also review the role of these MCMC algorithms in simulation, likelihood-based inference, identifying degeneracy of inference, and Bayesian formulations.

KEYWORDS: Random graph models; Markov Chain Monte Carlo; Bayesian statistics.

1. Introduction

Networks are a form of "relational data". Relational data arise in many social science fields and graph models are a natural approach to representing the structure of these relations. In these applications, the nodes usually represent people, and the edges represent a specified relationship between the people. This framework has many applications including, for example, the structure of social networks, the behavior of epidemics, the interconnectedness of the WWW, and long-distance telephone calling patterns.

We consider stochastic models for such graphs that form a statistical exponential family. This class has been referred to as the "p^*" class of models in the psychology and sociology literatures (Wasserman and Pattison, 1996). Given their general nature and applicability, we shall refer to them simply as random graph models. A much studied sub-class of models are the Markov random graph models introduced by Frank and Strauss (1986). These models attempt to model the stochastic mechanism that produces the social ties and so represent the complex dependencies so induced. There is a large social network literature on this area which we do not review here. See Wasserman and Faust (1994), and Pattison and Robins (2000) for detailed information. The topic has connections to a broad array of literatures and here we emphasize the links to spatial statistics, statistical exponential families, log-linear models and statistical physics.

The exploration of the properties of graph models has been limited by three factors. First the complexity of realistic models has limited the insight that has been gained by analytical methods. Most analytical work has focused on simple one or two parameter models with independence between the dyads (Wasserman and Faust 1994, Frank 1997). Second statistical methods for the stochastic simulation from general random graph models have not existed. Because of this the properties of general models (e.g., range of graphs represented, dependence among the parameters) can not be explored though simulation studies. Third the properties of statistical methods for estimating the parameters based on observed networks are poorly understood (we consider inference in Section 3). Hence the range of parameter values relevant to real networks is largely unknown. In this paper we improve understanding of the nature and properties of graph models important to social networks by further considering methods for the stochastic simulation of, and inference for, random graphs.

We address one aspect of modeling that has been a persistent obstacle in the work in this area: *inferential degeneracy*. Many previous attempts to develop MCMC based estimation for Markov models have found that the algorithms nearly always converge to degenerate graphs – graphs that are either empty or full, or the algorithms do not converge consistently. Using statistical exponential family theory, we show that this is a function of the form of the model and algorithm used.

In the next section we review the statistical theory of social network models expressed in exponential form. We also consider MCMC algorithms to simulate graphs from these models. In Section 3 we consider forms of inference for the parameters of the models with focus on likelihood-based forms and Bayesian methods in particular. In Section we consider *model degeneracy* and some possible solutions to it.

2. Review of theory

Let the random matrix **X** represent the incidence matrix of an undirected graph on n individuals. Thus **X** is an $n \times n$ symmetric matrix, each of whose entries is a Bernoulli random variable; we assume further that the diagonal elements of **X** are 0, which is to say that self-partnerships are disallowed. Suppose that X denotes the set of all possible graphs on the given n individuals. The multivariate distribution of **X** can be parameterized in the form:

$$P_{\theta}(X = x) = \frac{\exp\left[\theta^{T} t(x)\right]}{c(\theta)} \qquad x \in X \tag{1}$$

where $\theta \in \Theta \subseteq ¡^{q}$ is the model parameter and $t(x)$ is a q-vector of statistics based on the graph x. (Wasserman and Pattison, 1996). The denominator $c(\theta)$ is the constant that ensures the distribution sums to one: $c(\theta) = \sum_{y\in} \exp\left[\theta^{T} t(y)\right]$. Note that X contains at most

$N = n(n-1)/2$ graphs, and $\Theta = \{\theta : c(\theta) < \infty\}$. The dimension of Θ is at most $2^{N} - 1$ (for the "saturated" model), although is typically much smaller than this. The parameter and statistics that correspond to a given model for $\mathbf{X}$ can be identified using the Hammersley-Clifford theorem (Frank and Strauss 1986). Conversely, each choice of parameter and graph statistics $t(x)$ specifies a model for $\mathbf{X}$. For example, if the dyads X_{ij} are mutually independent the model can be written: $\log[P_\theta(X=x)] = \sum_{i<j} \theta_{ij} x_{ij} - \kappa(\theta), \quad x \in X$ where $\theta_{ij} = \text{logit}[P_\theta(X_{ij} = x_{ij})]$ and $\kappa(\theta) = \log[c(\theta)] = \sum_{i<j} \log[1+\exp(\theta_{ij})]$. Thus q=N and the elements of $t(x)$ are just x_{ij}. This model is often called a Bernoulli graph. In the special case where the dyads have a common probability, $\log[P_\theta(X=x)] = \theta t(x) - \kappa(\theta)$ where $q=1$, $t(x)$ is the number of partnerships in the graph, and θ can be interpreted as the common log-odds of partnership formation within a dyad. The mathematical properties of this *homogeneous Bernoulli graph* model has been extensively studied (see, e.g., Renyi and Erdos 1959), although its simplicity and homogeneity make it less useful as a realistic model for social phenomena.

An alternative specification of the model (1) clarifies the interpretation of the parameters. Let $X_{ij}^c = \{X_{kl} : kl \neq ij, k<l\}$, $x_{ij}^c = \{x_{kl} : kl \neq ij, k<l\}$, $x_{ij}^+ = \{x_{ij}^c \text{ and } x_{ij} = 1\}$, and $x_{ij}^- = \{x_{ij}^c \text{ and } x_{ij} = 0\}$. Thus, X_{ij}^c represents all elements in the graph excluding X_{ij}, while x_{ij}^+ and x_{ij}^- represent the graph with the x_{ij} equal to 1 and 0, respectively. The full conditional distributions of X_{ij} are given by

$$\text{logit}[pr(X_{ij} = 1 \mid X_{ij}^c = x_{ij}^c)] = \theta^T \delta(x_{ij}^c) \qquad x \in X \tag{2}$$

where $\delta(x_{ij}^c) = t(x_{ij}^+) - t(x_{ij}^-)$ (Strauss and Ikeda 1991). The statistic $\delta(x_{ij}^c)$ is the change in the graph statistics when x_{ij} changes from 0 to 1. Hence θ can be interpreted as the increase in the conditional log-odds of a partnership between individuals i and j induced by the formation of the partnership and conditional on all other ties remaining unchanged. In the homogeneous Bernoulli graph, for example, θ is the common log-odds of individual partnership formation.

Holland and Leinhardt (1981) appear to be the first to propose log-linear models for social networks. Suppose that the dyads are independent with

$$\Pr(X_{ij} = x, X_{ji} = y) = \begin{cases} m_{ij} & \text{if } x=1, y=l \\ a_{ij} & \text{if } x=0, y=l \\ n_{ij} & \text{if } x=0, y=0 \end{cases} \tag{3}$$

Thus each dyad can have its own probability distribution. Thus the model can represent arbitrary attractiveness between individuals and degree of reciprocity within relationships. However the dyad independence implies specific transitivity and higher-order interactions. The model can be expressed in log linear form as:

$$log\left[\Pr(X=x)\right] = \sum_{i<j} \rho_{ij} x_{ij} x_{ji} + \sum_{i \neq j} \theta_{ij} x_{ij} - \kappa(\theta) \qquad x \in X$$

They called this the p^1 model.

Based on developments in spatial statistics (Besag 1974), Frank and Strauss (1986) extended this work and introduced forms of dependence with Markov structure. Further extension were made by Wasserman and Pattison (1996) to incorporate actor attributes (Pattison and Wasserman 1999) and to allow explanatory and response variables (Robins, Pattison and Wasserman 1999), resulting in social influence (Robins, Pattison and Elliott 2000) and social selection models (Robins, Elliott and Pattison, 2000). These generalizations essentially allow

analysis of graphs with "colors" on the nodes, the coloring indicating the attribute. Recent developments have included new forms of dependency structures, to take into account social settings, and on the other hand a relaxation of Markovian dependence assumptions, allowing investigation of longer range configurations, such as longer paths in the network or larger cycles (Pattison and Robins, 2000). Models for bipartite (Faust and Skvoretz, 1999) and tripartite (Mische and Robins, 2000) graph structures have also been developed.
The incorporation of attribute information into the random graph model is straightforward. Suppose we wish to incorporate p exogenous covariates represented by a $n \times n \times p$ array of attributes W where the ijk^{th} element is the covariate for the pth attribute on the ij^{th} dyad. Note that this allows the covariates to be attributes of the pairs of individuals (e.g., age difference) as well as specific to the individual alone. The graph statistic $t(x)$ in (1) is then replaced by $t(x,W)$, indicating that the statistics depend on the attribute information in addition to the relationship information. In this sense, the statistic $t(\cdot)$ can be defined to reflect the attribute information. We consider an implementation of this in the next section.

2.1. Cross-sectional models for random graphs

The most common form of random graph models exhibit Markov dependence in the sense of Frank and Strauss (1986). For these models, dyads that do not share an individual are conditional independent: an idea analogous to the nearest neighbor concept in spatial statistics. Typically a homogeneity condition is added: all isomorphic graphs have the same probability under the model. Frank and Strauss (1986) show that homogeneous Markov graphs are exactly those having the *triangle parameterization*: $q = n,\ \theta \in \Theta = ¡^{N}$ and

$$t_k(x) = \frac{1}{k!}\sum_{i_0,\dots,i_k} x_{i_0 i_1}\dots x_{i_0 i_k} \qquad k = 1,\dots,n-1 \qquad t_n(x) = \frac{1}{6}\sum_{i,j,k} x_{ij}x_{jk}x_{kl},$$

where $t_k(x)$ is called a $k-$star and $t_n(x)$ is a count of the complete triads. An equivalent form is the degree distribution parameterization:

$$d_k(x) = \text{the proportion of individuals with exactly } k \text{ relationships} \quad k = 1,\dots,n-1$$

$$t_n(x) = \frac{1}{6}\sum_{i,j,k} x_{ij}x_{jk}x_{kl},$$

in which $d_k(x)$ counts the proportion of individuals with degree k. The degree distribution parameterization has the advantage that it is directly interpretable in terms of concurrency of partnerships (i.e. $d_m(x)$ for $m > 0$ counts the number of individuals with m concurrent partners).

A form of model that may realistically represent dependent social processes, reflect the impact of covariates is:

$$P(X = x) = \frac{\exp\left[x^T Z\beta + \sum_{k=0}^{n-1}\alpha_k d_k(x) + \theta^T t(x)\right]}{c(\alpha,\beta,\theta)} \qquad x \in X \qquad (4)$$

where x is the N-vector of the unique elements of X, $Z = \{z_{ij}\}_{N\times p}$ is a matrix of (exogenous) covariates on the ij^{th} dyad, $t(x)$ a q-vector of additional network statistics, β p-vector of regression parameters, α g-vector of degree parameters, and θ a q-vector of network structure parameters.

This model is an extension of equation (1) and contains a number of special cases that have been considered in separate literatures. First the homogeneous Markov graphs of Frank and Strauss (1986) correspond to the case where there are no covariates and the additional network statistic is the count of complete triads. Second, if there are no covariates and no additional network statistics the model corresponds to the random graphs with arbitrary degree distributions considered in Newman, Strogatz and Watts (2001). This model assumes that all graphs with the same degree distribution are equally likely. On particular interest are the various "scale-free," preferential attachment and power-law models popular in the physics literature (see, e.g., Newman 2002). Third, if there are no degree distribution parameters and no additional network statistics the model corresponds to the random graphs with independent dyads. The model still allows differential activity levels and assortative missing via the covariate parameters. Such models have been traditionally specified as log-linear models of mass action. See Morris, Goodreau and Koehly (2003) for an examination of the connections between the two.

As an example, consider a random graph model for a social network based on heterosexual partnerships. An example of a cross-sectional model that incorporates captures both concurrency and the assortative mixing based on race is:

$$P_\theta(X = x) = \exp\left[\sum_{k=1}^{4} \alpha_k d_k(x) + \beta \text{race}(x)\right] / c(\alpha, \beta, \theta) \qquad x \in X_{\text{h}}$$

$$P_\theta(X = x) = 0 \qquad x \in X / X_{\text{h}}$$

where race(x) is the proportion of partnerships where both partners say they are of the same race, X_{h} is the subset of graphs in X in which all ties are heterosexual, and $\alpha \in \mathbb{R}^4$. The parameter α_1 represents the propensity to form monogamous relationships. The parameters $\alpha_2, \ldots, \alpha_4$ represent the propensity to form concurrent partnerships with 2, 3 and 4 partners, respectively. Hence positive values for the latter parameters indicate the propensity of the graph toward higher degrees of concurrency. The parameter β represents the propensity for partnerships to be formed between individuals of the same race. Note that the graph and model reflect the heterosexual nature of the graph (i.e., $X_{ij} = 0$ unless i and j are of opposite sex). If $\alpha_1, \ldots, \alpha_4$ are zero the dyads are independent and the model is simply assortative mixing by race. The model can then be re-written as a contingency table form (Morris, Goodreau and Koehly 2003). If β is zero then there are no preferences for partnerships based on race. We consider alternative parameterizations for this model in Section 3.

These models have a form that is flexible enough to capture the structure of many real networks. However to be practically useful we need to be able to simulate graphs with these distributions, infer their parameters from real data and measure their overall and relative goodness-of-fit. We now turn to each of these topics.

2.2. Simulating random graph models

The mathematical form of the models (1) and (4) allow graphs to be generated from them using Markov Chain Monte Carlo (MCMC) algorithms. Indeed MCMC algorithms have been much studied and are a nature way to simulate social networks (e.g. Gilks *et. al.* 1996,

Newman and Barkema 1999). The basic idea is to construct a Markov Chain on X with $P(X = x)$ as the equilibrium distribution. This is operationalized by starting from a graph in X, and making a large number of Markov transitions until approximate convergence to $P(X = x)$ is reached. Subsequent transitions are sampled and form a (dependent) sample from the desired model. For details, see the extensive literature cited in the above books. Many chains are possible with vastly different statistical properties. However convergence is "ensured" under mild conditions on the Markov Chain (irreducibility and aperiodicity). For the social network representation (1) this process has been studied by Crouch, Wasserman and Trachtenberg (1998), Coriander et. al. (1998), and Snijders (2002).

The full-conditional MCMC for the model (1) and (4) has a simple form and is motivated by the auto-logistic representation (2). In this algorithm each dyad is updated separately based on the conditional probabilities given in (2). This so-called "Gibbs sampling" or "heat bath" algorithm chooses the dyads randomly, sequentially, or using some mixture of the two. Each update requires the difference $\delta(x_{ij}^c) = t(x_{ij}^+) - t(x_{ij}^-)$ to be determined. The speed of the calculation of $\delta(x_{ij}^c)$ is an important factor in the computational quality of the algorithm (i.e., speed of convergence to $P(X = x)$, the relative frequency of producing each graph in X). Alternative Metropolis algorithms propose transitions from $x_{current}$ to $x_{proposed}$ based on the unconditional probabilities require the determination of $t(x_{proposed}) - t(x_{current})$. These tend to perform better for the same amount of computation. More general Metropolis-Hastings algorithms choose $x_{proposed}$ from an ancillary stochastic process dependent on $x_{current}$ and aimed at either focusing the transitions or spreading them more broadly through X . The behavior of these algorithms is very dependent on the choice of statistics $t(x)$.

The papers that use MCMC algorithms to simulate social network models report difficulties in convergence to realistic distributions (Crouch, Wasserman and Trachtenberg 1998, Coriander et al 1998, and Snijders 2002). A typical occurrence is for the algorithm to produce graphs that are complete, empty, or else are extreme in related ways. Coriander et. al. 1998 consider algorithms that condition on the number of ties in the graph. This ensure that the realizations are not complete or empty graphs. However, in most circumstances the density of the graph is a product of the social process that produced it and can not be assumed to be known in advance. Snijders 2002 reports on a number of related odd properties. In some cases the sequences of realizations transition quickly between very different graphs after periods of minor variation. In Section 3 we indicate why these algorithms behave in this way, how it relates to the model and how it can be resolved.

3. Inference for random graph models

Statistical methods for estimating the parameters in a random graph model are underdeveloped. Developing inference with a likelihood framework has the advantage of being able to draw upon a statistical theory for closely related models in statistical physics and spatial statistics (Besag 1975, Geyer 1999). This framework is also compatible with the Bayesian paradigm (Gelman, Carlin, Stern and Rubin 1995). The likelihood framework makes available exploratory graphical tools useful for inference about the underlying random field (Handcock, Meier and Nychka 1994). These tools, for example, can identify when a maximum likelihood approach is insufficient for inferential purposes.

Major barrier to the application of random graph models to social networks has been the lack of a sound statistical theory to evaluate how closely the models capture the structure in the observed graphs. This has two dimensions to it: the degree to which the graph structure of the models matched that in the data, and second the degree to which disease propagation through the model matches that of the data. The likelihood-based approach allow one to measure the first dimension of "goodness-of-fit" using Monte-Carlo p-value statistics and Bayes Factors under the Bayesian paradigm (Gelfand 1996).

3.1. Likelihood inference for random graph models

In principal, likelihood inference is straightforward for exponential random graph models. In this section we describe the most fundamental ideas and why direct computation is difficult. The log-likelihood for model (1) is:

$$L(\theta;x) \equiv \log\left[P_\theta(X=x)\right] = \theta^T t(x) - \kappa(\theta) x \in X \tag{5}$$

where $\kappa(\theta) = \log[c(\theta)]$. Likelihood inference is difficult as direct evaluation of $L(\theta;x)$ requires calculating

$$c(\theta) = \sum_{x \in X} \exp[\theta^T t(x)] \cdot$$

For even simple and modest models this can be problematic. Table 1 gives the number of elements in X (i.e., 2^N) as the number of actors grows.

Table 1: Number of Graphs for Different Numbers of Actors

Number of Actors, n	Number of Elements in X.
3	8
6	32,728
10	1.24×10^{27}
25	2.307×10^{90}

3.2. Alternative inference for random graph models

Clearly for realistic graphs direct enumeration is not feasible. Many alternatives have been proposed. Frank (1971) and Frank and Strauss (1986) consider (linear) approximations to the cumulant generating function:

$$C(\psi) = E\left[\log(\psi t(X))\right]$$

as a means to solve the *likelihood equations*

$$E_\theta\left[t(X)\right] = t(x_{observed}) \tag{6}$$

This approach is generally difficult to apply to general multiparameter models unless supplemented by a means of simulation from the same network model (Coriander et al 1998).

One commonly used method is *pseudolikelihood* originally motivated by, and developed for, spatial models by Besag (1975). The idea is to use an alternative local version of the likelihood function defined the *pseudolikelihood*. The pseudolikelihood for model (1) is algebraically identical to the likelihood for a logistic regression of the unique elements of X on the design matrix with i th row $\delta(x_{ij}^c)$. The value of the maximum pseudolikelihood estimator for social networks can then be expediently found by using logistic regression as a computational device. Explicitly, the value of the maximum likelihood estimator for the logistic regression will also be the maximum pseudolikelihood estimator. Note, however, that the other characteristics of the maximum likelihood estimator do not necessarily carry over. In particular the standard errors of the estimates of θ from the logistic regression will not be appropriate for the maximum pseudolikelihood estimator. The statistical properties of pseudolikelihood estimators for social networks are only partially understood and are discussed in Handcock (2000). In the remainder of this paper we focus on likelihood based estimation.

3.3. Existence and uniqueness of MLE

The maximum likelihood estimator (MLE) for θ is:

$$\hat{\theta} = argmax_{\theta \in \Theta} L(\theta; x_{observed}) \tag{7}$$

Many properties of the MLE can be derived from statistical exponential family theory. Let C be the closed convex support of $t(X)$ - the convex hull of the discrete support points. Denote the interior of C by $int(C)$ and the boundary by ∂C.

Result:

a) If Θ is open, the MLE exists if, and only if, $t(x_{observed})$ is inside the interior of C.
b) If it exists, it is unique. In addition, when it exists, it can be found as the unique solution of (6) or equivalently as (7), the unique local minima of (5).
c) As the support of $t(X)$ is discrete, and $t(x_{observed})$ is in it, a necessary and sufficient condition for the MLE not to exist is that $t(x_{observed})$ falls on the boundary of the support and that boundary be part of C.

The result is a fundamental property of statistical exponential families (Barndorff-Nielsen 1978).

In practice this means that attempt to numerically maximize the likelihood leads to unbounded estimates when the observed graph has statistics falling on the boundary of C. This typically means the optimization algorithm does not converge. Simulation studies in Handcock (2000) show that this is common for realistic models. If $t(x_{observed})$ falls on the boundary of C it is still possible that subsets of θ have MLEs that exist. Let $t(x_{observed}) = (t_a(x_{observed}), t_b(x_{observed}))$ and $\theta = (\theta_a, \theta_b)$ be similar partitions of $t(x_{observed})$ and θ. Under mild conditions, if $t_a(x_{observed})$ is on the boundary of C and $t_b(x_{observed})$ is in the relative interior of the convex hull of $\{t(X) : t_a(X) = t_a(x_{observed})\}$ then the MLE of θ_b exists and is the unique local minima of the conditional likelihood equation:

$$CL(\theta; x,) \equiv \log\left[P_\theta(X = x \mid t_a(X) = t_a(x_{observed}))\right] = \theta^T t_b(x) - \kappa(\theta, t_a(x_{observed}))$$

$$x \in X : t_a(X) = t_a(x_{observed})$$

3.4. Likelihood inference based on MCMC algorithms

The difficulties in determining the normalizing function for the model (1) can be overcome using MCMC algorithms. The approach is based on the following idea: If a large number of simulations from a social network in the same ballpark as that of the observed network can be generated then these can be used to approximate the normalization function to a desired accuracy. Estimate the "population" value:

$$c(\theta) = \sum_{x \in X} \exp\left[\theta^T t(x)\right]$$

by the weighted "sample" mean:

$$\bar{c}(\theta) = |X| \sum_{M\ sampled\ graphs\ y} \exp\left[\theta^T t(y)\right] w(y)$$

where the sample weights $w(y)$ are internally normalized to sum to unity. We can use the MCMC approach of Section 2.2 to simulate a sample of graphs from a model similar to the true, but unknown, model. The approximation to the likelihood using this approach is called the *MCMC likelihood.* The MLE for the data is them approximated by the maximum of the of the MCMC likelihood (the MC-MLE). This idea has been made precise and studied by Geyer and Thompson (1992). They show the MC-MLE converges to the true MLE as the number of simulations increases. The procedure also produces estimates of the asymptotic covariance matrix, the size of the MCMC induced error, and other related quantities.

As the sampled graphs form the basis of a statistical exponential family with sample space the realized values and probabilities the empirical proportions, the existence and uniqueness of the MC-MLE can be understood:

Result:

Let CO be the convex hull of *sampled* sufficient statistics. In practice, there are two situations:

1) $t(x_{observed}) \in int(CO) \subseteq int(C)$: The MC-MLE exists and is unique. It is found as the unique maximum of the MCMC likelihood.
2) $t(x_{observed}) \notin int(CO)$ but is in $int(C)$: The MC-MLE does not exist, even though MLE does.
3) $t(x_{observed}) \notin int(C)$: Neither the MC-MLE nor the MLE exists.

This result explains why attempts to calculate MC-MLE estimates for social network models fail. If the model used to simulate the graphs is not close enough to produce realizations that cover the observed values of the statistics, the MC-MLE will not exist even in cases where the MLE does. This behavior is quite common. As we shall see in Section 3, it is magnified by properties of commonly used models that do not place probability mass broadly enough. In sum, the MC-MLE may not exist for at least two reasons. First, the MLE itself may not exist (in which case neither does the MC-MLE). Second, it is difficult to specify parameter values for commonly used models to produce realizations that cover the observed values of the network statistics. In particular, simulations in Handcock (2000) show that simulations based on the maximum pseudolikelihood estimates usually do not produce realizations sufficiently similar to those of the true values to support MC-MLE estimation. These properties of the models are very similar to those for spatial point processes considered in Geyer (1999).

3.5. Bayesian models and inference for random graph models

In random graph models of the form (1) the maximum likelihood estimator is not necessary optimal and, indeed, any point estimator of θ can be very poor. As such we need to move away from point estimators of θ and to frameworks for inference that naturally allow the uncertainty about the value of θ to be expressed.

We do this by supplementing likelihood-based inference with the Bayesian paradigm, mainly as it provides an elegant way of incorporating parameter uncertainty into the final inference and the incorporation of expert knowledge when it exists (Gelman, Carlin, Stern and Rubin 1995). Inference with the Bayesian paradigm, implemented via the now standard Markov Chain Monte Carlo (MCMC) methods can address, and even solve, many very difficult inferential problems, often making it the only realistic option.

Bayesian approaches to random graph models for social networks have received little attention (Wang and Wong 1987). We are in the process of developing Bayesian methodology for random graphs paying particular attention to the specification of prior distributions for the parameters that are meaningful for social networks. Under a Bayesian formulation, let $pr(\pi)$ be an arbitrary prior distribution for θ. The posterior distribution of θ is then $pr(\theta;X=x) = pr(\theta)P_\theta(X=x)/m(x)$ where $m(x) = \int_\Theta pr(\phi)P_\theta(X=x)d\phi$ can be interpreted as the apriori probability that $X=x$. $pr(\theta;.X=x)$ captures our knowledge about θ after the observed data (i.e., that is $X=x$) has been taken into account.

Note that $pr(\theta)$ may be chosen to restrict the parameter space to a subset of Θ by placing zero prior mass on the excluded values. Under these circumstances the posterior mass on these same values will always be zero regardless of their likelihood under the model and data. Computationally, Bayesian inference for an arbitrary prior is straightforward if MCMC simulation of the process is available. Conceptually this can be achieved by sampling a value θ^m from the prior distribution for $\theta, pr(\theta)$, and then sampling $\mathbf{X}^m$ from the distribution $P_{\theta^m}(X=x)$ using MCMC simulation. If this is repeated until $\mathbf{X}^m$ equals the observed graph x_{obs} then the corresponding value of θ^m, θ^m (say), is a random sample from the posterior $pr(\theta;X=x_{obs})$. By repeating this process, a large sample of values of θ from $pr(\theta;X=x_{obs})$ can be generated. The posterior mean of θ can then be estimated by the mean of the sample. The posterior density corresponding to $pr(\theta;X=x_{obs})$ can be estimated by a non-parametric density estimate based on the sample. Note that this applies even when θ is multivariate, and so the posterior dependence between the components of θ can also be determined. There are alternative computational methods that are vastly superior in terms of computational efficiency to the above algorithm. These alternatives will almost always be used in practice. However, the above algorithm does show how Bayesian inference is achieved using MCMC simulation.

The definition and properties of families of conjugate priors for exponential families has been addressed in Barndorff-Nielsen (1978), Diaconnis and Ylvisaker (1979) and, more recently,

Gutiérrez-Peña and Smith (1997). Of the many possible families possible, one of the most richest classes is discussed by Gutiérrez-Peña and Smith (1997). Let $g(\nu,\gamma)$ be the $(q+1)$ parameter exponential family with distributions:

$$\Pr(\theta;\nu,\gamma)=\frac{\exp\left[\nu^T\theta+\gamma\psi(\theta)\right]}{c(\gamma,\nu)}\qquad \theta\in\Theta,\ \gamma\geq 0$$

Thus $g(\nu,\gamma)$ has canonical statistics θ and $-\psi(\theta)$ and is minimal unless $\psi(\cdot)$ is a linear function of θ. Here $\psi(\cdot)$ is a prespecified function. The *hyperparameters* ν and γ specify, respectively, the location and scale of θ. If $\Theta = ¡\ ^q$ then this distribution is proper if, and only if, ν/γ is in the interior of the convex hull of the sample space of $t(X)$ and $\gamma > 0$. Suppose the prior for θ is chosen to be $g(\nu,\gamma)$ then, formally, the posterior for θ, having observed $X = x$, is $g(\nu+t(x),\gamma+1)$. That is,

$$\Pr(\theta;X=x;\nu,\gamma)=\frac{\left[(\nu+t(x))^T\theta+(\gamma+1)\psi(\theta)\right]}{c(\gamma+1,\nu+t(x))}\qquad \theta\in\Theta,\ \ \gamma\geq 0$$

This family can be generalized to a $p-$variate γ. Let $g(\nu,\gamma)$ be the $(q+p)$ parameter exponential family with distributions:

$$\Pr(\theta;\nu,\gamma)=\frac{\exp\left[\nu^T\theta+\gamma^T\psi(\theta)\right]}{c(\gamma,\nu)}\qquad \theta\in\Theta,\ \gamma_1\geq 0,\ldots,\gamma_p>0$$

Here $\psi(\cdot)$ is a prespecified $p-$variate function. Thus $g(\nu,\gamma)$ has canonical statistics θ and $-\psi(\theta)$ and is minimal unless some component of the $\psi(\cdot)$ is a linear function of θ. Suppose the prior for θ is chosen to be $g(\nu,\gamma)$ then, formally, the posterior for θ, having observed $X = x$, is $g(\nu+t(x),\gamma+1)$.

While inference for this family is quite tractable it is unclear under which circumstances the prior can be chosen to realistically represent knowledge about θ. It is more natural to choose the prior to reflect knowledge we do have and which is often quite strong. Examples include selectivity of graphs, degeneracy and stability. For these cases the prior family is unlikely to be conjugate.

4. Identifiability, Degeneracy and Stability for social networks models

The research reviews in the previous sections has allowed progress to be made in both the estimation and simulation of random graphs models. This work, and that of Besag (2000), has allowed provided insight into the properties of random graphs models. Two properties of random graph models that have a big impact on practice are *degeneracy* and *stability*. This builds on ideas of Ruelle (1969), Strauss (1986), Geyer (1999) and Baddeley (1999), Section 4. This work is in statistical physics and spatial point process theory.

The issue of what makes a useful model for a social network is a complex one. All models are representations of the manifestations of the social processes that produced the social network. Some models represent the proximate mechanisms of the formation of ties. This can be done by representation the temporal dynamics of the social process that produced the social network, or by direct representation of the network itself through appeal to concepts like structural balance and transitivity. Alternatively models may only aim at describing the probabilistic structure of the social ties. In all cases the models will be idealizations and simplification of the actual processes. Ultimately the answer to the question of what is a useful model is fundamentally dependent on the purpose for which the model is intended. Simple models are often adequate, and even desirable, if there is a simple objective (e.g., what is the density of ties in the network). For other purposes, such as understanding the dynamics of the spread of STDs over networks, more sophisticated models are necessary.

Here we consider a basic property that a useful model should have. Broadly speaking, useful stochastic models place a significant proportion of their probability mass on graphs that have high probability of being produced by the underlying social process. We define a random graph model to be *degenerate* if the model places almost all its probability mass on a small number of graph configurations in X . Hence degeneracy of a graph model occurs when the model places disproportionate probability mass on only a few of the possible graph configurations. A common case is where the distribution places almost all its mass on the empty graph (i.e., $X_{ij} = 0 \quad \forall i, j$), and/or the complete graph (i.e., $X_{ij} = 1 \, \forall i, j$). Such models are not useful for modeling networks as almost all realizations from these models will be empty or full. In addition is such a model is used for simulation and MCMC likelihood inference the approximations to the true model will be very poor.

4. Discussion and future work

While estimation techniques are often of little interest to non-statisticians, this case is an exception. The complete enumeration of all graphs required by the denominator in (1) makes simple maximum likelihood estimation impossible for graphs larger than about 30 nodes. In early applications a form of pseudo-likelihood was used to solve this problem (Besag 1974, Wasserman and Pattison 1996). More recent approaches, however, employ Markov Chain Monte Carlo (MCMC) methods (Geyer and Thompson 1992). This is particularly interesting for our purposes because MCMC methods effectively simulate the network over the space of possible graphs in order to maximize the likelihood. One can, however, just as easily use the MCMC algorithm to simulate the network given the parameter estimates, and this provides the solution to the problem of linking network data to the network simulation.

This paper address the question of what is a good model and in doing so helps resolve the dilemma lack of convergence when estimation or simulating using MCMC. Many of the models that are proposed in literature suffer from degeneracy. Further algorithms used for inferential purposes are often inadvertently based on degenerate forms resulting in inferential degeneracy. One implication of these results is that the *effective* parameter space of exponentially parameterized random graph models is bounded and a small subset of the theoretical parameter space. The Bayesian framework for inference promises to be very powerful in social network modeling. It facilitates the propagation of parameter uncertainty into the final inference and allowing the incorporation of expert prior knowledge when it exists.

The Key Player Problem[1]

Stephen P. Borgatti[2]

Introduction

The key player problem (KPP) consists of two separate sub-problems, which can be described at a general level as follows:

1. (KPP-1) Given a social network, find a set of k nodes (called a *kp-set* of order k) which, if removed, would maximally disrupt communication among the remaining nodes.

2. (KPP-2) Given a social network, find a kp-set of order k that is maximally connected to all other nodes.

Of course, these introductory definitions leave out what is meant precisely by "maximally disrupt communication" and "maximally connected". Part of the process of solving these problems is providing definitions of these concepts that lead to feasible solutions and useful outcomes. However, it would seem clear that KPP-1 involves fragmenting a network into components, or, failing that, making distances between nodes so large as to be practically disconnected. In contrast, KPP-2 involves finding nodes that can reach as many remaining nodes as possible via direct links or perhaps short paths.

The first problem, KPP-1, arises in a number of contexts. A prime example in the public health context is the immunization/quarantine problem. Given an infectious disease that is transmitted from person to person, and given that it is not feasible to immunize and/or quarantine an entire population, which subset of members should be immunized/quarantined so as to maximally hinder the spread of the infection? An example in the military context is target selection. Given a network of terrorists who must coordinate in order to mount effective attaches, and given that only a small number can be intervened with (e.g., by arresting or discrediting), which ones should be chosen in order to maximally disrupt the network?

The second problem, KPP-2, arises in the public health context when a health agency needs to select a small set of population members to use as seeds for the diffusion of practices or attitudes that promote health, such as using bleach to clean needles. In the organizational management context, the problem occurs when management wants to implement a change initiative and needs to get a small set of informal leaders on-board first, perhaps by running a weekend intervention with them. In the military context, KPP-2 translates to locating an efficient set of enemies to surveil, turn (into double-agents), or feed misinformation to.

At first glance, both KPP-1 and KPP-2 would appear to be easily solved by either employing some graph-theoretic concepts such as cutpoints and cutsets, or via the methods of social network analysis, such as measuring node centrality. It turns out, however, that none of the existing methods are adequate. This paper explains why and presents a new approach specifically designed for the key player problem.

---

[1] Acknowledgements: This research is supported by Office of Naval Research grant number N000140211032. Thanks to Scott Clair for leading me to this problem, Mark Newman for suggesting reciprocal distances, Kathleen Carley for useful discussions, and Valdis Krebs for providing illustrative data.

[2] Dept. of Organization Studies, Carroll School of Management, Boston College, Chestnut Hill, MA 02467

Centrality Approach

The centrality approach consists of measuring the centrality of each node in the network, then selecting the *k* most central nodes to comprise the kp-set. Since many measures of centrality exist, one question that arises is which measure to use. For KPP-1, we can expect the best measures to be those based on betweenness. For example, Freeman's betweenness measure sums the proportion of shortest paths from one node to another that pass through a given node. Thus, a node with high betweenness is responsible for connecting many pairs of nodes via the best path, and deleting that node should cause many pairs of nodes to be more distantly (if not completely disconnected).

For KPP-2, we can expect measures based on degree centrality and closeness centrality to be useful. Degree centrality is simply the number of nodes that a given node is adjacent to. Hence, depending on what the social relation represented by the graph is and assuming that adjacency implies potential for influence, a node with high degree can potentially directly influence many other nodes. Closeness centrality is defined as the sum of geodesic distances from a given node to all others, where geodesic distance refers to the length of the shortest path between two points. Thus, a node with a low closeness score (very central) should be able to influence, directly and indirectly, many others.

The centrality measures are plausible solutions for KPP. However, they are not optimal. There are two basic problems, which I refer to as the design issue and the group selection issue. Of the two, the group selection issue is the more serious.

The Design Issue

The design issue arises ultimately from the fact that centrality measures were not designed with KPP-1 and KPP-2 specifically in mind. Starting with KPP-1, consider the graph in Figure 1.

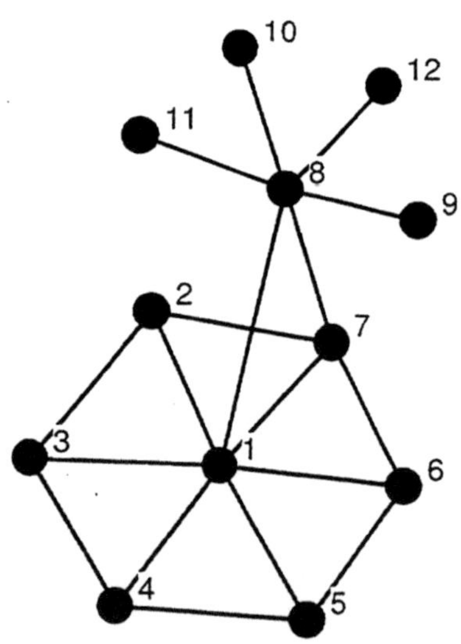

Figure 1.

Node 1 has the highest centrality on all considered measures, including betweenness centrality. Yet deleting node 1 has relatively little effect on the network. Distances between certain pairs of nodes do increase, but it is clear that communication among all points remains possible as there is no fragmentation. In contrast, deleting node 8, which does not have the highest betweenness, is more effective. Removing 8 splits the graph into five unconnected fragments (components).

For KPP-2, the picture is a little brighter. If we formulate KPP-2 in terms of reaching the most nodes directly, degree centrality is optimal. If we formulate it in terms of reaching the most nodes in up to *m* steps, then we can readily define a new measure of centrality ("*m*-reach centrality") that counts the number of nodes within distance *m* of a given node.

The Group Selection Issue

The group selection issue, discussed as the group centrality problem in Everett and Borgatti (1999), refers to the fact that selecting a set of nodes which, as an ensemble, solves KPP-1 or KPP-2, is quite different from selecting an equal number of nodes that individually are optimal solutions for KPP. To start with, consider KPP-1. Figure 2 shows a graph in which nodes *h* and *i* are, individually, the best nodes to delete in order to fragment the network. Yet deleting *i* in addition to *h* yields no more fragmentation than deleting *i* alone. In contrast, deleting *m* with *h* does produce increased fragmentation, even though individually *m* is not nearly as effective as *i*. The reason *i* and *h* are not as good together as *i* and *m* is that *i* and *h* are redundant with respect to their liaising role – they connect the same third parties to each other. In a sense, the centrality of one is due to the centrality of the other, with the result being that the centrality of the ensemble "control" is quite a bit less than the sum of the centralities of each.

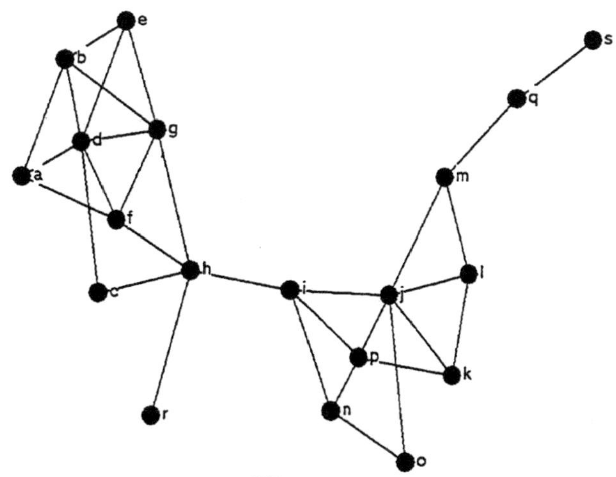

Figure 2

The redundancy principle also applies to KPP-2. Consider the graph in Figure 3. Nodes *a* and *b* are individually the best connected. Each reaches five other nodes, more than any other by far. But together they reach no more than either does alone. In contrast, if *b* is paired with *c* (which individually reaches only three nodes), the set reaches every node in the network.

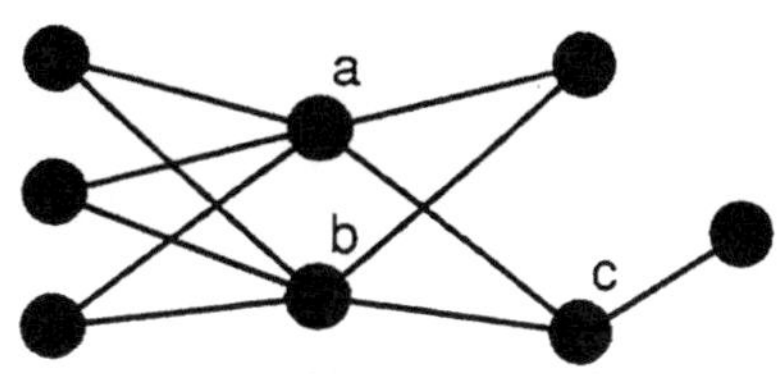

Figure 3.

Graph Theoretic Approaches

In addition to basic concepts such as components and distance, a number of graph-theoretic concepts are relevant to KPP. For KPP-1, the most obvious are the notions of cutpoint and bridge, which are nodes and lines respectively whose deletion would increase the number of components in the graph. These concepts do not address the group-selection issue. However, both have set-level counterparts in the form of cutsets. A cutset is a set of nodes (or lines) whose removal would increase the number of components in the graph. Most work has focused on minimum weight cutsets, which are smallest sets that have the cutset property. There are three difficulties with cutsets in the KPP context. First, we cannot specify the number of nodes in the set and then seek the set of that size that does the best job (rather, the measure of success is fixed and we are able to find a smallest set that achieves that level of success). In this sense, the graph theoretic approaches solve the inverse of the problem we seek to solve. Second, no account is taken of distances among nodes. Third, all solutions that increase the number of components are equal, even if one solution creates just two components while another creates ten.

For KPP-2, applicable concepts include vertex covers and dominating sets. A vertex cover is a set of nodes whose members are incident upon every edge in the graph. A dominating set is a set of nodes whose members are adjacent to all other nodes in the graph.[3] For our purposes these are equivalent and fail for exactly the same reasons as cutsets.

Measuring Success

In order to optimally solve KPP, we must have a clear definition of success. I propose that for KPP-1 there are two network properties we want to maximize by removing the kp-set: fragmentation and distance. For KPP-2, we want to measure the distance-based reach of the kp-set into the network around it. Therefore, we need measures for each of these concepts.

Fragmentation

Perhaps the most obvious measure of network fragmentation is a count of the number of components. If the count is 1, there is no fragmentation. The maximum fragmentation occurs when every node is an isolate, creating as many components as nodes. For convenience, we normalize the count by dividing by the number of nodes.

$$C = \frac{K}{n}$$

Eq. 1

The problem with this measure is that it doesn't take into account the sizes of the components. For example, in Figure 2, deleting node *m* would break the network into two components, but the vast majority of nodes remain connected. In contrast, deleting node *i* would also result in just two components, but more pairs of nodes would be disconnected from each other.

This suggests another measure fragmentation that simply counts the number of pairs of nodes that are disconnected from each other. Given a matrix *R* in which $r_{ij} = 1$ if *i* can reach *j* and $r_{ij} = 0$ otherwise, we can define the new measure as follows:

---

[3] Graph theorists differ on whether these sets are understood to be minimal or not.

$$F = 1 - \frac{2\sum_i \sum_{j<i} r_{ij}}{n(n-1)}$$

Eq. 2.

Since, by definition, nodes within a component are mutually reachable, the F measure can be rewritten more economically in terms of the sizes (s_k) of each component (indexed by k):

$$F = 1 - \frac{\sum_k s_k(s_k - 1)}{n(n-1)}$$

Eq. 3.

The F measure is remarkably similar to a diversity measure known variously as heterogeneity, the concentration ratio, the Hirschman-Herfindahl index, or the Herfindahl index. Applied to the current context it is defined as follows:

$$H = 1 - \sum_k \left(\frac{s_k}{n}\right)^2$$

Eq. 4.

One difference between F and H is that while both achieve minimum values of 0 when the network consists of a single component, when the network is maximally fragment (all isolates) the H measure can only achieve $1\text{-}1/n$. If we normalize H by dividing by $1\text{-}1/n$, we obtain the F measure (and seeing F as a normalization of H points us to a slightly faster computing formula).

An alternative approach is information entropy. Applied to this context, the measure is defined as

$$E = -\sum_k \frac{s_k}{n} \ln\left(\frac{s_k}{n}\right)$$

Eq. 5.

The measure is bounded from below at zero, but is unbounded from above. We can bound it by dividing it by its value when all nodes are isolates:

$$E = \frac{\sum_k \frac{s_k}{n} \ln\left(\frac{s_k}{n}\right)}{\sum_k \ln\left(\frac{s_k}{n}\right)}$$

Eq. 6.

Distance

While the fragmentation measure F is very satisfactory for what it does, it does not take into account the shape – the internal structure – of components. A network that is divided into two components of size 5 in which each component is a clique (Figure 4a) is seen as equally fragmented as a network divided into two components of size 5 in which each component is a line (Figure 4b). Yet distances and therefore transmission times are much higher in the latter network. Further, if we can delete only so many nodes, it may be that there is no possible selection of nodes whose removal would disconnect the graph. In such cases, we would still like some way of evaluating which sets are better than others.

An obvious solution would be to measure the total distance between all pairs of nodes in the network. However, this only works in the case where the graph remains connected. Otherwise, we must sum infinite distances. A practical alternative is to base the measure on sum the reciprocals of distances, observing the convention that the reciprocal of infinity is zero. In that case we can create a version of F, based on Equation 2, that weights by reciprocal distance.

$$^{D}F = 1 - \frac{2\sum_{i>j} \frac{1}{d_{ij}}}{n(n-1)}$$

Eq. 7.

The ^{D}F measure is identical to F when all components are complete (i.e. each component is also a clique). However, when distances within components are greater than 1, the measure captures the relative cohesion of the components. For example, the graph in Figure 4a has two components of size 5 and the ^{D}F measure is 0.556. The graph in Figure 4b, which is less cohesive, also has two components of size 5, but the ^{D}F measure is 0.715, indicating much less cohesion . Like the F measure, ^{D}F achieves its maximum value of 1.0 when the graph consists entirely of isolates.

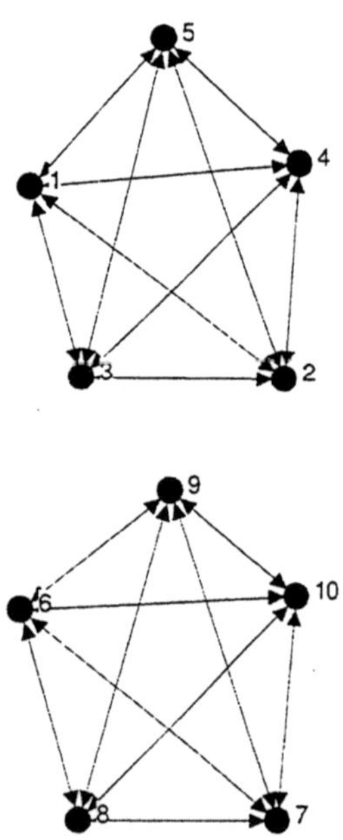

Figure 4a. ^{D}F = 0.556

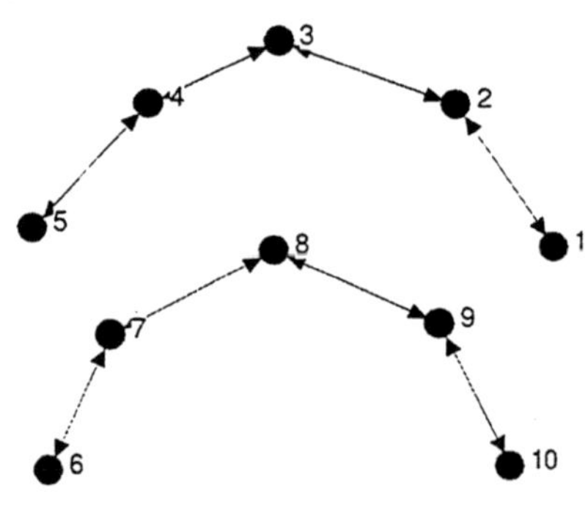

Figure 4b. ^{D}F = 0.715

Distance-Based Reach

The measures discussed for KPP-1 are graph-level measures that we apply to a kp-set by removing the set and measuring the fragmentation in the remaining graph. For KPP-2, we seek a set of nodes that, as a group, is maximally connected to all other nodes. Hence, we need a direct measure of the centrality of the kp-set as a group. The concept of group centrality has already been elaborated by Everett and Borgatti (1999), but only degree, closeness, betweenness and eigenvector group centrality measures have been discussed. As noted earlier, these measures are not optimal for the KPP-2 problem. Hence, we must develop new ones based on the concept of reach.

The simplest group reach measure, termed *m-reach*, is a count of the number of unique nodes reached by any member of the kp-set in m links or less. The advantage of this measure is its face validity. The disadvantage is that it assumes that all paths of length *m* or less are equally important (when in fact a path of length 1 is likely to be more important than a path of length 2) and that all paths longer than *m* are wholly irrelevant.

A more sensitive measure, called distance-weighted reach, can be defined as the sum of the reciprocals of distances from the kp-set *S* to all nodes (see Equation 8). As described by Everett and Borgatti (1999), the distance from a set to a node outside the set can be usefully defined in a number of ways, such as taking the maximum distance from any member of the set to the outside node, taking the average distance, or taking the minimum distance. For KPP-2, the minimum distance is appropriate since the fact that the distance to an outside node might be large for a given member of the set will usually be irrelevant.

$$^{D}R = \frac{\sum_j \frac{1}{d_{Sj}}}{n}$$

Eq. 8.

In the equation, the distance from kp-set *S* to node *j* is indicated by d_{Sj}. In addition, it should be noted that the summation is across all nodes and the distance from the set to a node within the set is defined to be 1. As before the reciprocal of an infinite distance is defined to be 0. Taking some interpretive license, we can view ^{D}R as the proportion of all nodes reached by the set, where nodes are weighted by their distance from the set and only nodes at distance 1 are given full weight. Hence, ^{D}R achieves a maximum value of 1 when every outside node is adjacent to at least one member of the kp-set (i.e., the kp-set is a dominating set). The minimum value of 0 is achieved when every node is an isolate.

Selecting a KP-Set

For KP-sets of size 1, the measures presented above can used straightforwardly to select key players by simply choosing the one with the highest score on any given measure. Thus, they can be regarded as new measures of node centrality that are optimized for the key player problem.

For kp-sets of size k > 1, however, there is no simple procedure for choosing an optimal set. Some heuristic procedures may be of value. For example, for KPP-2, we start by selecting the node with the highest ^{D}R score. Then, for each of the remaining k-1 selections, we choose the node with the highest score that is not adjacent to any of the nodes already selected. This algorithm, a variant of the first fit decreasing algorithm for the bin-packing problem, is fast and easy, but often yields solutions that are considerably less than optimal.

Other heuristic approaches specific to the KPP can be constructed, but the fact that we have clear measures of success that are easily computed recommends a generic combinatorial optimization algorithm, such as tabu-search (Glover, 1986), K-L (Kernighan and Lin, 1970), simulated annealing (Metropolis *et al*, 1953) or genetic algorithms (Holland, 1975). Initial experiments suggest that all of these do an excellent job on KPP, and so I present only a simple greedy algorithm. Figure 5 outlines the method, which is normally repeated using dozens of random starting sets.

1. Select k nodes at random to populate set S
2. Set F = fit using appropriate key player metric
3. For each node u in S and each node v not in S
   a. DELTAF = improvement in fit if u and v were swapped
4. Select pair with largest DELTAF
   a. If DELTAF <= then terminate
   b. Else, swap pair with greatest improvement in fit and set F = F + DELTAF
5. Go to step 3

Figure 5. Greedy optimization algorithm.

Empirical Trials

The operation of the algorithm is illustrated using two datasets drawn from the public health (AIDS) and military (terrorism) contexts. Both cases are approached from both KPP-1 and KPP-2 points of view.

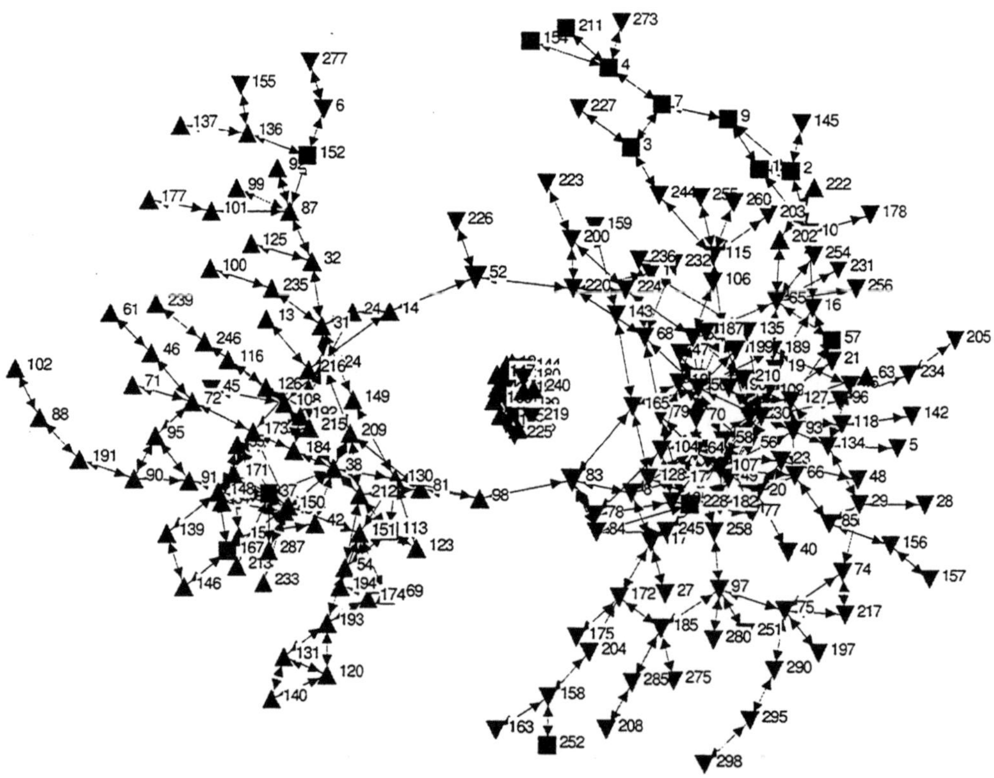

Figure 6. Acquaintance network. Upward triangles indicate African-Americans, downward triangles indicate Puerto-Ricans, and squares identify all others.

AIDS Example

The AIDS dataset consists of an acquaintance network among 293 drug injectors on the streets of Hartford, CT. The data are described in Weeks et al (2002). The network consists of one large main component (193 nodes), and many very small components. As shown in Figure 6, the main component of the network has a very clear structure. It consists of two groups, one african-american (with higher HIV+ proportion), and the other largely puerto-rican (with lower HIV+ proportion). Connection between the two groups is limited by just a few acquaintances and this bottleneck helps maintain the lower HIV+ rate in the Puerto-Rican part of the network. Whether through immunization (should that become possible) or quarantining, it is clear that one thing we would want to do early on is to isolate the two groups from one another, both because we want to maintain the low HIV+ rates in Puerto-Rican cluster, and because risk is a function of the size of the component a node is part of. Thus, we have a case of KPP-1.

The network provides a useful first test of the key player optimization algorithm for two reasons. First, the structure of the network makes it quite vulnerable to disconnection, and easy to check the results visually. If the algorithm fails this test, it is clearly not adequate. Second, the network is already fragmented, providing noise that could confuse some algorithms.

Based on visual inspection, it is clear that immunizing or quarantining just two nodes would separate the main component into two nearly equal halves. So for the first run of the algorithm we seek a kp-set of size 2. The starting fragmentation index for the graph is 0.567. The algorithm selected two nodes, identified in black in Figure 6, which, if deleted, would increase fragmentation to 0.658 (a proportional increase in fragmentation of 16%). The selected nodes match our intuition and divide the main component in two big chunks.

Turning to KPP-2, we are also interested in selecting a small group of nodes to be subjects of an intervention – specifically, to be trained as peer educators (known as Peer Health Advocates or PHAs) to disseminate and demonstrate HIV prevention practices. Weeks et al (2002) did this by hand, laboriously selecting the smallest group that could reach more than 50% of the main component of the network. The winning set contained 14 nodes. Running Key Player on the same data, yields the same result, as shown in Table 1.

Group Size	Number Reached	Percent Reached
1	16	8.3
2	27	14.0
3	36	18.7
4	43	22.3
5	49	25.4
6	55	28.5
7	61	31.6
8	67	34.7
9	72	37.3
10	77	39.9
11	82	42.5
12	87	45.1
13	92	47.7
14	97	50.3

Table 1.

As might be expected, the number of people reached increases as a fractional power of the group size, but fuller consideration of this phenomenon is outside the scope of this paper.

Terrorist Example

The terrorist dataset, compiled by Krebs (2001), consists of a presumed acquaintance network among 74 suspected terrorists. For the purposes of this analysis, only the main component is used, consisting of 63 individuals.

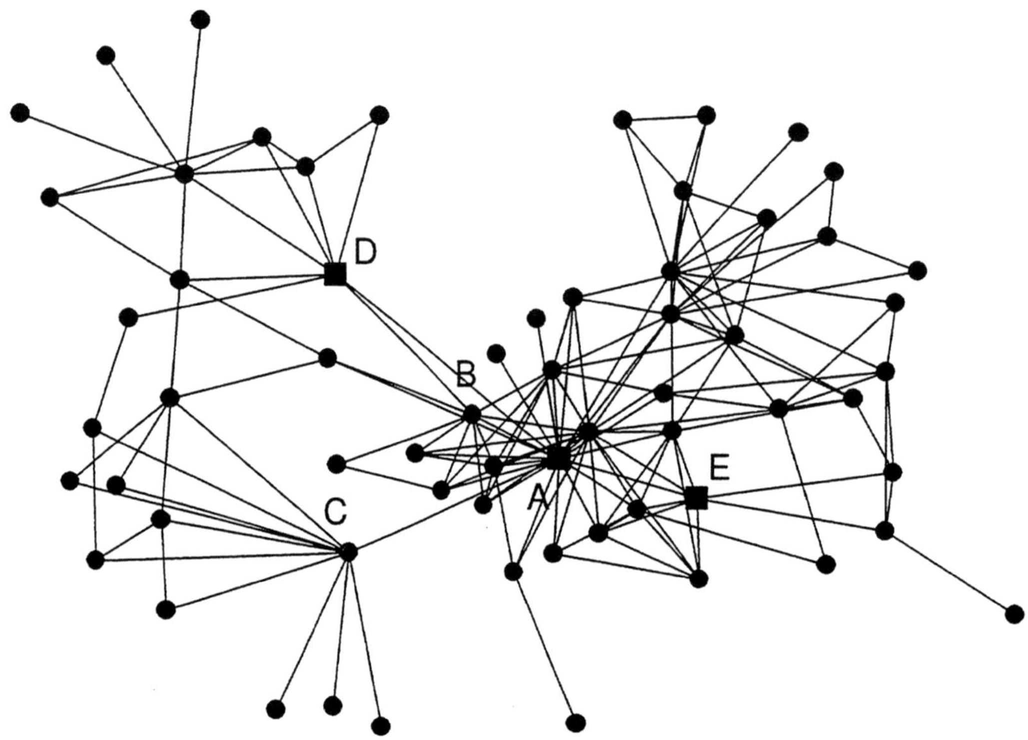

Figure 7. Terrorist network compiled by Krebs (2002).

The first question we ask is which persons should be isolated in order to maximally disrupt the network. Let us assume that we can only isolate three people. A run of the KeyPlayer program selects the three red nodes identified in red in Figure 7 (nodes A, B and C). Removing these nodes yields a fragmentation measure of 0.59, and breaks the graph into 7 components (including two large ones comprising the left and right halves of the graph).

The second question we ask is, given that we would like to diffuse certain information, which nodes would we want to be exposed to the information so as to potentially reach all other nodes quickly and with certainty? Let us assume that information that travels more than two links tends to degrade or be viewed with suspicion. Hence we want the smallest set of nodes that can reach all others within two links or less. The KeyPlayer algorithm finds that a set of three nodes (the square nodes in Figure 7, labeled A, C and D) reaches 100% of the network (including themselves).

Discussion

In this paper we have defined the KeyPlayer problem and demonstrated why the naïve centrality-based approach and more sophisticated graph-theoretic approaches fail to solve the problem. We have introduced new metrics for measuring success, and implemented a combinatorial optimization algorithm to maximize these quantities. Applications in both health and military areas were demonstrated.

The metrics for measuring success in the KPP-1 problem are essentially measures of graph cohesion that may be useful descriptively in a number of contexts besides the key player problem. Typical applications might be the comparison of similar organizations, or using cohesion as a predictor of group performance.

The fact that KPP-1 and KPP-2 have different solutions is interesting. For many, centrality is either a unitary concept with many highly correlated measures, or a fully multidimensional concept in which each measure indicates a different kind of centrality. I would suggest an intermediate view that divides notions of nodal importance into two basic types, corresponding to the KPP-1 and KPP-2 problems. KPP-1 measures quantify the extent to which a graph's cohesion is reduced by the removal of that node, while KPP-2 measures quantify the extent to which a node's ties reach into the network. It is the second type that is most directly about centrality: a node that is well-connected. The first type is not as much about the node's well-connectedness as about the connectedness of the rest of the graph in the absence of the node. From the graph's point of view, there is a loose analogy to the distinction in operant conditioning between positive reinforcement (KPP-2) and negative reinforcement (KPP-1): positive reinforcement provides benefit (connectivity) by directly providing a boon (the node's connections), while negative reinforcement provides benefit by relieving a stressor (the node holds together the otherwise fragmented graph). From the node's point of view, a node achieves its highest values on KPP-2 measures when the graph is highly cohesive. In contrast, high values on KPP-1 measures will normally occur only when the graph is not very cohesive. Actors high on KPP-2 measures lend themselves to maximizing utilization of resources flowing through the network, while actors high on KPP-1 measures lend themselves to maximizing the benefits of brokerage, gatekeeping and playing actors off each other.

Limitations and Next Steps

There are significant dimensions to the problem that I have ignored. Perhaps the most important is the issue of data quality. If this approach is to yield a practical tool, we cannot simply assume perfect data. Rather, the method should be robust in the face of errors in the data. Two approaches will be explored. First, there is the notion of not optimizing too closely to the observed dataset. If the data are known to vary from the truth by a given magnitude (e.g., 10% of observed ties don't actually exist and 10% of observed non-adjacent pairs are in fact adjacent), then we can randomly vary the data by this magnitude and optimize across a set of "adjacent" datasets obtained in this way. The result is a kp-set that is not necessarily optimal for the observed dataset, but will represent a high-quality solution for the neighborhood of the graph as a whole.

An alternative approach is to treat knowledge of ties as probabilistic, modifying the KeyPlayer metrics accordingly. For example, suppose we knew, for each pair of nodes, the independent likelihood that a tie exists between them. Then, in principle, we could work out the expected distance (including infinity) between the nodes across all possible networks.[4] KPP measures based on distance and reachability could then be computed substituting expected distance for observed distance. The practical challenge here is to find shortcut formulas for expected distance and connectedness that enable fast computation.

[4] Note that the problem being addressed is certainty of observed data values, not the existence of ties. It is assumed in this approach that ties are fixed and not probabilistically emerging as a function of node attributes or other ties. The dynamic nature of ties is a different phenomenon that wants its own models.

Another issue concerns the use of geodesic distance at all. As discussed by Borgatti (2002), different kinds of flows processes have different kinds of characteristic trajectories. For example, infections that immunize (or kill) the host don't return to nodes they have previously infected. Hence, they travel along graph theoretic paths. In contrast, gossip transmitted via email can easily reach the same node multiple times, but in general not from the same sources (i.e., a person doesn't usually tell the same confidential story to the same person more than once). Hence, stories travel along trails. Neither infections nor stories necessarily travel via the shortest paths to each node. Consequently, for those processes, the expected distance travelled by something flowing through the network is not equal to geodesic distance, and it would make sense to substitute this other expected distance in the equations.

For simplicity of exposition, this paper has assumed undirected simple graphs with non-valued edges. The extension to directed graphs is straightforward, but the extension to valued edges will require some development. An exception is the class of fragmentation measures, which generalize nicely along the lines of minimum weight cutsets, losing only the computational shortcuts available with non-valued data. The distance-based metrics will require different generalizations depending on the kinds of values, which could range from distances to capacities to probabilities of transmission. Multiple relations, recorded as separate graphs with a common node set, might be handled by summing the success criterion across all relations.

Finally, it may be of interest in the future to incorporate actor attributes. In the military context, communication among actors with redundant skills may sometimes be less important than communication between actors with complementary skills. In the public health context, it is helpful in slowing epidemics to minimize mixing of different populations (such as when married women are linked to commercial sex workers via their husbands). Hence, an additional criteria we would want to consider in fragmenting a network is maximizing separation of actors with certain attributes.

References

Borgatti, S.P. 2002. Stopping terrorist networks: Can social network analysis really contribute? *Sunbelt International Social Networks Conference.* 13-17 February. New Orleans.

Everett, M. G., & Borgatti, S. P. 1999. The centrality of groups and classes. *Journal of Mathematical Sociology.* 23(3): 181-201

Glover F., 1986, Future paths for integer programming and links to artificial intelligence, *Computers and Operations Research,* 5: 533-549.

Holland, J. 1975. *Adaptation in Natural and Artificial Systems.* University of Michigan Press.

Kernighan, B.W., and Lin, S. 1970. Efficient heuristic procedure for partitioning graphs. *Bell Systems Technical Journal.* 49(2): 291-297.

Krebs, V. 2002. Uncloaking terrorist networks. *First Monday* 7(4): April. http://www.firstmonday.dk/issues/issue7_4/krebs/index.html

Metropolis,N., A. Rosenbluth, M. Rosenbluth, A. Teller, E. Teller. 1953. Equation of state calculations by fast computing machines", *J. Chem. Phys.*,21, 6, 1087-1092.

Weeks, M.R., Clair, S., Borgatti, S.P., Radda, K., and Schensul, J.J. 2002. Social networks of drug users in high risk sites: Finding the connections. *AIDS and Behavior* 6(2): 193-206.

Balancing Efficiency and Vulnerability in Social Networks

Elisa Jayne Bienenstock
University of California, Irvine
Phillip Bonacich
University of California, Los Angeles

Abstract

Network centrality is thought to be crucial for the efficient distribution of information or resources through a social network. Inherent to this structure, the flow of information in high-centrality networks can be easily undermined. By introducing two concepts, network efficiency and vulnerability, we show that efficiency is compromised more in networks characterized by high degree centralization when degree and betweenness centrality are not distinct than in other networks, following the removal of network positions. Vulnerability is the loss in efficiency resulting from the elimination of nodes. The resiliency of a network was then assessed following progressive removal of nodes and all adjacent nodes. Nodes were removed in two ways: 1) randomly, which modeled incidental vulnerability; or, 2) based on the calculated centrality measures, which modeled vulnerability to a strategic attack. Our findings highlight the social impact of removing a person from a network, which is likely to disable, or make inactive, all direct ties to that individual. Such network analyses can be used to undermine or fortify existing network structures necessary for law enforcement and those concerned with national security.

Introduction

Social networks can be generally defined as a group of inter-connected individuals. The patterns of exchange of information or resources from person to person varies dependent on the inherent structure of the network. One simple network can be modeled as a pinwheel structure: each person, e.g., node, is connected to a common tie, which is the individual occupying the hub, or center, of the network (Fig. 1a). This structure has been shown to facilitate the flow of communication, since information from any location requires only two steps to saturate the network. If, however, the center node is removed the entire network collapses as the nodes occupying the periphery of this structure become isolated. As such, the pinwheel network is both very efficient and highly vulnerable as it is easily penetrated from an outside attack. The stability of a network is, therefore, dependent on its organization and ability to withstand such an attack.

Initial research found that networks with one, or several, central nodes were more efficient than networks in which the number of connections between nodes was more evenly dispersed (Bavelas, 1950). Freeman (1978) distinguished three conceptually different types of individual centrality: degree, betweenness and closeness, together with their corresponding system-wide, measure of the dispersion of the centrality, or centralization (Freeman, 1978:228). Degree is number of connections: a node with high degree has many connections. A network with high degree centralization is likely to have a few nodes with many ties and many nodes with few ties, such as the hub in a pinwheel structure. Betweenness measures the frequency with which a node is located on a path between other nodes: a node with high betweenness is in a position to act as either a bridge or a bottleneck. A network with high betweenness centralization is likely to have a few nodes that act as bridges. Closeness measures the degree to which a node is close to other nodes in the network. Centrality measures have been shown to be indicators of prestige or importance among actors in networks. Similarly, centralization has been associated with efficiency.

In another study (Cook, 1983), it was shown that, for tasks other than communication, centrality measures are not good indicators of who has power in the network. While local centrality measures predicts which individuals in a network have more control of the flow of information, and global centrality measures are good predictors of overall efficiency, this study (Cook, 1983) showed that in exchange networks, where the value of the commodity exchanged is lost to the person who relinquishes it, centrality measures do not predict who will have power to control resources. As an alternative to traditional centrality measures, this study (Cook, 1983) employed a vulnerability measure known as point vulnerability which measures the reduction in maximum resource flow (RMF) to the network that results when each position is removed. In an exchange network each individual adds value to the total value possible for the network, the network is vulnerable from the removal of an individual to the degree that value is lost to the network. This concept, point vulnerability did not do any better than centrality, ultimately, as a measure of power in exchange networks, so development of this measure was abandoned (Markovsky et al., 1988). Application of network methods to criminal and terrorists activity suggests that vulnerability may be an important and under-utilized network measure.

A recent report suggested that high degree centrality networks were both efficient and invulnerable to random attacks when compared to random networks (Barabasi 2002). This finding is in part a function of the definition used to define attack as the removal of one node from the network. Consider the pinwheel (Fig 1a). The only node essential for the functioning of the network is the central node and that node has only a 1/9 chance of being selected. The odds are good that the network can withstand a random attack. However, this report also notes that these networks are very susceptible to strategic attacks. If the network structure is known and centrality measures are calculated, then critical nodes are easily identified.

In this paper, we examine which network properties are required to design networks that are both efficient and resilient by comparing of networks based on the following four prototypes: random, scale-free, lattice and bipartite. We show that lattice structures and bipartite graphs that include a small proportion of random ties are the best at achieving enduring efficiency. While scale-free, high centrality networks do well when compared to random networks, they do not do well when compared with these other structures. We also expanded the scope of vulnerability, defining vulnerability as the removal of a node and all adjacent nodes. This models the likely effect of the removal of a node in a social network. When this more stringent type of vulnerability is considered the rewired lattice and rewired bipartite networks do well.

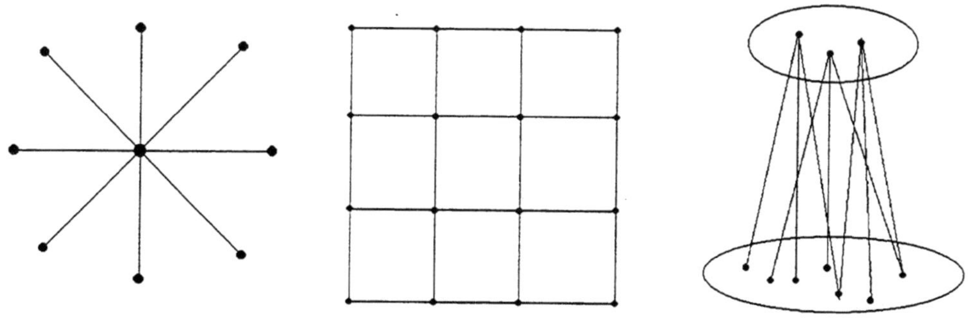

a. b. c.

Figure 1. A pinwheel, lattice, and bipartite graph.

Methods

Efficiency is defined as:

$$E = \frac{\sum_{i=1}^{n}\sum_{j>i}^{n} 1/d_{ij}}{n(n-1)}$$

E is the "efficiency" of a communications network; d_{ij} is the distance between vertices i and j. Shorter distances imply more effective communication and more efficient networks. When a network consists of more than one component such that i and j are not connected, d_{ij} is undefined. The reciprocal of the distance between nodes is zero for vertices in separate components and approaches one as the distance between two nodes diminishes. The denominator creates a measure that varies from zero to one where one is complete connectivity, all nodes are directly connected to all other nodes, and zero indicates the dissolution of the network into separate components.

Vulnerability (E_A) is a measure of the average decrease in efficiency of the network after attack and takes into account the entire history of the attack and the rapidity of the decline.

$$E_A = \frac{\sum_{i=1}^{K} E_i}{K}$$

Let $E_1, E_2, \ldots, E_K$ be the efficiency the network after the elimination of 1, 2, up to K nodes. E_A measures the average loss of efficiency during K attacks so that networks with a more rapid decline will have higher E_A scores. Efficiency and the reduction in efficiency were compared for ten networks of each type. The reduction in efficiency resulting from random attacks, attacks aimed against individuals with high betweenness centrality and attacks aimed against individuals with high degree were was calculated for each network. Table 1 summarizes the measures calculated for each network and compared in the analysis that follows.

Table 1. Measures compared: Efficiency, reduction in efficiency and centralization.

E	Initial efficiency. The range is from 0 to 1.
E_R	Recalculated efficiency after K attacks on randomly selected nodes. The range is from 0 to K.
E_B	Recalculated efficiency after K attacks on nodes with highest betweenness centrality. The range is from 0 to K.
E_D	Recalculated efficiency after K attacks on nodes with highest degree centrality The range is from 0 to K.
C_B	Betweenness centralization. The range is from 0 to 1.
C_D	Degree centralization. The range is from 0 to 1.

Networks

Four network structures were compared. Networks were the same with respect to size (N=100) and density (density = 4).

Random networks. Random networks serve as a baseline and have desirable properties of the own in terms of efficiency and vulnerability. Distances between vertices are short and they are decentralized and thus relatively invulnerable. To guarantee the connectedness of the network a circle frame network was imposed on 100 modes and 100 additional connections were randomly assigned.

Scale-free networks. Scale-free networks are networks characterized by having hubs (Fig 1a). Therefore, we predicted high degree centralization. Beginning with a small random network of ninety-five, additional positions with initial degree 2 were added using the scale-free algorithm;

the probability that a new node would connect to an existing node was proportional to the degree of the existing node.

Lattice networks. A ten by ten lattice network on a torus was created using the Von Neumann definition of neighbors (Fig 1b). As counterpoint to the scale-free network, lattice degree and betweenness centralization are zero. We also investigated a lattice that was rewired so that forty connections from the lattice network were replaced with randomly chosen connections, modeling a small world network (Watts, 1999). Since a lattice is not an efficient structure, but it is very resistant to attack, we predicted a rewired lattice to be more efficient then the lattice with no random connections (Watts, 1999). We hypothesized that this increase in efficiency would not undermine its resistance to attack in standard two-dimensional lattice. Lastly, we investigated the efficiency and resilience of three-dimensional lattices.

Bipartite networks. Bipartite networks were included because they modeled a structure that resembled real world criminal network structures. The network was composed of two types of actors. Actors can only be connected to members of the other class (Fig 1c). We were interested in a network that modeled a hierarchy where one class represented group leaders and the other the soldiers. The sizes of the two classes were twenty and eighty. Bipartite networks differ from actual criminal network insofar as in real networks members of the leadership are often directly connected. For that reason, bipartite network are likely less vulnerable than real life networks. In addition to strict bipartite networks we investigated bipartite networks that included some randomness. Forty edges from a bipartite network were randomly eliminated and replaced with 40 connections between positions in the larger class. We expected this to increase efficiency. To ensure networks were connected each of the eighty vertices in the larger class was randomly connected to one of the vertices in the smaller class and 120 additional randomly chosen edges were then added.

Results

Node Vulnerability

A comparison of the loss in efficiency for the random, scale free, rewired bipartite and rewired lattice structures to removal one node from the network, for five consecutive attacks confirm results of prior research that scale free networks are better than random networks at resisting random attacks, but they do not do better then a rewired bipartite graph structure. Values in table 2 and the error bars in Figure 2 indicate that scale free networks are the least resistant to strategic attacks that target nodes based on degree or betweenness centrality.

Table 2. Average Initial Efficiencies and Efficiencies Averaged over five attacks for ten networks of each type.

		Average Efficiency during 5 Attacks Criteria for Target Selection		
	Initial Efficiency	Random	High Betweenness	High Degree
Random	0.329	0.306	0.165	0.167
Scale-free	0.370	0.346	0.037	0.041
Bipartite Rewired	0.373	0.349	0.155	0.145
2D Lattice Rewired	0.307	0.286	0.181	0.179

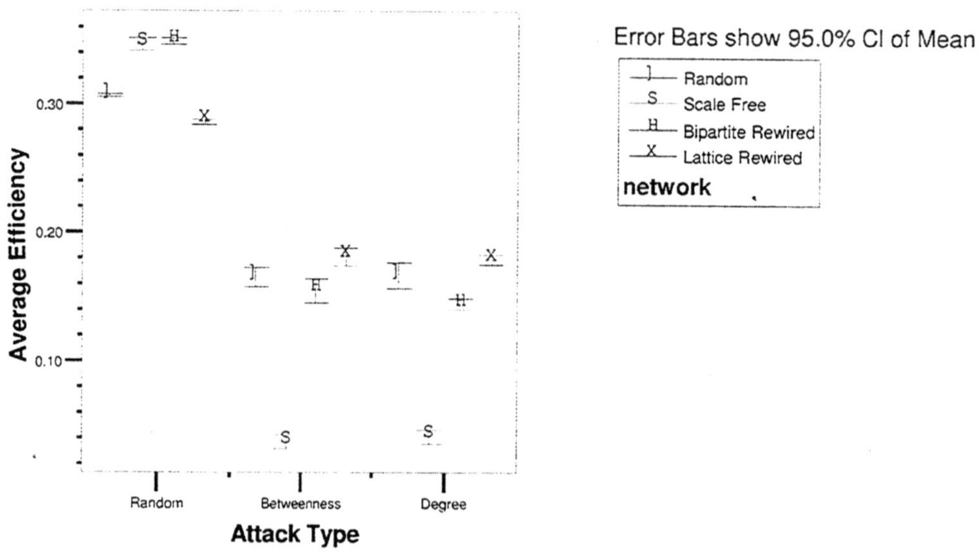

Figure 2. Average Efficiency during random, betweenness and degree based attacks for four network types.

Node Vulnerability vs. Neighborhood Vulnerability

The removal of a node from a graph is only the first step toward modeling the effect of the removal of an individual from a social network. The nature of human interaction is such that when one person is removed from a network, others, especially those who are directly connected to that person, are also affected. When considering the effect of the removal of an individual on network efficiency a model that focuses only on an isolated individual underestimates the impact that the loss a key person can have on a network. For example, in a criminal network, the arrest of one individual could result in a lull in the criminal activity simply because those connected to the arrested individual are alerted to the possibility that they may be under surveillance.

Alternatively, one network member's ability to function may be contingent on the presences of another, for example when there is a division of labor in an organization. In this case the removal of one network member can incapacitate many. To expand the scope of vulnerability accordingly we define vulnerability as the removal of a node and all adjacent nodes.

The following simulation illustrates the effect on network efficiency when vertices and their neighbors are eliminated by attacks rather than when vertices alone are eliminated. Random networks of size 15 with different average degrees were created and attacked either by eliminating the most central (betweenness) position or by eliminating the most central position plus its neighbors. Each cell table 3 is based on 10 simulations.

Table 3. Average degree and efficiency in random networks when position or position plus its neighbors eliminated.

Average degree	Efficiency	Nodal attack	Neighborhood attack
3	.534	.456	.249
4	.607	.520	.252
5	.663	.571	.199
6	.707	.612	.268
7	.750	.648	.191
8	.786	.683	.120

These results indicate that nodal vulnerability differs from neighborhood vulnerability. Depending on the research question the implications for vulnerability are different for different measures. As degree, or connectivity of the average node increases and high betweenness nodes are targeted the decrease in efficiency is minor. In fact, just as efficiency increases with degree so does efficiency in spite of nodal attack. However, if neighborhoods are implicated along with the node the opposite is true. As average degree increases network efficiency decreases. This is not only because more people are removed from the network, but also because there is an increasing likelihood that a random person will be connected to a person with higher degree centrality. The implication is that cells of criminal activity, connected by a few individuals with high betweenness are very vulnerable to the discovery of these individuals.

Centralization

For each structure type, ten networks were generated, each network containing 100 vertices with an average degree of 4 (200 edges). When networks were rewired (the bipartite and lattice networks), the number of rewired edges was 40. The maximum number of attacks was 5. An attack is the removal of a node along with all adjacent nodes. Criteria for node selection were 1) random, 2) high degree centrality, or 3) high betweenness centrality.

For most networks, there was no difference between betweenness and degree centralization. This is, in part, because for most networks betweenness and degree were highly correlated, as high betweenness is a function of high degree centrality. Networks in which these two centrality measures were not synonymous were likely to be most capable of balancing efficiency and invulnerability. For example, when correlations of nodal degree and betweenness were compared for three rewired-lattice networks, the correlations were 0.785, 0.729, and 0.753; for three scale-free networks the correlations were 0.943, 0.973, and 0.957.

Average values for initial efficiency, betweenness centralization and degree centralization for ten simulations runs for each type of network are presented in Table 4. The standard errors were small, so even small differences were significant. There was a relationship between centralization and efficiency: efficiency was related centralization as structures with high centrality also had high values for efficiency. The scale-free network, which is highest in both types of centralization, did not have the highest initial efficiency. Rather, the rewired bipartite graph had the highest initial efficiency score. Table 5 presents correlation coefficients for initial efficiency by betweenness and degree centralization.

Table 4. Initial efficiency, betweenness centralization and degree centralization with standard errors for six network structures.

Network	Initial Efficiency	Betweenness Centralization	Degree Centralization
Random	0.331	0.265	0.095
	0.000	0.020	0.006
Scale Free	0.357	0.613	0.345
	0.002	0.019	0.023
Bipartite	0.341	0.639	0.215
	0.001	0.038	0.008
Bipartite Rewired	0.373	0.449	0.196
	0.001	0.026	0.009
Lattice	0.258	0.000	0.000
	0.000	0.000	0.000
Lattice Rewired	0.307	0.238	0.048
	0.001	0.014	0.003

Table 5. Correlation of Initial efficiency, betweenness centralization and degree centralization for six network structures.

	Initial Efficiency	Betweenness Centralization	Degree Centralization
Initial Efficiency	1.000	0.751*	0.740*
Betweenness Centralization	0.751*	1.000	0.921**
Degree Centralization	0.740*	0.921**	1.000
*Correlation is significant at the 0.05 level (2-tailed)			
**Correlation is significant at the 0.01 level (2-tailed)			

Neighborhood Vulnerability to Attacks

To be invulnerable to attacks, networks must be able to sustain successive attacks and still remain a network. In others words the network should not disintegrate into many components. A network should also be able to continue functioning. Table 6 presents data from ten runs of six network types. Each network was subject to a five hits of three types. After each hit the efficiency of the remaining network was computed and averaged for all attacks (E_A). Values for random attacks, attacks based on degree centrality and attacks based on betweenness centrality are compared.

Table 6. Efficiency and average reduction in efficiency due to random and selective attacks based on betweenness and degree centrality by network type.

		Average Efficiency during 5 Attacks Criteria for Target Selection		
Network	Initial Efficiency	Random	Betweenness	Degree
Random	0.331 0.000	.238 0.016	.166 0.008	.165 0.009
Scale Free	0.357 0.002	.234 0.034	.058 0.014	.057 0.013
Bipartite	0.341 0.001	.207 0.021	.132 0.008	.138 0.020
Bipartite Rewired	0.373 0.001	0.220 0.018	0.146 0.007	0.146 0.009
Lattice	0.258 0.000	.186 0.003	.187 0.000	.205 0.000
Lattice Rewired	0.307 0.001	0.222 0.006	.182 0.006	.184 0.006

Scale-free networks are initially efficient, as are rewired bipartite graphs. The scale-free network is also more resistant than most other structures to random attacks (Figure 3) although again, not as resistant as random networks or the rewired lattices. The distinction between these structures becomes salient when strategic attacks are considered (Figure 4). Scale-free networks are the least resistant of all networks to strategic attacks. Adding random connections to the lattice and bipartite networks increases efficiency without sacrificing resilience. In fact the rewired bipartite network has higher efficiency after any type of attack then its rigidly structured counterpart. Graphs for degree vulnerability are not plotted since they do not differ significantly from the values for betweenness vulnerability.

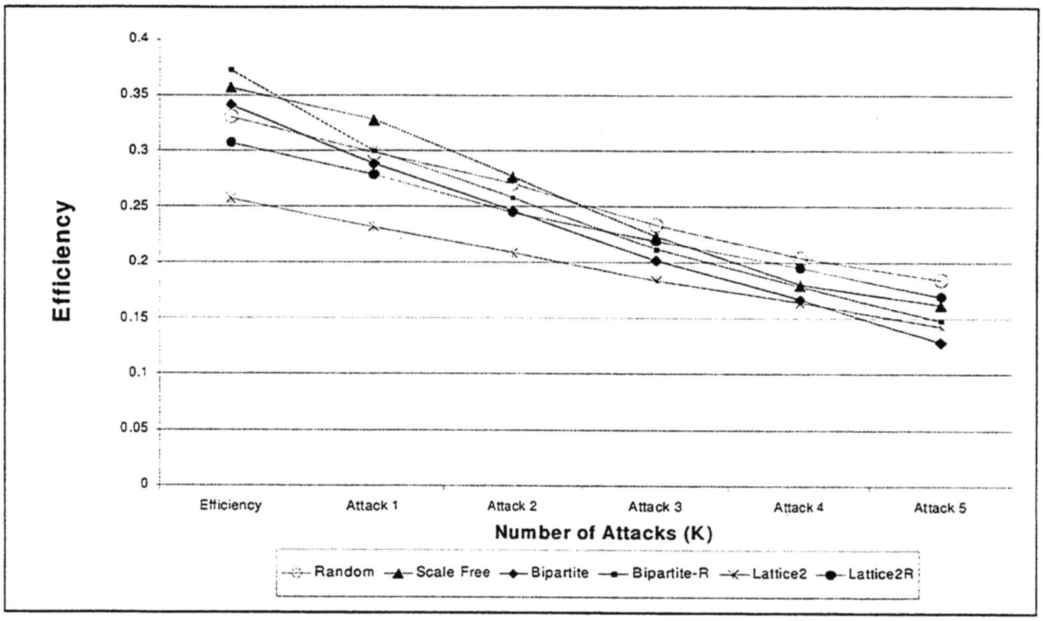

Figure 3. Loss of Efficiency resulting from 5 random hits.

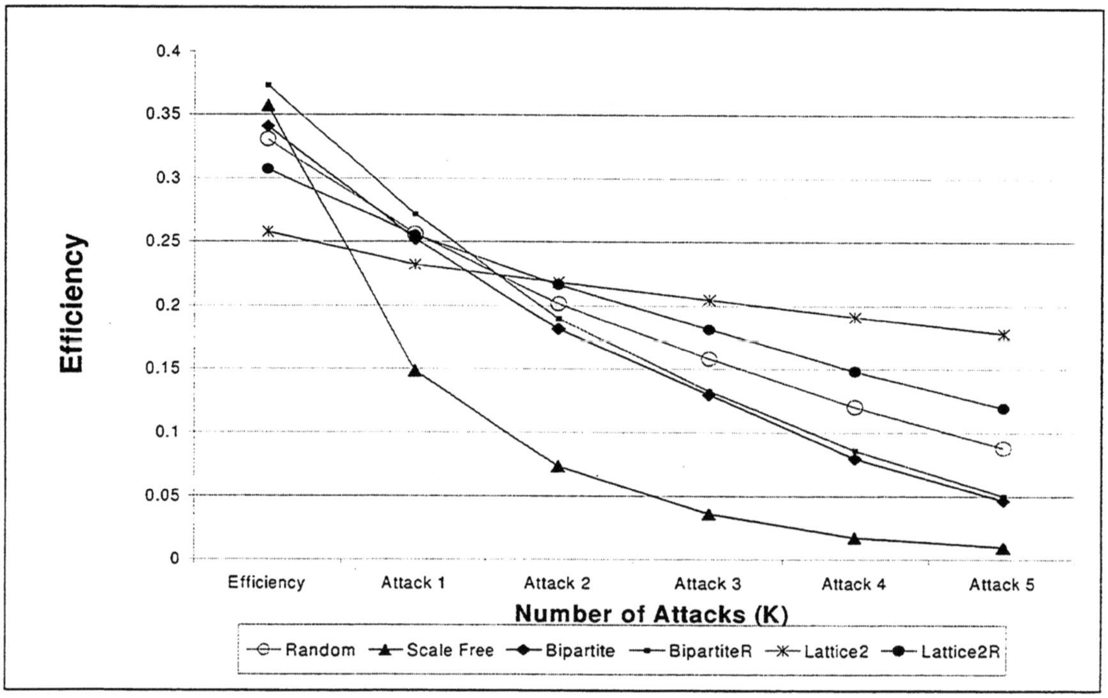

Figure 4. Loss of Efficiency resulting from 5 hits targeted at nodes with high betweenness.

Finally, the data clearly demonstrate that using centrality measures to select targets to weaken networks is beneficial. Table 5 presents the differences between measures of efficiency after attacks on targets chosen randomly or based on betweenness centrality. All but two values are positive indicating that efficiency levels after each attack are higher when the target is chosen randomly than when it is chosen strategically. In the two instances where this is not the case the values are nearly zero.

Table 7. Differences in efficiency between random and selective attacks by network structure

	Scale Free	Rewired Bipartite	Rewired Lattice
0	0.000	0.000	-0.001
1	0.045	-0.003	0.063
2	0.139	0.007	0.089
3	0.135	0.010	0.102
4	0.125	0.017	0.106
5	0.095	0.022	0.106

Conclusion

Insights from social network analysis may assist those who design networks in constructing structures that maximize communication yet minimize vulnerability. Designers of networks that may come under attack face two dilemmas. First, centralized networks are very efficient but also vulnerable to selective attacks on their most central members. Second, a high density of connections leads to shorter communication paths and less dependence on particular members but to ensure resistance to attack network members must be separated from one another so an attack on one member does not unravel the entire network. This paper explores classes of networks, random, scale-free, bipartite, and small-world, to explore what properties of networks obviate these dilemmas. The focus of this paper was on the resistance of networks to random attacks and attacks aimed at positions of high centrality. Future work will expand this to test network resilience to attacks based on other criteria. For example, selecting targets based on point vulnerability rather than centrality may prove detrimental to other structures.

This research provides insight into the relationship between network structure in terms of centrality, density, efficiency and vulnerability. Future work will test the robustness of these results by expanding the model and the analysis to include larger networks of varying densities. Understanding the relationship of standard network measure to efficiency and vulnerability is a first step toward designing organizational networks that maximize both efficiency and resistance to attack. This will allow researchers and analyst a systematic way to evaluate existing networks to uncover vulnerabilities.

References

Barabasi, A. 2002. Linked: *The New Science of Networks.* Perseus Publishing. Cambridge.

Bavelas, A. 1950. "Communication Patterns in Task-Oriented Groups." *The Journal of the Acoustical Society of America* 22 6: 725-730.

Cook, K. S., R,M. Emerson, M.R. Gillmore, and T. Yamagishi. 1983. "The Distribution of Power in Exchange Networks: Theory and Experimental Results." *American Journal of Sociology* 89:275-305.

Freeman, L., 1978. "Centrality in Social Networks: Conceptual Clarification." *Social Networks* 1:215-239.

Markovsky, B., D. Willer, and T. Patton. 1988. "Power Relations in Exchange Networks." *American Sociological Review* 53: 220-236.

Watts, D.J. Small Worlds: *The Dynamics of Networks between Order and Randomness.* Princeton University Press. New Jersey.

Data Mining on Large Graphs

Christopher R. Palmer
Computer Science Department
Carnegie Mellon University
Pittsburgh, PA
crpalmer@cs.cmu.edu

Phillip B. Gibbons
Information Sciences Research Center
Bell Laboratories
Murray Hill, NJ
gibbons@research.bell-labs.com

Christos Faloutsos*
Computer Science Department
Carnegie Mellon University
Pittsburgh, PA
christos@cs.cmu.edu

Abstract

Graphs are an increasingly important data source, with such important graphs as the Internet and the Web. Other familiar graphs include CAD circuits, phone records, gene sequences, city streets, social networks and academic citations. Any kind of relationship, such as actors appearing in movies, can be represented as a graph. This work presents a data mining tool, called ANF, that can quickly answer a number of interesting questions on graph-represented data, such as the following. How robust is the Internet to failures? What are the most influential database papers? Are there gender differences in movie appearance patterns? At its core, ANF is based on a fast and memory-efficient approach for approximating the complete "neighbourhood function" for a graph. For the Internet graph (268K nodes), ANF's highly-accurate approximation is more than **700 times faster** than the exact computation. This reduces the running time from nearly **a day to a matter of a minute or two**, allowing users to perform ad hoc drill-down tasks and to repeatedly answer questions about changing data sources. To enable this drill-down, ANF employs new techniques for approximating neighbourhood-type functions for graphs with distinguished nodes and/or edges. When compared to the best existing approximation, ANF's approach is both faster and more accurate, given the same resources. Additionally, unlike previous approaches, ANF scales gracefully to handle disk resident graphs. Finally, we present some of our results from mining large graphs using ANF.

---

*This material is based upon work supported by the National Science Foundation under Grants No. DMS-9873442, IIS-9817496, IIS-9910606, IIS-9988876, LIS 9720374, and by the Defense Advanced Research Projects Agency under Contracts No. N66001-97-C-8517 and N66001-00-1-8936. Additional funding was provided by donations from NEC and Intel. Any opinions, findings, and conclusions or recommendations expressed in this material are those of the author(s) and do not necessarily reflect the views of the National Science Foundation, DARPA, or other funding parties.

1 Introduction

Graph-based data is becoming more prevalent and interesting to the data mining community, for example in understanding the Internet and the WWW. These entities are modeled as graphs where each node is a computer, administrative domain of the Internet, or a web page, and each edge is a connection (network or hyperlink) between the resources. Google is interested in finding the most "important" nodes in such a graph [2]. Broder et al. studied the connectivity information of nodes in the Internet [13, 3]. The networking community has used different measures of node "importance" to build a hierarchy of the Internet [20]. Another source of graph data that has been studied are citation graphs [18]. Here, each node is a publication and each edge is a citation from one publication to another and we wish to know the most important papers. There are many more examples of graphs which contain interesting information for data mining purposes. For example, the telephone calling records from a long distance carrier can be viewed as a graph, and by mining the graph we may help identify fraudulent behaviour or marketing opportunities. DNA sequencing can also be viewed as a graph, and identifying common subsequences is a form of mining that could help scientists. Circuit design, for example from a CAD system, forms a graph and data mining could be used to find commonly used components, points of failure, etc.

In fact, any binary relational table is a graph. For example, in this paper we use a graph derived from the Internet Movie Database [10] where we let each actor and each movie be a node and add an undirected edges between and actor, a, and a movie, m, to indicate that a appeared in m. It is also common to define graphs for board positions in a game. We will consider the simple game of tic-tac-toe. From all of these data sources, we find some prototypical questions which have motivated this work:

1. How robust is the Internet to failures?
2. Is the Canadian Internet similar to the French?
3. Does the Internet have a hierarchical structure?
4. Are phone call patterns (caller-callee) in Asia similar to those in the U.S.?
5. Does a new circuit design appear similar to a previously patented design?
6. What are the most influential database papers?
7. Which set of street closures would least affect traffic?
8. What is the best opening move in tic-tac-toe?
9. Are there gender differences in movie appearances?
10. Cluster movie genres.

It is possible to answer all of these questions by computing three graph properties pertaining to the connectivity or neighbourhood structure of the graph:

Graph Similarity: Given two graphs, G_1 and G_2, do the graphs have similar connectivity / neighbourhood structure (independent of their sizes). Such a similarity measure is useful for answering questions 1, 4, and 5.

Subgraph Similarity: Given two subsets of the vertices of the graph, V_1 and V_2, compare how these two induced subgraphs are connected within the graph. Such a similarity measure is useful for answering questions 2, 4, 8, 9, and 10.

Vertex Importance: Assign an importance to each node in the graph based on the connectivity. This importance measure is useful for answering questions 1, 3, 6, and 7.

We answer questions 1, 7 and 10 in this paper, one from each of the three types. The remaining questions can be answered in a similar fashion, using various forms of the *Neighbourhood Function*. The basic neighbourhood function $N(h)$ for a graph, also called the *hop plot* [8], is the number of pairs of nodes within a specified distance h, for all distances h. In section 2 we will define this more formally and present a more general form of the neighbourhood function that can be used to compute all three graph properties.

The main contribution of this paper is a tool that allows us to compute these three graph properties, thereby enabling us to answer interesting questions like those we suggested. Beyond simply answering the questions, we want our tool to be fast enough to allow drill-down tasks. That is, we want it to be possible to interactively answer users requests. For example, to determine the best roads to close for a parade, the city planner would want to interactively consider various sets of street closures and compare the effect on traffic. Almost in contrast to the need to be able to run interactively on graphs, we also want a tool that scales to very large graphs. In [3, 13], measuring properties about the web required hardware resources that are beyond the means of most researchers. Instead, we produce a data mining tool that is useful given any amount of RAM. These two goals give rise to the following list of properties that our tool must satisfy when analyzing a graph with n nodes and m edges:

Error guarantees: estimates must be accurate at all distances (not just in the limit).

Fast: scale linearly with # of nodes and # edges (n, m).

Low storage requirements: use only $O(n)$ additional storage.

Adapts to the available memory: when the node set does not fit in memory, make effective use of the available memory.

Parallelizable: for massive graphs, must be able to distribute the work over multiple processors and/or multiple workstations, with low overheads.

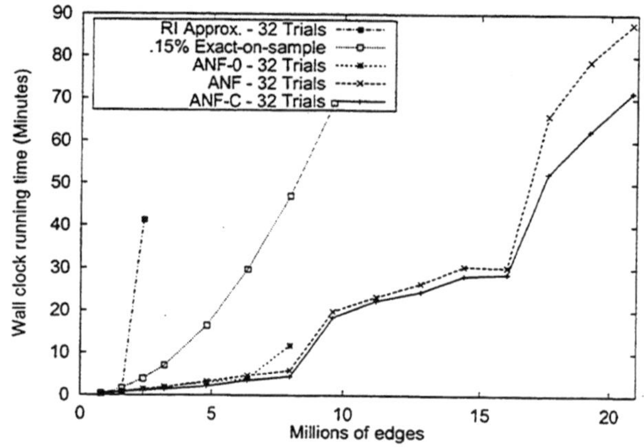

Figure 1: ANF algorithms scale but not the others

Sequential scans of the edge file: avoid random accesses to the graph. Random accesses exhibit horrible paging performance for the common case that the graph is larger than the available memory.

Estimates per node: must be able to estimate the neighbourhood function from each node, not just for the graph as a whole.

This paper presents such a tool, which we call ANF for *Approximate Neighbourhood Function*. In the literature, we have found two existing approaches that could prove useful for computing the neighbourhood function. We show that neither meets our requirements, primarily because neither scales well to very large graphs. This can be seen in Figure 1, which plots the running time versus the graph size for some randomly-generated graphs. The two existing approaches (the RI approximation scheme [4] and a random sampling approach) scale very poorly while our ANF schemes scale much more gracefully and make it possible to investigate much larger graphs. In section 2 we provide background material, definitions and a survey of the related work. In section 3 we describe our ANF algorithms. In section 4, we present experimental results demonstrating the scalability of our approach. In addition, we show that, given the same resources, (1) ANF is much more accurate and faster then the RI approximation scheme, and (2) ANF is more than 700 times faster than the exact computation for a snapshot of the Internet graph (268K nodes). In section 5, we use ANF to answer some of the prototypical questions posed in this introduction.

2 Background and Related Work

2.1 Definitions

Let $G = (V, E)$ be a graph with n vertices, V, and m directed edges, E. (Table 1 summarizes the symbols used in this paper.) Let $dist(u, v)$ be the number of edges on the shortest path from u to v. To answer our prototypical questions, we need a characterization of a node's connectivity and the connectivity within a graph, as a whole. Accordingly, we define the following forms of the

Table 1: Commonly used symbols

Name	Description
n	Number of vertices
m	Number of edges
V	Vertex set $\{0, 1, \cdots, n-1\}$
E	Edge set $\{(u, v) : u, v \in V\}$
d	Diameter of the graph
S	Starting set for the neighbourhood
C	Concluding set for the neighbourhood
r	Number of extra approximation bits
k	Number of parallel approximations

neighbourhood function:

Def. 1 *The* individual neighbourhood function *for u at h is the number of nodes at distance h or less from u.*
$IN(u,h) = | \{v : v \in V, dist(u,v) \leq h\} |$
Def. 2 *The* neighbourhood function *at h is the number of pairs of nodes within distance h.*
$N(h) = | \{(u,v) : u \in V, v \in V, dist(u,v) \leq h\} |$, *or*
$N(h) = \sum_{u \in V} IN(u,h)$.

To deal with subgraphs, we generalize these two definitions slightly. Let S be a set of *starting nodes* and C be a set of *concluding nodes*. We are interested in the number of pairs starting from a node in S to a node in C within distance h:

Def. 3 *The* generalized individual neighbourhood function *for u at h given C is the number of nodes in C within distance h.*
$IN^+(u,h,C) = | \{v : v \in C, dist(u,v) \leq h\} |$.
Note that $IN(u,h) = IN^+(u,h,V)$.
Def. 4 *The* generalized neighbourhood function *at h is the number of pairs of a node from S and a node from C that are within distance h or less.*
$N^+(h,S,C) = | \{(u,v) : u \in S, v \in C, dist(u,v) \leq h\} |$
$N^+(h,S,C) = \sum_{u \in S} IN^+(u,h,C)$.
Note that $N(h) = N^+(h,V,V)$.

In section 5 we will use the neighbourhood function to characterize graphs. We will compare $N_{G_1}(h)$ to $N_{G_2}(h)$ to measure the similarity in connectivity/neighbourhood structure of graphs G_1 and G_2. For example, if we want to know the structural similarly of the Web from 1999 to today's Web, we can compute their neighbourhood functions and compare them at all points. Comparing subgraphs induced by vertex sets V_1 and V_2 can be done by comparing $N^+(h,V_1,V_1)$ to $N(h,V_2,V_2)$. E.g., let V_1 be the routers in the Canadian domain and V_2 be the routers in the French domain. Finally, we will use the individual neighbourhood function for a node to characterize its importance, with respect to the connectivity. E.g., the most important router is the one that in some way reaches the most routers the fastest.

Thus, if we can compute all these variants of the neighbourhood function efficiently, then we can answer the graph questions that we posed in the introduction.

2.2 Related Work

It is trivial to compute $N(0)$ and $N(1)$, which are $|V|$ and $|V|+|E|$ respectively. $N(2)$ is reminiscent of the size of the (self-)join of the edge relation: each edge is viewed as a tuple with attributes "first" and "second" and $N(2) - N(1)$ is the size of the result of the query

```
select distinct E1.first, E2.second
from edge-rel E1, edge-rel E2
where E1.second = E2.first
```

Writing $N(2) - N(1)$ in this way illustrates the difficulty in efficiently computing $N(h)$ for any $h \geq 2$. The *distinct* means that we must know which of the n^2 possible pairs of nodes have already been counted and we must take care not to over count in the presence of multiple paths between the same pair of nodes. One approach to computing $N(h)$ is to repeatedly multiply the graph's adjacency matrix. Asymptotically, this could be done in $O(n^{2.38})$ time. Unfortunately, we would also require $O(n^2)$ memory, which is prohibitive. Instead, it is common to use breadth first searches in the graph. A breadth-first search beginning from u can easily compute $IN(u,h)$ for all h. We can compute $N(h)$ by running a breadth-first search from each node u and summing over all u. This takes only $O(n+m)$ storage but the worse case running time is $O(nm)$. For large, disk resident graphs, a breadth-first search results in an expensive random-like access to the disk blocks. This appears to be the state of the art solution for exact computation of $N(h)$.

The transitive closure is $N(\infty)$ or, equivalently, $N(d)$, where d is the diameter of the graph. Lipton and Naughton [14] presented an $O(n\sqrt{m})$ algorithm for estimating the transitive closure that uses an adaptive sampling approach for selecting starting nodes of breadth-first traversals. Motivated by this work, in section 4 we will experimentally evaluate a similar sampling strategy to discover that it scales poorly to large graphs and, due to the random-like access to the edge file, it does not scale to graphs larger than the RAM. Most importantly, however, we will find that the quality of this approximation can be quite poor (we show an example where even a sample as large as 15% does not provide a useful approximation!). Lipton and Naughton's work was improved by Cohen, who gave an $O(m)$ time algorithm using only $O(n+m)$ memory [4]. Cohen also presented an $O(m \log n)$ time algorithm for estimating the individual neighbourhood functions, $IN(u,h)$. This appears to be the only previous work which attempts to approximate the neighbourhood function. More details of this algorithm, which we refer to as the *RI approximation*, appear in section 4.1.1 when we experimentally compare it to our new approximation. Our experiments demonstrate that the RI approximation is ill-suited for large graphs; this is due to its extensive use of random-like access (for breadth first search, heap data structures, etc.).

The problems of random access to a disk resident edge file has been addressed in [15]. They find that it is possible to define good storage layouts for undirected graphs but that the storage blowup can be very large. Given that we are interested only in very large graphs and graphs with directed edges, this does not solve the problems related to large edge files. Instead, we will need to find a new computation strategy which avoids random access to disk.

State-of-the-art approaches to understanding/characterizing the Internet and the Web very often make use of neighbourhood information [3, 13, 1, 20]. Other recent work in data mining for graphs has focused on mining frequent substructures. Essentially, the problem of finding frequent

```
// Set 𝓜(x, 0) = {x}
FOR each node x DO
      M(x, 0) =   concatenation of k bitmasks
                  each with 1 bit set (P(bit i) = .5^(i+1))
FOR each distance h starting with 1 DO
   FOR each node x DO M(x, h) = M(x, h − 1)
   // Update 𝓜(x, h) by adding one step
   FOR each edge (x, y) DO
        M(x, h) = (M(x, h) BITWISE-OR M(y, h − 1))
   // Compute the estimates for this h
   FOR each node x DO
        Individual estimate IN̂(x, h) = (2^b)/.77351
        where b is the average position of the least zero bits
        in the k bitmasks
   The estimate is: N̂(h) = Σ_{all x} IN̂(x, h)
```

Figure 2: Introduction to the basic ANF algorithm

itemsets is generalized to frequent subgraphs. Systems for this include SUBDUE [5] and AGM [11]. Graphs have been used to improve marketing strategies [7]. A survey of work on citation analysis appears in [18].

3 Proposed Approximation to the Neighbourhood Function

We are given a graph $G = (V, E)$. We assume that $V = \{0, 1, \cdots, n-1\}$ and that E contains m directed edges. Undirected graphs can be represented using pairs of directed edges. We wish to approximate the function $N^+(h, S, C)$ and $IN^+(x, h, C)$ for a node x, allowing us to compute $N(h)$ and $IN(x, h)$. The approximation must be done accurately and in such a way that we will be able to handle disk resident graphs. In this section, we construct such an approximation gradually. First, we approximate $N(h)$ and/or $IN(x, h)$ assuming memory-resident data structures. We extend this algorithm to approximate $N^+(h, S, C)$ and $IN^+(x, h, C)$ but still requiring sufficient RAM for processing. Next, we move the data structure to disk and to create an algorithm that meets all of our requirements. Finally, we will extend this algorithm with bit compression to further increase its speed.

3.1 Basic ANF Algorithm (ANF-0)

A graph traversal effectively accesses the edge file in random order. Thus, if our algorithm is going to be efficient on a graph that does not fit in memory, we cannot perform any graph traversals. Instead, we are going to build up the nodes reachable from x within h steps by first finding out which nodes its neighbours can reach in $h-1$ steps. Slightly more formally, let $\mathcal{M}(x, h)$ be the set of nodes within distance h of x. Clearly, $\mathcal{M}(x, 0) = \{x\}$, since the only node within distance 0 of x is x itself. To compute $\mathcal{M}(x, h)$ we note that x can still reach in h or fewer steps the nodes it could reach in $h-1$ or fewer steps. But, x can also reach the nodes in $\mathcal{M}(y, h-1)$ if there is an edge from x to y. That is:

x	$M(x,0)$	$M(x,1)$	$\hat{IN}(x,1)$	$M(x,2)$	$\hat{IN}(x,3)$
0	100 100 001	110 110 101	4.1	110 111 101	5.2
1	010 100 100	110 101 101	3.25	110 111 101	5.2
2	100 001 100	110 101 100	3.25	110 111 101	5.2
3	100 100 100	100 111 100	4.1	110 111 101	5.2
4	100 010 100	100 110 101	3.25	110 111 101	5.2

Figure 3: Simple example of *basic ANF*

$\mathcal{M}(x,0) = \{x\}$ for all $x \in V$
FOR each distance h DO
  $\mathcal{M}(x,h) = \mathcal{M}(x,h-1)$ for all $x \in V$
  FOR each edge (x,y) DO
    $\mathcal{M}(x,h) = \mathcal{M}(x,h) \cup \mathcal{M}(y,h-1)$

This iterates over the edge set instead of performing a traversal. The trick will be to efficiently compute the number of distinct elements in $\mathcal{M}(x,h)$. One possibility is to use a dictionary data structure (e.g., a B-tree) to represent the sets $\mathcal{M}(x,h)$. However, this approach needs $O(n^2 \log n)$ time and space, which is prohibitive. An approach that people, particularly C hackers, often employ is to use bits to mark membership. That is, each node is given one of n bits and a set is a bit string of length n. To add a node to the set, we mark its bit. The union of two sets is the bitwise-OR of the bitmasks. Unfortunately, this approach still uses $O(n^2)$ memory, which will be prohibitive for large graphs.

Instead, we're going to use a clever probabilistic counting algorithm [9] to approximate the sizes of the sets using shorter bit strings ($\log n + r$ bits, for some small constant r). We refer to the bit string that approximates $\mathcal{M}(x,h)$ as $M(x,h)$. Instead of giving each node its own bit, we are going to give about half the nodes bit 0, a quarter of them bit 1, and so on (give a node bit i with probability $1/2^{i+1}$). We still mark a node by setting its bit and use bitwise-OR for the set-union. Estimating the size of the set from the small bit string is done based on the following intuition. If we expect 25% of the nodes to be assigned to bit 1 and we haven't seen any of them (bit 1 is not set), then we probably saw about 4 or less nodes. So, the approximation of the size of the set $\mathcal{M}(x,h)$ is proportional to 2^b, where b is the least bit number in $M(x,h)$ that has not been set. We refer the reader to [9] for a derivation of the constant of proportionality and a proof that this estimate has good error bounds.

A single approximation is obviously not very robust. We do k parallel approximations by treating $M(x,h)$ as a bit-string of length $k(\log n + r)$ bits. Figure 2 shows the complete algorithm implementing the edge-scan based ANF.

Example. Figure 3 shows the bitmasks and approximations for a simple example of our most basic ANF algorithm. The purpose is to clarify the concatenation of the bitmasks and to illustrate the computation. The input is a 5 node undirected cycle and we used parameters $k = 3$ and $r = 0$. The first `FOR` loop of the algorithms generates the table of random bitmasks $M(x,0)$. That is, using an exponential distribution, we randomly set one bit in each of the three concatenated bitmasks. (In the figure, bit 0 is the leftmost bit in each 3-bit mask.) Then, each iteration uses the `OR`

```
FOR each node x DO
    IF x ∈ C THEN
        Mcur(x) =   concatenation of k bitmasks each
                    with 1 bit set (P(bit i) = .5^(i+1))
FOR each distance h starting with 1 DO
    FOR each node x DO Mlast(x) = Mcur(x)
    FOR each edge (x,y) DO
        Mcur(x) = (Mcur(x) BITWISE-OR Mlast(y))
    FOR each node x DO
        IN^+(x,h,C) = (2^b)/.77351, where b is the average
        position of the least zero bit in the k bitmasks
    N^+(h,S,C) = Σ_{x∈S} IN(x,h,C)
```

Figure 4: ANF-0: In-core ANF

operation to combine the nodes that it could reach in $h-1$ steps plus the ones that its neighbours could reach in $h-1$ steps. For example, $M(2,1)$ is just $M(1,1)$ OR $M(2,1)$ OR $M(3,1)$, because nodes 1 and 3 are the neighbors of node 2. The estimates, for example $\hat{IN}(2,1)$, are computed from the average of the least zero bit positions ($2,1,1 = \frac{4}{3}$, and $2^{4/3}/.77359 = 3.25$).

The algorithm in Figure 2 uses an excessive amount of memory and does not estimate the more general forms of the neighbourhood function. Figure 4 depicts the same algorithm, with the following improvements:

- $M(x,h)$ uses $M(y,h-1)$ but never $M(y,h-2)$. Thus we use $Mcur(x)$ to hold $M(x,h)$ and $Mlast(y)$ to hold $M(y,h-1)$ during iteration h.
- The starting nodes, S, just changes the estimate by summing over $x \in S$ instead of $x \in V$. In terms of implementation, this can be done by extending $Mcur$ to hold a *marked* bit indicating membership in S.
- The concluding nodes change the $h=0$ case. Now $\mathcal{M}(x,0)$ is $\{\}$ if $x \notin C$ since it can reach no nodes in C in zero steps. Thus nodes not in C are initially assigned a bitmask of all 0s.

The ANF-0 algorithm meets all but one of the requirements set out in the introduction:

Error guarantees: each $IN^+(x,h,C)$ is provably estimated with low error with high confidence.

Fast: running time is $O((n+m)d)$ which we expect to be fast since d is typically quite small (verified in section 4).

Low storage requirements: only additional memory for $Mcur$ and $Mlast$.

Adapts to the available memory? No! We will address this issue in the next section.

Easily parallelizable: Partition the nodes among the processors and then each processor may independently compute $Mcur$ for each x in its set. Synchronization is only needed after each iteration.

Sequential scans of the edge file: Yes.

Estimates $IN(x, h)$: Yes, with provable accuracy.

3.2 ANF Algorithm

The ANF-0 algorithm no longer accesses the edges in random order, but we now access $Mcur$ and $Mlast$ in an effectively random order. When we see the edge (x, y) we read and write $Mcur(x)$ and read $Mlast(y)$. If these tables are larger than the available memory, swapping will kill performance. We propose a small amount of preprocessing, to make these accesses predictable. Our idea is to break the large bitmasks $Mcur$ and $Mlast$ into b_1 and b_2, resp., equal-sized pieces. We partition the edges into $b_1 \times b_2$ buckets. In most cases, a one pass bucket sort can be used to partition the edges. Given that we have partitioned the edges, we would like to run the following algorithm to update $Mcur$:

```
FOR each bucket i of Mcur DO
  Load bucket i of Mcur
  FOR each bucket j of Mlast DO
    Load bucket j of Mlast
    FOR each edge (x,y) in bucket (i,j) DO
      Mcur(x) = Mcur(x) OR Mlast(y)
  Write bucket i of Mcur
```

The cost of this algorithm is exactly the same cost as running ANF-0 plus the cost of the I/O (we have simply reordered the original computation). If $Mcur$ and $Mlast$ are N bytes long, then the cost of the I/O required to update the bitmasks is: $2N$ to load and store each bucket of $Mcur$ and b_1N to read $Mlast$ once for each bucket of $Mcur$. That is, the cost of this I/O is $(b_1 + 2)N$. Thus, we select b_1 and b_2 such that b_1 is minimal, given that we have enough file descriptors to efficiently perform the bucket sort in one pass.

Note that by reordering the computation to bucketize the edges, we now have very predictable I/O. Thus, we will insert *prefetching* operations which allows the computation and the I/O to be performed in parallel. The complete algorithm with prefetching appears in Figure 5.

This algorithm now meets all of our requirements.

3.3 Leading Ones Compressions (ANF-C)

ANF is an algorithm that will be dominated by the I/O costs for large data sets and by the cost of the bit operations for smaller data sets. In both cases, we can further improve ANF by reducing the number of bits of data that must be stored. First, observe that, as ANF runs, most of the

```
Select the number of buckets b1 and b2
Partition the edges into the buckets (sorted by bucket)
FOR each node x DO
    IF x ∈ C THEN
        Mcur(x) = concatenation of k bitmasks each
                  with 1 bit set (P(bit i) = .5^(i+1))
    IF x ∈ S THEN mark(Mcur(x))
    IF current buffer is full THEN
        switch buffers and perform I/O
Flush any buffers that need to be written
FOR each distance h DO
    Fetch the data for the first bucket of Mcur and Mlast
    Prefetch next buckets of Mcur and Mlast
    FOR each edge (x,y) DO
        IF Mcur(y) is not in memory THEN
            We have been flushing and prefetching it
            Wait for it if necessary
            Asynchronously flush modified buffer
            Begin prefetching next buffer
        IF Mlast(x) is not in memory THEN
            We have been prefetching it
            Wait for it if necessary
            Begin prefetching next buffer.
        Mcur(x) = (Mcur(x) OR Mlast(y))
    // Copy Mcur(u) to Mlast(u) as we stream through Mcur(u)
    // computing the estimate
    est = 0
    Fetch the data for the first bucket of Mcur
    FOR each node x DO
        IF Mcur(x) is not in memory THEN
            We have been prefetching it
            Wait for it to be available
            Start prefetching the next buffer
        Mlast(x) = Mcur(x)
        If x is the last element in its bucket of Mlast THEN
            Asynchronously flush the buffer
            Continue processing in the double buffer
        IF marked(Mcur(x)) THEN
            IN+(x,h,C) = (2^b)/.77351
            est += IN+(x,h,C)
                where b is the average position of the least zero
                bits in the k bitmasks
    output N̂+(h,S,C) = est
```

Figure 5: ANF: Disk based processing

bitmasks will gradually accumulate a relatively lengthy set of leading 1s. That is, the bitmasks are of the form:

$$1111111110xxxxxx$$

It is wasteful to apply the bit operations and to write these leading 1s to disk. Instead, we will compress them. Second, we can achieve even better compression by *bit shuffling*. We have k parallel approximations, each of which has many leading ones. Instead of compressing each mask individually, we interleave the bitmasks by taking the first bit of each mask, followed by the second bit of each, etc. For example, with 2 masks:

$$11010, 11100 \Rightarrow 1111011000$$

which gives rise to a larger number of leading ones. The ANF-C algorithm uses a counter of the leading ones to reduce the amount of I/O and the number of bit operations. Like the *mark* bit, this counter can be prepended to the bitmask. In our experiments, we will find that leading ones compressions provide a significant speed-up, up to 23% in Figure 1.

4 Experimental Evaluation

In this section we present an experimental validation of our ANF approximation. Two alternative approaches will be introduced and then we will describe our data sets. Next, we propose a metric for comparing two neighbourhood functions (functions over a potentially large domain). We conduct a sensitivity analysis of the parameter r. Then, we pick a value of r and we compare ANF to the approximation presented in [4] for various settings of the parameter k. We then show that sampling can provide very poor estimates and, finally, we examine the scalability of all approaches. The key results from this section are to answer these questions:

1. Is ANF sensitive to r, the number of extra bits?
2. Is ANF faster than existing approaches?
3. Is ANF more accurate than existing approaches?
4. Does ANF really scales to very large graphs? Do the others?

4.1 Framework

4.1.1 RI approximation scheme

The RI approximation algorithm is based on the approximate counting scheme proposed in [4]. To estimate the number of distinct elements in a multi-set, assign each a random value in $[0, 1]$ and record the least of these values added to the set. The estimated size is the reciprocal of the least value seen, minus 1. This approximate counting scheme was used to estimate the individual

Table 2: Data set characteristics

Name	(n) #Nodes	(m) #Edges	Degree Max.	Avg.	Prac. Diam.	Orient.
Cornell	844	1,647	131	1.95	9	Dir
Cycle	1,000	1,000	2	2.00	500	Undir
Grid	10,000	19,800	4	1.98	100	Undir
Uniform	65,378	199,996	20	3.06	8	Undir
Cora	127,083	330,198	457	2.60	35	Dir
80-20	166,946	449,832	723	2.69	10	Undir
Router	284,805	430,342	1,978	1.51	13	Undir

neighbourhood functions with the following algorithm. We need to know for each node, u the minimum value v_h of a node reachable from u in h hops. Then, the estimate for $IN(u,h)$ is $\frac{1}{v_h} - 1$. An equivalent, but more efficient algorithm was presented which uses breadth-first searches. It was shown that this improved procedure takes only $O(m \log n)$ time (with high probability). To reduce the variance in the estimates, the entire algorithm is repeated, averaging over the estimates.

4.1.2 Sampling

We can sample by selecting random edges, random nodes or random starting nodes for the breadth-first search. Randomly selecting a set of nodes (and all edges for which both end-points are in this set) and randomly selecting a set of edges is unlikely to produce a useful sample. For example, imagine sampling a cycle – anything but a very large sample will leave disconnected arcs which have very different properties. For completeness we verified that these approaches produced useless estimates. The last approach is much more compelling. It is akin to the sampling done in [14]. Recall that the neighbourhood function is: $N(h) = \sum_{u \in V} IN(u,h)$. Rather than summing over all nodes, u, we could sum over only a sample of the nodes while using breadth-first searches to compute the exact $IN(u,h)$. We call this method *exact-on-sample* and it has the potential to provide great estimates – a single sample of a cycle will provide an exact solution. However, experimentally we find that this approach also has the potential to provide very poor estimates. Additionally, we find that it does not scale to large graphs because of the random-like access to the edge file due to its use of breadth-first search.

4.1.3 Experimental Data Sets

We have collected three real data sets and generated three synthetic data sets. These data sets have a variety of properties and cover many of the potential applications of the neighbourhood function. Some summary information is provided in Table 2. "Prac. Diam." is the *Practical Diameter* which we use informally to mean the distance which includes most of the pairs of points. We use three real data sets:

Router: Undirected Internet routers data from ISI [19], including scans done by Lucent Bell Laboratories [12].
Cornell: A crawl of the Cornell web site by Mark Craven.

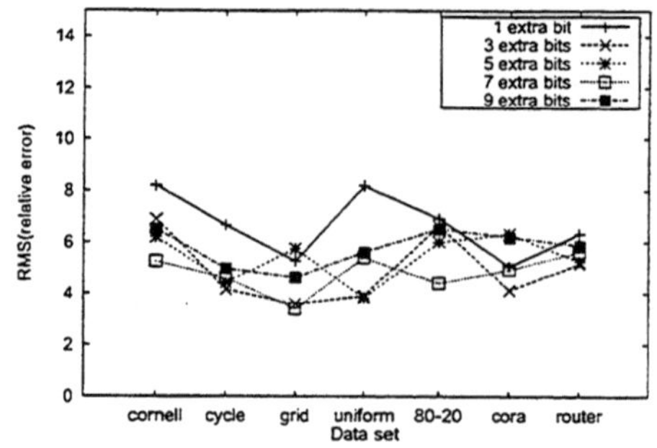

Figure 6: Results are not sensitive to r

Cora: The CORA project at JustResearch found research papers on the web and provided a citation graph [6].

and four synthetic data sets:

Cycle: A single simple undirected cycle (circle).
Grid: A 2D planar grid (undirected).
Uniform: Graph with random (undirected) edges.
80-20: Very skewed graph generated in an Internet like fashion with undirected edges using the method in [17].

4.1.4 Evaluation Metric

We are approximating functions defined over d points. Let N be the true neighbourhood function and $\hat{N}$ be the candidate approximation. To measure the error of $\hat{N}(h)$, we use the standard relative error metric. To measure the overall error of $\hat{N}$ we use the Root Mean Square (RMS) of point-wise relative errors. Thus, the error function, e, is:

$$rel(N(h), \hat{N}(h)) = \frac{|N(h) - \hat{N}(h)|}{N(h)}$$
$$e(N, \hat{N}) = \sqrt{\frac{\sum_{h=2}^{d} rel(N(h), \hat{N}(h))^2}{d-1}}$$

Note that the RMS is computed beginning with $h = 2$. Since $N(0) = |V|$ and $N(1) = |E|$ we do not require approximations for these points.

4.2 Results

4.2.1 Parameter Sensitivity

ANF has two parameters: the number of parallel approximations, k, and the number of additional bits, r. The number of approximations, k, is a typical trade-off between time and accuracy. We consider this in section 4.2.2 and fix $k = 64$ for the time being. Additional experiments were run with other values of k which produced similar results. To measure the sensitivity we averaged the RMS error over 10 trials for different values of r and the different data sets. These results appear in Figure 6 and we see that the accuracy is not very sensitive to the value of r. (The lines between the points are a visual aid only.) We find $r = 5$ or $r = 7$ provide consistent results.

4.2.2 Accuracy

We now examine the accuracy of the ANF approximation. To do so, we compare our accuracy with the RI approximation (the only existing approach). Now we fix $r = 7$ and consider three values of k: 32, 64 and 128. We average the error over 10 trials of each approximation scheme. The first row of Figure 7 shows the accuracy of each of the k values for each data set for each algorithm, while the second row shows the corresponding running times. We see that:

- ANF's error is independent of the data sets.
- RI approximation's error varies significantly between data sets.
- ANF achieves less than 10%, 7% and 5% errors for $k = 32$, $k = 64$ and $k = 128$, respectively.
- RI has errors of 27%, 14% and 12% for $k = 32$, $k = 64$ and $k = 128$, respectively.
- ANF is much faster than RI, particularly on the larger graphs, with up to 3 times savings.
- Using much less time, ANF is much more accurate than RI.

Thus, even for the case of graphs the may be stored in memory, we have a significant improvement.

4.2.3 Sampling

There are three problems with the described *exact-on-sample* approach. First, it has *heavy memory requirements* because fast breadth-first search requires that the edge file fit in memory. Second, the *quality is dependent on the graph* because there are no bounds on the error. Third, it is not possible to compute the *individual neighbourhood functions*. We now provide an example which demonstrates the first two problems. Figure 8(a) helps illustrate our example graph. First, create a chain of $d - 2$ nodes that start from a node r and end at a node x. Add N nodes to the center of the graph, each of which has a directed edge to r and a directed edge from x. This graph has diameter d and a neighbourhood function that is $O(N)$ for each distance less than d and $O(N^2)$ for distance d. Finally, define a set of s source nodes that have an edge to each of the N center nodes and a set of t terminal nodes that have an edge from each of the N center nodes. If $N \gg s$ and $N \gg t$, then the majority of the sampled nodes will be from the N center nodes and very few will be from the s source nodes. This will result in an error that is a factor of around s/p for exact-on-sample using a p% sample. We measure the error and the running time over 20 trials for a variety of sample sizes ranging from .1% to 15% on a graph generated with $N = 25,000$, $s = 100$, $t = 100$ and $d = 6$. Figure 8(b) shows the large errors, more than 20%, even for very large samples.

To illustrate the scalability issues for exact-on-sample, we constructed a graph with $N = 250,000$, $s = t = 5$ and $d = 6$. We then increase s and t proportionately to generate larger

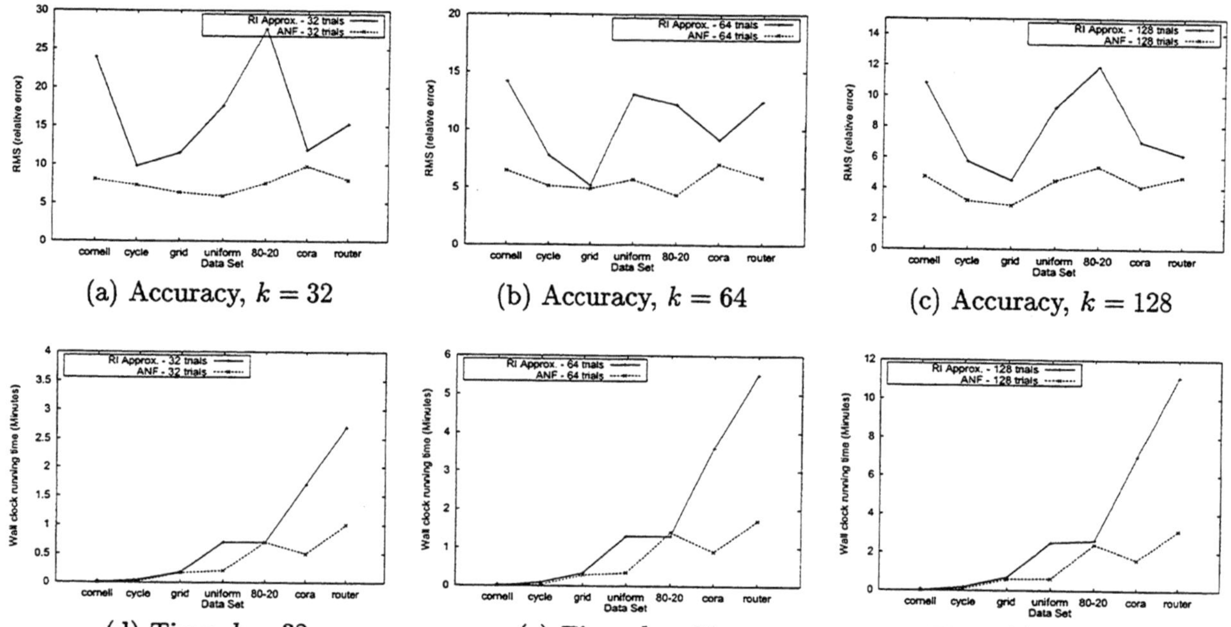

(a) Accuracy, $k = 32$ (b) Accuracy, $k = 64$ (c) Accuracy, $k = 128$

(d) Time, $k = 32$ (e) Time, $k = 64$ Time (f), $k = 128$

Figure 7: Our ANF algorithm provides more accurate and faster results than the RI approximation

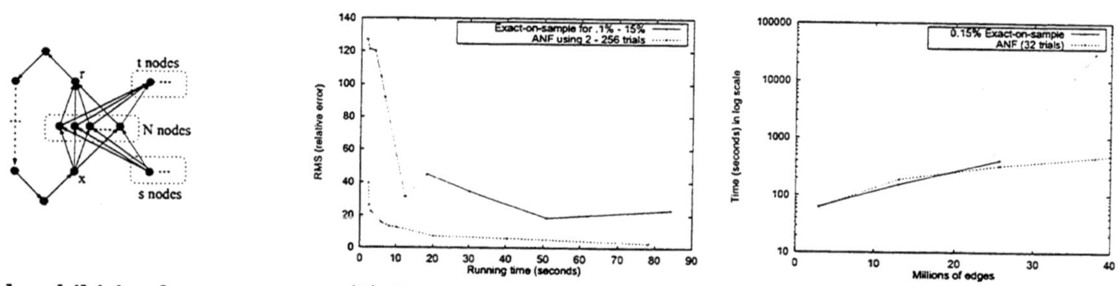

(a) Graph exhibiting huge errors (b) Error vs. Running time (c) Running time vs. # of edges

Figure 8: Sampled breadth-first search can provide huge errors and does not scale to very large edge files

graphs. Figure 8(c) shows that as the graph grows larger exact-on-sample scales about as well as ANF but as soon as the edge file no longer fits in memory (approximately 27 million edges) we see approximately a two order of magnitude increase in the running time of the exact-on-sample approach. Thus, we conclude that exact-on-sample scales very poorly to graphs that are larger than the available memory.

Table 3: Wall clock running time (minutes)

Data Set	BF (Exact)	ANF	Speed-up
Uniform	92	0.34	270x
Cora	6	1.4	4x
80-20	680	0.9	756x
Router	1,200	1.7	705x

4.2.4 Speed and Scalability

Table 3 reports wall-clock running times on an otherwise unloaded Pentium II-450 machine for both the exact computation (Breadth-First search) and ANF with $k = 64$ parallel approximations. We chose $k = 64$ since it provides much less than a 10% error, which should be acceptable for most situations. The approximations are quite fast and, for the *Router* data set, we have reduced the running time from approximately a day down to less than 2 minutes. This makes it possible to run drill down tasks on much larger data sets than before. Overall, we find that ANF is up to 700 times faster than the exact computation on our data sets.

ANF also scales to much larger graphs than the alternatives. We generated random graphs placing edges randomly between nodes. We increased the number of nodes and edges while preserving an edge:node ratio of 8:1 (based on the average degree found in two large crawls of the Web [3]). Figure 1 (in the introduction) shows the running times for the ANF variants, the RI approximation and example-on-sample. Parameters for each alternative were chosen such that they all had approximately the same running time for the first data point. These values are $k = 32$ for the ANF variants, $k = 8$ for RI and $p = 0.0015$ for exact-on-sample. We find that:

1. Exact-on-sample scales much worse than linearly. For a fixed sampling rate, we expect it to scale quadratically when we increase the number of nodes and edges.
2. RI very quickly exhausts its resources due to its data structures. Because RI was not designed to avoid the random accesses, it has horrible paging behaviour and, after about 2 million edges, we had to stop its timing experiment.
3. ANF-0 suffers from similar swapping issues when it exhausts the memory at around 8 million edges, and it too had to be stopped.
4. Approximate counting methods [9, 4] are not enough for disk resident graphs.
5. ANF/ANF-C scale the best, growing piece-wise linearly with the size of the graph. The break points are: all data fits in memory (about 8 million edges), $Mcur$ fits in memory (about 16 million edges) and neither fits in memory (the rest). This is as expected.
6. ANF-C offers up to a 23% speed-up over ANF.

Thus, ANF is the only algorithm that scales to large graphs and does so with a linear increase in running time.

2.50	2.37	2.50
2.36	**2.57**	2.36
2.50	2.36	2.51

(a) ANF importance

-.07	-.20	-.07
-.21		-.21
-.07	-.21	-.06

(b) Delta importance

Figure 9: ANF finds the best starting move for X

5 Data mining with our ANF Tool

With our highly-accurate and efficient approximation tool, ANF, it is now possible to answer some of the prototypical graph mining questions that we posed in the introduction. Due to the limits of page constraints and data availability, we will report on answers to only a representative sample of those questions. However, all 10 questions can be answered by the same approaches that we will now demonstrate. The approach is to compute various neighbourhood functions and then to compare them. Our tool allows for a detailed comparison of these functions. However, comparing neighbourhood functions requires that we compare two functions over potentially large domains (the domain is $\{1, 2, \cdots, d\}$). Instead, in this paper we will focus on a summarized statistic derived from the neighbourhood function, called the *hop exponent*. Many real graphs [8] have a neighbourhood function that follows a power law $N(h) \propto h^{\mathcal{H}}$. The exponent, $\mathcal{H}$, has been defined as the *hop exponent* (similarly, $\mathcal{H}_x$ is the *individual hop exponent* for a node x).

There are three interesting observations about the hop exponent that make it an appealing metric. First, if the power-law holds, the neighbourhood function will have a linear section with slope $\mathcal{H}$ when viewed in log-log space. Second, the hop exponent is, informally, the *intrinsic* dimensionality of the graph. A cycle has a hop exponent of 1 while a grid has a hop exponent of 2, which corresponds with some idea of their dimensionality. Third, if two graphs have different hop exponents, there is no way that they could be similar. While not all neighbourhood functions will actually follow a power-law, we have found that using the hop exponent still fairly reasonably captures the growth of the neighbourhood function.

To compute the hop exponent, we first truncate the neighbourhood function at , the *effective diameter*, then we compute the least-squares line of best fit in log-log space to extract the slope of this line. The slope is the hop exponent of the graph and we use it as our measure of the growth of a neighbourhood function. We define to be the least h such that it include 90% of the pairs of nodes. We use the individual hop exponent, $\mathcal{H}_x$, as a measure of a node's importance with respect to the connectivity of a graph. We can answer some of the proposed questions.

5.1 Tic-Tac-Toe

Tic-tac-toe is a simple game in which two players, one using X and the other using O, alternatively place their mark on an unoccupied square in a 3x3 grid. The winner is the first player to connect 3 of their symbols in a row, column or diagonal. The best opening move for X is the center square, the next best is any of the 4 corners and the worst moves are the 4 remaining squares. To verify that our notion of importance has some potential use, we will use our ANF tool to discover this same rule. Construct a graph where each node is a valid board and add an edge from board x to

Film-Noir
Animation Short
Adult
Fantasy Documentary Family
Mystery Musical Western War
Sci-Fi
Romance
Horror Adventure Crime Thriller Action
Comedy
Drama

Figure 10: Movie genre clusters sorted in increasing hop exponent value

board y to indicate that this is a possible move. Let C, the concluding set, be the set of all boards in which `X` wins. Compute the individual neighbourhood functions for each of the 9 possible first moves by `X`, which is their importance (speed at which they attain winning positions from each of these moves). Figure 9 shows these importances along with the difference between each and the best move. ANF determined the correct importance of each opening move. Using Figure 9(b), we see that the center is only slightly better than a corner square which is, in turn, much better than the remaining 4 squares. This shows both the correct ordering of the starting moves and the relative importance of each.

5.2 Clustering movie genres

The Internet Movie Data Base (IMDB) [10] is a collection of relations about movies. We will map a subset of the relations into graphs to illustrate questions that we can now answer thanks to our ANF tool. First, construct the `actor-movie` graph by creating a node for each actor and a node for each movie. An undirected edge is placed between an actor, a, and a movie, m, to indicate an appearance by a in m. Let S be the nodes we created for the actors. We now employ another relation of the IMDB. Each movie has been identified as being in one or more genres (such as documentaries, dramas, comedies, etc). For each genre, we take the set of movies in that genre and the set of actors which appear in one or more of those movies. We then cluster these graphs by computing the hop exponents and forming clusters that have similar hop exponents (less than 0.1 difference). This clustering appears in Figure 10. One interesting cluster is `mystery`, `musical`, `western`, `war` which actually corresponds to movies that are typically older. Finally, other fringe genres such as `Adult` turn out to be well separated from the others.

5.3 Internet Router Data

In the networking community, a study used an early version of our ANF tool (ANF-0) to look at the inherent robustness of the Internet. That is, the robustness that we observe from the topology itself. Each router was a node and edges were used to indicate communication links. Here we reproduce some of the results of this study, including Figure 11, from [16]. The goal is to determine how

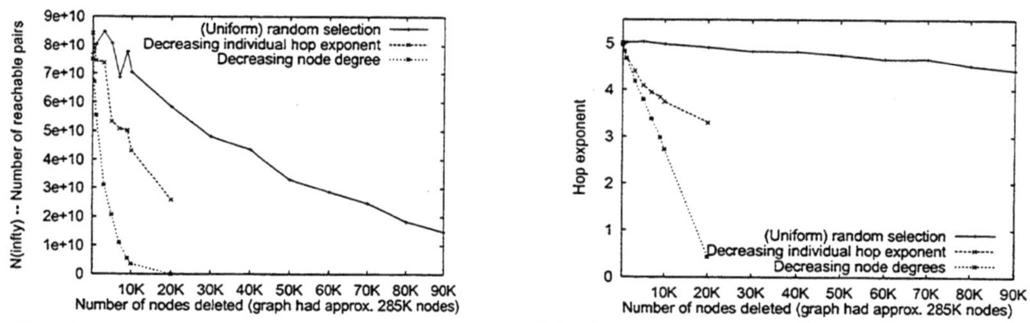

(a) Number of pairs of nodes that can communicate vs. number of deleted nodes

(b) Hop exponent of the Internet vs. number of deleted nodes

Figure 11: Effect of router failures on the Internet

robust the Internet is to router failures. As an experiment, we delete some number of routers and then measure the total connectivity (number of pairs of routers that are still able to communicate) and the hop exponent of the graph. The three lines differ in how the deleted routers are selected. First, randomly selected nodes are deleted. Second, nodes are deleted in decreasing order of their importance. Third, routers are deleted in decreasing order of their degree. Here we see some very interesting results:

1. Random failures do not disrupt the Internet.

2. It may be possible to take a random sample of the Internet by deleting random routers and adjacent edges. This appears possible because we found that the connectivity information (hop exponent) is not significantly changed under random deletions.

3. Targeted failures of routers can very quickly and very dramatically disrupt the Internet.

This type of study was infeasible before our ANF tool as an exact computation would have required over **a year of computation time**.

6 Conclusions

In this paper we presented 10 interesting data mining questions on graph data, proposed an efficient and accurate approximation algorithm that gives us the tool, ANF, we needed to answer these questions, and presented results for three of these questions on real-world data. We have found ANF to be quite useful for these and other questions that can be addressed by studying the neighbourhood structure of the underlying graphs (e.g., we have used ANF to study the most important movie actors). We experimentally verified that ANF provides the following advantages:

Highly-accurate estimates: Provable bounds which we also verified experimentally, finding less than a 7% error when using $k = 64$ parallel approximations (for all our synthetic and real-world data sets).

Is orders of magnitude faster: On the seven data sets used in this paper, our algorithm is up to 700 times faster than the exact computation. It is also up to 3 times faster than the RI approximation scheme.

Has low storage requirements: Given the edge file, our algorithm uses only $O(n)$ additional storage.

Adapts to the available memory: We presented a disk-based version of our algorithm and experimentally verified that it scales with the graph size.

Can be parallelized: Our ANF algorithm may be parallelized with very few synchronization points.

Employs sequential scans: Unlike prior approximations of the neighbourhood function, our algorithm avoids random access of the edge file and performs one sequential scan of the edge file per hop.

Individual neighbourhood functions for free: ANF computed approximations of the individual neighbourhood functions as a byproduct of the computation. These approximations proved to be very useful in identifying the "important" nodes in a graph.

Even for the case that graphs (and data structures) fit into memory, ANF represents a significant improvement in speed and accuracy. When graphs get too large to be processed effectively in main memory, ANF makes it possible to answer questions that would have been at least infeasible, if not impossible, to answer before. In addition to its speed, we found the neighbourhood measures to be useful for discovering the following answers to our prototypical questions:

1. We found the best opening moves to tic-tac-toe.
2. We clustered movie genres.
3. We found that the Internet is resilient to random failures while targeted failures can quickly create disconnected components.
4. We found that sampling the Internet actually preserves some connectivity patterns while targeted failures truly distort it.

References

[1] L. A. Adamic. The small world Web. In *Proceedings of the European Conf. on Digital Libraries*, 1999.

[2] S. Brin and L. Page. The anatomy of a large-scale hypertextual Web search engine. *Computer Networks and ISDN Systems*, 30(1–7):107–117, 1998.

[3] A. Broder, R. Kumar, F. Maghoul, P. Raghavan, and R. Stata. Graph structure in the Web. In *Proceedings of the 9th International World Wide Web Conference*, pages 247–256, 2000.

[4] E. Cohen. Size-estimation framework with applications to transitive closure and reachability. *Journal of Computer and System Sciences*, 55(3):441–453, December 1997.

[5] Cook and Holder. Graph-based data mining. *ISTA: Intelligent Systems & their applications*, 15, 2000.

[6] CORA search engine. `http://www.cora.whizbang.com`.

[7] P. Domingos and M. Richardson. Mining the network value of customers. In *KDD-2001*, pages 57–66, 2001.

[8] M. Faloutsos, P. Faloutsos, and C. Faloutsos. On power-law relationships of the internet topology. In *SIGCOMM*, 1999.

[9] P. Flajolet and G. N. Martin. Probabilistic counting algorithms for data base applications. *Journal of Computer and System Sciences*, 31:182–209, 1985.

[10] IMDB. `http://www.imdb.com`.

[11] A. Inokuchi, T. Washio, and H. Motoda. An apriori-based algorithm for mining frequent substructures from graph data. In *PDKK*, pages 13–23, 2000.

[12] `http://cs.bell-labs.com/who/ches/map/`.

[13] S. R. Kumar, P. Raghavan, S. Rajagopalan, D. Sivakumar, A. Tomkins, and E. Upfal. The Web as a graph. In *ACM SIGMOD-SIGACT-SIGART Symposium on Principles of Database Systems*, pages 1–10, 2000.

[14] R. J. Lipton and J. F. Naughton. Estimating the size of generalized transitive closures. In *Proceedings of 15th International Conference on Very Large Data Bases*, pages 315–326, 1989.

[15] M. H. Nodine, M. T. Goodrich, and J. S. Vitter. Blocking for external graph searching. In *Proc. ACM PODS Conference (PODS-93)*, pages 222–232, 1993.

[16] C. R. Palmer, G. Siganos, M. Faloutsos, C. Faloutsos, and P. Gibbons. The connectivity and fault-tolerance of the Internet topology. In *Workshop on Network-Related Data Management (NRDM-2001)*, 2001.

[17] C. R. Palmer and J. G. Steffan. Generating network toplogies that obey power laws. In *IEEE Globecom 2000*, 2000.

[18] G. Salton and M. McGill. *Introduction to Modern Information Retrieval.* McGraw-Hill, 1983.

[19] `http://www.isi.edu/scan/mercator/maps.html`.

[20] S. L. Tauro, C. Palmer, G. Siganos, and M. Faloutsos. A simple conceptual model for the Internet topology. In *IEEE Globecom 2001*, 2001.

SESSION IV

Networked Worlds

Data Mining in Social Networks

David Jensen and Jennifer Neville

Knowledge Discovery Laboratory
Computer Science Department, University of Massachusetts, Amherst, MA 01003
{jensen, jneville}@cs.umass.edu

Abstract. Several techniques for learning statistical models from relational data have been developed recently by researchers in machine learning and data mining. All of these techniques must address a similar set of representational and algorithmic choices and must face a set of statistical challenges unique to learning from relational data.

Introduction

Recent research projects in two closely related areas of computer science — machine learning and data mining — have developed methods for constructing statistical models of network data. Examples of such data include social networks, networks of web pages, complex relational databases, and data on interrelated people, places, things, and events extracted from text documents. Such data sets are often called "relational" because the relations among entities are central (e.g., acquaintanceship ties between people, links between web pages, or organizational affiliations between people and organizations).[1]

These algorithms differ from a substantially older and more established set of data mining algorithms developed to analyze propositional data. Propositional data are individual records, each of which can be represented as an attribute vector and each of which are assumed to be statistically independent of any other. For example, a propositional data set for learning medical diagnostic rules might represent each patient as a vector of diagnostic test results, and analysis would assume that knowing the disease of one patient tells you nothing about another patient. In contrast, analysis of a relational representation of the same data would retract this latter assumption and add information about familial relationships, workplace contacts, and other relationships among patients that might influence their medical status.

The handful of data mining techniques that have been developed recently for relational data include probabilistic relational models (PRMs) (Friedman, Getoor, Koller, and Pfeffer 1999), Bayesian logic programs (BLPs) (Kersting and de Raedt 2000), first-order Bayesian classifiers (Flach and Lachiche 1999), and relational probability trees (RPTs) (Jensen and Neville 2002). In each of these cases, both the structure and the parameters of a statistical model can be learned directly from data, easing the job of data analysts, and greatly improving the fidelity of the

[1] This meaning of "relational" should be distinguished from the more restrictive meaning of "data stored in relational databases." While relational databases can represent relational data, relational data can also be represented and accessed in other ways.

resulting model. Older techniques include inductive logic programming (ILP) (Muggleton 1992; Dzeroski and Lavrac 2001) and social network analysis (Wasserman and Faust 1994).

For example, we have employed relational probability trees (RPTs) to learn models that predict the box office success of a movie based on attributes of the movie and related records, including the movie's actors, directors, producers, and the studios that made the movie. We have also analyzed relational data in other ways to predict fraudulent cell phone use based on the calling patterns of individual phone numbers. Finally, we have produced models that predict the function and location of proteins in a cell based on network of interactions with other proteins.

Many of these techniques for relational learning share a common set of statistical challenges and design issues. In this paper, we survey these issues, using examples from our work on PROXIMITY, an integrated system for relational learning, and an algorithm for learning RPTs that we have incorporated into PROXIMITY. For each issue, we briefly discuss our design choices in PROXIMITY, and point to alternative approaches used by other systems.

We begin by describing a specific data set and an example analysis task — predicting the box-office receipts of movies — that we use throughout the remainder of the paper. Next, we describe some of the basic features of PROXIMITY and our approach to querying data and learning RPTs. The next several sections discuss a set of representational and algorithmic choices faced by techniques for relational learning and a set of statistical issues unique to relational data. We finish with some brief conclusions.

Example Data and Analysis Task

Consider the relational data shown schematically in Figure 1. The data consist of movies and associated objects including people (who act in, produce, or direct the movies), organizations (studios), events (releases of the movie), and other objects (awards). These objects are connected in the ways that you would expect (e.g., actors are linked to movies they act in) and in some occasionally unexpected ways (e.g., movies are linked directly to other movies that are remakes). In addition to the high-level structure of the database shown in Figure 1, the database contains attributes associated with each object, including the titles and genres of movies, the names and ages of persons, and the countries and box-office receipts of movie releases.

The data are drawn primarily from a large online resource, the Internet Movie Database (*www.imdb.com*) that makes its data public for research and other non-commercial purposes. In addition, we have added other data drawn from the Hollywood Stock Exchange (*www.hsx.com*), an artificial market where players trade in stocks that track the relative popularity of movie actors.

The data are voluminous, consisting of over 300,000 movies, 650,000 persons, and 11,000 studios. Those objects are connected by over 2.3 million acted-in links, 300,000 directed links, and 200,000 produced links. The available data on movies vary widely. For example, not all movies have releases, and HSX data are only available for a small percentage of actors in IMDb. Data are more complete for more recent movies and persons.

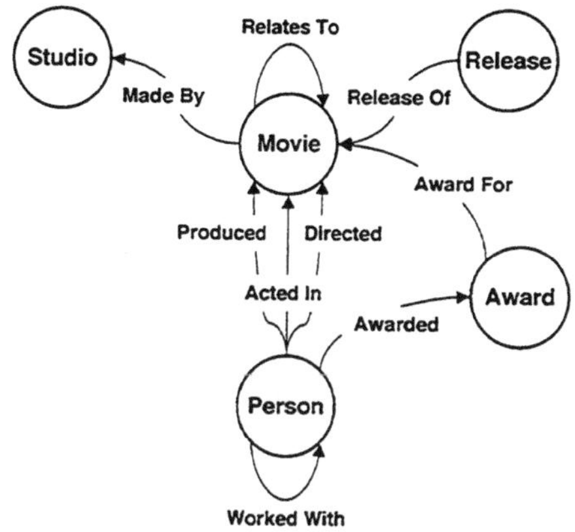

Figure 1: Example schema for data from the Internet Movie Database.

The movie data support a variety of interesting predictive modeling tasks. We have already mentioned one — predicting the opening weekend box office receipts of a movie — and we will use this task as an example throughout the paper. Specifically, we will focus on predicting a probability distribution over a simple binary attribute of movies — Does the movie make more than $2 million in its opening weekend? We will call this attribute *receipts*.

We could attempt to build models of other attributes of objects (e.g., a movie's genre or an actor's gender) or attributes of links (e.g, the type of a link between a person and a movie) with PROXIMITY. In addition to these, other types of prediction tasks are certainly possible. One could attempt to learn models that predict missing links between objects. For example, reviewers sometimes call a movie a "crypto-sequel" when it stars the same actors and has a similar plot line as another recent movie, but does not explicitly tie the two storylines. For example, the 1998 movie "You've Got Mail" starring Tom Hanks and Meg Ryan was said to be a crypto-sequel to the 1993 movie "Sleepless in Seattle" (as well as a remake of the 1940 movie "Shop Around The Corner" starring James Stewart and Margaret Sullavan). Given enough examples of crypto-sequels, a data mining algorithm could learn a predictive model from the movie data. Recent work by Getoor, Friedman, Koller, and Taskar (2001) has created models that predict the existence of missing links.

One could also attempt to learn models that predict an attribute of a subgraph, rather than only a single object or link. For example, the emergence of a highly paid Hollywood movie star may consist of a set of successful movies in which the actor had a starring role and one or more awards. Models of this pattern would consist of many objects and links, combined in a particular temporal sequence.

In this paper, we will focus almost exclusively on the task of learning probability distributions over the values of attributes of objects and links. While predicting link existence and classifying subgraphs are extremely interesting problems, the techniques learning probabilistic models for these tasks are much less numerous and much less well-developed than for simple attribute modeling.

One important input to relational learning algorithms is a *schema* or interpretation of the data that specifies a type system over the objects and links in the data. For example, Figure 1 above specifies one schema for the movie data, but others are possible. For example, an alternative schema might specify people as either actors, directors, or producers. Figure 2 provides a hierarchy of possible object types as well as two possible families of schemas constructed from those object types (a full schema would also specify a set of link types). Such a hierarchy is sometimes called an *ontology* (Gruber 1993).

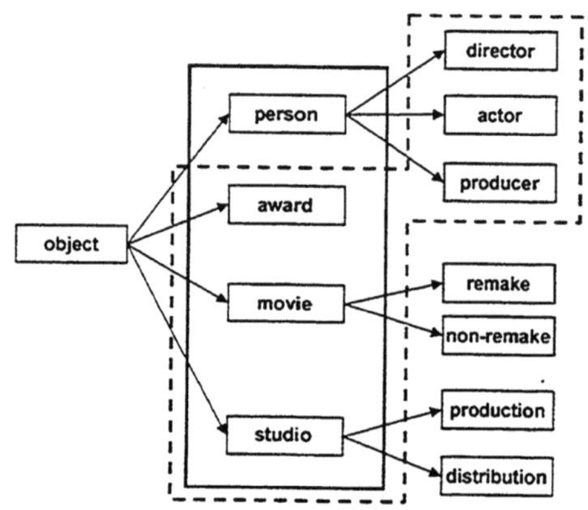

Figure 2: An example ontology of movie objects.

Querying and Learning

To address learning tasks of this kind, our research group is constructing PROXIMITY — a system for machine learning and data mining in relational data. The system is designed as a framework within which a variety of analysis tools can be used in combination. At the foundation of PROXIMITY is a graph database for storing semi-structured data that can be represented as a graph. The database can be accessed by tools for querying data, sampling data, and calculating attributes that depend partially or entirely on network structure (e.g., measures drawn from social network analysis). Sampled data can then be analyzed with tools that construct statistical models. Finally, all these tools can be called from a scripting language interface. In addition to these components, we are developing additional components for clustering, graph partitioning, and additional types of statistical modeling.

In this paper, we will focus on a relatively simple combination of two tools — our query language and one of our learning algorithms. The query language is a visual language for expressing queries to the graph database. The learning algorithm constructs relational probability trees (RPTs), a type of probabilistic classifier for relational data. The two components work in concert. The query language is used to extract subgraphs from a large network of data; the RPT algorithm is used to learn a model that estimates a conditional probability distribution for the value of an attribute of a class of objects or links represented in all those subgraphs. That estimate is conditioned on the attributes of other objects and links in the subgraph.

For example, a query might extract subgraphs consisting of a movie and all directly related actors, producers, directors, studios, and awards. An RPT could then be constructed to estimate the probability that a movie makes more than $2 million in its opening weekend (*receipts = True*), given attributes of the actors, producers, directors, studios, and awards. Note that different movies will have different numbers of related objects such as actors and awards. Thus, the subgraphs could not be represented directly as simple attribute vectors.

Our query language, QGraph, represents queries as graphs with associated attribute constraints and annotations on vertices and edges (Blau, Immerman, and Jensen 2002). For example, Figure 3 shows the query described above with a movie and all its related objects. The numeric annotation *[1..]* on the actor vertex specifies that a match must have one or more actors, and that all associated actors should be returned as part of each matching subgraph. Some object types and link types are left unspecified because of known connectivity constraints in the data. Matches to the query are shown in Figure 4. Actual names of people, studios, and movies are left out for simplicity. The first match has three actors and no award; the second has four actors and no award, and shares an actor and a studio with the first match; the third match has only a single actor, but won an award. The fact that entire subgraphs are returned as part of a match is a subtle, yet vital, feature of the language for our purposes. Other languages such as SQL, for example, can only return a single record as a match, not a record of variable size, such as a subgraph.

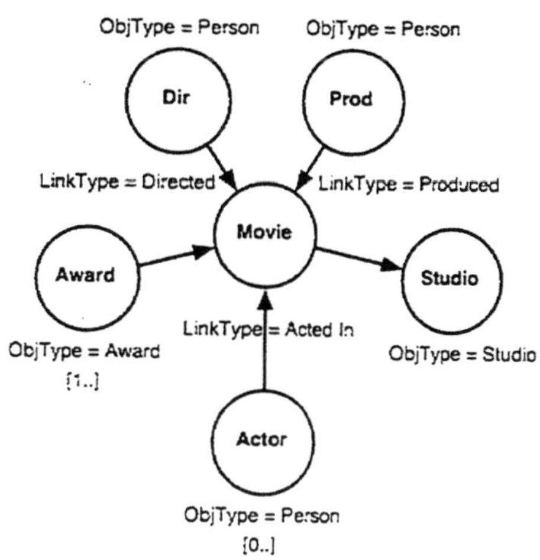

Figure 3: QGraph query for IMDb data.

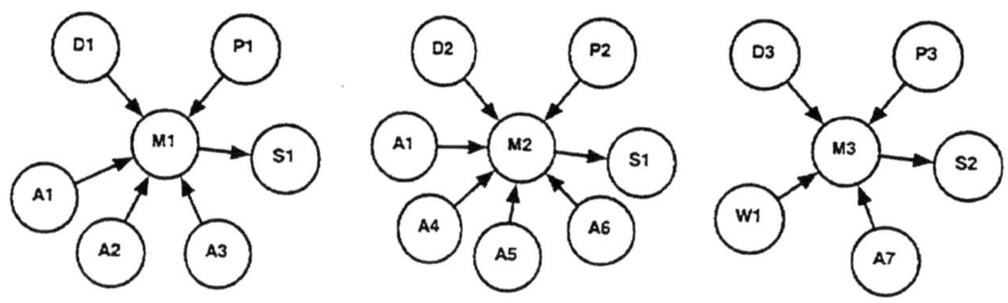

Figure 4: Matches to the query in Figure 3.

Our learning algorithm for relational probability trees constructs trees such as the one shown in Figure 5. The tree represents a series of questions to ask about any subgraph returned by the corresponding query. In this tree, the root node asks whether the movie has more than five actors born after 1943. If so, the subgraph travels down the left-hand branch to a node asking whether the movie at the center of the subgraph is a drama. The subgraph continues moving down appropriate branches of the tree until a leaf node is reached. The leaf nodes contain probability distributions over the values of the *receipts* attribute. Leaf nodes in Figure 5 shows the number of movie subgraphs of each class that reach the leaf, as well as their respective probabilities. The leftmost pair of numbers indicate the number and probability of movies with opening weekend box office receipts exceeding $2 million (*receipts = True*). The second numbers indicate the converse (*receipts = False*).

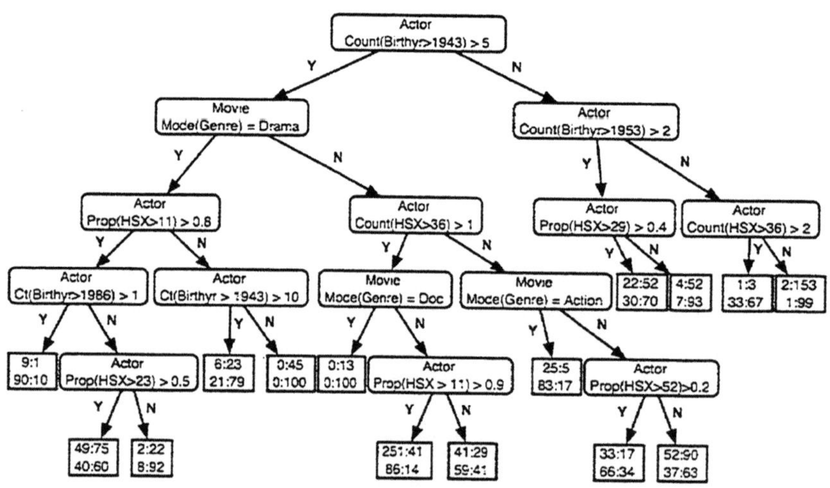

Figure 5: An example relational probability tree (RPT)

Our construction algorithm for RPTs is a recursive partitioning algorithm similar in spirit to CART (Breiman, Friedman, Olshen and Stone 1984), C4.5 (Quinlan 1993), and CHAID (Kass

1980). However, the RPT algorithm searches over the attributes of different object types in the subgraph and multiple methods of aggregating the values of those attributes and creating binary splits on those aggregated values. For example, for a numeric attribute such as birth year, it searches over splits such as *MEAN(birthyr)>x*, *PROPORTION(birthyr>x)>y*, *MAXIMUM(birthyr)>y*, *MINIMUM(birthyr)>x*, and *COUNT(birthyr>x)>y*. Our current approach continues partitioning the training data until a stopping criteria is reached. Our current stopping criteria uses a Bonferroni-adjusted chi-square test analogous to that used in CHAID. However, such methods face a variety of problems due to multiple comparison effects (Jensen and Cohen 2000), and we are exploring the use of randomization tests (Jensen 1992) to better adjust for such effects.

This two-step approach of querying and then learning is necessary because of the semi-structured data model that underlies Proximity. In Proximity's graph database, objects and links are not created with strong type information. Rather, data about each object or link is stored in zero or more attributes, name-value pairs such as *<age, 54>* or *<genre, comedy>*. Even type information (e.g., person or movie) is stored as an ordinary attribute without privledged status. As a result, attributes are not constrained to occur in particular combinations, in contrast to more conventional relational databases, where a static schema defines both type information and the fields (attributes) corresponding to each entity or relation type. If such structure is needed in Proximity, it can be imposed by a QGraph query. The labels in a query (e.g., the "movie", "actor", and other labels in Figure 3) are assigned to the matching portions of a subquery and remain on those elements for use by other algorithms such as the RPT construction algorithm. Similarly, we often employ particular schemas (such as the one shown in Figure 1) to aid communication, but this is a convenience, not a necessity.

This high degree of flexibility imposes a performance penalty for querying. However, such flexibility is essential for effective machine learning and data mining. First, practical data mining often involves the creation of many new attributes as a human data analyst tries alternative methods for understanding and modeling the data. Adding many attributes to a conventional database would require constant updates to its schema, a costly operation for traditional relational databases. Second, a particular schema is just one way of interpreting a given data set, and it can bias analysis in important ways. To enable truly effective data mining, analysts must be able to change the schema easily, and thus reconceptualize the domain (Jensen & Neville 2002b; Neville & Jensen 2002).

Design Choices: Data, Tasks, and Models

Techniques for relational learning can be better understood by examining them in the context of a set of design choices and statistical issues. This section describes several decision choices and the next section covers a small set of unique statistical issues facing relational learning algorithms.

Data characteristics

Network size — Raw size is one of the most obvious methods of characterizing a relational data set. PROXIMITY has been constructed and evaluated on relatively large networks. The largest data set we have analyzed (on wireless phone fraud) contains nearly 2 million objects and 7 million links. The complete IMDb data set contains over 1.1 million objects and over 3.1 million links. These fairly large data sets contrast with the relatively small networks typically examined by work in social network analysis and inductive logic programming.

Connectivity — The degree of connectivity among different portions of the data graph is another important characteristic of relational data sets. Our work focuses on networks consisting of a small number of large connected components. In contrast, much of the work in ILP and SNA has focused on many small disconnected components, each of which can be considered a data instance. For example, some work in ILP has analyzed the relational structure of molecules to predict their mutagenicity (Srinivasan, Muggleton, Sternberg, and King 1996). Each molecule is considered a single instance for purposes of learning. Some other work has focused on forms of relational data in which linkages are formed by space and time. However, these types of relations are highly homogeneous (e.g., a square spatial region is linked to eight adjoining regions), whereas the types of relations we consider can be highly irregular (e.g., a given movie might have only a few actors or a cast of thousands).

Homogeneity — Many techniques that analyze relational data assume the data consist of homogeneous objects. Such networks include sets of web pages, phone numbers, or persons within an organization. In contrast, several recently developed techniques, including our work on RPTs, can analyze sets of relational data with heterogenous objects, such as movies, people, and studios that make up the IMDb data.

Task

Level of relational dependence — The most commonly used modeling techniques from machine learning, data mining, and statistics analyze independent attribute vectors, thus assuming that relational dependencies are unimportant, or at least beyond the scope of analysis. Specialized techniques for spatial and temporal data have been developed that assume a highly regular type of relational dependence. In contrast, the work discussed here addresses relational data sets with potentially irregular relational structure, with variation in the number and type of links among objects, and these variations are assumed to have significance for modeling.

Type of task — Nearly all the algorithms discussed here focus on *supervised learning*. That is, they attempt to predict the value of some attribute whose true value is known in the data set. In contrast, some approaches focus on *unsupervised learning*, where the task is to discern some unknown structure in the data. Clustering algorithms are a form of unsupervised learning, and similar work has recently been undertaken for relational data (e.g., Taskar, Segal, and Koller 2001).

Level of determinism — RPTs, PRMs, and many of the other approaches discussed here attempt to learn *probabilistic* models of relational data. However, some techniques are specially adapted to learning in deterministic domains. For example, such techniques have been applied to chess, learning grammars for artificial and natural languages, and inducing computer programs from examples. Most work in inductive logic programming is focused on deterministic domains, though some recent work extends this work into probabilistic domains (Dzeroski and Lavrac 2001).

Locality of inference — PROXIMITY's combination of querying for subgraphs and learning based on those subgraphs assumes that all relevant relational information is preserved in the portion of the entire data set represented in the subgraph. If important information resides on elements outside the matched subgraph, then the RPT cannot capture it. The subgraph is assumed to represents the relevant "local neighborhood" of an object (e.g., a movie), and more global features of the graph are assumed to be unimportant. A user can choose to alter the query, thus forming subgraphs with smaller or larger local neighborhoods, depending on their beliefs about the size of the relevant neighborhood. Similar locality constraints apply explicitly or implicitly for most techniques, but the degree of these constraints can vary considerably.

Model Representation and Learning

Type of model — To date, we have incorporated modeling algorithms into PROXIMITY that construct conditional or discriminative models. This contrasts with other work focused on constructing generative models. Generative models define a probability distribution over the entire space of data instances. For example, for the problem of predicting the receipts of movies, a generative model would define the probability of all possible movie subgraphs along with a probability distribution over possible values of the receipts attribute. In contrast, a discriminative model defines a probability distribution over the values of receipts, given a particular subgraph. As with other types of Bayesian network models, PRMs are generative models. As with other types of tree-based models, RPTs are discriminative models. Generative models have a wider range of uses (such as detecting anomalies in a data set), provide a more complete description of the dependencies in a data set, and allow for more robust inference in the presence of missing data. However, their accuracy on purely discriminative tasks is often lower than models explicitly learned for that purpose, and they can be more difficult to learn.

Search over model structures — The RPT learning algorithm searches over a wide range of possible structures for the tree and for the attributes included in the tree. In contrast, some approaches to relational learning, including first-order Bayesian networks, PROXIMITY's own relational Bayesian classifer, and other techniques in social network analysis only learn the parameters for a model with fixed structure and attributes.

Attribute construction — RPT learning involves a limited form of attribute construction. Aggregate attributes (e.g., average actor age) are constructed and evaluated when constructing the tree. Some techniques such as ILP offer far more extensive search of such "constructed" attributes, greatly expanding the set of possible models that can be learned (Silverstein and Pazzani 1991). Other techniques do no search whatsoever, relying on the existing attributes on objects and links.

Use of background knowledge — Data analysts often have substantial background knowledge that can greatly assist model construction. Some techniques can used encoded background knowledge in the learning process. For example, background knowledge in first-order logic can be used by ILP approaches to improve both efficiency and the quality of induced models. Similarly, prior probability distributions can be used in Bayesian learning techniques. To date, PROXIMITY does not employ any explicit form of background knowledge in its learning algorithms.

Statistical Issues

Our recent work on relational learning has concentrated on the unique challenges of learning probabilistic models in relational data. Specifically, we are examining how particular characteristics of relational data affect the statistical inferences necessary for accurate learning. We have identified three features of relational data — concentrated linkage, degree disparity, and relational autocorrelation — and shown how they lead to two pathological behaviors in learning algorithms.

To explain more fully, the relevant features of relational data are:

Concentrated linkage — Real relational data sets can show striking non-uniformities in the concentration of linkage between different types of objects. For example, in our IMDb data, movies are linked to only a single primary studio, and each such studio is typically linked to many movies. We refer to this as *concentrated linkage* (Jensen and Neville 2002a). It contrasts with other situations where a smaller number of movies link to a single object (e.g., directors) or where many movies link to many objects of the same type simultaneously (e.g., actors). Figure 6 shows a schematic of the two situations. We have found concentrated linkage in many relational data sets. Perhaps the best example is publicly traded companies that each link to a single accounting firm, of which there are only a very small number.

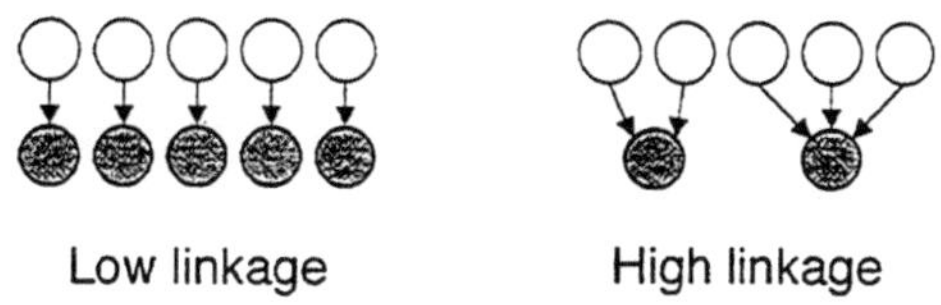

Figure 6: Concentrated linkage

Degree disparity — Another characteristic that occurs in some relational data sets is *degree disparity*. This condition arises when objects of different classes have widely different distributions of degree (the number links to objects of a particular type). For example, in IMDb, we found that US-based studios were systematically linked to a larger number of movies than foreign studios ($p<0.0001$). Figure 7 shows degree disparity schematically. We have found similar degree disparity in other data sets. For example, the number of owners differs systematically among publicly traded companies in different industries and the number of hyperlinks differs systematically among different classes of web pages at university web sites.

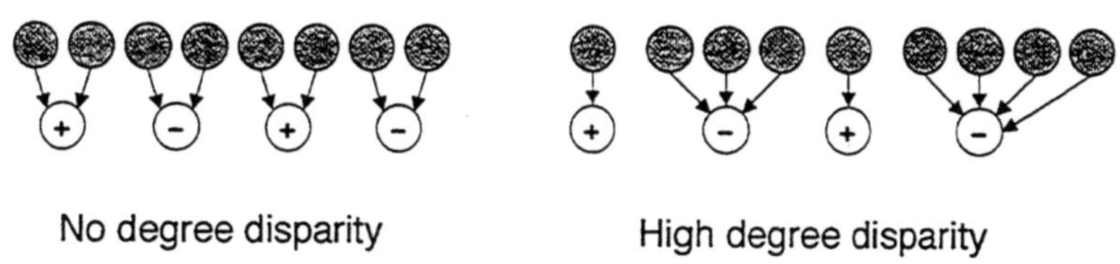

Figure 7: Degree disparity

Relational autocorrelation — Autocorrelation is the correlation among values of the same attribute for related objects. For example, temporal autocorrelation occurs when values of a given attribute (e.g., stock price) at time t tend to correlate highly with the value of the same attribute at time $t+1$. By analogy, we define *relational autocorrelation* as the correlation among values of given variable on objects that are nearby in graph space (Jensen and Neville 2002a). For example, the box office receipts of a movie tend to be highly correlated with the receipts of other movies made by the same director (correlation coefficient = 0.65) but not for movies starring the same actors (correlation coefficient = 0.17). Figure 8 shows autocorrelation schematically. We have found many other examples of autocorrelation, including correlation of the fraud status of interconnected wireless phone numbers and topics of interconnected web pages.

Figure 8: Relational autocorrelation

These three characteristics of relational data can greatly complicate efforts to construct good statistical models. Specifically, they can lead to:

Biased feature selection — Our recent work has shown that high levels of concentrated linkage and relational autocorrelation can cause data mining algorithms to select models that have the weakest, rather than the strongest, statistical support from the data (Jensen and Neville 2002a). This pathology occurs because linkage and autocorrelation combine to reduce the effective sample size of the data, thus increasing the variance of statistics used to assess the relatively utility of different components in learned models. Given that learning algorithms select the best component among many options, they can often select components with high variance, but low true utility, thus reducing the overall accuracy of the resulting model.

Spurious correlation — In other work, we demonstrate a pathology associated with building models that aggregate the values of many objects (e.g., the ages of many actors associated with a movie). This is a common method for simplifying relational data, and it is used in both RPTs and PRMs. When aggregation is used on data with degree disparity, it can lead data mining algorithms to include completely spurious elements in their models (Type I errors) and to completely miss very useful elements (Type II errors) (Jensen and Neville, in preparation). These errors occur with degree disparity because many aggregation functions (e.g., MAXIMUM) will produce apparent correlation between the aggregated values (e.g., maximum movie receipts) and a class label (e.g., studio location) whenever degree disparity occurs, regardless of whether movie receipts has any correlation with studio location.

Both of these effects show the problems associated with violating the assumption of independence among data instances that underlies so many of the techniques common to machine learning, data mining, and statistical modeling techniques. These results imply that new approaches are necessary to extend current techniques for data mining to relational data. We are developing one potentially promising class of techniques, based on randomization tests and resampling-based methods. We expect that these computationally intensive statistical procedures will allow us to adjust for the unique characteristics of a given relational data set, and make accurate parameter estimates and hypothesis tests. We are incorporating these approaches into our algorithm for constructing relational probability trees. We conjecture that similar approaches will need to be incorporated into all accurate techniques for building statistical models from relational data.

Conclusions

Recent work in machine learning and data mining has made impressive strides toward learning highly accurate models of relational data. However, little of this work has made good use of research in other areas, such as social network analysis and statistics. Cross-disciplinary efforts and joint research efforts should be encouraged to promote rapid development and dissemination of useful algorithms and data representations. In particular, this work should focus on the unique statistical challenges raised by relational data.

References

Blau, H., N. Immerman, and D. Jensen (2002). A Visual Language for Querying and Updating Graphs. University of Massachusetts Amherst Computer Science Technical Report 2002-037.

Breiman, L., J. Friedman, R. Olshen, and C. Stone (1984). *Classification and Regression Trees.* Belmont, CA: Wadsworth International Group.

Dzeroski, S. and N. Lavrac, (Eds.) (2001). *Relational Data Mining.* Berlin: Springer.

Flach, P. and N. Lachiche (1999). 1BC: A first-order Bayesian classifier. Proceedings of the Ninth International Workshop on Inductive Logic Programming (ILP'99). S. Dzeroski and Peter Flach (Eds.). Springer. 92-103.

Friedman, N., L. Getoor, D. Koller, and A. Pfeffer (1999). Learning Probabilistic Relational Models. In IJCAI'99. 1300-1309.

Getoor, L., N. Friedman, D. Koller, and B. Taskar (2001). Learning probabilistic models of relational structure. Proceedings of the Eighteenth International Conference on Machine Learning (ICML).

Gruber, T. (1993). Towards principles for the design of ontologies used for knowledge sharing. *Formal Ontology in Conceptual Analysis and Knowledge Representation.* Kluwer Academic Publishers. N. Guarino and R. Poli (Eds.).

Kass, G.V. (1980). An exploratory technique for investigating large quantities of categorical data. *Applied Statistics* 29:119-127.

Kersting, K. and Luc De Raedt (2000). Bayesian logic programs. Proceedings of the Work-in-Progress Track at the 10th International Conference on Inductive Logic Programming. J. Cussens and A. Frisch (Eds.). 138-155.

Jensen, D. (1992). Induction with Randomization Testing. PhD thesis. Washington University. St. Louis, Missouri.

Jensen, D. and P. Cohen (2000). Multiple comparisons in induction algorithms. *Machine Learning* 38: 309-338.

Jensen, D. and J. Neville (2002a). Linkage and autocorrelation cause feature selection bias in relational learning. Proceedings of the 19th International Conference on Machine Learning.

Jensen, D. and J. Neville (2002b). Schemas and models. Proceedings of the Multi-Relational Data Mining Workshop, 8th ACM SIGKDD International Conference on Knowledge Discovery and Data Mining.

Jensen, D. and J. Neville (in preparation). The effect of degree disparity on feature selection in relational learning.

Muggleton, S. (Ed.) (1992). *Inductive Logic Programming.* San Diego, CA: Academic Press.

Neville, J. and D. Jensen (2002). Supporting relational knowledge discovery: Lessons in architecture and algorithm design. Proceedings of the Data Mining Lessons Learned Workshop, 19th International Conference on Machine Learning.

Quinlan, J. R. (1993). *C4.5: Programs for Machine Learning.* San Mateo, CA: Morgan Kaufmann.

Silverstein, G. and Pazzani, M. (1991). Relational cliches: Constraining constructive induction during relational learning. Proceedings of the Eighth International Workshop on Machine Learning.

Srinivasan, A., S. Muggleton, M. Sternberg, R. King (1996). Theories for mutagenicity: A study in first-order and feature-based induction. *Artificial Intelligence* 85: 277-299.

Taskar, B., E. Segal, and Daphne Koller (2001). Probabilistic classification and clustering in relational data. Proceeding of the 17th International Joint Conference on Artificial Intelligence (IJCAI-01). 870-878.

Wassermann, S. and Faust, K (1994). *Social Network Analysis: Methods and Applications*. Cambridge: Cambridge University Press.

Acknowledgments

This research is supported by the Defense Advanced Research Projects Agency under contract numbers F30602-01-2-0566 and F30602-00-2-0597, respectively. The U.S. Government is authorized to reproduce and distribute reprints for governmental purposes notwithstanding any copyright notation hereon. The views and conclusions contained herein are those of the authors and should not be interpreted as necessarily representing the official policies or endorsements either expressed or implied, of DARPA or the U.S. Government.

Random Effects Models for Network Data

Peter D. Hoff*
Department of Statistics
University of Washington
Seattle, Washington
hoff@stat.washington.edu
www.stat.washington.edu/hoff

Abstract

One impediment to the statistical analysis of network data has been the difficulty in modeling the dependence among the observations. In the very simple case of binary (0-1) network data, some researchers have parameterized network dependence in terms of exponential family representations. Accurate parameter estimation for such models is quite difficult, and the most commonly used models often display a significant lack of fit. Additionally, such models are generally limited to binary data. In contrast, random effects models have been a widely successful tool in capturing statistical dependence for a variety of data types, and allow for prediction, imputation, and hypothesis testing within a general regression context. We propose novel random effects structures to capture network dependence, which can also provide graphical representations of network structure and variability.

1 Network Dependence

Network data typically consist of a set of n nodes and a relational tie $y_{i,j}$, measured on each ordered pair of nodes $i, j = 1, \ldots, n$. This framework has many applications, including the study of war, trade, the behavior of epidemics, the interconnectedness of the World Wide Web, and telephone calling patterns.

It is often of interest to relate each network response $y_{i,j}$ to a possibly pair-specific vector valued predictor variable $x_{i,j}$. A flexible framework for doing so is the generalized linear model (see, for example McCullagh and Nelder 1983), in which the expected value of the response is modeled as a function of a linear predictor $\beta' x_{i,j}$, where β is an unknown vector of regression coefficients to be estimated from the data. The ordinary regression model $E(y_{i,j}) = \beta' x_{i,j}$ is perhaps the most commonly used model of this type. A generalized linear model for binary (0-1) data is logistic regression, which relates the expectation of the response to the regression variable via the relation $g(E[y_{i,j}]) = \beta' x_{i,j}$, where $g(p) = \log \frac{p}{1-p}$.

*This research was supported by Office of Naval Research grant N00014-02-1-1011.

As an example of the use of such statistical models, consider the analysis of strong friendship ties among 13 boys and 14 girls in a sixth-grade classroom, as collected by Hansell (1984). Each student was asked if they liked each other student "a lot", "some", or "not much". A strong friendship tie is considered present if a student likes another student "a lot." Also recorded is the sex of each student. The data, presented in Figure 1, suggest a general preference for same-sex friendship ties. Of potential interest is statistical estimation of this preference, as well as a confidence interval for its value. One approach for such statistical analysis would be to formulate the logistic regression model $g(E[y_{i,j}|x_{i,j}, \beta]) = \beta_0 + \beta_1 x_{i,j}$, where $x_{i,j}$ is one if children i and j are of the same sex, and zero otherwise, and $\beta = (\beta_0, \beta_1)$

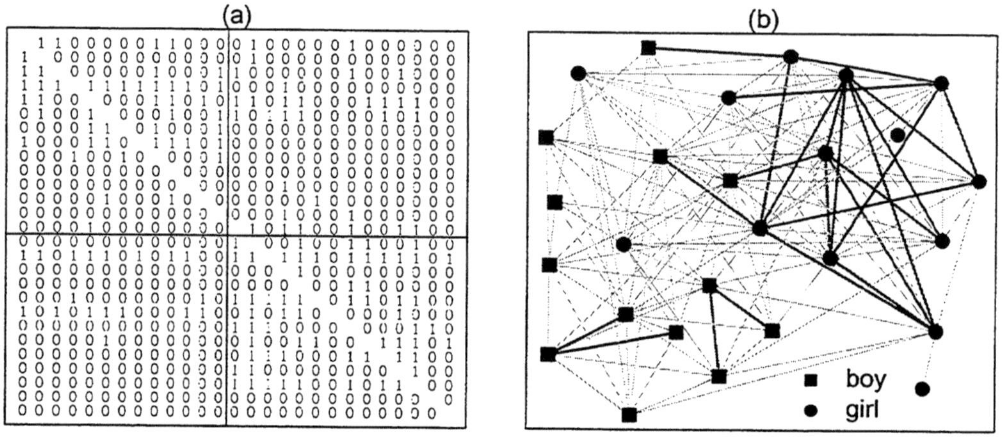

Figure 1: (a) Sociomatrix for friendship data: Rows and columns 1-13 are boys, 14-27 are girls; (b) Graphical representation of friendship data: Dark blue lines are reciprocated ties.

are parameters to be estimated.

Estimation of regression coefficients β typically proceeds under the assumption that the observations are conditionally independent given β and the $x_{i,j}$'s. However, this assumption is often violated by many network datasets. For example, the data on friendship ties display several types of dependence:

Within-node dependence: The number of ties sent by each student varies considerably, ranging from 0 to 19 with a mean of 5.8 and a standard deviation of 4.7 (the standard deviation of the number of ties received was 3.2). This node level variability suggests that responses from the same individual are positively dependent, in that the probability that $y_{i,j} = 1$ (i sends a tie to j), is high if we know $y_{i,k} = 1$ for lots of other nodes k, and lower if $y_{i,k}$ is mostly zero. More formally, we may wish to have a model in which $\Pr(y_{i,j} = 1|y_{i,1}, \ldots, y_{i,j-1}, y_{i,j+1}, \ldots, y_{i,n})$ is an increasing function of $y_{i,k}, k \neq j$.

Reciprocity: For directed relations, it is often expected that $y_{i,j}$ and $y_{j,i}$ are positively dependent. The classroom data exhibit a sizable degree of reciprocity, in that the number of pairs in which $y_{i,j} = y_{j,i} = 1$ is 24, which is more than we would expect due to just random chance: In only 11 of 500 (2.2%) random permutations of the network data, holding constant the number of ties sent by each student, did the number of such reciprocal dyads exceed 24. The average number of reciprocal dyads in the 500 permutations was 17.2. This suggests an appropriate model would be one which allowed for positive dependence between $y_{i,j}$ and $y_{j,i}$.

Transitivity and Balance: In many situations we expect that two nodes with a positive relation will relate similarly to other nodes. For relations which are positive or negative, this has led to the concept of "balance" in which a positive value for $y_{i,j}$ implies $y_{i,k}$ and $y_{j,k}$ are likely to be of the same sign for other nodes k. A related concept is transitivity, in which a large value of $y_{i,j}$ together with a large value of $y_{j,k}$ implies a large value of $y_{i,k}$ (see Wasserman and Faust, 1994, Chapter 6).

The classroom data exhibit a large degree of transitivity, in that the number of non-vacuously transitive ordered triples (see Wasserman and Faust, page 244), is 400. In 500 random permutations of the network data, holding constant the number of ties sent by each student, the largest observed number of transitive triples was 347. This indicates the data exhibit significantly more transitivity than would be expected due to just random chance and node-level variability, and an appropriate model should allow for some form of transitive dependence.

In this article, we discuss statistical regression models which can describe such types of network dependence. This is done by incorporating random effects structures in a generalized linear model setting. We discuss parameter estimation for these models in a Bayesian framework, and provide example statistical analyses of the classroom data described above and of a dataset on alliances and conflict among New Guinean tribes.

2 Network Random Effects Models

Generalized linear models, or glm's, are ubiquitous tools which extend linear regression models to non-normal data and transformably additive covariate effects (McCullagh and Nelder, 1983). A standard glm assumes the expectation of the response variable $y_{i,j}$ can be written as a function of a linear predictor $\eta = \beta' x_{i,j}$. Assuming observations are conditionally independent given the $x_{i,j}$'s and β, the model is:

$$\begin{aligned} \Pr(y_{1,2}, \ldots, y_{n,n-1}|X, \beta) &= \prod_{i \neq j} p(y_{i,j}|x_{i,j}, \beta) \\ g(E[y_{i,j}|x_{i,j}, \beta]) &= \eta_{i,j} = \beta' x_{i,j}. \end{aligned}$$

Examples of glm's include ordinary linear regression, logistic regression, Poisson regression, and quasilikelihood methods.

As discussed above, one feature that distinguishes network data is the likely dependence among the $y_{i,j}$'s. This lack of independence makes standard glm models inappropriate. In other settings which involve dependent data, a common approach to parameter estimation has been the generalized linear mixed-effects model (McCulloch and Searle, 2002) in which it is assumed the network observations can be modeled as *conditionally* independent, given appropriate random effects terms which can be incorporated into the glm framework. The model above becomes

$$
\begin{aligned}
\Pr(y_{1,2},\ldots,y_{n,n-1}|X,\beta,\gamma) &= \prod_{i\neq j} p(y_{i,j}|x_{i,j},\beta,\gamma_{i,j}) \qquad (1)\\
g(E[y_{i,j}|X,\beta,\gamma_{i,j}]) &= \eta_{i,j} = \beta' x_{i,j} + \gamma_{i,j},
\end{aligned}
$$

where $\gamma_{i,j}$ is an unobserved random effect. The distribution of and dependence among the $\gamma_{i,j}$'s determines the dependence among the $y_{i,j}$'s. For many kinds of network data, we may wish to find a form for the $\gamma_{i,j}$'s that induces the kinds of dependence described above, such as within-node dependence, reciprocity, transitivity, and balance.

A simple approach to modeling the node variability that gives rise to within-node dependence is the use of random intercepts, that is, to let $\gamma_{i,j} = a_i + b_j + \epsilon_{i,j}$, where a_i and b_j represent independently distributed sender- and receiver-specific effects. Such a distribution on the a_i's and b_j's induces a positive dependence among responses involving a common node. Typically, the distribution of these effects are taken to be normal distributions with means equal to zero, and variances to be estimated from the data.

Modeling other forms of network dependence is not as straightforward. In the case of binary logistic regression, Hoff, Raftery, and Handcock (2002) propose using a latent-variable approach as a means of modeling balance, transitivity, and reciprocity in network data. As applied to the glm above, such an approach presumes the error $\epsilon_{i,j}$ can be written as a function f of independent k-dimensional latent variables $z_i, z_j \in \mathbb{R}^k$ so that $\epsilon_{i,j} = f(z_i, z_j)$, $i, j = 1,\ldots,n$. The function f is chosen to be simple and to mimic the forms of network dependence described above. Incorporating both the random intercepts and the z_i's into the model, and assuming independent normal distributions, (1) becomes

$$
\begin{aligned}
\eta_{i,j} &= \beta' x_{i,j} + a_i + b_j + f(z_i, z_j)\\
a_1,\ldots,a_n &\sim \text{i.i.d. Normal}(0,\sigma_a^2)\\
b_1,\ldots,b_n &\sim \text{i.i.d. Normal}(0,\sigma_b^2)\\
z_1,\ldots,z_n &\sim \text{i.i.d. Normal}(0, I_k \times \sigma_z^2),
\end{aligned}
$$

where $\beta, \sigma_a^2, \sigma_b^2$, and σ_z^2 are parameters to be estimated, and I_k is the $k \times k$ identity matrix. Additionally, if the researcher is interested in local network structure, it may be desirable to estimate a_i, b_i, z_i for each node.

It remains to choose a suitable function f. One approach is to presume reciprocity, transitivity, and balance arise due to the existence of unobserved node characteristics, and that nodes relate preferentially to other nodes with similar values of those characteristics. This motivates letting f be a measure of "similarity" between the random effects z_i and z_j, which gives rise to a "latent position" interpretation as discussed in Hoff et al. (2002). For example, consider the following forms for f :

- (distance model) $f(z_i, z_j) = -|z_i - z_j|$;
- (inner product model) $f(z_i, z_j) = z_i' z_j$.

In the case of directed responses, each of the above functions induces a degree of reciprocity as $\epsilon_{i,j} = f(z_i, z_j) = f(z_j, z_i) = \epsilon_{j,i}$ due to the symmetry of f. The common error term induces a positive dependence between $y_{i,j}$ and $y_{j,i}$.

The above functions also give rise to higher-order dependence. For example, the distance model gives an error structure that is inherently transitive, since $|z_i - z_j| \leq |z_i - z_k| + |z_k - z_j|$ by the triangle inequality. The observation of strong ties from i to k and k to j suggests that $|z_i - z_k|$ and $|z_k - z_j|$ are small, and therefore $|z_i - z_j|$ cannot be too large and we might expect strong ties from i to j. The inner product model satisfies a similar but more complicated relation: in the special case that the vectors z_i are of unit length, $z_i'z_j \geq z_i'z_k + z_k'z_j - (1 + 2\sqrt{(1 - z_k'z_i)(1 - z_k'z_j)})$.

An undirected signed graph is said to be balanced if the product of the relations in all cycles is nonnegative, i.e. $y_{i_1,i_2} \times y_{i_2,i_3} \times \cdots \times y_{i_{k-1},i_k} \geq 0$ for all sequences of indices for which the corresponding data are available (Wasserman and Faust 1994, Chapter 6). As $f(z_i, z_j)$ exists in the model for each pair i, j, balance in terms of this random effect is equivalent to the balance of the complete graph formed by the sociomatrix with i, jth entry equal to $f(z_i, z_j)$. For a complete signed graph, all cycles are balanced if and only if each triad is balanced, i.e. $f(z_i, z_j) \times f(z_j, z_k) \times f(z_k, z_i) \geq 0$ for all triples i, j, k. Interestingly, this is satisfied by the inner product model in one dimension ($z_i \in \mathbb{R}$), as $(z_i'z_j) \times (z_j'z_k) \times (z_k'z_j) \geq 0$. For $z_i \in \mathbb{R}^k, k > 1$, these terms are not necessarily balanced, although they are "probabilistically" balanced in the following sense: if the directions of the z_i's are uniformly distributed, then the expected number of balanced triads exceeds the number of imbalanced triads, with the difference decreasing with increasing k. An additional feature of the inner product model is that if the directions of the $z_i's$ are uniformly distributed, then in general $E(z_i'z_j) = 0$. In particular, if each z_i is a vector of k independent normal random variables with mean 0 and variance σ_z^2, then $z_i'z_j$ will have mean 0 and variance $k\sigma_z^4$, furthering the interpretation of $z_i'z_j$ as an error term.

On the other hand,$-|z_i - z_j|$ is always negative, and so we lack this interpretation for the distance model. However, the distance model may be easier to interpret as a spatial representation of network structure: The z_i's can be interpreted as positions in a latent "social space," with nodes having strong ties to one another being estimated as close together, and subsets of nodes with strong within-group ties being estimated as clusters in this social space. Additionally, plotting estimates and confidence regions for the z_i's gives a graphical, model-based representation of the network data.

3 Parameter Estimation

Given network data $Y = \{y_{i,j}\}$ and possible regressor variables $X = \{x_{i,j}\}$, the goal is to make statistical inference on the unknown model parameters, which we generically denote as θ. The parameter θ may include the regression coefficients β, the variances of the random effects, and possibly the random effects themselves. We take a Bayesian approach to parameter estimation, in that we posit a (potentially diffuse) prior probability distribution $p(\theta)$, and base our inference on the posterior, or conditional distribution of the parameters given the information in the data, which is given by Bayes' rule, $p(\theta|Y) = p(Y|\theta) \times p(\theta)/p(Y)$. A closed form expression for the desired conditional distribution is generally unavailable, however we can make approximate random samples from this distribution using Markov chain Monte Carlo (MCMC) simulation (Gelfand and Smith 1990, Besag, Green, Higdon, and Mengersen 1995). MCMC-based inference constructs a dependent sequence of θ-values as follows: Given the lth-value θ_l in the sequence,

- sample a parameter value θ^* from a proposal distribution $J(\theta|\theta_l)$;
- compute the acceptance probability

$$r = \max\left(1, \frac{p(Y|\theta^*)p(\theta^*)J(\theta_l|\theta^*)}{p(Y|\theta)p(\theta)J(\theta^*|\theta_l)}\right);$$

- set $\theta_{l+1} = \theta^*$ with probability r, otherwise set $\theta_{l+1} = \theta_l$.

The particular details, such as the choice of the proposal distribution J, will depend on the model and the data. See Hoff et al. (2002) for MCMC algorithms designed specifically for such latent variable models.

The result of the algorithm is a sequence of θ values having a distribution that is approximately equal to the target distribution $p(\theta|Y)$. Statistical inference can be based on these samples. For example, a point estimate of θ is often taken to be the posterior mean, which is approximated by the average of the sampled θ-values. Posterior confidence intervals can be based on the sample quantiles.

4 Example Data Analyses

We now apply the methods described above to the statistical analysis of two example datasets. In the first example, we use the inner product model as a means of making inference on the preference for same sex friendship ties in Hansell's classroom data. In the second example, we use the distance model to make inference on the network of alliances among sixteen New Guinean tribes studied by Read (1954). Both datasets involve binary network data, although the methods are easily adapted to other types of network data via an appropriate generalized linear model.

4.1 Classroom Friendships

Hansell's (1984) data exhibit a tendency of children to form same sex friendship ties, in that 72% of the ties are same-sex. We consider a statistical analysis of this preference, in which we estimate the log odds of a same-sex tie, as well as make a confidence interval for its value. This is done via the logistic regression model with random effects described above,

$$g(E[y_{i,j}|\beta, x_{i,j}, \gamma_{i,j}]) = \beta_0 + \beta_1 x_{i,j} + \gamma_{i,j},$$

where $x_{i,j}$ is the indicator that i and j are of the same sex, $\beta = \{\beta_0, \beta_1\}$ are parameters to be estimated, and $\gamma_{i,j}$ is a random effect. In this parametrization, β_0 is the log odds of a friendship between children of opposite sexes, and $\beta_0 + \beta_1$ is the log odds for children of the same sex.

As described in the introduction, Hansell's (1984) classroom data exhibit several forms of network dependence, including node-level variability, reciprocity, and transitivity. This suggests we model the data with node-specific rates of sending and receiving ties, as well as a term which captures reciprocity and transitivity. We choose the following inner-product model with random sender and receiver effects:

$$\begin{aligned}
\log \text{odds}(y_{i,j}=1) &= \beta_0 + \beta_1 x_{i,j} + a_i + b_j + z_i' z_j \\
a_1, \ldots, a_n &\sim \text{i.i.d. Normal}(0, \sigma_a^2) \\
b_1, \ldots, b_n &\sim \text{i.i.d. Normal}(0, \sigma_b^2) \\
z_1, \ldots, z_n &\sim \text{i.i.d. Normal}(0, \sigma_z^2)
\end{aligned}$$

The parameters in this model are the regression coefficients β_0 and β_1, as well as the variance terms $\sigma_a^2, \sigma_b^2, \sigma_z^2$, which determine the dependencies between ties.

A Bayesian analysis was performed using the methods outlined in Section 3. The prior distributions for β_0 and β_1 were taken to be independent, diffuse normal distributions, both having mean zero and variance 100. The variance terms $\sigma_a^2, \sigma_b^2, \sigma_z^2$ were given diffuse inverse-Gamma(2,1) distributions, having an expectation of one but an infinite variance. An MCMC algorithm was used to obtain the 500,000 approximate samples from the posterior distribution $p(\beta_0, \beta_1, \sigma_a^2, \sigma_b^2, \sigma_z^2|Y)$. Marginal posterior distributions of $\beta_1, \sigma_a^2, \sigma_b^2, \sigma_z^2$ are presented in Figure 2. The results suggest a significant preference for same sex friendship ties, in that the posterior distribution for β_1 is centered around a median of 1.49, and a 95% quantile-based confidence interval for β_1 is (0.84, 2.11), which does not contain zero. The posterior distributions of σ_a^2 and σ_z^2 have deviated from their prior distributions and have moved to the right, giving evidence for sender-specific variability as well as the need for the latent variables $z_1, \ldots, z_n$. The posterior for σ_b^2 concentrates mass on low values, and is not much different from the prior distribution, indicating little evidence for strong receiver-specific variability.

In comparison, a naive approach to inference would be to treat each possible tie as a Bernoulli random variable, independent of all other ties. Using standard logistic regression, our estimate of β_1 is 1.3 with a standard error of 0.2, giving an approximate 95% confidence interval of (0.91,1.70), which is of substantially smaller width than the interval obtained with the random effects model. Of course, we might expect the confidence interval based on this naive analysis to be too small, as it incorrectly assumes all ties between individuals are independent and thus overestimates the precision of the parameter estimate.

4.2 Tribal alliances

Read (1954) describes a number of network relations between sixteen New Guinean tribes. Here we consider the network of alliances between tribes, letting $y_{i,j} = 1$ if tribes i and j have an alliance, and $y_{i,j} = 0$ otherwise. We analyze these data using the simple distance model with no covariates or separate sender- and receiver-specific random effects:

$$\log \text{odds } \Pr(y_{i,j} = 1|\beta_0, z_i, z_j) = \beta_0 - |z_i - z_j|,$$

where β_0 represents the baseline odds of a tie between two nodes that have the same latent position (i.e. β_0 the maximum log odds of a tie), and the z_i's are latent positions in $\mathbb{R}^2$.

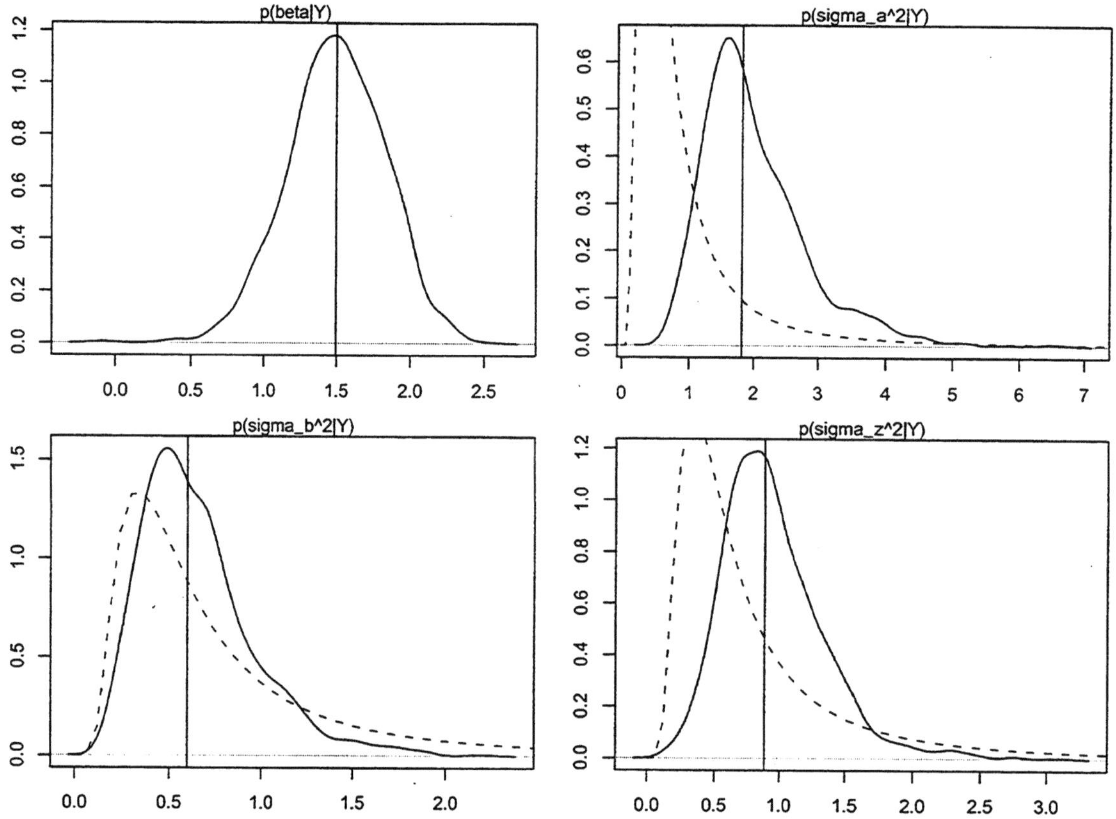

Figure 2: Marginal posterior distributions for the classroom data: Dashed lines represent the prior distributions for the variance parameters, solid lines the posterior. Vertical lines give the posterior median.

Without separate sender- and receiver-specific effects, we may expect that tribes with many alliances will be estimated as being more centrally located, and those with few ties as being on the periphery.

Bayesian estimates and confidence intervals for β_0 and the z_i's are obtained using the methods outlined in Section 3. In particular, samples of latent positions from the posterior distribution $p(z_1, \ldots, z_{16}|Y)$ are plotted in the first panel of Figure 1 (colors are chosen so that nearby node locations will have similar colors). Additionally, a black line drawn between nodes indicates the presence of an alliance.

Ad-hoc approaches, or simple point estimates of latent locations, might uncover some of the structure of the network. Our method goes beyond this by providing posterior confidence regions for node locations, which in turn give us a model-based measure of uncertainty about the network structure. Additionally, forms of predictive inference can be obtained from such a model. For example, suppose that the presence or absence of an alliance between pair (i, j) is unobserved or missing. The model can be fit with all available information (excluding the unknown $y_{i,j}$), and from the available information the posterior distributions of z_i and z_j can be obtained. From these, predictive inference about the value of $y_{i,j}$ can be made.

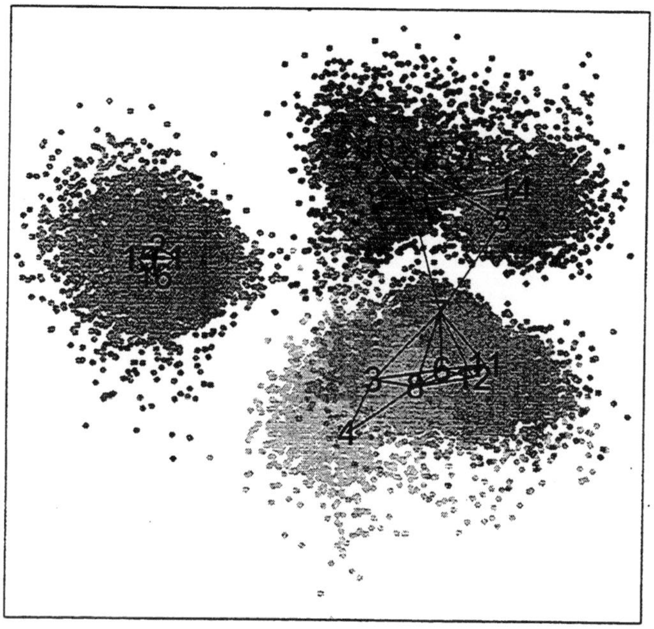

Figure 3: Tribal alliance network and marginal posterior distributions of locations.

Also collected by Read (1954) were data on conflicts between the tribes. It is interesting to note that, based on a clustering of nodes (1,2,15,16), (3,4,6,7,8,11,12), and (5,9,10,13,14), there were no within-cluster conflicts, even though not every tribe within a cluster had an alliance with every other cluster co-member. Additionally, node 7, towards the center of the alliance structure, had no conflicts with any of the other 15 tribes. We note that both responses (conflict and alliance) could be modeled concurrently by a similar method, in which a multinomial logistic random effects model is employed in place of the binary logistic random effects model above.

5 Discussion

This article proposes a form of generalized linear mixed-effects model for the statistical analysis of network data for which parameter estimation is practical to implement. The approach has some advantages over existing social network models and inferential procedures: the approach allows for prediction and hypothesis testing; lends itself to a model-based method of network visualization; is highly extendable and interpretable in terms of well known statistical procedures such as regression and generalized linear models; and has a feasible means of exact parameter estimation.

The models discussed here can capture some types of network dependence, although it is possible (or even likely) that in many datasets there are types of dependencies that cannot be well-represented with these models. It then becomes important to develop methods for assessing model lack of fit, and determining the effect of lack of fit on the estimation of regression coefficients. Furthermore, it may be useful to combine the types of random effects discussed here with other types of random effects, or latent variables. For example, Nowicki and Snijders (2001) discuss a latent class model, a useful model for identifying clusters of nodes that relate to others in similar ways. Their latent class model, combined with types of random effects models presented here and possibly other random effects structures, could provide a rich class of models for dependent network data.

References

Besag, J., Green, P., Higdon, D., and Mengersen, K. (1995), "Bayesian computation and stochastic systems," *Statist. Sci.*, 10, 3–66, With comments and a reply by the authors.

Gelfand, A. E. and Smith, A. F. M. (1990), "Sampling-based approaches to calculating marginal densities," *J. Amer. Statist. Assoc.*, 85, 398–409.

Hansell, S. (1984), "Cooperative groups, weak ties, and the integration of peer friendships," *Social Psychology Quarterly*, 47, 316–328.

Hoff, P. D., Raftery, A. E., and Handcock, M. S. (2002), "Latent Space Approaches to Social Network Analysis," *Journal of the American Statistical Association*, 97, to appear.

McCullagh, P. and Nelder, J. A. (1983), *Generalized linear models*, Chapman & Hall, London.

McCulloch, C. E. and Searle, S. R. (2001), *Generalized, linear, and mixed models*, Wiley Series in Probability and Statistics: Texts, References, and Pocketbooks Section, Wiley-Interscience [John Wiley & Sons], New York.

Nowicki, K. and Snijders, T. A. B. (2001), "Estimation and Prediction for Stochastic Block Structures," *Journal of the American Statistical Association*, 96, 1077–1087.

Read, K. (1954), "Cultures of the central highlands, New Guinea," *Southwestern Journal of Anthropology*, 10, 1–43.

Wasserman, S. and Faust, K. (1994), *Social Network Analysis: Methods and Applications*, Cambridge: Cambridge University Press.

Predictability of Large-scale Spatially Embedded Networks*†

Carter T. Butts‡

10/23/02

Abstract

Although it is well-known that there is a relationship between socio-physical distance and edge probability in interpersonal networks, the predictive power of such distances for total network structure has not been established. Here, it is shown that upper bounds on the marginal edge probabilities for far-flung dyads can be used to place a lower bound on the predictive power of distance, and one such bound is derived. Application of this bound to the special case of uniformly placed vertices on the plane suggests that only modest constraints are required for distance effects to dominate at large physical scales.

Keywords: social networks, spatial models, Shannon entropy, predictive power, distance

1 Introduction

Numerous studies show a strong relationship between physical distance and social structure (e.g., Merton (1948); Festinger et al. (1950); Caplow and Forman (1950); Blake et al. (1956); Whyte (1957); Sommer (1969); Snow et al. (1981); Latané et al. (1995)); arguably, few other findings in the social sciences can claim such a degree of strength and generality. While this is an interesting and important result in and of itself, it begs a critical question: assuming

*This material is based upon work supported by the National Science Foundation under Grant No. 0100999, as well as an NSF Graduate Research Fellowship. Additional support was provided by the Center for the Computational Analysis of Social and Organizational Systems and the Institute for Complex Engineered Systems at Carnegie Mellon University.

†I would like to thank Kathleen Carley, David Krackhardt, Shelby Stewman, David Rode, and Katie Faust for their comments and input.

‡Institute for Mathematical Behavioral Sciences and Department of Sociology, University of California-Irvine, Irvine, CA 92697, buttsc@uci.edu

that the distance/edge probability relationship is as it appears to be, to what extent can this account for the variability of social structure *writ large*? In his 1984 comment, "Chance and Necessity in Sociological Theory," Bruce Mayhew makes the characteristically bold claim that well over 90% of the variation in social structure is determined by physical space[1]. If Mayhew's assertion is correct, then we would expect for network models based on vertex position to allow us to develop extremely credible predictions of large-scale network structure. Since individual positions can be inferred from population data, such a result should (in principle, at least) allow us to reduce the problem of macrostructural prediction to one of spatial demography. If the assertion is false, by contrast, then other approaches will be required to effectively model the structure of social macrostructure.

While the "Mayhew question" is unlikely to be settled by a single paper, it is shown here that the requirements for predicting network structure from vertex layout are fairly modest. Fairly minimal constraints on the probability of edges between distant alters are sufficient to establish a lower bound on the predictive power of distance, where predictive power is defined in terms of reduction in the Shannon entropy of the total structure. Application of this bound to the special case of vertices in a planar region suggests that the requirements for strong distance effects (e.g., $> 90\%$ uncertainty reduction) are likely to be attainable in practice for moderate to large physical scales, and thus that it is reasonable to expect that large-scale spatially embedded social networks will be readily predictable from vertex position data.

2 Notation and Basic Assumptions

For the results which follow, we will focus exclusively on the case of a loopless undirected graph $G = (V, E)$ with known vertex set V and uncertain (i.e., random) edge set E. (For convenience, we denote the cardinality of V by $N = |V|$.) It is assumed further that G is spatially embedded, in the sense that there exists some space $\mathbb{S}$ and set $\mathbf{V} = \{\mathbf{v}_1, \ldots, \mathbf{v}_N\}$ such that $\mathbf{V} \subset \mathbb{S}$ and $\mathbf{v}_i$ is the *position* of vertex v_i. We assume that there exists some distance function, d, on $\mathbb{S}$, but do not require it to be a metric (i.e., it need not satisfy the triangle inequality). Substantively, the the most obvious interpretation of $\mathbb{S}$ is as a socio-physical space (often called a "Blau" space (Blau, 1977)); such a space may include both physical and demographic dimensions, including gender, age, race, and primary language. For the purposes of our present application, we will focus on a physical space interpretation of $\mathbb{S}$, but it should be emphasized that this is not required for the general result to apply.

[1]This, he quips, being an artificially low estimate due to measurement error.

3 Predictability of Spatially Embedded Networks

What, precisely, is meant by the "predictability" of spatially embedded networks? In the context of this paper, predictability is understood to be the extent to which our initial uncertainty regarding network structure is reduced by the provision of new information. Specifically, we are interested in the extent to which knowledge of vertex positions within $\mathbb{S}$ reduces our uncertainty regarding the edge set of G. A natural measure of uncertainty – and the one which we shall employ here – is the Shannon entropy, which can be interpreted as the expected length of an optimally encoded signal expressing the value of a random variable. Denoting the entropy function by I, we form the R^2-like predictability measure

$$\mathcal{P}(G|\mathbf{V}) \equiv 1 - \frac{I(G|\mathbf{V})}{I(G)} \tag{1}$$

which expresses the extent to which knowledge of the vertex position set, $\mathbf{V}$, can account for the total information content of G. With $\mathcal{P}$ as our notion of predictability, we can state the following general result:

Theorem 1 (Predictability). *Let $G = (V, E)$ be a spatially embedded random graph with vertex position set $\mathbf{V}$ and distance function d, and let G be distributed such that $p(\{v_i, v_j\} \in E(G)) \leq \epsilon \; \forall \; v_i, v_j : d(\mathbf{v}_i, \mathbf{v}_j) \geq r_c$, for some $\epsilon < 0.5$. Then $\mathcal{P}(G|\mathbf{V}) \geq p(d(\mathbf{v}_i, \mathbf{v}_j) \geq r_c)(1 - I_B(\epsilon))$, and $\lim_{\epsilon \to 0} \mathcal{P}(G|\mathbf{V}) \geq p(d(\mathbf{v}_i, \mathbf{v}_j) \geq r_c)$, where $\mathcal{P}(G|\mathbf{V}) = 1 - \frac{I(G|\mathbf{V})}{I(G)}$, I is the Shannon entropy, and $I_B(\epsilon) = -\epsilon \log_2 \epsilon - (1-\epsilon)\log_2(1-\epsilon)$.*

Proof. For convenience in notation, let $d_{ij} = d(\mathbf{v}_i, \mathbf{v}_j)$ and let $e_{ij} \equiv \{v_i, v_j\} \in E(G)$. We begin by assuming that, for actors within radius r_c, distance tells us *nothing* regarding edge probability; that is to say, $p(e_{ij}|d_{ij} < r_c) = 0.5$. Then it trivially follows from the definition of the Shannon entropy that $I(e_{ij}|d_{ij} < r_c) = 1$. For the complementary case, we begin by noting that $I(e_{ij}|d_{ij} \geq r_c) = -p(e_{ij}|d_{ij} \geq r_c)\log_2 p(e_{ij}|d_{ij} \geq r_c) - (1 - p(e_{ij}|d_{ij} \geq r_c))\log_2(1 - p(e_{ij}|d_{ij} \geq r_c))$. The fact that $p(e_{ij}|d_{ij} \geq r_c) \leq \epsilon < 0.5$ then implies that $I(e_{ij}|d_{ij} \geq r_c) \leq -\epsilon\log_2\epsilon - (1-\epsilon)\log_2(1-\epsilon) = I_B(\epsilon)$.

We now consider the entropy of the entire graph. Using the well-known result that $I(X, Y) \leq I(X) + I(Y)$ for (possibly dependent) random variables X, Y, we can bound the entropy of the graph by the sum of the (independent) edgewise entropies. Therefore we have

$$\begin{aligned}
I(G|\mathbf{V}) &\leq \sum_{\{i,j\}} I(e_{ij}|\mathbf{V}) \\
&\leq \sum_{\{i,j\}:d_{ij}<r_c} 1 + \sum_{\{i,j\}:d_{ij}\geq r_c} I_B(\epsilon) \\
&= \binom{|V(G)|}{2} p(d_{ij} < r_c) + \binom{|V(G)|}{2} p(d_{ij} \geq r_c) I_B(\epsilon) \\
&= \left[p(d_{ij} < r_c) + p(d_{ij} \geq r_c) I_B(\epsilon)\right] \binom{|V(G)|}{2} \\
&= \left[p(d_{ij} < r_c) + (1 - p(d_{ij} < r_c)) I_B(\epsilon)\right] \binom{|V(G)|}{2}.
\end{aligned}$$

Since the uninformative entropy of G is given by $I(G) = \binom{|V(G)|}{2}$, it follows that

$$\begin{aligned}
\mathcal{P}(G|\mathbf{V}) &= 1 - \frac{I(G|\mathbf{V})}{I(G)} \\
&\geq 1 - \frac{\left[p(d_{ij} < r_c) + (1 - p(d_{ij} < r_c)) I_B(\epsilon)\right] \binom{|V(G)|}{2}}{\binom{|V(G)|}{2}} \\
&= 1 - p(d_{ij} < r_c) - (1 - p(d_{ij} < r_c)) I_B(\epsilon) \\
&= p(d_{ij} \geq r_c) - p(d_{ij} \geq r_c) I_B(\epsilon) \\
&= p(d_{ij} \geq r_c)(1 - I_B(\epsilon))
\end{aligned}$$

which demonstrates the first portion of Theorem 1. To complete the proof, we allow $\epsilon \to 0$ and take the limit:

$$\begin{aligned}
\lim_{\epsilon \to 0} \mathcal{P}(G|\mathbf{V}) &\geq \lim_{\epsilon \to 0} p(d_{ij} \geq r_c)(1 - I_B(\epsilon)) \\
&= \lim_{\epsilon \to 0} p(d_{ij} \geq r_c)(1 + \epsilon \log_2 \epsilon + (1 - \epsilon) \log_2 (1 - \epsilon)) \\
&= p(d_{ij} \geq r_c).
\end{aligned}$$

□

This is a powerful and general result: it tells us that whenever we can place a reasonable upper bound on the marginal edge probability between distant vertices, we can use the quantiles of the distance distribution to place a lower bound on the predictive power of $\mathcal{V}$. Furthermore, when this bound on marginal edge probability becomes small, the predictive power of the position set becomes bounded by the probability that the distance between two randomly selected vertices will exceed the critical threshold. Thus, where the threshold distance is small relative to the overall distribution, we can *guarantee* that the total structure will be easily predicted from vertex position alone.

One important and somewhat counter-intuitive aspect of Theorem 1 is that it does not depend on N: the predictability of the total structure can be bounded by a function which depends only on the geometry of the population layout. Similarly, we did not have to assume dyadic independence to obtain this result (only bounds on the edgewise marginals). These two facts greatly facilitate the application of Theorem 1 in the field, where population distributions and some crude estimates of the distance/edge probability relationship may be all that is available. They also serve to reinforce the argument that the predictive power of distance is robust to varying assumptions about the precise determinants of network structure.

4 Uniform Population Distribution on the Plane

Consider the special case in which a population of arbitrary size is placed uniformly within a square region of size $\ell \times \ell$. Such a model may be thought of as a first approximation to a sparse population distribution in physical space, particularly over large areas. Here, we show the minimum threshold distances necessary to obtain a given level of predictive power for a structure on the plane, as a function of the linear scale (ℓ) of the embedding region. As will be shown, the only modest critical thresholds are required to guarantee high levels of predictability under uniform vertex placement.

4.1 Distribution of Inter-point Distances

In order to apply Theorem 1, we must first know the distribution of inter-point distances for square planar regions. Under the assumption that d is the euclidean distance, we derive this distribution in the following lemma:

Lemma 1. *Let $\mathbf{v}_i, \mathbf{v}_j$ designate two randomly selected points on a two-dimensional plane, with each coordinate being IID $U(0,\ell)$. Then the density function of $d(\mathbf{v}_i, \mathbf{v}_j)$ is given by*

$$f(d) = \begin{cases} 2d\left[\frac{\pi}{\ell^2} - \frac{4d}{\ell^3} + \frac{d^2}{\ell^4}\right] & 0 \le d \le \ell \\ 2d\left[\frac{2}{\ell^2}\sin^{-1}\left(\frac{2\ell^2-d^2}{d^2}\right) - \frac{4}{\ell^3}\left(\ell - \sqrt{d^2-\ell^2}\right) + \frac{2\ell^2-d^2}{\ell^4}\right] & \ell < d \le \sqrt{2}\ell\,, \\ 0 & \textit{otherwise} \end{cases}$$

with associated distribution function

$$F(d) = \begin{cases} 0 & d < 0 \\ 2\left[\frac{\pi d^2}{2\ell^2} - \frac{d^3}{3\ell^3} + \frac{d^4}{4\ell^4}\right] & 0 \leq d \leq \ell \\ \frac{1}{3} + \frac{2d^2}{\ell^2}\left[1 - 2\left(\frac{\ell^2 d^2 - \ell^4}{d^4}\right) + \sin^{-1}\left(\frac{d^2 - 2\ell^2}{d^2}\right)\right] + \frac{8\left(d^2-\ell^2\right)^{\frac{3}{2}}}{\ell^3} - \frac{d^4}{\ell^4} & \ell < d \leq \sqrt{2}\ell \\ 1 & d > \sqrt{2}\ell \end{cases}.$$

Proof. For the two-dimensional case, we may write the euclidean distance in terms of coordinate differences:

$$d\left(\mathbf{v}_i, \mathbf{v}_j\right) = \sqrt{\left((\mathbf{v}_i)_1 - (\mathbf{v}_j)_1\right)^2 + \left((\mathbf{v}_i)_2 - (\mathbf{v}_j)_2\right)^2}$$

By assumption, these coordinates are uniformly distributed on $[0, \ell]$. It can easily be shown that the difference between two such uniform deviates is distributed Triangular with lower bound $-\ell$, upper bound ℓ, and mode 0. Thus, we may simplify the distribution of d as follows:

$$\begin{aligned} d\left(\mathbf{v}_i, \mathbf{v}_j\right) &\sim \sqrt{\left(U(0,\ell) - U(0,\ell)\right)^2 + \left(U(0,\ell) - U(0,\ell)\right)^2} \\ &\sim \sqrt{\left(T(-\ell,\ell,0)\right)^2 + \left(T(-\ell,\ell,0)\right)^2} \end{aligned}$$

Note that $T(-\ell, \ell, 0)$ is symmetric about the origin; thus, it is a standard result that $F_{T^2}(x) = 2F_T\left(\sqrt{x}\right) - 1$, where F_{T^2} and F_T are the cumulative distribution functions of variates T^2 and T, respectively (Evans et al., 2000). For the distribution function of a Triangular deviate with lower bound a, upper bound b, and mode c we have

$$F_T(x) = \begin{cases} 0 & x < 0 \\ \frac{(x-a)^2}{(b-a)(c-a)} & 0 \leq x < c \\ 1 - \frac{(b-x)^2}{(b-a)(b-c)} & c \leq x \leq b \\ 1 & x > b \end{cases},$$

and hence

$$\begin{aligned} F_{T^2}(x) &= 2F_T\left(\sqrt{x}\right) - 1 \\ &= \begin{cases} 0 & \sqrt{x} < 0 \\ 2\frac{\left(\sqrt{x}-a\right)^2}{(b-a)(c-a)} - 1 & 0 \leq \sqrt{x} < c \\ 1 - 2\frac{\left(b-\sqrt{x}\right)^2}{(b-a)(b-c)} & c \leq \sqrt{x} \leq b \\ 1 & \sqrt{x} > b \end{cases} \end{aligned}$$

which, by symmetry, can be collapsed to

$$= 1 - \frac{2\left(b - \sqrt{x}\right)^2}{2bb}$$
$$= 1 - \frac{\left(b - \sqrt{x}\right)^2}{b^2}$$

(for $0 \leq x \leq b^2$).

To obtain the associated density function, $f_{T^2}(x)$, we simply differentiate:

$$\begin{aligned} f_{T^2}(x) &= \frac{\partial}{\partial x} F_{T^2}(x) \\ &= \frac{\partial}{\partial x}\left(1 - \frac{\left(b - \sqrt{x}\right)^2}{b^2}\right) \\ &= \begin{cases} \frac{1}{b\sqrt{x}} - \frac{1}{b^2} & 0 \leq x \leq b^2 \\ 0 & \text{otherwise} \end{cases} \end{aligned}$$

Having derived the density of a single T^2 variate, we now must consider the sum of two such (IID) variates. Since the variates in question are independent, their joint density is simply the product of their individual densities, and we may obtain the density of the sum via convolution. In this case, however, we note that the domain of $T^2 + T^2$ depends on the individual variates, and hence some care is needed in choosing the limits of integration. We divide the density at $x = b^2$ (the point beyond which both variates must be greater than 0), taking the lower region first:

$$\begin{aligned} f_{T^2+T^2}\left(x \left| 0 \leq x \leq b^2\right.\right) &= \int_0^x f_{T^2}(y)\, f_{T^2}(x-y)\, \mathrm{d}y \\ &= \int_0^x \left(\frac{1}{b\sqrt{y}} - \frac{1}{b^2}\right)\left(\frac{1}{b\sqrt{x-y}} - \frac{1}{b^2}\right) \mathrm{d}y \\ &= \frac{1}{b^2}\sin^{-1}\left(\frac{2y-x}{x}\right)\Bigg|_0^x - \frac{2\sqrt{y}}{b^3}\Bigg|_0^x + \frac{2\sqrt{x-y}}{b^3}\Bigg|_0^x + \frac{y}{b^4}\Bigg|_0^x \\ &= \frac{1}{b^2}\left[\sin^{-1}(1) - \sin^{-1}(-1)\right] - \frac{2\sqrt{x}}{b^3} - \frac{2\sqrt{x}}{b^3} + \frac{x}{b^4} \\ &= \frac{\pi}{b^2} - \frac{4\sqrt{x}}{b^3} + \frac{x}{b^4} \end{aligned}$$

Now, we consider the upper region:

$$
\begin{aligned}
f_{T^2+T^2}\left(x \,|b^2 < x \leq 2b^2\right) &= \int_{x-b^2}^{b^2} f_{T^2}(y)\, f_{T^2}(x-y)\, \mathrm{d}y \\
&= \int_{x-b^2}^{b^2} \left(\frac{1}{b\sqrt{y}} - \frac{1}{b^2}\right)\left(\frac{1}{b\sqrt{x-y}} - \frac{1}{b^2}\right) \mathrm{d}y \\
&= \frac{1}{b^2}\sin^{-1}\left(\frac{2y-x}{x}\right)\Big|_{x-b^2}^{b^2} - \frac{2\sqrt{y}}{b^3}\Big|_{x-b^2}^{b^2} + \frac{2\sqrt{x-y}}{b^3}\Big|_{x-b^2}^{b^2} + \frac{y}{b^4}\Big|_{x-b^2}^{b^2} \\
&= \frac{1}{b^2}\left[\sin^{-1}\left(\frac{2b^2-x}{x}\right) - \sin^{-1}\left(\frac{x-2b^2}{x}\right)\right] - \frac{2}{b^3}\left(b-\sqrt{x-b^2}\right) \\
&\quad + \frac{2}{b^3}\left(\sqrt{x-b^2}-b\right) + \frac{2b^2-x}{b^4} \\
&= \frac{2}{b^2}\sin^{-1}\left(\frac{2b^2-x}{x}\right) - \frac{4}{b^3}\left(b-\sqrt{x-b^2}\right) + \frac{2b^2-x}{b^4}
\end{aligned}
$$

Finally, putting this together, we obtain the complete density for a sum of two squared triangular variates:

$$
f_{T^2+T^2}(x) = \begin{cases} \frac{\pi}{b^2} - \frac{4\sqrt{x}}{b^3} + \frac{x}{b^4} & 0 \leq x \leq b^2 \\ \frac{2}{b^2}\sin^{-1}\left(\frac{2b^2-x}{x}\right) - \frac{4}{b^3}\left(b-\sqrt{x-b^2}\right) + \frac{2b^2-x}{b^4} & b^2 < x \leq 2b^2 \\ 0 & \text{otherwise} \end{cases}
$$

From the above, we may now derive the density of d. The last step in this process involves applying a positive square root transformation to the sum of squared triangular variates. This is a monotonically increasing one-to-one transformation, and we can thus derive the new density by a simple change of variables:

$$
f_{\sqrt{T^2+T^2}}(x) = f_{T^2+T^2}\left(x^2\right)|J|
$$

(where $|J|$ is the Jacobian determinant of the transformation)

$$
\begin{aligned}
&= f_{T^2+T^2}\left(x^2\right)2x \\
&= \begin{cases} 2x\left[\frac{\pi}{b^2} - \frac{4x}{b^3} + \frac{x^2}{b^4}\right] & 0 \leq x \leq b \\ 2x\left[\frac{2}{b^2}\sin^{-1}\left(\frac{2b^2-x^2}{x^2}\right) - \frac{4}{b^3}\left(b-\sqrt{x^2-b^2}\right) + \frac{2b^2-x^2}{b^4}\right] & b < x \leq \sqrt{2}b \\ 0 & \text{otherwise} \end{cases}
\end{aligned}
$$

To arrive at the distribution function of d, we need merely integrate $f_{\sqrt{T^2+T^2}}$ over the desired

Scale		$\mathcal{P}(G\|\mathbf{V})$		
ℓxℓ		90%	95%	99%
0.1x0.1 km	$r_c \leq$	0.019	0.013	0.006
1x1 km	$r_c \leq$	0.192	0.133	0.058
10x10 km	$r_c \leq$	1.924	1.331	0.578
100x100 km	$r_c \leq$	19.236	13.311	5.923
All r_c values given in kilometers.				

Table 1: Maximum Critical Radius as a Function of Scale and Uncertainty Reduction, Uniform Vertex Placement

range.

$$F_{\sqrt{T^2+T^2}}(x) = \begin{cases} 0 & x < 0 \\ \int_0^x 2x\left[\frac{\pi}{b^2} - \frac{4x}{b^3} + \frac{x^2}{b^4}\right] dy & 0 \leq x \leq b \\ \int_0^b 2x\left[\frac{\pi}{b^2} - \frac{4x}{b^3} + \frac{x^2}{b^4}\right] dy & \\ + \int_b^x 2x\left[\frac{2}{b^2}\sin^{-1}\left(\frac{2b^2-x^2}{x^2}\right)\right. & \\ \left. -\frac{4}{b^3}\left(b - \sqrt{x^2-b^2}\right) + \frac{2b^2-x^2}{b^4}\right] dy & b < x \leq \sqrt{2}b \\ 1 & x > \sqrt{2}b \end{cases}$$

$$= \begin{cases} 0 & x < 0 \\ 2\left[\frac{\pi x^2}{2b^2} - \frac{4x^3}{3b^3} + \frac{x^4}{4b^4}\right] & 0 \leq x \leq b \\ \frac{1}{3} + \frac{2x^2}{b^2}\left[1 - 2\left(\frac{b^2x^2-b^4}{x^4}\right) + \sin^{-1}\left(\frac{x^2-2b^2}{x^2}\right)\right] & \\ + \frac{8\left(x^2-b^2\right)^{\frac{3}{2}}}{b^3} - \frac{x^4}{b^4} & b < x \leq \sqrt{2}b \\ 1 & x > \sqrt{2}b \end{cases}$$

Substitution of d for x and ℓ for b completes the proof. □

4.2 Predictability

Using Lemma 1 together with Theorem 1, we may determine the maximum r_c value needed to guarantee that a given fraction of the uncertainty in G can be accounted for by the euclidean distances between vertex positions; these threshold values are shown in Table 1. As the table indicates, a critical radius at or below approximately %20 of the linear scale of the region is adequate for a %90 uncertainty reduction, with a reduction of %99 possible for radii of 0.06ℓ or less.

How do these threshold values compare to empirical assessments of the distance/edge probability relationship? Fits of dyadic edge models to existing data sets suggest that a low-probability threshold is attainable, but also clearly indicate that thresholds will depend upon relational content (Butts, 2002). Recalling that $\mathcal{P}(G|\mathbf{V}) \geq p\big(d(\mathbf{v}_i, \mathbf{v}_j) \geq r_c\big)\big(1 - I_B(\epsilon)\big)$, we can express the adequacy of the threshold approximation in terms of $I_B(\epsilon)$. In this regard, $\epsilon \leq 0.001$ is sufficient to bring the predictability bound within approximately 1% of the limit; such a bound is not hard to achieve in practice. Based on the Butts models, thresholds of as little as 0.05km may be reasonable approximations for face-to-face contact, with larger thresholds of approximately 0.25km and 18km for social friendship and telephone contacts, respectively. Although it may be possible to obtain *more* predictive power using these or other models than Table 1 would suggest, the lower bounds alone indicate that physical layout has the potential to account for the overwhelming majority of network structure at even modest spatial scales.

5 Conclusion

To summarize, then, it would seem that even a *very* modest null model based on physical distance (the threshold model) must account for the vast majority of network structure in large-scale networks, under quite minimal assumptions. Since fitted models have the capacity to be much more informative than the null model, they are expected to provide even more information about network macrostructure at even smaller scales. Thus, not only might one reasonably speculate that distance could account for most of the uncertainty in large-scale interpersonal networks, it almost *has* to do so. This would seem to vindicate the intuition of theorists such as Mayhew, who perceived that physical space was a critical structuring force, but who did not demonstrate the extent of that result.

References

Blake, R. R., Rhead, C., Wedge, B., and Monton, J. (1956). Housing architecture and social interaction. *Sociometry*, 19:133–139.

Blau, P. M. (1977). *Inequality and Heterogeneity.* Free Press, New York.

Butts, C. T. (2002). *Spatial Models of Large-scale Interpersonal Networks.* Doctoral Dissertation, Carnegie Mellon University.

Caplow, T. and Forman, R. (1950). Neighborhood interaction in a homogeneous community. *American Sociological Review*, 15:357–366.

Evans, M., Hastings, N., and Peacock, B. (2000). *Statistical Distributions.* John Wiley and Sons, New York, third edition.

Festinger, L., Schachter, S., and Back, K. (1950). *Social Pressures in Informal Groups.* Stanford University Press, Stanford, California.

Latané, B., Liu, J. H., Nowak, A., Bonevento, M., and Zheng, L. (1995). Distance matters: Physical space and social impact. *Personality and Social Psychology Bulletin*, 21(8):795–805.

Mayhew, B. H. (1984). Chance and necessity in sociological theory. *Journal of Mathematical Sociology*, 9:305–339.

Merton, R. (1948). The social psychology of housing. In Dennis, W., editor, *Current Trends in Social Psychology*, pages 163–217. University of Pittsburgh Press, Pittsburgh, PA.

Snow, D. A., Leahy, P. J., and Schwab, W. A. (1981). Social interaction in a heterogeneous apartment: An investigation of the effects of environment upon behavior. *Sociological Focus*, 14(4):309–319.

Sommer, R. (1969). *Personal Space.* Prentice-Hall, Englewood Cliffs, NJ.

Whyte, W. H. (1957). *The Organization Man.* Doubleday, Garden City, NY.

Using Multi-theoretical Multi-level (MTML) Models to Study Adversarial Networks

Noshir S. Contractor
Departments of Speech Communication & Psychology
Research Affiliate, Beckman Institute for Advanced Science & Technology
University of Illinois at Urbana-Champaign

Peter R. Monge
Annenberg School for Communication & Marshall School of Business
University of Southern California

Abstract

This paper applies the multi-theoretical multi-level (MTML) model to study the creation, maintenance and dissolution of adversarial communication and knowledge networks. It begins by identifying the theoretical mechanisms that influence the dynamics and co-evolution of communication and knowledge networks in general. Next it describes how examining adversarial social networks requires an extension to the MTML framework. In particular, we describe how community ecology theory helps us better understand how the network linkages in a focal network can be influenced by other networks within the same population as well as networks within other populations in the community. Finally, we briefly describe an analytic framework that we have developed to specify (i) multi-theoretical multi-level models for the evolution of these network, (ii) agent based computational models in *Blanche* to assess the transient and long-term implications of these theoretical mechanisms on the co-evolution of the networks, and (iii) p* analytic techniques to validate these predictions using empirical data.

Some of the material in this paper has been adapted from Monge & Contractor (2003). *Theories of Communication Networks*. New York: Oxford University Press.

Using Multi-theoretical Multi-level (MTML) Models to Study Adversarial Networks

Overview

To date, most network research has been limited by five major problems. First, it tends to be atheoretical, ignoring the various social theories that contain network implications. Second, it explores single levels of analysis rather than the multiple levels out of which most networks are comprised. Third, network analysis has employed limited theoretical insights from contemporary complex systems analysis and computer simulations. Fourth, it typically uses descriptive rather than inferential statistics, thus robbing it of the ability to make theoretical claims about the larger universe of networks. Finally, almost all the research is static and cross-sectional rather than dynamic. In our book, Theories *of Communication Networks* (2003), we propose solutions to all five problems. First, we have developed a multi-theoretical model that relates different social theories with different network properties. Second, the model is multi-level, offering a network decomposition that applies pertinent social theories at all network levels: individuals, dyads, triples, groups, and the entire network. Third, the model relies on a complex systems perspective, implementing *Blanche*, an agent-based network computer simulation environment, to generate and test theories and hypotheses. Fourth, the model utilizes the p^* family, a set of innovative tools for statistical network analysis, to provide a basis for valid multilevel statistical inferences. Finally, our model relates communication networks to other networks, enabling more sophisticated study of how dynamic organizational networks emerge.

This paper advances arguments in support of a multi-theoretical multi-level approach to study the emergence of adversarial networks. Recent advances in digital technologies invite consideration of organizing as a process that is accomplished by flexible, adaptive, and ad hoc networks that can be created, maintained, dissolved, and reconstituted with remarkable alacrity. We propose, and describe briefly, a Multi-theoretical Multi-level (MTML) framework -- based on network formulations of social theories -- to examine the mechanisms that influence people and organizations to forge network links with other individuals, organizations, as well as non-human agents (such as knowledge repositories). We extend the MTML framework to explicitly advance our understanding of adversarial networks.

Adversarial social networks are defined as the networks of multiple organizations within a population or the networks of multiple populations of organizations within a community (van Meter, 2001). These networks exist in the same or similar niches, competing for the same or similar resources, and seek to drive out their competitors, thus dominating the community. The relations among these nodes represent ties that vary in the extent to which they may be "adversarial." For instance, the multiple intelligence gathering organizations within the US (such as the CIA, FBI, and the NSA) are populations of organizations that are sometimes collectively referred to as the "intelligence community." The relationships between these populations range from being cooperative to competitive. Also included within the "intelligence community." are additional populations including intelligence gathering organizations of "friendly" countries as well as the intelligence gathering organizations of hostile countries and non-sovereign entities. This conceptualization of adversarial networks includes communities (or populations of organizations) within a variety of contexts including the telecommunications industry, the Wi-Fi landscape, biological warfare, the film industry, and even the development and distribution of retail consumer products. Arquilla and Ronfeldt (2001) identify several recent social movements and ideological campaigns that they identify as "netwars" in which "numerous dispersed small groups using the latest communications technologies could act conjointly across great distances" (p. 2). The groups they consider include terrorists, criminals, separatists, drug cartels, radical activists, non-government organizations (NGOs) and civil society advocates. They noted similar adversarial network patterns when they examined the organizational forms of seemingly disparate activities such as the al-Qaeda network's terrorist operations (see also Krebs, 2001), the Chechen effort to secede from Russia, the Direct Action Network's operations during the 1999 World Trade Organization summit in Seattle, Greenpeace, the International Campaign to Ban Landmines (ICBL), and the Zapatista National Liberation Army. Therefore, although the notion of adversarial networks has captured a great deal of attention in the context of terrorist networks, the theoretical scope is increasingly relevant to a much wider cast of social contexts, many of which do not carry the same illegal and illicit connotations (Bryant, Shumate, & Monge, 2002).

From "Networks in Organizations" to "Networks as Organization"

Network forms of organization are neither vertically organized hierarchies like their bureaucratic predecessors nor are they unorganized marketplaces governed by supply and demand (Powell, 1990; Williamson, 1996). Rather, network organizational forms are built on *generalized* structures that link people and knowledge in all parts of the organization to one other, while simultaneously tying them to multiple external contacts. These new forms are knowledge intensive (Badaracco, 1991), agile (Goldman, Nagel, & Preiss, 1995), and are constantly adapting as new links are added and dysfunctional ones are dropped. Thus, the evolving network form *is* the organization.

Knowledge networks by themselves and as organizational forms are understood as general concepts. Knowledge circulates throughout network organizations in a variety of forms: as individual and cognitive networks (Carley, 1995); as distributed work team networks (Hollingshead, 1998); as internal organization-wide networks enabled by Intranets (Monge & Contractor, 2001; 2003); and as external network connections via Extranets (Bar, 1995). Further, these networks are highly interdependent and co-evolve with the network forms of which they are a part. In fact, because knowledge work consists primarily of linking and integrating the various components of knowledge together, it is crucial for scholars to examine all parts of the entire knowledge network concurrently over time. This includes efforts to compile, extend, test and refine current understanding of (i) how best to characterize knowledge networks at various levels and measure their state and dynamic evolution; and (ii) the theoretical mechanisms that explain the evolution of these networks.

Multi-Theoretical Multi-level (MTML) Model for Studying the Emergence of Networks

Monge and Contractor (2003) have proposed a multi-theoretical multi-level (MTML) model to study the creation, maintenance, development, and reconstitution of network linkages in organizational and inter-organizational contexts. In general terms, we ask the question: "What are the social mechanisms that help us understand why individuals (or aggregates of individuals) seek to forge, sustain, or dissolve our network ties with other human and non-human agents?" As developments in information and communication technologies continue to reduce or eliminate the potential *logistic* barriers to our network relations, it becomes increasingly important to identify the various *social* factors that enable or constrain the development of these network linkages. Monge and Contractor (2003) identify a wide array of theories that can be used to develop network formulations. The theories and their theoretical mechanisms are summarized in Table 1. In the interest of brevity, the following summary does not include citations to the various scholars who have contributed to these theories. Details about the theories and their intellectual proponents can be found in Monge and Contractor (2003).

Theories of self-interest focus on how actors (people, organizations, etc.) make choices that favor their personal preferences and desires (Bourdieu & Wacquant, 1992; Coleman, 1986). That is, Person *i*'s decision to forge a tie with another Person *j* is motivated entirely by Person *i*'s self-interest and ability in seeking a resource that Person *j* possesses. Two primary theories in this area are the theory of social capital (Burt, 1992, 2001; Lin 2001) and transaction cost economics (Williamson, 1975, 1985). Distinct from human capital, which describes individual personal characteristics, social capital focuses on the properties of the communication networks in which people are embedded. Structural holes in the network provide people opportunities to invest their information, communication, and other social resources in the expectation of reaping profits. Transaction cost economics examines the information and communication costs involved in market and organizational transactions as well as ways in which to minimize these costs. Network forms of organization provide an alternative to markets and hierarchy, which focuses on embeddedness in complex networks (Powell, 1990). Information flows are essential in determining to whom a firm should link and joint value maximization offers an alternative principle to minimizing transaction costs (Zajac & Olsen, 1993). Self-interest mechanisms are likely to foster the formation of separate adversarial networks. These theories suggest that each network will invest its own social capital to expand its own network. They also suggest that each network will seek to exploit the structural holes of its adversaries.

Theories of mutual interest and collective action examine how coordinated activity produces outcomes unattainable by individual action (Marwell & Oliver, 1993).

That is, Individual *i*'s and Individual *j*'s decision to forge a tie is motivated by their belief that it serves their mutual (or collective) interest in accomplishing common or complementary goals. One theory that exemplifies this perspective is public goods theory (Hardin, 1982; Samuelson, 1954), which examines the communication strategies that enable organizers to induce members of a collective to contribute their resources to the

Table 1. Selected Social Theories and their Theoretical Mechanisms

Theory	Theoretical Mechanism
Theories of Self-Interest	
Social Capital	Investments in opportunities
Structural Holes	Control of information flow
Transaction Costs	Cost minimization
Mutual Self Interest & Collective Action	Joint value maximization
Public Good Theory	Inducements to contribute
Critical Mass Theory	Number of people with resources & interests
Cognitive Theories	Cognitive mechanisms leading to:
Semantic/knowledge Networks	Shared interpretations
Cognitive social structures	Similarity in perceptual structures
Cognitive Consistency	
Balance theory	Drive to avoid imbalance & restore balance
Cognitive Dissonance	Drive to reduce dissonance
Contagion Theories	Exposure to contact leading to:
Social Information Processing	Social influence
Social Learning Theory	Imitation, modeling
Institutional Theory	Mimetic behavior
Structural Theory of Action	Similar positions in structure and roles
Exchange and Dependency	Exchange of valued resources
Social Exchange Theory	Equality of exchange
Resource Dependency	Inequality of exchange
Network Exchange	Complex calculi for balance
Homophily & Proximity	Choices based on similarity
Social Comparison Theory	Choose comparable others
Social Identity	Choose based on own group identity
Physical proximity	Influence of distance
Electronic Proximity	Influence of accessibility

Theories of Network Co-evolution	Variation, Selection, Retention
Organizational ecology	Competition for scare resources
NK(C)	Network density and complexity
Community ecology	Commensalist/Symbiotic relns b/w populations

realization of a public good. Mutual interest often conflicts with the individual self-interests of the members of a collective and sometimes leads to free riding (Olson, 1965) and other social and communication dilemmas (Bonacich & Schneider, 1992; Kalman, Monge, Fulk, & Heino, 2002). Network relations are often essential to the provision and maintenance of the good. Mutual interest theories apply largely to the separate adversaries, as they seek to foster their own agendas in consort with those of like minds. Insight can be gained by analyzing what the various networks define as their collective goods and bads, and the strategies and enticements they use to induce others in join their networks or at least support their separate causes.

Contagion theories address questions pertaining to the spread of ideas, messages, attitudes, and beliefs through some form of direct contact (Carley, 1991; Contractor & Eisenberg, 1990). For instance, Person *i*'s decision to forge a tie with another Person *j* is motivated by others in Person *i*'s network who have forged ties with Person *j*. Contagion theories are based on a disease metaphor, where exposure to communication messages leads to "contamination." Inoculation theory (McGuire, 1966) provides strategies that can be used to prevent contamination. Two competing contagion mechanisms have received considerable attention in the research literature. Contagion by cohesion implies that people are influenced by direct contact with others in their communication networks (Erickson, 1988). Contagion by structural equivalence suggests that those who have similar structural patterns of relationships within the network are more likely to influence one another (Burt, 1987). Social information processing (social influence) theory (Fulk, Schmitz, & Steinfield, 1990) suggests that the attitudes and beliefs of people become similar to those of the others in their communication networks. Social cognitive theory (Bandura, 1986) and institutional theory (DiMaggio & Powell, 1983; Meyer & Rowan, 1977) posit that mimetic processes lead to contagion, whereby people and institutions imitate the practices of those in their relevant networks. Contagion theories apply to adversarial networks in at least three ways. First, each contending network attempts to extend itself by acquiring and linking new members that accept its core identity. Second, they seek to infect the members of their adversaries' networks with messages, information, and ideologies that will undermine or destroy them. Finally, the adversaries seek to defend themselves by inoculating the members of their own networks against their rivals' efforts to infect them.

Cognitive theories explore the role that meaning, knowledge, and perceptions play in communication networks. Individual *i*'s decision to forge a tie with another Person *j* is motivated by who Individual *i* thinks Person *j* knows or what *i* thinks *j* knows or possesses. *Semantic networks* are created on the basis of shared message content and similarity in interpretation and understanding (Carley, 1986; Monge & Eisenberg, 1987). A complementary perspective views interorganizational networks as *structures of knowledge* (Kogut, Shan, & Walker, 1993). Creating interorganizational alliances requires building extensive knowledge networks among prospective partners and maintaining them among current partners. These knowledge networks are the mechanisms though which organizations share both explicit and tacit knowledge. *Cognitive communication structures* represent the perceptions that people have about their communication networks, that is, about who in their networks talk to whom (Corman & Scott, 1994). These individual cognitive communication networks can be aggregated to provide a collective or consensual view of the entire network (Krackhardt, 1987). Cognitive consistency theory examines the extent to which the attitudes, beliefs, opinions and values of network members are governed by a drive toward consistency or balance (Heider, 1958). The theory suggests that network members tend toward cognitive similarity as a function of the cognitive balance in their networks rather than alternative mechanisms such as contagion (Davis & Leinhardt, 1972; Holland & Leinhardt, 1975). *Transactive memory systems* consist of knowledge networks in which people assume responsibility for mastery among various aspects of a larger knowledge domain. In this way the collective is more knowledgeable than any component (Hollingshead, 2000, Moreland, 1999; Wegner, 1987). Knowledge repositories linked to the larger knowledge network facilitate knowledge storage and processing (Wegner, 1995). While knowledge flow is essential to an effective knowledge network, communication dilemmas sometimes lead people to withhold potentially useful information (Kalman, et al., 2002). These theories offer insights into adversarial networks. Competitors often develop differing semantic networks based on ingroup-outgroup polarization. While developing their own knowledge networks, competitors seek to undermine the knowledge networks of others, often by disseminating misinformation and faulty knowledge to their opponents, including their cognitive communication structures. Finally transactive memory systems help identify where crucial expertise lies within knowledge networks, thus helping adversaries to build their own expertise and to mount attacks their opponents.

Exchange and dependency theories seek to explain the emergence of communication networks on the basis of the distribution of information and material resources across the members of a network (Emerson, 1962, 1972a, 1972b; Homans, 1950). That is, Person *i*'s decision to forge a tie with another Person *j* is motivated by *i*'s interest in seeking a resource that *j* possesses, and in exchange offering Individual *j* some resource that *i* possesses and is of interest to *j*. People seek what they need from others while giving what others also seek. The exchange form of this family of theories is based largely on equality, assuming that giving and getting generally balances out across the network (Bienenstock & Bonacich, 1992; Cook, 1982). The dependency form emphasizes inequality and focuses on how those who are resource rich in the network tend to dominate those who are resource poor (Benson, 1975; Freeman, 1977, 1979). Consequently, power, control, trust, and ethical behavior are central issues to both theories (Oliver, 1991). Adversaries seek to dominate each other, perhaps to the point of destroying all opponents. While they are likely to utilize exchange mechanisms within their own networks, adversarial networks are dominated by attempts to assert dependency relations on their competitors.

Homophily and proximity theories account for network emergence on the basis of the similarity of network members' traits (Brass, 1995) as well as their similarity of place (Homans, 1950). Agent *i*'s decision to forge a tie with another Agent *j* is motivated by *i* and *j* sharing common traits (gender, tenure, etc.) or being proximate in physical or electronic spaces. Traits represent a variety of personal and demographic characteristics such as age, gender, race, professional interests, etc. (Carley, 1991; Coleman, 1957, Marsden, 1988) Social comparison theory suggests that people feel discomfort when they compare themselves to others who are different because they have a natural desire to affiliate with those who are like themselves (Festinger, 1954). Of course, this ignores the old adage that opposites attract, which would argue for a heterophily mechanism. Proximity theories argue that people communicate most frequently with those to whom they are physically closest (Monge, et al, 1985). The theory of electronic propinquity extends this to the realm of email, telephones and other forms of electronic communication (Contractor & Bishop, 2000;Korzenny & Bauer, 1981; Wellman, 2001). Homophily theory suggests that networks engaged in adversarial relations are likely to be comprised of people and organizations who are more similar to each other than to the members of their competitors' networks. A block model of all adversarial networks (in a given adversarial community) combined into a supra-network would reveal greater similarity within than between blocks. Proximity theory indicates that competing adversarial networks should exist in separate physical and electronic spaces. Yet similarity of traits and space also predicts likely points of contact between competitors and possible locations for penetration of one network by another, both overt and covert.

Coevolutionary theory extends traditional evolutionary theory that posits aspirations towards "fitness" based on mechanisms of variation, selection, retention, and struggle or competition (Aldrich, 1999; Campbell, 1965; Hawley, 1986). For example, Entity *i*'s decision to forge a tie with Entity *j* is motivated entirely by *i*'s belief that the network linkage will increase *i*'s fitness (measured as performance, survivability, adaptability, robustness, etc.; Hannan & Freeman, 1977). Random or planned variations in organizational traits occur, which are selected and retained on the basis of their contribution to organizational fitness and survival(Baum, 1996; Nelson & Winter, 1982). Coevolutionary theory articulates how communities of organizational populations linked by intra-and-interpopulation networks compete and cooperate with each other for scare resources (Astley, 1985; Kauffman, 1993). In order to survive, organizational networks must adapt to the constantly changing environmental niches in which they find themselves while also attempting to influence the ways in which their environments change (McKelvey, 1997).

In most social contexts, more than one of the theoretical mechanisms reviewed above simultaneously influence people. In some cases different theories, some using similar theoretical mechanisms, offer similar explanations but at different levels of analysis. For instance, contagion mechanisms help explain the emergence of networks among individuals as well as among adversarial organizations. In other cases, different theories offer contradictory explanations for the emergence of networks. For instance, theories of self-interest would suggest that adversarial networks create links with others who are indirectly connected to their adversaries, thereby increasing the amount of nonredundant information that can be gleaned. On the other hand, cognitive theories of balance suggest that people seek to be friends with enemies of their enemies thereby increasing their cognitive need for balance.

EXTENSIONS TO MTML MODEL FOR THE STUDY OF ADVERSARIAL NETWORKS: A COMMUNITY ECOLOGY PERSPECTIVE

The MTML model proposed by Monge and Contractor (2003) focused largely on the social mechanisms that explain the creation, maintenance, and dissolution of network linkages within *single* networks. It does so by examining the structural tendencies of various relations (such as communication linkages, knowledge linkages, trust relations) among the actors within that network and the attributes (such as gender, level in the hierarchy, and level of expertise) of the actors within that *same* network. Also included in that model, though not extensive explored, was the influence of other networks on the focal network as well as the influence of the focal network at previous points in time. These relations are summarized in Figure 1. In the case of adversarial networks it is

Figure 1. The MTML network structuring process

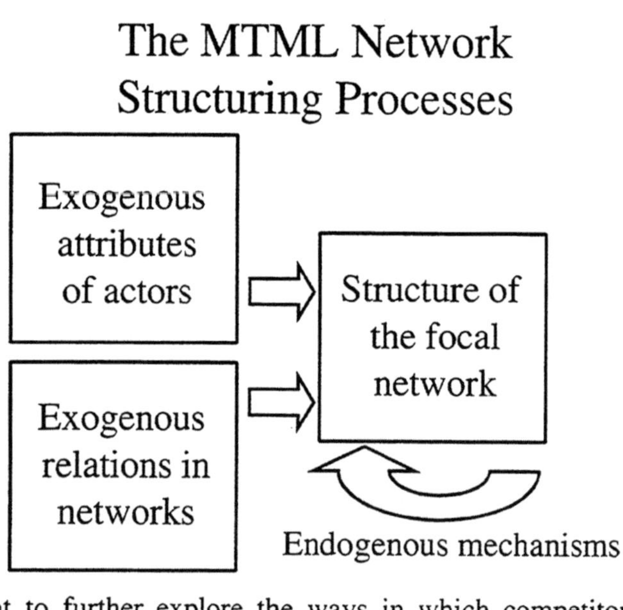

important to further explore the ways in which competitors influence each other and coevolve within the community.

There are several examples of how adversarial networks influence the structuring of ties within a focal network. For instance, Baker and Faulkner (1993) note that the activation of ties within a covert network are often constrained by the structure and scope of ties within the adversaries' networks. The desire to communicate, share information, and coordinate within a covert network have to be reconciled with the desire to shield the identity, structure and content of the focal network --- that is, the very survival of the covert network. Indeed as Weiser (2001) says a recently uncovered terrorist manual notes explicitly the premium put on secrecy over communication. Further, as Rothenberg (2001, p. 41) states, the viability of terrorist networks is specifically enhanced by other networks in the community – "the American democratic system that they seek to destroy, a system that permits open movement, freedom of choice, and respects privacy." As described earlier, many of the MTML mechanisms (such as self-interest, social exchange, and proximity) can account for how competing networks configure themselves to advance their position in the community while decreasing the viability of their competitors.

Community ecology theory (Aldrich, 1999; Baum & Singh, 1994; Hawley, 1950) provides a framework to explain the coevolution of populations of adversarial networks within a community. Community ecology examines multiple populations of differing organizations as well as the various niches in which they occur. Organizations must typically compete with others in their own populations to acquire the resources they need to survive in their selected environments. For example, Barnett (1990) studied the competition among the members of the population of the telephone companies in Pennsylvania from 1879-1934, until one company AT&T dominated the market. And Staber (1989) studied the emergence or worker and consumer coops showing how they competed for customer loyalty. Likewise members of the population of US intelligence organizations (such as the FBI, CIA, NSA) compete with each other for resources, jurisdiction, and legitimacy. But internal competition is not the only challenge that populations face. They must deal with the members of other populations of friendly and adversarial intelligence organizations outside the US as well as of non-governmental organizations that coexist in their niche. For example, Haveman (1992) studied the competition between banks and savings and loan associations for customers and their funds under changing regulatory conditions. And Carroll and Swaminathan (1992) examined the emergence of microbreweries and brewpubs who competed with the mass producers. Often organizations must compete, but under some conditions organizations from different populations can also *cooperate*, seeking mutually beneficial outcomes, a fact that Kauffman (1995, p. 215) says is much more commonly recognized now than in earlier theorizing. Aldrich (1999, citing Hawley, 1950) argues that two types of interdependence drive community dynamics: commensalism and symbiosis. "*Commensalism* refers to competition and cooperation between similar units, whereas *symbiosis* refers to mutual interdependence between dissimilar units" (p. 298, italics in the original). Thus, in large part, relations both within and among populations govern communities. The first relation is the degree to which similar populations in the same niches compete or cooperate and the second is the degree to which different populations in the same or different niches support each other.

An important issue that has arisen with regard to community ecology is how to define a community (Aldrich, 1999; DiMaggio, 1994). Hawley's (1950) original sociological work on community ecology focuses relationships within geographically and temporally bound communities. As community ecology has been refitted for organizational scholarship, the definitions of community have taken a more functional approach (Ruef, 2000). That is not to say, however, that organizational scholars completely agree on how community should be defined, operationalized, or analyzed. Astley's (1985) organizational model of community focuses on the technology-based interrelationships between populations. Barnett and his colleagues (Barnett, 1994; Barnett & Carroll, 1987; Barnett, Mischke, & Ocasio, 2000) define community on the basis of commensalist and symbiotic relationships between organizations. Hannan and Carroll (1995) broaden the scope of this definition, asserting that community "refers to the broader set of organizational populations whose interactions have a systemic character, often caused by functional differentiation" (p. 30). Rosenkopf and Tushman (1994) add that context is important, in their case the technological context. Aldrich (1999) and Ruef (2000) add that the populations in a community should be organized around a "core," whether it be technological, normative, functional, or legal-regulatory. Ruef (2000) goes about organizing his community of health care populations by focuses on four main functions of the health care field. Aldrich (1999, p. 301) proffers this succinct definition: "An organizational community is a set of coevolving organizational populations joined by ties of commensalism and symbiosis through their orientation to a common technology, normative order, or legal-regulatory regime." (p. 301).

Aldrich (1999, p. 302) proposes a taxonomy of eight possible relations between organizational populations based on the effects these relations have on each of the population. Aldrich proposes 6 types of commensalist relations (those that occur among similar units): full competition (where each population negatively impacts the other); partial competition (where only one of the populations has a negative effect on the other); predatory competition (where one population has a positive effect on the other while the latter has a negative impact on the former); neutrality (where neither population has a positive or negative impact on the other); partial mutualism (where one has a positive effect on the other, but the latter has no impact on the former), full mutualism (where both have positive impacts on each other). While full mutualism is defined as a commensalist relation (between similar populations), symbiosis is defined as a mutually beneficial relation between dissimilar populations. Finally, Aldrich (1999; p. 302) defines a dominance relation where a "dominant population controls the flow of resources to other populations (Hawley, 1950). The structure of the community and the coevolution of the populations of networks that comprise it depend on the outcome of commensalistic and symbiotic relations."

Aldrich's (1999) review illustrates several research examples for each of these intra- and inter-population relationships. However, most of the extant research in this area has examined only two populations at a time. Clearly, the community ecology theory posits an examination of multiple (not just two) populations within the community and their co-evolving influences on one another. Social network analysis in general, and the MTML framework proposed here, is particularly well-suited to this task. For instance, we can begin to hypothesize and empirically test how the populations within the community co-evolve when relations *among* the competing populations are considered at the triadic, sub-groups, and global levels. To what extent is the creation of ties within adversarial networks influenced by their common technology, normative order, or legal-regulatory regime? And, to what extent are the creation, maintenance, and dissolution of network relations within focal adversarial networks influenced by the various commensalist relations (within other organizations in the same population) and symbiotic relations with other populations within the community? Thus community ecology theory provides an important addition to the previously described MTML mechanisms in explaining the emergence of adversarial networks.

ANALYTIC FRAMEWORK FOR STUDYING MTML MODELS

The previous section has described theoretical mechanisms that offer explanations for the co-evolution of communication and knowledge networks. The schematic in the following figure describes a comprehensive analytic methodology developed by Contractor et al (1999) as part of our ongoing NSF-funded research to computationally model, empirically assess, and statistically validate the multiple theories that explain co-evolution of knowledge networks. These include changes resulting from the interventions of technologies. The schematic shows the relationship among the key elements of the analytic framework approach: (1) theory building/hypothesis formulation about mechanisms of network co-evolution; (2) computational modeling/simulation of those mechanisms and how they produce emergent behavior; (3) collection and analysis of empirical data, and (4) development and deployment of novel "community-ware" knowledge network enabling tools. The new kinds of data analysis and theory validation are enabled by (5) advances in p* statistical techniques for modeling and analyzing network data.

Table 2 provides an illustration of how p* network analytic techniques can be used to simultaneously test multiple theories at multiple levels (Contractor, Wasserman, & Faust, 2002). Table 2 summarizes various genres of network hypotheses in terms of the probabilities of graph realizations exhibiting the hypothesized relational property. In each case, the hypothesis is that graph realizations with the hypothesized property have larger probabilities of being observed. In other words, the probability of ties being present or absent in the graph reflects the hypothesized relational property. The table begins by distinguishing endogenous and exogenous variables that influence the probability of ties being present or absent in the focal network. It should be noted that the exogenous-endogenous distinction being made here is not equivalent to similar terminology used in the development of causal models in general and structural equation models in particular. Unlike its use in causal modeling, endogenous variables here are not predicted by exogenous variables. Here, both explain structural tendencies of the network.

Endogenous variables (Rows 1 through 4 in Table 2) refer to various relational properties of the focal network itself that influence the probability of ties being present or absent in the same network. From a meta-theoretical perspective, these endogenous variables capture the extent to which relational properties of the network influence its self-organization. *Exogenous variables* (Rows 5 through 11 in Table 2) refer to various properties outside the specific relation within the focal network that influence the probability of ties being present or absent in the focal network. Hence exogenous variables include the attributes of the actors in the network, additional network relations among the actors, the same network relation at previous points in time, as well as other networks within the same population or other populations. Within each of these two categories (i.e., endogenous and exogenous variables), the table offers a further sub-classification based on the extent to which the probability of ties being present or absent in the network are influenced by properties at the actor, dyad, triad, and global levels. In addition to including genres of network hypotheses, the third column in Table 2 also

Figure 2. Analytic framework to study the coevolution of adversarial networks

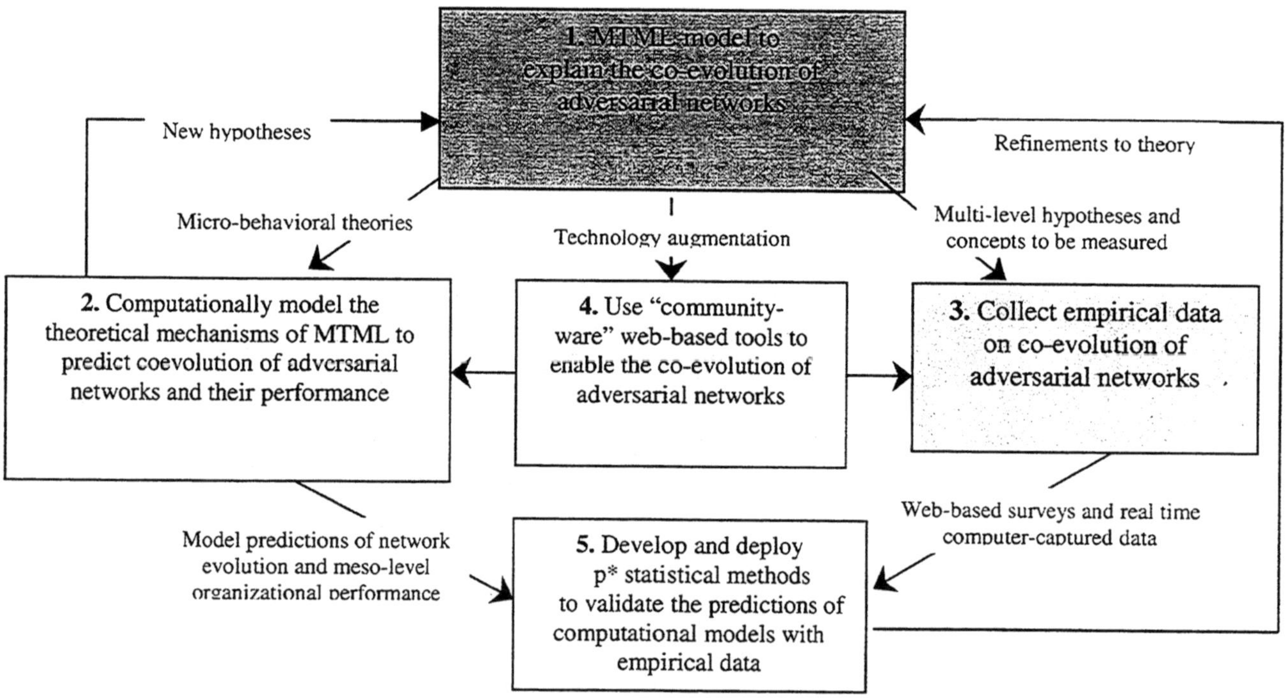

Endogenous variables (Rows 1 through 4 in Table 2) refer to various relational properties of the focal network itself that influence the probability of ties being present or absent in the same network. From a meta-theoretical perspective, these endogenous variables

capture the extent to which relational properties of the network influence its self-organization. *Exogenous variables* (Rows 5 through 11 in Table 2) refer to various properties outside the specific relation within the focal network that influence the probability of ties being present or absent in the focal network. Hence exogenous variables include the attributes of the actors in the network, additional network relations among the actors, the same network relation at previous points in time, as well as other networks within the same population or other populations. Within each of these two categories (i.e., endogenous and exogenous variables), the table offers a further sub-classification based on the extent to which the probability of ties being present or absent in the network are influenced by properties at the actor, dyad, triad, and global levels. In addition to including genres of network hypotheses, the third column in Table 2 also includes specific theories, previously discussed in the MTML models that might provide support for hypotheses. As such it demonstrates a close coupling between the MTML model and p* as a confirmatory analytic technique for empirically testing the model.

Table 2. Summary of a multilevel multi-theoretical framework to test hypotheses about adversarial networks (Variable of interest: Probability of the realizations of a graph)

Independent variable	**Examples of specific measures**	**Hypotheses:** Graph realizations where there is greater likelihood of ...
1. Endogenous (same network): *Actor level*	Actor centrality, structural autonomy.	... high actor centrality have higher probabilities of occurring *(e.g., Theory of structural holes)*
2. Endogenous (same network): *Dyad level*	Mutuality, Reciprocation	... high mutuality have higher probabilities of occurring *(e.g., Exchange Theory)*
3. Endogenous (same network): *Triad level*	Transitivity, cyclicality	... high cyclicality have higher probabilities of occurring *(e.g., Balance Theory)*
4. Endogenous (same network): *Global level*	Network density, centralization	... high centralization have higher probabilities of occurring. *(e.g., Collective action theory)*
5. Exogenous: Actor attributes (*Actor level*)	Age, gender, organization type, education	... ties between actors with similar attributes have higher probabilities of occurring *(e.g., Theories of homophily)*
6. Exogenous: Actor attributes (*Dyad level*)	Differential mutuality and reciprocation	... mutual ties between actors with similar attributes have higher probabilities of occurring *(e.g., Exchange Theory)*
7. Exogenous: Actor attributes (*Triad level*)	Differential transitivity and cyclicality	... transitive (or cyclical) ties between actors with similar attributes have higher probabilities of occurring. *(e.g., Balance Theory)*
8. Exogenous: Actor attributes (*Global level*)	Differential network density, centralization	... network centralization among actors with similar attributes have higher probabilities of occurring. *(e.g., Collective action theory)*
9. Exogenous: Network *(Other relations)*	Advice, friendship network	... communication ties co-occurring with ties on a second relation have higher probabilities of occurring. *(e.g., Cognitive theories)*
10. Exogenous: Network *(Same relation at previous point in time)*	Communication network	... ties between actors co-occurring with ties at preceding points in time have higher probability of occurring. *(e.g., Evolutionary theories)*
11. Exogenous: Other networks (*Within the same population and in other populations*)	Actor, dyad, triad, and global metrics in other networks	... ties between actors co-occurring due to structural properties of other networks within the same population and other populations within the community (e.g., *Community Ecology theory*)

References

Aldrich, H. (1999). *Organizations evolving*. Thousand Oaks, CA: Sage.

Arquilla, J., & Ronfeldt, D. (2001). The advent of netwar (revisited). In J. Arquilla & D. Ronfeldt (Eds.), *Networks and netwars: The future of terror, crime, and militancy* (pp. 1-25). Santa Monica, CA: Rand.

Astley, W. G. (1985). The two ecologies: Population and community perspectives on organizational evolution. *Administrative Science Quarterly, 30*, 224-241.

Badaracco, J. L., Jr. (1991). *The knowledge link: How firms compete through strategic alliances*. Boston, MA: Harvard Business School Press.

Baker, W. E., & Faulkner, R. R. (1993). The social organization of conspiracy: Illegal networks in the heavy electrical equipment industry. *American Sociological Review, 58*, 837-860.

Bar, F. (1995), Intelligent Manufacturing in the Global Information Economy, in *The Transition to a Global Economy: Challenges for United States and the World*, W. Drake ed., New York, NY: 20th Century Fund.

Bandura, A. (1986). *Social foundations of thought and action*. Englewood Cliffs, NJ: Prentice-Hall.

Barnett, W. P. (1994). The liability of collective action: Growth and change among early American telephone companies. In J. A. C. Baum & J. V. Singh (Eds.), *Evolutionary dynamics of organizations* (pp. 337-354). New York: Oxford University Press.

Barnett, W. P., & Carroll, G. R. (1987). Competition and mutualism among early telephone companies. *Administrative Science Quarterly, 32*, 400-421.

Barnett, W. P., Mischke, G. A., & Ocasio, W. (2000). The evolution of collective strategies among organizations. *Organization Studies, 21*, 325-354.

Baum, J. A. C. (1996). Organizational ecology. In S. Clegg, C. Hardy, & W. Nord (Eds.), *Handbook of organization studies* (pp. 77-114). Thousand Oaks, CA: Sage.

Baum, J. A. C., & Singh, J. V. (1994). Organizational hierarchies and evolutionary processes: Some reflections on a theory of organizational evolution. In J. A. C. Baum & J. V. Singh (Eds.), *Evolutionary dynamics of organizations* (pp. 3-20). New York: Oxford University Press.

Benson, J. K. (1975). The interorganizational network as a political economy. *Administrative Science Quarterly, 20*, 229-249.

Bienenstock, E. J., & Bonacich, P. (1997). Network exchange as a cooperative game. *Rationality and Society, 9*, 37-65.

Bonacich, P., & Schneider, S. (1992). Communication networks and collective action. In W. B. G. Liebrand, D. M. Messick, & H. A. M. Wilke (Eds.), *Social dilemmas:*

Theoretical issues and research findings (pp. 225-245). New York: Pergammon Press.

Bourdieu, P., & Wacquant, L. J. D. (1992). *An invitation to reflexive sociology.* Chicago, IL: University of Chicago Press.

Brass, D. J. (1995). A social network perspective on human resources management. *Research in Personnel and Human Resources Management, 13*, 39-79.

Bryant, A., Shumate, M., & Monge, P. (2002). Globalization and coevolving communities: The legitimate, illegitimate, and legal. Paper under publication review.

Burt, R. S. (1987). Social contagion and innovation: Cohesion versus structural equivalence. *American Journal of Sociology, 92*, 1287-1335.

Burt, R. S. (1992). *Structural holes: The social structure of competition.* Cambridge, MA: Harvard University Press.

Burt, R. S. (2001). Structural holes versus network closure as social capital. In N. Lin, K. Cook, & R. S. Burt (Eds.), *Social Capital: Theory and Research,* (pp. 31-56) New York: Aldine de Gruyter.

Campbell, D. T. (1965). Variation and selective retention in socio-cultural evolution. In H.R. Barringer, G.I. Blanksten, & R. Mack (Eds.), *Social change in developing areas: A reinterpretation of evolutionary theory* (pp. 19-49). Cambridge, MA: Schenkman.

Carley, K. (1986). An approach for relating social structure to cognitive structure. *Journal of Mathematical Sociology, 12,* 137-189.

Carley, K. (1991). A theory of group stability. *American Sociological Review, 56*, 331-354.

Carley, K. M. (1995). Communication technologies and their effect on cultural homogeneity, consensus, and the diffusion of new ideas. *Sociological Perspectives, 38(4),* 547-571.

Carroll, G. R., & Swaninathan, A. (1992). The organizational ecology of strategic groups in the American brewing industry from 1975-1990. *Corporate and Industrial Change, 1*, 65-97.

Coleman, J. S. (1957). *Community conflict.* New York: Free Press.

Coleman, J. S. (1986). *Individual interests and collective action: Selected essays.* New York: Cambridge University Press.

Contractor, N., & Bishop, A.. P. (2000). Reconfiguring community networks: The case of PrairieKNOW. In T. Ishida (Ed.), *Digital cities: Technologies, experiences, and future perspectives. Lecture Notes in Computer Science* (pp. 151-164). Berlin: Springer-Verlag.

Contractor, N. S., Carley, K., Levitt, R., Monge, P., Wasserman, S., Bar, F., Fulk, J., Hollingshead, A., & Kunz, J. (1999). *Co-Evolution of Knowledge Networks and Twenty-First Century Forms: Computational Modeling and Empirical Testing.* Research proposal funded by the National Science Foundation (Grant # IIS-9980109).

Contractor, N. S., & Eisenberg, E. M. (1990). Communication networks and new media in organizations. In J. Fulk & C.W. Steinfield (Eds.), *Organizations and communication Technology* (pp. 143-172). Newbury Park, CA: Sage.

Contractor, N. S., Wasserman, S., & Faust, K. (2002). *Testing multi-theoretical multilevel hypotheses about organizational networks: An analytic framework and empirical example.* Paper under publication review.

Cook, K. S. (1982). Network structures from an exchange perspective. In P. V. Marsden & N. Lin (Eds.), *Social structure and network analysis* (pp. 177-218). Beverly Hills, CA: Sage.

Corman, S. R., & Scott, C. R. (1994). Perceived networks, activity, foci, and observable communication in social collectives. *Communication Theory, 4*, 171-190.

Davis, J., & Leinhardt, S. (1972). The structure of positive interpersonal relations in small groups. In J. Berger (Ed.), *Sociological theories in progress.* (Vol. 2, pp. 218-251). Boston, MA: Houghton-Mifflin.

DiMaggio, P. (1994). The challenge of community evolution. In J. A. C. Baum, & J. V. Singh (Eds.), *Evolutionary dynamics of organizations* (pp. 444-450). New York: Oxford University Press.

DiMaggio, P.J., & Powell, W. W. (1983). The iron cage revisited: Institutional isomorphism and collective rationality in organizational fields. *American Sociological Review, 48*, 147-160.

Emerson, R. M. (1962). Power-dependence relations. *American Sociological Review, 27*, 31-41.

Emerson, R.M. (1972a). Exchange theory, part I: A psychological basis for social exchange. In J. Berger, M. Zelditch, & B. Anderson (Eds.), *Sociological theories in progress* (Vol. 2, pp. 38-57). Boston, MA: Houghton Mifflin.

Emerson, R.M. (1972b). Exchange theory, part II: Exchange relations and networks. In J. Berger, M. Zelditch, & B. Anderson (Eds.), *Sociological theories in progress* (Vol. 2, pp. 58-87). Boston, MA: Houghton Mifflin.

Erickson, B. (1988). The relational basis of attitudes. In S. D. B. B. Wellman (Ed.), *Social structures: A network approach*, (pp. 99-121,): Cambridge: Cambridge University Press.

Festinger, L. (1954). A theory of social comparison processes. *Human Relations, 7*, 114-140.

Freeman, L. (1977). A set of measures of centrality based on betweenness. *Sociometry, 40*, 35-41.

Freeman, L. (1979). Centrality in social networks: I Conceptual clarification. *Social Networks, 1*, 215-239.

Fulk, J., Schmitz, J., & Steinfield, C. W. (1990). A social influence model of technology use. In J. Fulk & C. W. Steinfield (Eds.), *Organizations and communication technology* (pp. 117-140). Newbury Park, CA: Sage.

Goldman, S. L, Nagel, R. N., & Preiss, K. (1995). *Agile competitors and virtual organizations: Strategies for enriching the customer.* New York: Van Nostrand Reinhold.

Hannan, M. T., & Freeman, J. (1977). The population ecology of organizations. *American Journal of Sociology, 82*, 929-984.
Hardin, R. (1982). *Collective action.* Baltimore, MD: John Hopkins University Press.
Haveman, H. A. (1992). Between a rock and a hard place: Organizational change and performance under conditions of fundamental environmental transformation. *Administrative Science Quarterly, 37*, 48-75.
Hawley, A. (1950). *Human ecology: A theory of community structure.* New York: Ronald Press.
Hawley, A. (1986). *Human ecology: A theoretical essay.* Chicago: University of Chicago Press.
Heider, F. (1958). *The psychology of interpersonal relations.* New York: John Wiley.
Holland, P. W., & Leinhardt, S. (1979). *Perspectives on social network research.* New York: Academic Press.
Hollingshead, A. B. (1998). Distributed expertise and communication processes ingroups. In E.A. Mannix, M. A. Neale, D. H Gruenfeld, *Research on Managing in Groups and Teams.* (Volume 1). Greenwich, CN: JAI Press.
Hollingshead, A.B. (2000). Perceptions of expertise and transactive memory in work relations. *Group Processes and Intergroup Relations, 3*, 257-267.
Homans, G. C. (1950). *The human group.* New York: Harcourt Brace.
Kalman, M. E., Monge, P. R., Fulk, J., & Heino, R. (2002). Resolving communication dilemmas in database-mediate collaboration. *Communication Research, 29*, 125-154.
Kauffman, S.A. (1993). *The origins of order: Self-organizing and selection in evolution.* New York: Oxford University Press.
Kauffman, S. A. (1995). *At home in the universe: The search for the laws of self-organization and complexity.* New York: Oxford University Press.
Kogut, B., Shan, W., & Walker, G. (1993). Knowledge in the network and the network as knowledge: Structuring of new industries. In G. Grabher (Ed.), *The embedded firm: On the socioeconomics of industrial networks* (pp. 67-94). New York: Routledge.
Korzenny, F. & Bauer, C. (1981). Testing the theory of electronic propinquity: Organizational teleconferencing. *Communication Research, 8*, 479-498.
Krackhardt, D. (1987). Cognitive social structures. *Social Networks, 9*, 109-134.
Krebs, V. (2001). Mapping networks of terrorist cells. *Connections, 24*, 43-52.
Lin, N. (2001). Building a network theory of social capital. In N. Lin, K. Cook, R. S. Burt (Eds.), *Social Capital: Theory and Research* (pp. 3-30). New York: Aldine de Gruyter.
Marsden, P. V., (1988). Homogeneity in confiding relations. *Social Networks, 10*, 57-76.
Marwell, G., & Oliver, P. (1993). *The critical mass in collective action: A micro-social theory.* Cambridge, MA: Cambridge University Press.
McGuire, W. J. (1966). Attitudes and opinions. *Annual Review of Psychology, 17*, 475-514.

McKelvey, B. (1997). Quasi-natural organization science. *Organization Science, 8*, 352-380.

Meyer, J. W., & Rowan, B. (1977). Institutionalized organizations: Formal structure as myth and ceremony. *American Journal of Sociology, 83*, 340-363.

Monge, P. R., & Contractor, N. S. (2001). Emergence of communication networks. In F. Jablin, & L. L. Putnam (Eds.), *The new handbook of organizational communication* (pp. 440-502). Thousand Oaks, CA: Sage.

Monge, P. R., & Contractor, N. S. (2003). *Theories of communication networks*. New York: Oxford University Press.

Monge, P. R., & Eisenberg, E. M. (1987). Emergent communication networks. In F. M. Jablin, L.L. Putnam, K.H. Roberts, and L.W. Porter, (Eds.), *Handbook of organizational communication* (pp. 304-342). Newbury Park, CA: Sage.

Monge, P. R., Rothman, L.W., Eisenberg, E.M., Miller, K.I., & Kirste, K.K. (1985). The dynamics of organizational proximity. *Management Science, 31*, 1129-1141.

Moreland, R. L. (1999). Transactive memory: Learning who knows what in work groups and organizations. In L. Thompson, D. Messick, & J. Levine (Eds.), *Sharing knowledge in organizations* (pp. 3-31). Mahwah, NJ: Lawrence Erlbaum.

Nelson, R. R., & Winter, S. G. (1982). *An evolutionary theory of economic change*. Cambridge, MA: Belknap Press of Harvard University Press.

Oliver, C. (1991). Network relations and loss of organizational autonomy. *Human Relations, 44*, 943-961.

Olson, M., Jr. (1965). *The logic of collective action*. Cambridge, MA: Harvard University Press.

Powell, W. W. (1990). Neither market nor hierarchy: Network forms of organization. In L.L. Cummings & B. Staw (Eds.), *Research in organizational behavior* (pp. 295-336). Greenwich, CT: JAI Press.

Ruef, M. (2000). The emergence of organizational forms: A community ecology approach. *American Journal of Sociology, 106*, 658-714.

Samuelson, P. (1954). The pure theory of public expenditure. *Review of Economics and Statistics, 36*, 387-389.

Staber, U. H. (1989). Age dependence and historical effects of the failure rates of worker cooperatives. *Economic and Industrial Democracy, 10*, 59-80.

Rosenkopf, L., & Tushman, M. L. (1994). The coevolution of technology and organization. In J. A. C. Baum & J. V. Singh (Eds.), *Evolutionary dynamics of organizations* (pp. 403-424). New York: Oxford University Press.

Rothenberg, R. (2001). From whole cloth: Making up the terrorist network. *Connections, 24*, 36-42.

van Meeter, K. M. (2001). Terrorists/Liberators: Researching and dealing with adversary social networks. *Connections, 24*, 66-78.

Wegner, D. M. (1987). Transactive memory: A contemporary analysis of the group mind. In B. Mullen & G. R. Goethals (Eds.), *Theories of group behavior* (pp. 185-208). New York: Springer-Verlag.

Wegner, D. M. (1995). A computer network model of human transactive memory. *Social Cognition, 13*, 319-339.

Weiser, B. (October 28, 2001). Captured terrorist manual suggests hijackers did a lot by the Book. *New York Times*.

Wellman, B. (2001). Computer networks as social networks. *Science*, 293, 2031-2034.

Williamson, O. E. (1975). *Markets and hierarchies: Analysis and antitrust implications, a study of the economics of internal organization*. New York: Free Press.

Williamson, O. E. (1985). *The economic institutions of capitalism: Firms, markets, relational contracting*. New York: Free Press.

Williamson, O. E. (1996). Economic organization: The case for candor. *Academy of Management Review, 21,* 48-57.

Zajac, E. J., & Olsen, C. P. (1993). From transaction cost to transactional value analysis: Implications for the study of interorganizational strategies. *Journal of Management Studies, 30*, 131-145.

IDENTIFYING INTERNATIONAL NETWORKS: LATENT SPACES AND IMPUTATION

Michael D. Ward
Political Science
University of Washington
Seattle, Washington
98195

Peter D. Hoff[1]
Statistics
University of Washington
Seattle, Washington
98195

Corey Lowell Lofdahl
Simulation & Information
Technology Operations
SAIC
Burlington, MA 01803

Introduction

Most analyses of world politics and studies of national security policies recognize the *interdependence* among the salient actors across the salient issues. Traditionally, international politics has been defined as the scope and extent of the relations among independent countries, thought to be the most important elements in world politics. This means that actors as well as their actions are strategically interdependent (Signorino 1999). Ignoring the interdependence among these phenomena would appear to be a serious oversight that plague attempts to understand, let alone predict, the course of national security policy and world politics more generally. With very few exceptions, *quantitative, systematic* studies of international relations and national security have assumed that the major actors and actions that comprise world politics consist of unconnected actions and actors. Game theoretic models are legion, but rarely deal with more than two actors at a time. Some beginning attempts to model the interdependency in international relations have appeared in the literature (Ward and Kirby 1987; Gleditsch and Ward 2001; Gleditsch and Ward 2001; Ward and Gleditsch 2002; Gleditsch 2002; Lofdahl 2002), but as yet network models have yet be widely applied in scholarly or policy work on international politics. This is somewhat surprising, since it is evident at first blush that international politics is about the interdependence that appears around the world.

Social network analysis is one technique that has been developed to map and measure the relationships and flows among agents. The nodes in the network are the individuals and groups and the links among them illustrate their interdependencies, both in terms of structure and in terms of the flows of information from one node to others. Since the development of the sociogram (Moreno 1934), sociologists among others have been interested in analyzing the linkages among individuals and groups. An interesting early example is found in the early work of Coleman, Katz and Menzel (1957). Most early theoretical advances were based on graph theory as developed and advanced by Frank Harary and his students and collaborators (Harary 1959; Harary 1969; Harary, Norman and Cartwright 1965). The so-called "Columbia school" worked throughout the 1960s and beyond to further advance the substantive findings in this arena of sociology (White 1963; White, Boorman and Breiger 1976). Broader dissemination of these ideas came much more recently with didactic writings (Knoke and Kuklinski 1982; Scott 1991) as well as early

[1]Peter Hoff's research is supported by Office of Naval Research grant N00014-02-1-1011.

applications that are by now canonical (Padgett and Ansell 1993; Hansell 1983). Indeed, social network analysis has become even more fashionable as outside of sociology in technical fields, and has spread to the wider press as an important method for understanding an increasingly perplexing and complicated social environment (Garreau 2001). However, it is somewhat ironic that to date there are no published applications of network analysis to the study of international relations.[2]

Hoff, Raftery and Handcock (2002 in press) developed probabilistic models of links among actors based on latent positions of actors in an unobserved "social space." We apply such a model a large database on international relations that is typical for the national security and international politics literatures, and discuss making predictive inference on links that are missing at random. In particular, we analyze the interactions among important social actors in Central Asia, using data taken from the Kansas Event Data Survey an automated textually oriented data generating process (Schrodt, Davis and Weddle 1994; Gerner, Schrodt, Francisco and Weddle 1994), specifically the CASIA database, available from the KEDS Web site at http://www.ku.edu/ keds/data.html. This database captures the daily ebb and flow of cooperative and conflictual events among important political and economic agents (typically called "actors" in the international relations literature) in the Central Asian region.

Our main purpose is to illustrate the value in using a latent space approach to understanding network structure in an applied, international relations context.

Event Data on International Relations among Central Asian Countries

Event data are nominal or ordinal codings of the recorded interactions of international actors.[3] Berelson (1952) introduced the concept of content analysis to the social sciences, but it was North, Holsti, Zaninovich and Zinnes (1963) that pioneered its use in studies of world politics . Event data have been widely used in quantitative international relations research and in policy research for four decades, following their introduction, event data in international relations were widely used (North 1967; McClelland and Hoggard 1969; Azar 1980). Until the development of machine coding the World Event Interaction Survey (WEIS) and Conflict on Peace Databank (COPDAB) were the two dominant schema. The contemporary, state-of-the-art is found in the Kansas Event Data System (KEDS) which uses automated coding of English-language news reports to generate political event data (Schrodt 2000; Schrodt, Davis and Weddle 1994).

According to Schrodt, there are three major steps involved in creating event data.

[2]Steven J. Brams (1966; 1968) and later Schofield (1972) tried to estimate linkages among countries, but this line of research was not pursued. Some work with elementary graph theory in the field of international relations has appeared more recently (Lai 1995), but like most of the early work, this applies to a small number of actors, typically three.

[3]This section is taken and adapted with permission from the KEDS Web site at http://www.ku.edu/ keds/intro.html.

1. First, a source of news is identified. Typically a news summary is used, ideally one that is already available in a machine readable format. The two current *de facto* publically available standards are the Reuters news service lead paragraphs or the Foreign Broadcast Information Service (FBIS)[4]

2. Second, a coding system is developed, or one of the extant coding systems such as the World Events Interaction Survey (aka WEIS), the Conflict and Peace Data Bank (COPDAB), or CAMEO (a KEDS coding schema (Gerner, Schrodt, Ömür Yilmaz and Abu-Jabr 2002)) is chosen. This coding system must specify what types of interactions constitute an "event." This requires the specification of which actors will be coded, for example, whether nonstate actors such as NATO and the United Nations or guerilla movements or salient individuals will be included. At the same time the coding rules must specify what basic issue areas will be included. The COPDAB data set includes a general "issue area" which describes whether an action is primarily military, economic, diplomatic or one of five other types of relationship. In contrast, WEIS also had a few specific "issue arenas" such as the Vietnam War, Arab- Israeli conflict, and SALT negotiations.

3. The coding rules themselves may be developed in terms of a manual that is given to human coders or more frequently is encapsulated in a computer program such as KEDS, which uses extensive dictionaries to identify actors and events and associate these with specific numerical codes. These dictionaries are developed theoretically by specification and tuned practically by coding a large number of test sentences from the actual data and adding the appropriate vocabulary when the machines makes an observed error.

Table 1 shows a sample of the lead sentences of reports on the Reuters newswire that preceded Iraq's invasion of Kuwait in August 1990. Generally each lead corresponds to a single event, though some sentences generate multiple events. For example, the lead sentence for July 23, 1990 is "Iraqi newspapers denounced Kuwait's foreign minister as a U.S. agent Monday." This corresponds to WEIS category 122, defined as "Denounce; denigrate; abuse". In this event, Iraq is the source (actor) of the action and Kuwait is the target. Together, these generate the event record that corresponds to an event in which Iraq denounces Kuwait.[5]

The WEIS codes and associated Goldstein (1992) weights are given in 2 for some of the WEIS categories. Goldstein scores are psychometrically determined weights, where a positive weight means that the event has positive affect; conversely, a negative Goldstein score indicates negative affect.

Table 3 shows the Reuters stories converted to WEIS events. Event data analysis relies on a large number of events to produce meaningful patterns of interaction. The information

[4]FBIS is available at `http://199.221.15.211/`, while Reuters can be contacted via `www.reuters.com`.

[5]This gives "900723 IRQ KUW 122" where "900723" is the date of the event, IRQ is a standard code for Iraq, KUW is the code for Kuwait, and 122 is the WEIS category.

Table 1: *Reuters Chronology of 1990 Iraq-Kuwait Crisis, adapted from Schrodt (http://www.ku.edu/ keds/intro.html), with permission. The Iraqi denunciation of Kuwati on July 23, 1990 is a typical conflict event.*

Date	Headline	Lead Sentence
July 17, 1990	RESURGENT IRAQ SENDS SHOCK WAVES THROUGH GULF ARAB STATES	Iraq President Saddam Hussein launched an attack on Kuwait and the United Arab Emirates (UAE) Tuesday, charging they had conspired with the United States to depress world oil prices through overproduction.
July 23, 1990	IRAQ STEPS UP GULF CRISIS WITH ATTACK ON KUWAITI MINISTER	Iraqi newspapers denounced Kuwait's foreign minister as a U.S. agent Monday, pouring oil on the flames of a Persian Gulf crisis Arab leaders are struggling to stifle with a flurry of diplomacy. (I.e., Iraq Denounces Kuwait.)
July 24, 1990	IRAQ WANTS GULF ARAB AID DONORS TO WRITE OFF WAR CREDITS	Debt-burdened Iraq's conflict with Kuwait is partly aimed at persuading Gulf Arab creditors to write off billions of dollars lent during the war with Iran, Gulf-based bankers and diplomats said.
July 24, 1990	IRAQ, TROOPS MASSED IN GULF, DEMANDS $25 OPEC OIL PRICE	Iraq's oil minister hit the OPEC cartel Tuesday with a demand that it must choke supplies until petroleum prices soar to $25 a barrel.
July 25, 1990	IRAQ TELLS EGYPT IT WILL NOT ATTACK KUWAIT	Iraq has given Egypt assurances that it would not attack Kuwait in their current dispute over oil and territory, Arab diplomats said Wednesday.
July 27, 1990	IRAQ WARNS IT WON'T BACK DOWN IN TALKS WITH KUWAIT	Iraq made clear Friday it would take an uncompromising stand at conciliation talks with Kuwait, saying its Persian Gulf neighbor must respond to Baghdad's "legitimate rights" and repair the economic damage it caused.
July 31, 1990	IRAQ INCREASES TROOP LEVELS ON KUWAIT BORDER	Iraq has concentrated nearly 100,000 troops close to the Kuwaiti border, more than triple the number reported a week ago, the Washington Post said in its Tuesday editions.
August 1, 1990	CRISIS TALKS IN JEDDAH BETWEEN IRAQ AND KUWAIT COLLAPSE	Talks on defusing an explosive crisis in the Gulf collapsed Wednesday when Kuwait refused to give in to Iraqi demands for money and territory, a Kuwaiti official said.
August 2, 1990	IRAQ INVADES KUWAIT, OIL PRICES SOAR AS WAR HITS PERSIAN GULF	Iraq invaded Kuwait, ousted its leaders and set up a pro-Baghdad government Thursday in a lightning pre-dawn strike that sent oil prices soaring and world leaders scrambling to douse the flames of war in the strategic Persian Gulf.

Table 2: *Selected WEIS action categories and Goldstein Scores.*

Yield (1.0)	Surrender (0.6)	Retreat (0.6)
Retract (2.0)	Accommodate, Cease Fire (3.0)	Cede Power (5.0)
Comment (0.0)	Decline Comment (-0.1)	Pessimist Comment (-0.4)
Neutral Comment (-0.2)	Optimist Comment (0.4)	Explain Position (0.0)
Consult (1.0)	Meet (1.0)	Visit (1.9)
Receive (2.8)	Vote, Elect (1.0)	Approve (3.5)
Praise (3.4)	Endorse (3.6)	Rally (3.8)
⋮	⋮	⋮
Kidnap, Jail (-2.5)	Spy (-5.0)	Force (-9.0)
Non-Injury Destruction (-8.3)	Non-Military Destruction (-8.7)	Military Engagement (-10.0)
Riot, Violent Clash (-7.0)	Assassinate Torture Execute (-9.0)	Coup Attempted (-8.0)

provided by any single event is very limited; single events are also affected by erroneous reports and coding errors. However, important events trigger other interactions throughout the system. For example while Iraq's invasion of Kuwait by itself generates only a single event with WEIS code 223–military force–the invasion triggers an avalanche of additional activity throughout the international system as states and international organizations denounce, approve or comment, so the crisis is very prominent in the event record. This kind of implicit triggering is analyzed and described in Schrodt and Mintz (1988) and Ward and House (1988).

Table 3: *Coding of the 1990 Iraq-Kuwait Crisis, using WEIS coding scheme. These events appear in textual format in Table 1, above.*

Date	Actor	Target	WEIS Action Code	Type of Action
900717	IRQ	KUW	121	CHARGE
900717	IRQ	UAE	121	CHARGE
900723	IRQ	KUW	122	DENOUNCE
900724	IRQ	ARB	150	DEMAND
900724	IRQ	OPC	150	DEMAND
900725	IRQ	EGY	054	ASSURE
900727	IRQ	KUW	160	WARN
900731	IRQ	KUW	182	MOBILIZATION
900801	KUW	IRQ	112	REFUSE
900802	IRQ	KUW	223	MILITARY FORCE

Data generated in this fashion are exactly the same kind of data that are used to represent social networks. Yet, to date, despite the widespread use of such data in international relations, there are no published studies which analyze these kind of data from a social network perspective. We turn to the application of latent space analysis of social networks using these data in the following sections.

Latent Space Models of Network Structures

Let $y_{i,j}$ denote the value of a relationship between agent i and agent j; these relationships may be measured discretely or continuously. The matrix Y is variously called a *transaction* matrix, a *sociomatrix*, or a *spatial weights* matrix. Let X comprise observed characteristics (co-variates) that can be specific to the agents i or j, or specific to their interaction i, j.[6]

The observed network is assumed to be a function of all relevant co-variates, observed or not observed. The presence of important non-observed co-variates often leads to dependencies in the network Y. The models of (Hoff, Raftery and Handcock 2002 in press) assume the dependencies in the data can be represented via a latent, unrealized position or characteristic z_i for each node i, and that the network responses are conditionally independent given the set of latent positions. Given this assumption, we can express the probability of the given network conditional on the latent positions of the agents and their characteristics as

$$P(Y|Z, X, \theta) \quad = \quad \prod_{i \neq j} P(y_{i,j}|z_i, z_j, x_{i,j}, \theta, \sigma^2). \tag{1}$$

Unconditional on the z_i's, the data are dependent.

If the data are binary, Equation (1) can be parameterized as a logistic regression model in which the probability of linkage depends on some projected closeness between the agents (z_i and z_j) and covariates such that:

$$\eta_{i,j} \quad = \quad \log \text{odds}(y_{i,j} = 1|z_i, z_j, x_{i,j}, \alpha, \beta, \sigma^2) = \alpha + \beta' x_{i,j} + z_i' z_j, \tag{2}$$

where z_i and z_j represent the projected positions of actors i and j in the latent space. Suppose that each actor i has an associated vector z_i of characteristics. Each vector can be thought of as comprising a position on a k-dimensional sphere of unit radius (the direction of the z_i), as well as an "activity level" (the length of z_i). In the model above, agents i and j are more likely to have linkages if they have simliar locations on the sphere, and they are "active," that is, if $z_i' z_j$ is large and positive.

This leads to a (log) probability of the sociomatrix specified as:

$$\log P(Y|\eta) \quad = \quad \sum_{i \neq j} (y_{i,j}(\alpha + \beta' x_{i,j} + z_i' z_j) - log(1 + e^{(\alpha+\beta' x_{i,j}+z_i' z_j)})). \tag{3}$$

[6]Most of the notation (but not necessarily the terminology) herein follows (Hoff, Raftery and Handcock 2002 in press).

Maximum likelihood and Bayesian estimates for the parameters in this model can be obtained in a straightforward way. First, the maximum likelihood estimates of the parameters are formed by direct maximization of Equation (3). Then, with this estimate as a starting value and with diffuse prior distributions over the model parameters, a Markov chain is constructed to generate samples of the parameters from the posterior distribution. Such a sample is generated by drawing proposal values from a symmetric proposal distribution, and accepting the proposal with an appropriate probability. For example, in sampling a new Z value at the kth stage of the chain, we sample a proposal value $\breve{Z}$ from a proposal distribution $J(Z|Z_k)$, where Z_k is the most recently sampled value. The proposal is accepted as the new value Z_{k+1} with probability $\frac{p(Y|\breve{Z},\alpha_k,\beta_k,\sigma_k^2,X)}{p(Y|Z,\alpha_k,\beta_k,\sigma_k^2,X)}\frac{\pi(\breve{Z})}{\pi(Z_k)}$, where $\pi(Z)$ is the prior distribution for Z. If the proposal is not accepted, then Z_{k+1} is set equal to Z_k. This approach has been used by Hoff, Raftery and Handcock (2002 in press) to estimate several of the classic social network analysis data sets.[7] The basic setup is quite general and can be even more widely employed.

Estimation of Network Links in CASIA database

We use this framework to estimate the network structure of the political interactions of the primary actors in Central Asian politics over the period from 1989 through 1999. This region has a great deal of conflict and spotty coverage in English language media, despite its contemporary salience. Based on the CASIA database, there are 113 such actors which have been deemed by substantive experts to be significant. Of these, there are 51 country level actors that have interactions with one another during this eleven year period. We sum the paired interactions among these 51 countries across the eleven year period. A link is deemed to occur for any interaction between two countries during this period. Thus, our data is a 51×51 sociomatrix in which an entry is 1 if and only if there is an interaction between i and j in the CASIA database between 1989 and 1999; otherwise it is 0. We use a single covariate for this analysis: $x_{i,j}$ is the distance in thousands of kilometers between the capital city of each of the countries. Distance is widely employed as an indicator of interaction in international relations: countries closer together have higher probabilities of having linkages.

We have glossed over the important content of the interactions. Some will have been cooperative and others highly conflictual. There are many debates in the national security literature about reciprocity. It turns out that countries that have high levels of cooperative interactions also *tend* to have high levels of conflictual interactions. So this seems a reasonable approximation, though it is certainly possible to disaggregate these data by event type, issues, and time.

Treating all years in one aggregation is not optimal perhaps, but it does reduce considerably the sparseness of the data. We also recognize that some pairs of countries will have

[7]These are the *drosophila melanogaster* of social network analysis, the so-called Monk data (Sampson 1968), as well as data on Florentine marriage patterns among Medici families (Padgett and Ansell 1993), and data on classroom friendship networks (Hansell 1983).

many more interactions. Examination of the histograms of the actual data suggested to us that most of the information about the linkages was captured in the dichotomy; most of the responses were zero and the second most likely value was 1.

Equation 3 was estimated using direct optimization of the maximum likelihood to generate starting values for the MCMC. One million iterations of the chain were run to obtain estimates of the parameters α and β as well as the latent positions Z and their underlying variance σ^2. The negative coefficient for the distance covariate indicates a lower probability of interaction at greater distances, consistent with many published results from different contexts. These estimates are presented in Table 4.

Table 4: *Maximum Likelihood and MCMC estimates of parameters for the sociogram of the 51 countries involved in Central Asian politics over the period from 1989-1999. Quantile based confidence intervals are provided for the MCMC estimates.*

			95% Confidence Interval	
Parameter	MLE	MCMC	2.5%	97.5%
α	-4.32	-4.20	-4.69	-3.06
β	-0.26	-0.25	-0.40	-0.21
σ^2		5.82	4.48	10.53

Figure 1 illustrates the trajectories of the log likelihood and the parameters $\hat{\alpha}$, $\hat{\beta}$, and $\hat{\sigma}^2$ over the 10^6 scans of the Markov chain. These plots suggest that the chain mixes reasonably well for all the estimated parameters. The density of these estimated distributions are

Figure 1: *MCMC Diagnostic plots of parameter estimation via* 10^6 *scans of Markov Chain.*

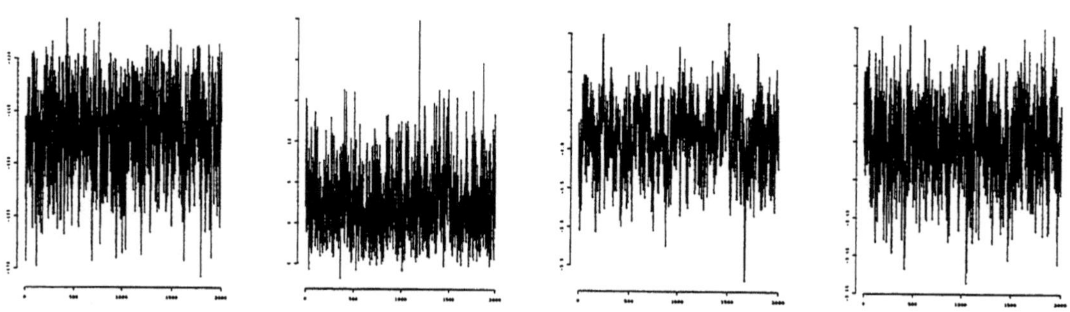

(a) MCMC $\mathcal{L}$ (b) $\hat{\sigma^2}$ (c) $\hat{\alpha}$ (d) $\hat{\beta}$

presented in Figure 2. These represent the marginal posterior densities, with vertical lines representing the maximum likelihood estimate. Each of these densities presents a fairly narrow bandwidth.

Figure 2: *Marginal Posterior Densities of the Estimated Parameters. Vertical lines present the MLE.*

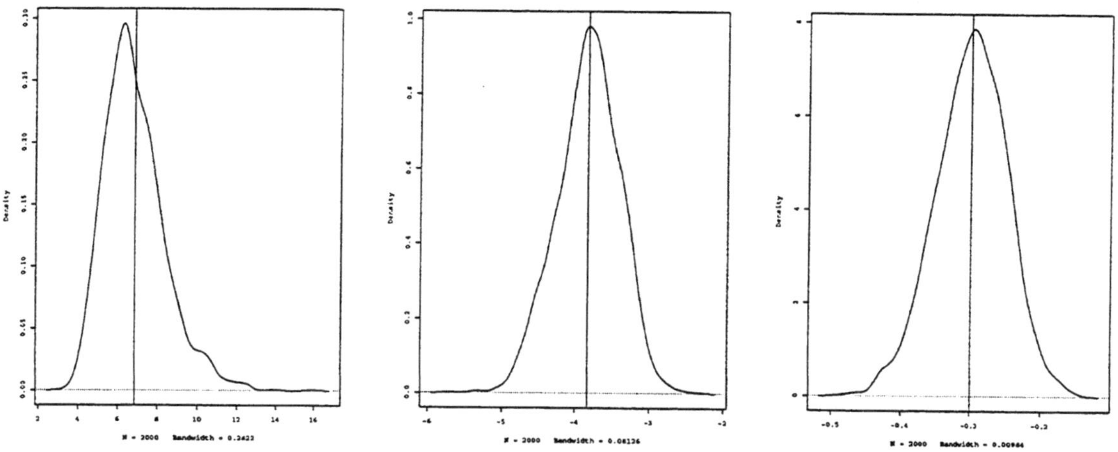

(a) $\hat{\sigma}$ (b) $\hat{\alpha}$ (c) $\hat{\beta}$

As interesting as these estimates and diagnostics are, the most interesting output of a latent space analysis is the position of the actors in the latent space. Figure 3 illustrates these positions for the 51 countries analyzed. Figure 4 displays the relative, latent positions of countries projected onto a circle. Countries that are close together on this circle have higher probability of sharing a link. Since this set of countries shares many ties, many countries are close to one another in latent space.

Imputation of Missing Network Linkages in CASIA

Gauging whether a network is completely sampled is perhaps the holy grail of network analysis. As yet there is no simple solution to this perplexing problem. We offer no complete solution here. However, practically, it may be useful to use imputation methods along with the latent space estimates to gauge whether or not a link that does not turn up actually may be missing at random.

We conduct an experiment using the CASIA database through the following procedure:

1. Randomly assign NA to 100 $y_{i,j}$'s , keeping track of the 100 actual values of these "missing" data;

2. Fit the model using the non missing data;

3. For each missing $y_{i,j}$, use the parameter estimates to the calculate predicted probability $\hat{p}_{i,j}$ that each missing value $y_{i,j}$ equals one, i.e. is a hidden links;

4. Compute the number of correct and incorrect predictions, using as a first cut a 0.5 threshold;

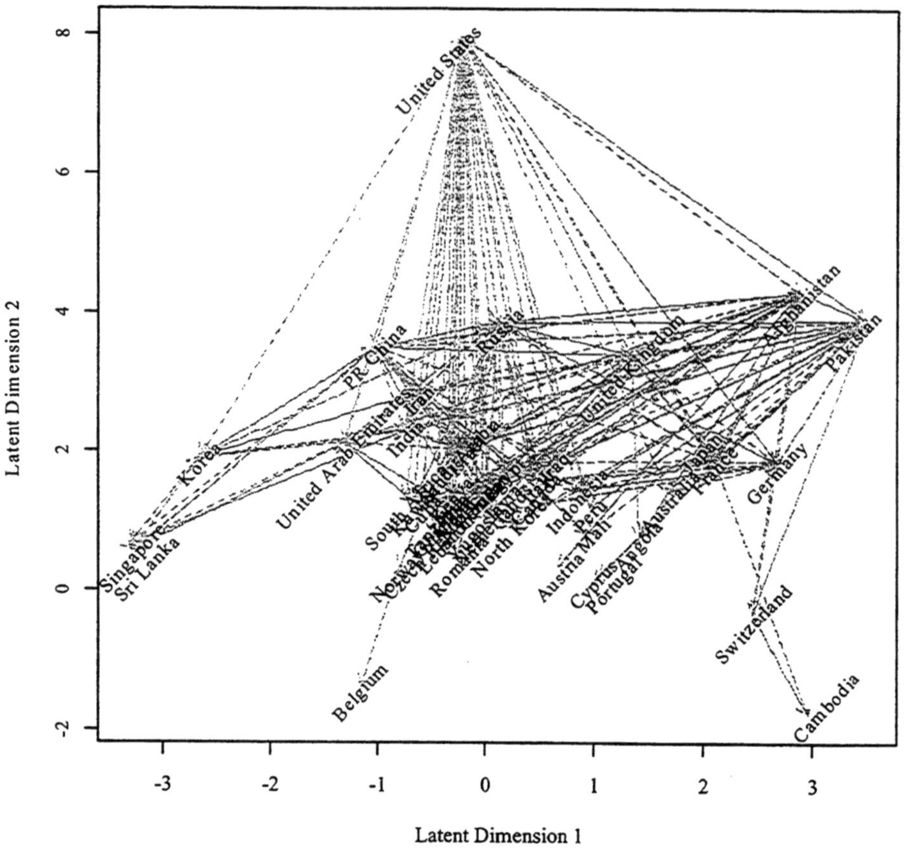

Figure 3: *The Latent Positions of 51 Countries as a function of their interactions in Central Asia. The United States has links to many of the other countries, as do Pakistan, Afghanistan, China, Russia, and India.*

5. Compute the Brier score (Brier 1950): $(n(n-1))^{-1}\sum_{i\neq j}(\hat{p_{i,j}} - y_{i,j})^2$.

6. Repeat the above steps 200 times; and finally,

7. Compare these results to a standard, logistic framework with the same covariates.

The results of this experiment are quite supportive of using latent space to predict non-sampled or hidden network linkages. For the 200 runs, the average Brier score was 0.087, which is quite low. The proportion of correctly predicted observations was 0.88. The original sociomatrix has about four non-links for every link. This means that a modal guess of 0 would result in correctly predicting about 0.80 of the observations. Thus, the latent space approach improves significantly upon that result, garnering an *additional* 8 of the remaining 20 percent. Specifically, conditional on the true value being no linkage, the predicted value is 0 with probability of 0.95. Given that the true value is 1 (i.e., linkage), the predicted value is 1 with probability of 0.67.

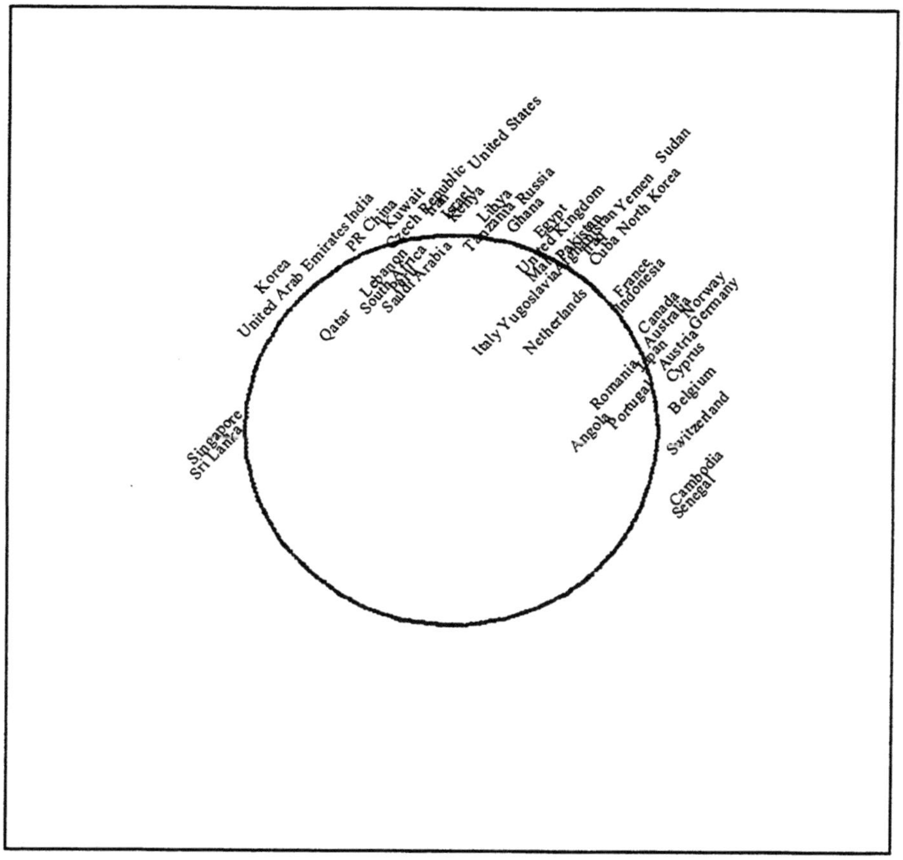

Figure 4: *The latent positions of countries is projected on a unit circle. Because many of the positions are very close to one another, the positions have been loosely jittered so that the overlap of country labels is reduced.*

In comparison, a logistic model using the same geographic covariate, the average Brier score is almost twice as high (0.17); higher Brier scores indicate poorer predictive performance. A logistic model, as is typical of this approach, will correctly predict all the zeros and none of the links, because it, like the modal guess, always predicts 0.

The upshot of this experiment is the important implication that if we sample network ties at random, then estimate the latent positions, this approach can be used to predict the $y_{i,j}$ that were not sampled.

Although quantitative models in international relations that make actual predictions are themselves rare (Schrodt 2000; King and Zeng 2001; Ward and Gleditsch 2002) for a variety of reasons (Schrodt 2002), these results are strong in comparison. More broadly this approach identifies an effective way to sample networks.

Conclusion

The latent space approach to social network analysis seems promising. It performs quite well in identifying observed, complete networks in the national security realm. It does so in a way that embraces the interdependence of the network data, rather than assuming that it is generated randomly. Moreover, the approach facilitates the presentation of network positions in an intuitively satisfying way, mapped into a small number of dimensions. These locations incorporate measures of uncertainty. Perhaps most importantly this approach is quite general, since it encapsulates a broader class of models. Specifically, a variety of discrete and continuous specifications can easily be adapted, depending upon the data generating process. Finally, our experiments on using the latent space positions to impute missing at random network links proved to be remarkably productive, especially given the absence of any substantive covariates. This leads to the exciting result that it may be possible to use this approach to sample network ties at random, then estimate the latent positions in order to predict network ties that were not initially sampled.

References

Azar, Edward. 1980. "The Conflict and Peace Data Bank (COPDAB) Project." *Journal of Conflict Resolution* 24:143–152.

Berelson, Bernard. 1952. *Content Analysis in Communication Research.* Glencoe, IL: Free Press.

Brams, Steven J. 1966. "Transaction Flows in the International System." *American Political Science Review* 60:880–898.

Brams, Steven J. 1968. "DECOMP: A Computer Program for the Condensation of a Directed Graph and the Hierarchical Ordering of Its Strong Components." *Behavioral Science* 13:344–345.

Brier, G.W. 1950. "Verification of forecasts expressed in terms of probabilities." *Bulletin American Meteorological Society* 78:1–3.

Coleman, James S., Elihu Katz and Herbert Menzel. 1957. "The Diffusion of an innovation among physicians." *Sociometry* 20:253–70.

Garreau, Joel. 2001. "Disconnect the Dots: Maybe We Can't Cut Off Terror's Head, but We Can Take Out Its Nodes." *Washington Post* September 17:C–01.

Gerner, Deborah J., Philip A. Schrodt, Ömür Yilmaz and Rajaa Abu-Jabr. 2002. Conflict and Mediation Event Observations (CAMEO): A New Event Data Framework for a Post Cold War World. Annual Meetings of the American Political Science Association Boston, MA: .

Gerner, Deborah J., Philip A. Schrodt, Ronald Francisco and Judith L. Weddle. 1994. "The Analysis of Political Events using Machine Coded Data." *International Studies Quarterly* 38:91–119.

Gleditsch, Kristian S. and Michael D. Ward. 2001. "Measuring Space: A Minimum Distance Database and Applications to International Studies." *Journal of Peace Research* 38(6):749–768.

Gleditsch, Kristian Skrede. 2002. *All International Politics is Local: The Diffusion of Conflict, Integration, and Democratization.* Ann Arbor, MI: University of Michigan Press.

Goldstein, Joshua. 1992. "A Conflict-Cooperation Scale for WEIS International Events Data." *Journal of Conflict Resolution* 36(2):369–385.

Hansell, Stephen. 1983. "Cooperative Groups, Weak Ties, and the Integration of Peer Friendships." *Social Psychology Quarterly* 47(4):316–328.

Harary, Frank. 1959. "Graph theoretic methods in the management sciences." *Management Science* 5:387–403.

Harary, Frank. 1969. *Graph Theory.* Reading, MA: Addison-Wesley.

Harary, Frank, Robert Norman and Dorwin Cartwright. 1965. *Structural Models.* New York: Wiley.

Hoff, Peter D., Adrian E. Raftery and Mark S. Handcock. 2002 in press. "Latent Space Approaches to Social Network Analysis." *Journal of the American Statistical Association* tba(tba):tba.

King, Gary and Langche Zeng. 2001. "Improving Forecasts of State Failure." *World Politics* 53(4):623–658.

Knoke, David and James H. Kuklinski. 1982. *Network Analysis.* Beverly Hills, CA: Sage.

Lai, David. 1995. "A Structural Approach to Alignment: A Case Study of the China-Soviet-U.S. Strategic Triangle, 1971-1988." *International Interactions* 20(4):349–374.

Lofdahl, Corey L. 2002. *Environmental Impacts of Globalization and Trade: A Systems Study.* Cambridge, MA: The MIT Press.

McClelland, Charles A. and Gary Hoggard. 1969. Conflict patterns in the interactions among nations. In *International Politics and Foreign Policy*, ed. James N. Rosenau. New York: The Free Press pp. 711–724.

Moreno, Jakob L. 1934. *Who Shall Survive?* Washington, D.C.: Nervous and Mental Disease Publishing Company.

North, Robert C. 1967. "Perception and Action in the 1914 Crisis." *Journal of International Affairs* 21:103–122.

North, Robert C., Ole R. Holsti, M. George Zaninovich and Dina A. Zinnes. 1963. *Content Analysis: A Handbook with Applications for the Study of International Crisis.* Chicago: Northwestern University Press.

Padgett, John F. and Christopher K. Ansell. 1993. "Robust Action and the Rise of the Medici, 1400-1434." *American Journal of Sociology* 98:1259–1319.

Sampson, S.F. 1968. A Novitiate in a Period of Change: An Experimental and Case Study of Relationships, unpublished Ph. D. Dissertation, Department of Sociology, Cornell University, Itaca, NY.

Schofield, Norman J. 1972. "A Topological Model of International Relations." *Peace Research Society, Papers* 18:93–112.

Schrodt, Philip A. 2000. "Forecasting conflict in the Balkans using Hidden Markov Models." Presented at the Annual Meetings of the American Political Science Association, Washington, D.C.

Schrodt, Philip A. 2002. Forecasts and Contingencies: From Methodology to Policy. Annual Meetings of the American Political Science Association Boston, MA: .

Schrodt, Philip A. and Alex Mintz. 1988. "A Conditional Probability Analysis of Regional Interactions in the Middle East." *American Journal of Political Science* 32(1):217–230.

Schrodt, Philip A., Shannon G. Davis and Judith L. Weddle. 1994. "Political Science: KEDS-A Program for the Machine Coding of Event Data." *Social Science Computer Review* 12(3):561–588.

Scott, John. 1991. *Social Network Analysis: a Handbook.* Newbury Park, CA: Sage.

Signorino, Curtis. 1999. "Strategic Interaction and the Statistical Analysis of International Conflict." *American Political Science Review* 92(2):279–298.

Ward, Michael D. and Andrew M. Kirby. 1987. "Re-examining Spatial Models of International Conflict." *Annals of the American Association of Geographers* 77:86–105.

Ward, Michael D. and Kristian Skrede Gleditsch. 2002. "Location, Location, Location: An MCMC Approach to Modeling the Spatial Context of War and Peace." *Political Analysis* 10(3):244–260.

Ward, Michael D. and Lewis L. House. 1988. "A Theory of Behavioral Power of Nations." 32(1):3–36.

White, Harrison. 1963. *An Anatomy of Kinship: Mathematical Models for the Structure of Cumulated Roles.* Englewoods Cliffs, NJ: Prentice Hall.

White, Harrison, Scott Boorman and Ronald Breiger. 1976. "Social Structure From Multiple Networks; Blockmodels of Roles and Positions." *American Journal of Sociology* 81:730–799.

SUMMARY

Themes, Issues, and Applications

Linking Capabilities to Needs

Kathleen M. Carley
Institute for Software Research International
Carnegie Mellon University

Abstract

Social network analysis is an established field with a wealth of theory, method, and tools for handling network or relational data. Recent advances have expanded this repertoire to include larger scale more dynamic networks under conditions of uncertainty. This moves the field closer to the needs of the defense department and intelligence agencies. However, the needs are not completely met. This paper briefly outlines where the field is, what it has to offer, and where the needs are not being met.

Acknowledgement

The research reported herein was supported by the National Science Foundation NSF IRI9633 662, the NSF IGERT in CASOS, the Office of Naval Research (ONR) Grant No. N00014-97-1-0037 and Grant No. 9620.1.1140071, Additional support was provided by the NSF IGERT 9972762 for research and training in CASOS and by the center for Computational Analysis of Social and Organizational Systems at Carnegie Mellon University (http://www.casos.ece.cmu.edu). The views and conclusions contained in this document are those of the authors and should not be interpreted as representing the official policies, either expressed or implied, of the Office of Naval Research, the National Science Foundation or the U.S. government.

Citation

Kathleen M. Carley, forthcoming, "Linking Abilities to Needs" in the Summary of the NRC workshop on Social Network Modeling and Analysis, Ron Breiger and Kathleen M. Carley (Eds.), National Research Council.

Linking Capabilities to Needs

The increase in concerns with terrorism world wide have led the researchers, policy makers, the defense community and the intelligence community to ask – what techniques, tools, methods, findings can help defeat terrorism. Social network analysis is one area that shows promise. The recent press on "linking the dots" and the "new" science of networks has brought this area into the limelight. In attempt to determine whether is a match between capabilities and needs an NRC workshop on Social Network Modeling and Analysis was run.

The purpose of this paper is to juxtapose the work discussed and not discussed at this meeting with the needs of the defense and intelligence community to the extent that is possible at the unclassified level. This will be done first by describing what the social networks area, broadly defined, has to offer particularly with respect to data collection, analysis, special training, intelligence and policy needs, and effects based operations. This is followed by a short description of what was missed. Finally, a few concluding comments are provided on what can be done to reduce the mismatch between capabilities and needs.

What Social Networks Has to Offer

Most work in social network analysis (SNA) has focused on small, bounded networks, with 2-3 types of links (such as friendship and advice) among one type of node (such as people), at one point in time, with close to perfect information. The research presented here is striving to overcome these limitations. As such it is increasingly useful to members of the defense and intelligence community. For in those communities, data is rarely complete, often there are massive quantities of data, relevant relational information is both multi-modal and multi-link, and the networks range in size from smaller command and control teams, to international terrorist networks. Recent work is helping to reduce this gap between capabilities and needs. In particular there are four areas where network analysis, such as that described in this workshop, is particularly relevant. These are data collection, analysis, special training, intelligence and policy needs, and effects based operations. Cross cutting these areas the work on networks has been done on the micro, meso and macro levels. At each level, issues of diffusion and so information warfare arise. At each level, issues of power, influence, control, and the role of technology arise. And, at each level issues of governance arise. The upshot is that network tools, techniques and theories can be used at each of these levels and across these levels to inform policy makers.

Data Collection

Much of the recent work provides some guidance for data collection. One of the key concerns with SNA is that it is data greedy and requires intensive effort. The image is of questionnaires to small groups asking each person who interacts with whom generating full information. However, the work presented herein suggests that full information is not needed, that the data can be collected in a more automated fashion, that it is possible to estimate the whole network from parts of it, and that it is key to collect new types of relational data.

We see here new techniques for collecting data. For example, by focusing on the paths among the key actors, data can be collected on the core of the network rapidly (Klovdahl, Borgatti). We can think of this as "socially informed" search. Another difference here is the emphasis on new types of data such as the meta-matrix (Carley), role data (Johnson), internet ties (Faloutsos), and multiple types of relations such as finance plus communication (Jensen, Morris, Contractor). A third difference is the growing emphasis on collecting indicators of the shape and nature of networks rather than on collecting the exact networks. Examples here are the work on spatial and proximity effects (Butts) and temporal issues (Morris). Another implication of the work on large scale and functional networks is that general demographic data and the nature of the tasks being done place constraints on the resulting networks limiting the forms that they can take on (Jensen, Carley). These factors pave the way for expanding the area to collect the type of data useful in defense and intelligence contexts.

Nevertheless, there is much to be done. It is still the case that most data collection techniques are too personnel intensive. What is needed are additional tools for doing rapid assessment and for collecting vast quantities of data. In terms of rapid assessment the issue is what high level indicators can be quickly gathered that indicate the overall shape of the network and the key actors within it. Tools for estimating the size, shape and other key dimensions of networks from leading indicators are needed. The key scientific question is from the space of possible networks, what key indicators suggest which portion of this space the network of interest is in. A related question is what constraints due institutions, social conventions, cognitive limitations and capabilities, geography, etc. place on the shape and structure of the social networks.

As to more automated data collection several things are needed. New non-invasive tools for data capture need to be developed and deployed so that they can be easily used in organizational and social analysis. These range from automatic data capturing tools, to automated text analysis (such as KEDDS, automap, etc.), to tools for turning standard data such as web pages, etc. into network data. Further, an inventory needs to be conducted of standard currently collected data to determine which data can be used and converted into network data. Examples of such data are web pages, HR reports, personnel records, phone logs. Then shareable tools need to be developed so that researchers can take the extant data and generate a network from it. For example, since KEDDS extracts events, techniques for inferring interactions and so networks from these events are needed (Ward, Hoff and Lofdahl).

In many cases, there is a need to reason about networks and how they will change where there is little actual data. To address this problem, two possible approaches were described. On the one hand, computational techniques can be used to enumerate and analyze classes of networks with specific properties (Bienenstock and Bonacich, Wasserman). Here, statistical models can be used to characterize distributions (Hockman). Then computational techniques can be used to generate sample networks with these characteristics.

On the other hand, computational techniques can be used to grow networks from limited data and basic principles about the way networks evolve. A variety of principles for how networks evolve were discussed including changes in interaction due to changes what is known or owned, relative similarity (homophilly), relative expertise, co-work on same tasks, contributions to the public good, who else is around, changes in status or role (Carley, Contractor and Monge, Freeman, Borgatti, Friedkin). Given these principles, computational techniques can be used to both generate networks consistent with these principles and then evolve them over time. Using such techniques it then possible to address questions such as how and to whom information will diffuse (Carley), how contagious diseases will spread (Morris), how cultures will evolve (Macy), how to destroy and preserve networks (Carley, Stanley and Havlin). From a data collection standpoint, such tools can be used in many ways, including to provide guidance on new data collection efforts, to generate hypothetical data that can be used for planning when actual data is not available (as in the case of biological and chemical attacks), and to supplement real data by filling gaps or suggesting trends.

Analysis

Advances in analysis have been moving on a number of dimensions. Advances in statistical approaches for analyzing networks are expanding our ability to formally handle relational data and to utilize more realistic network distributions (Hoff, Hockman, Snijders, Wasserman). Advances in visualization techniques are enabling greater understanding of the shape of networks and the impact of various change strategies (Borgatti, Richards). Meanwhile work on large-scale networks suggests that there is little information content or variability in existing measures, or that existing tools are computationally slow when faced with large networks. Thus, leading to a quest for alternative measures, metrics that scale well, increased concern with optimized or parallelizable code, fast algorithms, and estimation techniques (Stanley, Faloutsos). Work on scale free networks is one possible avenue (Faloutsos) although questions abound on the relevance of such work to traditional social networks such as friendship. That is, are such networks good enough approximations to be useful?

All this being said there are quite a few questions left unanswered that are critical in the current context. For example, for each of the existing measures, what is its robustness, resistance and sensitivity (Bienenstock and Bonacich, Borgatti, Butts, Carley, Pattison, Snijders, Wasserman). How do different measures behave for networks drawn from different distributions? How does the distribution of nodal characteristics relate to the overall structure (Snijders)? How do the various measures correlate, and how does this change as a function of the error in information, the size and density of the network. It would benefit the area to identify a few distinct core measures that are consistent and robust indicators of the shape of the underlying network.

With the movement to new types of data there is a corresponding movement to apply old metrics in new contexts to see how they behave and to develop new metrics specifically tuned to the underlying type of data. Measures that link multiple networks together such as cognitive load (Carley) or that indicate specific temporal patterns of ties such as sequences of financial transactions (Jensen) are particularly promising. A great deal of fundamental work needs to be done in the area of metrics, algorithms and the assessment of metrics.

In many cases, computational approaches, particularly simulation is playing a key role in analysis. Such work is enabling a greater understanding of the way in which networks evolve under standard and attack conditions (Macy, Carley), the way in which influence, ideas, and diseases propagates (Friedkin, Morris). In this sense simulations can be used to put "probabilities" on possible futures – suggesting not only that the network might change but how and the likelihood of such change. Further, simulations can be used to suggest areas where data might be missing. An example of this would be to turn KeyPlayer around (Borgatti) and ask where might there be a key player that we are not observing. Simulations can also be used to suggest when is it worth gathering more information as in the DyNet model (Carley). A key avenue that will increase the value of these uses of simulation would be to place the simulation in a decision context and ask what are the cost and benefits of such additional data collection and the chance of being wrong.

Special Training, Intelligence and Policy Needs

A key need in the defense and intelligence communities is for tools to help with training, intelligence, and policy analysis. In particular tools that enable the analyst to utilize the bits and pieces of disparate information in a systematic, and if possible, quantitative fashion that moves the analysis beyond informed guess work. Here, to the extent that network tools are combined with computational modeling techniques, simulation tools can be created for doing "what if" scenario analysis and suggesting possibilities. Such tools are "thinking tools" for reasoning about events. The use of such tools would not be to predict specific events but to reduce the likelihood of being "surprised." Such tools may be particularly useful in reasoning about and planning operations related to the destabilization of networks, the impact of changes in trade or cooperative agreements on inter-national, inter-state, and inter-agency behavior, understanding inter-player coordination in situations other than war, knowledge management within and among agencies, and so on. Work on governance (Lazer), influence (Friedkin), and network stability (Carley, Stanley, Borgatti, Bienenstock and Bonacich) are key in this context.

Combining network techniques with computational techniques can thus promote Effects Based Planning (EBP). Effects based planning is, according to the Joint Forces Command Glossary "an operational planning process to conduct effects based operations within rapid decisive operations. ... EBP closely mirrors the current joint planning process, yet focuses upon the linkage of actions to effects to objectives. ... It employs virtual, near-simultaneous planning at all echelons of command."

Using dynamic network models in effects based planning will require researchers to seriously address the issue of realism. How real is real enough in these models? Are simplistic models based on central social science principles sufficient or are social network flight simulators necessary? If the latter, a core area to address is how the simulation models can meaningfully make use of abstract data, easily available data, and data at varying levels of fidelity.

Core concerns in developing such models include the following. It is imperative for validation, development of metrics, and usefulness of results that the data collected from the computational model and the data collected from the real world are the same kind of data and at the same level of granularity. Second, the models should be easy to use. In part this means greater attention to user-interfaces that are rarely developed by academicians. To facilitate this, funding agencies need to provide funds not just for the basic model but also for the development of the interface, the development of ontologies and the development of links to other programs. Finally, the computational tools need to include "meaningful" variables. To aid in this, subject matter experts should be consulted to develop a vocabulary for the tool that maps from the academicians ideas to the terms of the user.

Effects Based Operations

Network techniques can also enable certain types of effects based operations. Effects based operations, according to the Joint Forces Command Glossary, is "a process for obtaining a desired strategic outcome or 'effect' on the enemy, through the synergistic, multiplicative, and cumulative application of the full range of military and nonmilitary capabilities at the tactical, operational, and strategic levels." Many types of effects are particularly amenable to being planned for using network techniques and models – destabilization of the adversaries networks, reducing the ability of the adversary to acquire intelligence or coordinate, decreasing/increasing trust in the adversaries leaders or key operators (information warfare effects), and reduction in the adversaries "reach."

In order to use network analysis for effects based operations a number of advances are needed. First, network analysis need to move beyond characterizing the structure to understanding its dynamics and how to influence it. Further, in this area particularly, it is important to link the social, anthropological and communication approach so common in social networks with the understanding of events and actions coming out of political science. This will enable the analyst to ask, what types of networks can be handled through diplomacy, war, operations other than war and with what effects. This may be particularly important when the adversary is not a nation-state.

Is There Anything Else?

While the work covered at this meeting addressed many of the core areas in social networks, there are still areas left uncovered. It is not my intent to comprehensively review these. Rather, I will mention only a few where the tools may have direct relevance in the defense and intelligence communities.

Network analysis can be used to characterize difference across cultures and to suggest strategies for changing the underlying culture. One way in which culture can be viewed is as the distribution of knowledge, beliefs, and norms across people – i.e., the knowledge network. Work melding social networks and knowledge networks demonstrates that the underlying culture can be changed through the flow of targeted information. The basic idea is that as individuals interact through the social network, they learn, thus changing the knowledge network, and so the overall culture. Basically, the co-evolution of social structure (the social network) and culture (the knowledge network) can be managed. In this area, individuals interested in communication, organizational knowledge management, and social networks are coming together to ask questions such as – how can we identify the culture-change agent in the social network?, what is the core piece of knowledge that needs to be changed?, and how can we rapidly assess the culture? Such work provides new tools of use in the area of information warfare.

Network techniques are also being used to analyze coded texts. Work is being conducted to create automated tools for analyzing texts as networks of concepts (often called mental models) and for extracting social, knowledge and event networks from texts. Postprocessors are then storing the coded data in formats that can be analyzed using standard network analysis tools like Mage, Pajek, Ucinet. One of the key possible uses of these tools is to facilitate rapid first past coding of intelligence reports. Another use here is to contrast differences in the structural properties of the mental models of experts with novices, or to contrast the reports of different intelligence officers.

Another area of advancement is in the area of visualizing networks. Here research is on-going on how to simultaneously represent nodes and "meta-nodes" and automatically create meta-nodes. A meta-node is a node containing a set of other nodes that have some structural property in common. Simultaneous representation of multiple networks, zooming in and out in extremely large networks, and graphic representation of critical nodes are all key aspects of the new visualization techniques.

The final area I want to mention is health. New epidemiological models now take not only geographic factors but the networks in to account. This has profound implications for estimating the size of potentially exposed populations and evaluating prevention, containment and treatment policies. Such models are useful in combating bio-terrorism.

Finally, and it is important to stress this point, tools and techniques for dealing with relational data are currently being developed in a number of fields. In this workshop there was a small representation of the work in computer science and physics on graphs, networks, and relational data. In addition to this, there is on going work in other areas of computer science, information science, electrical engineering, biology and chemistry that is of value here. Major advances may well require linking network analysis to other techniques such as data-mining, data-fusion, and machine learning. The key here, is that there are an increasing number of applications as the field moves from standard network analysis to dynamic network analysis, from looking at small to large networks, from looking at static to dynamic networks, from looking at single mode (e.g. people) to multi-mode (e.g., people and knowledge) networks. Dynamic network analysis and the associated tools and techniques will be useful in addressing both tactical and strategic issues. Further, it will be useful in looking at both short and long term issues; e.g., in how to destabilize a covert network and in how to alter the underlying culture to reduce the possibility of new recruits.

Outreach – Connecting the Dots

As we have seen, many of the ideas, measures, and tools being developed hold promise relative to the needs of the defense and intelligence community. However, there is still large gap. Filling this gap is not simply a straightforward excursion moving the theoretical to the applied. Rather, it requires fundamental new science on dynamic networks under varying levels of uncertainty. Further, it requires channel through which the needs of the intelligence and defense community can be better expressed to the scientific community.

On the academic side, it would benefit the field, the government and the economy if a larger number of masters and Ph.D. students were trained in formal (statistical, mathematical and computational) network techniques. In fields where the link between science and government is tighter, roughly 50% of the students graduating go into industry or government positions rather than academics. In contrast, not only are fewer graduate students produced in the social network area (almost an order of magnitude fewer) but many fewer go into non-academic positions (almost two orders of magnitude).

Further the two key factors academics need to consider are scale and communication. That is, the network community needs to take seriously whether the data collection techniques, measures, methods, algorithms scale with the size of the network. It is imperative that the issue of scale be addressed so that the academic researcher and government analyst can utilize the ideas, theories, tools etc. regardless of the size of the network. One thing the community needs to be concerned with is collecting and sharing databases of networks of varying sizes – from the tiny, 4 nodes, to the mega, millions of nodes – that can be used to test all theories, measures, algorithms, etc.

The second key factor is communication. The way in which academics in this field ask questions are often tied to the body of theory rather than the needs of the time. It is important when doing research to ask both – how do I ask my questions among academic peers – and – how do I ask my question from an applied angle. Or in other words – "why should defense or intelligence agencies care?".

On the part of the defense and intelligence community there is also work to be done. Here, personnel should go to training courses or bring in faculty to run short courses. In network analysis there are a number of training courses – such as that at the ISPCR in Michigan, the CASOS summer institute, the training sessions at the Sunbelt Social Networks Meetings and the Academy of Management. Having even a rudimentary training would help with communication as more terms of art would be shared. Another key point is that this applied community needs to provide more detailed guidance as to the level and types of measures needed and to questions of concern. It is not sufficient to tell the academician – well what you have is not quite right. Rather, ways of discussing needs, without compromising national security, must be found. This is very possible and is done quite well in other areas, such as technology design, data mining, and engineered systems. Techniques that might help in this regard include getting academicians in the area to help write the broad area announcements, sending personnel to spend one term on a campus as a visitor, creating cleaned or hypothetical datasets that can be shared with the academic community, and of course, workshops like this where the two communities can exchange views.

Appendixes

A

Workshop Agenda

WORKSHOP ON DYNAMIC SOCIAL NETWORK ANALYSIS
AGENDA
November 7-9, 2002

Thursday, November 7

Welcome
Anne Mavor, National Research Council
Rebecca Goolsby, Office of Naval Research

Opening Address
"Emergent Themes in Social Network Analysis: Results, Challenges, Opportunities"
Ronald L. Breiger, Workshop Chair, University of Arizona

Session I: Social Network Theory Perspectives
Ronald L. Breiger, Moderator and Discussant

- *Linton C. Freeman, University of California, Irvine*—Finding Social Groups: A Meta-Analysis of the Southern Women Data

- *Harrison C. White, Columbia University*—Modeling Entrepreneurial Agency within Networks of Markets

- *Noah E. Friedkin, University of California, Santa Barbara*—Social Influence Network Theory: Toward a Science of Strategic Modification of Interpersonal Influence Systems

- *David Lazer, Harvard University*—Information and Innovation in a Networked World

Discussion and Roundtable Themes, Issues, and Applications
Ronald L. Breiger, Moderator and Discussant

Session II: Dynamic Social Networks
Stanley Wasserman, Moderator and Discussant

- *Jeffrey C. Johnson, East Carolina University*—Informal Social Roles and the Evolution and Stability of Social Networks (coauthors Lawrence A. Palinkas, University of California, San Diego, and James Boster, University of Connecticut)

- *Kathleen M. Carley, Carnegie Mellon University*—Dynamic Network Analysis

- *Tom A.B. Snijders, ICS University of Groningen, The Netherlands*—Accounting for Degree Distributions in Empirical Analysis of Network Dynamics

- *Michael W. Macy, Cornell University*—Culture Wars and Dynamic Networks: A Hopfield Model of Emergent Structure (coauthors James A. Kitts, University of Washington, and Andreas Flache, University of Groningen)

- *Martina Morris, University of Washington*—Local Rules and Global Properties: Modeling the Emergence of Network Structure

Friday, November 8

Session II: Dynamic Social Networks (continued)

- *H. Eugene Stanley, Boston University*—Threat Networks and Threatened Networks: Interdisciplinary Approaches to Stabilization and Immunization (coauthor Shlomo Havlin, Bar-Ilan University)

Discussion and Roundtable Themes, Issues, and Applications
Stanley Wasserman, Moderator and Discussant

Session III: Metrics and Models
Pip Pattison, Moderator and Discussant

- *Stanley Wasserman, University of Illinois*—Sensitivity Analysis of Social Network Data and Methods: Some Preliminary Results (coauthor Douglas Steinley, University of Illinois)

- *Andrew J. Seary and William D. Richards, Simon Fraser University*—Spectral Methods for Analyzing and Visualizing Networks: An Introduction

- *Mark S. Handcock, University of Washington*—Assessing Degeneracy in Statistical Models for Social Networks

- *Stephen P. Borgatti, Boston College*—The Key Player Problem

- *Elisa Jayne Bienenstock, University of California, Irvine, and Phillip Bonacich, University of California, Los Angeles*—Balancing Efficiency and Vulnerability in Social Networks

- *Christos Faloutsos, Carnegie Mellon University*—Finding Patterns in Large, Real Networks

Discussion and Roundtable Themes, Issues, and Applications
Pip Pattison, Moderator and Discussant

Session IV: Networked Worlds
David Lazer, Moderator and Discussant

- *Alden S. Klovdahl, Australian National University*—Large Social Networks in Contemporary Societies
- *David Jensen, University of Massachusetts, Amherst*—Data Mining in Social Networks (coauthor Jennifer Neville, University of Massachusetts, Amherst)
- *Peter D. Hoff, University of Washington*—Random Effects Models for Network Data

Saturday, November 9

Session IV: Networked Worlds (continued)

- *Carter T. Butts, University of California at Irvine*—Predictability of Large-Scale Spatially Embedded Networks
- *Noshir S. Contractor, University of Illinois*—Using Multi-Theoretical Multi-Level (MTML) Models to Study Adversarial Networks (coauthor Peter R. Monge, University of Southern California)
- *Michael D. Ward, University of Washington*—Identifying International Networks: Latent Spaces and Imputation (coauthor Peter D. Hoff and Corey Lowell Lofdahl, SAIC)

Discussion and Roundtable Themes, Issues, and Applications
David Lazer, Moderator and Discussant

Summary of Workshop Themes, Issues, and Applications
Kathleen M. Carley, Carnegie Mellon University

B

Biographical Sketches

WORKSHOP CHAIR

Ronald L. Breiger is professor of sociology at the University of Arizona. His research is in the areas of social network analysis, stratification, mathematical models, theory, and measurement issues in cultural and institutional analysis. His Ph.D. is from Harvard University. A list of recent publications is available at *www.u.arizona.edu/~breiger/*.

PRESENTERS

Elisa Jayne Bienenstock is a visiting assistant professor at the Department of Sociology at the University of California at Irvine. Her research integrates social networks with game theory and social psychology. Her current focus is on developing formal and experimental models of exchange processes and their relation to the emergence of power, status, inequality, conflict, cooperation, and coalition formation. She has a Ph.D. in sociology from the University of California, Los Angeles. A current vita is available at *http://hypatia.ss.uci.edu/sociology/Bienenstock/VitaWeb01.htm.*

Stephen P. Borgatti is professor of organization studies at the Carroll School of Management at Boston College. His research focuses on social networks, most recently with application to knowledge flows in organizations. He has a Ph.D. in mathematical social science from the University of California, Irvine. A current vita is available at *http://www.analytictech.com/borgatti.*

Carter T. Butts is assistant professor of sociology the University of California, Irvine. His current research focuses on methods for network measurement and comparison, spatial models of network structure, and decision-theoretic models of organizational change. He received his B.S. from Duke University and his Ph.D. from Carnegie Mellon University. A current vita and additional information are available on his Web page, at *http://hypatia.ss.uci.edu/sociology/Butts/buttsprof.html.*

Kathleen M. Carley is a professor at the Institute for Software Research International in the School of Computer Science and director of the Center for Computational Analysis of Social and Organizational Systems at Carnegie Mellon University. Her research areas include computational social and organization theory; dynamic social networks; multiagent network models; group, organizational, and social adaptation and evolution; statistical models for dynamic network analysis and evolution, computational text analysis, and the impact of telecommunication technologies on communication and information diffusion within and among groups. She received an S.B. in political science and an S.B. in economics from Massachusetts Institute of Technology, and a Ph.D. in sociology from Harvard University. Her vita, papers, and abstracts can be found at *http://hss.cmu.edu/departments/sds/faculty/carley.html, http://www.epp.cmu.edu/people/bios/carley.html, http://www.heinz.cmu.edu/researchers/faculty/carley.html*).

Noshir S. Contractor is professor of speech communication and psychology at the University of Illinois at Urbana-Champaign and a research affiliate at the Beckman Institute for Advanced Science and Technology. His research applies theories of complexity to communication and knowledge networks within and between organizations. He has a B. Tech. (1983) in electrical engineering from the Indian Institute of Technology, Madras, and a Ph.D. (1987) in communication from the Annenberg School for Communication at the University of Southern California. For more information and publications, see *http://www.uiuc.edu/ph/www/nosh.*

Christos Faloutsos is a professor at Carnegie Mellon University. His research interests include data mining for streams and networks, fractals, indexing methods for spatial and multimedia bases, and database performance. He has a Ph.D. in computer science from the University of Toronto, Canada. A current vita is at *http://www.cs.cmu.edu/~christos/short-cv.txt.*

Noah E. Friedkin is professor of sociology at the University of California, Santa Barbara. His current research focuses on the development and application of social influence network theory. He received his B.A. in 1969 and Ph.D. in 1977 from the University of Chicago. A complete vita and selected reprints are available on his Web site: *http://www.soc.ucsb.edu/faculty/friedkin/.*

Linton C. Freeman is a research professor of sociology in the Institute for Mathematical Behavioral Sciences and the Department of Sociology at the University of California, Irvine (UCI). He has taught at UCI for 24 years and has served as dean of the School of Social Sciences. His primary focus is in the area of social network analysis. His recent work has focused on graphic representations of network structure. His vita, including publications, is available online at *http://moreno.ss.uci.edu/vita.html.*

Mark S. Handcock is a professor of statistics and sociology at the Center for Statistics and the Social Sciences, University of Washington, Seattle. His work focuses on the development of statistical models for the analysis of social network data, spatial processes and longitudinal data arising in labor economics. He received his B.Sc. from the University of Western Australia and his Ph.D. from the University of Chicago. His vita is available online at *http://www.stat.washington.edu/~handcock/.*

Peter D. Hoff is assistant professor of statistics and biostatistics and a member of the Center for Statistics and the Social Sciences at the University of Washington. His current research involves dyadic data, latent variable models, and nonparametric Bayesian methods. He has a Ph.D. in statistics from the University of Wisconsin, Madison. More information on his research can be obtained at *http://www.stat.washington.edu/hoff.*

David Jensen is research assistant professor of Computer Science and Director of the Knowledge Discovery Laboratory at the University of Massachusetts, Amherst. His research focuses on machine learning, knowledge discovery, and data mining in large relational databases. He received his D.Sc. in engineering and policy from Washington University in St. Louis. A current vita is available at *http://kdl.cs.umass.edu/people/jensen/.*

Jeffrey C. Johnson is a senior scientist at the Institute for Coastal and Marine Resources, professor in the Department of Sociology, and adjunct professor in the departments of Anthropology, Biology, and Biostatistics at East Carolina University. He received his Ph.D. in social science from the University of California, Irvine, and is currently interested in the evolution and stability of social networks and in network models of complex biological systems. A current vita is available at *http://personal.ecu.edu/johnsonje/*.

Alden Klovdahl is a sociologist at the Australian National University in Canberra. He has a longstanding interest in the scientific study of large social networks in the real world, tools for more efficient processing of large amounts of network data, and harnessing the power of visual representations for analyses of complex networks. A focus of much of his research has been the spread of human pathogens and the design of more effective methods for infectious disease control. He received his Ph.D. in sociology from the University of Michigan, Ann Arbor. Contact information and a listing of publications can be found at *http://arts.anu.edu.au/Arts/SSSchool/Sociology/klovdahl.htm*.

David Lazer, assistant professor of public policy, teaches courses on management and executive branch politics. He is associate director of the National Center for Digital Government Research and Practice and co-chair of the Cambridge Colloquium on Complexity and Social Networks. He is currently completing an edited volume titled *The Technology of Justice: DNA and the Criminal Justice System* and is launching an NSF-funded project to study how a Web-based system might facilitate the sharing of information about this policy area (the dnapolicy.net initiative). He holds a Ph.D. in political science from the University of Michigan. A current vita, with papers, is available at *www.ksg.harvard.edu/davidlazer*.

Michael W. Macy is professor and chair of sociology at Cornell University. His current research focuses on agent-based models of dynamic social networks, with application to diffusion of norms and beliefs. He has a Ph.D. in sociology from Harvard University. A current vita is available at *http://www.people.cornell.edu/pages/mwm14/* .

Martina Morris is the Blumstein-Jordan Professor of Sociology and Statistics at the University of Washington. Her research focuses on social network epidemiology and methods, with a focus on HIV and STI transmission dynamics. She has an M.A. in statistics and a Ph.D. in sociology from the University of Chicago. A current vita is available at *http://faculty.washington.edu/morrism*.

Philippa (Pip) Pattison is a professor in the School of Behavioural Science at the University of Melbourne. Her current research focuses on mathematical models for social networks and network-based processes. She holds a Ph.D. in mathematical psychology from the University of Melbourne.

William D. Richards is professor of communication at the Simon Fraser University in Burnaby, British Columbia. With Andrew Seary, Richards has been investigating spectral analysis and its application to large complex networks since 1988. They have developed the MultiNet program to make these analytic tools available for network researchers. He received his Ph.D. in communication research in 1976 from Stanford University. Information about his software and his research is available at *http://www.sfu.ca/~richards* and *http://www.scu.ca/insna*.

Andrew J. Seary is a research associate and Ph.D. graduate student at Simon Fraser University. His research topic is application of methods of mathematical physics to large networks, with emphasis on analysis and visualization. He has a B.Sc. in mathematical physics from McGill University, Montreal. He has over 25 years experience in applied mathematics and interactive graphical programming and has developed software for large networks that is freely available at *http://www.sfu.ca/~richards*.

Tom A.B. Snijders is professor of methodology and statistics at the Department of Sociology of the University of Groningen, The Netherlands, and scientific director of the research and graduate school ICS (Interuniversity Center for Social Science Theory and Methodology). His main research interests are social network analysis and multilevel analysis. He holds a Ph.D. in mathematical statistics from the University of Groningen. More information about his activities is available at *http://stat.gamma.rug.nl/snijders/*.

H. Eugene Stanley is university professor and professor of physics at Boston University. His research focuses on complex systems in physics, biology, and social science, including a focus on complex networks. He has a Ph.D. in theoretical physics from Harvard University. A current vita for him is available at *http://polymer.bu.edu/hes*, which also includes pdf files of all his papers.

Michael D. Ward is professor of political science at the University of Washington, Seattle, and holds a Chaire Municipale in the faculty of economics at the University of Pierre Mendes France in Grenoble, France. His research focuses on democratization and international conflict, with emphasis on political geography and economics. He has a Ph.D. from Northwestern University. He may be reached at *mdw@u.washington.edu*.

Stanley Wasserman is professor of psychology, statistics, and sociology at the University of Illinois, as well as professor in the Beckman Institute for Advanced Science and Technology at the university. His research focuses on social networks and applied statistics. He has a Ph.D. in statistics from Harvard University. A current vita is available at *http://kentucky.psych.uiuc.edu*, and a brief overview of his recent research can be found at *http://kentucky.psych.uiuc.edu/pstar*.

Harrison C. White is acting chair, Department of Sociology, and Giddings Professor of Sociology, Columbia University. One line of his current research melds economic sociology with mathematical modeling (*Markets from Networks*, Princeton University Press, 2002); another meshes social network with discourse analyses. He has a Ph.D. in theoretical physics from the Massachusetts Institute of Technology and a Ph.D. in sociology from Princeton University.

Planning Subcommittee

Daniel R. Ilgen (*Chair*) is the John Hannah Professor of Psychology and Management at Michigan State University. His background is in industrial/organizational psychology. His work focuses on work motivation, individual, and social perspectives and models of small group/team behavior, particularly team decision making.

John M. Carroll is the director of the Center for Human-Computer Interaction, and a professor of computer science, education, and psychology at Virginia Polytechnic Institute in Blacksburg. He has researched human learning and problem-solving in human-computer interaction contexts for two decades. His long-term interests are in methods of remote collaboration and in team and organizational communications.

Martha Grabowski, professor of management information systems at LeMoyne College and research professor at Rensselaer Polytechnic Institute, has expertise in management information systems, expert systems, decision support systems, telecommunications and networking, organizational impact of information technology, technology and organizational strategy, use of information systems for competitive advantage, and interface of technology with marketing and manufacturing.